# THE INTERNATIONAL HANDBOOK ON GENDER, MIGRATION AND TRANSNATIONALISM

INTERNATIONAL HANDBOOKS ON GENDER

Series editor: Sylvia Chant, *FRSA, Professor of Development Geography, London School of Economics and Political Science, UK*

International Handbooks on Gender is an exciting new Handbook series under the general editorship and direction of Sylvia Chant. The series will produce high quality, original reference works offering comprehensive overviews of the latest research within key areas of contemporary gender studies. International and comparative in scope, the Handbooks are edited by leading scholars in their respective fields, and comprise specially commissioned contributions from a select cast of authors, bringing together established experts with up-and-coming authors and researchers. Each volume offers a wide-ranging examination of current issues to produce prestigious and high quality works of lasting significance.

Individual volumes will serve as invaluable sources of reference for students and faculty in gender studies and associated fields, as well as for other actors such as NGOs and policymakers keen to engage with academic discussion on gender. Whether used as an information resource on key topics, a companion text or as a platform for further study, Elgar International Handbooks on Gender aim to provide a source of definitive scholarly reference.

Titles in the series include:

The International Handbook on Gender, Migration and Transnationalism
Global and Development Perspectives
Edited by Laura Oso and Natalia Ribas-Mateos

The International Handbook on Gender, Migration and Transnationalism

Global and Development Perspectives

Edited by

Laura Oso

Universidade da Coruña, Spain

and

Natalia Ribas-Mateos

Universidade da Coruña, Spain

INTERNATIONAL HANDBOOKS ON GENDER

Edward Elgar
Cheltenham, UK • Northampton, MA, USA

© Laura Oso and Natalia Ribas-Mateos 2013

All rights reserved. No part of this publication may be reproduced, stored in a retrieval system or transmitted in any form or by any means, electronic, mechanical or photocopying, recording, or otherwise without the prior permission of the publisher.

Published by
Edward Elgar Publishing Limited
The Lypiatts
15 Lansdown Road
Cheltenham
Glos GL50 2JA
UK

Edward Elgar Publishing, Inc.
William Pratt House
9 Dewey Court
Northampton
Massachusetts 01060
USA

A catalogue record for this book
is available from the British Library

Library of Congress Control Number: 2013932983

This book is available electronically in the ElgarOnline.com
Social and Political Science Subject Collection, E-ISBN 978 1 78195 147 7

ISBN 978 1 78195 146 0 (cased)

Typeset by Servis Filmsetting Ltd, Stockport, Cheshire
Printed and bound in Great Britain by T.J. International Ltd, Padstow

Contents

List of figures viii
List of tables and boxes ix
List of contributors xi

1 An introduction to a global and development perspective: a focus on gender, migration and transnationalism 1
   Laura Oso and Natalia Ribas-Mateos

PART I FRAMEWORK OF CHANGES IN GENDER, MIGRATION AND TRANSNATIONALISM FROM THE VANTAGE POINTS OF GLOBALIZATION AND DEVELOPMENT

2 Gender and international migration: globalization, development and governance 45
   Lourdes Benería, Carmen Diana Deere and Naila Kabeer

3 Talking culture: new boundaries, new rhetorics of exclusion in Europe 69
   Verena Stolcke

4 The long shadow of 'smart economics': the making, methodologies and messages of the *World Development Report 2012* 97
   Sylvia Chant

PART II NEW THEORETICAL AND METHODOLOGICAL ISSUES IN THE STUDY OF FEMALE MIGRATION AND DEVELOPMENT

5 Gender, Andean migration and development: analytical challenges and political debates 127
   Almudena Cortés

6 Theoretical debates on social reproduction and care: the articulation between the domestic and the global economy 145
   Christine Verschuur

PART III GENDER, MIGRATION AND DEVELOPMENT THROUGH DIFFERENT CASE STUDIES

7 Gender, development and Asian migration in Spain: the Chinese case   165
   Amelia Sáiz López

8 Back to Africa: second chances for the children of West African immigrants   185
   Caroline H. Bledsoe and Papa Sow

9 Transnational return and pendulum migration strategies of Moroccan migrants: intra-household power inequalities, tensions and conflicts of interest   208
   Hein de Haas and Tineke Fokkema

PART IV A PERSPECTIVE ON MIGRATION AND TRANSNATIONALISM

10 New directions in gender and immigration research   233
   Pierrette Hondagneu-Sotelo

11 Women, gender, transnational migrations and mobility: focus on research in France   246
   Christine Catarino and Mirjana Morokvasic

12 The gendered dynamics of integration and transnational engagement among second-generation adults in Europe   268
   James D. Bachmeier, Laurence Lessard-Phillips and Tineke Fokkema

13 Gendered and emotional spaces: Nordic–Hellenic negotiations of ethno-cultural belongingness in narrating segmented selves and diasporic lives of the second generation   294
   Anastasia Christou

14 Bolivian migrants in Spain: transnational families from a gender perspective   312
   Sònia Parella

PART V GLOBAL PRODUCTION

15 The internationalization of domestic work and female immigration in Spain during a decade of economic expansion, 1999–2008 337
Elena Vidal-Coso and Pau Miret-Gamundi

16 Towards a gender-sensitive approach to remittances in Ecuador 361
Diana Mata-Codesal

17 Remittances in the Spain–Ecuador corridor: a gendered estimation through Bayesian networks 376
Pilar Campoy-Muñoz, Melania Salazar-Ordóñez and Carlos R. García-Alonso

PART VI GLOBAL CARE CHAINS

18 Care and feminized North–South and South–South migration flows: denial of rights and limited citizenship 397
María Luisa Setién and Elaine Acosta

19 What has Polanyi got to do with it? Undocumented migrant domestic workers and the usages of reciprocity 420
Anna Safuta and Florence Degavre

20 Temporary female migrations through transnational family networks: the ethnographic case of the caregiver in Riffian Imazighen women 439
Irina Casado i Aijón

21 Transnational mobility and family-building decisions: a case study of skilled Polish migrant women in the UK 453
Anna Cieslik

Index 471

Figures

12.1	Predicted probability of return by economic integration and sex	285
15.1	Female occupational structure by birthplace, Spain (1999–2008)	346
15.2	Female occupational structure by area of birthplace, Spain (1999–2008)	348
15.3	Immigrant–native rates in occupational categories	350
15.4	Age and educational structure of cleaning and domestic employed women by birthplace (2008)	352
17.1	Bayesian network for remittance flows and gender: complete (a) and simplified (b) models	379
17.2	Remittance flows Rm_t in Spain–Ecuador corridor: estimated values	388
17.3	Estimated values of some relevant variables: WDE_t, PRm_t, UD_t and Nm_t	390

Tables and boxes

TABLES

12.1	Weighted means and percentages of variables used in analyses of transnationalism among second-generation adults in Europe (2006–2008)	280
12.2	Coefficients from negative binomial models of the number of visits (A) and from logit models of remitting (B) to parents' country of birth among second-generation adults in Europe	282
12.3	Coefficients from multinomial logit models of origin country return intentions among second-generation adults in Europe	284
12A.1	Results from principal components analysis of indicators of ethno-cultural and economic integration among second-generation adults in Europe	293
14.1	Basic data on Bolivian migrants in Barcelona	320
14.2	Transnational practices of Bolivian migrants by sex and family structure	322
15.1	Absolute and relative growth of female employment by area of birthplace, Spain (1999–2008)	345
15.2	Absolute and relative growth of cleaning and domestic female employment in Spain (1999–2008)	355
17.1	Dependence relationships in the Bayesian network: simplified model	385
17.2	Expert-based structure of input variables in the Bayesian network	386
17.3	Characteristics of dependence relationships: outputs and structure	387
17.4	Characteristics of dependence relationships: inputs and structure	387
18.1	Rights and duties with regard to care	403
18.2	Most relevant indicators of increased feminine migratory presence in Spain and Chile	405
18.3	Spheres of violation of labour rights in care work and their relationship with other rights, as perceived by immigrant caregivers and employers	412

BOXES

4.1	The 'globalization' of 'smart economics'?	101
4.2	Extracts from April 2011 draft WDR 2012	105
4.3	'Smart economics' remains! Extracts from WDR 2012	110
4.4	Internal World Bank appraisal of WDR 2012	111

Contributors

Elaine Acosta Elaine is a sociologist from the University of Havana, Cuba. She holds an MA in Latin American Studies from the Alberto Hurtado University in Chile and a doctorate in International and Intercultural Studies from the University of Deusto, Bilbao, Spain. Her research interests range from care work and international female migrations – including rights, citizenship and gender – to female labour market issues and, recently, transnational family networks. Currently, she collaborates with the International Migration Research Unit at the University of Deusto and also works in the Department of Sociology at Alberto Hurtado University.

James D. Bachmeier James is Assistant Professor in the Department of Sociology at Temple University, Philadelphia, USA. His research focuses on Mexican migration to the United States, the sociology of immigrant incorporation in the United States and Europe, and the dynamics of immigration and health.

Lourdes Benería Lourdes is Professor Emerita at Cornell University and is associated with IIEDG, Barcelona. An economist, her work on gender and international development began in 1977–79, as coordinator of the Program on Rural Women at the International Labour Office in Geneva. Since then, she has continued to be involved with projects at UN-related and other international institutions. She is the author of *Gender, Development and Globalization* (Routledge, 2003), and other authored or edited books such as the three-volume *Feminist Economics for the 21st Century*, with Ann Mari May and Diana Strassmann, Edward Elgar Economics Series. She is a former president of the International Association for Feminist Economics (IAFFE), an associate editor of *Feminist Economics* and the *European Journal of Development Research*, and a member of the editorial board of *Economia Crítica*.

Caroline H. Bledsoe Caroline was awarded a doctorate in Anthropology by Stanford University and is currently the Herskovits Professor of African Studies and Anthropology at Northwestern University in Evanston (Illinois, USA). Her research topics include cultural visions of reproduction and conjugal union in West Africa, as well as among Africans in Spain and, for comparison, in the US. Specific themes have been: marriage, contraception, ageing, child fostering and education. A more recent project has concerned the development of obstetrics in the US.

Pilar Campoy-Muñoz Pilar received a BA in Business Administration in 2005 and an MA in Research Methods on Economics and Business Sciences in 2011, both from the University of Córdoba, Spain. She is currently pursuing a doctorate and working as a researcher in the Department of Economics of Loyola University, Andalucía, Spain. Her current research interests include labour migrations, gender differences and computational economics.

Irina Casado i Aijón Irina is Lecturer in Anthropology at the Universitat Autònoma de Barcelona. She is also a member of GRAFO (Fundamental and Oriented Anthropology Research Group) and GETP (Study Group of Cross-cultural Kinship). She has done fieldwork in Oslo (Norway), focusing her research on motherhood, fatherhood and the socio-cultural organization of childcare and upbringing. She completed research in the Àneu Valleys (Catalonian Pyrenees) on kinship organization and domestic structures as well as the construction processes of individual and collective identities that arise from societies in a high mountain landscape. She has been carrying out fieldwork with the Amazigh Rif immigrant population in Catalonia since 2006, focusing on medical pluralism and the construction of therapeutic itineraries, paying special attention to sexual, reproductive and paediatric health.

Christine Catarino Christine holds a PhD in Sociology from the University of Paris I Panthéon-Sorbonne, and is an associate member of the Institut des Sciences sociales du Politique – Université Paris Ouest – Nanterre La Défense. Her areas of investigation include migration studies and intersectionality. She has worked as a contractual researcher on two European projects looking at the integration of ethnic entrepreneurs' families and female migrants. Among her recent publications are 'Family matters: migrant domestic and care work and the issue of recognition', with Maria Kontos and Kyoko Shinozaki, in F. Anthias, M. Kontos and M. Morokvasic-Müller (eds), *Female Migrants in Europe: The Paradoxes of Integration* (Springer, 2013, pp. 133–52) and 'Politiques migratoires et politiques d'emploi: la flexibilité sexuée en Europe', *Cahiers du Genre*, **51**, December, 2011, 93–112.

Sylvia Chant Sylvia is Professor of Development Geography at the London School of Economics and Political Science, UK, where she is Director of the MSc in Urbanisation and Development. She was elected as a Fellow of the Royal Society of Arts (FRSA) in 2011 on the grounds of her 'expertise and exploration of gender in geographical development', and she has conducted research in Mexico, Costa Rica, the Philippines and The Gambia. Her main interests are in gender and poverty, female employment and urban labour markets, rural–urban migration, housing and female-headed households. Author of over a dozen books, her latest titles include *Gender, Generation and Poverty: Exploring the Feminisation of Poverty in Africa, Asia and Latin America* (Edward Elgar, 2007), and *The International Handbook of Gender and Poverty: Concepts, Research, Policy* (Edward Elgar, 2010).

Anastasia Christou Anastasia is Reader in Sociology, Middlesex University, UK. She has previously been Senior Lecturer in Cultural Geography, University of Sussex; Visiting Assistant Professor, University of Aalborg; Postdoctoral Researcher at the Academy for Migration Studies in Denmark, and Visiting Research Fellow at the Wissenschaftszentrum Berlin für Sozialforschung in Germany. She has conducted multi-sited, multi-method and comparative ethnographic research in the United States, Germany, Denmark, Greece and Cyprus and has published widely on issues of diasporas; migration/return migration; the second generation and ethnicity; space and place; transnationalism and identity; culture and memory; gender and feminism; home and belonging; and emotion and narrativity.

Anna Cieslik Anna is an Assistant Professor at New Jersey City University and a research fellow at Max Planck Institute for the Study of Religious and Ethnic Diversity. She is an urban geographer with an interest in gender, immigration and diversity in urban contexts. She received her doctorate from Clark University (2011) where she worked on Polish migration to London and migrants' perceptions of urban environments. Her current research investigates the social and spatial patterns that arise under conditions of superdiversity in Astoria, NY and is part of the GlobalDivercities project, funded by the European Research Council, which compares superdiverse neighbourhoods in Singapore, Johannesburg and New York City.

Almudena Cortés Almudena is Lecturer in Social Anthropology at the Complutense University in Madrid (Spain). In 2010, she was awarded a doctorate with honours in Social Anthropology (Autonomous University of Madrid). She has been Visiting Scholar at the Danish Institute for International Studies, FLACSO-Ecuador and the Latin American Studies Institute (Freie Universität, Berlin). Her fieldwork focuses on 'migration', development and governance migration patterns, consisting of values, standards and cultural representations of migration and based on multi-sited, transnational work in different places in Ecuador and Spain from 2004 to 2009. She has published her research findings nationally and internationally in a wide range of prestigious, peer-reviewed journals, as well as individual and collective books.

Hein de Haas Hein is co-director of the International Migration Institute at the University of Oxford and Lecturer in Migration Studies. His research focuses on the links between migration and broader development processes, primarily from the perspective of migrant-sending societies. He did extensive fieldwork in the Middle East and North Africa and, particularly, Morocco. He has published on a wide range of issues including migration theory, migration and development, remittances and transnationalism, migration determinants and policies. He has regularly acted as consultant or adviser to national governments and international organizations including UNDP, UNRISD, IOM and the EU.

Carmen Diana Deere Carmen is Distinguished Professor of Latin American Studies and Food and Resource Economics at the University of Florida and former director of the UF Center for Latin American Studies. She holds a doctorate in Agricultural Economics from the University of California, Berkeley. She is a past president of the Latin American Studies Association (LASA) and an associate editor of *Feminist Economics*. She is the co-author (with Magdalena León) of *Empowering Women: Land and Property Rights in Latin America* (University of Pittsburgh Press, 2001), winner of LASA's Bryce Wood Book Award, and co-editor of special issues of *Feminist Economics* on gender and international migration and on women and wealth.

Florence Degavre Florence is a socio-economist, researcher at the Centre Interdisciplinaire de Recherches Travail, Etat et Société, and an Assistant Professor at the Catholic University of Louvain, Belgium. Her main research interest is social policy, in particular, marketization and defamilialization in European care regimes. She studies elderly care from a Polanyian and feminist perspective. She also conducts research on gender and social enterprise.

Tineke Fokkema Tineke is a Senior Researcher at the Netherlands Interdisciplinary Demographic Institute in The Hague. Her research interests include the determinants of remittances and immigrant integration, gender and generational dynamics of migration, the contested links between integration and transnationalism, return migration and the reintegration of returnees into society and their extended families.

Carlos R. García-Alonso Carlos received his BSc in Engineering in 1985 and doctorate in Agricultural Engineering in 1988, both from the Polytechnic University of Madrid. He is currently Operations Research and Information Systems Professor in the Department of Quantitative Methods at Loyola University in Andalucía, Spain. His current research interests include operational research (simulation and data envelopment analysis), artificial intelligence (fuzzy logic and evolutionary algorithms), and information systems in order to design simulation-based and artificial intelligence-based models in economics.

Pierrette Hondagneu-Sotelo Pierrette is Professor in the Department of Sociology at the University of Southern California. She is the author or editor of eight books, the most recent of which are *God's Heart Has No Borders: How Religious Activists are Working for Immigrant Rights* (University of California Press, 2008), *Nation and Migration, Past and Future*, co-edited with David Gutierrez (Johns Hopkins University Press, 2009), and *Domestica: Trabajadoras Inmigrantes a Cargo de la Limpieza y el Cuidado a la Sombra de la Abundancia* (Mexico: Porrua Editorial, 2011). She is currently writing a book about migration and transformations of garden landscapes.

Naila Kabeer Naila is Professor of Gender and Development at the Gender Institute, London School of Economics and Political Science, University of London, UK. She is a social economist working on the social and economic interactions between households, communities and the wider economy. Areas of specialization include: poverty, social exclusion and gender in relation to labour markets and livelihood strategies in the context of globalization. Her main areas of research have been in South and Southeast Asia. She has been active in developing frameworks and methodologies for integrating gender concerns into policy and planning and, recently, has been working with the UN Division for the Advancement for Women (DAW) as the lead author on 'The World Survey on Women and Development, 2009'.

Laurence Lessard-Phillips Laurence is a research associate at the Institute for Social Change, University of Manchester (UK). Her research focuses on the dimensionality of immigrant adaptation from a comparative perspective; the academic, policy and public perspectives of immigration adaptation; ethnic inequalities in education and the labour market; the cumulative dynamics of international migration and their effect; and the impact of immigration and diversity on social cohesion.

Diana Mata-Codesal Diana is a postdoctoral researcher at UNAM, Mexico and at the University of Deusto, Spain. She holds a doctorate in Migration Studies from the University of Sussex, UK. She has a multidisciplinary background (BA in Economics and Anthropology) and research experience in mobility-related issues. She is interested in Latin American migrations to Europe and the US. She has carried out research on the food practices of Ecuadorian migrants abroad and on social and material remittances in rural Highland Ecuador.

Pau Miret-Gamundi Pau is a researcher at the Centre for Demographic Studies (CED) at the Autonomous University of Barcelona (UAB). He obtained a BSc in Sociology at UAB in 1989, a post-graduate diploma in Demography at CED in 1991, and a PhD in Sociology from Spain's Universidad Nacional de Educación a Distancia. He has worked in the Cathie Marsh Centre for Census and Survey Research (Manchester, UK) and in the Department of Social Statistics at the University of Southampton (UK). He was a Ramón y Cajal Fellow from 2005 to 2009 at the UAB's Department of Geography. His main areas of study are the effects of education and migration on family formation and labour force participation.

Mirjana Morokvasic Mirjana is a Research Director and Professor Emeritus at the Centre National de la Recherche Scientifique, Paris. She has taught at universities in France – including the Lille University and Paris X–Nanterre University – and abroad, as the Marie Jahoda Professor at the Ruhr Universität Bochum, Germany, and as Guest Professor at the Institute for Gender Studies, Ochanomizu University, Tokyo. Her research focuses on migration, identity processes, transnationalism and gender, and privileges a comparative perspective. Her numerous publications are in several languages and her latest book, co-edited with Floya Anthias and Maria Kontos, is *Paradoxes of Integration: Female Migrants in Europe* (Springer, 2013).

Laura Oso Laura holds doctoral degrees in Sociology from the University of La Sorbonne (2002) and the University of A Coruña (1997). She is currently Senior Lecturer at the Faculty of Sociology at the University of A Coruña, where she coordinates ESOMI (Research Group on the Sociology of International Migrations). She has worked as a consultant for various international organizations, including the OECD and the European Union. Her research has focused mainly on gender and migration and the insertion of immigrant populations in labour markets, covering domestic service, prostitution and ethnic entrepreneurship. In recent years she has coordinated the Research Projects 'The Impact of Migration on Development: Gender and Transnationalism' (SEJ2007/6379) (2007–10) and 'Gender, Transnationalism and Inter-Generational Strategies for Social Mobility' (FEM2011-26210) (2011–2014) from the Ministerio de Economía y Competitividad, Spain. Her numerous publications include: 'From sex to gender: the feminisation of migration and labour-market insertion in Spain and Portugal', *Journal of Ethnic and Migration Studies*, **39** (4), 2013 (co-authored with Christine Catarino); 'Tortoises and elephants in the fight for family social mobility: second-generation Spanish migrants in France and their desire to "return"', *Journal of Mediterranean Studies*, **20** (2), 2011; and 'Money, sex, love and the family: economic and affective strategies of Latin American sex workers in Spain', *Journal of Ethnic and Migration Studies*, **36** (1), 2010.

Sònia Parella Sònia is Associate Professor in the Department of Sociology at the Autonomous University of Barcelona. She holds a PhD in Sociology from the UAB (2002). She is a Senior Researcher at the GEDIME (Centre for Immigration and Ethnic Minorities Studies) at the UAB. Her primary research interests and publications focus on gender, migration and domestic work; ethnic entrepreneurship; transnational families and cross-border social practices. Most of these studies involve Latin American groups in Spain.

Natalia Ribas-Mateos Natalia holds a BA from the Complutense University of Madrid in 1988, and a doctorate from the Autonomous University of Barcelona, where she conducted research and taught in the Sociology Department until 2001. In 2001 she obtained a Marie Curie Fellowship at the University of Sussex and then a second Marie Curie Fellowship at the CNRS, Aix-en-Provence. She is now a Ramón Cajal Fellow at ESOMI (Research Group on the Sociology of International Migrations, University of A Coruña). She has six single-authored books, one of them published in the United States in 2005, entitled *The Mediterranean in the Age of Globalization: Migration, Welfare and Borders* (New Brunswick, NJ: Transaction).

Anna Safuta Anna is Research Fellow of the Belgian National Fund for Scientific Research (FNRS) and a PhD student at the Catholic University of Louvain-la-Neuve (UCL) in Belgium. Her doctorate is a study of domestic services as performed by first-generation migrants in Belgium and Poland, in particular, home-based elderly care. Previously a researcher at the European Social Observatory in Brussels (OSE), Anna has authored publications on social and health policy in Europe. Her current research interests include social policy, migration and gendered approaches of theory and methodology in the social sciences.

Amelia Sáiz López Amelia is a sociologist and Lecturer in East Asian Studies at the Autonomous University of Barcelona. She is also co-director of the Red de Investigaciones sobre Comunidades Asiáticas en España (RICAE) at the Cidob Foundation in Barcelona. Over the last decade she has completed many research projects on gender and East

Asian migration in Spain and in East Asian Women Studies. Her major publications include *Utopía y género: Las mujeres chinas en el siglo XX* (Barcelona: Edicions Bellaterra, 2001); *Mujeres asiáticas: cambio social y modernidad* (Barcelona: CIDOB, 2006); and *Empresariado asiático en España* (Barcelona: CIDOB, 2009). She has also published book chapters and articles such as 'Transnationalism, motherhood, and entrepreneurship: Chinese women in Spain', in M.T. Segal, E.N. Chow and V. Demos (eds), *Social Production and Reproduction at the Interface of Public and Private Spheres* (Bingley, UK: Emerald, 2012).

Melania Salazar-Ordóñez Melania received an MA in Regional Development in 2007 and her doctorate in Economic Science and Business Administration in 2009, both from the University of Seville, Spain. She is currently an applied economics researcher at the Department of Economics, Loyola University, Andalucía, Spain. Her current research interests include labour migrations, labour market and computational economics.

María Luisa Setién María Luisa is Lecturer in Sociology at the University of Deusto, Bilbao, Spain. She is also director of the Research Team on Social and Cultural Challenges of a World in Transformation. Her main research areas focus on international migrations, inter-ethnic relations, social welfare and values.

Papa Sow Papa gained his doctorate in Human Geography from the Autonomous University of Barcelona. He is a former Marie Curie Fellowship holder at the University of Warwick, and is currently a senior researcher in the Cultural and Social Change Department at the Centre for Development Research (ZEF) at the University of Bonn, Germany. His research has concerned the international migration of Senegalese and Gambians to Spain and France. He has studied the connections that immigrants strike up, through family, trade and communication technologies; and the socioeconomic, environmental and demographic changes that continue to unfold in the post-colonial era, both within and between Africa and Europe.

Verena Stolcke Verena is Professor Emeritus of Social Anthropology at the Autonomous University of Barcelona. Born in Germany in 1938, she was educated at Oxford University (DPhil, 1970). She conducted field and archival research in Cuba in 1967–68 and in São Paulo, Brazil between 1973 and 1979, while she taught at the Universidade Estadual de Campinas. She is the author of *Marriage, Class, and Colour in Nineteenth-Century Cuba* (Cambridge: Cambridge University Press, 1974, reprinted by the University of Michigan Press in 1989 and 2003). Her research in

São Paulo was published in *Cafeicultura: Homens, Mulheres e Capital (1850–1980)* (São Paulo: Editora Brasiliense SA, 1986), which appeared in English under the title *Coffee Planters, Workers, and Wives: Class Conflict and Gender Relations on São Paulo Plantations, 1850–1980* (Oxford: St Antony's/Macmillan, 1988). She has also published on sex and gender, nationality and identity, and identifications. Some of the articles are: 'Is sex to gender as race is to ethnicity?', in *Gendered Anthropology*, edited by Teresa del Valle (London: Routledge, 1993) and 'The "nature" of nationality', in *Citizenship and Exclusion*, edited by Veit Bader (London: Macmillan, 1997). A new line of research has been published as 'Los mestizos no nacen sino que se hacen', in *Identidades Ambivalentes en América Latina (Siglos XVI–XXI)*, edited by herself and Alexandre Coello, and her most recent article is 'Homo clonicus', in *Clones, Fakes and Posthumans: Cultures of Replication*, edited by Philomena Essed and Gabriele Schwab (Amsterdam and New York: Editions Rodopi, 2012).

Christine Verschuur Christine is an anthropologist and was awarded a PhD in Socioeconomic Development by the Paris 1–Sorbonne University in 1983. She is a Senior Lecturer at the Graduate Institute of International and Development Studies in Geneva where she is also Director of the Gender and Development Programme. She is also Director of the *Cahiers Genre et Développement* collection for L'Harmattan, Paris. Her areas of focus are gender and development, decolonial feminist studies, urban popular movements, migration, rural development and peasant organizations. Recent publications include: 'Raccommodages de la pauvreté ou engagements féministes dans les quartiers populaires de San Cayetano et Gamboa en Amérique latine', *Autrepart* (61), 2012, 175–90, and 'Féminismes décoloniaux, genre et développement', *Revue Tiers Monde* (209), 2012, with B. Destremau.

Elena Vidal-Coso Elena is a Post-doctoral Research Fellow at the Socio-Demography Group in the Department of Political and Social Sciences of the Pompeu Fabra University in Barcelona. She obtained her PhD in Demography from the Autonomous University of Barcelona in 2009 on the subject of 'Labour and Socio-demographic complementarity between immigrant and non-immigrant women in Spain'. From 2004 to 2010 she worked at the Centre for Demographic Studies (CED) as a researcher on several projects about female labour supply, on the dilemmas of reconciling family and work, and on the impact of international migration on the Spanish labour market. Her current research interests are the dynamics of labour supply and integration in the employment structure of female immigrants, and the intra-household specialization of immigrant families.

1 An introduction to a global and development perspective: a focus on gender, migration and transnationalism
*Laura Oso and Natalia Ribas-Mateos**

INTRODUCTION

This first chapter to the handbook encourages readers to conceptualize the introduction of a gender perspective on mobilities into a cartography of global chains and circuits. This is done in order to present a particular field on gender and migration studies, specifically in relation to the important works, concepts, debates and trends found in the different chapters and which we think should constitute a comprehensive overall work for many years to come. This introduction addresses the challenge of summarizing extensive areas of literature as well as describing the written work from which it is drawn, It provides an extensive bibliography, which also indicates further reading in the selected topics of interest.

Our point of departure is that this new phase in the study of global mobilities follows on from considering previous studies, first within the scope of gender and development, and second in terms of gender and migration analysis. More specifically, this introduction examines the connections between gender, migration, development and transnationalism in the context of globalization. The contributions in this volume address, one way or another, the terms of such connection between the different axes, which have somehow become parts of the book. Theoretically and operationally, such connections are strategic and capable of illuminating the issues at hand. They provide the elements that will enable us to explore the contents of the handbook, be they theoretical or empirical, by introducing a vast range of case studies, examples drawn from around the world. Each of the chapters presented here illustrates in different ways gender and mobilities in the processes of globalization.

Over the past two decades there has been growing academic and policy interest in gender and migration, resulting, as we shall see, in a very productive literature. Research has centred mainly on the analysis of the reproductive role of migrant women, as domestic servants, sex workers and caregivers within the process of globalization (Truong, 1996; Hochschild, 2000; Parreñas, 2001a; Ehrenreich and Hochschild 2002; among others).

Literature also expanded around the issue of the transnational family (Grasmuck and Pessar, 1991; Levitt and Sørensen, 2004; among others). Some more recent works have been compiled from a feminist policy approach, which consider the gendered nature of the meanings we give to migration (Palmary et al., 2010), or focus on the diversification and stratification of gendered migratory streams, as shown in the work edited by Piper (2008a), which analyses the extent to which the level of skill, legal status, country of origin and mode of entry constitute key axes of differentiation between male and female migrants. In addition, some other publications adopt a historical perspective, reflecting on the differences between men and women in terms of their participation in the labour market, the creation of networks and the processes involved in immigrant organization, belonging, diaspora and vulnerability (Schrover and Yeo, 2011). They also fall within the historical, legal, political and cultural framework of European Migration (Stalford et al., 2009). Nevertheless, published work to date has spent far less time considering gender and migration in the nexus of migration and development (Sørensen, 2005; Piper, 2008b; among others). Thus, one of the main contributions that this handbook makes to this body of literature is that it addresses the issue of gender and migration from a migration–development nexus. Furthermore, our main thesis covers the influence of global changes, which represents the work's principal analytical approach, namely the analysis of transnational migration flows from the perspective of the articulation of production and reproduction chains.

Thus, the thematic connection between gender, migration, development and transnationalism will be dealt with analytically, as follows: Part I: Framework of changes in gender, migration and transnationalism from the vantage points of globalization and development; Part II: New theoretical and methodological issues in the study of female migration and development; Part III: Gender, migration and development through different case studies; Part IV: A perspective on migration and transnationalism; Part V: Global production; and Part VI: Global care chains.

Together, these parts reflect a comprehensive discussion of the interplay between the various sections in this introduction. First we shall discuss the links between globalization and the various social processes that are fundamental to the migration–development nexus.

Second, this introduction will analyse the gender and migration axis, giving a chronological order to the presentation of the debates. We shall examine detailed accounts of the periods informing discussion on the uses of gender in migration studies to be able to understand the social thought and conceptualization of today's debates.

Third, we shall discuss how contemporary issues of development have been affected by the policy discourse regarding international migration – especially female migration – focusing on the complex intersection between development studies, migration studies and gender. Although there are multiple visions of development, we shall focus on the migration–development nexus. We shall consider – again by giving a chronology – the different development visions and interests of varying stakeholders used in the field of what we loosely term 'gender and development', and also include current discussions about gender and postcolonialism. We shall then examine such issues within the circuits of production and reproduction in the global era, ending with a brief conclusion.

THE GLOBAL CONTEXT AND ITS MOBILITIES

Globalization as a Point of Entry

Globalization provides the general context in which to understand international migration. Globalization forces backed up by neoliberal ideologies about market-oriented growth have been key in many aspects of what we nowadays call the 'global era'. However, such neoliberal ideology has to be considered from before the crisis in 2008, as well as by its nature, which is historically specific and unevenly developed (Brenner et al., 2010).

The persistent disparities and asymmetries are important when regarding the mobility of not only capital but also labour around the around the world. One of the strong impacts of globalization is the increasingly precarious conditions for workers worldwide, which has a huge effect on the conditions where contemporary mobilities take place.

Mapping an Articulated Geography

Nevertheless, the global shift is a complex process and even when we consider migration spaces, globalization should not be viewed, therefore, as an undifferentiated unity but rather as a 'geographically articulated patterning' of global capitalist activities and relations (Cox, 1997). Thus, when we refer to a 'geographically articulated patterning' we take into consideration the uneven geographical development that takes place on a number of scales.

The global-economic features such as hypermobility and time–space compression are not self-generative. They need to be produced and such a feat of production requires capital fixity (Harvey, 1982), vast concentrations of highly mobile material and less-mobile facilities and infrastructures. Thus, even if state and territory continue to play an important role, state territorial power is rearticulated and reterritorialized in relation to both sub- and suprastate scales (Brenner, 1999, p. 433) Here, the nation-state reproduces both old and new roles of administrative forms, including categories and subcategories of classifying mobilities and populations.

In this volume we are able to pin down such an articulated geography with reference to many different case studies, so the reader will be able to consider them across different scales and places. Such examples alert us to the existence of a whole battery of reading about globalization scales, as does Chapter 2 by Benería, Deere and Kabeer, which also makes available a full perspective on a regional-wide variation of case studies.

The National and the Global

Thus globalization is definitely challenging the state-centric model or the territorial focus of social sciences, thereby highlighting the importance of mobilities in contemporary societies and in social theory (Bauman, 1998; Held and McGrew, 2000; among others). In contrast to the ongoing attention reserved for a variety of classic perspectives on integration (which may be called 'assimilation' or 'adaptation', and refers to the idea of settlement), and the predominance of a unilocal, unilineal, undirectional and ethnocentric approach, the existence of various and multidirectional human mobilities typical of the global era – of varying durations and in different directions, even in opposing directions (hence the idea of circularity) – tends to be overlooked.

Much of social science has operated with the assumption of the nation-state as a container, representing a unitary spatio-temporality. However, authors such as Sassen (2000) try to shed light on current discussions regarding such supposed achieved territorial-time fixity as they argue that modern nation-states themselves never achieved spatio-temporal unity and the global restructurings of today threaten to erode the usefulness of this proposition for what is an expanding arena of sociological reality. This corresponds to most of Sassen's effort in her works when she tries to explain the dynamics of the national–global overlap and interaction.

Another problem added to the role of the nation-state is fully developed by Stolcke in Chapter 3. She unveils the political background, namely, the articulation of the nation-state in which transnationalism operates. In addition she shows how the financial and economic world crisis has brought to light within the European Union endless quarrels inspired by new and old fears about the loss of national sovereignty. The author uncovers the production of the discourse on immigrants as a threat to cultural integrity of the nation. The collective identity would then be constructed in terms of ethnicity, culture, heritage, tradition, memory and difference, with only the occasional reference to 'blood' and 'race'. Culturally different 'aliens' would be ratified through appeals to basic human instincts in terms of a pseudo-biological theory. Racism has usually provided a rationalization for class prerogatives by naturalizing the socio-economic inferiority of the underprivileged (to disarm the political) or claims of national supremacy (Blanckaert, 1988, quoted by Stolcke in Chapter 3).

Turning it through the contemporary debate we could then underline two main ideas brought to the fore by Stolcke. First, that modern racism constitutes an ideological sleight-of-hand for reconciling the irreconcilable – a liberal meritocratic ethos of equal opportunity for all in the marketplace and socio economic inequality – which, rather than being an anachronistic survival of past times during the era of slavery and/or European colonial expansion and the ascriptive ordering of society, is part and parcel of liberal capitalism. Second, the new global order, in which both old and new boundaries, far from being dissolved, are becoming more active and exclusive, poses formidable new questions for anthropology. We would even contend that it also poses formidable new questions for the study of globalization and development.

Introducing the Global Assembly Line

There are three prevailing components to delocalization: decentralization from nationally oriented bureaucratic regimes; devolution from the public to the private sector; and deterritorialization of formerly place-fixed production and institutions. Globalization is not simply the delocalization into placeless fluidity, but a reterritorialization into new configurations – whether they are multiscalar (where the urban and supranational gain prominence), public–private partnerships or new spatial forms of organization. Something new is being laid out, using the raw materials of a nationally oriented mode of accumulation and regulation.

The bigger question we wish to address here is how to relate our work to global commodity chains. We could relate it to different global chains, which in principle could range from finance, to kinship and care. A commodity[1] chain consists of a series of linkages stretching from raw-material production at one end through manufacture and assembly, to wholesale and retail distribution at the other, and generally encompasses important segments of a limited number of interdependent industries. The process of industrial transformation can be understood in terms of the relations between these chains. Restructuring and job loss in the garment industry has accompanied North–South trade liberalization in the search for a low-cost production site.

Consider this example. Flexible production has had a major impact on US garment workers and on the once-powerful unions. Wages have dropped and sweatshops are once again to be seen in US cities, often staffed by foreign, undocumented workers. There, workers slave long hours for piecerate wages (that is, payment by the piece instead of by the hour) without the basic protections of minimum wage, overtime, the prevention of industrial homework or child labour, or benefits of any kind (Bonacich, 2002, p. 123).

Another aspect of such flexibilization is the fact that the garment industry is more advanced than most in terms of outsourcing and offshore production, although it is also true that other sectors are gradually moving in a similar direction. Reactions against these practices are ongoing protests from anti-globalization movements. The anti-sweatshop campaign has been among the most visible and successful of efforts to forge a cross-border movement based on solidarity between First World consumers and workers in so-called developing countries.

This global stage, driven by the internationalization of production, finance, banking and services, coupled with cheap labour, takes full advantage of information technology and weakens the role of the state in decisions on where to locate production plants. In many parts of the world, this location has been a female-led industrialization in export processing zones, particularly in countries such as Bangladesh, Morocco, Mexico and Singapore. Nevertheless, these processes of industrial delocalization and the emergence of export zones were particularly intensified in certain regions of the world, namely Southeast Asia, Latin America and the Caribbean. It was what some authors have labelled as 'the global assembly line' (Fernández-Kelly, 2006).

However this is not completely new. During the 1980s and early 1990s, economic recession in northern countries had a major impact on southern nations – those of the Global South – specialized in export manufacturing industries, which led to a reduction in overall household income. In addition, structural adjustment programmes further worsened women's social situation, leading to a sharp rise in female migration (for example, Sassen, 1988).

Some authors have explained the participation of women in international migration as the result of the recomposition of capital on a worldwide scale. In particular, the impact of economic globalization on developing economies can be associated with an increase in their foreign debt (especially in light of the World Bank's and the International Monetary Fund's (IMF) structural adjustment programmes), the increase in unemployment rates and cuts in social spending, as well as the closure of companies that traditionally targeted local and domestic sectors due to the growth in export industries (Fernández-Kelly, 1983; Salzinger, 2003; Sassen, 2005, p. 523).

But such chains are much more complex, as we shall unveil in this introduction. In this respect we base our conceptualization on Sassen (2000), because she provides us with a framework in which to understand the profound transformations of the economic globalization processes (structural adjustment programmes, opening up to foreign capital and removal of state subsidies) which match the growing significance of female international migration as a way of activating household survival strategies – from domestic work to industrial cleaners, from searching for marriage partners to sex work – from many of those sectors where the global economy is present. Such sectors are utilizing the specific circuits that connect labour demand and supply. Through such circuits they are able to connect labour and capital from the Global North to investing in multiple ways in their own households of origin in the Global South.

Highlighting the Fordist Migration Model

We cannot possibly review all of the emerging migration patterns here. However, we do want to look more closely at a change in the migration process that impinges most directly upon the ways we understand contemporary international migration. Fordism, as described by Harvey, is not only a system of production, but also – we should bear in mind – a society defined by mass consumption, a new system of labour power reproduction, a new politics of labour control and management, a new aesthetic and psychology, a new kind of rationalized, modernist and populist democratic society (Harvey, 1990).

In the Fordist period, international migration was seen as peripheral, as the national industrial society was seen as the 'container' for all aspects of social being, and crossing borders was the exception and a deviation from the nation-state model (Castles, 2008). During that time, studies on migration and development, despite being strategic policies for many 'Third World countries' had only scant influence on social theory. In terms of the European experience during the industrial era, migratory movements from the South reached the factories of European cities (especially in France, Belgium, the UK and Germany), contributing to the expansion of the Fordist cycle. This migration cycle in Europe started as early as the First World War and acquired mass proportions after the Second World War, completing the cycle until the crisis in the 1970s and the obsolescence of Fordism in Europe's industrial regions. The state changed from being hospitable and charitable to being repressive, and was constructed by the restriction of borders (Ribas-Mateos, 2013b), converting integration into a residual symbolic measure.

Introducing Transnationalism as Opposition to the Fordist Migration Model

Globalization has been challenging the state-centric model or the territorial focus of social sciences, which finally stress the importance of mobilities in contemporary societies and in social theory (as mentioned above). Although transnationalism is not a completely new phenomenon, it did reach a particularly high degree of intensity on a global scale at the end of the twentieth century as a result of globalization, technological changes and decolonization processes. Transnationalism implies people building their lives around references to the various social worlds, imagined in a scope that goes beyond national borders, in which they spend considerable amounts of time. Peraldi (2001) believes that contemporary migrations cannot really be considered as a single unequivocal form of mobility, in the sense of an institutionally organized social destiny. While 'controlled migration' (using Sayad's terminology) characterizes the essential nature of labour migrations during the Fordist age, today they have changed radically. There are a number of reasons for these changes: on the one hand, there are those who consider the entire range of forms of movement, and on the other, those who look at the fluidity and types of involvement in the economy. In other words, according to Peraldi, if we consider the Malthusianism of the receptor states, we should then replace migratory movements with a typology of social forms of mobility.

Catarino and Morokvasic, in reference to previous works (Morokvasic, 1999, 2004), highlight in their chapter (ch. 11, this volume) the fact that migrants are more anxious to 'settle in mobility' than to settle in the receiving country. Mobility therefore becomes an alternative to migration; migrants attempt to remain mobile in order to guarantee the standard of living in their country of origin. As a result, mobility is seen as a resource and a dimension of migrants' social capital.

Pointing Out Sharp Asymmetries as Global Contradictions

In Chapter 2, Benería et al. bring to the fore certain aspects of globalization that are crucial in understanding the rapidly growing pace of labour migratory movements. They show first how globalization forces, backed up by neoliberal ideologies on market-oriented growth, have been crucial in many aspects of what is today termed the 'global era'. According to these authors, migration is also impacted by the global crisis that has been affecting many high-income countries since 2008, whose roots lie in the excesses of financial globalization and other neoliberal policies, which have generated high unemployment. So, they also show how the globalization impact results in a widening gap in inequalities between low- and high-income areas; the development of international networks (non-profit, country-based, international associations, commercial, family); and the intensification of interregional migrations: the 'care crisis'.

These authors have drawn attention to a clear contradiction: while globalization has increased the opportunities to which individuals can aspire in various countries, it has also created a context in which these opportunities are tinged with vulnerability and precariousness. Therefore we witness the growth of social inequalities within and across countries, as well as the persistence of abject poverty in many locations.

In short, increased circularity is to be considered one of the elements of global migration. The participation of women in international mobilities is another of its key features, covering new regions and migration poles (West Africa, Southern Europe, the Gulf, China), as well as emerging new countries of emigration–immigration and spaces of transit (Sub-Saharan Africa, Maghreb, Turkey, Mexico). Women now cover all the global parameters of migration: the structure of the global care chains and new transnational practices (related to remittances, subjective transnationalism and transnational identity) (Ribas-Mateos, 2013a).

THE GENDER–MIGRATION AXIS

In principle, women's growing participation in labour-based migratory flows is largely due to the globalization of production and worsening labour conditions in the Global South, as well as to the transfer of social reproduction fomented by the demand in developed countries for women willing to take on work classified on the bottom rungs of the labour market in terms of its social value (domestic service, personal care services and sex work). As a consequence, several authors in this handbook have chosen the context of globalization to provide a general framework in which to understand the conditions of foreign and ethnic minority women working in the international division of reproductive work.

As mentioned above, industrial delocalization processes have brought with them a fall in the need for foreign labour for the North's industrial activities, as production processes are increasingly being transferred to southern countries. The rapid growth of duty-free zones has brought with it an increase in female migratory flows in developing countries, particularly in Latin America, Asia and the Caribbean (Sassen, 1988). But this model was easily replicated in many areas of the world, such as in the Mediterranean (Ribas-Mateos, 2005).

In the North, the growing involvement of migrant women in paid work was mainly the result of an increase in the demand for labour in unskilled and poorly paid jobs in the services sector in migrant-receiving countries. Domestic service, catering, personal and sex work cannot be exported in the same way as industrial activity and therefore results in the recourse to foreign labour and the development of exclusively female migratory flows (Sassen, 1988). Immigrant women work in those jobs that are scorned by their autochthonous counterparts and carry out the work required for social reproduction in a commodified manner. We are therefore witnessing an international South/North transfer of reproductive work, a process that runs parallel to the transfer of productive activities on a global scale (Truong, 1996).

Some researchers refer to 'global chains of care' in order to explain the way in which, in a global context, women replace one another in those tasks traditionally associated with personal care and affection: the autochthonous woman is replaced by the immigrant woman, whose place in turn is filled by other women who take charge of her children in her country of origin (grandmothers, sister and so on) (Hochschild, 2000; Ehrenreich and Hochschild, 2002).

In turn, Sassen discusses the South–North female migratory flows to work in the informal economy within a framework that she refers to as the 'counter-geographies of globalization'. She considers that these circuits generate major economic resources that very often remain invisible (Sassen, 2003). Benería et al. (ch. 2, this volume) speak of the 'commodification of care work on a global scale'. They highlight the way in which changes in fertility rates and life expectancy, as well as the sharp rise in the female workforce, have contributed to the 'care crisis', leading to a demand for immigrant women to work in paid care work (paid domestic work, childcare and nursing). Such global commodification of care would then be a part of the globalization of the labour force.

From the perspective of the Global South countries, following the intensification of economic informalization trends, the neighbourhood and the household have re-emerged as strategic localizations of migrant and non-migrant economic activity, often operating in spatial and temporary organizations, and often of a circular nature. In this context, new questions emerge, such as how international migration alters gender patterns and how the formation of transnational households can empower women. All these issues have taken on an added complexity, with many migrants living their lives and planning their futures within the parameters of transnational circuits. It is within this matrix that we understand the complexities surrounding the various types of migration in our selected cases in the different chapters – as we shall show later – due to processes of internal, return and temporary migration. Furthermore, these are some of the issues that have fuelled the debate surrounding the gender–migration axis as we shall see next.

From 'Birds of Passage are also Women' to 'A Glass Half Full?'[2]

As social science literature has revealed, up until around three decades ago female migration was largely overlooked, with the focus of study centring mainly on male migratory flows. Based on previous works, the treatment of female migration can be classified into three major historical periods (Golub et al., 1997). If one wonders why we decide to review such historical periods, it is because they are determinant in understanding today's conceptualization debates.

The first period, would last up until the mid-1970s, and is characterized by the almost complete absence of studies on female migration. Scientific production has repeatedly shown that immigrant women have been largely overlooked because of the predominance of the patriarchal family model. This model sees women as dependent on men, the principal breadwinners and heads of the household (Morokvasic, 1984). Up until the late 1960s, the stereotyped image of women as being economically inactive prevails in the academic discourse of various fields of study, including economics, sociology and history (Borderías and Carrasco, 1994), thereby influencing classical migration theories.

In addition, traditional analytical approaches to the study of population movements, namely those focused on analysing demographic movements from the point of view of the rational decisions of the individual (the neoclassical perspective), and those based on the perspective of the macro-structural factors behind migration (the structural approach) – influenced by classic development paradigms – (modernization and dependency), have generally tended to overlook gender. Indeed, as Scott shows in her analysis of women's role in the theory of modernization, development has been conceptualized as being opposed to the traditional household. Modernity requires the appearance of rational, industrial beings that emigrate to urban environments. This is achieved through a market-based system, which enables competitive and enterprising men to triumph. While men dominate a city's public space, women are associated with nature and relegated to the private, rural and tribal space, which are considered impediments to development (Scott, 1995).

In connection with the socioeconomic constraints of migration the dependency theory could be highlighted, especially in the case of Latin America: a more exhaustive world systems theory focused on the way less-developed 'peripheral' regions were incorporated into a world economy controlled by 'core' capitalist nations. In such analyses, the presence of multinational corporations in less-developed economies accelerated rural change, leading to poverty, the displacement of workers, rapid urbanization and the growth of informal economies. Again in keeping with the findings of Scott, the approach to dependency focuses on public production as the key to development, based on the subordination of the periphery to the centre in the global capitalist economy, where men are perceived as the agents of development and revolutionaries, and women are confined to the private sphere of the home (ibid.).

As stated earlier, these two paradigms of development influenced classic migration theories. Consequently, they coincide in highlighting the figure of the migrant as a source of labour, a worker and an economic actor, while choosing to overlook the role played by women. These paradigms, in turn, relegated women to the private space of the home and their economic contribution to society is largely ignored.

The second period begins with the closure of European borders (1974–75) and the emergence of the figure of the visible female migrant, who, as yet, remains limited to a stereotyped image of the reunited woman, economically inactive who accompanies and is dependent on the male migrant. Following the implementation in Europe of restrictive immigration policies, women have dominated entry flows, although they continue to represent a minority in terms of the stock of immigrants (Zlotnik, 1995). There is a growing awareness that immigration is far from being a merely temporary phenomenon, and instead involves family groups settling in the receiving country, which naturally includes women. The figure of the female immigrant therefore makes its appearance, albeit restricted to the perspective of the reunited wife rather than as playing a relevant role as an economic and social actor (Morokvasic, 1984; Golub et al., 1997). Yet beyond the invisible nature of female migration, which has been amply brought to our attention in social sciences literature, how and why does the figure of the immigrant woman appear?

In the third period, from the 1980s onwards, the active role played by female migration begins to emerge. A series of publications are brought out, which draw our attention to the underestimation of the numbers of migrant women and are considered classics within their field, including Morokvasic's article, 'Birds of passage are also women' (1984). This growing awareness of the figure of the immigrant woman is partly attributable to a more open analytical approach within the field of social studies that allows the economic contribution of women to be brought to the fore. New theoretical approaches begin to appear that highlight the problems involved in domestic work, such as the new family economy (Borderías and Carrasco, 1994) or Delphy's belief that in addition to capitalist production, which produces goods under (formal) industrial methods, there is an alternative type of production, creating domestic service and goods within the (informal) family sphere, and which is responsible for the biological and social reproduction of the group (Delphy, 1970).

Consequently, female migration begins to emerge on a parallel with the increasingly visible phenomenon of the working woman, which in turn coincides with a new, more comprehensive approach to the analysis of migratory phenomena. Traditional approaches, which focused almost exclusively on the figure of the male immigrant worker, are left aside in favour of theoretical considerations that take other more sociological conditioning factors into account when considering population flows. As a result, new perspectives also arise that refer to macro- and micro-determining factors when describing and explaining migratory processes (Massey et al., 1987).

Within such a new perspective, the focus on networks as well the focus on household has been decisive. Thus, the new wider theoretical approach to the analysis of networks as a factor behind migratory phenomena now extends to the role of women in population flows. A further factor that favours the increased visibility of female immigration is that migratory phenomena are no longer considered to be the result of an individual decision, but rather as part of family and community strategies (Stark, 1984), together with the growing importance of considering the 'household' as a unit of analysis in the study of population flows (Boyd, 1989; Grasmuck and Pessar, 1991; Hondagneu-Sotelo, 1991; among a vast international literature on this topic). In short, there is a shift from the individual male to the household and the community as the driving forces behind geographical movements. This means that the woman becomes visible and is no longer seen merely as a dependant but also as an actor within migration processes.

Consequently, there is a growing awareness that migratory processes do not have the same effect and impact on men as on women and, by focusing on the male migrant only, we fail to fully understand the complexities involved in migration. So, what are the principal lines of research addressed in recent years in terms of gender and migration? There are two contributions to this book that enable us to move forward in a very complete review of such a rich bibliography (Hondagneu-Sotelo, ch. 10 and Catarino and Morokvasic, ch. 11).[3]

New Debates on Gender and Migration

In order to give some clues to the general debate we shall now consider a number of axes that we have chosen as being more relevant to the contemporary debates on gender and migration, by mainly describing the organization of references used by Hondagneu-Sotelo and Catarino and Morokvasic in this volume, and we could also add the work by Sørensen (2011).

Thus, we structure such a new debate on the following items: the controversy around the feminization of migration; the gender perspective; the axis of care work; sexualities and sex trafficking; the transnational household as a unit of study; the implications of a focus on agency; and, finally, the emerging debates on intersectionality.

The feminization of migration discourse: from migrant women to gender and migration studies

Since the 1990s, immigrant women have acquired a degree of visibility. As Oso and Catarino pointed out (2012), the discourse surrounding the feminization of migration is now an international phenomenon, as revealed in some international reports (United Nations, 2006). These authors tend to refer to the work of Zlotnik, to show that the percentage of women among international migrants grew a mere two percentage points between 1960 and 2000 (rising from 46.6 to 48.8 per cent). This increase 'is small compared to the high level of feminization that already existed in 1960' (Zlotnik, 2003, p.1). Nevertheless, Morrison et al. (2008) refer to more-recent data, according to which in 2005 women made up 49.6 per cent of the migrant population (Oso and Catarino, 2012).

Catarino et al. (2005), were the first to note the recurrent discourse regarding the feminization of migration as part of an academic ritual consisting of drawing attention to women's previous invisibility. A revision of such invisibility studies would highlight data that would show the relevance of female migration. Besides, as Oso and Garson state, discourse regarding the feminization of migration appears to have anticipated the statistical trend. Indeed, rather than a sharp rise in the number of women opting to migrate, they noted a 'feminization of migratory discourse' (Oso and Garson, 2005). These authors formulated their work in response to descriptions of the feminization of migration that did not necessarily correspond to empirical findings.

So, we could say that instead of emphasizing the feminization of migration discourse it might be more interesting to highlight the interest in including the gender perspective in the analysis of international migration. On this trend, Hondagneu-Sotelo (ch. 10) refers to the special issue of *International Migration Review*, published in 2006 and dedicated to gender and migration studies (Donato et al., 2006), to show how, from the 1990s onwards, the research focus shifts from the study of migrant women to the analysis of 'migration as a gendered process'. Below is an overview of the principal debates on gender and migration generated in the late twentieth and early twenty-first centuries.

Migration and care work

According to Hondagneu-Sotelo, one of the principal areas of debate considers the connection between women's migration, paid domestic work and family care. The key concepts addressed in literature include 'care work', 'global care chains', 'care deficits', 'transnational motherhood' and 'international social reproductive labour'. Reference to these works has already been made in the previous section on global context and mobilities. These issues make up much of the literature on gender and migration from the 1990s onwards (see Vidal-Coso and Miret-Garamundi (ch. 15). Setién and Acosta (ch. 18), Safuta and Degavre (ch. 19) and Casado i Aijón (ch. 20)). However, as Catarino and Morokvasic claim, there is another, less positive side to this line of research, namely the reproduction of stereotypes through the analysis of migrant women essentially in their reproductive role.

Sexualities and sex trafficking

The sexualities-based approach would include work on 'gay and queer identities, as well as heteronormativity and compulsory heterosexuality, employed both as a form of legal immigration exclusion as well as inclusion' (Hondagneu-Sotelo, ch. 10, p. 237). This author posits that such an approach is more developed in the United States than in Europe, although Catarino and Morokvasic (ch.11) show how in France:

> the emphasis has shifted from (unpaid) work to sexual/sexualized issues and from class *per se* to ethnicity . . . Indeed, feminist debates and research rather concentrate on different forms of sexuality and gender, thereby increasingly questioning the heterosexual norms of society. At the same time, research has demonstrated that questions about sexuality are racialized and racial issues sexualized. (Ch. 11, pp. 253, 254).

Both reviews in this handbook provided by Hondagneu-Sotelo and Catarino and Morokvasic reveal that the question of trafficking is also an emerging issue. They refer to several works in which discourse on trafficking moves beyond a criminalizing and victimizing approach (see for example, Guillemaut, 2006; Agustín, 2007).

Transnational households

During the 1990s burgeoning literature on migrants' transnational connections in the global era (Glick Schiller et al., 1992; Levitt et al., 2003; Vertovec, 2004) would provide a further angle on the subject of gender and migration. Within such literature, an interest in the transnational family emerges. The participation of women in migration gave rise to a particular formation of transnational families in many different intra-family processes which would affect gender roles and the children and adults left behind, family reunion processes, changes in care roles, the role of remittances and household allocation, and so on.

Parella (ch. 14) reviews the concept of the transnational family, quoting Herrera (2005a, p. 12), 'the transnational family should be understood as a locus of social and emotional support, but also as a field of conflictive power relations between its members'. That definition allows her to avoid approaching the family as a uniform entity or unified object of analysis, and to take into account the unequal power relations within it (gender relations, intergenerational relations), as well as the differentiated allocation of roles in processes of identity construction and in the reproduction of the welfare of its members.

Bledsoe and Sow (ch. 8) refer to a particular case of such transnational practices: the possibility that African families must try to protect their children in the West by sending them away underscores the need to probe beneath vague rationales of sending children back home to know their kin or to become familiar with the traditions of the homeland. They explain why West Africans living in Europe or North America, places often identified as the global centres of safety and opportunity for children, are then not there when they want to send their children back to live in Africa. Why might they send children to West Africa at a crucial moment in their educational trajectories, when the children should be preparing most intensively to succeed in the new home their parents have tried so hard to create for them? The materials these authors have found tell a remarkably consistent story of West African immigrant parents' despair at being denied adequate disciplinary means to protect their children from what they see as Western society's indulgent attitude towards children.

The agency-based approach
This transnational approach, in turn, leads to a recurrent question in gender and migration studies, namely the impact of migration on the status of migrant women. Does it transform gender relations? And what can be said of the process of empowerment?

One characteristic of scientific production in the last decade has been the impact of the agency-based approach, namely the role played by immigrant women as agents of empowerment. The aim is to try to shed the stereotyped image of a passive female immigrant who is dependent on the male migrant. Nevertheless, as already pointed out in this introduction there is a new tendency showing that despite the current focus on agency and empowerment-based discourse, studies continue to be centred on the reproductive sphere (domestic service, personal services and sex work). Indeed, only a few researchers have opted to look into the way women set up their own empowerment strategy within the framework of other economic areas of activity such as ethnic entrepreneurship or skilled labour (Catarino et al., 2005). In this area, mention must be made of the research into qualified migrant women by Erel and Kofman (2003) or early literature addressing the issue of ethnic entrepreneurship and gender (for example, Morokvasic, 1991; Anthias and Mehta, 2002; Apitzsch and Kontos, 2003).

Furthermore, certain academic and political circles would seem to have established a linear link between the supposed 'feminization' of migration, the role of women as agents in the migration processes, and empowerment. It is important to note that even though immigrant women participate in the economies of their country of origin and destination by sending large remittances and maintaining transnational households, this role as social and economic agents does not necessarily imply an increase in their status or empowerment (Oso, 2002). The same issue is also raised by Catarino and Morokvasic (ch. 11), focusing on France. They discuss the fact that in recent years, research in France has focused on women who migrate alone, who are considered autonomous, in contrast to women who form part of family migratory projects.

Intersectionality theory

The key concepts that are referred to in a number of contributions in this volume, such as care work, care deficits, transnational motherhood, production and reproduction work, are also connected with contemporary studies on intersectionality. Studies on black feminism (Crenshaw, 1989) led to a line of research that aims to focus on this approach.

Thus, Hondagneu-Sotelo (ch. 10) describes how the development of this literature has been made possible by theories of intersectionality. She shows the origins of the debate from the 1970s, when feminist research projects started to emphasize the ways in which institutions and social privileges are constructed in ways that favour men. Since then, most feminist-oriented scholars have dispensed with unitary concepts of 'men' and 'women'. Multiplicities of femininities and masculinities are recognized today as interconnected, relational and intertwined in relations of class, race-ethnicity, nation and sexualities.

Over the past four decades, studies of race, gender and class have criticized conceptualizations of identity as discrete or additive, and of oppression as consisting of types of discrimination and the effects of the burdens of disadvantage simplistically added together (Lurbe, 2011). Current scholars of inequality and discrimination have found the application of an intersectional approach appealing, to overcome the problem of reductionism, whereas social practice tends to be much more complex, comprising multilayered social relations, contested concepts of identity and multiple social roles. Thus, for Lurbe, cultural patterns of oppression are not only interrelated, creating a system that reflects intertwined, multiple forms of discrimination; they are also bound together and influenced by the intersectional systems of society, where any particular individual stands at the crossroads of multiple groups. Lurbe's reading of intersectionality emphasizes the identity categories and social positions that are found when multiple forms of subordination occur simultaneously, the 'intercategorical' approach adopts existing categories to investigate the multiple and conflicting dimensions of inequality among them. This relational version of intersectionality begins by identifying the processes, such as dichotomizing gender and racializing selected ethnicities, that interact to produce dynamic and complex patterns of inequality for everyone, not merely the most disadvantaged (Hancock, 2007, quoted by Lurbe, 2011). Struggles and conflicts, rather than groups, are the preferred focus of study for Lurbe because these are understood as both ubiquitous and informative. A context-dependent, relational intersectionality approach applied to specific fields of migration research on local integration and social exclusion, to which Lurbe's study on extremely marginalized minorities, particularly Roma, in France, seeks to solve one of the fundamental problems of migration research: how to reconcile structure and agency without promoting cultural essentialism.

In conclusion, during the last decade, the efforts of scientific production have been successful in shedding the cape of invisibility that has tended to shroud immigrant women and the secondary role to which history has traditionally relegated them. Growing awareness of the female migrant figure is due to a number of social science analyses that bring female workers to the fore, combined with the appearance of new approaches that focus on micro and macro factors when addressing migratory processes.

Together with the importance of the household, we have been guided in the past by the reassurance, through migration research, that the answer to many of our questions lay in household dynamics, especially when focusing on gender and migration and in relation to the formation of transnational families. However, research has mainly considered the role of migrant women in worldwide care chains, revealing, albeit to a lesser extent, their influence on production chains within the framework of globalization. The major global chain is hence of a reproductive nature and relates primarily to care.

The identification of such care chains shows us how gender divisions of labour are incorporated into uneven economic development processes. The connection between migrant care work, globalization and the privatization of social reproduction has been variously designated as the 'new domestic world order', the 'new international division of reproductive labour', or the 'transnational economy of domestic labour'. Nevertheless, some questions still remain less developed.

Several of such questions have already been highlighted by the 2004 World Survey on the Role of Women in Development: Women and International Migration (United Nations, 2005). How can migrant women best contribute to the development of their country of origin, particularly through mechanisms such as remittances, temporary and permanent return and the skills and financial resources of diaspora communities? How can women best benefit from economic, political and social development so that they can obtain employment opportunities, education, healthcare and other services in their home community without being forced to migrate? This brings us to the nexus between gender, migration and development, which we address below.

ADDING DEVELOPMENT AS A RESULT

First, we should consider the concept of development, although reviewing all the given definitions is not possible here. Even so, we do want to look more closely at how we can apply the concept in a way that results in connecting it to migration outcomes. Cortés (ch. 5) gives some hints on such a discussion when present in the different development visions and interests of different stakeholders that are conducted through their daily livelihood activities or institutional initiatives. These stakeholders would be government actors (government officials, regional and/or municipal), technicians of nongovernmental organizations (NGOs) working in migratory contexts, as well as the migrants themselves. The development stakeholders have different visions of development, power and influence in order to enforce them. In this regard, as we shall discuss below, the European conceptions of the link between migration and development are based on a modernizing vision of this relationship, which defines development exclusively within economic paradigms. These visions do not incorporate critical development reviews, nor do they include new proposals such as human development, or the progress already made on the topic of gender and development. We could even consider co-development, which for Cortés would be to generate patterns of governance on migration and would consist of values, norms and cultural representations on migration and 'suitable' ways for their management, facilitated by the relationship established between the state and civil society organizations. And, if referring to concrete projects, would be very varied: voluntary return, migrant associations and, especially, financial remittances from migrants, and so on.

Second, if we think again in terms of a chronological perspective, Benería's work presents an overview of the conceptual approaches that have been used in the field of what we loosely term 'gender and development' (Benería, 2011). During the 1970s there was great emphasis on the domestic labour debate and the significance of reproduction and women's unpaid work and criticism of the neoclassical model.

Beginning briefly with Ester Boserup's modernization approach and the different frameworks that sprang from the critique of her work, Benería goes on to consider the conceptual transformations that took place in the 1980s, particularly the significance of introducing a 'gender perspective' and the postmodern influences that followed throughout the 1990s. Her interest continued during work on building safety nets within the structural adjustments of the early 1990s. Feminist post-development thought would also be included. It was then the time to review the postcolonial condition, by tackling gender analysis in a time of growing inequalities. Finally, her chronology explores present conceptual currents underpinning the multiple aspects of work being carried out, including: neoliberalism, the human development/capabilities approach, the social reproduction framework and human rights approaches.

Third, we should consider from which point of view we talk about women and development. Current discussions about gender and postcolonialism have resurrected concern about what type of feminism we refer to. Jabardo (2011) introduces the perspective of black feminism into African female migratory flow analysis, by showing how the categories used to construct gender relations in Western feminism have concealed the practices and social agendas of female migrants of African origin. In this sense, she places the theoretical nexus in both gender–development–migration and multiculturalism and gender. In a return to the concept of social agency posited by Saba Mahmood, understood as the capacity for action created and recreated by certain relations of subordination, she reinterprets the practices of African female migrants from the conceptualization of the feminine as a new sphere, which although removed from the public arena, extends beyond the private one. For that reason she shows how in a number of theoretical contributions the concept central to feminist theory is problematized in application to the life of black women: 'family, patriarchy, reproduction' (Carby, 1982 quoted by Jabardo, 2011). It is around these three concepts that 'black British Feminism' articulates the criticism on the adoption of 'inclusive' arguments of socialist feminism (Parmar, 1982; Amos and Parmar, 1984; Bhavnani and Coulson; 1986; Knowles and Mercer, 1992; all cited in Jabardo, 2011).[4]

Fourth, we should see such issues under the context of migration and development literature. Prior to the 1990s, gender was relatively overlooked in studies of the links between migration and development; indeed, the book published by Chant in 1992 (*Gender and Migration in Developing Countries*) was a pioneer in this field. The start of the twenty-first century has seen a growing body of literature on the topic of gender, migration and development (see, for example, Salih, 2001; Elhariri, 2004; Escrivá and Ribas-Mateos, 2004; Monquid, 2004; Zapata and Saurez, 2004; Herrera, 2005b; Ramírez et al., 2005; Semyonov and Gorodzeisky, 2005; Sørensen, 2005; Amuedo-Dorantes and Pozo 2006; Gainza, 2006; King et al., 2006; Kunz, 2008; Pauli, 2008; Kunz, 2008; Piper, 2008b; Ribas-Mateos and Basa, 2013), including INSTRAW publications that take an in-depth look at gendered patterns in the sending, reception, use and management of remittances (for example, INSTRAW, 2006, 2007, 2008, 2010), and which highlight how remittances may act as a means for the transformation of relations between men and women in a developing context. The evolution of these gender-focused studies is linked to the development of a more open analytical approach to the debate addressing the migration–development nexus. Therefore, we require further elaboration of the development and migration relation to bring us up to date with the topic at hand. As indicated by de Haas (2010), over the last five decades, analysis of the migration–development nexus has shifted considerably, from the debates of the 'migration optimists' which lasted up until the early 1970s, to those of 'migration pessimists' (until the 1990s). These outlooks in turn form part of the legacy of the two great paradigms of the social sciences (functionalist versus structuralist), and also of the theories of development (balanced growth versus asymmetric development paradigms). Recent years have seen a return to an optimistic vision (ibid., pp. 229–30).

During the 1980s and 1990s empirical research revealed the heterogeneous and non-deterministic nature of the impact of migration on development. This falls within the emergence of more pluralist and hybrid approaches to social theory that attempt to integrate the impact of structure and agency in their analyses. Consequently, the New Economics of Labour Migration (NELM), the livelihood approaches, as well as sociological and anthropological research on migrant transnationalism 'provide a more nuanced perspective on reciprocal migration and development interactions, which integrates structure and agency perspectives, and gives sufficient analytical room for explaining the heterogeneous relationship between migration and wider development processes' (ibid., p. 242). According to de Haas, the NELM sees migration as risk-sharing behaviour undertaken by families and households, whereby households diversify their resources, such as labour, in order to minimize income risks. Then, the livelihood approaches consider migration as a strategy that employs households 'to diversify, secure and potentially, durably improve, their livelihoods'. In turn, the transnational perspective enables us to understand 'migrant engagement with origin countries is not conditional on their return, but can be maintained through remitting money and ideas, telecommunications, holiday visits and pendular migration patterns' (ibid., p. 247).

As a result, households and transnational communities (or diasporas) are becoming increasingly important units of analysis, in their capacity as social actors of development. This has also broadened the gender approach when analysing the migration–development nexus. On the other hand, international institutions – through specific programmes – have made NGOs and households themselves the key actors of such a desired social development.

De Haas and Fokkema (ch. 9) develop the framework of transnational return and pendulum migration strategies. The case study is that of Moroccan migrants from the Todgha valley, by examining intra-household power inequalities, tensions and conflicts of interest in migration decision making and the consequences of migration strategies for intra-household power relations. These authors conclude that although this migration is part of a household-livelihood strategy of improvements in standards of living, not all members of the household are on an equal footing when it comes to the material and non-material benefits of this strategy. Far from being a consensus-based decision, migration instead reflects intra-households' inequalities along lines not only of gender but also of generation.

Taking the European context as their reference, Bachmeier, Lessard-Phillips and Fokkema's[5] results (ch. 12) show how, in the first generation, transnationalism is the exception rather than the rule, as most second-generation adults are oriented overwhelmingly towards life in their country of origin. Indeed, transnational engagement is complementary to host-country economic integration among members of the second generation. Integration and transnationalism are also gendered processes as the second generation also seem to show, but different. They reveal that second-generation women are relatively more integrated ethno-culturally and economically than their adult male counterparts. Therefore that makes important differences to their transnational behaviour on the development of the countries of origin: remittances, transnational practices and so on. Furthermore, they also suggest that the more economically integrated second-generation women are less likely to sustain origin country attachments while more economically integrated men are more likely to sustain meaningful attachments. So they conclude by pointing out that it is possible that development strategies focused on second-generation migrants may have little impact on gender-relations regimes in origin countries.

Following the same topic of generations in Europe, Christou (ch. 13) brings us the case of the Greek–Danish second generation by using ethnographic and life history data with a gendered and affective approach. She examines women's portrayals of their fluid sense of self and blurred sense of place in negotiating their emotions and their impact on their diasporic lives. She considers the way in which intimate attachments, desires and emotionalities shape mobility experiences, addressing issues of cultural marginality and the emotionally embodied context of belonging. The author reveals how gendered identities are appropriated within gendered (power) diasporic relations and how cultural processes take place in diasporic settings. Ultimately she analyses women's sense of self and identity, considering that the journey of counter return to the ancestral homeland is still an expectation for a future life. In her conclusion she notes:

> As the participants are still shuffling the fragments of memory of an ancestral past Greek life while coping with the present life of Danish/Greek context, the ultimate expectation is the attainment of equilibrium between the 'cultural stuff' of Danishness and of Greekness that gets in the way of finally accepting the self, neither coherent, nor split but in the making. After all, isn't this the pathway of adulthood as the life course progresses and stages follow one after the other, don't we all yearn to 'settle' somewhere and somehow? (Christou, ch. 13, pp. 307–8)

International Institutions and Stakeholders

Another approach to understanding the migration–development nexus can be found in the new roles of international institutions. Castles (2008) cites the example of the British government suggesting that the UN Refugee Convention of 1951 was no longer appropriate because, in a situation of enhanced global migration flows, it was creating the conditions for the misuse of the asylum system by economic migrants. To save the Convention, then UN Refugee Commissioner, Rudd Lubbers, suggested 'Convention Plus': a set of measures to safeguard asylum while also addressing the issue of 'mixed flows' and the causes of forced migration. Similar objectives were to be found in the French approach adopted of *co-développement*, which would afterwards spread throughout Southern Europe, by seeking to link development measures for African and Latin American countries to measures designed to encourage return or managing remittances as shown in Cortés (ch. 5).

This line of analysis is also adopted by Chant (ch. 4). In her opinion, gendered migration and mobility receives scant attention in the *World Development Report 2012*. The author notes that this publication makes a passing reference to the topic of 'migration and social norms', highlighting that migration can broaden women's social networks and also reduce preference for sons (in certain countries such as China). More generally, migration can also lessen gendered constraints; however, it may also strengthen social conservatism. The economic crisis in countries such as Georgia has brought about the migration of women who send higher remittances than their male counterparts. The first World Development Report devoted to gender largely overlooks the topic of gender and migration, a notable omission that is highlighted by this author who questions whether the 'WDR 2012 is likely to aid or abet the struggle to achieve gender justice in development' (Chant, ch. 4, p. 97). She also draws attention to the fact that while 'huge strides' have been achieved for gender and development (GAD) since the United Nations (UN) Decade for Women, the encroaching dominance of the World Bank's 'smart economics' rationale for 'investing in women', has led primarily to 'building women's capacities in the interests of development than with promoting women's rights for their own sake' (ibid., ch. 4, p. 97).

Cortés (ch. 5) highlights the fact that the Spanish cooperation policy for development has adopted the Women in Development approach (WID), which excludes the analysis of gender and power relations and their economic, social, cultural and political impact in order to comply with the rights of women focusing on positive action measures as a function or merely formal equality, without questioning the structures that cause inequality. This policy, through remittances, has put migration on the 'development agenda' within the framework of co-development projects. The creation of these projects is justified by a discourse that claims that migration has led to the dismantling of families in the country of origin, and also the misuse of remittances spent on non-productive activities. As a result, migrant families and women are instrumentalized with the aim of implementing initiatives designed to slow down migration. Development projects attempt to redirect remittances to productive activities in order to prevent international migration and encourage return, in such a way that 'women would become a means of contributing to the reduction in migration, instead of the project activities being aimed at strengthening the rights, projects and needs of these migrant women' (ibid., p. 140). Her case study on the development visions of staff members from NGOs in Ecuador and Spain reveals the tensions between development discourses and the reinforcement of class, gender, generation and ethnic hierarchies, not only in the societies of origin but also in host societies.

The chapters by Chant and Cortés show how development policies – either from a gender and development approach (smart economies), or the migration–development nexus (through co-development projects) – have largely instrumentalized women, yet have failed to take into consideration the aim of improving women's rights to any effective degree.

In short, in recent years, a more pluralistic approach to the migration–development nexus revealing the articulation between structure and agency has allowed for the development of the issue of gender in studies addressing the issue of migration and development. However, such studies have generally limited their scope to the descriptive differences in remittances sent by men and women, such as their use and management, analysing the transformation of roles and the impact of remittances on gender relations. Considerably less attention has been paid to the analytical framework on the nexus between migration, gender and development from the perspective of the articulation between productive and reproductive strategies, within the framework of global capitalism. This is precisely one of the main objectives of this book and one that is developed in the next section.

IDENTIFYING KEY CHAINS FOR THE GMD (GENDER, MIGRATION AND DEVELOPMENT) NEXUS

Our crucial issue has been to address the core debates surrounding topics of gender, migration, transnationalism and development, articulating analyses of global production and reproduction chains (and in particular, so-called 'global care chains') with new models developed around the emerging trends played out by women in contemporary mobility flows. The scope of the book is ambitious; it presents evidence of the importance of extended geographical chains that allow us to tackle gender in global migration processes. Such extended geographical chains encompass North Africa (Northern and Southern Morocco), West Africa, Asia (China), Latin America (Bolivia, Chile, Ecuador), Northern and Southern Europe (Belgium, the UK, France, Germany, Austria, the Netherlands, Switzerland, Sweden, Denmark, Greece, Spain), and Eastern Europe (Poland).

Classic Production Chains

Production chains relate principally to consumer commodities, such as clothing, footwear, toys and electronic appliances for the international market. Such manufacturing industries, especially in China, have created a continuous demand for labour, including many young peasant women. Nevertheless, similar processes have been developed in many other areas of the Global South. In such chains, smaller manufacturers may also decide to subcontract to other manufacturers or homeworkers. These forms of industrial development have been the basis of advocacy strategies to develop educational programmes around workers' rights in industry. As discussed earlier by Sassen (2003), *inter alia*, migrant women have become crucial agents in 'global survival circuits'.

In relation to labour production, Vidal-Coso and Miret-Gamundi (ch. 15) highlight just such a process. By using Spanish Labour Force data from the recent period of economic growth, 1999–2008, they study the dynamics of labour supply and integration in the employment structure of female immigrants from developing countries. The existence of labour complementarities by birthplace explains why while young Spanish women are mainly employed in skilled occupations, immigrant women, regardless of their human capital, are overrepresented in more unskilled, feminized, labour positions. The second hypothesis they give is the existence of a process of socio-demographic substitution in domestic occupations: from mature and less-skilled native women to younger and more-skilled immigrant women. Finally, the authors hypothesize that the initial demand for domestic help is not sufficient to explain the acceleration of female immigrant flows during recent years in Spain. It is the arrival of a low-cost and available migrant labour force that has caused an additional effect, generalizing the hiring of domestic workers within the middle classes and multiplying the demand for this type of labour. On the supply side, economic trends such as growing inequalities between high- and low-income countries and insecurity, vulnerability and instability due to economic crises, together with gender-related factors such as abuse, family conflict and discrimination have led to an increase in the numbers of women who migrate in order to obtain paid work.

Production Chains and Remittances

We also consider an overview of the importance of remittances as a new global trend. The link between transnational migration, remittances and the processes of change and development in the places of origin and transit for migration is a relatively new issue on the political and research agenda in many parts of the world. As already mentioned, remittances are a key factor in the survival of household, community and country in a number of developing countries and exporting workers is one means by which governments cope with unemployment and foreign debt.

Literature points to a widely held belief that women send a larger percentage of their income to their household of origin. Indeed, the stream of remittances sent by women is both more constant and continued over time, and as they are also the principal recipients of remittances (Gregorio Gil, 1998; INSTRAW, 2006, 2007), families may even actively encourage women to migrate, as they are more responsible than men in sending money back to their country of origin (Tacoli, 1999; Parreñas, 2001a and b; Ribas-Mateos, 2004; Ramírez et al., 2005). On the other hand, we must note that a study carried out into remittance trends among Filipino men and women revealed that men send higher amounts of money, as their incomes are higher (Semyonov and Gorodzeisky, 2005).

The figure of women as the recipients of remittances sent by male migrants has also been the object of study. Pribilsky's research highlights the way that Ecuadorian women achieve a position of greater authority thanks to the control they exert over their husbands' remittances (Pribilsky, 2004). However, very few studies have actually managed to quantify the sending of remittances from a gendered perspective. This is the main aim of the work carried out by Campoy-Muñoz, Salazar-Ordóñez and García-Alonso (ch. 17), and which considers one of the principal corridors from Latin America, between Ecuador and Spain. Using a Bayesian framework, the chapter describes the cause–effect relationships among the key factors that determine remittance flows. In the absence of robust data, Monte-Carlo simulations and 'fuzzy logic' confirm that Ecuadorian migrant women who reside in Spain display a greater propensity to send remittances in comparison with their male counterparts. During the 2000–10 period, Ecuadorian men's propensity to send money varied from 10 per cent to 15 per cent, while women's propensity to remit rose from 20 per cent to 30 per cent at the end of the period, results that indicate the relevant contribution of Ecuadorian females in supporting their families back home even though they have been severely affected by the economic crisis.

Similar attention is also focused on this corridor in Mata-Codesal (ch. 16), who opens the black box of households to explore the negotiations, tensions, continuities and changes triggered by remittances. She sheds light on the family dynamics of remittance sending and receiving practices in two contrasting rural settings in Southern Highland Ecuador (Xarbán and Pindo). She operationalizes the concept of 'remittance dyads', which are contrary to traditional approaches (that focus either on remittance senders or receivers), and considers the relationship between remittance sender(s) and receiver(s). The work takes into account the gender of the receivers and the gendered effects of material remittances, as well as the power, emotional and symbolic negotiations taking place between remittance senders and receivers, considering gender as a key variable of negotiations. She also differentiates between two types of remittances: 'emic remittances' and savings. The former consists of small amounts of money sent periodically to pay for food, utilities and cover the expenses for the basic physical reproduction of the household members (including children's education and small medical expenses). She also shows how these remittances have dramatically increased well-being among residents. Such remittances comprise to any money transfer not intended to cover the daily expenses of the receiving household. The chapter concludes with an explanation of how the effects of remittances are gendered.

Reproduction Chains and Care

The second major chain is of a reproductive nature and relates primarily to care. Recent and contemporary studies, such as the works of Truong (1996) in the 1990s on the internationalization of reproduction, reveal how care is increasingly set up in complex diasporic and interfamily settings (as also shown by Sørensen, 2011), and that the consideration of professional women and their interaction between the productive and reproductive spheres is a key element in explaining transnational mobility patterns (as also shown by Cieslik, ch. 21).

Verschuur's (ch. 6) theoretical contribution offers us a critical review of the concept of social reproduction and, particularly, that of care in the global context. Feminist studies have conceptualized those activities and relations that are indispensable for social reproduction, as well as the role of women migrant workers in the new global economy, articulated with the domestic economy. Women's work is connected to processes of globalization and considerable research has been conducted into women and work and into the shifting divisions of productive and reproductive labour globally, particularly in development studies. She opens up the discussion on the opposition between market/non-market production (often associated with male/female), which shows that it is not the nature of production that makes the difference, but the problem of the appropriation of the work – paid or unpaid – of individuals. She considers that when commodities are produced outside the family, the work to produce them is paid. When commodities are produced in the framework of domestic-type relations and exchanged on the market, the work is generally not remunerated or not adequately remunerated.

Verschuur's primary interest is testing the theoretical implications of the notion of care. For her, care consists of activities such as physical care and attention to close persons, family members, children and the elderly. It also includes caring for non-dependent persons, which is not always taken into account in studies. Care includes unpaid tasks such as preparing meals, cleaning, washing clothes, shopping and so on. In countries with limited infrastructure, care work may also include fetching water and collecting wood, all of which form part of social reproduction. Care can be paid or unpaid.

For Verschuur the concept of care, associated with the reflections on migration, has also shown the links between the domestic and the global economy. However, the concepts of social reproduction and care cannot be merged. While the concept of care has widened the focus of analysis of social reproduction, she sheds light on some important limitations in the context of gender, development and migration studies. These are especially relevant when taking into account both the increase of social and gender inequalities, and the subjective dimensions, emotion or intimacy. The concept of care has been useful in illuminating them but they are not fully acknowledged or taken into consideration in the debates on social reproduction. Furthermore, care, be it conceptualized as ethics of care, mainly perceived as a relational activity, or in the frame of research on social policies, is associated with reflections on migration, as a growing part of care work is commoditized and undertaken by migrant women from different classes or races.

Logically, problematization is even harder when we consider the concept of the care chain. The identification of care chains shows us how gender divisions of labour are incorporated into uneven economic development processes. The connection between migrant care work, globalization and the privatization of social reproduction has been variously designated the 'new domestic world order', the 'new international division of reproductive labour', or the 'transnational economy of domestic labour'. On the demand side, the participation of women in migration is fuelled by the increase in women's labour force participation, falling fertility rates, increasing life expectancy, changes in family structure, shortages of public care and the increasing commodification of care in the North.

Migration not only has implications for policies designed to reconcile paid employment and care responsibilities in both host and home countries, but it also has sharp contradictory impacts. As already indicated, the employment of migrant women to perform care work in the receiving countries of the North is an individual and privatized solution to the broader problem of combining paid work with unpaid care work. Since this solution is only an option for families who can afford it, lower-income families are left in a difficult position. In fact, as Benería (2008, p.10) points out, 'the employment of migrant women from the South might contribute to a vicious circle in the host country, in which private solutions delay collective efforts to search for appropriate public policies'. As it is mostly women who move in to assume the family roles of migrant females, there is a growing need for reconciliation policies in the South. While women's decisions to migrate can increase their financial autonomy and enable them to contribute to their household through remittances, their absorption into the care markets of the North reinforces the gendered nature of care. Thus, not only do global care chains illustrate the ways in which unequal resources are distributed globally, they also reveal the gendered nature of this inequality.

Access to citizenship by immigrant women employed in care work is another issued addressed in this book. Setién and Acosta[6] (ch. 18) explore the rights and obligations involved in working in the care sector, with a special focus on care provided by immigrant women. The assessment and perception of how rights are achieved and exercised in the social relationship of care provide evidence of the denial of rights under such conditions, as found in other studies. This results in the exercise of limited citizenship in the case of women immigrant carers as well as dependants, who find themselves in the most precarious of situations.

Safuta and Degavre (ch. 19) also consider the problems of domestic work through the study of undocumented migrant women, albeit from a different perspective, namely that of the use of reciprocity and redistribution. Their chapter focuses on the informal home-based provision of paid care for the elderly by migrant women in Poland and in Belgium. It maps the combination of socioeconomic principles presiding over this type of care provision and identifies the resources that each of these principles (as well as their combination) offers migrant care providers.

Safuta and Degavre's work throws light on how, in contemporary market societies, men and women are expected to be 'commodified' – to survive on resources stemming primarily from what Karl Polanyi (1944) called 'market exchange'. Redistribution (the welfare state) and reciprocity (social links and obligations) are said only to supplement or temporarily replace market resources when individuals are unable to take part in market exchange. Because they do not have access to the safety net offered to citizens and legal residents by redistribution, reciprocity is of utmost importance for undocumented migrants. In this chapter the authors thus examined the usages of Polanyian reciprocity by undocumented migrants, focusing on those who are or have in the past been employed in domestic services.

Based on Degavre and Nyssens's (2008, 2009) pioneering application of Polanyi's transactional modes (reciprocity, redistribution, the market and householding) to the analysis of elder care provision, Chapter 19 shows the ways in which migrant women (can) make the most of each principle when creating their migration and empowerment strategies. The resources offered by the socioeconomic principles under consideration can be both of a monetary or non-monetary nature. Monetary resources are mainly wages (stemming from the market or, in the case of cash-for-care allowances, from redistribution), but literature cites other monetary means, such as the case of employers financing the education or holidays of the migrant care worker's child. Non-monetary resources available to migrant care providers can stem from the market (such as the room and board in live-in provision) or reciprocity (for example, when employers help their undocumented migrant employee to obtain a stay permit). Through in-depth interviews with migrant providers and elderly receivers of informal home-based care, the chapter contributes to the scholarly debate on the effects of employment in predominantly 'migrant' sectors. In particular, it aims to test empirically the 'paradoxical effects of care' concept developed by Degavre and Langwiesner (2011, p. 3), who posit that a job in the care sector can simultaneously contribute to the worker's emancipation but can also be a socioeconomic trap.

Furthermore, care work for migrant women has also brought with it new forms of mobility through transnational family networks, as in the case of the population studied by Casado i Aijón (ch. 20). This author analyses the temporary migrations of Riffian women between Nador (located in the Rif, Northern Morocco), Catalonia and Europe. As a result of the intensification of contemporary migrations carried out by this population during the second half of the twentieth century, today we can draw a map whereby extended families are found practically throughout Europe – in Catalonia, Belgium, Germany, the Netherlands, France – and also in Morocco. It is in such a context that we witness heterogenic migration processes in which we can highlight a specific type of migration, namely that the maintenance of the female role of employment of migrant women from the South might contribute to a vicious circle in a Riffian family, and the usage of the transnational network that the settlement of diverse domestic units of the extended family has configured. The specificity of those migrations highlights three different characteristics, differentiating them from other migration projects from the Rif: they have a temporal delimitation; they are clearly feminine – integrated by women who travel, very often alone; and the objectives of these temporary migrations are assistance, support and care in cases of sickness of family members, but especially during and after pregnancy of any family members in general, but particularly sisters. The transnational nature of extended families also has clear consequences, involving the perception of tasks attributed to women and the maintenance of family principles of family role organization and status according to specific notions of maternity, feminine solidarity and family functions.

Towards an Articulationist Approach

Beyond a focused approach on care chains, this introduction and the whole book aim to highlight the relevance of analysing the interaction between the productive and reproductive spheres.[7] And it is precisely this articulation to which we wish to draw attention through the remaining contributions to this book.

The need to articulate the analysis focused on the GMD nexus, from the perspective of production chains and remittances in relation to care and reproduction chains, is revealed through some of the empirical studies presented in this book, including the chapters by Sáiz López (ch. 7), Parella (ch. 14) and Cieslik (ch. 21).These chapters will provide three different European realities, that of the Chinese and Bolivian communities in Spain and that of Polish migrants in the UK.

Sáiz López (ch. 7) gives an Asian perspective, more precisely, a Chinese one, based on migrants originating from Qingtian, Wenzhou (Zhejiang province) and Changle (Fujian province) and living in Spain, in a 'family migration' pattern. The Chinese diaspora is analysed from two angles: on the one hand, the transnational practices of the family business, differentiated between men and women; and on the other, the economic, social and symbolic dimensions of monetary transactions between origin and destination. Such an analysis helps us to understand the value and significance of gender relations as well as how they affect families and developing communities. It is interesting how Sáiz López is able to link through a very specific case study the articulation of both the production and the reproduction cases. She sheds light on the combination of the economic insertion in Europe, as a model of upward social mobility (with a rural family-based culture) with a social system where behaviour, norms, ideals, attitudes and values are linked by kinship and marriage. Furthermore, in such a model, both men and women participate in the securing of success and, by extension, in migration. Familism also explains the involvement of women throughout the family business cycle, from the accumulation of capital and the business consolidation phase, to business expansion.

Parella (ch. 14) covers the experiences of Bolivian migrants in Spain from a methodological approach based on a transnational perspective, which involves the study of the arrangements that diasporic families generate in terms of productive links (remittances), provision of care (caring work) and kin-keeping support (kin work). The chapter begins with a theoretical discussion of the concept of the 'transnational family', aimed at identifying the dimensions that are most relevant for the analysis of the geographical separation of families from a gender perspective.

However, beyond family economic transfers, Parella underlines the other types of existing links, grounded in the overlapping of the productive and reproductive spheres (management of affect and care, also known as caring work) and kin work towards the maintenance of kinship bonds within the family group. Furthermore, in the case of Bolivia, the influence of gender should be framed in the context of the recent feminized migratory patterns from Bolivia to Spain (and Europe), which have substantially altered the canons of Bolivian society's 'migratory culture', characterized by its masculinization, its circularity and its intra-regional character. In general terms, Parella overviews the impact of migration in the development of transnational links (remittances, trips to Bolivia), accompanied by the migrants' desire to return. However, there are considerable differences between men and women. For the latter, according to her results, migration is motivated more by family welfare than by individual advancement, which results in a greater capacity for saving and the sending of remittances, which are used mainly for family consumption and children's education.

Decisions concerning childrearing also influence the transnational mobility of skilled women, as shown by Cieslik (ch. 21). On the basis of research into skilled Polish migrants in the United Kingdom, the chapter considers if and how family planning decisions influence international migration trajectories. The 'if' part of the question highlights women's expectations regarding their future mobility and how such expectations are modified by their plans to have children. The 'how' considers the migrants' emotional ties to places, their beliefs about the right places for raising children and the role of family as a support system in childrearing. Research findings suggest that an important factor influencing the mobility of skilled migrant women lies in the perceived advantages and disadvantages of having children in Poland and the UK. A primary consideration pulling them back to Poland is the availability of childcare help from parents and grandparents. The UK, on the other hand, is an attractive location because of the child-friendly provisions offered by most employers. Emotional attachment to home and family tends to tip the scales towards returning to Poland. The free movement of people in the EU market is directly linked to reproductive choices made by skilled migrant women, frequently on the basis of emotional rather than 'rational' calculations. As can be seen, this chapter also reveals the gap in the social sciences literature concerning professional migrant women and the interaction between the productive and reproductive spheres.

CONCLUSION: LINKING PRODUCTION AND REPRODUCTION CHAINS IN CONTEMPORARY MOBILITY

This introduction has proposed a means of linking production and reproduction chains in contemporary gender mobility, by considering its extended connection with development. Our starting point was provided by the framework of globalization. Authors such as Mittelman (2000) draw our attention to the contradictory trends of globalization, revealing how cross-border flows of undocumented workers and instant telecommunications are positioned outside the effective control of state regulatory bodies. In keeping with this perspective, globalization also represents a dialectical set of continuities and discontinuities, an intensification of previously established models, as well as new features of a system that is lacking in effective regulatory measures.

Such a global context has allowed us to specify the processes that constitute the link between the different types of global changes through a particular type of conceptualization that brings to the fore how women's strategic migration projects have emerged in the play of global chains. Conceiving of globalization along these lines confronts theory and research with fresh challenges related to transnational migration.

It is in this global context that we have located the persistent disparities and asymmetries regarding the mobility not only of capital but also of labour around the world. Some of the topics covered in Part I – the global context and its mobilities – were the notion of the global assembly line and the change from the Fordist migration model to transnationalism. We then understood the mobility of people as a fundamental resource of mobility chains when considering it in different scales and places provided by a number of case studies in this handbook.

Second, we focused on gender and the migration axis. Meanwhile in migration studies, traditional approaches, which almost exclusively emphasize the figure of the male immigrant worker (the *homo economicus* interpretation), have given way to contemporary ones that focus on more sociological conditioning factors when considering population flows. As a result, new perspectives arise that refer to macro- and micro-determining factors when describing and explaining migratory processes. We have considered all such issues of the new debates: migration and care work, sexualities and sex trafficking, the transnational approach, the agency-based approach and the intersectionality theory related to migrant women status. This contemporary scope has led us to introduce a more combined approach, which we think we can solve through linking production and reproduction chains.

An introduction to a global and development perspective 35

Third, we covered development as a result – Part II – of the perspective on policy discourse regarding international migration – especially female migration – focusing on the complex intersection between development studies, migration studies and gender. Starting from a critical conceptualization of gender as well as gender and migration, we have seen – with our contributors' help – that the cases can be heterogeneous, even by using examples from the same country and by acknowledging that the impact of migration on development is far from being a deterministic model. This again has driven us to reflect on a more combined approach of structure and agency, which we think we can solve through linking production and reproduction chains.

Lastly, we have tried to deconstruct the key chains for the GMD nexus, by articulating analyses of global production and reproduction chains (and in particular, so-called 'global care chains') with new models developed around the emerging trends played out by women in contemporary mobility flows. By examining them we have revealed an articulation based on the complex interaction of productive and reproductive systems.

NOTES

* This publication was made possible by the generous support of the research projects of the Ministerio de Economía y Competitividad: The Impact of Migration on Development, Gender and Transnationalism (SEJ2007/6379); Gender, Transnationalism and Inter-Generational Strategies for Social Mobility (FEM2011-26210, FEM20/1002/E), Network Gender, Migration and Development (SEJ2007-30782-E) and FEM2010-10702-E which funded part of the English editing of the book, as well as different seminars and meetings related to the theme of the handbook. We benefited greatly from these discussions.

The English editing of the book was also made possible by the 2011 call for consolidating and structuring competitive research units (ref. CN2011/03 for ESOMI, University of A Coruña), (Department of Education and University System of Galicia, co-financed by the Regional Development Fund of the EU).

We are grateful for the comments and constructive criticism that we received from the editors at Edward Elgar and for their support and that of their staff. Thanks to Sarah Moss for translating some parts of the introduction from Spanish into English, and to Montse Golias and Sofía Laiz for last-minute help with formatting. We are also grateful for the feedback from Caroline Bledsoe, Sylvia Chant and Ivan Light, and last, but not least, to Ali Stewart for translating some parts of the Introduction and for editing the manuscript as well as for her continuous and engaging support throughout the whole process.

1. We are aware that it is a complex conceptualization. The contrast between the concept of gift and commodity has many sources: as Appadurai indicates, 'among them are the tendency to romanticize small-scale societies; to conflate use value (in Marx's sense) with *gemeinschaft* (in Tönnies' sense)' (1986, p. 42), where gifts and reciprocity often appear to clash with the profit-oriented, self-centred and calculated spirit that fires the circulation of commodities. The issue of the 'objectivization of persons' also has to be taken into account in cross-cultural perspectives. However, Marxist approaches have focused on the production-dominated view of the commodity while overlooking the consumption

facet. What Appadurai's analysis reveals is the commoditization (after lengthy explanations) that lies at the complex intersection of temporal, cultural and social factors.
2. This title refers to two previous articles, both published in special issues of the *International Migration Review* (Morokvasic, 1984; Donato et al., 2006).
3. We have opted not to cite the wealth of literature addressing each of these issues, as it can be consulted in the chapters by Hondagneu-Sotelo, and Catarino and Morokvasic.
4. See Jabardo (2011) for extensive literature on this issue.
5. They interpret the data of the TIES survey (the Integration of the European Second Generation), carried out in 15 cities across eight European countries (France, Germany, Spain, Austria, the Netherlands, Belgium, Switzerland and Sweden). They focus on three expressions of second-generation transnational engagement (visiting, remitting and return intention), in order to examine the extent to which second-generation transnational engagements, from the perspective of gender, are associated with host-country incorporation outcomes.
6. The study is based on 67 in-depth interviews held with different actors involved in the social scope of care (women immigrant carers, employers and dependents) in both Spain and Chile.
7. Other works have also highlighted the relevance of this articulationist approach in gender and migration studies (Catarino and Oso, 2012).

BIBLIOGRAPHY

Agustín, L. (2007), *Sex at the Margins: Migration, Labour Markets and the Rescue Industry*, London: Zed Books.
Amos, V. and P. Parmar (1984), 'Challenging imperial feminism', *Feminist Review*, **17**, 3–19.
Amuedo-Dorantes, C. and S. Pozo (2006), 'Migration, remittances, and male and female employment patterns', *American Economic Review*, **96** (2), 222–6.
Anthias, F. and N. Mehta (2002), 'Gender, migration and self-employment: gender divisions and ethnic enterprise, *International Review of Sociology*, **2**, 123–44.
Apitzsch, U. and M. Kontos (eds) (2003), 'Self-employment, gender and migration: women in non-privileged self-employment', *International Review of Sociology*, **13** (1), 67–76.
Appadurai, A. (1986), 'Introduction, commodities and the politics of value', in A. Appadurai (ed.), *The Social Life of Things: Commodities in Cultural Perspective*, Cambridge: Cambridge University Press, pp. 3–63.
Bauman, Z. (1998), *Globalization: The Human Consequences*, New York: Columbia University Press.
Benería, L. (2008), 'The crisis of care, international migration, and public policy', *Feminist Economics*, **14** (3), 1–21.
Benería, L. (2011), 'Gender and development: where are we now?', paper presented at Linking Production and Reproduction Chains in Contemporary Mobility Conference, Maó, Menorca, 6–8 October.
Bhavnani, K. and M. Coulson (1986), 'Transforming socialist feminism: the challenge of racism', *Feminist Review*, **23**, 81–92.
Blanckaert, C. (1988), 'On the origins of French ethnology: William Edwards and the doctrine of race', in G.W. Stocking Jr (ed.), *Bones, Bodies, Behavior Essays on Biological Anthropology*, Madison, WI: University of Wisconsin Press, pp. 18–55.
Bonacich, E. (2002), 'Labor's response to global production', in G. Gereffi, D. Spener and J. Bair (eds) *Free Trade and Uneven Development: The North American Apparel Industry after NAFTA*, Philadelphia, PA: Temple University Press, pp. 123–35.
Borderías, C. and C. Carrasco (1994), 'Las mujeres y el trabajo: aproximaciones históricas, sociológicas y económicas', in C. Borderías, C. Carrasco and C. Alemany (eds), *Las mujeres y el trabajo: rupturas conceptuales*, Madrid: Icaria, pp. 15–110.
Boyd, M. (1989), 'Family and personal networks in international migration: recent

developments and new agendas', *International Migration Review*, **23** (3), Special Silver Anniversary Issue: International Migration an Assessment for the 90s (Autumn), 638–70.

Brenner, N. (1999), 'Globalisation as reterritorialisation: the re-scaling of urban governance in the European Union', *Urban Studies*, **36** (3), 431–51.

Brenner, N., J. Peck and N. Theodore (2010), 'After neoliberalization?', *Globalizations*, **7** (3) 327–45.

Carby, H. (1982), 'White women listen: black feminism and the boundaries of sisterhood', in Centre for Contemporary Cultural Studies, University of Birmingham (ed.), *The Empire Strikes Back: Race and Racism in 70s Britain*, London: Hutchinson, pp. 211–32.

Castles, S. (2008), 'Development and migration – migration and development: what comes first?', paper presented at the Social Science Research Council Conference Migration and Development: Future Directions for Research and Policy, New York, 28 February–1 March.

Catarino, C., M. Morokvasic and M.A. Hily (eds) (2005), 'Femmes, genre, migration et mobilités', *Revue Européenne des Migrations Internationales*, **21** (1), 7–27.

Catarino, C. and L. Oso (2012), 'Production et reproduction: une analyse à partir du nexus Migrations Femmes/Genre et Développement', paper presented at the *Sous le développement, le genre conference*, Geneva, 27–28 September.

Chant, Silvia (ed.) (1992), *Gender and Migration in Developing Countries*, London: Belhaven Press.

Cox, K. (ed.) (1997), *Spaces of Globalization: Reasserting the Power of the Local*, New York: Guilford Press.

Crenshaw, K.W. (1989), 'Demarginalizing the intersection of race and sex: a black feminist critique of antidiscrimination doctrine, feminist theory and antiracist politics', University of Chicago Legal Forum, Chicago, IL.

De Haas, H. (2010), 'Migration and development: a theoretical perspective', *International Migration Review*, **44** (1), 227–64.

Degavre, F. and G. Langwiesner (2011), 'Le care dans les stratégies migratoires au début du XXIème siècle: quel gain d'autonomie pour les femmes migrantes en Belgique?', in M.-P. Arrizabalaga, D. Burgos and M. Yusta (eds), *Femmes et stratégies transnationales (XVIIIe-XXIe siècles)*, Brussels: Pieter Lang, pp. 67–91.

Degrave, F and M.Nyssens (2008), 'L' innovation sociale dans les services d'aide à domicile: les apports d'une lecture polanyienne et féministe', *Revue français de socio-économie*, **2** (2), 79–98.

Degavre, F. and M. Nyssens (2009), 'L'innovation sociale dans les services d'aide à domicile: normes et processus', in C. Nicole-Drancourt and I. Jonas (eds), *Conciliation famille/travail: Attention Travaux!*, Paris: L'Harmattan, pp. 145–54.

Delphy, C. (1970), 'L'énnemie principal', *Partisans, Libération des Femmes, année zero* (54–5), 157–72.

Donato, K., M.D. Gabaccia, J. Holdaway, M. Manalansan and P.R. Pessar (2006), 'A glass half full? Gender in migration studies', *International Migration Review*, Gender and Migration Revisited, **40** (1), February, 3–26.

Ehrenreich, B. and A.R. Hochschild (eds) (2002), *Global Woman: Nannies, Maids and Sex Workers in the New Economy*, New York: Henry Holt.

Elhariri, S. (2004), 'Les transferts monétaires et commerciaux des Marocaines et le développement local au Maroc', *Revue Passerelles*, **28**, Spring–Summer, 69–79.

Erel, U. and E. Kofman (2003), 'Professional female immigration in post-war Europe: counteracting an historical amnesia', in R. Ohliger, K. Schönwalder and T. Triadafilopoulos (eds), *European Encounters 1945–2000: Migrants, Migration and European Societies since 1945*, Aldershot and Burlington, VA: Ashgate, pp. 71–95.

Escrivá, A. and N. Ribas-Mateos (eds) (2004), *Migración y desarrollo: estudios sobre remesas y otras prácticas transnacionales*, Córdoba: Consejo Superior de Investigaciones Científicas e Instituto de Estudios Sociales de Andalucía.

Fernández-Kelly, M.P. (1983), *For We Are Sold, I and My People: Women and Industry in Mexico's Frontier*, Albany, NY: SUNY Press.

Fernández-Kelly, M.P. (2006), 'The global assembly line in the new millennium', CMD Working paper 06–05, Princeton University, Princeton, NJ, June.
Gainza, P. (2006), 'Feminización de las remesas, familias transnacionales y comercio nostálgico', *Revista Tercer Mundo Económico*, 204, May, Montevideo, available at: http://old.redtercermundo.org.uy/tm_economico/texto_completo.php?id=3043.
Glick Schiller, N., L. Basch and C. Blanc-Szanton (eds) (1992), *Towards a Transnational Perspective on Migration: Race, Class, Ethnicity and Nationalism Reconsidered*, New York: Academy of Sciences.
Golub, A., M. Morokvasic, and C. Quiminal (1997), 'Evolution de la production des connaissances sur les femmes immigrées en France et en Europe', *Migrations Société*, 9 (52), July–August, 19–36.
Grasmuck S. and P. Pessar (1991), *Between Two Islands: Dominican International Migration*, Berkeley, CA: University of California Press.
Gregorio Gil, C. (1998), *La migración femenina y su impacto en las relaciones de género*, Madrid: Narcea de ediciones.
Guillemaut, F. (2006), 'Victimes de trafic ou actrices d'un processus migratoire? Saisir la voix des femmes migrantes prostituées par la recherche action (enquête)', *Terrains & Travaux*, 1 (10), 157–76.
Hancock, A.M. (2007), 'When multiplication doesn't equal quick addition: examining intersectionality as a research paradigm', *Perspectives on Politics*, 5, 63–79.
Harvey, D. (1982), *The Limits to Capital*, Chicago, IL: University of Chicago Press.
Harvey, D. (1990), *The Condition of Postmodernity*, Cambridge, MA, Blackwell.
Held, D. and A. McGrew (eds) (2000), *The Global Transformations Reader: An Introduction to the Globalization Debate*, Cambridge: Polity Press.
Herrera, G. (2005a), 'Mujeres ecuatorianas en las cadenas globales del cuidado', in G. Herrera, C. Carrillo and A. Torres (eds), *Migración ecuatoriana: Redes, transnacionalismo e identidades*, Quito: FLACSO-Plan Migración Comunicación y Desarrollo, pp. 281–304.
Herrera, G. (2005b), 'Remesas, dinámicas familiares y estatus social: una mirada de la emigración ecuatoriana desde la sociedad de origen', in Zuñiga García-Falces (ed.), *La migración, un camino entre el desarrollo y la cooperación*, Madrid: Centro de Investigación para la paz (CIP-FUHEM), Comunidad de Madrid, pp. 149–62.
Hochschild, A.R. (2000), 'Global care chains and emotional surplus value', in W. Hutton, and A. Giddens (eds), *On the Edge: Living with Global Capitalism*, New York: Free Press, pp. 130–46.
Hondagneu-Sotelo, P. (1991), 'Family and community in the migration of Mexican undocumented immigrant women', in M.T. Segal, V. Demos and D. Hills (eds), *Ethnic Women: A Multiple Status Reality*, New York: General Hall, pp. 173–85.
INSTRAW (2006), *El caso de la migración femenina de Vicente Noble, República Dominicana*, Santo Domingo: INSTRAW.
INSTRAW (2007), *Género y Remesas. Migración colombiana del AMCO hacia España*, Santo Domingo: INSTRAW.
INSTRAW (2008), *Gender, Remittances and Development: The Case of Filipino Migration to Italy*, Santo Domingo: INSTRAW. Author: Natalia Ribas-Mateos.
INSTRAW (2010), *Migration, transferts et développement local sensible au genre: le cas du Sénégal*, Santo Domingo: INSTRAW.
Jabardo, M. (2011), 'From black feminism: a look at gender and migration', paper presented at the Linking Production and Reproduction Chains in Contemporary Mobility Conference, Maó, Menorca, 6–8 October.
King, R., M. Dalipaj and N. Mai (2006), 'Gendering migration and remittances: evidence from London and northern Albania', *Population, Space and Place*, 12, 409–34.
Knowles, C. and S. Mercer (1992), 'Feminism and antiracism', in J. Donald, and A. Rattansi (eds), *Race, Culture and Difference*, London: Sage, pp. 104–25.
Kunz, R. (2008), "Remittances are beautiful?" Gender implications of the new global remittances trend', *Third World Quarterly*, 29 (7), 1389–409.

Levitt, P., J. De Wind and S. Vertovec (2003), 'Perspectives on transnational migration: an introduction', *International Migration Review*, **37** (3), 565–75.
Levitt, P. and N.N. Sørensen (2004), 'The transnational turn in migration studies', *Global Migration Perspectives*, **6**, 2–13.
Lurbe, K. (2011), 'On Roma's migrants' development capability in France: a class, gender and race intersectional approach', paper presented at the Linking Production and Reproduction Chains in Contemporary Mobility Conference, Maó, Menorca, 6–8 October.
Massey, D.S., R. Alarcón, J. Durand and M. González (1987), *Return to Aztlan: The Social Process of International Migration from Western Mexico*, Berkeley, CA: University of California Press.
Mittelman, J. (2000), *The Globalization Syndrome: Transformation and Resistance*, Princeton, NJ: Princeton University Press.
Monquid, S. (2004), 'Les femmes émigrés vecteur de modernisation? Le rôle occulté des femmes émigrés dans le développement du pays d'origine: le cas marocain', *Revue Passerelles*, **28**, Spring–Summer, 59–68.
Morokvasic, M. (1984), 'Birds of passage are also women', *International Migration Review*, **18** (68), 886–907.
Morokvasic, M. (1991), 'Roads to independence: self-employed immigrants and minority women in five European states', *International Migration*, **29** (3), September, 235–314.
Morokvasic, M. (1999), 'La mobilité transnational comme ressource: la cas des migrants de l'Europe de l'Est', *Cultures and Conflits*, 33–4, Spring/Summer 105–22.
Morokvasic, M. (2004), 'Settled in mobility: engendering post-wall migration in Europe', *Feminist Review*, **77** (1), 7–25.
Morrison, A.R., M. Schiff and M. Sjöblom (eds) (2008), *The International Migration of Women*, Basingstoke: Palgrave Macmillan and Washington, DC: World Bank.
Oso, L. (2002), 'Stratégies de mobilité sociale des domestiques immigrées en Espagne', *Revue Tiers Monde*, **43** (170), April–June, 287–305.
Oso, L. and C. Catarino (2012), 'From sex to gender: the feminisation of migration and labour-market insertion in Spain and Portugal', *Journal of Ethnic and Migration Studies*, **18** December (online), 13 March (print).
Oso, L. and J.P. Garson (2005), 'Migrant women and the labour market: diversity and challenges', Paper presented at the OCED and European Commission Seminar, Brussels, 26–27 September.
Palmary, I., E. Burman, K. Chantler and P. Kiguwa (eds) (2010), *Gender and Migration: Feminist Interventions*, London: Zed Books.
Parmar, P. (1982), 'Gender, race and class: Asian women's resistence', in Centre for Contemporary Cultural Studies, University of Birmingham (ed.), *The Empire Strikes Back: Race and Racism in 70s Britain*, London: Hutchinson.
Parmar, P. (1990), 'Black feminism: the politics of articulation', in J. Rutherford (ed.), *Identity: Community and Difference*, London: Lawrence and Wishart.
Parreñas, R. (2001a), *The Global Servants: Migrant Filipinas Domestic Workers in Rome and Los Angeles*, Palo, Alto, CA: Stanford University Press.
Parreñas, R. (2001b), *Servants of Globalization: Women, Migration and Domestic Service*, Stanford, CA: Stanford University Press.
Pauli, J. (2008), 'House of one's own: gender, migration, and residence in rural Mexico', *American Ethnologist*, **35** (1), 171–87.
Peraldi, M. (with A. Bettaieb and V. Manry) (2001), 'L'esprit de bazaar. Mobilités transnationales maghrébines et sociétés métropolitaines: les routes d'Istambul', in Peraldi (ed.), *Cabas et containers. Activités marchandes informelles et réseaux migrants transfrontaliers*, Paris: Maisonneuve & Larose, pp. 329–81.
Piper, N. (ed.) (2008a), *New Perspectives on Gender and Migration: Livelihood, Rights and Entitlements*, New York: Routledge.
Piper, N (2008b), 'Gender, Migration and Development: Trends and Issues', Situation Report on International Migration in East and South East Asia, UNIFEM, Bangkok.

Polanyi. K (1944), *The Great Transformation: The Political and Economic Origins of our Time*, New York: Farrar & Rinehart.
Pribilsky, J. (2004), '"Aprendemos a convivir": conjugal relations, co-parenting, and family life among Ecuadorian transnational migrants in New York and the Ecuadorian Andes', *Global Networks*, **4** (3), July, 313–34.
Ramírez, C., M. García and J. Míguez (2005), *Cruzando fronteras: Remesas, género y desarrollo*, Santo Domingo: INSTRAW.
Ribas-Mateos, N. (2004), 'Barrios y familias tangerinas dependientes de remesas', in A. Escrivá and N. Ribas-Mateos (eds), *Migración y desarrollo: estudios sobre remesas y otras prácticas transnacionales*, Córdoba: Consejo Superior de Investigaciones Cientificas e Instituto de Estudios Sociales de Andalucía, pp. 257–312.
Ribas-Mateos, N. (2005), *The Mediterranean in the time of Globalization: Migration, Borders and Welfare*, New Brunswick, NJ: Transaction Publishers.
Ribas-Mateos, N. (2013a), 'Introduction: Réflexions sur la place des femmes et des mobilités dans la globalisation', in Ribas-Mateos and V. Manry (eds), *Mobilités au féminin*, París: Karthala.
Ribas-Mateos, N. (2013b), *The Border Shift*, Aldershot, UK and Burlington, VA: Ashgate.
Ribas-Mateos, N. and C. Basa (2013), *How Filipinos Immigrants in Italy Send Money Back Home: The Role of Cross-Border Remittances in the Global Economy*, London and New York: Mellen Press.
Rotkirch, A. (2005), '"Sauver ses fils": migrations trans-européennes comme stratégies maternelles', *Migrations Société*, **17** (99–100), May–June, 161–72.
Salih, R. (2001), 'Moroccan migrant women: transnationalism, nation-states and gender', *Journal of Ethnic and Migration Studies*, **27** (4), 655–71.
Salzinger, L. (2003), *Genders in Production. Making Workers in Mexico's Global Factories*, Berkeley, CA: University of California Press.
Sassen, S. (1988), *The Mobility of Labour and Capital: A Study in International Investment and Labor Flow*, New York: Cambridge University Press.
Sassen, S. (2000), 'The global city: strategic site/new frontier', *American Studies*, **42** (2/3), 79–95.
Sassen, S. (2003), 'The feminisation of survival: alternative global circuits', in M. Morokvasic-Müller, U. Erel and K. Shinozaki (eds), *Crossing Borders and Shifting Boundaries, Vol. I. Gender on the Move*, Opladen: Leske & Budrich, pp. 59–77.
Sassen, S. (2005), 'When national territory is home to the global: old borders to novel bordering', *New Political Economy*, **10**, December, 523–41.
Schrover, M. and E. Yeo (2011), *Gender, Migration, and the Public Sphere, 1850–2005*, London and New York: Routledge.
Scott, C.V. (1995), *Gender and Development, Rethinking Modernization and Dependency Theory*, Boulder, CO: Lynne Rienner.
Semyonov, M. and A. Gorodzeisky (2005), 'Labor migration, remittances and household income: a comparison between Filipino and Filipina overseas workers', *International Migration Review*, **39** (1), Spring, 45–68.
Sørensen, N. (2005), 'Migrant Remittances, Development and Gender', DIIS Brief, Danish Institute for International Studies, Copenhagen.
Sørensen, N. (2011), 'Who cares? Transnational family life and development', paper presented at the Linking Production and Reproduction Chains in Contemporary Mobility Conference, Maó, Menorca, 6–8 October.
Stalford, H., S. Currie and S. Velluti (2009), *Gender and Migration in 21st Century Europe*, Ashgate: Dartmouth.
Stark, O. (1984), 'Discontinuity and the theory of international migration', *Kyklos*, **37** (2), 206–22.
Tacoli, C. (1999), 'International migration and the restructuring of gender asymmetries: continuity and change among Filipino labour migrants in Rome', *International Migration Review*, **33** (3), 658–82.
Truong, T. (1996), 'Gender, international migration and social reproduction: implications

for theory, policy, research and networking', *Asian and Pacific Migration Journal*, **5** (1), 27–52.
United Nations (2006), *2004 World Survey on the Role of Women in Development: Women in International Migration*, New York: United Nations.
Vertovec, S. (2004), 'Trends and impacts of migrant transnationalism', Center on Migration, Policy and Society, University of Oxford, Working Paper 3, WP-04-03, Oxford.
Zapata, E. and B. Suárez (2004), *Remesas, Milagros y mucho más, realizan mujeres indígenas y campesinas*', México: Editorial GIMTRAP-Fundación Ford-Fundación Rockefeller, Serie PEMSA.
Zlotnik, H. (1995), 'The south to north migration of women', *International Migration Review*, **29** (1), 229–54.
Zlotnik, H. (2003), 'The global dimensions of female migration', *Migration Information Source*, 1 March, available at: www.migrationinformation.org.

PART I

FRAMEWORK OF CHANGES IN GENDER, MIGRATION AND TRANSNATIONALISM FROM THE VANTAGE POINTS OF GLOBALIZATION AND DEVELOPMENT

Gioconda Herrera

→ feminization of most migrator flows
family + gender roles
international division of labor

2. Gender and international migration: globalization, development and governance*

Lourdes Benería, Carmen Diana Deere and Naila Kabeer

INTRODUCTION

Since the late 1980s, international migration has been one of the most debated of the diverse processes through which globalization has taken place. With an estimated 210 million people living outside their country of origin (ILO, 2010), international migration has touched the lives of almost everyone in both the sending and receiving countries of the Global South and the Global North. It has also generated major tensions in politics and policies that have, in turn, affected the ways in which migration has been experienced by different social groups and by men and women. From a gender perspective, we have witnessed the feminization of most migration flows, especially since the 1990s, with profound transformations in the structure of families and gender roles in the international division of labour. Sociologists and anthropologists provided some of the initial studies on international migration from a gender perspective (Ehrenreich and Hochschild, 2002; Parreñas, 2005; Herrera, 2006). Economists have subsequently contributed to the multi- and interdisciplinary character of these studies (Benería, 2008; Pérez Orozco, 2009; Lyberaki, 2011).

Globalization provided the context in which international migration has been on the rise, especially since the 1980s. Certain aspects of globalization have been particularly prominent in accelerating the movement of labour. First, huge changes in technology and communications have contributed to the dissemination of information and have affected people's perceptions of life options. Knowledge of living standards and social conditions across countries has become increasingly more available, especially through travel; both the real and symbolic reduction of time and distance have created powerful incentives for people to move.

Second, structural transformations in many countries, particularly those leading to rural–urban migration and the informalization of production during the neoliberal period, have generated strong pressures to search for paid work and better living conditions, often leading to international migration. This includes structural change intensified by trade and agreements such as the North American Free Trade Agreement, which, in Mexico for instance, has resulted in a large outflow of labour from rural areas. The number of countries sending large numbers of their citizens abroad has gradually been increasing, while many of them are also receiving migrants, from Argentina and Russia to China, Italy and Spain (Yakovlev, 2010).

Third, despite relatively high levels of growth in many southern countries in recent years, inequalities between low- and high-income areas have continued to grow and to provide further incentives for international migration. As the United Nations Development Programme's Human Development Report 2010 documents, between 1970 and 2010 human development indices show substantial progress in most countries (UNDP, 2010), but this has not had any effect on bridging the gap between poorer and richer nations. On the contrary, the gap has increased. According to UNDP estimates, in 1970 the average income of countries in the highest 25 per cent GDP group was 23 times higher than that of the lowest 25 per cent group; this figure increased to 29 times by 2010 (ibid., p. 42), thus increasing the economic incentive to migrate.

Fourth, the formation and expansion of international networks has also provided the knowledge and support often needed in making decisions to migrate, at the individual, family or group levels. This includes non-profit country-based or international associations as well as commercial networks involved with facilitating labour flows at different levels. The latter include various businesses that have proliferated to handle the many legal and organizational aspects of migration. Family networks have been intensified with the formation of transnational families, whose members live and engage in paid work in different countries following a variety of arrangements and survival strategies.

Fifth, a rapid increase in women's labour force participation in high-income countries, together with demographic changes in fertility rates and life expectancy, have contributed to the care crisis in many northern countries and generated high levels of demand for paid care work, which has been supplied mostly by immigrant women from lower-income countries. To a large extent, the global commodification of care has been part of the globalization of the labour force, but it has also contributed to the feminization of international migration.

Sixth, globalization has also intensified interregional migration, including flows between southern countries responding to different levels of development and wages. Such is the case with migratory flows in South and Central America, with Asian migration to the Middle East, or with the influx of labour from Eastern to Western Europe.

Finally, the global crisis affecting many high-income countries since 2008, with roots in the excesses of financial globalization and other neoliberal policies, has generated high levels of unemployment with an impact on international migration. On the one hand, the crisis has tended to generate reverse migration and to slow down immigration rates. On the other, in countries with very high youth unemployment rates, such as Ireland and Spain, it is creating new migration flows of young and qualified labour to widely different destinations such as Australia, Germany, Argentina and China (Del Barrio, 2010; Díaz-Varela, 2011).

While many of the forces driving international migration are rooted in longstanding disparities between the poor and affluent countries of the world, these forces of globalization have been shaped in recent decades by neoliberal ideologies about market-oriented growth. Market liberalization and deregulation have given rise to a marked asymmetry in the mobility of capital and labour across national boundaries. Most of the obstacles to the free movement of capital have gradually been removed. While the roots of financial liberalization can be traced back to the formation of the eurodollar market in the 1960s, the neoliberal policies of the 1980s and 1990s represented a giant step forward in removing the barriers to capital mobility. In high-income countries, deregulation became a dominant force in economic policy, giving rise to the development of the risky financial instruments and practices that played a key role in the bursting of the bubble that generated the 2008 economic crisis. In developing countries, structural adjustment policies of the 1980s and 1990s were used to open doors for international capital and to globalize financial markets.

With the financialization of the economy worldwide, the financial sector has become dominant and influential over total economic policy (Epstein et al., 1993). In the United States, for example, it is well documented that Wall Street had much to do with the policies that eliminated financial regulations during the 1990s, including some that had been in place since the 1929 crisis (Financial Crisis Inquiry Commission, 2011). Debates about the need to regulate the movement of capital, particularly financial flows, across borders have not been absent although they have not had the prominence in everyday public discourse that immigration has. The call for capital controls, particularly for short-term speculative flows, has been reactivated as a result of financial crises. Even the International Monetary Fund (IMF) has recommended a permanent infrastructure for the control of these flows in order to prevent speculative runs, and Brazil has become a leading proponent of these types of control (Leahy, 2011). However, taxes and regulations on financial transactions face the powerful opposition of financial elites. As a result, the widely supported 'Tobin tax' that could be applied to international capital flows has not come close to being taken up as a serious policy measure. While the European Parliament approved the so-called 'Podimata Report' advocating a tax on financial flows worldwide in March 2011, it is likely to remain a mere political move as long as it is not backed by the power of law. The history of this type of tax, advocated since the 1970s, provides an example of the ways in which capital has continued to prevail in its strong opposition to financial market regulations.

By contrast to the freedom enjoyed by capital, the movement of labour across national boundaries continues to face many obstacles. Migrant-receiving countries have shaped their policies in contradictory directions in their attempt to respond to various domestic interests by curtailing the duration of migrant work contracts. The overall effect of these policies has been to severely reduce the international mobility of labour relative to capital. Investment capital has been able to take advantage of wide differences in labour costs across the world by shifting from higher to lower wage economies, but this has not been matched by commensurate ability on the part of labour in low-wage economies to move towards higher-wage contexts. The constant threat of shifting investment to ever-lower cost areas has served to erode the economic and political power of labour relative to capital and undermine its capacity to bargain for a fairer share of the benefits of globalization. Likewise, capital has benefited from the insecurity that immigrant labour faces in receiving countries since this insecurity weakens workers' ability to voice their demands and contributes to precarious labour conditions. The current global crisis is likely to reinforce these tendencies.

The consequence of these asymmetries and of the pressures resulting from global competition has been the prevalence of labour market conditions tending towards the lowest common denominator regarding precarious working conditions, wages and other production costs. The multiple processes leading to the relocation of production, deregulation of labour markets, and the increasing informality of employment have reinforced this tendency, with an adverse impact on labour standards both in high- and low-income countries. Many of the social gains that had been obtained over the years, for example in terms of wage levels and labour rights, have been rolled back. Since the 1970s there has been a steady decrease in the share of the total income going to labour relative to capital (ILO and ILS, 2008). As the ILO report points out, in 54 out of the 73 countries included in the study, the share of wages to total income declined during the two decades previous to the study. At the same time, income disparities within countries have risen as a result of the growing polarization in returns to labour, exacerbating inequalities across the board (UNDP, 2010). Current evaluations of the economic crisis indicate that these tendencies are intensifying rather than reversing (Reich, 2010).

Thus, an increase in labour market vulnerability and insecurity for a large proportion of the world's population has accompanied globalization in the current period, leading to the formation of what Standing (2011) and others have called the 'precariat' – the large number of workers surviving under very precarious working conditions and low levels of social protection worldwide. This group includes the large proportion of migrant workers who work under temporary and/or part-time conditions of employment. As a result, across the world, the informal economy has become a prevalent and permanent feature of national economies. It can no longer be viewed as a separate 'sector' that would fade away with economic development (ILO and ILS, 2010).

This, then, is the general context in which the growth of international migration and its feminization since the last decades of the twentieth century need to be located. Globalization has increased the possibility of taking advantage of differences and opportunities across countries that represent an incentive for people to improve their lives. However, vulnerability and precariousness have accompanied this context of possibilities, leading to the contradictory results and multiple effects analysed in this handbook.

GLOBALIZATION AND THE 'FEMINIZATION' OF INTERNATIONAL MIGRATION

The feminization of international migration – a key aspect of migration, particularly since the 1990s – has given rise to new debates on migration, gender and globalization. By 2006, women represented almost half of the total number of international migrants, with many women now migrating on their own rather than in association with other family members (UNFPA, 2006). They have constituted what the UNFPA's report calls a 'silent and mighty river' that has been growing since the 1980s (p. 1). The reasons for this increase in women's migration are multiple; they range from women's conditions in sending countries – including lack of opportunities to engage in paid work and life options, divorce or separation, women's desire for greater autonomy, and a decrease in social restrictions on women's mobility – to knowledge of employment opportunities in receiving countries. The result has been an increasing recognition of the importance of gender dimensions in international migration. Feminist analysis – and, more specifically, feminist economics literature – has focused on a variety of aspects, ranging from the employment of women migrants across sectors worldwide to the effects of women's migration on gender roles, immigrant women's wages and gender discrimination in labour markets, the formation of transnational families, and the differences between men's and women's remittance behaviour, among others.

Women migrants tend to be located in the lower echelons of labour markets. This is the case for manufacturing employment as well as for employment in the service and care sectors. Immigrant women's employment opportunities tend to be in temporary and unstable jobs. Many governments, in both sending and receiving countries, are involved in some form of regulation of migrant labour, but this does not change the informal and mostly precarious character of women's migration. Employment contracts tend to be temporary and unstable, both in high- and low-income countries. Although contracts can be extended, this temporary nature often becomes a source of instability and concern in the lives of immigrants and their families. The precariousness of paid work in the care economy has been analysed extensively and in the context of a great variety of countries (Razavi and Staab, 2010; Razavi, 2011). The same can be said for industrial employment, which has often used national and international migrant labour.

Immigrant women face a high level of occupational segregation in labour markets. First, they are found in extreme forms of segregated paid work often linked to migration, such as in prostitution or other forms of sex work. Second, they tend to be employed within workplaces highly segregated by gender. A good proportion of women's migration is highly linked with paid work opportunities in the care economy, an issue that has been widely explored in feminist literature. The variety of factors explaining the growing demand for care services in high-income countries during the past decades is well known: a rapid increase in women's labour force participation, particularly in countries where the rate had been relatively low, such as in Southern Europe; higher life expectancy; and extremely low fertility rates lowering the capacity of families to care for their own families (Benería, 2008; Lyberaki, 2011). The result has been the further commodification of care and increasing reliance on immigrant women for paid care work, including paid domestic work, childcare and nursing. To provide this labour, immigrant women often leave their own family care behind, thus creating new care needs in their family and country of origin. This phenomenon has generated empirical studies on different regions, often focusing on the formation of 'care chains', which link a variety of care arrangements on a global scale, in sending and receiving countries. The importance of immigration for paid care work can also be viewed from the conceptual framework of social reproduction. Not only is paid and unpaid care work a basic ingredient in the social reproduction of any society, but it can also be crucial to deal with more specific crises of reproduction. In many northern countries, low fertility rates and shortages of caring labour threaten their ability to reproduce the labour force necessary for the economy as a whole or for specific sectors or families. At the same time, many families cannot afford paid care, and this in turn has a negative repercussion on their decision to have children – hence the importance of immigrant labour to deal with the shortage of care labour. The lowest fertility rates across countries are found in very different parts of the world, from Japan and South Korea in Asia to Italy, Spain and other southern Mediterranean countries, with multiple repercussions involving the ways in which countries have dealt with this issue (Kabeer, 2007; Benería, 2009). In some Asian societies, low fertility rates accompanied by shortages of women in the population have generated an international demand for marriageable women.

The feminization of migration has reinforced the formation of transnational families, giving rise to many questions regarding intra-family dynamics, changing gender roles and forms of gender in/equality, effects on children and adults left behind, involvement of non-emigrant women in family care, the role of remittances, household allocation of resources and family reunification (Schmalzbauer, 2004; Parreñas, 2005; UNFPA, 2006). Parreñas, for example, provided one of the initial studies of the effects of a father's or mother's migration on their children left in the Philippines, showing how the effects might be different by gender of the parent.

Finally, women are also prominent actors in intra-regional migration, including Global South–South migration. Examples include the migration of women from Burma to Thailand; from Southeast Asia to Korea; from the Philippines, Malaysia and Indonesia to Hong Kong and the Middle East; and in Latin America, from Bolivia to Argentina, Peru to Chile, Nicaragua to Costa Rica, and Guatemala to Mexico. While the specific dynamics differ, such as whether migration is facilitated by guest worker and other specific recruitment programmes or motivated by the market in brides, what these migration flows share is that they are rooted in the differences and asymmetries among countries of the Global South – thus linking countries with lower wages with those where wages and standards of living are relatively higher.

Intra-regional migration bears a number of other similarities to Global South–North migration. For one, migrants also tend to enter gendered labour markets: agriculture and construction for men; domestic service and other care occupations for women; and garment and hotel and restaurant sectors for both men and women, depending on the country. Finally, intra-regional migration is sometimes also characterized by a divide between documented and undocumented migration, with skilled migrants generally comprising the majority of the documented migrants who are attracted by higher salaries in specific industries.

MIGRATION, GENDER AND DEVELOPMENT

Does migration undermine development in sending countries or speed it up? And, conversely, does development slow down or encourage international migration? There is very little agreement on these questions (Sutcliffe, 1998). In the debates in the literature on these questions the meaning of 'development' is rarely made explicit, although generally, development is assumed to be equivalent to steady increases in gross domestic product (GDP) per capita. Although it would be more interesting to use, for example, the notion and indices of human development, in the following we review the literature on its own terms to highlight the gender aspects of the migration–development nexus.

Does Migration Undermine Development?

It is generally accepted that international migrants tend to be among the better qualified of a sending country's citizenry, for international migration involves monetary costs and knowledge networks that exclude the very poor. Much of the early literature on international migration was focused on the 'brain drain', since one of the first manifestations of globalization was the development of an international labour market for highly educated, skilled labour (Bhagwati and Hamada, 1974). If skilled labour could not earn internationally competitive salaries or have similar opportunities for professional development at home, there was strong motivation for such people to leave. The implication was that investments in education, particularly secondary and tertiary education, in developing countries might not lead to faster economic growth (Carrington and Detragiache, 1999). In other words, as a result of the brain drain, sending countries incur the costs of reproduction – absorbing the costs of education, healthcare and maintenance up to the age of migration – while receiving countries reap the benefits. This outcome has also been linked to the development model implemented in the Global South, whereby state policies are geared to imitate the development path of advanced countries (Sutcliffe, 1998).

Little attention was given to the gender dimensions of the brain drain in this debate in part because sex-disaggregated data on the educational level of international migrants were rarely available. In a large-scale study with data from around 2000, Dumont et al. (2007) found that the average emigration rate of tertiary-educated women from non-OECD countries was 17.6 per cent, exceeding that of men, which was 13.1 per cent. In contrast, among those with only primary education, there is no gender gap in emigration rates. The gender gap in emigration rates of skilled labour in favour of women differs across regions of the world, but is especially large for Africa and Latin America. This is a particularly interesting finding since women's access to higher education differs considerably in these two regions, with women in Latin America, but not in Africa, having surpassed parity in tertiary enrolment rates. It suggests that irrespective of their access to higher education, women in these two continents share similar obstacles in finding educationally appropriate employment opportunities at home, providing an incentive for their international migration.

It is not uncommon for international migration to involve a de-skilling process for women, as they end up in jobs for which they are overqualified, such as domestic or other caring labour (Altman and Pannell, 2012). Thus while migrant women may gain individually by the higher wages that they may earn abroad as compared to educationally commensurate paid work at home, overall there seems to be an implicit net global social welfare loss.

Also, the trend to favour or limit legal permanent migration to highly educated workers in specific technical and professional occupations has an implicit gender bias since they tend to favour occupations in fields that men dominate, such as information technology and engineering. Thus this shift reduces the opportunities for women to migrate legally on their own. It also leads to the concentration of legal women migrants among those whose migration is tied to family circumstances, so-called 'tied movers', and relegates many women migrants to the ranks of the undocumented. Since this trend paralleled the increase in the demand for women migrants due to the care crisis in high-income countries, a high number of care workers have been either undocumented or the wives of legal migrants. Little research has been done to date on whether there is a gender difference in the likelihood of migrating with or without legal documents. Katharine M. Donato's (2010) study of Latin American migration to North America found different patterns depending on the country. These different patterns lend weight to the argument that the individual costs and benefits from international migration are gendered (including by the policies of labour-importing countries), suggesting that the consequences in countries of origin will be gendered as well.

While higher incomes and remittances resulting from migration might be beneficial to the individual and potentially to her or his household in the sending country, the brain-drain argument implies that, because migrants have left, development has slowed down or been undermined. This incongruity has been raised, for example, in the analysis of the 'care deficit' in the Philippines (Yeates, 2009).

Other negative impacts of international migration that have been noted in the literature include the overall disruptive effect of migration on families and of changing gender roles. In the case of the migration of married men, the focus has been on the women 'left behind' to raise children on their own and assume new responsibilities, whether managing agricultural production or pursuing new income-generating activities until remittances (which are never a sure thing) begin to arrive. Whether these changes are empowering for women, as they exercise greater agency in household and agricultural decision making, or simply represent an increase in their responsibilities and total labour time worked, is a source of contention in the literature (Jolly, with Reeves, 2005; UNFPA, 2006; Ghosh, 2009; UNDP, 2009). These changes in gender roles brought about by international migration can also have macro consequences, such as a shift from market to subsistence agricultural production, reducing overall national food sufficiency (Preibisch et al., 2002).

The recent trend towards the increased migration of women on their own, including mothers, has raised another set of issues in terms of what this means for the welfare of the children left behind (Moran-Taylor, 2008; Yeates, 2009). There may be different short-versus long-term effects of women's migration on the acquisition of skills and educational levels and, thus, on human development as well as GDP growth rates.

In their econometric analysis of emigration from developing countries, Dumont et al. (2007) found that the rate of emigration of highly educated women as compared to men was negatively associated with infant mortality, under-five mortality, and secondary school enrolment rates of girls and boys. They also found that the emigration of women with only a primary education had a positive effect on some of these health and education indicators, suggesting that remittances play a differential role depending on household income levels. Since they also found the emigration rate of highly skilled women to be higher the poorer their country of origin, this suggests that the negative, gendered impact of the brain drain may be greatest in the poorest countries.

The crucial issue in the debate over the brain drain is whether or not international migrants could have been productively employed at home. This is an open question. It may well be that the answer to this question is gendered, if, for example, women with tertiary degrees are more likely than men to migrate because of cultural barriers or labour market discrimination at home, issues that require further research.

Does Migration Speed Up Economic Development?

The potential positive effect of international migration on the development of sending countries rests on three arguments: the positive effect of the absence of migrants on the opportunities of those who stay behind, the contribution of remittances, and the positive contribution of returned migrants to economic development (Sutcliffe, 1998).

Labour market impacts

In theory, an exodus of labour due to international migration should lead to rising wages in the country of origin, hence increasing national income and eventually bringing about a convergence of living standards between sending and receiving countries. But as we know, labour is not perfectly mobile and markets do not always function as expected. In many cases, globalization has created a dual international labour market, characterized by mobility for the highly educated and skilled but predominantly national and restricted with respect to unskilled labour. Migration processes can also potentially lead to a drain of unskilled labour, through either guest worker programmes or undocumented migration flows. In theory this should have a positive effect on development, by raising wages in the agricultural or construction sectors in the sending country and leading to higher incomes. But it can also produce other outcomes, such as interregional relay or chain migration (Durand and Massey, 2010). Thus the potential positive effects of migration on labour markets depends not only on whether labour shortages lead to higher wages, but also on interlinked regional labour markets.

Remittances

One of the main trends since 2000 has been the spectacular growth in the volume of international remittances. Between 2000 and 2008, the total volume of remittances to all developing countries increased from US$81.3 billion to US$324.8 billion (World Bank, 2011). Remittances now far exceed the level of total direct foreign assistance and, for some countries, are equivalent to their export earnings from commodity production (UNDP, 2009). Remittances may contribute to development in several ways. As a source of foreign exchange, remittances contribute to macroeconomic stability and allow countries to better manage their external debt. As a source of investment funds, they directly contribute to GDP growth. And, as a source of consumption, they also potentially contribute to GDP growth through their impact on aggregate demand and hence employment. Moreover, remittances may serve as a mechanism for poverty reduction by raising the incomes of migrant households, particularly in countries where the migration of unskilled labour dominates; this mechanism also serves to reduce income inequality.

For all these reasons remittances have become the new development panacea, garnering the attention of international financial institutions (IFIs), such as the World Bank and the various regional development banks, and a good number of governments that now explicitly encourage or facilitate the migration of their citizens as development policy, such as the Philippines, Sri Lanka and Indonesia (Rosewarne, 2012). In this context, IFIs and governments view the feminization of migration flows positively because they assume that women are motivated by a higher sense of commitment to family well-being and thus are more likely to remit.

The question then is whether remittances are in fact so favourable for development in the Global South. At the macro level, there is no consistent relation empirically between the volume of remittances and the growth or level of fixed capital formation or GDP (UNDP, 2009). Remittances are overwhelmingly used for consumption purposes or poverty alleviation. This is, of course, a beneficial outcome, since poverty alleviation is an important objective of development. The main argument is that for remittances to fuel development, a high level of remittances must be maintained and this depends on two factors: women must continue to be an important share of migrants, since women tend to remit a higher share of their income than do men; and migration must maintain its temporary character, since the share of income remitted is positively related to the expectation of return to the home country and inversely related to the length of stay in the destination country. Both IFIs and human rights activists have failed to see that the temporariness of migrant labour is not only what secures the remittance flow, but also what allows women's migrant labour (particularly contract labour in the Asian cases he focuses on) to be highly exploitable (Rosewarne, 2012).

Family position, gender roles, and the motivation for migration appear to be highly correlated with remittance behaviour. For example, sometimes mothers migrate alone with the explicit purpose of financing the education of the children they left behind (Ribas-Mateos, 2013). This makes them highly likely to remit and provides a strong motivation to remit a high share of their income.

Holst et al. (2012) contribute an added dimension to the classical studies of remittances – using the case of Germany: the role played by migrant networks (or the structure of the transnational family) and how this varies with the length of migration and citizenship status. Due to the gender wage gap resulting from both gender and migrant occupational segregation, one would expect that women remit less than men in absolute terms.

But, in addition, they note that women are more likely than men to send income in kind to family members in the country of origin, whether food, clothes, or other consumer items. Since surveys rarely ask about non-monetary transfers, measures of cash remittances alone might introduce a downward bias in the contribution of women migrants. There are also differences in remittance behaviour between foreign nationals and citizens in terms of migrants' networks, which they define in terms of the relative balance of a migrant's immediate and extended family and friends in the country of residence versus country of origin.

Whether remittances are consumed or saved and invested matters for GDP growth rates, although perhaps not for human development. Thus it is important to consider whether migrants themselves make the decision on how remittances are used or whether the person receiving the remittances makes this decision. This raises the question of whether the gender of the person remitting or receiving matters with respect to how remittances are utilized, a topic that has been insufficiently addressed in the literature. Petrozziello's (2011) case study of Honduran migrants to the US suggests that it is the family's needs in the country of origin rather than migrant aspirations that are paramount in this decision. She also cautions against considering the use of remittances that go toward consumption, including education and health expenses, as 'unproductive', since they enhance human development and are the primary reason why people migrate internationally. Her concern, is that in the 'remittances for development' approach promoted by IFIs and others, migrant women are seen 'as instruments for development rather than resourceful actors in their own right' (2011, p. 54).

Turning to the impact of remittances on poverty and inequality, there is a general consensus that remittances play an important role in poverty alleviation internationally, even if spatially concentrated in only a subset of countries. There is also some evidence that remittances contribute towards reducing national income inequality. In Mexico, for example, over the 2000–07 period, remittances contributed to closing the gap between urban and rural household per capita incomes (López-Calva and Lustig, 2010). However, as noted earlier, the role of remittances in poverty alleviation depends on the socioeconomic background of those who moved, and this varies among countries (UNDP, 2009). Remittances may also generate considerable differences in living standards between those who receive them and those who do not, making those who receive remittances a new kind of elite, such as in the case of Cuba (Blue, 2004). This may lead to family and community tensions at the point of origin as Ribas-Mateos (2013) found in her analysis of rural Philippines.

Another concern refers to the stability of remittances and whether gains in poverty alleviation may turn out to be short-lived if remittances go primarily to support consumption. The volume of remittances depends crucially on the vigour of the economies of destination countries and, in times of crisis, remittances can also be 'transmission belts' of international crisis (Herrera, 2012). The 2007 financial crisis led to high rates of unemployment in destination countries, particularly among immigrant communities, and took a toll on the volume of remittances, which fell from US$325 billion in 2008 to US$307 billion in 2009 for all developing countries (World Bank, 2011).

The argument for returned migrants' positive contribution to development focuses on the knowledge and experience that migrants gain abroad that, along with their savings, might be harnessed for development efforts at home. And indeed, some governments of sending countries, such as Ecuador, are trying to harness this potential through state-sponsored inducements to return migration (Margheritis, 2011). However, this argument does not take into account the potential de-skilling often involved in the migration process, particularly for women. While there is little question that international migration broadens an individual's horizons (and in the specific case of women migrating on their own, may enhance their sense of independence, autonomy and self-esteem), it is not clear that their labour market experience in the country of destination will have a pay-off once they return home.

The impact of development on migration: does it slow it down or speed it up?

One argument claims that the best way to stop undocumented migration to the US, Europe and elsewhere is to channel more resources, such as foreign assistance, towards the economic development of countries in the Global South. Implicitly assumed is a negative relation between the level of development (as measured by GDP per capita) and international migration. The greater the opportunities and relative wage levels are at home, the less likely that people seek their fortunes elsewhere.

According to UNDP (2009), the relationship between the level of development (as measured by the Human Development Index: HDI) and international migration is best described by an inverse U-shape. In countries with very low levels of HDI, people are too poor to migrate, since international migration is costly and requires information networks. As income and educational levels rise, so too does international migration, with rates peaking at medium levels of HDI. A reading of such aggregate country-level data thus suggests that development increases but then eventually reduces migration. The UNDP report thus concludes that, 'these results shed strong doubts on the idea, often promoted in policy circles, that development in countries of origin will reduce migratory flows' (2009, p. 25).

Rao and Presenti (2012) test whether the sexual trafficking of women follows a similar pattern. Their study confirms an inverse U-shaped relationship between the level of income and trafficking, suggesting that trafficking and undocumented migration in general are driven by similar conditions. Contrary to expectations, trafficking is more likely not in countries with greater gender inequality, but rather, in those where women have achieved some level of economic mobility.

Changing gender roles are among the factors that explain why increasing levels of per capita income would be positively associated with international migration. As women's education and labour force participation increase, women's mobility tends to increase as well. In general, international migration is positively associated with all the factors associated with changes in traditional modes of life and rising expectations, particularly rural–urban migration and hence structural change.

There is every reason to expect that globalization, to the extent that it leads to rising income levels internationally but maintains the basic asymmetry in income levels between the Global North and the Global South, will continue to fuel migration (Sutcliffe, 1998). Increased trade, investment and telecommunications all foster an enhanced flow of information, knowledge and contacts. These, in turn, contribute to ever-rising expectations, and, combined with cheaper transport, also enhance mobility. Thus, as the UNDP study concludes 'the data indicate that income incentives to move from poor to rich countries have strongly increased' (2009, p. 33). Moreover, it is likely that the top of the inverse U-curve will keep shifting successively upward as long as living standards between the Global North and the Global South continue to diverge so substantially.

Summary

To summarize then, there is a better understanding of the effect of development on migration than there is regarding the impact of international migration on the level of economic development of sending countries. The latter debate is still under way. Of the three arguments examined here – the impact of migration on the labour market in sending countries, the benefits of remittances, and return migration – the one regarding the impact of remittances seems to be the most important and worthy of further study, particularly in terms of what tips the balance in the use of remittances from consumption towards investment. A gendered perspective – one that takes into account the combined effect of motivation, family position and gender – is absolutely necessary to move this debate forward. In particular, it implies looking into the extent to which migration contributes to changing gender roles, women's empowerment and gender equality.

MIGRATION AND GOVERNANCE

As discussed earlier, marked asymmetry in the international mobility of capital and labour has accompanied late twentieth-century globalization. This asymmetry reflects a regulatory environment that has consistently favoured the interests and mobility of capital – including deregulation of the financial sector, intellectual property rights, and trade dispute resolutions through the World Trade Organization (WTO) – but has undermined the rights and mobility of labour through various controls and restrictions. However, there are also important asymmetries in the international mobility of labour itself. As argued above, immigration policies in the wealthy labour-receiving countries of the world generally seek to encourage the immigration of highly educated workers who have the personal funds necessary to obtain and maintain residence and work permits and can make up skills deficits in the knowledge economy. The same policies seek to impose tight controls to keep out 'the others' or only allow them entry on short-term contracts that underline their status as temporary workers dependent on the goodwill of employers to remain in the country. Those without the funds or skills to secure legal entry migrate through undocumented channels and remain vulnerable to violence, abuse and constant fear of deportation for much of their stay abroad.

This asymmetry in the terms on which different categories of labour are able to migrate has broadly gendered consequences. We have pointed out that, in general, it is largely male workers who fit the desired skill categories, while the kinds of skills that women acquire tend to fall outside these skill definitions – although there are some important exceptions, such as nurses. However, a closer analysis of the immigration policies of wealthy destination countries suggests that they cannot be reduced to a simple dichotomy between permitting some forms of labour and keeping out others. Official policies may ostensibly be designed around such a dichotomy, but in reality they do accommodate a variety of different and contradictory pressures.

These contradictory impulses and policies in the field of migration policies have given rise to immigration governance regimes that are characterized by a considerable degree of incoherence. A diverse range of actors, both state and non-state, are in a position to exercise arbitrary authority over the status and lives of people who lack clear legal protection. But they do so within an official framework that lends itself to highly selective interpretations as to when the law applies, to whom it applies and what exceptions to the law can be permitted.

Flexibility of policy allows affluent countries to adapt their immigration laws to different needs at different times and thus take advantage of the benefits associated with permitting increased entry in times of economic boom, and expelling migrants in times of crisis. Such flexibility is built into low-skilled migration through insistence on the temporariness of migrant workers and the institutionalization of circular migration, bringing in migrant labour on a temporary but repeated basis.

Flexibility is also built in through the combination of official insistence on closed and tightly policed borders and an unofficial policy of considerable porousness that allows in a steady flow of undocumented migrants. Points of entry and closure are not confined to national borders but operate through a variety of state and non-state gatekeepers, such as police officers, lawyers, judges, translators and local officials.

Finally and importantly, flexibility allows countries to respond to humanitarian concerns through recognition of exceptions. Such exceptions often relate to situations where migrants can be defined as victims, and labour market disadvantage can be cast as a 'moral concern'. These situations relate primarily to sex work and trafficking but also, as in Spain, to victims of domestic violence. These various forms of flexibility have instrumental value in permitting countries a supply of low-cost migrant labour while at the same time placating anti-migration interests. But their political consequences – for migrants as a group and for the societies in question – are profound. The practice of official resistance to migration combined with tacit acceptance denies migrants important protections allowed to other workers. Restrictions on workers' rights – and curbs on their human rights – differentially disadvantage women because they compound the physical and social isolation in which most migrant women engage in paid work, making them more subject to physical, psychological and sexual abuse: the denial of one's liberty, being subject to compulsory pregnancy and other medical tests and restrictions on the right to interact socially with family and friends can have devastating consequences for an individual's mental health and well-being.

The resulting stereotypes and systemic misrecognition of migrants' contributions to the economy of the receiving country and to the well-being and care of its citizens contribute to persistence of xenophobia and to periodic backlash, particularly in times of economic crisis. While most women workers in the more hidden niches of the economy – paid domestic work in particular – are denied protection and rights, it is the foreignness of migrant women, particularly undocumented ones, that puts them in a particularly precarious position since they do not have the rights of citizens or of workers.

Similar contradictions and incoherence can be observed at the international level, rooted in cross-cutting the concerns of rich, labour-receiving countries and less-affluent, labour-sending ones. We can see two sides of the larger neoliberal agenda, which celebrates the lifting of controls over the global movement of finance and investment capital: the first is related to restriction and neoliberalism; the second to the protection of migrant rights. A large number of organizations at the international, regional and national levels have been engaged in promoting this agenda. Given its standard-setting role with regard to workers' rights, the ILO can be regarded as the only agency with a constitutional mandate to protect migrant workers. It carries out its initiatives via formal standard setting through conventions and non-binding recommendations. The United Nations Educational, Scientific and Cultural Organization (UNESCO) has taken a specific interest in the 1990 UN International Convention on the Protection of the Rights of All Migrant Workers and Members of their Families. UNESCO functions mainly through commissioning studies on the obstacles to, and opportunities for, the ratification of the UN convention in various countries as well as active involvement in the Global Migration Group, an inter-agency group seeking to promote wider application of relevant international and regional instruments and norms relating to migration. The United Nations Development Fund for Women (UNIFEM) is also active in protecting and promoting the rights of women migrant workers, predominantly in the Southeast and East Asia region, although its promotion of standard contracts for all foreign domestic workers in Jordan and Lebanon has provided a good practice model for countries of destination elsewhere.

At both the international and national levels, non-governmental organizations (NGOs) have been very active in the defence of immigrants' rights as citizens and workers. The People's Global Action on Migration, Development and Human Rights Forum articulates migrant workers' rights as part of a human rights agenda. We can also add to the list the role of Amnesty International, the Euro Mediterranean Human Rights Network, the European Women's Lobby and RESPECT, a European network for migrant domestic workers' organizations, in fighting violence and discrimination against migrant workers. Despite these efforts, progress has been slow. The main labour-importing countries have not ratified UN or ILO conventions on migrant workers, so no legal or moral obligation binds them to migrant worker protections. The governments of labour-export countries must rely on the discretion and goodwill on the part of host governments to implement bilateral agreements and this cannot always be assured. International organizations' (IOs') success in drawing attention to the need for migrant worker protections is rarely matched by concrete programmes on the ground. Migrant workers' organizations, often supported by IOs, such as the ILO, the International Organization for Migration (IOM) and UNIFEM, have generally been more successful in pressuring labour-exporting countries and encouraging programmes such as pre-departure programmes designed to familiarize migrant workers with their employment rights as well as their responsibilities and the cultural contexts in which they will be working.

The crucial problem is that where the agendas of regulation and rights conflict, as in other areas of international governance, rights tend to be subordinated to market imperatives. This partly reflects the fact that most IOs depend on their funding from national governments and mainly from the wealthier donor countries that have spearheaded the rise of global neoliberalism.

At the international and national levels, there is a disproportionate focus on trafficking as the exceptional form of migration, with greater stress on the criminal activities of traffickers than on the rights-based protection of trafficked victims. The US in particular has used its annual Trafficking in Persons Report as a major tool in spearheading its global leadership role in the fight against trafficking. Its influence explains the large amounts of global funding available for anti-trafficking programmes, despite the fact that there is little, if any, clear evidence that trafficking is the most pressing concern in international migration. The disproportionate focus on trafficking serves to detract attention from the violations and abuses suffered by the larger stream of migrants.

Basok and Piper (2012) argue that the IOM exemplifies these tensions at the international level. The IOM is financially dependent on the rich industrialized countries that are interested in the regulation and control of migration flows but it is also an international apparatus with strategic priorities and relative autonomy from member states. The IOM articulates the rhetoric of migrant workers' rights but a great deal of its practice falls into the area of migration control (for example, through so-called 'voluntary' repatriation programmes, administration of detention and deportation camps). By prioritizing the regulation over the rights agenda, the IOM tends to interpret the protection of the rights of migrant women predominantly from the trafficking or violence against women perspectives. The IOM's priorities are well illustrated in its 2009 report, which dealt with addressing and preventing violence against women migrant workers. The report was organized around a number of themes: promoting legal and safe migration; regulating migrant recruitment and deployment; promoting and protecting migrants' human rights; researching and collecting data on women and international labour migration; fostering interstate dialogue as well as cooperation at the bilateral, regional and international levels; and counter-trafficking activities. It is noteworthy, and, among these activities, even those seemingly unrelated to trafficking include a reference to trafficking.

In summary, we can frame the issue of international migration at both the national and international levels has served to simultaneously sideline the exploitative conditions under which most migrant workers are routinely employed and to focus inordinate attention on a few. The attention given to the rights of migrant workers in exceptional cases, most frequently defined in terms of the trafficking of women and children and violence against women, allows the injustices and violence perpetrated on other 'illegal aliens' to go unchecked. And finally, the trafficking frame that dominates the international discourse on migration promotes a selective perspective that sees the abuse of migrant workers' rights as the fault of traffickers rather than as the byproduct of the asymmetries in the mobility of capital and labour juxtaposed with the vast economic disparities between rich and poor countries and the dynamics of immigration politics at the country level.

CONCLUSION

This chapter addresses the importance of gender awareness for understanding the multiple aspects of international migration. From labour-market dynamics to remittances, development and governance, any analysis of migration will miss important insights if gender divisions and asymmetries are not considered. Our introduction provides an analysis on the usefulness of incorporating gender analysis and gender-related variables that open up information leading to policy and action. They highlight the fact, for example, that women do not escape the gender segmentation of labour markets by migrating from their home country but simply experience it in a different, often intensified, form in the receiving country. In fact, their labour-market segregation in the latter is generally greater than that experienced by migrant men as well as by native women. The intersection of global and local inequalities has given rise to the irony that educated women are relatively more likely than educated men to migrate, presumably because of more limited opportunities at home, but they generally end up in jobs for which they are overqualified.

A gender analysis of international migration also makes visible the increasing commodification of care work on a global scale. The emergence of care deficits in some of the world's wealthier countries, itself partly a reflection of women's entry into the labour market in these countries, has in turn given rise to the well-known phenomenon of care chains that straddle richer and poorer countries located in different regions of the world. Studies have shown that many of the women migrating as part of the care chain are able to fulfil their unpaid care responsibilities to their children and families only by leaving them behind to take on paid care responsibilities for the children and families of others. This in turn creates new care needs within their own families and gives rise to care deficits within the larger society. Other factors that add to care deficits within sending countries arise from the emigration of skilled and unskilled women who might otherwise have worked in the paid care economy: the negative gendered impact of this brain drain appears to be greater in poorer countries, but more research is needed along these lines. In any case, it is clear that migration contributes to the social reproduction not only of individual families but also of affected countries as a whole.

Furthermore, a gender perspective highlights the ways in which the organization of families is changing as a result of migration. The rise of transnational families, including transnational mothering, has been studied and much debated since the late 1990s although more research is needed to understand, for example, the effects on children who are part of these transnational ties. One recent aspect of this is the study of marriage migration in a variety of countries. While marriage migration is ostensibly a response to demographic factors such as internal migration and the emergence of deficits of women in the marriage market in certain countries in the world, it appears also to be acting as a means to address care deficits in relation to the growing proportion of elderly. It has given rise to what the Korean government has dubbed 'the multicultural family'. Current research and comparative analysis on this topic, particularly in Asia, is likely to throw light on the different factors contributing to this phenomenon.

Gender also defines how different categories of migrants enter policy discourse. For instance, there is growing evidence of migrant women's contribution to remittance flows that are relatively, and sometimes absolutely, greater than that of men migrants. Women have therefore featured very positively in the migration and development policy discourse, often constructed as the more altruistic members of their family, motivated by a greater sense of commitment to family well-being than men. While women's greater contribution may reflect a variety of factors, not only a sense of altruism but also greater pressure to meet familial obligations than men, it may also reflect the greater temporariness of their status as migrants – since temporary workers are more likely to send remittances home. The possibility of achieving legal and permanent status is much more likely for occupations staffed by men, relegating disproportionate numbers of women to the ranks of temporary, often undocumented migrants. It also leaves women far more easily exploited under precarious working conditions.

Finally, while international migration generally presents a number of challenges to nation-based notions of citizenship, particularly in the receiving countries, gender inflects this challenge in a number of ways. Women migrants are far more likely than men to be in isolated jobs that have little or no social or legal protection: paid domestic work and sex work are obvious examples. They are more likely to be on temporary contracts that tie them to particular employers. While they may sometimes be singled out for special treatment, it is largely as victims who invoke moral concerns: as victims of domestic violence who may be treated as exceptions to efforts to regulate migration or as victims of trafficking who must be rescued and returned to their home country. What policy makers have generally failed to do, however, is to address the rights violations that most temporary migrants, and women in particular, experience on a daily basis. This work represents a step further in understanding these issues theoretically, empirically and as a basis for policy and action.

NOTE

* The original version of this chapter first appeared in *Feminist Economics*, **18** (2), 2012, 1–33, under the same title. This amended version is reproduced here with the kind permission of the copyright holder, IAFFE. Details are available at http://www.feministeconomics.org.

REFERENCES

Altman, Meryl and Kerry Pannell (2012), 'Policy gaps and theory gaps: women and migrant domestic labour', *Feminist Economics*, **18** (2), 291–315.
Basok, Tanya and Nicola Piper (2012), 'Management versus rights: women's migration and global governance in Latin America and the Caribbean', *Feminist Economics*, **18** (2), 35–61.
Bener´ıa, Lourdes (2008), 'The crisis of care, international migration, and public policy', *Feminist Economics*, **14** (3), 1–21.
Bener´ıa, Lourdes (2009), 'Globalization, women's work, and care needs: the urgency of reconciliation policies', *North Carolina Law Review*, **88** (5), 1501–25.
Bhagwati, Jagdish and Koichi Hamada (1974), 'The brain drain, international integration of markets for professionals and unemployment: a theoretical analysis', *Journal of Development Economics*, **1** (1), 19–42.
Blue, Sarah A. (2004), 'State policy, economic crisis, gender, and family ties: determinants of family remittances to Cuba', *Economic Geography*, **80** (1), 63–82.

Carrington, William J. and Enrica Detragiache (1999), 'How extensive is the brain drain?', *Finance & Development: A Quarterly Magazine of the IMF*, **36** (2), 46–9.
del Barrio, Ana (2010), 'Los nuevos emigrantes' (The new emigrants), *El Mundo*, 22 July.
Díaz-Varela, Mar (2011), 'La salida de inmigrantes reducirá los parados en medio millónen el 2012' (The exit of immigrants will reduce the number of unemployed by half a million in 2012), *La Vanguardia*, 28 November.
Donato, Katharine M. (2010), 'US Migration from Latin America: gendered patterns and shifts', *The ANNALS of the American Academy of Political and Social Science*, **630** (1), 78–92.
Dumont, Jean-Christophe, John P. Martin and Gilles Spielvogel (2007), 'Women on the move: the neglected gender dimension of the brain drain', IZA Discussion Paper 2920, Institute for the Study of Labour (IZA), Bonn.
Durand, Jorge and Douglas S. Massey (2010), 'New world orders: continuities and changes in Latin American migration', *The ANNALS of the American Academy of Political and Social Science*, **630** (1), 20–52.
Ehrenreich, Barbara and Arlie Russell Hochschild (eds) (2002), *Global Woman: Nannies, Maids, and Sex Workers in the New Economy*, New York: Metropolitan Books.
Epstein, Gerald, Julie Graham and Jessica Gordon Nembhard (eds) (1993), *Creating a New World Economy: Forces of Change and Plans for Action*, Philadelphia, PA: Temple University Press.
Financial Crisis Inquiry Commission (2011), *The Financial Crisis Inquiry Report: Final Report of the National Commission on the Causes of the Financial and Economic Crisis in the United States*, Washington, DC: US Government Printing Office.
Ghosh, Jayati (2009), 'Migration and Gender Empowerment: Recent Trends and Emerging Issues', Human Development Research Paper 2009/4, Human Development Reports, United Nations Development Programme (UNDP), New York.
Herrera, Gioconda (2006), 'Mujeres ecuatorianas en las cadenas globales del cuidado' (Ecuadorian women in global care chains), in Herrera and María Moreno-Ruiz (eds), *Cohesión social, políticas conciliatorias y presupuesto puúblico: Una mirada desde el género* (Social cohesion, reconciliation policies and the public budget: a gender perspective), Mexico City: UNFPA and GTZ, pp. 118–26.
Herrera, Gioconda (2012), 'Starting over again? Crisis, gender, and social reproduction among Ecuadorian migrants in Spain', *Feminist Economics*, **18** (2), 125–48.
Holst, Elke, Andrea Schäfer and Mechthild Schrooten (2012), 'Gender and remittances: evidence from Germany', *Feminist Economics*, **18** (2), 201–29.
International Labour Organization (ILO) (2010), *International Labour Migration: A Rights-Based Approach*, Geneva: ILO.
International Labour Organization (ILO) and International Institute for Labour Studies (ILS) (2008), *World of Work Report 2008: Income Inequalities in the Age of Financial Globalization*, Geneva: ILO.
International Labour Organization (ILO) and International Institute for Labour Studies (ILS) (2010), *World of Work Report 2010: From One Crisis to the Next?*, Geneva: ILO.
International Organization for Migration (IOM) (2009), 'Working, to Prevent and Address Violence Against Women Migrant Workers', IOM, Geneva.
Jolly, Susie, with Hazel Reeves (2005), *Gender and Migration: Overview Report*, Brighton BRIDGE and Institute of Development Studies.
Kabeer, Naila (2007), 'Marriage, motherhood and masculinity in the global economy: reconfigurations of personal and economic life', IDS Working Paper 290, Institute of Development Studies (IDS), University of Sussex, Brighton.
Leahy, Joe (2011), 'Don't improvise capital controls, IMF says', *The Financial Times*, 29 May.
López-Calva, Luis F. and Nora Lustig (2010), 'Explaining the decline in inequality in Latin America: technological change, educational upgrading, and democracy', in López-Calva and Lustig (eds), *Declining Inequality in Latin America: A Decade of Progress?*, New York and Washington, DC: United Nations Development Programme (UNDP) and Brookings Institution Press, pp. 1–24.

Lyberaki, Antigone (2011), 'Migrant women, care work, and women's employment in Greece', *Feminist Economics*, **17** (3), 101–31.
Margheritis, Ana (2011), '"Todos somos migrantes": the paradoxes of innovative state-led transnationalism in Ecuador', *International Political Sociology*, **5** (2), 198–217.
Moran-Taylor, Michelle J. (2008), 'When mothers and fathers migrate North: caretakers, children, and child rearing in Guatemala', *Latin American Perspectives*, **35** (4), 79–95.
Parreñas, Rhacel Salazar (2005), *Children of Global Migration: Transnational Families and Gendered Woes*, Stanford CA: Stanford University Press.
Pérez Orozco, Amaia (2009), 'Global perspectives on the social organization of care in times of crisis: assessing the situation', trans. Laura Olsen, Working Paper 5, Gender, Migration and Development Series, United Nations International Research and Training Institute for the Advancement of Women (INSTRAW).
Petrozziello, Allison J. (2011), 'Feminised financial flows: how gender affects remittances in Honduran–US transnational families', *Gender & Development*, **19** (1), 53–67.
Preibisch, Kerry L., Gladys Rivera Herrejón and Steve L. Wiggins (2002), 'Defending food security in a free-market economy: the gendered dimensions of restructuring in rural Mexico', *Human Organization*, **61** (1), 68–79.
Rao, Smriti and Christina Presenti (2012), 'Understanding human trafficking origin: a cross-country empirical analysis', *Feminist Economics*, 18 (2), 231–63.
Razavi, Shahra (2011), 'Rethinking care in a development context: an introduction', *Development and Change*, **42** (4), 873–903.
Razavi, Shahra and Silke Staab (2010), 'Underpaid and overworked: a cross-national perspective on care workers', *International Labour Review*, **149** (4), 407–22.
Reich, Robert B. (2010), 'How to end the Great Recession', *The New York Times*, 3 September.
Ribas-Mateos, N. (2013), *How Filipino Immigrants in Italy Send Money Back Home: The Role of Informal Cross-Border Money Remittances in the Global Economy*, Lewinston, Queenston and Lampeter: Edwin Mellen Press.
Rosewarne, Stuart (2012), 'Temporary international labour migration and development in South and Southeast Asia', *Feminist Economics*, **18** (2), 63–90.
Schmalzbauer, Leah (2004), 'Searching for wages and mothering from afar: the case of Honduran transnational families', *Journal of Marriage and Family*, **66** (5), 1317–31.
Standing, Guy (2011), *The Precariat: The New Dangerous Class*, London: Bloomsbury.
Sutcliffe, Bob (1998), *Nacido en otra parte: Un ensayo sobre la migración internacional, el desarrollo y la equidad* (Born elsewhere: An essay on international migration, development and equity), Bilbao: Hegoa.
United Nations Development Programme (UNDP) (2009), *Human Development Report 2009: Overcoming Barriers: Human Mobility and Development*, New York: UNDP.
United Nations Development Programme (UNDP) (2010), *Human Development Report 2010: The Real Wealth of Nations: Pathways to Human Development*, New York: UNDP.
United Nations Population Fund (UNFPA) (2006), *State of World Population 2006: A Passage to Hope: Women and International Migration*, New York: UNFPA.
World Bank (2011), *Migration and Remittances Factbook 2011*, 2nd edn, Washington, DC: World Bank.
Yakovlev, Petr (2010), 'Los problemas clave de las migraciones internacionales' (Key problems in international migration), in Carmen de la Céamara (ed.), *Ensayos de economía crítica en homenaje a Benjamin Bastida* (Essays in critical economics in homage to Benjamin Bastida), Barcelona: Publicacions I Edicions de la Universitat de Barcelona, pp. 198–201.
Yeates, Nicola (2009), 'Women's migration, social reproduction and care', in Shahra Razavi (ed.), *The Gendered Impacts of Liberalization: Towards 'Embedded Liberalism'?*, New York: Routledge, pp. 219–43.

3 Talking culture: new boundaries, new rhetorics of exclusion in Europe*
Verena Stolcke

Es gibt zwei Sorten von Ratten, die hungrigen und die satten; die Satten bleiben vergnügt zuhaus, die Hungrigen wandern aus . . . Oh weh, sie sind schon in der Näh. (There are two kinds of rat, the hungry ones and the well fed ones; the well fed stay happily at home while the hungry ones emigrate . . . Oh dear! They are already approaching).

Heinrich Heine (translated by the author)

The uniqueness of European culture, which emerges from the history of the diversity of regional and national cultures, constitutes the basic prerequisite for European Union.

Commission of the European Communities (1987)

PREFACE 2012

I first published this work in 1995. As it has turned out, it was sadly prophetic. Little research was then and still is available on the political background, namely the nation-state, in which transnational migration takes place and by which it is regulated, controlled and migrants are symbolized. At the time readers did not quite understand my central argument about the ideological assumptions on which growing rejection and aggression of non-European immigrants were based. As I contended then, in the contemporary debate about the problems that transnational migrants who hoped to settle in Europe posed, the idea of the boundedness of cultures and cultural differences had gained new prominence. By now, however, it is not only the political right in Europe that employs a political rhetoric of exclusion in which non-European immigrants, who proceed in part from its ex-colonies, are construed as posing a threat to the national identity and unity of the receiving countries because they are culturally different. In addition, this rhetoric of exclusion has generally been branded as a new form of racism. I argued, however, that rather than asserting different endowments of human races, this discourse postulated instead a xenophobia supposedly innate in human nature, that is, a propensity of human nature to reject strangers. This assumption underlies radical opposition between nationals and immigrants as foreigners precisely informed by a reified notion of bounded and distinct, localized national–cultural identity and heritage that is employed to rationalize the call for restrictive immigration policies. My conclusion was that what I called 'cultural fundamentalism' of the political right is, with respect to traditional racism, both old and new. It is old in that it draws for its argumentative force on the unresolved contradiction in the modern conception of the nation-state between an organicist and a voluntarist idea of belonging. It is new in that, because racism has become discredited politically in Europe, cultural fundamentalism attributes the alleged incompatibility between different cultures to an incapacity of different cultures to communicate that which is inherent to human nature. Furthermore, the very idea of 'human nature' is part and parcel of Cartesian dualism, that is, the binary opposition between nature and culture so ingrained in modern ontology, which allows for essentializing attitudes that can be demonstrated to be political such as the antagonism and discrimination towards non-European immigrants.

But what have been the changes with regard to transnational migration that have taken place since the original publication? On the one hand, the belief that globalization was in the process of bringing about a post-national world, has proved to be an illusion. Financial capital and goods do, indeed, circulate ever more freely and speedily around the globe. And the paradox of walls and fences being built in this global world to contain the 'invasion' of migrants who challenge the borders of the wealthy countries – for example, in the south of Spain between Morocco, Melilla and Ceuta or between Mexico and the United States – has made the unrelenting political function of state borders to control the entrance of migrants all the more evident (*El País*, 17 October 2012, p. 14). Besides, the financial and economic world crisis has brought to light within the European Union endless quarrels inspired by new and old fears about the loss of national sovereignty.

On the other hand, however, there is no doubt that transnational migration is at once both a cause and an effect of the progressive expansion in the past four decades of an internationalized labour market. Because my aim has been to examine the ideological reactions to transnational migrants in Europe, I have hardly dealt with the composition by origin, sex, family status and so on, of transnational migration. However, abundant research is now available, not least in this volume, which shows that transnational migrants have never been only archetypical young single males.

Women transnational migrants were initially largely invisible in research because they were regarded as family dependants. Yet, thanks to properly focused gender-oriented research the rising proportion of women migrants, be they married or single, not least in response to specific job opportunities in care work has been documented in relation to family migratory projects, migration chains, gender relations, and so on. As a consequence of the composition of transnational migration by sex and the gendered nature of work opportunities and conditions in the receiving country, the internationalized labour market is, moreover, doubly segmented, namely by sex and by the legal status of migrants according to whether they have access to residence and work permits – another effect of the operation of state and border controls.

Robert Frost's metaphorical poem *Mending Wall* (1914) sums up well the socio-political backdrop of contemporary transnational migration:

> ... Before I built a wall I'd ask to know
> What I was walling in or walling out ...

BUILDING WALLS IN A GLOBAL WORLD

As anthropology gradually outgrows postmodernist self-scrutiny and cultural self-examination and moves back into the real world, neither the world nor the discipline is any longer the same. Anthropologists have learned to be more sensitive to the formidable difficulties involved in making sense of cultural diversity without losing sight of shared humanity. At the same time, the notions of culture and cultural difference, anthropology's classical stock-in-trade, have become ubiquitous in the popular and political language in which Western geo-political conflicts and realignments are being phrased. Anthropologists in recent years have paid heightened critical attention to the many ways in which Western economic and cultural hegemony has invaded the rest of the world and to how 'other' cultures have resisted and reworked these insidious influences. How these 'others' are being politically and culturally rethought by the West, where the idea of cultural distinctness is being endowed with new divisive force has, however, attracted surprisingly little interest among anthropologists. I want to address one major instance of contemporary culture-bounded political rhetoric.

The alarming spread of hostility and violence in Europe against immigrants from the Third World has provoked much soul-searching in the past decade over the resurgence of the old demon of racism in a new guise. I propose, however, that a perceptible shift in the rhetoric of exclusion can now be detected. From what were once assertions of the differing endowment of human races there has risen since the 1970s a rhetoric of inclusion and exclusion that emphasizes the distinctiveness of cultural identity, traditions and heritage among groups and assumes the closure of culture by territory (Soysal, 1993). In this chapter, first I shall examine the nature of this shift in the way in which European anti-immigrant sentiment is phrased, and then I shall trace the social and political roots and the implications of this new rhetoric.

The formation of liberal states and notions of belonging has, of course, been quite different from one Western European country to another. History may explain the origins of these different political traditions, but it is not the cause of their continuity; each period interprets history according to contemporary needs. Therefore, I shall conclude by contrasting the ways in which the national political repertoires of Britain and France have shaped and been employed to legitimate mounting animosity against immigrants.

The building of Europe is a twofold process. As intra-European borders become progressively more permeable, external boundaries are ever more tightly closed. Stringent legal controls are put in place to exclude what have come to be known as 'extra-communitarian' immigrants as parties of the right appeal for electoral support with the slogan 'Foreigners Out!'. There is a growing sense that Europeans need to develop a feeling of shared culture and identity of purpose in order to provide the ideological support for European economic and political union that will enable it to succeed. But the idea of a supranational, culturally integrated Europe, and how much space is to be accorded to national and regional cultures and identities, are matters of intense dispute because of the challenge to national sovereignties they are variously felt to pose (Gallo, 1989; Commission of the European Communities, 1987, 1992; Cassen, 1993). By contrast, immigrants, in particular those from the poor South (and, more recently, also from the East) who seek shelter in the wealthy North, have all over Western Europe come to be regarded as undesirable, threatening strangers, aliens. The extra-communitarian immigrants already 'in our midst' are the targets of mounting hostility and violence as politicians of the right and conservative governments fuel popular fears with a rhetoric of exclusion that extols national identity predicated on cultural exclusiveness.

The social and political tensions that extra-communitarian immigration has provoked in a context of successive economic crises have been accompanied by a heightened concern over national cultural identities which has eroded the cosmopolitan hopes professed in the aftermath of the deadly horrors of the Nazi race policies of the Second World War. The demons of race and eugenics appeared to have been politically if not scientifically exorcised partly by the work done by UNESCO and other bodies in defence of human equality in cultural diversity in the Boasian tradition after 1945 (Lévi-Strauss, 1978, 1985; Haraway, 1988; Nye, 1993, p. 669). Yet cultural identity and distinctiveness, ideas which until then seemed to be a peculiar obsession only of anthropologists, have now come to occupy a central place in the way in which anti-immigration sentiments and policies are being rationalized.

There is a growing propensity in the popular mood in Europe to blame all the socioeconomic ills resulting from the recession and capitalist readjustments – unemployment, housing shortages, mounting delinquency, deficiencies in social services – on immigrants who lack 'our' moral and cultural values, simply because they are there (see Taguieff, 1991, for a detailed analysis and challenge of these imputations in the case of France). The advocates of a halt to immigration and like-minded politicians have added to the popular animosity towards immigrants by artificially increasing the scale of the 'problem'. Allusions to an 'immigration flood' and an 'emigration bomb' serve to intensify diffuse popular fears, thereby diverting spreading social discontent from the true causes of the economic recession. Opponents of immigration often add to this the neo-Malthusian argument which attributes declining socioeconomic opportunities and poverty and the consequent desire or need to migrate to the 'population bomb' ticking away in the Third World, which is blamed especially on its women's reproductive improvidence. They thereby mask the economic–political roots of modern poverty and instead justify aggressive population control programmes whose targets are women in the poor South. Advocates of a halt to immigration talk of a 'threshold of tolerance', alluding to what ethologists have called the, 'territorial imperative' – the alleged fact that populations (note, among animals) tend to defend their territory against 'intruders' when these exceed a certain proportion estimated variously at 12–25 per cent, because otherwise severe social tensions are bound to arise (Erdheim, 1992, p. 19; Zungaro, 1992). The media and politicians allude to the threat of cultural estrangement or alienation (Kallscheuer, 1992; Winkler, 1992). In other words, the 'problem' is not 'us', but 'them'. 'We' are the measure of the good life which 'they' are threatening to undermine and this is so because 'they' are foreigners and culturally 'different'. Although rising unemployment, the housing shortage and deficient social services are obviously not the fault of immigrants, 'they' are effectively made into the scapegoats for 'our' socioeconomic problems. This line of argument is so persuasive because it appeals to the 'national habitus', an exclusivist notion of belonging and political and economic rights conveyed by the modern idea of the nation-state (Elias, 1991) central to which is the assumption that foreigners, strangers from without, are not entitled to share in 'national' resources and wealth, especially when these are apparently becoming scarce. It is conveniently forgotten, for example, that immigrants often do the jobs that natives won't. Similarly overlooked are the otherwise much bemoaned consequences of the population implosion in the wealthy North, that is, the very low birthrates in an ageing Europe, for the viability of industrial nations and the welfare state ('Below-replacement fertility', 1986; Berquó, 1993). The question why, if there is a shortage of work, intolerance and aggression are not directed against one's fellow citizens is never raised.

The meaning and nature of these rationalizations of animosity towards immigrants and the need to curb extra-communitarian immigration have been highly controversial. I shall here analyse the political centre's and right's rhetoric of exclusion rather than examining the logic of popular anti-immigrant resentment. Popular reactions and sentiments cannot simply be extrapolated from the discourse of the political class.

IMMIGRANTS: A THREAT TO THE CULTURAL INTEGRITY OF THE NATION

In the early 1980s, Dummett identified a change in Britain in the idiom in which rejection of immigrants was being expressed when she drew attention to the tendency to attribute social tensions to the *presence* of immigrants with *alien cultures* rather than to racism (Dummett and Martin, 1982, p. 101, my emphasis; see also Dummett, 1973). As early as in the late 1960s the right in Britain was exalting 'British culture' and the 'national community', distancing itself from racial categories and denying with insistence that its hostility towards immigrant communities and its call for a curb on immigration had anything to do with racism (see Asad, 1990, on the idea of Britishness, constructed out of the values and sensibilities of the English dominant class; see also Dodd, 1986). People 'by nature' preferred to live among their 'own kind' rather than in a multicultural society, this attitude being, after all, a natural, instinctive reaction to the presence of people with a different culture and origin. As Alfred Sherman, director of the rightwing Institute for Policy Studies and one of the main theoreticians of this doctrine, elaborated in 1978, 'National consciousness is the sheet anchor for the unconditional loyalties and acceptance of duties and responsibilities, based on personal identification with the national community, which underlie civic duty and patriotism' (quoted in Barker, 1981, p. 20; see also Barker and Beezer, 1983; Barker, 1984). Immigrants in large numbers would destroy the 'homogeneity of the nation'. A 'multiracial' society would inevitably endanger the values and culture of the white majority and unleash social conflict. These were non-rational, instinctual fears built around feelings of loyalty and belonging (Barker and Beezer, 1983, p. 125).[1] As Enoch Powell had argued in 1969, 'an instinct to preserve an identity and defend a territory is one of the deepest and strongest implanted in mankind . . . and . . . its beneficial effects are not exhausted' (quoted in Barker, 1981, p. 22).

Until the late 1970s such nationalist claims were put forward only by a few (though vociferous) ideologues of the right who went out of their way to distance themselves from the overt racism of the National Front, morally discredited by its association with Nazi ideology. By the 1980s, with mounting economic difficulties and growing animosity against immigrants, in an effort to gain electoral support the Tory party had adopted a discourse of exclusion which was similarly infused by expressions of fear for the integrity of the national community, way of life, tradition and loyalty under threat from immigrants (Barker, and Beezer, 1983; Barker, 1984). One symptomatic example of this ideological alignment of the Tory party with its right is Margaret Thatcher's much-quoted statement of 1978:

> People are really rather afraid that this country might be swamped by people with a different culture. And, you know, the British character has done so much for democracy, for law, and done so much throughout the world, that if there is a fear that it might be swamped, people are going to react and be hostile to those coming in. (Quoted in Fitzpatrick, 1987, p. 121)

To protect 'the nation' from the threat immigrants with alien cultures posed for social cohesion, their entry needed to be curbed.

A similar shift in the rhetoric of exclusion has also been identified within the French political right. Taguieff (1987) is probably the most detailed, though controversial, analysis of ideological developments among the various tendencies of the French right since the 1970s. It is controversial because the author at once harshly criticizes antiracist organizations for invoking, in their defence of immigrants' right to difference, what he regards as an equally essentialist conception of cultural difference (see also Duranton-Crabol, 1988). The French right began orchestrating its anti-immigrant offensive by espousing what Taguieff has termed a 'differential racism', a doctrine which exalts the essential and irreducible cultural difference of non-European immigrant communities whose presence is condemned for threatening the 'host' country's original national identity. A core element of this doctrine of exclusion is the repudiation of 'cultural miscegenation' for the sake of the unconditional preservation of one's own original, purportedly biocultural, identity. In Taguieff's terms, by contrast with earlier 'inegalitarian racism', rather than inferiorizing the 'other' it exalts the absolute, irreducible difference of the 'self' and the incommensurability of different cultural identities. A key concept of this new rhetoric is the notion of *enracinement* (rootedness). To preserve both French identity and those of immigrants in their diversity, the latter ought to stay at home or return there. Collective identity is increasingly conceived in terms of ethnicity, culture, heritage, tradition, memory and difference, with only occasional references to 'blood' and 'race'. 'Differential racism' constitutes a strategy designed by the French right to mask what has become a 'clandestine racism' (Taguieff, 1987, pp. 330–37).

Notwithstanding the insistent emphasis on cultural identity and difference, scholars have tended to identify a 'new style of racism' in the anti-immigrant rhetoric of the right (Barker, 1981, 1984; Taguieff, 1987; Solomos, 1991; Wieviorka, 1993). Several related reasons have been adduced for this. Analysts in France no less than in Britain attribute this culturalist discourse of exclusion to a sort of political dialectic between antiracists' condemnation of racism for its association with Nazi race theories and the right's attempts to gain political respectability by masking the racist undertones of its anti-immigrant programme. Besides, ordering humans hierarchically into races has become indefensible scientifically (Barker, 1981; Taguieff, 1987), and it is a mistake to suppose that racism developed historically only as a justification of relations of domination and inequality (Barker, 1981). Lastly, even when this new 'theory of xenophobia' (ibid.) does not employ racial categories, the demand to exclude immigrants by virtue of their being culturally different 'aliens' is ratified through appeals to basic human instincts, that is, in terms of a pseudo-biological theory. Even though the term 'race' may, therefore, be absent from this rhetoric, it is racism none-the-less, a 'racism without race' (Rex, 1973, pp. 191–2; Balibar, 1988 [1991]; Gilroy, 1991, pp. 186–7; Solomos, 1991).

CULTURAL FUNDAMENTALISM: A NEW CONSTRUCTION OF EXCLUSION

However, the emergence of culture as the key semantic terrain (Benthall and Knight, 1993, p. 2) of political discourse needs to be explored more carefully. I want to argue that it is misleading to see in the contemporary anti-immigrant rhetoric of the centre and right a new form of racism or a racism in disguise. This is, of course, no mere quibble over words. Not for a moment do I want to trivialize the socio-political import of this novel exaltation of cultural difference, but in order to combat the beast we need to know what sort it is. To this end we need to do more than uncover the strategic motives for the right's disavowal of racism and analyse the conceptual structure of this new political discourse and the repertoire of ideas on which it draws.

A substantive conceptual shift that can be detected among political rightists and conservatives towards an anti-immigrant rhetoric predicated on cultural diversity and incommensurability is, in fact, informed by certain assumptions implicit in the modern notions of nationality, citizenship, national identity and the nation-state. Even if this celebration of national-cultural integrity instead of appeals to racial purity is a political ploy, this does not explain why the right and conservatives, in their efforts to protect themselves from accusations of racism, should have resorted to the invocation of national-cum-cultural identity and incommensurability to do this. This culturalist rhetoric is distinct from racism in that it reifies culture conceived as a compact, bounded, localized and historically rooted set of traditions and values transmitted through the generations by drawing on an ideological repertoire that dates back to the contradictory nineteenth-century conception of the nation-state.[2]

Rather than asserting different endowments of human races, contemporary cultural fundamentalism (as I have chosen to designate this contemporary anti-immigrant rhetoric) emphasizes differences of cultural heritage and their incommensurability. The term 'fundamentalism' has conventionally been reserved for describing anti-modern, neo-traditionalist religious phenomena and movements, interpreted as a reaction to socioeconomic and cultural modernization. As I shall argue, however, the exaltation in the contemporary secular cultural fundamentalism of the right of primordial national identities and loyalties is not pre-modern, for the assumptions on which it is based form a contradictory part of modernity (Dubiel, 1992; Klinger, 1992). There is something genuinely distinct from traditional racism in the conceptual structure of this new doctrine, which has to do with the apparently anachronistic resurgence, in the modern, economically globalized world, of a heightened sense of primordial identity, cultural difference and exclusiveness. What distinguishes conventional racism from this sort of cultural fundamentalism is the way in which those who allegedly threaten the social peace of the nation are perceived. The difference between these two doctrines resides, first, in the way in which those who are their respective targets are conceptualized – whether they are conceived as naturally inferior members or as strangers, aliens, to the polity, be it a state, an empire, or a commonwealth. Cultural fundamentalism legitimates the exclusion of *foreigners, strangers*. Racism has usually provided a rationalization for class prerogatives by naturalizing the socioeconomic inferiority of the underprivileged (to disarm them politically) or claims of national supremacy (Blanckaert, 1988). Second, whereas both doctrines constitute ideological themes that 'naturalize' and thereby aim to neutralize specific socio-political cleavages whose real roots are economic–political, they do this in conceptually different ways. Equality and difference tend to be arrayed against each other in political discourse in both cases, but the difference which is invoked and the meaning with which it is endowed differ. There may be occasional references to 'blood' or 'race', but there is more to this culturalist discourse than the idea of insurmountable essential cultural differences or a kind of biological culturalism (Lawrence, 1982, p. 83), namely, the assumption that relations between different cultures are by nature hostile and mutually destructive because it is in human nature to be ethnocentric; different cultures ought, therefore, to be kept apart for their own good.

Homo Xenophobicus

An assumption regarding human nature can, in effect, be found in political as well as popular discourse on extra-communitarian immigration in the 1980s. Newspaper headlines, politicians and scholars invoke the term 'xenophobia' along with racism to describe mounting anti-immigrant animosity. In 1984, for example, the European Parliament convened a committee of inquiry to report on the rise of fascism and racism in Europe in a first attempt to assess the extent and meaning of anti-immigrant hostility. In 1985 the committee concluded that 'a new type of spectre now haunts European politics: xenophobophilia'. The report described xenophobia as 'a latent resentment or "feeling", an attitude that goes before fascism or racism and can prepare the ground for them but, in itself, does not fall within the purview of the law and legal prevention' (Evregenis, 1985, p. 60). The components of this more or less diffuse feeling and of increasing tensions between the national and immigrant communities and their association with a general sense of social malaise, it was argued, were admittedly difficult to identify, but one element was 'the time-honoured distrust of strangers, fear of the future combined with a self-defensive reflex' (p. 92). One outcome of the committee's work was a Declaration against Racism and Xenophobia made public in 1986 (European Parliament, 1986). In 1989 the Parliament set up yet another committee of inquiry, this time into racism and xenophobia. Its task was to assess the efficacy of the declaration and to update the information on extra-European immigration in the light of the extension of freedom of movement within Europe to be introduced in 1992–93 (European Parliament, 1990). The notion of xenophobia was thus incorporated, without any further attempt to dispel its ambiguities, into European Parliament parlance. The media and politicians have equally picked up the idea and it has captured the European imagination in general. It was this terminological innovation which first made me wonder whether there was not something distinct to the rhetoric of exclusion whereby anti-immigrant sentiment in Western Europe is justified.[3]

Xenophobia literally means 'hostility toward strangers and all that is foreign' (*Le Petit Robert*, 1967). Cashmore, in his 1984 *Dictionary of Race and Ethnic Relations*, still dismissed the term as a 'somewhat vague psychological concept describing a person's disposition to fear (or abhor) other persons or groups perceived as outsiders' because of its uncertain meaning and hence its limited analytical value in that it presupposes underlying causes which it does not analyse; therefore, he thought (as it has turned out, wrongly), 'it has fallen from the contemporary race and ethnic relations vocabulary' (p. 314). Either the root causes of this attitude are not specified or it is taken for granted that people have a natural propensity to fear and reject outsiders because they are different.[4] The right's explicit sympathy and the affinity of its argument with key postulates of human ethology and socio-biology have been noted repeatedly (Barker, 1981, ch. 5; Duranton Crabol, 1988, pp. 44, 71–81). The scientific weaknesses of notions of human nature based on biological principles such as the territorial imperative and the tribal instinct, according to which humans no less than animals have a natural tendency to form bounded social groups and for the sake of their own survival to differentiate themselves from and to be hostile to outsiders have been reiterated (see, for example, Sahlins, 1976; Gould 1981; Lowentin et al., 1984). The point here is, however, to show why a belief in *Homo xenophobicus* has so much commonsense appeal.

Striking in that it suggests that this assumption is not restricted to the scientific or political right is, for example, Cohn-Bendit and Schmid's (1991, p. 5, my translation and emphasis) argument:

> The indignation over xenophobia (*Fremdenhass*), which suggests as an antidote a policy of open borders, is somehow false and dangerous. *For if history has taught us one thing, then it is this: in no society has a civil intercourse with foreigners been inbred. Much indicates that the reserve* vis-à-vis *the foreigner constitutes an anthropological constant of the species*: and modernity with its growing mobility has made this problem more general than it was before.[5]

This claim is as politically dangerous as it is scientifically indemonstrable, for history, by contrast, for example, with biology, is unable to prove human universals, at least as far as our contemporary understanding of the human experience goes. Besides, it is not difficult to come up with examples showing the fallacy of the idea that xenophobia is part of the human condition. The war in Bosnia provides probably the most tragic contemporary instance. Until Serbian radical nationalism tore them apart, Muslims, Serbs and Croats had lived together as neighbours in their acknowledged religious and other cultural differences.

Xenophobia, an attitude supposedly inherent in human nature, constitutes the ideological underpinning of cultural fundamentalism and accounts for people's alleged tendency to value their own culture to the exclusion of any other and therefore be incapable of living side by side.

Contemporary cultural fundamentalism is based, then, on two conflated assumptions: that different cultures are incommensurable and that, because humans are inherently ethnocentric, relations between cultures are by nature hostile. Xenophobia is to cultural fundamentalism what the bio-moral concept of 'race' is to racism, namely, the naturalist constant that endows truth with value and legitimates the respective ideologies.

RACISM VERSUS CULTURAL FUNDAMENTALISM

A systematic comparison of the conceptual structures of traditional racism and this cultural fundamentalism may render clearer the distinctness of what are alternative doctrines of exclusion.[6] They have in common that they address the contradiction between the modern universalist notion that all humans are naturally equal and free and multiple forms of socio-political discrimination and exclusion, but they do so differently. Both doctrines derive their argumentative force from the same ideological subterfuge, namely, the presentation of what is the outcome of specific politico-economic relationships and conflicts of interest as natural and hence incontestable because it, as it were, comes naturally.

Modern Western racism rationalizes claims of national superiority or socio-political disqualification and economic exploitation of groups of individuals within a polity by attributing to them certain moral, intellectual or social defects supposedly grounded in their 'racial' endowment which, by virtue of being innate, is inevitable. The markers invoked to identify a 'race' may be phenotypic or invented. Racism thus operates with a particularistic criterion of classification, namely, 'race', which challenges the claim to shared humanness by dividing humankind into inherently distinct groups ordered hierarchically, one group making a claim to exclusive superiority. In this sense racist doctrines are categorical, concealing the socio-political relationships that generate the hierarchy. 'Race' is construed as the necessary and sufficient natural cause of the unfitness of 'others' and hence of their inferiority. Socio-political inequality and domination are thereby attributed to the criterion of differentiation itself, namely, 'their' lack of worth, which is in 'their' race. As a doctrine of asymmetric classification racism provokes counter-concepts that demean the 'other' as the 'other' could not demean the 'self'. Mutual recognition is denied precisely because the 'racial' defect, being relative, is not shared by the 'self'. And that is the point. By attributing unequal status and treatment to its victims' own inherent shortcomings, this doctrine denies the ideological character of racism itself.

Of course, this raises the important question of the place of an idea of social status inscribed in nature, rather than resulting from contract, in modern society, otherwise conceived of as consisting of self-determining individuals born equal and free. Modern racism constitutes an ideological sleight-of-hand for reconciling the irreconcilable – a liberal meritocratic ethos of equal opportunity for all in the marketplace and socioeconomic inequality – which, rather than being an anachronistic survival of past times of slavery and/or European colonial expansion and the ascriptive ordering of society, is part and parcel of liberal capitalism (Goldberg, 1993; Stolcke, 1993; Fitzpatrick, 1987).

At different moments in history systems of inequality and oppression have been rationalized in distinct ways. Racist doctrines are only one variation of the same theme, namely, the endeavour to reconcile an idea of shared humanity with existing forms of domination. Early modern colonial encounters with 'primitives' intensely exercised European minds. Initially it was not their phenotypic diversity which haunted the European imagination but their different religious-cum-moral attitudes which were felt to challenge Christian hegemony. How, if God had created 'man' in His image, could there be humans who were not Christians? Nineteenth-century scientific racism was a new way of justifying domination and inequality inspired by the search for natural laws that would account for the order in nature and society. Striking in the nineteenth-century debate over the place of humans in nature is the tension between man's faith in free will unencumbered by natural constraints, in his endeavour as a free agent to master nature, and the tendency to naturalize social man. Social Darwinism, eugenics and criminology provided the scientific legitimization for consolidating class inequality. Their first targets were the dangerous labouring classes at home (see, for example, Chevalier, 1958 [1984]). If the self-determining individual, through persistent inferiority, seemed unable to make the most of the opportunities society purported to offer, it had to be because of some essential, inherent defect. The person or, better, his or her natural endowment – be it called racial, sexual, innate talent, or intelligence – rather than the prevailing socioeconomic or political order was to be blamed for this. This rationale functioned both as a powerful incentive for individual effort and to disarm social discontent. Physical anthropology at the same time lent support both to claims of national supremacy among European nations and to the colonial enterprise by establishing a hierarchy of bio-moral races (Blanckaert, 1988; Brubaker, 1992, pp. 98–102).

Cultural fundamentalism, by contrast, assumes a set of symmetric counter-concepts, that of the foreigner, the stranger, the alien as opposed to the national, the citizen. Humans by their nature are bearers of culture. But humanity is composed of a multiplicity of distinct cultures which are incommensurable, the relations between their respective members being inherently conflictive because it is in human nature to be xenophobic. An alleged human universal – people's natural propensity to reject strangers – accounts for cultural particularism. The apparent contradiction, in the modern liberal democratic ethos, between the invocation of a shared humanity which involves an idea of generality so that no human being seems to be excluded and cultural particularism translated into national terms is overcome ideologically: a cultural 'other', the immigrant as foreigner, alien, and as such a potential enemy who threatens 'our' national-cum-cultural uniqueness and integrity, is constructed out of a trait which is shared by the 'self'. In a further ideological twist, national identity and belonging interpreted as cultural singularity becomes an insurmountable barrier to doing what comes naturally to humans, in principle, namely, communicating.

Instead of ordering different cultures hierarchically, cultural fundamentalism segregates them spatially, each culture in its place. The fact that nation-states are by no means culturally uniform is ignored. Localized political communities are regarded by definition as culturally homogeneous. Presumed inherent xenophobic propensities – though they challenge the supposed territorial rooting of cultural communities, since they are directed against strangers 'in our midst' – re-territorialize cultures. Their targets are uprooted strangers who fail to assimilate culturally.

Being symmetrical, these categories are logically reversible – any national is a foreigner to any other nation in a world of nation-states, for to possess a nationality is in the nature of things. This formal conceptual polarity – nationals as against foreigners – is charged with political meaning. By manipulating the ambiguous link between national belonging and cultural identity, the notion of xenophobia infuses the relationship between the two categories with a specific and substantive political content. Because the propensity to dislike strangers is shared by foreigners, it also becomes legitimate to fear that the latter, by their disloyalty, might threaten the national community. When the 'problem' posed by extra-communitarian immigration is conceptualized in terms of self-evident cultural difference and incommensurability, the root causes of immigration, namely, the deepening effects of North–South inequality, are explained away.

Cultural fundamentalism invokes a conception of culture paradoxically inspired by both the universalist Enlightenment tradition and German romanticism that marked much of nineteenth-century nationalist debate. By building its case for the exclusion of immigrants on a trait shared by all humans alike rather than on an unfitness allegedly intrinsic to extra-communitarians, cultural fundamentalism, by contrast with racist theories, has a certain openness which leaves room for requiring immigrants, if they wish to live in our midst, to assimilate culturally. And because of the other important idea in modern Western political culture, namely, that all humans are equal and free, anti-immigrant rhetoric is polemical and open to challenge, which is why existing forms of exclusion, inequality and oppression need to be justified ideologically.

At the core of this ideology of collective exclusion predicated on the idea of the 'other' as a foreigner, a stranger, to the body politic is the assumption that formal political equality presupposes cultural identity and hence cultural sameness is the essential prerequisite for access to citizenship rights. One should not confuse the useful social function of immigrants as scapegoats for prevailing socioeconomic ills with the way in which immigrants as foreigners are conceptualized. Rather than being thematized directly, immigrants' socioeconomic exclusion is a consequence of their political exclusion (*Le Monde Diplomatique*, 1993). Opponents of immigration on the right may object to granting immigrants the social and political rights inherent in citizenship on economic grounds. Immigration is construed as a problem, however, because it allegedly threatens national identity and integrity on account of immigrants' cultural diversity because the nation-state is conceived as founded on a bounded and distinct community which mobilizes a shared sense of belonging and loyalty predicated on a common language, cultural tradition and beliefs. In a context of economic recession and national retrenchment, appeals to primordial loyalties fall on fertile ground because of the ordinary taken-for-granted sense of national belonging that is the common idiom of contemporary political self-understanding (Weber, 1976, cited by Brubaker, 1992).

Immigrants are seen as threatening to bring about a 'crisis of citizenship' (Leca, 1992, p. 314)[7] in both a juridical and a politico-ideological sense. In the modern world nationality as the precondition for citizenship is inherently bounded as an instrument and an object of social closure (Brubaker, 1992). In this respect, nationality is not all that different from the kinship principles that operated in so-called 'primitive societies' to define group membership. In the modern world of nation-states, nationality, citizenship rights, cultural community and state are conflated ideologically (Beaud and Noiriel, 1991, p. 276) and endow immigrants' cultural distinctiveness with symbolic and political meaning.

It may be objected that not all immigrants or foreigners are, of course, treated with animosity. This is obviously true. But then, equality and difference are not absolute categories. The politico-ideological repertoire on which the modern nation-state is built provides the raw materials from which cultural fundamentalism is constructed. Specific power relationships with the countries from which extra-communitarian immigrants proceed and the exploitation they have undergone explain why 'they' rather than, for example, North Americans are the targets in Europe of this rhetoric of exclusion. Hostility against extra-communitarian immigrants may have racist overtones, and metaphors can certainly be mixed. Yet, as somebody remarked to me recently, immigrants carry their foreignness in their faces. Phenotype tends now to be employed as a marker of immigrant origin rather than 'race' being construed as the justification for anti-immigrant resentment.

FRENCH REPUBLICAN ASSIMILATION VERSUS BRITISH ETHNIC INTEGRATION

For the sake of clarity I have so far neglected major differences in dealing with the immigration 'problem' among European countries that have been pointed out repeatedly (Lapeyronnie, 1993 Rouland, 1993, Wieviorka, 1993; pp. 16–17). 'It is an almost universal activity of the modern state to regulate the movement of the people across its national boundaries' (Evans, 1983, p. 1), but this can be done in diverse ways. The Dutch and the British governments were the first to acknowledge the presence in their countries of so-called 'ethnic minorities'. All Western European states were, by the 1980s, curbing immigration and attempting to integrate immigrants already in their midst. Depending on their political cultures and histories, different countries designed their immigration policies differently. The French model, informed by the traditional Republican formula of assimilation and civic incorporation, contrasted sharply with the Anglo-Saxon one, which left room for cultural diversity, although by the 1980s a confluence could be detected between the two countries' anti-immigrant rhetoric and restrictive policies.

The entry and settlement of immigrants in Europe poses again the question of what constitutes the modern nation-state and what are conceived as the prerequisites for access to nationality as the precondition for citizenship. Three criteria – descent (*jus sanguinis*), birthplace (*jus soli*), and domicile combined with diverse procedures of *naturalization* (note the term) – have usually been wielded to determine entitlement to nationality in the modern nation-states. *Jus sanguinis* constitutes the most exclusive principle. However, the priority given historically to one or another criterion has depended not only on demographic–economic and/or military circumstances and interests but also on conceptions of the national community and the substantial ties of nationhood. The classical opposition between the French *Staatsnation* and the German *Kulturnation* (Meinecke, 1919; Guiomar, 1990, pp. 126–30) has often obscured the essentialist nationalism present also in nineteenth-century French thought and debate on nationhood and national identity and hence the part played by the Republican formula of assimilation in the French conception of the Republic.[8] Almost from the start there has been a tension between a democratic, voluntarist and an organicist conception of belonging in the continental European model – by contrast with the British tradition – of the modern nation-state which, depending on historical circumstances, has been drawn on to formulate and rationalize a more or less exclusive idea of the nation and of citizenship. A comparison of French and British post-war experiences and treatments of the immigration problem will serve to make this point (see Lapeyronnie, 1993, for a different interpretation).

The French debate over immigration since the 1970s reveals the ambivalence underlying the Republican assimilationist conception of nationality and citizenship. The first genuine French nationality code was enacted in 1889, at a time when foreigners, predominantly of Belgian, Polish, Italian and Portuguese origin, had a large presence in the country, by contrast with Germany. The code drew a sharp line between nationals and foreigners.[9] It consecrated *jus sanguinis*, that is, descent from a French father and, in the case of an illegitimate child, from the mother, as the first criterion of access to French nationality, but simultaneously it reinforced the principle of *jus soli*, according to which children of foreigners born on French soil were automatically French (Brubaker, 1992, pp. 94–113, 138–42; see also Noiriel, 1988, pp. 81–4). The relative prominence given to *jus soli* in the code has been interpreted as a liberal, inclusive solution (ibid., p. 83; Brubaker, 1992). On closer inspection this combination of descent and birthplace rules can also be read, however, as a clever compromise struck for military and ideological reasons (in the context of the confrontation over Alsace-Lorraine following the French defeat in the Franco-German War and the establishment of the German Empire) between an organicist and a voluntarist conception which, though contradictory, are intrinsic to the French conception of the nation-state.

The nationality code of 1889 did not apply to the French colonies until French citizenship was extended to all colonial territories after the Second World War (Werner, 1935). As soon as Algeria gained its independence, however, Algerians became foreigners, while inhabitants of the French overseas departments and territories remained fully French, with right of entry into France. Those Algerians who were living in France at independence had to opt for French or Algerian citizenship. For obvious political reasons most of them rejected French nationality, though their French-born children continued to be defined as French at birth, as were the French-born children of the large numbers of immigrants to France in the decade following the war of independence (Weil, 1988). By the mid-1970s the regulation of French nationality and citizenship became inseparable from immigration policy. As opinion grew more hostile towards immigrants, especially from North Africa, *jus soli* came under increasing attack from the right for turning foreigners into Frenchmen on paper without ensuring that they were 'French at heart' (Brubaker, 1992, p. 143). A controversial citizenship law reform submitted in 1983 and designed to abolish the automatic acquisition of French nationality by French-born children of immigrants, requiring an explicit declaration instead, was nevertheless defeated in 1986 because of strong opposition to the traditional French assimilationist conception by pro-immigrant organizations and the left. In 1993 the new conservative government finally succeeded, however, in passing a reform to the same effect, which restricts the *jus soli* rule, thereby giving new prominence to *jus sanguinis*.[10]

Until the mid-1980s and in response to the right's cultural fundamentalism the antiracist movement and pro-immigrant organizations in France had advocated a multicultural model of integration based on respect for immigrants' cultural diversity. The heated debate over immigrants' 'right to difference' was typically French.[11] Thereafter progressive opinion began to swing around, calling for 'a return to the old republican theme of integration according to which membership in the nation is based not on an identity but on citizenship, which consists in individual adherence to certain minimal but precise universal values' ('Dossier', 1991, pp. 47–8). The 'republican model of integration' which conditions citizenship on shared cultural values and demands cultural assimilation became the progressive political alternative to the right's cultural fundamentalism.[12]

British immigration debate and experience developed quite differently. According to the traditional nationality law of England, later extended to Britain, every person born within the domain of its king was a British subject. Nineteenth-century French advocates of *jus sanguinis* had already rejected as inappropriate the British unconditional *jus soli* rule because for them citizenship reflected an enduring and substantial rather than merely accidental connection to France as well as the will to belong and because of its expansiveness and feudal roots (Brubaker, 1992, p. 90). But the meaning and consequences of legal norms depend on their historical context. The traditional British concept of subjecthood based on birth on British soil, which established an individual vertical bond of allegiance to the crown and its parliament, unaltered until 1962, allowed immigrants from the colonies free entry into the country as British subjects regardless of their cultural and/or phenotypic difference.[13] The Home Office (quoted by Segal, 1991, p. 9) argued in the 1930s as follows:

> It is a matter of fundamental importance both for the United Kingdom and for the Empire as a whole, if there is to be such an organization at all based in the last resort on a common sentiment of cohesion which exists, but cannot be created, that all British subjects should be treated on the same basis in

the United Kingdom. . . . It is to the advantage of the United Kingdom that persons from all parts of the Empire are attracted to it.

Despite post-war concerns over free and unrestricted immigration's lowering the quality of the British people (Dummett and Nicol, 1990, p. 174), the British Nationality Bill of 1948 ruled that British subjecthood was acquired by virtue of being a citizen of a country of the Commonwealth. Yet, as large numbers of immigrants arrived and demands for control increased, the Commonwealth Immigrants Act of 1962 introduced the first special immigration controls. It did not explicitly discriminate against non-white immigrants, but it left a large amount of discretion for immigration officers to select immigrants at a time when it went without saying that Commonwealth immigrants were not white (Dummett and Nicol, 1990, pp. 183–7; Segal, 1991, p. 9). In 1981, finally, the Conservative government passed the British Nationality Act, which brought nationality law in line with immigration policy and limited the ancient unconditional *jus soli*, concluding the process of *alienation* of New Commonwealth immigrants by transforming them into aliens (Evans, 1983, p. 46; Dummett and Nicol, 1990, pp. 238–51). Those who had been rejected earlier as 'black subjects' are now excluded as 'cultural aliens'.[14]

Britain's common law tradition and the absence of a code of citizenship rights had provided space for immigrant subjects' cultural values and needs. Tolerance for cultural diversity formed part of the history of Britain, acknowledged as a multicultural polity, until in the late 1970s an English-centric reinvention of that history took place (Clark, 1991a, b; Kearney, 1991). This does not mean that Britain's post-war immigration experience was not beset with social conflict. Anti-immigrant sentiment was alive and aggressions were frequent, but they were racist. Until the late 1970s the controversy over immigration was predominantly phrased in racist terms. As Dummett and Nicol (1990, p. 213) have pointed out:

> Just as the advocates of strict immigration control were exclusively concerned with non-white immigration, so the supporters of liberalisation attacked racial discrimination first and foremost and perceived immigration policy as the driving force behind this discrimination. It had become psychologically impossible for both sides to think of 'immigration' in any sense, or any context, except as a verbal convention for referring to the race situation in Britain.

Legal provisions to combat discrimination typically aimed at ensuring subjects from the ex-colonies equal opportunities independent of their 'race'.[15] As long as immigrants from the ex-colonies were British subjects they were fellow citizens, albeit considered as of an inferior kind.

Anti-immigrant prejudice and discrimination were rationalized in classical racist terms. Formal legal equality was not deemed incompatible with immigrants' different cultural traditions as long as these traditions did not infringe basic human rights. The right's demand for cultural assimilation constituted a minority opinion. Liberals defended integration with due respect for cultural diversity and the particular needs of 'ethnic' minorities. A key instrument of liberal integration policy was multicultural education. As I have shown above, when the Tory government took up the banner of curbing immigration it began to rationalize it, invoking, by contrast with earlier racist arguments, national-cum-cultural unity and calling for the cultural assimilation of immigrant communities 'in our midst' to safeguard the British 'nation' with its shared values and lifestyle. Immigrant communities needed to be broken up so that their members, once isolated, would cease to pose a cultural and political threat to the British nation. Immigrant children were to receive a standard English education, and uniform legal treatment was to be accorded them (Parekh, 1991). Thus as Europe appeared to evolve into a supranational polity, a continental nation-state paradoxically emerged out of the ashes of the British multicultural though racist empire.

THE NATION WITHIN THE STATE

As I indicated earlier, the debate over immigrants' 'right to difference' unleashed singular passions in France. The character and reasons for this controversy transcend the polarized political climate over the immigration problem. They reveal a historical tension inherent in the French universalistic Republican conception of the modern nation-state. In a world of emerging nation-states, the early cosmopolitan revolutionary spirit was soon eroded by a crucial dilemma, namely, how to build a nation-state endowed with a distinct and bounded citizenry. Ethnic group differences were, in principle, alien to the revolutionary democratic point of view. But, as Hobsbawm (1990, p.19, added italics; see also Cranston, 1988, p.101) has identified the problem:

> The equation nation = state = people, and especially sovereign people, undoubtedly linked nation to territory, since structure and definition of states were now essentially territorial. It also implied a multiplicity of nation states so constituted, and this was indeed a necessary consequence of popular self determination. . . . But it said little about what constituted *the people*. In particular there was no logical connection between a body of citizens of a territorial state, on one hand, and the identification of a *nation* on ethnic, linguistic or other grounds or of other characteristics which allowed collective recognition of group membership.

The advocates of an idea of the *nation* based on a freely entered contract among sovereign citizens usually invoke Renan's celebrated metaphor: 'The existence of a nation is a plebiscite of every day'. Renan's *Qu'est-ce qu'une nation?* (1882 [1992])[16] is in fact often taken for the expression of a conception of the nation particularly well suited to modern democratic individualism.[17] They tend to overlook, however, that Renan simultaneously uses another culturalist argument to resolve the difficulty of how to circumscribe the 'population' or 'people' entitled to partake in this plebiscite (ibid., p. 54):

> A nation is a soul, a spiritual principle. Two things which in reality make up no more than one constitute that soul, that spiritual principle. One is in the past, the other in the present. One is the shared possession of a rich heritage of memories; the other is the present consent, the desire to live together, the will to continue to sustain the heritage one has received undivided. . . . The nation, the same as the individual, is the realization of an extended past of endeavours, of sacrifice and of devotion. The cult of the ancestors is among all the most legitimate; the ancestors have made us what we are . . .

Two contradictory criteria, one political (free consent) and one cultural (a shared past), are thus constitutive of the *nation* (Noiriel, 1988, pp. 27–8; Todorov, 1989, pp. 165–261; see also Gellner, 1987, pp. 6–28 for a different, functionalist interpretation and, for a witty take-off of French republican mythology, Gatty, 1993).

Renan's difficulty in defining the 'nation' in purely contractual, consensual terms is just one illustration of a fundamental dilemma that has beset continental European state building. The principle of nationality, which identified the state, the people, and the law with an ideal vision of society as culturally homogeneous and integrated, became the novel, though unstable, form of legitimization in nineteenth-century struggles for state formation.

Contemporary cultural fundamentalism unequivocally roots nationality and citizenship in a shared cultural heritage. Though new with regard to traditional racism, it is also old, for it draws for its argumentative force on this contradictory nineteenth-century conception of the modern nation-state. The assumption that the territorial state and its people are founded on a cultural heritage that is bounded, compact and distinct is a constitutive part of this, but there is also, as I have argued, an important conceptual difference. Nineteenth-century nationalism received enormous reinforcement from the elaboration of one central concept of social theory, 'race'. With heightened enmity between nation-states, nationalism was often activated and ratified through claims to racial superiority of the national community. Because racist doctrines were discredited by the horrors of the Second

World War, cultural fundamentalism informed by the nineteenth-century cultural conception of the nation-state came in handy to underwrite the contemporary rhetoric of exclusion of extra-European immigrants, instead, by reifying cultural cum state boundaries and difference.

CONCLUSION

Not for a moment do I mean to deny different ways of organizing the business of life and different systems of meaning. Humans have, however, always been on the move, and cultures have proved fluid and flexible. The new global order, in which both old and new boundaries, far from being dissolved, are becoming more active and exclusive, also poses formidable new questions for anthropology. A crucial issue that should concern us is, then, the circumstances under which culture ceases to be something we need for being human to become something that impedes us from communicating as human beings. It is not cultural diversity *per se* that should interest anthropologists but the political meanings with which specific political contexts and relationships endow cultural difference. Peoples become culturally entrenched and exclusive in contexts where there is domination and conflict. It is the configuration of socio-political structures and relationships both within and between groups that activates differences and shapes possibilities and impossibilities of communicating. In order to make sense of contemporary cultural politics in this interconnected and unequal world, we need to transcend our sometimes self-serving cultural relativisms and methodological uncertainties and proceed to explore, in a creative dialogue with other disciplines, 'the processes of production of difference' (Gupta and Ferguson, 1992, pp. 13–14).

Genuine tolerance for cultural diversity can flourish without entailing disadvantages only where society and polity are democratic and egalitarian enough to enable people to resist discrimination (whether as immigrants, foreigners, women, blacks) and develop differences without jeopardizing themselves and solidarity among them. I wonder whether this is possible within the confines of the modern nation-state or, for that matter, of any state.

NOTES

* This is a revised and updated version of my 1995 article published as 'Talking culture: new boundaries, new rhetorics of exclusion in Europe', *Current Anthropology*, **36** (1), 1–24.

Talking culture 91

1. Barker (1981, p. 22) summed up what he called 'the new racism' as follows: 'Immigrants threaten to "swamp" us with their alien culture: and if they are allowed in large numbers they will destroy the "homogeneity of the nation". At the heart of this "new racism" is the notion of culture and tradition. A community is its culture, its way of life and its traditions. To break these is to shatter the community. These are non-rational (and indeed in the fully fledged version, instinctual), built around feelings of loyalty and belonging'.
2. For a different interpretation of British identity that attempts to reconcile a defence of British cultural values with tolerance for cultural diversity in the aftermath of the Rushdie affair received with approval by liberal opinion outside the Conservative party, see Asad (1990).
3. Scholars have noted increasingly frequent reference to xenophobia. Because hostility towards immigrants is, in practice, selective Taguieff (1987, p. 337, my translation), for example, has argued for the French case that 'in sum, the xenophobic attitude indicates only a limit; it never manifests itself in a strict sense (as the rejection of the foreigner as such) but results from a more or less explicit hierarchy of rejected groups. It is not a rejection of the "other" which does not choose among its "others" and does not presuppose a set of values which authorize discrimination. Any xenophobia in this sense constitutes a latent racism, a nascent racism'. Taguieff therefore also disagrees (pp. 80–81) with Lévi-Strauss's celebrated though controversial distinction between ethnocentrism as a universal attitude of cultural self-preservation and creativity and racism as a doctrine that justifies oppression and exploitation, which gained new prominence in the French debate over immigration. Others have interpreted xenophobic claims as a second-level racist discourse (Langmuir, 1978, p. 182 and Delacampagne, 1983, pp. 42–3, cited by Taguieff, 1987, pp. 79–80, 509). For a critique of Lévi-Strauss's cultural relativism, see Geertz (1986). More recently, Todorov (1989, pp. 81–109) has taken Lévi-Strauss to task for radical relativism and extreme cultural determinism. See also Lévi-Strauss (1994, pp. 420–26).
4. Béjin (1986, p. 306, my translation), for example, has asked in a critique of antiracists, 'Why has this natural and even healthy ethnocentrism which has been generated in Europe in recent years produced expressions of exasperation? It is the antiracists themselves who provide us with an adequate, even obvious, answer to this question when they insist that allegedly "racist" politicians experience an increase in their audiences under conditions and in regions where there is a strong, important and, in the event of apathy on the part of the "corps social", irreversible influx of immigrants of extra-European origin. They thus acknowledge, I presume involuntarily, that this exasperation is a *reaction of defence* by a community that senses that its identity is threatened, a reaction which presents analogies with the resistance this or that occupation by foreign armed forces has provoked in the past. This rejection might even, if international tensions intensify, become more profound as immigrants concentrate, modifying in a more irreversible way a country's identity than would occupation forces, which do not intend to settle and reproduce' (Layton-Henry, 1991, p. 169, added italics).
5. Cohn-Bendit was at the time the head of the Department of Multicultural Affairs of the city of Frankfurt, and Schmid was his assistant. This article was written in support of a shift in the Green party's immigration policy towards a system of immigration quotas (for a more cautious argument, see Cohn-Bendit and Schmid, 1992). Enzensberger (1992, pp. 13–14, my translation) argued similarly that 'every migration, independent of its causes, its aims, whether it be voluntary or involuntary, and its magnitude, leads to conflicts. Group selfishness and xenophobia constitute anthropological constants which precede any rationalization. Their universality suggests that they are older than any known form of society. Ancient societies invented taboos and rituals of hospitality in order to contain them, to prevent recurrent bloodbaths, to allow for a modicum of exchange and communication between different clans, tribes, ethnicities. These measures do not, however, eliminate the status of alien. On the contrary they institutionalize it. The guest is sacred but may not stay'. Another way of naturalizing and thus universalizing

what can be shown to be attitudes shaped by history consists in arguing that racism is universal. Thus Todorov (1989, p. 114, my translation) has argued that racism as a form of behaviour, as opposed to racialism as a pseudoscientific doctrine, is 'an ancient behaviour and probably a universal one; racialism is a current of opinion born in Western Europe whose heyday extends from the 18th to the middle of the 20th century'.

6. I draw here on Koselleck's (1985) important analysis of political counter-concepts.
7. Leca distinguishes between two ways of conceiving nationality as a condition of citizenship, one *biological* and another *contractual*, but does not pursue the politico and ideological implications of these distinct modalities.
8. By distinguishing between 'ethnic moments' (understood as racist) and 'assimilationist moments' in nineteenth-century French formulations of nationality law, in his comparative study of citizenship in France and Germany, Brubaker (1992, esp. ch. 5) disregards the fundamentalist assumption on which the assimilationist idea rests, namely, that formal legal equality among citizens presupposes cultural homogeneity.
9. The term '*étranger*' was introduced during the 'glorious revolution' to designate political enemies, traitors to the revolutionary cause – the French nobility plotting against the *patriotes* and the British suspected of conspiring to impose royal rule in Paris again. The assumption that the *étrangers* are bound to be disloyal to the nation has been especially powerful in times of war (Wahnich, 1988).
10. Charles Pasqua, the Gaullist French Minister of the Interior who drafted the reform, was also a staunch opponent of the Maastricht agreement and European political integration during the campaign in France for its approval by referendum with the revealing argument that: 'In France, the right to vote is inseparable from citizenship and this from nationality. There are 5 million foreigners here, 1.5 million of them communitarians. Our communitarian guests are welcome, but we are not willing to share our national sovereignty with them. France is an exceptional people and not an amalgam of tribes' (*El País*, 14 September 1992, p. 41).
11. Guillaumin (1992, p. 89) points to an important political distinction between the claim to 'a right to difference', which implies an appeal by immigrants for authorization by the state to be different from nationals, and 'the right of difference', which assumes a universal, inherent right.
12. In 1991 the socialist government set up a Ministry of Social Affairs and of Integration and a State Secretariat for Integration to promote immigrants' assimilation (Perroti and Thépaut, 1991, p. 102).
13. In the late 1960s the former liberal Tory Home Secretary, Reginald Maudling, revealingly argued that 'while one talked always and rightly about the need to avoid discrimination between black and white it is a simple fact of human nature that for the British people there is a great difference between Australians and New Zealanders, for example, who come of British stock, and people of Africa, the Caribbean, and the Indian Sub-Continent who are equally subjects of the Queen and entitled to total equality before the law when established here, but who in appearance, habits, religion and culture were totally different from us. The problem of balancing the moral principle of non-discrimination with the practical facts of human nature was not an easy one, and the dangers that arise from mistakes of policy in this field were very real indeed' (Evans, 1983, p. 21).
14. In 1969 Enoch Powell proposed a Ministry of Repatriation and referred to Commonwealth immigrants as 'aliens' in the cultural sense (Dummett and Nicol, 1990, p. 196).
15. To outlaw racial discrimination in public places, housing and employment, successive British governments passed a series of Race Relations Acts in 1965, 1968 and 1976 (Dummett and Nicol, 1990; Layton-Henry, 1991; Parekh, 1991). The 1976 Race Relations Act repealed earlier laws and created the Commission for Racial Equality, an administrative body responsible for implementing the equal opportunities policies laid down in the act (Walker and Redman, 1977 Lustgarten, 1980; Jenkins and Solomos, 1987).

16. Renan wrote this essay at the time of the Franco-German war over Alsace-Lorraine, claimed by Germany on the grounds that its population was of German culture and spoke the German language.
17. Louis Dumont, the prominent French anthropologist, is illustrative of those who overlooked the organicist elements in Renan when he contrasted that scholar's writings with those of Johann Gottfried Herder and Johann Gottlieb Fichte and emphasized an unwarrantedly sharp contrast between French voluntarist theory and the German ethnic conception (Dumont, 1979; also 1991).

BIBLIOGRAPHY

Asad, T. (1990), 'Multiculturalism and British identity in the wake of the Rushdie affair', *Politics and Society*, **18**, 455–80.
Balibar, E. (1988 [1991]), 'Existe un neoracismo?', in Balibar and I. Wallerstein (eds), *Raza, nación, y clase*, Madrid: IEPALA.
Barkan, E. (1992), *The Retreat of Scientific Racism: Changing Concepts of Race in Britain and the United States between the World Wars*, Cambridge: Cambridge University Press.
Barker, M. (1981), *The New Racism*, London: Junction Books.
Barker, M. (1984), 'Racism: the new inheritors', *Radical Philosophy*, **21**, 2–17.
Barker, M. and A. Beezer (1983), 'The language of racism: an examination of Lord Scarman's report on the Brixton riots', *International Socialism*, **2** (18), 108–25.
Beaud, S. and G. Noiriel (1991), 'Penser l'intégration des immigrés', in P.-A. Taguieff (ed.), *Face au racism*, vol. 2, *Analyses, hypothèses, perspectives*, Paris: Éditions La Découverte/Essais, pp. 261–82.
Béjin, A. (1986), 'Réflexions sur l'antiracisme', in Béjin and J. Freund, *Racismes, antiracismes*, Paris: Librairie des Méridiens, pp. 303–26.
'Below-replacement fertility in industrial societies: causes and consequences' (1986), *Population and Development Review*, **12**, suppl.
Benthall, J. and J. Knight (1993), 'Ethnic alleys and avenues', *Anthropology Today*, **9** (5), 1–2.
Berquó, E. (1993), 'La cuestión demográfica: Confrontación Sur-Norte', *Mujeres y política de población*, Oaxetepec, Mexico: Red de Salud de las Mujeres Latinoamericanas y del Caribe.
Blanckaert, C. (1988), 'On the origins of French ethnology: William Edwards and the doctrine of race', in G.W. Stocking Jr (ed.), *Bones, Bodies, Behavior Essays on Biological Anthropology*, Madison, WI: University of Wisconsin Press, pp. 18–55.
Brubaker, R. (1992), *Citizenship and Nationhood in France and Germany*, Cambridge, MA: Harvard University Press.
Bunyan, T. (1991), 'Towards an authoritarian European state', *Race and Class*, **32** (3).
Cashmore, E.E. (1984), *Dictionary of Race and Ethnic Relations*, London: Routledge.
Cassen, B. (1993), 'Culture et pouvoir', *Le Monde Diplomatique*, **40** (32), 474.
Chevalier, L. (1958. [1984]), *Classes laborieuse et classes dangereuses à Paris, pendant la première moitié du XIX siècle*, Paris: Hachette.
Clark, J.C.D. (1991a), 'Britain as a composite state: sovereignty and European integration', *Culture and History*, **9–10**, 55–84.
Clark, J.C.D. (1991b), 'Sovereignty: the British experience', *Times Literary Supplement*, 29 November, 15–16.
Cohn-Bendit, D. and T. Schmid (1991), 'Wenn der Westen unwiderstehlich wird', *Die Zeit*, 22 November, 5.
Cohn-Bendit, D. and T. Schmid (1992), *Heimat Babylon: Das Wagnis der multikulturellen Demokratie*, Frankfurt a.M.: Hoffman & Campe.
Commission of the European Communities (1987), 'A fresh boost for culture in the European Community', *Communication*, 14 December.

Commission of the European Communities (1992), 'New prospects for community cultural action', *Communication*, 29 April.
Cranston, M. (1988), 'The sovereignty and the nation', in C. Lucas (ed.), *The French Revolution and the Creation of Modern Political Culture*, vol. 2, *The Political Culture of the French Revolution*, Oxford: Pergamon Press, pp. 97–104.
Delacampagne, C. (1983), *L'invention du racisme: Antiquité et Moyen Age*, Paris: Fayard.
Dodd, P. (1986), 'Englishness and the national culture', in R. Colls and Dodd (eds), *Englishness: Politics and Culture 1880 to 1920*, London: Croom Helm, pp. 1–28.
'Dossier-Immigrés: Les 5 tabous' (1991), *L'Express*, 8 November, 47–8.
Dubet, F. (1989), *Immigration: Qu'en savons-nous? Un bilan des connaissances*, Notes et Études Documentaires 4887, Paris: La Documentation Française.
Dubiel, H. (1992), 'Der Fundamentalismus der Moderne', *Merkur*, **46** (9–10), 747–62.
Dummett, A. (1973), *A Portrait of English Racism*, Harmondsworth: Penguin.
Dummett, A. and I. Martin (1982), *British Nationalism: The AGIN Guide to the New Law*, London: Action Group on Immigration and Nationality/National Council for Civil Liberties.
Dummett, A. and A. Nicol (1990), *Subjects, Citizens, Aliens and Others: Nationality and Immigration Law*, London: Weidenfeld & Nicolson.
Dumont, L. (1979), 'Peuple et nation chez Herder et Fichte', *Libre*, **6**, 233–50.
Dumont, L. (1991), *L'idéologie allemande: France-Allemagne et retour*, Paris: Gallimard.
Duranton-Crabol, A.-M. (1988), *Visages de la nouvelle droite: Le GRECE et son histoire*, Paris: Presses de la Fondation Nationale des Sciences Politiques.
Elias, N. (1991), *La société des individus*, Paris: Fayard.
Enzensberger, H.M. (1992), *Die grosse Wanderung: 33 Markierungen*, Frankfurt a.M.: Suhrkamp.
Erdheim, M. (1992), 'Fremdeln, kulturelle Unverträglichkeit und Anziehung', *Kursbuch*, **107**, 19–32.
European Parliament (1986), *Declaration against Racism and Xenophobia*, Brussels.
European Parliament (1990), *Bericht im Namen des Untersuchungsausschusses Rassismus und Ausländerfeindlichkeit*, DOC-DE-RR-93062, Brussels, 23 July.
Evans, J.M. (1983), *Immigration Law*, London: Sweet & Maxwell.
Evregenis, M.D. (1985), 'Report Drawn up on Behalf of the Committee of Inquiry into the Rise of Fascism and Racism in Europe on the Findings of the Committee of Inquiry', PE DOC A 2-160/85, Brussels, 25 November.
Fitzpatrick, P. (1987), 'Racism and the innocence of law', in Fitzpatrick and A. Hunt (eds), *Critical Legal Studies*, Oxford: Basil Blackwell, pp. 119–21.
Frost, R. (1914), 'Mending Wall'.
Gallo, M. (1989), 'L'Europe sans nations, cet artifice, ce mirage dangereux', *Le Monde Diplomatique*, **36**, 420.
Gatty, J. (1993), 'Les soucis d'Ernest Renan', *Les Temps Modernes*, **48** (558), 1–11.
Geertz, C. (1986), 'The uses of diversity', *Michigan Quarterly Review*, Winter, 105–23.
Gellner, E. (1987), 'Nationalism and the two forms of cohesion in complex societies', in *Culture, Identity, and Politics*, Cambridge: Cambridge University Press, pp. 6–28.
Gilroy, P. (1991), 'Le fin de l'antiracisme', *Les Temps Modernes*, **46** (540–41), 186–7.
Goldberg, D.T. (1993), *Racist Culture: Philosophy and the Politics of Meaning*, Oxford: Blackwell.
Gord, G. (1991), 'There is a rising tide of racism sweeping across Europe', *The Courier* **129**, September–October.
Gould, S.J. (1981), *The Mismeasure of Man*, New York: Norton.
Guillaumin, C. (1992), *Sexe, race et pratique du pouvoir: L'idée de nature*, Paris: Côté Femmes.
Guiomar, J.-Y. (1990), *La Nation entre l'histoire et la raison*, Paris: Éditions La Découverte.
Gupta, A. and J. Ferguson (1992), 'Beyond "culture": space, identity, and the politics of difference', *Cultural Anthropology*, **7**, 6–44.
Haraway, D.J. (1988), 'Remodelling the human way of life: Sherwood Washburn and

the new physical anthropology, 1950–1980', in G.W. Stocking Jr (ed.), *Bones, Bodies, Behavior: Essays on Biological Anthropology*, Madison, WI: University of Wisconsin Press, pp. 206–59.
Herskovits, M. (1964), *Cultural Dynamics*, New York: Knopf.
Hobsbawm, E.J. (1990), *Nations and Nationalism since 1780*, Cambridge: Cambridge University Press.
Jenkins, R. and J. Solomos (eds) (1987), *Racism and Equal Opportunities Policies in the 1980s*, Cambridge: Cambridge University Press.
Kahn, J. (1989), 'Culture: demise or resurrection?', *Critique of Anthropology*, **9** (2), 5–25.
Kallscheuer, O. (1992), 'Fremde Götter oder die Grenzen der Toleranz', *Kursbuch*, **107**, 51–67.
Kearney, H. (1991), 'Nation-building – British style', *Culture and History*, **9–10**, 43–54.
Keesing, R.J. (1994), 'Theories of culture revisited', in R. Borofsky (ed.), *Assessing Cultural Anthropology*, New York: McGraw-Hill, pp. 301–12.
Klinger, C. (1992), 'Faschismus: Der deutsche Fundamentalismus?', *Merkur*, **46** (9–10), 782–98.
Koselleck, R. (1985), 'The historical–political semantics of assymmetric counterconcepts', in *Futures Past: On the Semantics of Historical Time*, Cambridge, MA: MIT Press, pp. 159–97.
Langmuir, G.I. (1978), 'Qu'est-ce que "les Juifs" signifiaent pour la société médiévale?', in L. Poliakov (ed.), *Ni Juif ni Grec: Entretiens sur le racisme, Antiquité et Moyen Age*, Paris: Mouton.
Lapeyronnie, D. (1993), *L'Individu et les minorités: La France et la Grande-Bretagne face à leurs immigrés*, Paris: Presses Universitaires de France.
Lawrence, E. (1982), 'Just plain common sense: the "roots" of racism', in Centre for Contemporary Cultural Studies (ed.), *The Empire Strikes Back: Race and Racism in '70s Britain*, London: Hutchinson.
Layton-Henry, Z. (1991), 'Race and immigration', in D.W. Urwin and W.E. Paterson (eds), *Politics and Western Europe Today: Perspectives, Policies, and Problems since 1980*, London: Longman, pp. 162–81.
Le Monde Diplomatique (1993), *Le temps des exclusions*, vol. 20 of Manière de voir.
Leca, J. (1992), 'La citoyennté en question', in P.-A. Taguieff (ed.), *Face ou racisme*, vol. 2, *Analyses, hypothèses, perspectives*, Paris: Éditions La Découverte/Essais, pp. 311–36.
Lévi-Strauss, C. (1978), *Structural Anthropology*, Vol. 2, Harmondsworth: Penguin.
Lévi-Strauss, C. (1985), 'Race and culture', in *A View from Afar*, New York: Basic Books.
Lévi-Strauss, C. (1994), 'Anthropology, race, and politics: a conversation with Didier Eribon', in R. Borofsky (ed.), *Assessing Cultural Anthropology*, New York: McGraw-Hill, pp. 420–26.
Lowentin, R.C., S.Rose and L.J. Kamin (eds) (1984), *Not in Our Genes: Biology, Ideology, and Human Nature*, Harmondsworth: Penguin Books.
Lustgarten, L. (1980), *Legal Control of Racial Discrimination*, London: Macmillan.
Meinecke, F. (1919), *Weltbürgertum und Nationalstaat*, 5th edn, Munich: Oldenburg.
Noiriel, G. (1988), *Le creuset français: Histoire de l'immigration XIXe-XXe siècle*, Paris: Éditions du Seuil.
Nye, R.A. (1993), 'The rise and fall of the eugenics empire: recent perspectives on the impact of biomedical thought in modern society', *Historical Journal*, **36** (3).
Parekh, B. (1991), 'La Grande-Bretagne et la logique sociale du pluralisme', *Les Temps Modernes*, **46** (540–41), 83–110.
Perroti, A. and F. Thépaut (1991), 'Revue de press: Immigration, le fracas dans les discours, la contradiction dans les faits', *Migrations-Société*, **3** (16–17), 93–116.
'Quels discours sur l'immigration?' (1988), *Plein Droit*, **3**, 2–37.
Renan, E. (1882 [1992]), *Qu'est-ce qu'une nation?*, edited by Joël Roman, Paris: Presses Pocket.
Rex, J. (1973), 'Race as a social category', *Race, Colonialism, and the City*, London: Routledge & Kegan.

Rouland, N. (1993), 'La France s'interroge sur la meilleure manière d'intégrer les étrangers', *Le Monde Diplomatique*, **40** (475), 16–17.
Sahlins, M. (1976), *The Use and Abuse of Biology: An Anthropological Critique of Sociobiology*, Ann Arbor, MI: University of Michigan Press.
Segal, D.A. (1991), '"The European": allegories of racial purity', *Anthropology Today*, **7** (5), 7–9.
Silverman, M. (1992), *Deconstructing the Nation: Immigration, Racism, and Citizenship in Modern France*, London: Routledge.
Solomos, J. (1991), 'Les formes contemporaines de l'idéologie raciale dans la société britannique', *Les Temps Modernes*, **46** (540–41), 65–82.
Soysal, Y.N. (1993), 'Construction of immigrant identities in Europe', paper presented at the conference 'European Identity and its Intellectual Roots', Cambridge, 6–9 May.
Stolcke, V. (Martinez-Alier) (1974), *Marriage, Class and Colour in Nineteenth-century Cuba: A Study of Racial Attitudes and Sexual Values in a Slave Society*, Cambridge: Cambridge University Press.
Stolcke, V. (1993), 'Is sex to gender as race is to ethnicity?', in Teresa del Valle (ed.), *Gendered Anthropology*, London: Routledge, pp. 17–37.
Taguieff, P.-A. (1987), *La force du préjugé: Essai sur le racisme et ses doubles*, Paris: Éditions La Découverte.
Taguieff, P.-A. (1991), *Face ou racisme*, Vol. 1, *Les moyens d'agir*, Paris: Éditions La Découverte/Essais.
Todorov, T. (1989), *Nous et les autres: La réflexion française sur la diversité humaine*, Paris: Éditions du Seuil.
Turner, T. (1993), 'Anthropology and multiculturalism: what is anthropology that multiculturalists should be mindful of it?', *Cultural Anthropology*, **8**, 411–29.
Wahnich, S. (1988), 'L'étranger dans la lutte des factions: Usage d'un mot dans une crise politique', *Mots*, **16**, special issue: *Langages: Langes de la Revolution Française*, 111–13.
Walker, D.J. and M.J. Redman (1977), *Racial Discrimination: A Simple Guide to the Provisions of the Race Relations Act of 1976*, London: Shaw.
Weber, E. (1976), *Peasants into Frenchmen: The Modernization of Rural France, 1870–1914*, Stanford, CA: Stanford University Press.
Weil, P. (1988), 'La politique française d'immigration (entre 1974 et 1986) et la citoyenneté', in C. Wihtol de Wenden (ed.), *La citonyenneté*, Paris: Edilig/Fondation Diderot, pp. 190–200.
Werner, A.-R. (1935), *Essai sur la réglementation de la nationalité dans le droit colonial français*, Paris: Librairie du Recueil Sirey.
Wieviorka. M. (ed.) (1993), *Racisme et modernité*, Paris: Éditions La Découverte.
Winkler, B. (ed.) (1992), *Zukunftsangst Einwanderung*, Munich: C.H. Beck Verlag.
Zungaro, E.G. (1992), 'Die Barbaren kommen: Ein Gespräch mit Piero Bassetti über Einwanderung und Invasion', *Kursbuch*, **107**, 120–30.

4 The long shadow of 'smart economics': the making, methodologies and messages of the *World Development Report 2012*
Sylvia Chant

INTRODUCTION

Following on from Benería et al. (ch. 3 in this volume), and recognising the huge strides that have been made in respect of gender and development (GAD) policy since the United Nations (UN) Decade for Women, my contribution focuses on the current state of play through the World Bank's *World Development Report 2012* (World Bank, 2011a, b, henceforth WDR 2012) on Gender Equality and Development.[1] What does WDR 2012 – the first ever World Development Report devoted to gender – represent in terms of progressing gender justice in development? More particularly, are there signs of change in the Bank's 'smart economics' approach, which has gathered ever more momentum in recent decades, was the zeitgeist of the Bank's Gender Action Plan (GAP) 2007–10, and has conventionally been associated more with building women's capacities in the interests of development than with promoting women's rights for their own sake?

My chapter is divided into four main sections. First, I locate 'smart economics' in a brief historical retrospective, identifying its correspondence with the 'efficiency approach' to gender planning of the 1980s. Second, I offer thoughts on the WDR 2012 consultation process in which I was personally involved. Third, I review the evolution of WDR 2012 from its first appearance in draft form on a dedicated Bank website in March 2011 to final publication six months later. Aside from discussing continuities and change in 'smart economics' language and philosophy, I draw attention to some notable omissions, including the comparative neglect of gendered migration. Finally, I reflect upon whether WDR 2012 is likely to aid or abet the struggle to achieve gender justice in development.

'SMART ECONOMICS': A BRIEF RETROSPECTIVE

'Smart economics' rationalises 'investing' in women and girls for more effective development outcomes. Its roots extend back until at least the

1980s, when, in the context of post-oil crisis recession and structural adjustment policies (SAPs), it became clear that women, individually and collectively, were picking up the shortfalls of SAP-related tendencies such as rising male un- and underemployment, the declining purchasing power of household incomes, and dwindling public sector service provision. Through women's efforts, both in the form of increased participation in remunerative activities, usually of an informal nature, and intensified unpaid labour at domestic and community levels, household members were 'cushioned' to a substantial degree from the worst effects of 1980s and 1990s neoliberal restructuring (see for example, Elson, 1989, 1991; Moser, 1989a, 1997; Benería, 1991; Benería and Feldman, 1992; Chant, 1994, 1996; González de la Rocha, 1994). In gender planning terms, recognition of the utility of harnessing the benefits of women's predominantly unpaid and largely 'voluntaristic' contributions translated into what Caroline Moser dubbed the 'efficiency approach' (Moser, 1989b, 1993). The latter has been strongly aligned with what Lourdes Benería (2012, p.175) describes as a tradition of 'fairly notorious' World Bank thinking on, and policy towards, gender issues, 'characterised . . . by an economistic and functionalist perspective on the integration of women in development'.

A landmark moment in the World Bank's pursuit of gender equality as a strategy for development effectiveness came in 1995 with its publication for the Fourth United Nations World Conference in Beijing: *Enhancing Women's Participation in Economic Development* (World Bank, 1995). In a chapter rather bluntly entitled 'The pay-offs to investing in women', the Bank claimed:

> Investing in women is critical for poverty reduction. It speeds economic development by raising productivity and promoting the more efficient use of resources; it produces significant social returns, improving child survival and reducing fertility, and it has considerable inter-generational pay-offs. (p. 22)

As Rianne Mahon (2012, p.173) points out with reference to Kate Bedford's (2009) dedicated research on the World Bank, gender equity became part and parcel of the agenda of the post-Washington Consensus. This process is evidenced, *inter alia*, by mounting reference to gender in mainstream Bank publications in the late twentieth and early twenty-first centuries (ibid., p.173), and to the parallel process of inserting 'smart economics' in its gender publications and policy statements. Indeed 'smart economics' assumed what I have termed 'full-blown' status (Chant, 2012, p.200) when the Bank's GAP 2007–10 was named 'Gender Equality as Smart Economics', and declared as its main objective: 'to advance women's economic empowerment by enhancing women's ability to participate in land, labour, financial and product markets, thus promoting shared growth and accelerating the implementation of MDG 3' (World Bank, 2006, p. 9).

The apparent importance to the Bank of advancing 'smart economics' through alignment with the third Millennium Development Goal (MDG 3), 'Promoting Gender Equality and Women's Empowerment', is revealed not only in repeated reference to MDG 3 in GAP 2007–10, but in several other Bank publications as well. This includes the *Global Monitoring Report* of 2007 (World Bank, 2007) which was dedicated to both gender and 'fragile states', and in which fulfilment of MDG 3 is deemed not just as a desirable outcome in and of itself, but also a means by which (neoliberal) economic development can be better assured (Chant and Sweetman, 2012). This is typified by statements such as: '(i)n the long run . . . greater gender equality in access to opportunities, rights and voice can lead to more efficient economic functioning and better institutions, with dynamic benefits for investment and growth. The business case for investing in MDG 3 is strong – it is nothing more than smart economics' (World Bank, 2007, p. 145; see also Buvinic and King, 2007).

Yet one might well ask why Bank gender discourse has accorded so much headroom to MDG 3 when the latter has been the subject of such intense debate in wider feminist circles, particularly in respect of its narrow indicators of female educational enrolment, share of non-agricultural employment, and parliamentary representation. These measures not only exclude large numbers of women, particularly in the Global South, but also constitute a decidedly insipid amalgam of objectives when compared with the considerably more far-reaching feminist agenda of the Beijing Platform for Action (BPFA) (see, for example, Barton, 2005; UNMP/TFEGE, 2005; Saith, 2006; Chant, 2007; Johnsson-Latham, 2010). Indeed, Peggy Antrobus (2004) has felt moved to suggest that the abbreviation MDG might better be described as 'Major Distracting Gimmick'! In a sense, then, it becomes less surprising that the World Bank has ostensibly chosen to channel its ('smart economics') gender work in the service of MDG 3. Given the Bank's historical hesitance in advancing a notably radical or rights-based approach when it comes to gender (or most other 'development' issues for that matter), the rather conservative remit of MDG 3 is entirely in keeping with this proclivity. On top of this, association with a UN-agreed goal for the first decades of the twenty-first century provides added legitimacy to the World Bank's gender programming, despite the irony that the Bank's 'endless policy conditionalities' at the macroeconomic level are likely to thwart the attainment even of the limited objectives of MDG 3 (Zuckerman, 2007, p. 1; see also Mblinyi, 2004; Painter, 2004; Schech and Dev, 2007; Woodford-Berger, 2007).

The 'endless policy conditionalities' to which Elaine Zuckerman refers have undoubtedly played a part in strengthening the ascendance of 'smart economics', since, in a neoliberalising and globalising macroeconomic context, women's routinely unpaid and (under)paid responsibilities become ever more critical (Chant and Sweetman, 2012).

Notwithstanding a pervasive need for tactical slogans to garner international support for gender – as I have previously argued in relation to the 'feminisation of poverty' (Chant, 2008) – soundbites on 'smart economics' as the rationale for investing in women have been used in a striking number of policy and advocacy campaigns, publications and web-based media in the past few years (see Box 4.1). That so many non-Bank GAD stakeholders have latched on to 'smart economics' as their mantra, and in so doing helped to popularise it, remains puzzling. While admitting that some might see some intrinsic good sense in 'smart economics', it is perhaps also important here to flag the pressure on smaller players in the international development field to stay 'hand in (financial) glove' with big donors. As articulated most succinctly by Robert Chambers (2010, p. 14): 'Recipients do not tell donors what they experience. They think about future funding'.

Despite widespread take-up of 'smart economics' as a rationale for investing in women and girls, and that everybody nominally stands to gain in its win–win scenario, one surely has to ask whether the goal of female investment is primarily to promote gender equality and women's 'empowerment', or to facilitate development 'on the cheap'. Regardless of the motives behind 'smart economics' adoption, one notable new strand in the picture has been the inclusion of girls. In Plan International's 'The State of the World's Girls 2009', for instance, quotes from two senior World Bank personnel are used to throw weight behind the message that 'girls matter'. One is provided by Dr Ngozi Okonjo-Iweala, then Managing Director of the World Bank,[2] who claims that, 'Investing in girls is the right thing to do. It is also the smart thing to do'. The second citation comes from incumbent World Bank President, Robert B. Zoellick,[3] who affirms that, 'Investing in adolescent girls is precisely the catalyst poor countries need to break intergenerational poverty and to create a better distribution of income. Investing in them is not only fair, it is a smart economic move' (see Plan International, 2009). One of the promotional videos of the Nike 'Girl Effect' campaign (Box 4.1), takes the message of investing in girls to perhaps even more extreme lengths by proposing that once these investments are made girls will 'do the rest', 'change the course of history' and safeguard the 'future of humanity' (Chant, 2012, p. 202).[4] One wonders, of course, why, in this cross-generational broadening of beneficiaries, gender remains exclusively identified with women and girls, and leaves men and

BOX 4.1 THE 'GLOBALIZATION' OF 'SMART ECONOMICS'?

'CARE works with women's aid. Women are one of the largest underutilised resources we have. When CARE invests in women, the entire world receives the value of that money . . . Today, more than 75% of the poor in the world are women. Women produce more than half of the world's food, but own only 1% of the farmed land in the world. Women are the key to raising education levels, countering the spread of HIV and AIDS, increasing access to clean water and good sanitary standards, better economic possibilities and protecting national resources . . . Poverty has a woman's face. But she has the power to change that. You have the power to help her do that' (Care Norway, available at: http://www.care.no, accessed 13 November 2008).

'Investing in women pays!' (Norwegian Agency for Development Cooperation, available at: http://www.norad.no, accessed 13 November 2008).

The 'Double Dividend of Gender Equality', sub-title of UNICEF, *State of the World's Children 2007*, New York: UNICEF (available at: http://www.unicef.org).

Gender Equality for Smarter Cities, Nairobi: UN-HABITAT (available at: www.un-habitat.org).

'Investing in girls has the potential to save the world' (Nike Foundation, 'Girl Effect', available at: http://www.youtube.com/watch?v=WIvmE4_KMNw).

Source: Chant (2012, p. 201, Table 1).

boys out of the picture. Is this because investments in men and boys are regarded as already sufficient? Or is it because the prospective 'returns to development' from male investments might be less than those in their female counterparts? If the latter is so, what does this signify in respect of the primacy of gender justice and rights *vis-à-vis* macroeconomic growth and/or to promote further economic liberalization? In the World Bank's first-year progress report on GAP 2007–10 (World Bank, 2008), for example, the aim of 'making markets work for women' was reiterated, but given the emphasis on investing in women to reduce poverty, to promote growth, and to benefit others, one gets the sense that this is much more about 'making women work for markets'.[5] In a similar vein, 'smart economics' is probably very 'smart' from the perspective of development agencies and wider society, but arguably less so when it comes to poor women and girls.

One case in point is provided by conditional cash transfer (CCT) programmes, which, in line with the instrumentalization of gender associated with 'smart economics', consign women to the role of what Maxine Molyneux (2006) has termed a 'conduit for policy'. Despite the nominally 'empowering' process of putting money in the hands of women in poor households, the underlying agenda is that women work in the service of others. In the particular case of CCTs, female 'beneficiaries' have to ensure that their sons and daughters remain healthy and stay in school, as well as to collaborate in various types of community work. Although some positive intergenerational impacts of CCTs have been noted, especially for girls (see, for example, González de la Rocha, 2010 on Mexico; Harman, 2010 on Malawi and Tanzania), this may come at the cost of increased time and work burdens for their mothers, the perpetuation of gender divisions of labour, and the (re)entrenchment of essentialising maternalist and 'female altruist' stereotypes (Molyneux, 2006, 2007; Bradshaw, 2008; Chant, 2008; Brickell and Chant, 2010; Tabbush, 2010; see also Roy, 2002, 2010; Mayoux, 2006). From such a vantage point it is no surprise that Elaine Zuckerman from the IFI-watching, Washington DC-based NGO Gender Action, complains that in GAP 2007–10 the World Bank's 'business case ignores the moral imperative of empowering women to achieve women's human rights and full equal rights with men' (Zuckerman, 2007, p. 1).

Although some positive signs came with GAP 2007–10's successor, 'Applying GAP Lessons: A Three-Year Road Map for Gender Mainstreaming 2010–13', insofar as it vowed to strengthen gender mainstreaming in Bank operations, to focus more attention on maternal mortality and reproductive health, and to introduce more comprehensive plans for gender-focused monitoring and evaluation (see Arend, 2010), the Bank continues to be reticent on how it actually incorporates 'gender issues' in projects with 'gender coverage' and how these have actually benefited women (see Bedford, 2009). Another major problem is the pernicious, if not explicitly articulated, presence of 'smart economics' in GAP 2010–13, which prioritises the 'need to build and disseminate a solid business rationale for gender equality [which is] the basic incentive for Bank staff to mainstream gender issues and for client countries to demand gender equality work' (Arend, 2010).

The long shadow of 'smart economics' 103

Given these caveats, preparations for WDR 2012, coming just before GAP 2010–13's mid-term point, provided a potentially fruitful space for reflection and re-consideration. This was especially so given the World Bank's apparent enthusiasm for consulting a wide variety of stakeholders internationally, including myself and colleagues.

THE MAKING OF WDR 2012: A PERSONAL ENCOUNTER WITH WORLD BANK CONSULTATION

In October 2010 I was approached by the World Bank about the prospect of discussing the remit of WDR 2012. Given the Bank's general influence in the international development field, and the likely impact WDR 2012 would have on shaping gender analysis and policy around the world, I seized the opportunity and offered to convene a group of interested and research-active colleagues. The meeting that ensued was hosted by the LSE Gender Institute and comprised a total of nine LSE staff and affiliates and three members of the Bank's Core WDR 2012 Team (including one of its two-co-directors, Dr Sudhir Shetty – see Chant, 2012 for further details).

Yet despite the rich and diverse array of gender expertise gathered at this meeting, it became clear from an early stage that it might be difficult to steer a new course of action. Indeed, in accordance with the rather dubious record of the World Bank in ensuring genuine (non-tokenistic/rubber-stamping) stakeholder participation in such arenas as Poverty Reduction Strategy Papers (PRSPs) (see, for example, Bradshaw and Linneker, 2003, 2010) and PPAs Whitehead and Lockwood, 1999; Kabeer, 2003, p. 99 ff; see also Schech and Dev, 2007), events as they unfolded could perhaps better be described not so much as 'surprises', as 'self-fulfilling prophecies' (Chant, 2012, p. 204). This was double-underlined by my own experience of working with the Bank in the late 1990s on the topic of men and masculinities in GAD which had indicated that there was probably a predetermined line to tow that could not be shaken by dissonant voices (ibid.).[6]

Among the main problems attached to the consultation were the short notice provided for reading briefing documents, that a draft of WDR 2012 had already been prepared (and this as yet without the results of a major field survey which was not due for completion until the very time (February 2011) when the final draft of the report was scheduled),[7] and that no post-meeting minutes or feedback were ever received (despite being promised).

It was only in April 2011, six months after our face-to-face consultation, that I learned from the Bank that an updated version of the WDR 2012 outline was available on a dedicated page of its website (launched 8 March 2011 to coincide with the 100th anniversary of International Women's Day).

Growing Concerns: WDR 2012 in the Making as of April 2011

On the surface, the World Bank website on WDR 2012 as of April 2011 offered some signs of hope. For example, rights ostensibly had a more prominent place than in the heyday of explicit 'smart economics' advocacy, as indicated by statements such as 'WDR 2012 Gender Equality and Development . . . will argue first that gender equality is a core development issue – a primary objective in its own right. Following Sen (1999) and others, the point of departure for the Report is a view of development as a process of expanding freedoms equally for men and women'.[8]

However, as revealed in various items on the website, such as the blog posted by the World Bank's chief economist, Justin Yifu Li, 'smart economics' thinking seemed very much alive and thriving:

> Gender was chosen as the focus for next year's WDR in part because gender equality can lead to better development outcomes and because, as Amartya Sen asserted, development is a process of expanding freedoms equally for all individuals. This view assumes that gender equality is a core goal in and of itself and that people's welfare shouldn't be determined by their birthplace or whether or not they were born male or female.

Although reference to Amartya Sen and the priority given to gender equality as 'a core goal in and of itself' were to be applauded, I remained concerned about what might be termed 'clever conflations' (or even 'cunning conflations'), where, much as in earlier promotional gambits for 'smart economics', gender equality becomes completely intertwined with gender instrumentality, as typified by selected extracts from the WDR 2012 draft (see Box 4.2). A big question here is how such oxymorons might hold up in practice? Is it really possible to promote equality through utilitarianism and, if so, what guarantee is there that gender equality – which as far as I can see occupies a somewhat secondary role – will necessarily be achieved? (see also Mayoux, 2006 on how women's 'empowerment' occupies a similar position in relation to poverty reduction).

However all was perhaps not lost, since the website maintained not only that WDR 2012 would be utilizing its firsthand survey of grassroots consultations with women and men around the world (see note 7), but would also 'analyse the wide swath [sic] of literature on gender and development'. Another beacon was that there appeared to be a number of people with considerable gender expertise engaged directly by the Bank in the WDR 2012 process.

The long shadow of 'smart economics' 105

BOX 4.2 EXTRACTS FROM APRIL 2011 DRAFT WDR 2012

'On the one hand, it [WDR 2012] will assess the extent to which sustained income growth ... contributes to greater gender equality ... On the other, it will explore whether and how greater gender equality can itself contribute to economic growth and development'

'The Bank recognises the importance of gender equality for poverty reduction and development effectiveness'

'One rationale for policies aimed at improving gender equality has been that such policies, if successful, will yield a large dividend in terms of economic growth'

Composition of WDR 2012 Teams

The World Bank WDR 2012 website was refreshingly transparent about the members of its three component teams. This allowed for some illuminating enquiry into who was where in the process of shaping the report, even if it was difficult to determine exactly what everyone was contributing at different levels. At first glance, and especially when considering the 'advisory board', there seemed to be a buoyant clutch of eminent female scholars and policy professionals with redoubtable gender expertise. Many men were on board too, which was potentially encouraging, even if their credentials as GAD specialists proved somewhat obscure. Indeed, as opposed to having dedicated experience of and expertise in gender, the male advisory board members tended to hail from mainstream economics backgrounds, with a slightly more forensic exploration of where they were represented giving rise to some concerns as to balance in gender and disciplinary provenance in the overall hierarchy of personnel. Not only were most members of the three teams economists by profession (especially if one includes individuals with a Master's degree in Public Administration – MPA), but, perhaps more significantly, there was a general rise in the male and economist quotient upwards through the 'core' and 'extended teams', to the advisory board.

From web details on the members of the 13-member WDR 2012 'core team', which was responsible for the day-to-day work on the report, I drew some crude, but perhaps interesting, summary observations. For example, while Sudhir Shetty shared his co-directorship with a woman, Ana Revenga – like him, an economist – there was only one designated 'gender specialist' (a junior woman) in the whole team and although 31 per cent of members were male, the five rank-and-file research analysts were all female. Not only was leadership exclusively in the hands of economists, but the approximate overall economist quotient (including MPAs) was also 75 per cent. And in terms of 'race' and geographical origins of team personnel there was no one from Sub-Saharan Africa or Southeast Asia.

The WDR 2012 'extended team' comprised 11 members, one of whom was Carolyn Turk, a senior Bank social development specialist who was involved in the methodology for the 'Defining Gender in the 21st Century' survey. The proportion of economists at this level dropped to about 60 per cent (although they were still in a clear majority), but the male quotient rose to 36 per cent, and members from Sub-Saharan Africa and Southeast Asia remained conspicuous by their absence.

The male quotient and the economist quotient were at their highest levels – at 40 per cent and about 90 per cent, respectively – when it came to the 10-member WDR 2012 advisory board, where the inclusion of an African male economist meant at least some representation from one of the regions hitherto excluded. Another problem, however, was that although some big gender names featured in the line-up, including Professor Naila Kabeer, Professor Bina Agarwal, Dr Alison Evans and Dr Geeta Rao Gupta, all but one of the six women (Rao Gupta) on the Advisory Board were practising economists or economists by training. Notwithstanding the strongly established engagement of these women with feminism and broader social science scholarship, one question that struck me was why recruitment had not been from a wider body of disciplines. This seemed to stand in stark relief to the fact that the post-1975 feminist agenda worldwide has been driven by a diverse constituency of academics, policy makers, practitioners and activists with professional formations in anthropology, sociology, psychology, geography, political science, area studies, cultural studies, gender/women's studies and so on.

THE EVOLUTION OF WDR 2012: FROM DRAFT TO COMPLETION

Tracing the evolution of WDR 2012 from draft form to final publication is an interesting exercise, not least because although some of the caveats noted in the former were addressed during this interlude, one or two of the more promising strengths in the draft version were actually lost.

WDR 2012 at Draft Stage

It was encouraging to see no explicit mention of 'smart economics' in the draft version of WDR 2012[9] nor any obvious exhortation to 'invest' in women and girls on grounds of greater development efficiency, except as retrospective reference to GAP 2007–10. None the less, despite regular reference in the WDR 2012 draft and accompanying website items to the fact that gender equality was a goal in itself, through the 'clever conflations' alluded to earlier, the links with 'economic growth' – and poverty reduction – were never far behind.

On top of this, a clutch of major omissions in the draft version were in evidence, one being that there was scarcely any reference to unpaid care work and time-use data (or crucial pertinent sources on these phenomena such as UNRISD's (2010) impressively detailed recent flagship report 'Combating Poverty and Inequality') or to comparable publications by other major agencies pertaining to gender, poverty and/or inequality (for example, UN-DESA/UNDAW 2009; CPRC, 2010; UN-DESA, 2010; UNDP, 2010).

Another problem with the draft report was its rather 'first principles', assumption-based nature which displayed neglect of crucial 'real-world' realities. For example, there was persistent reference to economic growth (normative), but scant mention of the (actual) current global economic crisis – with limitation to one paragraph (out of 160) hardly being appropriate for a global economics watchdog (Chant, 2012, p. 208). Indeed, one wondered why, with so many economists spread across the WDR 2012 team and advisory personnel, this rather major issue had not been elaborated in more detail.

Also disturbing in the pre-published version of WDR 2012 was its resolutely female focus. Boys and men tended only to be referred to as comparators to women, with as few as two to three paragraphs out of 160 in the entire draft document addressing the problems of gender stereotyping for males. There was also no obvious appeal to enjoin men in gender equality efforts, a caveat that was perhaps all the more surprising given that the theme of Plan International's 'State of the World's Girls 2011' was 'What About the Boys?', and as already discussed, an earlier report by this organization had been liberally endorsed by Bank personnel (see Plan International, 2009, 2011). Yet if men and boys were scarcely visible in the WDR 2012 draft, an even less visible constituency were non-heterosexuals (both female and male). Lack of even lip service to sexual diversity suggested that the Bank was out of touch with a major and burgeoning new area of research and debate in the GAD field (Armas, 2007; Cornwall et al., 2008; Bedford, 2009).

Also of concern was the unproblematised 'MDG-centrism' of the WDR draft, with little to no mention made of feminist critiques regarding the limitations for women compared with BPFA (Antrobus, 2004; Barton, 2004, 2005; Alpízar Durán, 2010), nor of the menu of additional strategic priorities and indicators for the MDGs proposed by the UN Millennium Project's Task Force on Education and Gender Equality (see UNMP/TFEGE, 2005). This narrowness was compounded by an equally unproblematised 'World Bank-centrism'. There was no mention of the newly consolidated UN Women as a potential driver of change nor of the Commission on the Status of Women (CSW) and its highly relevant key foci in respect of economic decision making such as unpaid care work (2009) and 'decent work' (2011). Moreover, despite the predominantly self-referential approach which carried through to the final version of WDR 2012, as Diane Elson (2012, p.182) points out:

> The World Bank itself is absent as a player in this text; it is not one of the institutions that are subject to scrutiny. . . . The report must not be allowed to become a figleaf that obscures the ways in which Bank operations and policies are themselves obstacles to the achievement of gender equality.

In many respects this selective self-referentialism links into the rather limited bibliography of the WDR 2012 draft document. Not only did this appear to pay no heed to specific references suggested at or after the LSE consultation, but there was also a relative dearth of peer-reviewed publications compared with World Bank own documents. Indeed, near the header of the bibliography a disclaimer was made that 'The word processed [*sic*] described [*sic*] informally reproduced works that may not be commonly available through libraries' (World Bank, 2011a, p.42).[10] Notwithstanding that many developing countries do not possess well-stocked or accessible libraries, a major question here was how useful a bibliography comprising numerous in-house Bank documents and elusive mimeos would be to academics and stakeholders possessing inadequate technical, administrative and logistical resources with which to track down such literature.

Broader reading would certainly have offered scope to avoid some rather superficial and/or wanly substantiated statements which paid little heed to the rich historical legacy of feminist scholarship and debate in the past 30–40 years. Some statements grated on account of their naked simplicity and/or impossibly voluntaristic assumptions, as in the idea that social processes might have an impact on gender, and that somehow employment might be an 'optional extra' for poor households (see Chant, 2012,

p. 209). Other proclamations gave cause for concern because they made no gesture to debates on hotly contested terms such as 'empowerment', or alternative interpretations of programmes and policies on which there has been considerable difference of opinion such as CCTs. In light of earlier discussion in this chapter, for example, the following statement reads as definitively underproblematised: 'conditional cash transfer programmes have not only had a positive impact on school enrolment and attendance, especially among girls, but have also increased women's empowerment by placing cash in the hands of mothers' (World Bank, 2011a, p. 38).

Indeed, at virtually every major point I came to in the draft document, my immediate reaction was why, with so many people involved in writing the report, had no one picked up on any literature that might qualify the one-sided interpretations that the Bank was propounding.

WDR 2012 at Publication

In the final published version of WDR 2012, which appeared in September 2011, 'smart economics' was again back into the language of the report and sometimes as a headlining term. Indeed, not only is 'smart economics' mentioned on the back cover, but it also features twice in the report's brief foreword and then in the very first paragraph of 'main messages' (see World Bank, 2011b; also Box 4.3).

Continued subscription to the terminology and underlying philosophy of 'smart economics' in WDR 2012 is even more apparent when taking into account a paper on the latter's implications prepared for the September 2011 Joint Ministerial Committee of the Boards of Governors of the Bank and the Fund on the Transfer of Real Resources to Developing Countries (World Bank, 2011c; see also Box 4.4).

Although the emphasis on rights between the draft and the final version remained, critical reactions to the latter reflect some equivocation. Shahra Razavi (2011) from UNRISD, for instance, talks about WDR 2012 as an opportunity that is both 'welcome' and 'missed'. In Razavi's view WDR 2012 is welcome because, *inter alia*, 'the value of gender equality seems . . . to have triggered some interest in gender equality as a political project' (p. 3), because it demonstrates that economic growth is not necessarily linked with the narrowing of gender gaps (p. 4), and because it accords attention to factors such as gender disparities in land and property ownership, political 'voice', and social policy. 'Missed' opportunities, however, abound in respect of the narrowness of social policy attention (reduced effectively to a discussion of CCTs) and in the lack of 'serious engagement with the gender biases of macro-economic policy agendas' (p. 11). This last point is echoed by Alice Evans (2012), in her paper entitled

BOX 4.3 'SMART ECONOMICS' REMAINS! EXTRACTS FROM WDR 2012

- *Two mentions in Foreword by Robert Zoellick*

  ' ... greater gender equality is also smart economics, enhancing development productivity and improving other development outcomes, including prospects for the next generation and for the quality of societal policies and institutions'

  'Gender equality is at the heart of development. It's the right development objective and it's smart economic policy'

- *Opening lines paragraph 1 in 'Main Messages of WDR 2012'*

  'Gender equality is a core development objective in its own right. It is also smart economics'

- *Overview*

  'Gender equality matters intrinsically ... (and) instrumentally' (p. 3)

  'Gender equality matters for development – It is smart economics ... an instrument for development'

- *Chapter 5: Gender differences in employment and why they matter*

  'The business case for gender equality'

- *Throughout*

  '.... considerable reference to 'smart', 'gender-smart' policies, e.g., 'helping adolescent girls make smart reproductive decisions'

Source: Chant (2012, p. 210, Table 3).

The long shadow of 'smart economics' 111

BOX 4.4   INTERNAL WORLD BANK APPRAISAL OF WDR 2012

- *Executive Summary – Opening lines paragraph 1*

    'Gender equality is a core development objective in its own right. It is also smart economics. It can enhance productivity, improve prospects for future generations, and make institutions and societies more representative' (p. ii)

- *Executive Summary*

    'Gender equality is a longer-term driver of competitiveness and equity that is even more important in the midst of global economic crisis. No country can afford to fall behind because it is failing to enable women and men to participate equally in the economy and society' (p. iii)

- *Section III: Strategic Direction for the World Bank Group*

    'The launch of the WDR 2012 offers a significant opportunity to increase awareness, especially among economic policymakers in client countries, that Gender Equality is Smart Economics' (p. 5).

Source: World Bank (2011c).

'WDR 2012: radical redistribution or just tinkering with the template?'. Although Evans applauds the World Bank's quite radical stance on active labour market policies, which includes recommendations not only on non-stereotypical vocational training for women but also on wage subsidies and gendered employment quotas, she also cautions:

> The WDR seems to focus on ways to unlock women's potential to work for economic development, rather than make development more conducive to gender equality. For example, the WDR disregards unproductive women who cannot work due to old age or disability. Further, although the WDR champions women in non-stereotypical work, there is no suggestion of parallel sponsorship for media programmes that might normalise men's sharing of unpaid reproductive work . . . So the World Bank's macro-economic template

remains unshaken, albeit engendered by its support for radical affirmative action. (p. 137)

Like Razavi and Evans, Benería's (2012) measured appraisal of WDR 2012 also finds pluses and minuses. On one hand she concludes that, 'this is an interesting report, not only for its content, but also for its symbolic value since it goes beyond the earlier "WB approach" on gender issues' (p. 177). By the same token, Benería finds this 'somewhat contradictory since the basic neoliberal paradigm of the Bank still predominates' (ibid.; see also Elson, 2012)

Between Draft and Finalisation of WDR 2012: What Was Lost and What Was Gained?

Aside from the restitution of 'smart economics' in the vocabulary of WDR 2012, a rather mixed bag of gains and losses occurred between preparation and the eventual publication of the report.

On the 'gains' front, it was welcome to see considerably more reference to unpaid domestic labour and care work in the final version of WDR 2012, albeit on the basis of Bank background papers rather than already published, and indeed classic, sources (see also Bedford, 2012).

The 'female focus' alluded to in my critique of the draft was also somewhat attenuated by more reference to men and boys, including dedicated boxes on 'What it means to be a "good wife" and a "good husband"' (World Bank, 2011b, p. 172, Box 4.5) and on 'Masculinity and its impacts on roles, preferences and behaviours' (p. 173, Box 4.6).

Yet on a more negative note, there remains little discussion of the current global financial crisis and this is mainly limited to the fall-out effects on employment, something which has been particularly injurious to poor women in developing countries (see Floro et al., 2010; Horn, 2010; Bedford, 2012; Tacoli, 2012). As Diane Elson (2012, p. 181) observes, the neoclassical economic theory subscribed to by the vast majority of Bank economists makes it no surprise that 'globalisation is seen as an essentially benign process which just needs to be complemented by public policies to ensure that the benefits extend to all women'.

Although sexuality does make an appearance in the published version of WDR 2012, it is overwhelmingly dealt with in passing only – usually in the form of 'sexual orientation' being added to a stock-in-trade list of factors differentiating women, but not in any depth in its own right. The BPFA remains in the shadow of the MDGs and reference to other major actors on the gender and development scene, such as UN Women, persists in being parlous in the extreme. Indeed, despite the considerable potential to WDR 2012 offered by the rich information and advocacy presented in UN Women's (2011) *Progress of the World's Women 2011–2012*, which appeared sufficiently in advance of the Bank's final publication deadline to have been incorporated, there is only one reference to the latter in WDR 2012's total of 372 pages – a factual background note on a women's resource centre in Lahore (see World Bank, 2011b, p. 328n).

From the particular perspective of the present volume, it is also important to point out that there is only very limited reference to gendered migration and mobility in WDR 2012. The sole direct entry in the index is on 'migration and social norms' which links to a few paragraphs in Chapter 4 which point out how, in countries such as China, women who move can broaden their social networks and also reduce son preference (ibid., p. 175), and more generally the ways in which rural–urban and international migration can simultaneously release women from gendered constraints, but also reinforce social conservatism (p. 176). Other than this, there is merely a brief case study provided in Chapter 8 on how economic crisis in Georgia has induced women and men to migrate and how women's remittances are on average higher than men's (p. 332, Box 8.1). In the appendices, there is also one table, on Trade, Aid and Finance, which includes a column on net migration (p. 400, Table 5).

These are slim pickings when considering not only that women are nearly half the world's international migrants, and in many developing countries the majority of rural–urban movers, but that the topic of gendered mobility was the theme of UNFPA's *State of the World's Population 2006* (UNFPA, 2006). Entitled *A Passage to Hope: Women and International Migration*, the UNFPA report gave balanced treatment to the benefits and drawbacks of female migration across national borders, while raising clear concerns, among other things, about the inequalities attached to globalisation, about forced and irregular migration, about the exploitation of domestic workers from developing countries in advanced economies, and about migrant health and social diversity. Many of these themes were also touched upon in the UNDP's *Human Development Report 2009: Overcoming Barriers: Human Mobility and Development* (UNDP, 2009). In the same year migration also featured substantially in the context of the Bank's own *World Development Report 2009: Reshaping Economic Geography* (World Bank, 2009). Although discussion of migration in WDR 2009 was typically more oriented to the economics of national and international movements and not especially gender sensitive, one would have thought that the Bank's usual practice of citing its own sources would have meant rather greater coverage of a topic absolutely intrinsic to macroeconomic development at a global level.

In a more practical vein, according to WDR 2012's Bibliographical

Note, which lists authors' names for the 50-plus background papers for WDR 2012, the latter are nominally available from the WDR 2012 website (www.worldbank.org/wdr2012) or through the World Development Report office (see World Bank, 2011b, p. 373). So far, however, I have been unable to locate a site containing even a small collection of these papers and even individual papers are immensely difficult to find. The usual scenario is that 'all roads lead to Rome' where one's searches end up back at a specific chapter of WDR 2012. To be meaningful for the vast community of scholars and activists concerned to explore the bases of the Bank's messages on gender, one can only hope that a more dedicated and user-friendly web resource will be provided in the near future. This also applies to raw data from the survey 'Defining Gender in the 21st Century' which, one year on from WDR 2012's publication remains, too, something of a pot of gold at the end of the rainbow.

WDR 2012: STEPPING FORWARD OR STANDING STILL?

The fact that WDR 2012 is the first ever of its annual flagship publications on gender is, as Razavi (2011, p. 2) describes, 'a welcome opportunity for widening the intellectual space'. It indicates that the Bank is taking gender seriously and this is bound to have an impact on the broader development community (ibid.; see also Bedford, 2012; Evans, 2012). However, in summing up, I feel it necessary to reiterate some of my principal concerns about the WDR 2012 preparatory process in relation to the prospects for taking the underlying impetus for gender and development policy beyond 'smart economics', and in being a convincing and enriching exercise for those involved in the actual making of the report, and for its intended beneficiaries.

First, there is a big question around timing and phasing. I am fully aware that the World Bank is not the only development organization with such a strong political mandate or agenda that decisions are made on key messages it wishes to convey prior to any fact-finding or opinion-eliciting mission has occurred. However, simply doing as others do is no excuse for the post hoc nature of the Bank's consultative stakeholder exercise in this instance. For example, why did the Bank not engage with the broader community of scholars and activists before the first draft of the Report was written and, perhaps more importantly, before the grassroots survey of how women and men 'do gender' was designed for application in the field? Or perhaps the Bank did, but we just do not know yet who, or what, was involved in that process (see also note 7). Additional qualms pertain to the dubious value of a 'rapid assessment methodology' for a 'fact-finding' grassroots survey that was only scheduled for completion when the 'final' draft of the Report was due for submission to the Bank's Board of Executive Directors. How much store should be set by a methodology that effectively uses empirical work to illustrate a priori conclusions?

Related to this, another of my original concerns was how the results of the qualitative gender survey 'Defining Gender in the 21st Century' would be presented, especially given the treatment of the Voices of the Poor exercise in WDR 2000/01, which amounted to being not only rather incidental, but characterised by somewhat 'patronising "box-friendly" padding' (Chant, 2011). This has mercifully not proved to be the case with WDR 2012, which actually contains a relatively minimal scattering of either straightforward quotes from respondents, or amalgamated boxes or tables, for example on time use (World Bank, 2011b, Box 5.8). Indeed, compared with calculations from Demographic and Health Survey data there are relatively few references to the Bank's own multi-country study.

Yet this, in turn, raises the question of how well money has been spent. Presumably the total expenditure incurred by the Bank on WDR 2012 has been considerable when taking into account not only the training, accommodation and support of field officers for its multi-country qualitative assessment, but also stakeholder consultations (complete with overseas travel and subsistence for permanent members of its teams and fees for senior advisers), and the commissioning of dedicated background papers, not to mention numerous WDR 2012 launch events around the world.[11] On the matter of the qualitative survey specifically, a synchronic cross-country fact-finding exercise is clearly of immense potential value in terms of drawing international comparisons about how women and men at the grassroots 'do gender', but could the Bank have perhaps spent rather less doing its 'own thing' and instead drawn empirical and analytical substance from a veritable wealth of statistics and pertinent literature already in existence? While at some level I accept Elson's (2012, p. 178) view that [t]he report does bring together large amounts of useful, interesting and well-presented information that can be deployed without accepting its interpretative framework', I remain disappointed by what I regard as several omissions of major bodies of data, such as that gathered on household decision making by the International Food and Policy Research Institute (IFPRI). Also conspicuous by their absence are the rich reserves of data and analysis on issues of poverty, gender, land rights, time-use and work, collated by the Chronic Poverty Research Centre (CPRC) of the Overseas Development Institute, the Food and Agriculture Organization (FAO), the United Nations Division for Economic and Social Affairs (UN-DESA), and the United Nations Research Institute for Social

Development (UNRISD). In addition, although quantitative gender indicators such as the Gender Inequality Index (GII), the Global Gender Gap Index (GGGI), and the Social Institutions and Gender Index (SIGI) may not be especially revealing of the situation of grassroots women, or of the processes which disadvantage them, there are legion academic case studies and research reports – a number of which are comparative in scope – which could have fed into a properly triangulated and comprehensive overview of gender differences and injustices at an international scale. One at least hopes, therefore, that in the spirit of transparency and proper gender accounting, a comprehensively detailed budget for WDR 2012 will be publicly available in due course. Ideally, and in line with the Bank's new Open Data initiative,[12] this should specify expenditure incurred for different elements of the preparatory process, and invite opinions from the international community of GAD scholars and activists as to the value yielded, especially in terms of the likely impacts on women's and men's lives 'on the ground' (see also Bedford, 2012). Indeed, acknowledging that some basic needs and interests could readily be fulfilled with quite small injections of cash, how might World Bank resources be used more effectively to promote gender equality at the grassroots in future and, especially, to resolve some of the 'sticky' domains it refers to so frequently in respect of eradicating gender inequalities? Do people themselves know best or do decisions on major international disbursements need to be retained in the hands of 'professionals', many of whom are not even based in the Global South (see Chambers, 2010)?

Last, but not least, I remain sceptical of the Bank's bid for legitimacy and kudos through consultations with numerous scholars in institutions whose inputs have been largely disregarded.

In summing up, I confess to remaining lukewarm about what can be learned from WDR 2012 with regard to cutting-edge debates and how the report will more effectively promote a rights-based approach to gender and development. Much as widespread allegations about how PRSPs were effectively SAPs in a new guise (see Ruggeri Laderchi et al., 2003, p.26), I fear that there is a similar process of window dressing in operation here. As concluded in a recent paper I co-authored with Caroline Sweetman: 'The smart economics approach represents, at best, pragmatism in a time of economic restructuring and austerity. Without reform of the institutions whose decisions and resource distribution shape their lives, women and girls are set up for exhaustion and failure' (Chant and Sweetman, 2012, p.524).

Although 'smart economics' may be more muted in WDR 2012, its nomenclature and conceptual and political underpinnings persist and I have doubts about whether this is the most appropriate route to gender justice. For the foreseeable future and especially in light of the global financial crisis which is endemic to the economic growth models championed by the World Bank, real improvements in women's lives within developing countries and for those who have migrated to the purportedly 'greener pastures' of the Global North, are likely to remain elusive.

NOTES

1. This chapter draws heavily on two previous papers. The first was a presentation at the Gender and Social Policy in Latin America Workshop organised by Maxine Molyneux and Jasmine Gideon at the Institute for the Study of the Americas, University of London, 10 May 2011 (Chant, 2011) when WDR 2012 was still in its preparatory phase. The second was an article based on this presentation and including reflections on the final version of WDR 2012, which was published in *Global Social Policy* (Chant, 2012).
2. In July 2011, Dr Ngozi Okonjo-Iweala left the World Bank to become Minister of Finance in Nigeria in the new administration of President Goodluck Jonathan.
3. Robert Zoellick was appointed as 11th President of the World Bank in 2007.
4. Interesting reactions to the Nike 'Girl Effect' campaign can be read on Aid Watch blog on 'So now we have to save ourselves and the world too? A critique of the "Girl Effect"' at: http://aidwatchers.com/2011/01/so-now-we-have-to-save-ourselves-and-the-world-too, and on *Contestations, Dialogues on Women's Empowerment*, 4, March 2011 at: http://www.contestations.net/.
5. This echoes the notion that the incorporation of women into development policy has been often more a case of getting women to work for development, than to get development working for women (Elson, 1989, 1991; Moser, 1993, pp. 69–73; Kabeer, 1994, p. 8; Blumberg, 1995, p. 10). Rianne Mahon (2012, p. 174) suggests that 'the state', too, is a major beneficiary.
6. In 1999, Matthew Gutmann and I were approached by the World Bank to compile a report on bringing men into gender and development (GAD). To this end we arranged consultations with 30 development agencies and NGOs in the UK and the US aiming to elicit opinions on the desirability of incorporating men in GAD and best practices to date. Through extensive team discussion and analysis of several pages of interview transcripts, we drew the general conclusion that the principle was sound but, in practice, would require a phasing-in that was gradual and that would not threaten the quite limited resource pools built up for women over several years. However, despite its methodological and academic integrity, our report was dismissed by the Bank at an early stage on grounds of being 'too feminist' which was not the line it wished to pursue (see Bedford, 2009, p. 55 onwards). Fortunately we were still given permission to publish the material elsewhere, which we did in the form of an Oxfam Working Paper, with a due disclaimer that the findings, interpretations and conclusions were entirely our own and 'should not be attributed in any manner to the World Bank, its affiliated organisations, the members of its Board of Executive Directors, or the countries they represent' (Chant and Gutmann, 2000, p. v). Somewhat ironically perhaps, our work was referred to under the auspices of a 'World Bank draft report' by Joyce Jacobsen (2006) in her introductory chapter to the Bank's subsequent in-house publication on men and development (see Bannon and Correia, 2006).
7. In a tradition that started with the World Bank's Millennium World Development Report 2000/2001 on 'Attacking Poverty', in which the Bank funded a major 'Voices of the Poor' project comprising group-based Participatory Poverty Assessments (PPAs) with a total of 60,000 individuals in 23 countries (see World Bank, 2000), the Bank also organised a major field survey for WDR 2012. This took place between June 2010 and February

2011 in 19 countries in six developing regions, and involved local researchers convening a total of 500 meetings with small groups of women or men from three generations. A total of 4,000 respondents were included in this qualitative 'rapid assessment methodology', which aimed 'to hear first hand about how men and women "do gender" in their everyday lives' (Chant, 2012, p. 206). Some details of this survey, which as from June 2011 acquired a name on the website – 'Defining Gender in the 21st Century: Conversations with Men and Women Around the World' – can be found at: http://siteresources.worldbank.org/INTWDR2012/Images/7778104-1300295445126/data-collection-table.gif (accessed 23 June 2011). Unfortunately, however, the site does not identify why consultation with academic and other stakeholders took place after the survey had been designed and embarked upon, nor why the survey was not completed until the same month (February 2011) as the 'final' draft of WDR 2012 was due. These are important issues giving rise to the concern that the major lead would not be taken so much from deductive research as from 'first principles' (Chant, 2012, p. 206).
8. This refers to Amartya Sen.
9. I consulted the World Bank WDR 2012 website at regular intervals between April and June 2011.
10. This phrase, which first appears at the top of the references itemized at the end of the Overview chapter in the final published version of the WDR 2012 (and is thereafter repeated for all chapters), is corrected to: 'The word *processed* describes informally reproduced works that may not be commonly available through libraries' (World Bank, 2011b, p. 40). While the correction makes grammatical sense, the 'processed' tag is used rather sparingly from the perspective of the difficulties of locating so many items in the bibliography, as discussed further later in the chapter.
11. From what I had been able to discern from exhaustive web searching, as of March 2012 expenditure by that date seems to have reached around US$600,000.
12. In a press release (2012/148/CTR) issued on 9 November 2011 entitled 'The World Bank's Financial Data, Open and Transparent', the Bank reports that since 2008 it has been 'working to make its operations and research more open, transparent and accountable' through making its data freely available on http://data.worldbank.org, and more recently by disclosing financial information via an open data website at: (http://web.worldbank.org/WBSITE/EXTERNAL/NEWS/0,,contentMDK:23043906~pagePK:64257043~piPK:437376~theSitePK:4607,00.html, (accessed 24 March 2012).

REFERENCES

Alpízar Durán, Lydia (2010), 'Beijing +15 from hopes to disappointment and non-accountability', *Development*, **53** (2), 202–9.
Antrobus, Peggy (2004), 'MDGs – the most distracting gimmick', in Women's International Coalition for Economic Justice (WICEJ) (ed.), *Seeking Accountability on Women's Human Rights: Women Debate the UN Millennium Development Goals*, New York: WICEJ, pp. 14–16.
Arend, Elizabeth (2010), 'Critique of the World Bank's Applying Gender Action Plan Lessons: A Three-Year Road Map for Gender Mainstreaming (2011–2013)', mimeo, Gender Action, Washington, DC.
Armas, Henry (2007), 'Whose sexuality counts? Poverty, participation and sexual rights', IDS Working Paper 294, University of Sussex, Brighton.
Bannon, Ian and Maria Correia (eds) (2006), *The Other Half of Gender: Men's Issues in Development*, Washington, DC: World Bank.
Barton, Carol (2004), 'Introduction', in Women's International Coalition for Economic Justice (WICEJ) (ed.), *Seeking Accountability on Women's Human Rights: Women Debate the UN Millennium Development Goals*, New York: WICEJ, pp. 3–5.

Barton, Carol (2005), 'Where to for women's movements and the MDGs?', in Caroline Sweetman (ed.), *Gender and the Millennium Development Goals*, Oxford: Oxfam, pp. 25–35.

Bedford, Kate (2009), *Developing Partnerships: Gender, Sexuality and the Reformed World Bank*, Minneapolis, MN: University of Minnesota Press.

Bedford, Kate (2012), 'Gender, WDR limits, gaps, and fudges', Bretton Woods Project: Critical Voices on the World Bank and the IMF, Update 79, available at: http://www.brettonwoodsproject.org/arrt-569646 (accessed 4 March 2012).

Benería, Lourdes (1991), 'Structural adjustment, the labour market and the household', in Guy Standing and Victor Tokman (eds), *Towards Social Adjustment: Labour Market Issues in Structural Adjustment*, Geneva: ILO, pp. 161–83.

Benería, Lourdes (2012), 'The World Bank and gender inequality', *Global Social Policy*, **12** (2), 175–8.

Benería, Lourdes and Shelley Feldman (eds) (1992), *Unequal Burden: Economic Crises, Persistent Poverty, and Women's Work*, Boulder, CO: Westview.

Blumberg, Rae Lesser (1995), 'Introduction: engendering wealth and well-being in an era of economic transformation', in Blumberg, Cathy Rakowski, Irene Tinker and Michael Monteón (eds), *Engendering Wealth and Well-Being: Empowerment for Global Change*, Boulder, CO: Westview, pp. 1–14.

Bradshaw, Sarah (2008), 'From structural adjustment to social adjustment: a gendered analysis of conditional cash transfer programmes in Mexico and Nicaragua', *Global Social Policy*, **8** (1), 188–207.

Bradshaw, Sarah and Brian Linneker (2003), *Challenging Women's Poverty: Perspectives on Gender and Poverty Reduction Strategies from Nicaragua and Honduras*, London: Catholic Institute of International Relations (now Progressio).

Bradshaw, Sarah and Brian Linneker (2010), 'Poverty alleviation in a changing policy and political context: the case of PRSPs with particular reference to Nicaragua', in Sylvia Chant (ed.), *The International Handbook of Gender and Poverty: Concepts, Research, Policy*, Cheltenham, UK and Northampton, MA, USA: Edward Elgar, pp. 516–21.

Brickell, Katherine and Sylvia Chant (2010), 'The unbearable heaviness of being: reflections on female altruism in Cambodia, Philippines, The Gambia and Costa Rica', *Progress in Development Studies*, **10** (2), 145–59.

Buvinic, Mayra and Elizabeth M. King (2007), 'Smart economics: more needs to be done to promote the economic power of women', *Finance and Development*, **44** (2), available at: http://www.imf.org/external/pubs/ft/fandd/2007/06/king.htm (accessed 20 June 2011).

Chambers, Robert (2010), 'Paradigms, poverty and adaptive pluralism', IDS Working Paper 344, Institute of Development Studies, University of Sussex, Brighton, available at: www.ids.ac.uk/ids/bookshop (accessed 4 January 2011).

Chant, Sylvia (1994), 'Women, work and household survival strategies in Mexico, 1982–1992: past trends, current tendencies and future research', *Bulletin of Latin American Research*, **13** (2), 203–33.

Chant, Sylvia (1996), 'Women's roles in recession and economic restructuring in Mexico and the Philippines', *Geoforum*, **27** (3), 97–127.

Chant, Sylvia (2007), 'Gender, cities, and the Millennium Development Goals in the Global South', New Series Working Paper, Issue 21, LSE Gender Institute, London, available at: http://www.lse.ac.uk/collections/genderInstitute/pdf/CHANT%20GIWP.pdf.

Chant, Sylvia (2008), 'The "feminisation of poverty" and the "feminisation" of anti-poverty programmes: room for revision?', *Journal of Development Studies*, **44** (2), 153–86.

Chant, Sylvia (2011), 'The disappearing of "smart economics"? Brief reflections on WDR 2012 proposals and consultation', paper presented at 'Gender and Social Policy in Latin America: Current Research Directions' workshop, Institute for the Study of the Americas (ISA), University of London, 10 May.

Chant, Sylvia (2012), 'The disappearing of "smart economics"? The World Development Report 2012 on Gender Equality: some concerns about the preparatory process and the prospects for paradigm change', *Global Social Policy*, **12** (2), 198–218.

Chant, Sylvia and Matthew Gutmann (2000), *Mainstreaming Men into Gender and Development: Debates, Reflections and Experiences*, Oxford: Oxfam.
Chant, Sylvia and Caroline Sweetman (2012), 'Fixing women or fixing the world? "Smart economics", efficiency approaches and gender equality in development', *Gender and Development*, **20** (3), 517–29.
Chronic Poverty Research Centre (CPRC) (2010), *Stemming Girls' Chronic Poverty*, London: ODI, available at: http://www.chronicpoverty.org/publications/details/stemming-girls-chronic-poverty (accessed 20 November 2010).
Cornwall, Andrea, Sonia Côrrea and Susie Jolly (eds) (2008), *Development with a Body: Sexuality, Human Rights and Development*, London: Zed Books.
Elson, Diane (1989), 'The impact of structural adjustment on women: concepts and issues', in Bade Onimode (ed.), *The IMF, The World Bank and the African Debt. Volume 2: The Social and Political Impact*, London: Zed Books, pp. 56–74.
Elson, Diane (1991), 'Structural adjustment: its effects on women', in Tina Wallace with Candida March (eds), *Changing Perceptions: Writings on Gender and Development*, Oxfam: Oxford, pp. 39–53.
Elson, Diane (2012), 'Review of World Development Report 2012: Gender Equality and Development', *Global Social Policy*, **12** (2), 178–83.
Evans, Alice (2012), 'WDR 2012: radical redistribution or just tinkering with the template?', *Development*, **55** (1), 134–7.
Floro, Maria Sagrario, Emcet Oktay Tas and Annika Törnqvist (2010), *The Impact of the Global Economic Crisis on Women's Wellbeing and Empowerment*, Stockholm: SIDA.
González de la Rocha, Mercedes (1994), *The Resources of Poverty: Women and Survival in a Mexican City*, Oxford: Blackwell.
González de la Rocha, Mercedes (2010), 'Gender and ethnicity in the shaping of differentiated outcomes of Mexico's "Progresa-Oportunidades" conditional cash transfer programme', in Sylvia Chant (ed.), *The International Handbook of Gender and Poverty: Concepts, Research, Policy*, Cheltenham, UK and Northampton, MA, USA: Edward Elgar, pp. 248–53.
Harman, Sophie (2010), *Why Conditional Cash Transfers Matter for HIV*, London: City University, available at: http://www.city.ac.uk/intpol/policy-briefs/harman-conditional-cash-transfers-HIV.html (accessed 4 March 2011).
Horn, Zoe Elena (2010), 'The effects of the global economic crisis on women in the informal economy: research findings from WIEGO and the Inclusive Cities Partners', *Gender and Development*, **18** (2), 263–76.
Jacobsen, Joyce P. (2006), 'Men's issues in development', in Ian Bannon and Maria Correia (eds), *The Other Half of Gender: Men's Issues in Development*, Washington, DC: World Bank, pp. 1–28.
Johnsson-Latham, Gerd (2010), 'Power, privilege and gender as reflected in poverty analysis and development', in Sylvia Chant (ed.), *The International Handbook of Gender and Poverty: Concepts, Research, Policy*, Cheltenham, UK and Northampton, MA, USA: Edward Elgar, pp. 41–6.
Kabeer, Naila (1994), *Reversed Realities: Gender Hierarchies in Development Thought*, London: Verso.
Kabeer, Naila (2003), *Gender Mainstreaming in Poverty Eradication and the Millennium Development Goals: A Handbook for Policy-makers and Other Stakeholders*, London: Commonwealth Secretariat.
Mahon, Rianne (2012), 'Introduction: the World Bank's new approach to gender equality?', *Global Social Policy*, **12** (2), 173–4.
Mayoux, Linda (2006), 'Women's empowerment through sustainable micro-finance: rethinking "best practice"', Discussion Paper, Gender and Micro-finance website, available at: http://www.genfinance.net (accessed 30 June 2007).
Mbilinyi, Marjorie (2004), 'Lessons of civil society engagement', in Women's International Coalition for Economic Justice (WICEJ) (ed.), *Seeking Accountability on Women's Human Rights: Women Debate the UN Millennium Development Goals*, New York: WICEJ, pp. 10–12.

Molyneux, Maxine (2006), 'Mothers at the service of the New Poverty Agenda: PROGRESA/ Oportunidades, Mexico's Conditional Transfer Programme', *Journal of Social Policy and Administration*, **40** (4), 425–49.

Molyneux, Maxine (2007), 'Change and continuity in social protection in Latin America: mothers at the service of the state?', Gender and Development Paper no. 1, UNRISD, Geneva, available at: http://www.unrisd.org (accessed 4 January 2008).

Moser, Caroline (1989a), 'The impact of structural adjustment at the micro-level: low-income women, time and the triple role in Guayaquil, Ecuador', in UNICEF (ed.), *Invisible Adjustment*, vol. 2, New York: UNICEF, Americas and Caribbean Office, pp. 137–62.

Moser, Caroline (1989b), 'Gender planning in the Third World: meeting practical and strategic gender needs', *World Development*, **17** (11), 1799–825.

Moser, Caroline (1993), *Gender Planning and Development*, London: Routledge.

Moser, Caroline (1997), *Household Responses to Poverty and Vulnerability. Volume 1: Confronting Crisis in Cisne Dos, Guayaquil, Ecuador*, Washington, DC: World Bank, Urban Management Programme.

Painter, Genevieve (2004), 'Gender, the Millennium Development Goals, and Human Rights in the Context of the 2005 Review Processes', report for the Gender and Development Network (GADN), London.

Plan International (2009), 'Because I am a Girl: The State of the World's Girls 2009. Girls in the Global Economy. Adding it All Up', Plan International, London, available at: http://www.ungei.org/resources/files/BIAAG_Summary_ENGLISH_lo_resolution.pdf (accessed 5 March 2010).

Plan International (2011), 'Because I Am a Girl: The State of the World's Girls 2011: So What About Boys?', Plan International, London, available at: http://plan-international. org/girls/resources/what-about-boys-2011.php (accessed 30 May 2011).

Razavi, Shahra (2011), *World Development Report 2012: Gender Equality and Development: An Opportunity Both Welcome and Missed (An Extended Commentary)*, Geneva: UNRISD, available at: http://www.unrisd.org/80256B42004CCC77/(httpInfoFiles)/E90 770090127BDFDC12579250058F520/$file/Extended%20Commentary%20WDR%202012. pdf (accessed 1 October 2011).

Roy, Ananya (2002), 'Against the Feminisation of Policy', Comparative Urban Studies Project Policy Brief, Woodrow Wilson International Center for Scholars, Washington DC, available at: http://www.wilsoncenter.org/topics/pubs/urbanbrief01.pdf (accessed 6 February 2008).

Roy, Ananya (2010), *Poverty Capital: Microfinance and the Making of Development*, New York: Routledge.

Ruggeri Laderchi, Caterina, Ruhi Saith and Frances Stewart (2003), 'Everyone agrees we need poverty reduction, but not what this means', paper prepared for the Inequality, Poverty and Human Well-Being Conference, World Institute for Development Economics Research, United Nations University, Helsinki, 30–31 May.

Saith, Ashwani (2006), 'From universal values to Millennium Development Goals: lost in translation?', *Development and Change*, **37** (6), 1167–99.

Schech, Susanne and Sanjugta Vas Dev (2007), 'Gender justice: the World Bank's new approach to the poor?', *Development in Practice*, **17** (1), 14–26.

Tabbush, Constanza (2010), 'Latin American women's protection after adjustment: a feminist critique of conditional cash transfers in Chile and Argentina', *Oxford Development Studies*, **38** (4), 437–51.

Tacoli, Cecilia (2012), 'Urbanisation, gender and urban poverty: paid work and unpaid carework in the city', Urbanisation and Emerging Population Issues Working Paper 7, International Institute of Environment and Development, London, available at: http:// pubs.iied.org/10614IIED.html (accessed 30 May 2012).

United Nations Children's Fund (UNICEF) (2007), *State of the World's Children 2007: The 'Double Dividend' of Gender Equality*, New York: UNICEF, available at: http://www. unicef.org (accessed 1 January 2008).

United Nations Department for Economic and Social Affairs (UN-DESA) (2010), *Report on*

the World Social Situation 2010: Rethinking Poverty, New York: UN-DESA, available at: http://www.un.org/esa/socdev/rwss/docs/2010/fullreport.pdf (accessed 30 August 2010).
United Nations Department for Economic and Social Affairs (UN-DESA) and United Nations Division for the Advancement of Women (UNDAW) (2009), *World Survey on the Role of Women in Economic Development 2009*, New York: UN-DESA/UNDAW, available at: http://www.unorg/womenwatch (accessed 2 February 2010).
United Nations Development Programme (UNDP) (2009), *Human Development Report 2009. Overcoming Barriers: Human Mobility and Development*, New York: UNDP, available at: http://hdr.undp.org/en/reports/global/hdr2009/ (accessed 3 February 2010).
United Nations Development Programme (UNDP) (2010), *Human Development Report 2010. The Real Wealth of Nations: Pathways to Human Development*, UNDP: New York, available at: http://hdr.undp.org/en/reports/global/hdr2010/ (accessed 3 January 2011).
United Nations Fund for Population Activities (UNFPA) (2006), *State of the World's Population 2006: A Passage to Hope: Women and International Migration*, New York: UNFPA, available at: http://www.unfpa.org/swp/2006.pdf (accessed 2 January 2007).
UN-HABITAT (2010), *Gender Equality for Smarter Cities; Challenges and Progress*, Nairobi: UN-HABITAT, available at: http://www.unhabitat.org (accessed 2 January 2011).
United Nations Millennium Project Task Force on Education and Gender Equality (UNMP/TFEGE) (2005), *Taking Action: Achieving Gender Equality and Empowering Women*, London: Earthscan.
United Nations Research Institute for Social Development (UNRISD) (2010), 'Combating Poverty and Inequality: Structural Change, Social Policy and Politics', UNRISD, Geneva, available at: http://www.unrisd.org (accessed 30 November 2010).
UN Women (2011), *Progress of the World's Women 2011–2012: In Pursuit of Gender Justice*, New York: UN Women, available at: http://progress.unwomen.org (accessed 30 May 2011).
Whitehead, Ann and Matthew Lockwood (1999), 'Gendering poverty: a review of six World Bank poverty assessments', *Development and Change*, **30** (3), 525–55.
Woodford-Berger, Prudence (2007), 'Gender mainstreaming: what is it (about) and should we continue doing it?', in Andrea Cornwall, Elizabeth Harrison and Ann Whitehead (eds), *Feminisms in Development: Contradictions, Contestations and Challenges*, London: Zed Books, pp. 122–34.
World Bank (1995), *Enhancing Women's Participation in Economic Development*, Washington, DC: World Bank.
World Bank (2000), *World Development Report 2000/2001: Attacking Poverty*, New York: Oxford University Press.
World Bank (2006), *Gender Equality as Smart Economics: A World Bank Action Plan (Fiscal Years 2007–10)*, Washington, DC: World Bank.
World Bank (2007), *Global Monitoring Report 2007: Confronting the Challenge of Gender Equality and Fragile States*, Washington, DC: World Bank, available at: http://web.worldbank/org (accessed 30 November 2007).
World Bank (2008), 'Gender equality as smart economics: World Bank Group Gender Action Plan. First Year Progress Report (Jan 2007–Jan 2008)', mimeo, World Bank Washington, DC, available at: http://web.worldbank.org/WORLDBANKSITE/EXTERNAL/NEWS/0,,contentMDK:20127207~menuPK:34 (accessed 28 November 2008).
World Bank (2009), *World Development Report 2009: Reshaping Economic Geography*, Washington, DC: World Bank, available at: www.worldbank.org (accessed 30 October 2009).
World Bank (2011a), *World Development Report 2012: Gender Equality and Development*, outline, Washington, DC: World Bank, available at: http://www-wds.worldbank.org/external/default/WDSContentServer/WDSP/IB/2010/11/03/000334955_20101103062028/Rendered/PDF/576270WDR0SecM1e0only1910BOX353773B.pdf (accessed 30 June 2011).
World Bank (2011b), *World Development Report 2012: Gender Equality and Development*, Washington, DC: World Bank, available at: http://econ.worldbank.org/WBSITE/

EXTERNAL/EXTDEC/EXTRESEARCH/EXTWDRS/EXTWDR2012/0,,contentMD K:23004468~pagePK:64167689~piPK:64167673~theSitePK:7778063,00.html (accessed 30 October 2011).

World Bank (2011c), 'Implications of the World Development Report 2012: Gender Equality and Development for the World Bank Group', Development Committee paper, available at: http://siteresources.worldbank.org/DEVCOMMINT/Documentation/23004019/DC2011-0011(E)WDR2012_Gender.pdf (accessed 30 October 2011).

Zuckerman, Elaine (2007), 'Critique: gender equality as smart economics: World Bank Group Gender Action Plan (GAP) (Fiscal years 2007–10)', mimeo, GenderAction, Washington, DC, available at: http://www.genderaction.org (accessed 3 March 2012).

PART II

NEW THEORETICAL AND METHODOLOGICAL ISSUES IN THE STUDY OF FEMALE MIGRATION AND DEVELOPMENT

5. Gender, Andean migration and development: analytical challenges and political debates
Almudena Cortés

INTRODUCTION

In the context of the European Union, Spain has been the most important recipient of Latin American and Caribbean migration since 2000 (López de Lera and Oso, 2007). This fact is especially significant when we look at the Andean countries of Bolivia, Colombia, Ecuador and Peru since, by 2011, these four countries represented 16.8 per cent of the foreign population residing in Spain. Within these national groups the data for 2012 indicate that the immigration figure for Bolivian women represented 59 per cent, Colombian women 58 per cent, Ecuadorian women 52.3 per cent, and Peruvian women 54.1 per cent (INE, 2012).

Scientific literature has reflected a great deal of interest in understanding this South–North female migration as a result of the transformation of structural factors linked to the global economy's development and the dislocation of productive activities on an international scale. This has, in many cases, resulted in female labour in the informal economy. For Sassen, these labour circuits generate important economic resources that often remain invisible (Sassen, 2003). These studies have shown that the lack of gender redistribution of social reproduction work has generated the demand for a female labour force from the South to the North, and a global transfer of care, domestic tasks and sexual activities (Truong, 1996; Ehrenreich and Hochschild, 2002).

Furthermore, there has been a growing scientific interest in the topics of migration, gender and development and, more specifically, in analysing remittances using a gender approach (Sørensen, 2004; Ramírez et al., 2005; Semyonov and Gorodzeisky, 2005; Gainza, 2006; Parella and Cavalcanti, 2009; Oso, 2011), highlighting the works published by the International Research and Training Institute for the Advancement of Women (INSTRAW), examining gender patterns in the remittance, receipt, use and management of the remittances (INSTRAW, 2006, 2007), and showing how remittances can be a vehicle for transforming relations between women and men.

Little attention, however, has been paid to the negotiations about different development visions and to the interests of different stakeholders that are conducted through their daily livelihood activities or institutional initiatives. These stakeholders would be government actors (government officials, regional and/or municipal), technicians of nongovernmental organizations (NGOs) working in migratory contexts, as well as the migrants themselves. The development stakeholders have different visions of development, power and influence in order to enforce them. In this regard, as we shall discuss below, the European conceptions of the link between migration and development are based on a modernizing vision of this relationship, which defines development exclusively within economic paradigms. These visions do not incorporate critical development reviews, nor do they include new proposals such as human development, or the progress already made on the topic of gender and development. This is surprising since, by the 1980s, the feminist critique of development discourse had already managed to make gender a cross-cutting item on all development agendas. The European Union incorporated the subject of Gender Equality after the United Nations Decade for Women (1975–1985), and the Third World Conference on Women held in Nairobi in 1985 (Debusscher, 2011, p. 39). In this way, the European Commission incorporated the 'Women in Development' (WID) approach, which in 1995, was replaced by 'Gender and Development' (GAD). This was a response to feminist critiques that considered the first programme as ineffective and conservative because of its focus on 'women' rather than on unequal gender relations. In the case of Spain, cooperation policies for development have adopted the GAD approach with instruments such as the Gender Sectoral Plan and its inclusion in the Guiding Plan for Spanish Cooperation (2009–12). With regard to migration, cooperation policies have incorporated Spanish co-development as a more thematic content in their guiding plans for areas such as democratic governance, rural development and gender in development. As we have shown in other studies, the main objective of co-development would be to generate patterns of governance on migration and would consist of values, norms and cultural representations on migration and appropriate ways for their management, facilitated by the relationship established between the state and civil society organizations (Cortés, 2011b). With regard to the co-development projects, various areas have been addressed – voluntary return, migrant associations and, especially, financial remittances from migrants – but there are very few co-development projects from a gender perspective (Giménez et al., 2006).

In fact, co-development policies do not acknowledge the relationship between co-development and gender, which are treated as two separate fields. This dynamic is channelled and materializes through development visions 'embodied' by the members of the NGOs who work in the countries that have high migration to Spain.

Given the above, my interest in this chapter is to analyse which gender model is present in the migration and development nexus driven by Spanish cooperation. I shall explore whether the visions of gender-related development and migration policies of cooperation include women in economic development without further discussion (the WID approach), or understand that women live their lives connected to three power systems: class, racial/ethnic and gender (GAD).

Therefore I shall start with the ethnographic fieldwork undertaken for five years in Ecuador. My aim is to analyse the political and cultural construction of the migration and development nexus between Ecuador and Spain, as well as pay special attention to the role carried out by the technical advisers of Ecuadorian and Spanish NGOs. First, I shall examine the migration and development model that underpins these co-development projects, starting from the financial remittances and the use of stigmatizing visions of Ecuadorian female migration within a logic of control and security over the migrant flows from Southern Europe.

THE POLITICAL CONSTRUCTION OF THE MIGRATION–DEVELOPMENT NEXUS

One of the most dynamic elements that have become part of the relation between the European Union and the migrants' country of origin has been the migration–development nexus. This debate was very active in the 1970s and 1980s, based on pessimistic views of the impact of migration on the drive for development in the countries of origin.

Recently, this debate has been reactivated, possibly for two reasons: the relevance achieved by international remittances, and the strong concern about immigration control. On the one hand, the interest in international financial remittances has enabled a greater importance to be given to the economic perspective of the relation between migration and development. Over time we have witnessed a proliferation of studies, consultations, reports and publications focused on analysing the purely economic dimension of the remittances that the immigrants settled in Europe, and the world, send to 'their country of origin'. The prevailing optimism on the relations between international remittances and economic development is reproducing the modernization approaches,[1] by defining economic development and the transfer of capital as the chief element in the meaning of development. As a sector, financial remittances far exceed development aid to the countries of the OECD (Faist, 2008, p. 22), which has enabled them to be seen as a tool for the redistribution of income, reduction of poverty and economic growth (de Haas, 2010, p. 228).

The way of understanding development in the nexus of migration and development has allowed the transferral of agency to individual migrants so that they are an agent of their own development. In this regard, special attention was given to the role of the highly qualified migrant male, at the expense of the less-qualified female migrant (Piper, 2008, p. 1288; Dannecker, 2009, p. 121).

The conception of the migration processes as economic facts, which are only viewed as such, falls, according to de Haas (2010, pp. 229–41), into the interpretation framework under which different theories have been used to explain the relation between migration and development. Both the neoclassical and the development-oriented theories that were optimistic about the role of migrants, as well the structuralist theories (dependence), were inspired by accumulative causation that conceives migration as an aggravating cause of underdevelopment and a playback mechanism for the reproduction of global capital. These theories are by nature deterministic and circular, incorporating characteristics that prevent or explain the heterogeneity of the relationship between migration and development. That is to say, we may find cases in which the relation can actually be negative, but there are also examples of a positive relation between migration and development. Therefore, we examine not only the controversy between optimistic and pessimistic positions, but also different paradigms. Thus, it is considered that the relation between one and the other has been established unequally and is characterized by *strong ideological positions* (Abad, 2008, p. 718). In other words, the problem of the relation between migration and development is social and political and not just economic (de Haas, 2010, p. 253).

Second, the interest in this subject also results from the growing interest in migration in a world preoccupied with the paradigm of security. Northern-led development is understood in the South as the element that can halt the northward migration, resulting in power technologies that prevent migration flows (Cortés and Torres, 2009; Raghuram, 2009, p. 113; Cortés, 2011b). Thus, the relationship between migration and development according to this perspective would take migration as something that can be contained, controlled, influenced and thus 'prevented', and development as the tool for this type of intervention would be something normatively good. In the case study of co-development between Ecuador and Spain, Cortés (2011a, p. 45) has shown that the wide range of stakeholder actors (governments involved, development cooperation technicians, development agencies, and even migrant leaders), has as a starting point the conviction that migration can be prevented or controlled through development aid.

TRANSNATIONAL MIGRATION, DEVELOPMENT AND GENDER

Since the 1990s, with the emergence of the transnational perspective, the existing link between migration and development has been incorporated as an emerging field of study. Therefore we are still facing a process of construction for this scientific and political agenda. However, we can already identify three elements of this research agenda in progress that are still unsolved: how to understand the nature of the link between migration and development; the absence of a gender perspective; and the lack of other ways of understanding development.

First, and as we saw in the previous section, the most abundant literature on this subject has tended to an economic, security and teleological reductionism with respect to understanding the link. However, one of the features that characterize this relationship is precisely its diverse nature. What has been documented in the work carried out within the transnationalism agenda is the heterogeneity of the interactions between migration and development, that is, 'contingency time scales of analysis does not allow definitive statements about it' (de Haas, 2010, p. 253). This heterogeneity, on the other hand, has established that there is no causal relationship between migration and development or vice versa, but rather that the relationship must be considered from a reciprocity viewpoint, rather than from the impact of one on the other, from the interactions, rather than from dependence on one another. In fact, we tend to think of the 'impact' of migration on development and vice versa, thus establishing a cause–effect relationship: either the migration is due to conditions of 'underdevelopment' or rather, migration has positive effects or negative development, when what is proposed is a view that establishes a relationship and enables a different range of cases.

Second, several authors state that the analytical category of gender has become part of the discussion of the migration–development nexus despite the work already done on gender and development (Benería and Sen, 1983; Moser, 1991, 1993; Benería and Roldan, 1993; Hondagneu-Sotelo, 2000; Chant, 2003; Kofman, 2004; Piper, 2005); and on remittances (Sørensen, 2004) The stratified, gendered nature of migration has implications for men's and women's incorporation in the labour market and for their claims of social, civil and political rights. However, more attention has been paid to immigration policies, immigration controls and the causes of the inflows and outflows of migrants, ignoring other relevant policy areas. The gender lens allows the redirection of significant analysis to broader social factors that influence the roles of men and women and their access to resources, facilities and services. This has implications for the issue of development and has reignited the ongoing debate on the migration–development nexus, which tends to be dominated by macroeconomic concerns (especially remittances), and is broadly based and sustained on scarce empirical evidence derived mostly from migration flows from South to North. As a result, the social dimensions of the migration–development nexus, which incorporate the potential to explore whether we can speak of contexts, experiences and tactics over equality, and take in a look at human relations based on class, ethnicity and gender, are virtually absent from the discourses and narratives. Thus, when the gender dimension is incorporated into the analysis, it implies placing the social dimensions of the issues under discussion at the centre of the debate, as well as questioning the power relations established.

Third, the way the migration–development nexus has been understood has received criticism from critical development sectors. In the first instance, the concept of development has not been viewed as a multi-dimensional process (Dannnecker, 2009, p. 119). The most widespread views do not include those critical of development; nor do they include new proposals such as human development[2] or those already made by the feminist movement. Thus, the migrants (women and men) would not be single players with a single development vision. And the gender dimension allows us to understand why some visions of development could be more egalitarian than others.

Current discussions fail to incorporate the various negotiations on development visions and interest carried out by the different stakeholders involved in development. In addition, these visions of migrant men's and women's development are built not only on an economic meaning, but also on a social and cultural context that must be taken into account. The social and cultural dimension of development and the interrelationship between the different dimensions of development have not been sufficiently examined. In discussions on the link between migration and development, development is not perceived as multidimensional or multiscalar. The analysis does not incorporate multilevel negotiations between different stakeholders, institutions and organizations (Faist, 2008) or between different social and cultural forces (Nederveen Pieterse, 2001, p. 17). As we have shown above, men and women experience transnational migration differently and also have different relationships in their homes. The question of how this affects the development process, the visions of development and the possibilities of negotiating these visions have been out of the focus of scientific and policy discussions. Through migration, social and cultural visions of development emerge differently between men and women, as well as the ability to negotiate and articulate these visions. Development cannot be conceptualized simply as a result of the processes of migration and remittances, but should be taken as an area of conflict where different actors are involved in trying to establish their views of development and change. For example, Dannecker has shown in his research how the meanings of development may change through the experience of migration, and migrants are understood as a set of beliefs and imaginings about how life should be. This concept ranges from a specific social and economic interest to wider social transformations. This may differ according to the actors: families, governments and institutions can also become the cause of conflicts.

However, this invisibility of the structural conditions of the contemporary discourse – the migration–development construct – also implies a neglect of the key elements in this relationship, such as knowing the role of ethnic inequalities, class, gender and age group, historically being built in both country of origin and of destination. And most importantly, it should be borne in mind how socio-cultural categories can be operated through this link in order to sort, manage and establish hierarchies on migrants who are involved in a migration process (Duffield, 2006).

With regard to the emergence of migrant women within the set of new development actors, a number of studies have been developed concerning so-called 'social remittances'. In scientific literature this term refers to the circulation, between the origin and destination countries, of ideas, practices, identities and social capital, carried out through various communication mechanisms deployed by migrants, such as the internet, letters, telephone or travel, which may have an impact on development and on gender relations and the construction of race and class identities. It includes regulatory structures, such as ideas, values and beliefs, and norms of behaviour, principles of community participation and social mobility aspirations (Levitt and Sørensen, 2004; Oso, 2011). Some studies suggest that changes in gender ideologies that occur with migration can have, with social remittances, an impact on the communities of origin (INSTRAW, 2006). Thus, social remittances could become a factor in development.

In short, most of the studies that have addressed the issue of migration, gender and development efforts have focused mostly on studying how remittances made by men and women vary, and the use and management of the same, examining the transformations of roles and the impact of remittances on gender relations.

THE FEMINIZATION OF ANDEAN MIGRATION TO EUROPE AND ITS DEVELOPMENT: THE NEED FOR A GENDER PERSPECTIVE

While the main destination for migrants from Latin America and the Caribbean is still the United States, where roughly three-quarters of all migrants in the region remain, it should be noted that we are facing a change in trends of Latin American migration, a change that chooses certain EU countries as a destination. The migration from Andean countries in recent decades reflects this change in trend, intensifying towards EU countries, especially Spain where, by 2009, this group was already one of the largest, reaching a total of 1,255,489 citizens from that region (INE, 2009). However, this figure drops to 965,518 for 2011 (the latest for which data are available), possibly because of the access to Spanish nationality for a part of this population, the ongoing process of return and an increased new mobility in a European context following the Spanish economic downturn.

According to the latest data available for the year 2012 (INE, 2012), Andean women in Spain consisted of 113,385 from Bolivia, 214,776 from Colombia, 245,567 from Ecuador and 106,967 from Peru, most of whom were concentrated in three of Spain's Autonomous Communities: Madrid, Catalonia and Valencia. With regard to their original locations, Bolivian female immigrants in Spain came primarily from the cities of La Paz, Cochabamba and Santa Cruz; the most regular flows of Colombian women were from the Valley of Cauca (23.1 per cent), Bogotá (17.6 per cent), Ontario (13.7 per cent) and Gauteng (7 per cent); Ecuadorian women are mainly from the cities of Guayaquil, Quito, Cuenca and Machala, and in the case of Peru, the majority of immigrants were from Lima and Callao, with smaller proportions coming from Tacna (6.9 per cent), Arequipa (5.6 per cent), Puno (4 per cent), Piura (3.9 per cent) and Trujillo (3.5 per cent) (Oxfam, 2010, p. 12).

Unlike the previous decades' flows, the most recent ones largely comprise urban women from the poorest socioeconomic strata. In fact, these clusters range in age between 23 and 35, of which the majority have completed secondary school, and a significant proportion have technical or academic degrees. Despite these relatively high levels of education, the work that they do in Spain is almost entirely unqualified, focusing on reproductive activities in the domestic household and care services and, to a lesser extent, in the cleaning, trade, hotels and catering industries, tourism and prostitution.

Andean migratory policies have been transformed to try to reflect the change in trend experienced by the migrations coming from each of their states. But if we look closely at these policies, we can see that they are characterized by a specialization in very specific subjects or aspects in 'reaction' to demands and certain situations such as the transfer or investment of remittances, the problems of obtaining legal documents, or the return. That is, these policies are characterized by the incorporation of a preventive outlook in the relation between migration and development. This has resulted in a work-area segmentation that is not always in tune with the migratory cycle in all its diversity and complexity, which is expressed both inside and outside the national borders (Oxfam, 2010, pp. 8–9; Cortés, 2011b, p. 68). Thus, although the majority of Andean countries have developed extraterritorial policies linking their nationals in EU countries, this situation has not yet been expressed transversally either from a gender and human rights perspective, or in the policies or public administration of each country. One of the most significant issues when speaking of gender, migration and development is that of remittances. With regard to the four Andean countries analysed, Andean migratory policies would appear not to be conforming to the Montevideo Commitment on Migration and Development that, along with Spain, they signed in Uruguay in 2006. The signatory countries promised clearly to 'facilitate' the flow of remittances, working to reduce their cost. Notwithstanding this, three of the Andean countries have ignored what was agreed: Bolivia imposed a 1 per cent tax on remittances in October 2007, although some months later made it applicable only to remittances over US$1,000, a measure that banks have generally not respected. For years Colombia has been collecting a tax of 0.4 per cent on the remittances that its citizens have been sending, while in Peru remittances are subject to a tax of 0.07 per cent that must be added to the commission charged by the financial intermediary. Only in Ecuador is there no type of tax or financial levy on remittances. Note that this tax is particularly negative and unfair to migrant women since, in general, they not only receive very low salaries (below those of migrant men), but also tend to send smaller amounts with a greater frequency.

One of the most significant aspects of the feminization of Andean migrations is the impact on the composition and sending of remittances. Thus, although women receive lower salaries than men, they send more money, more often, to their families in their country of origin, compared to their male counterparts. The study 'Migrant Andean Women' (Oxfam, 2010) shows that women not only contribute around 60 per cent of the transfers that immigrants send to their countries of origin, but this constitutes approximately 40 per cent of their salary, while men send only around 14 per cent of their salary. This situation would be partially explained by the fact that many men – having arrived at the start of the intensification of the migratory flow to Spain – have been able to regroup their families, and therefore no longer need to send large sums of money to those remaining behind. But basically it is because a significant share of the migrant women in the most recent flows are either heads of household or have migrated independently. They are taking charge not only of improving current living conditions for their family group in the short term, but also of the group's savings project over a much longer term.

In the set of Latin American remittances, the same study shows that the total from Bolivian women is the highest, reaching an average of US$568. Of the number of dispatches to Bolivia, 73.3 per cent are made by women whose contribution represents 73.6 per cent of the total sent to the country. The impact of Bolivian women's remittances is important for the country's economy, since they represent around 5.95 per cent of the national GDP, compared to 8.2 per cent of total income that Bolivia receives from migrants' remittances.

In turn, among the main female immigrant communities in Spain, the Colombian group occupies first place with regard to the number of remittances sent and the amounts thereof. The percentage of remittances of Colombian women (67 per cent) surpasses the female average of the other collectives mean of 61 per cent. The average remittance of Colombian women is US$349, with that of the men (US$400) being noticeably higher. It is estimated that in 2006, Colombian women's contribution to national treasury funds amounted to US$1,090 million, representing 0.8 per cent of the national GDP, while total remittances from Spain were 1.2 per cent.

In the case of Ecuador, although the average of the remittances made by men is US$470 a month and by women is US$412, the number of dispatches made by women is much higher, which results in 64.2 per cent of the total sent by Ecuadorian migrants of both genders in Spain being made by women. The impact of female remittances on Ecuador's economy is considerable: the amount sent by the collective residing in Spain represents 3.51 per cent of the Ecuadorian GDP; of this, women contribute 2.13 per cent and men 1.38 per cent.

The composition of remittances made by Peruvian immigrants in Spain is somewhat atypical compared to the other Andean countries. Although the dispatches by women – which average US$346 – clearly surpass the average of US$305 sent by the men, the difference with the other countries is rooted in the fact that the difference between the number of dispatches made by men and those made by women is not very great: women represent 50.5 per cent, and men 49.5 per cent. Thus, by comparison with the other Andean countries, women's contribution in terms of remittances is less than the average per country (60.3 per cent), as it represents only 50.5 per cent of the total. Even so, women's contribution to the Peruvian economy is relevant, since they contribute somewhat more than half of the 0.31 per cent of the total impact on the country's GDP made by remittances coming from Spain.

As we have shown, the role of women in sending remittances constitutes a strategic element in gender, migration and development. However, from the analysis of migratory policies and NGOs, we shall see that the projects that have been implemented are significantly supported by objectives, interests and development visions. They are more concerned with the coherence of first-phase control and security policies, than the articulation of heterogeneity between migration and development or reinforcing the role of women as development stakeholders. The next section will explore these issues, starting with the role played by Spanish and Ecuadorian NGOs in the context of the intensification of Ecuadorian migrant flows to Spain.

THE ROLE OF STEREOTYPES THROUGH CO-DEVELOPMENT FROM A GENDER PERSPECTIVE

The analysis of the migration and development nexus from a gender perspective has produced a set of functional stereotypes in a discourse quite distant from a transforming vision of gender relations. Thus, co-development projects have been boosted while plans and policies were being designed that have laid the foundations for the subject of gender and development in Spain: the Master Plan for Spanish Cooperation (2005–08, 2009–12) (AECID, 2005, 2009), the Gender Strategy in Development in Spanish Cooperation (AECID, 2007) and the Sectoral Gender and Development Action Plan of Spanish Cooperation (AECID, 2012). Therefore, co-development actions were based on the migration and development nexus prior to the institutionalization of the GAD approach in Spanish cooperation, and incorporate certain stereotypes about migration and gender. Possibly the most important is based on the relation between the dismantling of the family structure and migration, and it is implemented by the operators of the cooperation projects, that is, the Spanish and Ecuadorian technicians who design, execute and take on the projects:

> [W]hat we are trying to do is create projects . . . so that . . . those that live in this area do not have to leave, neither the mother nor the father, that the children do not have to remain in charge of the grandmother and that at three years of age are drug addicts, have committed suicide and such . . . the problem that has arisen in Ecuador with emigration is tremendous, that is, the level of suicides that it has generated at the level of children is striking, the grandparents are

not capable of maintaining any control over the children, the mothers are here with total psychological problems, the husband is there seeing other women or he has stayed and is spending all the money with the new woman, that is to say, there are problems . . . and no one seems to worry about them. (Cooperation technician, Spanish NGO, Madrid, 2007)

This type of discourse operates with the mobility logic that NGOs have attempted to disseminate through co-development projects: migration must be prevented by means of development whenever this does not take place along the legal channels established for it. Thus, from the very beginning these projects were linked to the logic of the return, which has reinforced the idea that the migrants must return home. The strategy for doing this has been to link the return to productive projects fed by the remittances of the migrants themselves. Thus, with co-development we have observed an unusual proliferation of projects that deal with the remittances, their management and their channelling towards productive initiatives. This is a result of two factors: first, the paradigmatic change of direction of the Official Development Aid patterns for the purpose of reorienting it towards establishing regulation and governance mechanisms (local, national and global) demanded by globalization, and second, the extension of a specific 'migration and development' model, which deals with linking remittances to migration management via productive initiatives.

With regard to the first factor, the in-depth discussion that marked the change of Official Development Aid rests historically and politically on the idea that poor countries must accelerate their integration process into the global markets as the sole means of overcoming underdevelopment. The institutions that have safeguarded this approach have been, primarily, the OECD and the World Bank. From the political and institutional viewpoint, a new development strategy was needed, based on the harmonization of governmental policies with market forces – a state 'market-friendly' approach. At the same time that the world economy went through a phase of acute transformation, international development also entered a new stage. None the less, a free market strategy was not proposed but rather a selective state intervention strategy. In addition, government had to open itself to greater private participation in sectors such as education, health, legal and tax infrastructure and environmental protection. Along with these sectors, that of migration and remittances has had great relevance in the last decade. In the case of Ecuador, it is undeniable that the impact of remittances has given stability to the Ecuadorian economy throughout the first decade of the twenty-first century. But Ecuador has also gone from being an oil and development-oriented state (in the 1970s) to being a state increasingly indebted to international agencies such as the IMF.

Thus, Ecuador has been obliged to depend on external investment and international financing. This implies two things: the agency of progress was transferred from the development-oriented state to the 'individual entrepreneur', and the dependence of global financial flows pushed the state to subject its administrative apparatus to an emerging global governmentality (Gupta, 1998).

The second factor, remittances and migration management, is illustrated by the case of co-development. Migration, through remittances, has become a subject on 'the development agenda', which is specified through co-development projects. In this type of project, the migrant is usually presented as an investor who must link part of 'his/her remittances' to productive projects that would help to generate the return of those who had migrated. In this regard, the technicians of the co-development projects usually refer to the use migrants make of the remittances, as that is how it is registered in the 'dichotomous' debates on migrants' money (Cortés, 2011b, p. 322). The discourses on the good or bad use of the remittances has resulted in the idea that they should be redirected. Thus both the sending and receiving immigration states, in their multiple forms of government (on a national, regional and local level), and different international institutions, are being legitimized to 'intervene' in the destination of the remittances and to dedicate them to projects in which they also take part (Guarnizo, 2004, pp. 63–4).

Therefore, in this context marked by the modernizing and economic logic of development, one of the most common resources from the discursive viewpoint has been the proliferation of stigmatizing visions on the 'dismantling of the family structure' and the misuse of the remittances, as an argument to justify the actions of the cooperation technicians for development:

> [The migrants' children] are left alone, they take on roles that do not correspond to them, they have money and they give money to their friends . . . but of course, the people use the remittances poorly due to lack of advice. (Technician of the Catholic Church, Loja, 2005)

Thus, the problem for these technical advisers is that the families do not use their money productively, they do not invest it in businesses but rather the money is wasted on activities that are not productive:

> The migrants' project, the idea, although I don't know if it will be achieved in the long term, is to try to get people to return to their country of origin by giving them businesses . . . I see that, a little, it is so they do not waste the money that their family members send them, the remittances, but rather tell them about these businesses so that they may have and produce something. Because the time will come when the money that the migrants send is a bag that

has been broken, it will have gone and it will not have been good for anything. (Guayaquil, representative of Ecuadorian NGO, 2007)

These visions, however, do not consider the impact of the remittances on development and their characterization by gender. Herrera observed differences of gender in remittance use, such that the women tend to send fewer collective remittances and direct their shipments to their families and especially to their children. The men also send to the family, but in addition they also send some for the well-being of the community (Herrera, 2006, p. 214). As Herrera indicates, expenditure is dedicated above all to food, health, clothing, education and the payment of debts. That is to say, remittances would contribute to the well-being of the family. These amounts are increased in the case of the women when the money is sent for health, education and food, while the men send higher amounts for the payment of debts, construction of homes, farming and so on. Women who send remittances do so in defiance of the hegemonic discourses on remittances and families (transnational) in Ecuadorian society. In this regard, the valuations of the destination and use of the remittances has at its heart a gender-based judgement; on the positive side, the male uses of money lean towards what is productive, while the negative would be sending money for reproductive purposes, which is mainly done by Ecuadorian female migrants. These valuations are made clear from positions of class, race and gender on how the money is used by the indigenous and mixed-race emigrées of middle/low class to further the interests of their families.

Thus, one of the risks is the instrumentalization of the families and of the women, in order to generate initiatives that alleviate migration. This problem has been introduced onto the development agenda. By conceiving such a relation between migration and development, activities and training workshops have been designed, as well as meetings held, that aim to redirect the remittances towards productive activities that serve to prevent more Ecuadorians from leaving and/or to promote their return. Thus, women would become a means of contributing to the reduction in migration, instead of the project activities being aimed at strengthening the rights, projects and needs of these migrant women. This shows that the uses of remittances are being constrained within some margins of reductionist meanings such that other social and cultural meanings of the remittances are not taken into account by the different actors.

As important as what the money is used for, is who manages the remittances. Ecuador follows the same pattern as other countries, that is, mothers who have stayed in the home country manage the money, followed by parents, sisters and brothers (Herrera, 2006, p. 216). This trend has also been found in the case of remittances that are managed in savings and credit cooperatives, although these types of financial, productive and political organizations have also allowed the bypassing of traditional forms of patriarchal control over the money that women send. Cortés and Ortega (2008, p. 46) found that the savings and credit cooperatives made it easier for women to control what the money was used for, whether it came from Spain, Italy or the United States.

However, the co-development projects, far from incorporating these considerations, are based more on stereotypes such as that of the dismantling of the family structure, which has made possible the emergence of programmes and policies that can skip over gender-related aspects. There can be no doubt that this reflects, on the part of those responsible for public policies on development cooperation, a certain degree of reticence in tackling the question of the relation between gender and migration in a context of development, more than that of migrant women. This has assisted in the creation of meta-groups outside the organizations that have been working on the country's human rights or in peasant organizations, since it has been much more convenient to work with target groups and with less-expensive strategies. This is because work aimed at goals and results is a neoliberal tool that enables the reduction of public spending on universal social programmes, favouring more effective schemes according to poverty reduction costs and/or those that promote development (Chant, 2002).

CONCLUSION

This chapter has focused on the link between migration and development from a gender perspective. From the case of the Andean migrations to Europe, and the co-development between Ecuador and Spain, the analysis has shown that the cooperation policy for Spanish development could be experiencing a return to the WID approach. This approach excludes the analysis of gender and power relations and their economic, social, cultural and political impact in order to comply with the rights of women focusing on positive action measures as a function of merely formal equality, without questioning the structures that cause inequality.

We have identified emerging subjects on this agenda from a gender perspective (the social remittances and stereotyping of families and migrant women). But an emerging field of study, analysis and understanding illuminates the contemporaneous political and socio-cultural processes that situate the role of the male and female migrants from their agency for development, that is, from their capacity to bypass limitations and improve their conditions of subsistence. It is also one that analyses the structural constrictions that historically have been, and continue to be constructed, inequalities of class, race, ethnicities, gender and age groups, in both societies of origin and of destination.

NOTES

1. For a historic discussion on the theories of migration and development, see the seminal paper by Michael Kearney (1986). According to Kearney, the theories that have been dedicated to this question can be classified into three areas: the theory of modernization, the theory of dependence and the theory of articulationism; for a review of these theories from a gender perspective, see Carmen Gregorio's groundbreaking book (1998).
2. We here echo other proposals posed by authors critical of development that go even beyond this concept, and propose new concepts such as post-development. It deals with visions that are based on the rejection of the way in which the idea of development has been extending as a promise of emancipation for everyone, up to the point of becoming something obligatory and indisputable (for example, Escobar, 1997; Rist, 2002).

REFERENCES

Abad, Luis V. (2008), 'Emigración y desarrollo: Un enfoque desde las condiciones iniciales', in J. García Roca and Joan Lacomba (eds), *La inmigración en la sociedad española: Una radiografía multidisciplinar*, Barcelona: Bellaterra, pp. 717–50.
Benería, Lourdes and Martha Roldan (1993), *Las encrucijadas de clase y género*, Mexico: El Colegio de Mexico and FCE.
Benería, Lourdes and Gita Sen (1983), 'Accumulation, reproduction and women's role in economic development: Boserup revisited', in Eleanor Leacock and Helen Safa (eds), *Women's Work: Development and the Division of Labor by Gender*, South Hadley, MA: Bergin & Garvey, pp. 141–57.
Chant, Sylvia (2002), 'Whose crisis? Public and popular reactions to family change in Costa Rica', in Christopher Abel and Colin Lewis (eds), *Exclusion and Engagement: Social Policy in Latin America*, Washington, DC: Brookings Institution, pp. 349–77.
Chant, Sylvia (2003), 'Nuevas contribuciones al análisis de la pobreza: desafíos metodológicos y conceptuales para entender la pobreza desde una perspectiva de género', *Mujer y Desarrollo*, **47**, 47–78.
Cortés, Almudena. (2011a), 'The transnational governance of Ecuadorian migration through co-development', *International Migration*, **49** (3), 30–51.
Cortés, Almudena (2011b), *Estados, Cooperación para el desarrollo y Migraciones: el caso del codesarrollo entre Ecuador y España*, Madrid: Entimema.
Cortés, Almudena and Alicia Torres (2009), 'Introducción. La migración y el codesarrollo: campos sociales de acción transnacional', in Cortés and Alicia Torres (eds), *Codesarrollo en los Andes: contextos y actores para una Acción transnacional*, Quito: FLACSO Ecuador, Instituto Universitario de Investigación sobre Migraciones, Etnicidad y Desarrollo Social and Ayuntamiento de Madrid, pp. 9–30.
Cortés, Almudena. and Carlos Ernesto Ortega (2008), 'Si ellas no vieran por mí, no tuviera nada: remesas y estructuras financieras locales en el Austro ecuatoriano. Una mirada transnacional al dinero de los migrantes', *Migración y Desarrollo*, **11**, 31–53.
Dannecker, Petra (2009), 'Migrant visions of development: a gendered approach', *Population, Space and Place*, **15**, 119–32.

de Haas, Hein (2010), 'Migration and development: a theoretical perspective', *International Migration Review*, **44** (1), Spring, 227–64.
Debusscher, Petra (2011), 'Mainstreaming gender in European Commission development policy: conservative Europeanness?', *Women's Studies International Forum*, **34**, 39–49.
Duffield, Mark (2006), 'Racism, migration and development: the foundations of planetary order', *Progress in Development Studies*, **6** (1), 68–79.
Ehrenreich, Barbara and Arlie Russell Hochschild (2002), *Global Woman: Nannies, Maids and Sex Workers in the New Economy*, New York: Henry Holt.
Escobar, Arturo (1997), 'Anthropology and development', *International Social Science Journal*, **154**, 497–516.
Escrivá, Ángeles and Natalia Ribas-Mateos (eds) (2004), *Migración y desarrollo*, Córdoba: CSIC.
Faist, Thomas (2008), 'Migrants as transnational development agents: an inquiry into the newest round of the migration–development nexus', *Population, Space and Place*, **14**, 21–42.
Gainza, Patricia (2006), 'Feminización de las remesas, familias transnacionales y comercio nostálgico', *Revista Tercer Mundo Económico*, **204**, May, available at: http://old.redtercermundo.org.uy/tm_economico/texto_completo.php?Id=3043 (accessed 10 September 2012).
Giménez, Carlos, Julio Martínez, Mercedes Fernández and Almudena Cortés (2006), *El codesarrollo en España: protagonistas, discursos y experiencias*, Madrid: Los Libros de la Catarata.
Gregorio, Carmen (1998), *Inmigración femenina: su impacto en las relaciones de género* (Women's migration: its impact on gender relations), Madrid: Narcea.
Guarnizo, Luis Eduardo (2004), 'Aspectos económicos del vivir transnacional', in A. Escrivá and N. Ribas-Mateos (eds), *Migración y desarrollo*, Córdoba: CSIC, pp. 55–86.
Gupta, Akil (1998), *Postcolonial Developments: Agriculture in the Making of Modern India*, Durham, NC: Duke University Press.
Herrera, Gioconda (2006), 'Precarización del trabajo, crisis de reproducción social y migración femenina: ecuatorianas en España y Estados Unidos', in Herrera (ed.) *La persistencia de la desigualdad. Género, trabajo y pobreza en América Latina*, Quito: CONAMU, FLACSO-Ecuador and Secretaria Técnica del Frente Social, pp. 199–223.
Hondagneu-Sotelo, Pierrette (2000), 'The international division of caring and cleaning work', in Mona Harrington (ed.) *Care Work, Gender Labor and Welfare State*, New York: Routledge, pp. 149–62.
Instituto Nacional de Estadística (INE) (2009, 2012), 'Población por nacionalided, país de nacimiento y sexo', available at: http://www.ine.es (accessed 10 September 2012)
INSTRAW (2006), *El caso de la migración femenina de Vicente Noble, República Dominicana*, Santo Domingo: INSTRAW.
INSTRAW (2007), *Género y Remesas. Migración colombiana del AMCO hacia España*, Santo Domingo: INSTRAW, PNUD.
Kearney, Michael (1986), 'From the invisible hand to visible feet: anthropological studies of migration and development', *Annual Review of Anthropology*, **15**, 331–61.
Kofman, Eleonore (2004), 'Gendered global migration', *International Feminist Journal of Politics*, **6** (4), December, 643–65.
Levitt, Peggy and Ninna Sørensen (2004), 'The transnational turn in migration studies', *Global Migration Perspectives*, **6**, 2–13.
López de Lera, Diego and Laura Oso (2007), 'La inmigración latinoamericana en España: Tendencias y estado de la cuestión' in Gioconda Herrera and Isabel Yépez del Castillo, *Nuevas migraciones latinoamericanas a Europa: Balances y desafíos*, Quito: FLACSO Sede Ecuador, Observatorio de las Relaciones Unión Europea – América Latina, Universidad de Lovaina and Universitat de Barcelona, pp. 31–67.
Ministerio de Asuntos Exteriores y de Cooperación (2005), *Master Plan of Spanish Cooperation, 2005–2018*, Madrid: AECID.
Ministerio de Asuntos Exteriores y de Cooperación de España (2007), *Estrategia de Género en Desarrollo en la Cooperación Española*, Madrid: AECID.

Ministerio de Asuntos Exteriores y de Cooperación de España (2009), *Master Plan of Spanish Cooperation 2009–2012*, Madrid: AECID.
Ministerio de Asuntos Exteriores y de Cooperación de España (2012), *Plan de Actuación Sectorial de Género y Desarrollo*, Madrid: AECID.
Moser, Caroline (1991), 'La planificación de género en el Tercer Mundo: enfrentando las necesidades prácticas y estratégicas de género', in Virginia Guzmán, Patricia Portocarrero and Virginia Vargas (eds), *Una nueva lectura: género en el desarrollo*, Lima: Flora Trastán, pp. 55–124.
Moser, Caroline (1993), *Gender Planning and Development: Theory, Practice and Training*, London: Routledge.
Nederveen Pieterse, Jan (2001), *Development Theory. Deconstructions/Reconstructions*, London, Thousand Oaks, CA and New Delhi: Sage.
Oso, Laura (2011), 'Plata y/o amor: remesas, acumulación de activos y movilidad social de las familias de migrantes ecuatorianos', in Jorge Ginieniewicz (ed.), *La migración latinoamericana a España: una mirada desde el modelo de acumulación de activos*, Quito: Flacso Ecuador, Global Urban Research Centre, pp. 129–49.
Oxfam (2010), *Mujeres Migrantes Andinas*, Santiago de Chile.
Parella, Sònia and Leonardo Cavalcanti (2009), 'Una aproximación cualitativa a las remesas de los inmigrantes peruanos y ecuatorianos en España y a su impacto en los hogares transnacionales', *Revista Española de Investigaciones Sociológicas*, **116**, 241–57.
Piper Nicola (2005), 'Gender and migration', Background paper for Global Commission on International Migration (GCIM) and appendix to the GCIM Global Report on Migration, Recommendations to the Secretary-General.
Piper, Nicola (2008), 'Feminisation of migration and the social dimension of development: the Asian case', *Third World Quarterly*, **29** (7), 1287–303.
Raghuram, Parvati (2009), 'Which migration, what development? Unsettling the edifice of migration and development', *Population, Space and Place*, **15**, 103–17.
Ramírez, Carlota, Mar García Domínguez and Julio Míguez Morais (2005), *Cruzando fronteras: Remesas, género y desarrollo*, Santo Domingo: INSTRAW.
Rist, Gilbert (2002), *El desarrollo: historia de una creencia occidental*, Madrid: Los Libros de La Catarata.
Sassen, Saskia (2003), *Contrageografías de la globalización: Género y ciudadanía en los circuitos transfronterizos*, Madrid: Traficantes de Sueños.
Semyonov, Moshe and Anastasia Gorodzeisky (2005), 'Labor migration, remittances and household income: a comparison between Filipino and Filipina overseas workers', *International Migration Review*, **39** (1), Spring, 45–68.
Sørensen, Ninna (2004), 'Globalización, Género y Migración Transnacional', in A. Escrivá and N. Ribas-Mateos (eds), *Migración y desarrollo*, Córdoba: CSIC, pp. 87–109.
Truong, Thanh-Dam (1996), 'Uncertain horizon: the women's question in Vietnam revisited', Institute of Social Studies, The Hague, 1–28.

6 Theoretical debates on social reproduction and care: the articulation between the domestic and the global economy
Christine Verschuur

INTRODUCTION

Women's work is connected to globalization processes. Considerable research has been conducted on women and work and on the shifting divisions of labour globally, particularly in development studies. The activities and relations indispensable for social reproduction have been conceptualized by feminist studies and the place of women migrant workers in the new global economy has been articulated in relation to the domestic economy. In this context, the concept of care has also been associated with reflections on migration and on the links between the domestic and the global economy. However, the concepts of social reproduction and care cannot be merged and furthermore, in the context of gender, development and migration studies, has some limitations. Therefore it is very important to deepen the question on the articulation of production and social reproduction in the context of globalization, within which care is included, in order to contribute to explaining the increase in social and gender inequalities in development. This chapter will shed light on these theoretical debates.

I shall start by presenting some reflections on the (re)production and circulation of the labour force in the global economy and continue with a brief analysis of the feminization of migration and the globalization of social reproduction. I shall then briefly present some feminist theoretical debates on work, clarifying differences and relations between domestic work, unpaid and paid work, care activities and social reproduction, and in particular discuss the issues of social reproduction and care in relation to the migration and development debate. Finally I shall discuss the articulation of the social relations in the domestic and capitalist spheres, in whose framework reproductive activities are carried out, as well as the way in which the globalization of social reproduction and migration processes contribute to the global economy. The chapter illuminates the production–reproduction debate, which, I argue, should not focus on the nature of the work carried out, but on the articulation of different social relations that predominate in the domestic and capitalist spheres where productive and reproductive activities are undertaken. I argue that gender and race, as socially constructed power relations, serve as 'magical tools' to maintain the capitalist system.

Gender is defined as a way of expressing power relations: 'Changes in the organization of social relationships always correspond to changes in the representation of power' (Scott, 1986, p. 1067). As a constitutive element of social relationships, it involves symbolic, normative, institutional and individual dimensions (Scott, 1986). Gender also has a strong legitimizing function. It explains how certain activities are considered, at specific moments and places, according to cultures, classes and races, as masculine or feminine: 'The sex-segregated labour market is a part of the process of gender construction' (ibid., p. 1068). In addition, the process of how gender relationships are constructed can be used to discuss race as a social construct which expresses power relations because understanding how *racial discourses* organize the world's population in an international division of labour is a requirement for understanding global capitalism. In this respect, Aníbal Quijano has shown how since the sixteenth century, the exploitation of the Global South by the Global North has been based on ethnic and racial organization (see Castro-Gómez and Grosfoguel, 2007).

Gender is a powerful tool to define the division of labour, at both the domestic and the global level. The reorganization of gender is part of the global strategy of capitalism. Women workers of a particular class/caste, race, are necessary for the capitalist global economy. They are present in the global economy as workers in industry, in the informal economy and in agricultural enterprises, but also in the less visible side of the economy, namely the reproductive sector: 'Making gender and power visible in the processes of global restructuring demands looking at, naming and seeing the raced and classed communities of women from poor countries, as they are constituted as workers in sexual, domestic, and service industries; as prisoners; and as household managers and nurturers' (Mohanty, 2002, p. 526). Anti-globalization movements have recognized the centrality of class and gender in the critique against capitalism and the new international division of labour. However, 'racialized gender is still an unmarked category' in the majority of the literature on anti-globalization movements (ibid., p. 530).

In this chapter I shall show how the debates on social reproduction and care contribute to illustrate the centrality of the category of gender and to a better understanding of the global economy. Can gender and race power relations change? Can new forms of legitimation be found through revision of the terms of gender and race? New kinds of symbols may emerge. Normative visions can be put into question, as a result of a global crisis. Different forms of how social reproduction is organized could open different possibilities for the construction of subjectivity, new areas of activity and social relations.

(RE)PRODUCTION AND CIRCULATION OF THE LABOUR FORCE, GLOBALIZATION OF CAPITALISM AND THE NEW INTERNATIONAL DIVISION OF LABOUR

Feminist movements and women's movements have played a central role in the critical analysis of the ideological, political, economic, environmental, social, familial and gender order, upon which the globalization of capitalism has rested for the past half century and which has been termed 'development' in what was called the Third World and is now called the Global South. They contested the sexual and racial division of labour and the inequalities in the new international division of labour, a decrease in state intervention in social policies, environmental degradation, inequalities and obstructions in accessing forums of power and decision making.

The extraction of labour, goods and services from the Global South to the Global North has been the object of critical development studies. The world-system perspective (Wallerstein, 1979) has centred on the analysis of the international division of labour and the geo-political military struggles in the processes of global capitalist accumulation (Castro-Gómez and Grosfoguel, 2007, p.14). While the world-system perspective emphasizes the economic structures, 'Anglo-Saxon postcolonial studies criticize developmentalism, euro-centric forms of knowledge, gender inequalities, racial hierarchies and cultural/ideological processes that favour the subordination of the periphery to the capitalist world system' (p.14, my translation) emphasizing the cultural agency of the subjects. In bringing back debates on colonialism, philosophy of liberation, pedagogy of the oppressed and theories of dependency, Latin American scholars propose a decolonized perspective that tries to integrate both dimensions. Decolonial feminisms integrate this double perspective, analysing the new international division of labour while at the same time recognizing women's and men's agency. It is this perspective that I adopt to reflect on the articulation of both domestic and global economies and on the debates about social reproduction and care.

First, to understand the globalization of capitalism and what has been called 'development', feminist scholars have underlined the importance of invisible productive and reproductive work (Boserup, 1970; Benería, 1982) and of the new international division of reproductive labour (Federici, 1999). The decolonial perspective considers that global capitalism is based on gender and racial discourses that organize the international division of labour (Castro-Gómez and Grosfoguel, 2007). In order to explain the roots of underdevelopment, economic anthropologists analysed the articulation between the sphere of reproductive labour – where domestic-type relations of production predominate, and the productive sphere of labour – where capitalist relations of production predominate.

This articulation of productive–reproductive spheres is 'the essential cause of underdevelopment as well as of the prosperity of the capitalist sector' (Meillassoux, 1975, p. 149, my translation). Other scholars (Delphy, 1970; Rey, 1976) have also shown the importance of maintaining domestic-type relations of production for the development of the capitalist economy. For instance, Meillassoux argues that the domestic economy is part of the *sphere of circulation* of capitalism, supplying it with labour force and goods, but that it remains outside the capitalist *sphere of production*. It is by maintaining these organic links between the capitalist and the domestic economies that the former ensures its growth and prosperity. The domestic economy permits the production and reproduction of the labour force at a low price for the capitalist economy. To maintain this, it is necessary to preserve the former – to continue extracting its substance – in order to supply the latter. This means that the domestic sphere has to be kept out of the capitalist sphere of production, while maintaining the organic links between them. It is in this perspective that one can situate temporary and circular labour migrations. 'The preservation and exploitation of the domestic agricultural economy' (Meillassoux, 1975, p. 165, my translation) in the southern countries, and generally the domestic economy in all its activities, ensures not only the production but also the reproduction and maintenance of this migrant labour force.

Second, I address the colonial order. The economic restructuring of the last four decades has created, according to Silvia Federici (1999), a new colonial order. Increasing poverty and inequalities, a drop in states' commitment to invest in labourers' reproduction (with cuts to social budgets, monetary devaluations, privatization and liberalization), decreasing salaries and work incomes, have all created a crisis of social reproduction in the Global South. Many women look elsewhere for income to ensure the maintenance and reproduction costs of their family members. These women may also leave to pursue their dreams, build new social relations and personal projects (Sanghera, 2004).

Lastly, I take a look into the new international division of labour, where studies have emphasized the *production* of goods and services more than the *reproduction* of labour. However, as Federici highlights, 'a significant part of the reproduction work necessary to produce the metropolitan work-force is performed by third-world women. Behind emigration, in fact, an immense "gift" of domestic labor is hidden' (Federici, 1999, p. 57), a gift by women of the Global South to the rich countries, by responding to the need for 'ready made workers' (Marx, cited by Meillassoux, 1975, p. 161). 'Through emigration, third-world women directly contribute to the accumulation of wealth in the "advanced" capitalist countries' (Federici, 1999, p. 57). For Federici, labour is the most important commodity exported by the Global South to the Global North.

The global economic restructuration is accompanied by changes in gender relations linked to the new division of labour. This is linked to the feminization of the workforce in delocalized manufacturing industries or agro-industrial industries, the growing number of women in the informal economy in cities or in petty agricultural commodity production, and the feminization of migration (Benería, 1982; Morokvasic, 1984; Kabeer, 1995; Federici, 1999; Sassen, 2005).

FEMINIZATION OF MIGRATION AND GLOBALIZATION OF SOCIAL REPRODUCTION

Women and men have always migrated. The circulation of people, even when it is not regulated or officially encouraged – except for very qualified migrants – is widespread. In 2010, the number of women migrants was estimated at 105 million and the number of male migrants was 109 million. Within 20 years, both numbers have increased by 38 per cent. Since 1975, the number of migrants has more than doubled (OIM, 2010).

First, the feminization of migration does not refer to the fact that women were not migrating before or are now migrating more than men. Figures show that women have always migrated, as men have, with many variations according to historical contexts, countries or according to their social and racial belonging (Moreno Fontes-Chammartin, 2002; Catarino et al., 2005; Oso-Casas and Garson, 2005; Verschuur and Reysoo, 2005). We have to understand this feminization in the context of the global increase in migration, of both men and women. As an example, OECD data on the proportion of immigrant women who, in 2004, had lived for five years or more in a country indicated a noticeable increase compared with 1994. This was particularly the case in Poland, Italy, the Netherlands, Portugal, Greece and Canada (Oso-Casas and Garson, 2005, p. 8). In

Spain, data from 2004 indicated that 86 per cent of immigrant women had arrived during the previous 10 years. While much data (as in OIM, 2010; see also Oso-Casas and Garson, 2005) confirm increasing migration of both women and men in many countries, 'feminization of migration' refers to a specific process, namely, that of women increasingly migrating as independent workers, not necessarily with their family.

Gender, migration and development studies have analysed the changes in the representation of the female migrant, as have 'gender and development' studies in general (Verschuur, 2009), when analysing the changes in women's representation in 'development' programmes since the Second World War. Represented only as 'mothers', women were at first absent from development studies and programmes, their work in productive and reproductive spheres being invisible. In a second phase, represented as 'workers' only, the accent was on the productive sphere, since their (formerly invisible) work was considered to be a useful resource for development, reproductive activities being still invisible. In a third phase, the accent was on their multiple identities, including the intersection of gender, race and class. People were represented as subjects of their own history. Women were no longer represented as victims, even if they were heroic ones (Agustín, 2005). While claiming their rights as waged or informal workers, they also made claims to be recognized in their social reproductive activities. Some of these activities are organized in collective ways (associations, groups, movements) where new spaces of resistance are emerging, new proposals to claim rights are arising and new power relations at the local level are slowly being constructed (Verschuur, 2012). The focus has thus shifted from being on women as only 'mothers', to women as mainly 'workers', to now being on women as subjects, where productive and reproductive activities and the social relations they need to carry them out are intertwined. Links are made between the new international division of labour in the global capitalist system, the cultural agency of the subjects and their concrete social struggles.

In migration and development studies, under pressure from feminist scholars and movements, discourses have changed in a similar way (Oso-Casas and Garson, 2005). In the first phase, women were invisible among migrant people and absent from studies on migration. Later on, women migrants were represented only as part of family reunification processes, never as economic agents. Women were considered as 'mothers' only and as passive, accompanying migrants. The fact that even when women migrated within the framework of family reunification many of them were also integrated in the labour market, was not recognized. Finally, women have been considered as active persons in the migration process, playing a role as economic agents and in reproductive activities.

The shift in the representation of migrant women has contributed to the deconstruction of the image of the victimized woman, without agency, which does not correspond to reality. The migratory route demands courage, nerve and skills. It is, without doubt, the strong women and/or those who have some resources (higher education, some means) who leave. Whatever the conditions of exploitation, they construct life projects, crossing borders, constituting themselves into subjects, here and there, in transnational networks. They participate in the subtle transformation of gender relations, organizing themselves to claim for their rights in the country of arrival, weaving links with organizations and reviving debates on the unequal sexual division of labour in the domestic sphere and on the development of social policies.

Second, a deconstruction of the representation of people who migrate contributes to a better analysis of the process. The image of the male migrant corresponding to the stereotype of the male breadwinner, the head of the household, explains why the woman migrant was often left in the shadows. The image of the female migrant as a 'caregiver only' is also a stereotype. Increasingly women are migrating independently and alone to earn money in paid jobs, which does not fit with the dominant image of a 'traditional' woman in a 'traditional family'. New family compositions are at work. Some migrant women choose to bring selected relatives, composing new unconventional units, or create new bonds in the country of arrival. While some migrant women are unmarried or separated, others are leaving behind a partner or a husband and their children in their country of origin. They take care of their families from a distance, with the help of new communication technologies, and sometimes arrange for members of their families to join them later. They develop strategies as subjects of their own lives, and are employed in paid jobs. Although often badly paid (OIT, 2010a), they send remittances to their countries, contributing to the GNP. They are far from being confined to the role of mother or the role of caregiver for others.

Sectors employing migrant women are primarily the service sector, including domestic work, personal care (children and the elderly, health services, sex work), cleaning and other services in hotels, restaurants and retail work (Moreno Fontes-Chanmmartin, 2002). These niches of work take place in homes or private, public and associate institutions and are frequently – but not only – occupied by migrant, often highly qualified women. In Spain, for instance, 63 per cent of Peruvian domestic workers have a university degree (Oso-Casas, 2002). This characteristic makes them particularly valued when it comes to taking care of children or the elderly, apart from the fact that they also meet the criteria of the so-called 'feminine qualities' sought after for these kinds of jobs (loving, patient, pious, with 'good reputation').

Domestic work is an important niche of work for migrant female workers, but some male migrants are also employed in domestic work (as gardeners, cleaners, cooks and so on). Localized studies show convergent tendencies. A study in Sri Lanka in 2001 showed that 83 per cent of female migrants worked as domestic workers, although they were highly educated (Moreno Fontes-Chammartin, 2002, p. 45). In Latin America, internal women migrants tend to be concentrated in three sectors: commerce, services and domestic work. On average,[1] between 75 and 80 per cent of women migrants who are employed are occupied in these sectors, and most are in domestic services (Tokman, 2010, p. 8). There are country differences. In Argentina, 78 per cent of women immigrants are employed in domestic services, while in Costa Rica and Chile, the shares were 47 and 37 per cent, respectively. In several Latin American countries most of the women in domestic work are immigrants. In Argentina, Chile, Brazil and Paraguay, between 90 and 96 per cent are migrants (ibid.). 'Worldwide, 17–25 million female migrants are estimated to work in the sector', according to Panell and Altman (2007, cited in Schwenken and Heimeshoff, 2011, p. 12). However, it is extremely difficult to evaluate precisely the number of female migrant workers in this sector due to the different definitions and sources of information and, particularly, to the fact that many migrant workers are illegal and many domestic workers 'unrecorded'.

Female migrant labour is not limited to domestic and care work. In the new international division of labour, industries are employing a large number of women who come from other regions or countries. Since the late 1980s, in many middle-income countries, the demand for women's labour (often internal migrants) in export-oriented manufacturing has been weakening, as export production has become more skill and capital intensive (Razavi, 2002). However, the representation of the migrant female worker has sometimes been reduced to that of the 'export-oriented manufacture worker' (*maquilas*, free economic zones), in the garment or electronic industries. As was the case in the 'women as workers only' phase of gender and development studies, the accent on this representation of women's work in the new international division of labour has led to an underestimation of their contribution to globalized social reproduction work. On the other hand, some researchers have placed emphasis on 'global care chains', underestimating migrant women's productive work and limiting women's contribution to their reproductive work. There is a need to consider the articulation of both productive and reproductive spheres, which are intimately intertwined.

RECOGNITION OF DOMESTIC WORK, CARE AND SOCIAL REPRODUCTION

Theoretical feminist debates on work have underlined the male bias attached to the concept of work. Not only was waged work thought of as male but also, for a long time, classical economics did not consider work that was unpaid or carried out in the domestic sphere. Since the 1960s, feminist movements have highlighted the issue of unpaid work carried out by women, invisible, not for oneself but for others, 'in the name of nature, love or maternal duty' (Kergoat, 2000). Feminist researchers have theorized on 'domestic work' and intense debates have taken place on the 'domestic mode of production' (Delphy, 1970).

Domestic work includes all the activities related to caring for people, accomplished within the framework of family. It can be carried out for free or by salaried people. It has been defined as 'the act of putting specifically women to work in the private sphere as the principal place of the care of persons' (Fougeyrollas-Schwebel, 2000, p. 237). Studies have analysed the particular link that is constituted between persons in domestic work and have shed light on 'the permanent availability of women's time to the benefit of the family' (ibid.), while at the same time analysing how this work is linked to institutions of social reproduction other than the family. The question of whether domestic work should be analysed as production or as reproduction was central to feminist debates.

The discussion often advanced on the opposition between market/non-market production (often associated with male/female) shows that it is not the nature of production that makes the difference, but the problem of the *appropriation* of the work – paid or unpaid – of individuals. When commodities are produced outside the family, the work to produce them is paid. When commodities are produced in the framework of domestic-type relations and exchanged on the market, the work is generally not remunerated or not adequately remunerated.

Unpaid work thus includes work in the domestic framework or in a family business; tasks such as collecting water, fodder, wood for personal consumption, or the unpaid care of relatives and loved ones. For many years (1993, just before the Beijing Conference on Women), some elements of this unpaid work were included in the National Accounts Systems (for instance, work in family businesses and fetching water), but a good deal was not, such as the preparation of meals, shopping and caring for relatives. The work of feminist economists, who have for a long time criticized the fact that unpaid work in the economy is not taken into account, have contributed to making part of this work recognized and included in the National Accounts Systems. An OECD report from

2011 has indicated that 'the value of unpaid work is considerable – more or less one third of Gross Domestic Product (GDP) in OECD countries ... constituting an important contribution to the well-being of societies in OECD'.

Care consists of activities such as physical care and concern for persons known to the carer, family members, children and the elderly. It also includes caring for non-dependants, which is not always taken into account in studies. Care includes unpaid tasks such as preparing meals, cleaning, washing clothes, shopping and so on. In countries with limited infrastructure, care work may also include fetching water, collecting wood, all of which form part of social reproduction. Care can be paid or unpaid. *Unpaid care work* is primarily done in the framework of the family, but also in the wider framework of family relations, the community, in the neighbourhood and in associations. Care work is difficult to separate from domestic work. The line between 'non-material' care, requiring a higher level of intimacy (washing a person, talking to him/her, cuddling) and 'material' care (preparing a meal, washing his/her clothes) is blurred. Preparing a meal can have a 'non-material' dimension (preparing a delicious dish for a loved person). Domestic workers who are doing housework while at the same time undertaking care work (keeping an eye on a child) are not considered as being paid to do care work. The subjective dimensions, emotion or intimacy, that the concept of care has illuminated are useful but are not fully acknowledged and taken into consideration in the debates on social reproduction. Care, be it conceptualized as ethics of care, mainly perceived as a relational activity, or in the frame of research on social policies, is associated with reflections on migration, as a growing part of care work is commoditized and undertaken by migrant women from different classes or races.

The concept of *global care chains* (Hochschild, 2002) illustrates the transnational links which connect the different homes that supply and demand care, from the countryside to the big cities in poor countries, and the metropoles of richer countries, taking into consideration the intersection of gender, class and race in this process. However, most analysis of the global care chains is limited to the study of care in the domestic and private sphere. But the global market of domesticity and care is a growing phenomenon, not only in terms of individual demands but also in terms of institutional demands. It is necessary to recognize that paid care work has become a growing sector of the economy. The adoption of the International Convention on Decent Work for Domestic Workers by the ILO in 2011 is a sign of how the growth of this sector has increased its importance. This particularly feminized work is not well recognized socially, is badly protected and poorly paid. Many migrant women workers, especially those working for individuals, are triply invisible: they are non-existent as workers, employed in a private space and doing work that is poorly or completely unaccounted for in the national economy (Destremau and Lautier, 2002).

The concept of social reproduction is crucial for the understanding of care. Such a concept offers us a useful conceptual framework in which unpaid work by women is a central element. *Social reproduction* includes 'the demographic and economical renewal of the workforce and the reconstitution of relations and social institutions that organize individuals according to the characteristics of the considered system' (Meillassoux, 1991, p. 15). One can distinguish between biological reproduction, workforce reproduction and social reproduction, also defined as 'all activities and relations aiming at maintaining the individuals in good conditions, day to day and from one generation to the other' (Nakano, 2010; see also 1992). Social reproduction is not only fulfilled in the private space, an important part is realized elsewhere in other institutions – public, associative or private. Reproduction also includes production work, such as agriculture to feed close family or petty commodity production that is also used to cover daily needs.

However, the distinction between productive and reproductive work has long been debated by feminists. To my understanding, what should be under discussion is not the *nature* of the work realized, but the social relations within the framework in which they are realized, and how the productive and reproductive spheres – in which different types of social relations predominate – are articulated. The domestic economy is part of the sphere of the circulation of capitalism (Meillassoux, 1975), supplying the global economy with a workforce, goods and services. These are objects of *appropriation* by the global economy, through the articulation of the sphere where capitalist relations of production predominate with that where domestic-type social relations of production predominate. The globalization of reproductive work tends to move along these lines. However, when domestic workers are employed and carry out reproductive activities within the framework of capitalist social relations, their work is not considered the same as any other type of waged work. It is badly paid and is often supposed to include non-material dimensions. 'Helping' for long hours because it is presented as being part of the family is far from unusual (see OIT, 2010a). Even if salaried, the work tends to have a dimension of domestic social relations. The articulation of different types of social relations is still present at the transnational level, since other domestic economies, in the migrant worker's place of origin, carry out work in non-capitalist social relations, allowing the migrant worker to work abroad in capitalist social relations.

DISCUSSING CARE AND SOCIAL REPRODUCTION

With the crisis of social reproduction in the Global North (cuts in public services, insertion of women into the labour market, unquestioned sexual division of labour at home between men and women, an ageing population), there is a growing need for migrants to realize these activities. Social reproduction is globalizing and the concept of care has gained a lot of attention. However, the concept of care does not merge with the concept of social reproduction and has its limitations.

Care has been extremely useful as a concept to highlight the relational character of reproductive activities and the impossibility of separating material and non-material labour. But it has several limitations. First of all, different activities and institutions where the activities are fulfilled, such as those mentioned above (agricultural production, petty commodity production, and so on) and which are part of reproductive activities, are generally not included in the studies on care. Second, studies on care are mainly centred on care of dependants (children, the elderly, sick or less able persons, and so on). In other words, focused on only a certain category of people, those who will constitute or have constituted the potential workforce, they generally do not pay attention to the entire workforce. But people in good health and with the capacity to work, even if at some point they have been or will be dependent, are also cared for. Furthermore, care analysis does not always conceptualize the extension of the relations and activities in the neighbourhood (service close by, activities of the social economy sector) as being part of reproductive work. These are places where unequal gender and racial relations are reproduced and reinforced, but which can also provide opportunities to reorganize gender and race relations, opening spaces of resistance, allowing for a transformative approach towards people participating in these sorts of activities, seeing them as subjects of change and not as victims. These could be spaces to construct non-capitalistic ways of organizing relations and activities of social reproduction, other than those provided by states and markets (Barbagallo and Federici, 2012).

Another limitation of care studies is that they do not analyse why these activities have been displaced from an unpaid logic, in the domestic sphere, to a paid logic, partially or totally (Kofman, 2008). They do not pay attention to the articulations and interactions between these two logics. Furthermore, they do not explain the inequalities of gender, class, race and nation in the organization of care regimes. They do not give satisfactory explanations that comprehend the strong female and racial dimension of care work and ignore the fact that men, too, carry out this type of work.

The concept of global care chains reveals the transnational nature of care work that is commoditized and is becoming an important sector of the economy. The limitations of this concept, as already mentioned, are that it often restricts itself to the study of care in the domestic sphere. Furthermore, it fails to emphasize the point of the contribution of the different links of the chain to the production of wealth. Migrant domestic workers employed by privileged social classes to perform domestic work free up working time for the women employers, who in turn can be employed in more highly valued sectors that will be better taken into account in the calculation of national wealth, or contribute more to it. The time these women dedicated, unpaid, to the domestic sphere before they employed 'help' was not accounted for in wealth production. Also, it is widely recognized (Razavi, 2007) that caregivers in the Global North have become a central element of the social protection systems and in this way also contribute to the wealth of the global economy.

Finally, care studies do not include an analysis of the different type of social relations (domestic and capitalist) within the framework in which activities are carried out, nor how they are articulated. They do not reflect on how global capitalism is based on the gendered and racialized international division of labour, as decolonial feminist studies have done. Gender and race as expressions of power relations are key to understanding these mechanisms at global and local levels.

GLOBALIZATION OF SOCIAL REPRODUCTION AND THE CONTRIBUTION OF MIGRANT WOMEN WORKERS TO THE PRODUCTION OF WEALTH AND TO THE GLOBAL NORTH'S SYSTEM OF PROTECTION

To sum up, in the context of 'development' and of the changes in the international division of labour, the organization of social reproduction is globalizing. People, generally young women and men, migrate temporarily to other countries or regions as a result of the organization and of the crisis of social reproduction in the countries or regions of origin and in the Global North. The domestic economies are thus articulated with the global economy. Migrants and, in particular, women have become an essential link in how social reproduction systems function in the Global North, in both private and public spheres, as well as in the associative or private institutions of social reproduction. They are present in the functioning throughout the whole social protection system in the Global North.

First, importing domestic and care work allows the receiving states to save on the expense of making these systems work, as another way of organizing the system would be much more expensive. So the social protection systems in the Global North benefit greatly from these migrant workers. Some social policy scholars even ask themselves whether migrant workers can cover the huge and growing needs of care in the Global North. Others ask themselves how care, extracted from the Global South to cover needs elsewhere, in particular in the Global North, is supplied in the countries where the migrant caregivers come from (Razavi, 2007). In the southern countries, the population is ageing too, public systems of care are weakened, major health crises are taking place, and the need for caregivers is growing. The extraction or transfer of care has been described as a 'care drain', akin to a 'brain drain' (Hochschild, 2002). Care drain has consequences for the social protection systems in the countries of origin and, subsequently, weakens them. The social reproduction crisis is amplified by the women's departure.

Second, the remittances sent by migrant workers to their country of origin represent huge amounts (World Bank, 2010[2]) and contribute to the cost of social reproduction. Studies indicate that the money sent to their families by women migrant workers is principally used to cover expenses in social reproduction in their country of origin. A study in Latin America has shown, for instance, that 88 per cent of the remittances was used for reproductive expenses (food, housing, clothes, education, health), 10 per cent was used for community projects, and only 2 per cent was put towards productive projects (Marin, 2006). Other localized studies seem to show the same tendencies. Social reproduction work performed 'in another's home', paid, provides income that is spent on items either produced in the country of origin, or imported from more industrialized countries (gadgets for instance). This economy is situated in the *sphere of circulation* of capitalism, while part of it remains outside the *sphere of production*.

In such an overall articulation we can thus observe a social, economic, cultural and moral system of organizing social reproduction that includes care and involves goods and services linked to the capitalist economy (Anderson, 2011), while at the same time remaining partially outside it. In this new global economic order, characterized by the new international division of labour, the articulation between the domestic and the capitalist economies is taking new forms. But it still relies on the organization of all the activities and relations indispensable for social reproduction, beyond frontiers, in transnational networks. In this system, women, and particularly racialized migrant women, predominate, and spheres where domestic social relations are predominant have to be maintained. The organization of this system constitutes the base for the prosperity of the Global North.

Thus, women migrant workers should not be represented only as caregivers, since they are also directly inserted in productive systems (factories, informal urban economy, agriculture and so on), and some are integrated in highly skilled jobs (Nedelcu, 2004), thereby contributing to the prosperity of the global economy.

Finally, the central question for understanding the persistence of social and gender inequalities is that of the articulation of domestic-type social relations and capitalist social relations, in the Global North and the Global South, at the transnational level and in the context of the new international division of labour. Gender, as a powerful 'magic' tool, intersected with class and race, permits the maintenance of this unequal organic link.

NOTES

1. The data on domestic service workers in Tokman's paper are from household surveys in the CEPAL database and cover 18 countries during the 1990–2008 period.
2. According to the World Bank, the money sent as remittances by women and men migrant workers in 2008 represented an amount of US$444 billion (101 billion in 1995), of which US$338 billion went to developing countries. Amounts sent via informal channels could increase the official estimate by at least 50 per cent. This represents around double the amount spent on public development and is a major source of external financing. Women are considered to send a higher proportion of their income than men.

REFERENCES

Agustín, L.M. (2005), 'Cessons de parler de victimes, reconnaissons aux migrants leur capacité d'agir', in C. Verschuur and F. Reysoo (eds), *Genre, nouvelle division internationale du travail et migrations*, Cahiers Genre et Développement, Vol. 5, Genève, Paris: L'Harmattan, pp. 109–15.
Anderson, J. (2011), 'Care and social reproduction in Pamplona, a poor neighbourhood in Lima', paper presented at DESCO conference, Lima, 31 August.
Barbagallo, Camille and Silvia Federici (2012), 'Introduction', *The Commoner, Care Work and the Commons*, no. 15, Winter, 1–21.
Benería L. (ed.) (1982), *Women and Development: The Sexual Division of Labor in Rural Societies*, New York: Praeger.
Boserup, E. (1970), *Women's Role in Economic Development*, London: Earthscan.
Castro-Gómez, S. and R. Grosfoguel (2007), *El giro decolonial: Reflexiones para una diversidad epistémica más allá del capitalismo global*, Bogotá: Iesco-Pensar-Siglo del Hombre Editores.
Catarino, C., M. Morokvasic and M.-A. Hily (eds) (2005), 'Femmes, genre, migration et mobilités', *Revue Européenne des Migrations Internationales*, **21** (1), 7–27.
Delphy, C. (1970), 'L'ennemi principal', *Partisans, numéro spécial Libération des Femmes*, 54–5, July–October; reprinted in Delphy (1998), *L'Ennemi principal: économie politique du patriarcat*, vol. 1, Paris: Éditions Syllepse.

Destremau, B. and B. Lautier (eds) (2002), 'Femmes en domesticité: les domestiques du Sud, au Nord et au Sud', *Revue Tiers Monde*, Paris.
Federici, S. (1999), 'Reproduction and feminist struggle in the new international division of labor', in M. Dalla Costa and G.F. Dalla Costa (eds), *Women, Development and Labor of Reproduction: Struggles and Movements*, Eritrea: Africa World Press, pp. 47–83.
Fougeyrollas-Schwebel, D. (2000), 'Le travail domestique', in H. Hirata, F. Laborie, H. Le Doaré and D. Senotier (eds), *Dictionnaire critique du féminisme*, Paris: PUF, pp. 235–40.
Hochschild, A.R. (2002), 'Love and gold', in B. Ehrenreich and Hochschild (eds), *Global Woman: Nannies, Maids and Sex Workers in the New Economy*, London: Granta Books, pp. 15–30.
Kabeer, N. (1995), 'Necessary, sufficient or irrelevant? Women, wages and intra-household power relations in Urban Bangladesh', Institute of Development Studies Working Paper 25, University of Sussex, Brighton.
Kergoat, D. (2000), 'Division sexuelle du travail et rapports sociaux de sexe', in H. Hirata, F. Laborie, H. Le Doaré and D. Senotier (eds), *Dictionnaire critique du féminisme*, Paris: PUF, pp. 35–44.
Kofman, Eleonore (2008), 'Genre, migrations, reproduction sociale et *Welfare State*', in *Femmes, genre, migrations et mondialisation: Un état des problématiques*, Paris: Cahiers du CEDREF, Université Paris Diderot, pp. 101–25.
Marin, P. (2006), *Remesas de mujeres migrantes colombianas en Lausanne, un análisis sobre los sueños y realizaciones en proyectos economicos y sociales*, Genève: Mémoire de DEA, IUED.
Meillassoux, C. (1975), *Femmes, greniers et capitaux*, Paris: Maspéro.
Meillassoux, C. (1991), 'La leçon de Malthus: le contrôle démographique par la faim', in F. Gendreau, C. Meillassoux, B. Schlemmer and M. Verlet (eds), *Les Spectres de Malthus: Déséquilibres alimentaires, déséquilibres démographiques*, Paris: ORSTOM.
Mohanty, C. (2002), '"Under Western eyes revisited": feminist solidarity through anticapitalist struggles', *Signs, Journal of Women in Culture and Society*, **28** (2), 499–535.
Moreno Fontes-Chammartin, C. (2002), 'La féminisation des migrations internationales', *Travailleurs et travailleuses migrants: Education ouvrière*, 2002/4, 129, OIT, Genève.
Morokvasic, M. (1984), 'Birds of passage are also women', *International Migration Review*, **18** (68), 886–907.
Nakano, G. (1992), 'From servitude to service work: historical continuities in the racial division of paid reproductive labor', *Signs*, **18** (1), 1–43.
Nakano, G. (2010), Unpublished paper, presented at the Migration, Domestic Workers and the Intersection of Race, Gender and Class Oppression Conference, Roman Swiss Gender Doctoral School, Viège, 11 November.
Nedelcu, M. (2004), 'La composante féminine des migrations roumaines qualifiées à Toronto: visibilités, rôles et stratégies', in C. Verschuur and F. Reysoo (eds), *Femmes en mouvement: genre, migrations et nouvelle division internationale du travail*, Genève: Comission nationale suisse pour l'UNESCO-DDC-IUED, pp. 202–23.
Organisation for Economic Co-operation and Development (OECD) (2011), *Society at a Glance – OECD Social Indicators*, Paris.
Organisation internationale pour les migrations (OIM) (2010), *Etat de la migration dans le monde en 2010*, Genève.
Organisation internationale du travail (OIT) (2010a), *Travail décent pour les travailleurs domestiques*, Rapport 4 (1), Conférence internationale du Travail, 99th session.
Organisation internationale du travail (OIT) (2010b), *Travail domestique: Note d'information*, 4, Genève.
Oso-Casas, L. (2002), 'Domestiques, concierges et prostituées: migration et mobilité sociale des femmes immigrées, espagnoles à Paris, colombiennes et équatoriennes à Madrid', doctoral thesis, IEDES, Paris.
Oso-Casas, L. and J.-P. Garson (2005), *The Feminisation of International Migration: Migrant Women and the Labour Market, Diversity and Challenges*, OECD and European Commission Seminar, Brussels, 26–27 September, Room Documents 1, OECD.

Razavi, S. (2002), 'Globalisation, emploi et droits des femmes', in C. Verschuur (ed.) with F. Reysoo, *Genre, mondialisation et pauvreté*, Cahiers Genre et Développement, Vol. 3, Genève, Paris: L'Harmattan, pp. 35–44.
Razavi, S. (2007), *The Political and Social Economy of Care in a Development Context*, Geneva: UNRISD.
Rey, P.-P. (ed.) (1976), *Capitalisme négrier*, Paris: Maspéro.
Sanghera, J. (2004), 'Floating borderlands and shifting dreamscapes. The nexus between gender, migration and development', in F. Reysoo and C. Verschuur (eds), *Femmes en mouvement: genre, migrations et nouvelle division internationale du travail*, Genève: DDC/UNESCO/IUED, pp. 59–71.
Sassen, S. (2005), 'Restructuration économique mondiale et femmes migrantes: nouveaux espaces stratégiques de transformation des rapports et identités de genre', in C. Verschuur and F. Reysoo (eds), *Genre, nouvelle division internationale du travail et migrations*, Cahiers Genre et Développement, Vol. 5, Genève, Paris: L'Harmattan, pp. 103–9.
Schwenken, H. and L.M. Heimeshoff (eds) (2011), *Domestic Workers Count: Global Data on an Often-invisible Sector*, Kassel: Kassel University Press.
Scott, J. (1986), 'Gender: a useful category of historical analysis', *American Historical Review*, **91** (5), December, 1053–75.
Tokman, V. (2010), 'Domestic workers in Latin America: statistics for new policies', WIEGO Working Paper 17, Harvard Kennedy School, Cambridge, MA.
Verschuur, C. (2009), 'Quel genre? Résistances et mésententes autour du mot genre dans le développement', *Revue Tiers Monde* (200), October–December, Paris, 785–803.
Verschuur, C. (2012), 'Raccommodages de la pauvreté ou engagements féministes dans les quartiers populaires de San Cayetano et Gamboa en Amérique latine', *Autrepart* (61), 175–90.
Verschuur, C. and F. Reysoo (eds) (2005), *Genre, nouvelle division internationale du travail et migrations*, Cahiers Genre et Développement, Vol. 5, Genève, Paris: L'Harmattan.
Wallerstein, I. (1979), *The Capitalist World-Economy*, Cambridge: Cambridge University Press.
World Bank (2010), *Implications économiques des envois de fonds et de la migration*, Washington, DC.

PART III

GENDER, MIGRATION AND DEVELOPMENT THROUGH DIFFERENT CASE STUDIES

7. Gender, development and Asian migration in Spain: the Chinese case*
Amelia Sáiz López

INTRODUCTION

In recent decades, the scientific literature on migration in Europe has revealed two phenomena that have acquired relevance: the feminization of migration flows and the fundamentally economic nature of these flows. Feminized migration flows are usually explained by the development of the process of the globalization of social reproductive tasks (Anthias and Lazaridis, 2000). Many of these migration flows, so visible in the contributions of contemporary research, correspond to the profile of female heads of households who become transnational mothers when their natal family left behind in the community of origin is economically dependent on their money transfers. In fact, money transfers by women constitute a large proportion of the global circulation of remittances (Parreñas, 2002).

Numerous recent studies, in addition to that of Parreñas, have focused on the analysis of the women migrants' productive role (Ehrenreich and Hochschild, 2002; Parreñas, 2001), as well as on their contribution to development (INSTRAW, 2006, 2007). In these studies the use of the remittances is emphasized through a gender perspective, especially for Latin American countries. Most research on migration and development in Asia, on the other hand, does not incorporate the gender differences, as seen, for example, in recent works by the International Organization for Migration (IOM), or the study by Asis et al. (2010).

In the context of China, the literature that studies the relation between migration and development does not usually take into account the gender differences (Murphy, 2002, 2005, 2008; Ping and Zhan, 2005), and those that link Chinese internal migration with gender do not introduce the development perspective (Jacka, 2009; Luo, 2006). On the other hand, studies on Chinese migration in Europe that examine the effect of remittances on origin use a macro perspective, which is linked to the politics of migration (Pieke, 2004) or to the local economic impact (Beltrán Antolín, 2004). In fact, there are few studies that connect Chinese international migration, gender and development analysed through a transnational perspective – something that this chapter seeks to redress.

Chinese migration to Europe is characterized by its marked familial nature. Men, women and children first arrived in stages, forming a tapestry of families settled across much of Southern Europe. Most came from small, localized regions of China, a country the size of a continent. These zones are called *qiaoxiang* (侨乡), and comprise communities specialized in international migration whose primary source of income is the emigration of people of working age. Those located in the province of Guangdong have traditionally been the focus of research into Chinese migration (Douw et al., 1999; Hoe, 2004). Qingtian and Wenzhou in the south of Zhejiang province have also been the object of investigation by European experts (Pieke and Malle, 1999; Beltrán Antolín, 2003; Hoe, 2004), as well as certain regions of Fujian province (Pieke et al., 2004), such as the district of Changle, the origin of one of the most recent family migration chains in Spain.

The principal Chinese migratory model consists of the pursuit of economic success through the ownership and management of businesses and commercial activities. It has a distinctly familial nature and is best described as overlapping the productive and reproductive dimensions of the family business. In this context, gender relations are subject to both family and work spheres. The role of women in both is blurred by the ideology of the family system that gives structure to the principles of Chinese kinship. The Chinese example provides the opportunity to analyse aspects of migration, gender and development, in a context that contrasts strongly with the family and work patterns of the main migration communities in Spain, which are markedly different from the Chinese case.

This chapter analyses, from a transnational perspective, the economic practices of Chinese families from Qingtian, Wenzhou (Zhejiang province) and Changle (Fujian province) resident in Spain, and the relationship between their monetary transfers, management, use and social value. First, an overview of the Chinese presence in Spain is presented in order to understand the logic behind the migratory pattern and the importance of family in each of the phases of the development of the family business. The transfer of money to the country of origin by transnational households and family businesses has various consequences from the point of view of capital, social status and gender.

THE CHINESE IN SPAIN: AN OVERVIEW

Although China's presence in Spain dates back to the early twentieth century, the country did not become a preferred destination for Chinese migration until the 1980s, with a significant increase in immigration from the mid-1990s. During this time Spain became established as a host country for people from various continents. Asian migration to Spain currently accounts for 6.6 per cent of the total, a small percentage, when compared with immigrants from Latin America and Northwest Africa. The arrival in Spain of men, women, adolescents and young children of Chinese origin from China and Europe grew steadily over the final two decades of the twentieth century, culminating in something of a watershed at the end of the first decade of the twenty-first century. According to official data, on 31 December 2011 there were 170,164 Chinese residents in Spain, of whom 79,609 (46.8 per cent) were women and 39,083 (23.2 per cent) children younger than 15.

Migration Flows

The Chinese presence in Spain is heterogeneous, with regard to both the arrival period of the flow and its origin. The main, and oldest, originates from south Zhejiang province, more specifically from Qingtian district and the neighbouring municipality of Wenzhou.[1] People born in *qiaoxiang* areas have been raised and socialized with the idea that upward social mobility is possible in Europe, where it is feasible to obtain economic success by controlling the means of production, that is, as self-employed entrepreneurs (Li, 1999). The route to achieving this is outlined and circumscribed within the Chinese ethnic niche established in European countries through the family business (Reis, 2010).

The ethnic niche offers several advantages. First, it welcomes new arrivals by providing work and lodging in societies where they are generally unfamiliar with the languages and mode of operating. Second, it serves to train Chinese entrepreneurs. Due to the low level of professional qualifications of the first generation of migrants, experience gained working for others, whether or not they are members of the extended family, is the key means of acquiring the skills and knowledge necessary for the success of their future business. Through direct experience of wage labour in the ethnic niche they learn to operate businesses (managing procurement, suppliers, contacts and so on) and the specific legal requirements (law, regulations, taxes and so on) of the host society where they settle. Business independence is achieved when the accumulation of capital – obtained through their own work, alongside that provided by members of the extended family and the ethnic network – is sufficient to establish a family business. In short, it facilitates the recruitment of cheap labour, which is usually composed of relatives and fellow citizens from the country of origin, and also provides the training necessary for the future business careers of employees.

Third, the ethnic niche proposes a model of economic success based on the family business that offers continuity because the family and co-ethnic network share the financial risk of the potential failure of bankrupt business ventures (Beltrán Antolín and Sáiz López, 2009), and they incorporate their children as a human resource in the company. There is a clear generational division of labour: parents initiate the chain of migration and the task of accumulating the initial capital, while school-age offspring are responsible for learning the local languages as well as the values of the destination society at school (Sáiz López, 2006). Similarly, those children who complete academic studies usually supplement the family estate by creating new businesses in which they implement the theoretical knowledge they have acquired through higher education (Sáiz López, 2010).

This Chinese system of economic insertion into Europe and into Spain is based primarily on the family business. The combination of the economic model of upward social mobility with a rural family-based culture, a social system where behaviour, norms, ideals, attitudes and values centre on the welfare of, or are directed towards, those who are linked by kinship and marriage, explains why both men and women participate in the securing of success and, by extension, in migration. Both can equally be the protagonists and the driving force to the extent that they have the means, the conditions and the opportunity to initiate a migration project. Familism also explains the involvement of women throughout the family business cycle, from the accumulation of capital and the business consolidation phase, to business expansion (Sáiz López, 2007). In each of the phases of the business cycle the contribution of the wife is as necessary as that of the husband and, on occasion, even more so. Women are also promoted by the ethnic niche (Ceccagno, 2007). However, their work and value do not result, in the questioning of family gender relations where women have traditionally occupied a subordinate position to adult males and to their husband. On the contrary, it is interpreted as being in line with family values. Women themselves positively value having a business because it increases their economic value within the family. However, the logic of familism provides the ideal framework to ensure that the presence of women in the productive sphere does not alter the gender system, as it is the obligation of parents to provide their children with the best living conditions within their reach (Sáiz López, 2007).

Another Chinese migration flow into Europe proceeds from the provinces of Heilongjiang, Jilin, Liaoning (*dongbei*, northeast China) and Shandong, and dates back to the late 1990s. The economic reforms undertaken by the Chinese government since the early 1980s eventually led to a major restructuring of state enterprises, with many of them being transferred into private hands or held under semi-private regimes, and others being closed down. This process was accelerated in urban areas in 1997–98 resulting in approximately 20 million unemployed (Sáiz López, 2001). Migration to Europe was presented as an alternative to unemployment. Insertion into the labour market has followed a dual path, with people working either as employees for the Chinese natives of Zhejiang province already settled in Europe, or for European employers. In the absence of an ethnic niche of their own, natives of *dongbei* have a different migration pattern from that discussed above. The lack of a historical settlement limits the likelihood of a community of extended families with collective economic development projects. For the majority of people from these provinces, of urban origin and with a work history of employment in state factories, the pattern of migration is individual or involves only the nuclear family, with its single child.

The lack of a family or co-ethnic network in the country of destination is not an impediment to employment. Labour mobility is made possible by access to job vacancies. In the absence of a network of their own, bulletin boards in Chinese grocery shops and other services located in co-ethnic residential areas, together with the Chinese-language newspapers published in Europe, are the usual means of hearing about the various job offers. Women from the Northeast tend to work in garment manufacturing, catering, shops, and domestic service for southeastern Chinese families, and use the same routes to obtain work as their male compatriots. In summary, in the Chinese ethnic niche, rather than employment discrimination based on gender, there is, in some occupations, a division of labour along lines of gender.

Natives of China's big cities, who constitute an indeterminate migratory collective, share with the previous group a migratory pattern that is personal or involves only the nuclear family. Married, single and divorced people decide to leave their country to pursue a professional activity or to bring about a change in their personal life. Generally, they cannot count on prior family or co-ethnic networks to facilitate their exit or their insertion into their destination country, but they have a level of professional training that gives them access to jobs and skilled occupations. Included in this group are highly skilled workers, a flow that is gradually increasing in volume in Spain, but continues to be very much a minority of all Chinese residents. These new migratory groups are in addition to those mentioned above. They are of an individual or nuclear family nature, but are not connected to the family and community codes, including economic practices, followed by their fellow citizens from Wenzhou, Qingtian and Changle.

FAMILIES IN THE TRANSNATIONAL MIGRATORY CONTEXT[2]

According to a previous analysis of the different migration flows from China into Spain, not all Chinese residents form part of productive domestic groups or transnational families. As they do not belong to the previous categories, the impact of their economic practices in their country of origin is strongly influenced by the situation in the destination country. When migration occurs as a personal project from places with no tradition of collective migration, links to the country of origin are limited to a family relationship of a private nature, so there is no direct relationship with local development since this does not form part of the migration agenda.

Qingtian, Wenzhou and Changle share a migration pattern based on achieving upward social mobility through economic activities of an entrepreneurial nature which draw on both sexes. The Chinese business community in Spain is mainly composed of family businesses. Chinese familism is present in the migration of the *qiaoxiang*, which centres on the nuclear and extended family with both entities being involved in different phases of the family business cycle. The importance of the family in the establishment and development of businesses permits analysis of both as single entities, a characteristic element of the business network of the Chinese community settled in Spanish and European territories. The business involves the whole family and requires all of its members to maximize the human resources at its disposal, with men and women contributing to the household economy equally.

These migration patterns follow transnational practices in the spheres of family, work and economy. However, not all families form the same type of domestic–economic unit, differing in their transnational economic activity and in their local impact. Chinese families present in Spain can, therefore, be classified into two types: transnational households and transnational family businesses.

Transnational Chinese Households

Transnational households are those where the nuclear family is residentially divided: the parents in their country of destination (Spain), the sons and daughters in the parental country of origin (China). Chinese families comprise two types of transnational household: those where the country of origin of parents and children is the same, namely China, and those where parents and children do not share a country of birth, that is, the sons and daughters were born in Spain.

Transnational households, whose parents and children share a country of birth can be temporary or permanent. If temporary, this means that there will be family reunification in Spain. Family migration begins with the father, mother or both, departing for a Western European country, leaving their children in the care of the extended family. In the accumulation of capital phase – wage labour for Chinese employers, usually within the Chinese ethnic niche where employers and employees share the same country of origin – the parents work long hours and staying in shared lodgings with either relatives or fellow citizens, to reduce the reproductive costs of labour. Family reunification is postponed until the opening of the family business, whether the sons and daughters are of working age or not. Thus, (nuclear) family reunification is a staggered practice, subject to the needs of the family business, to the stage it is at and to the ethnic social resources available. Therefore the variety in migration strategies has a significant bearing on the future of the family business: who should migrate first, where they should go, what kind of work they should look for and where, and the different migration flows and patterns of reuniting, for example, children who re-group pre-adolescence, those who reunite with their parents and those who re-group post-adolescence.

During this period of physical family separation, pre-reunification, the person working in the destination country financially maintains the rest of the family in the country of origin. This is the case for Mr Wang, a native of Changle, who arrived in Spain six years ago, leaving his wife and children in their village. For the first 18 months he worked in a restaurant, earning a monthly salary of €1,000, and sent €700 a month to China. This money was administered by his wife in China and covered the daily living expenses (food, clothing, study, and so on) of his wife and two children. At that time his wife was not working in China, so the family depended on the money that Mr Wang sent each month. Since the family's arrival in Spain, he has stopped sending money regularly and now only occasionally sends money to his parents in Changle.

But there are families who, despite owning businesses, choose not to reunite with their children. These remain in the care of the extended family, generally, but not always, in the paternal family home or at private boarding schools. In these permanent transnational households remittances are regular and, for the most part, are intended to cover the children's living expenses and education.

Currently, the number of children born in Spain to Chinese mothers is increasing.[3] This, however, is not an impediment to maintaining the structure of the transnational nuclear family. Once they are registered and the opportunity to travel occurs, these babies 'migrate' to the parental country of origin, where they remain until they reach school age, at which point they return to their country of birth to enrol in school. However, circumstances do not always permit this and reunification might take longer. This occurs when the birth of a child coincides with the implementation phase of the family business, a time during which none of the adult members of the nuclear family can be released from productive work to perform the reproductive work. The transnationalization of reproductive labour (re)appears to be the most profitable option for the family business, as much from the emotional as the economic standpoint:

> Since I have not had a very good time here, I mean, I haven't had much success in my work, I devote all my time to my work. I have little time to care for my son or my family. We have to work hard to save a little money, so I have no time to look after him. I think that my son lacks nothing in the material sense, and it is much better for him to stay in China. With respect to his relationship with his parents, it's a shame; however, he has a relationship with his grandparents. If he were here, we would live together. But I do not have the time or experience to attend to his behaviour and education. (Wife of the Zhou family, arrived in 2004)

The relatives in charge of raising children in China receive remittances from their sons and daughters – the infants' parents – intended for reproductive work. The money is administered by grandparents, according to the organizational criteria of the intra-familial relationships of the Chinese extended family, that is, according to the criteria of generation, gender and age.

In Chinese migration to Europe the transnationalization of reproductive labour is present at all stages, adapting to the production needs of the nuclear family at each stage by the (re)direction of the infant migration: from origin to destination country to be reunited with their parents, and from destination to origin country to be raised by their grandparents. This model of transnational motherhood where the country of destination is not the location of family reunification, but rather that of the transnationalization of the nuclear family, is unique among the various migrant groups in Spain.

Transnational Family Businesses

Transnational family businesses operate in Spain and maintain productive and/or financial links with the country of origin. However, this analysis will not address transnational productive links. The subject of this research is the investment in the origin country and the role of families in this process.

Chinese settlement in Spain has occurred in stages, which is why there are currently families and businesses at different stages of the family–business cycle. For example, existing simultaneously in the same place are established family businesses with adult children that have been in operation for more than five years, businesses importing and exporting

Chinese products owned by families with adolescent children, small family grocery shops with infant children in the country of origin, and so on. The combination of the family–business cycle and the length of settlement in the country of origin provide a complicated map of businesses of Chinese origin since, according to this model, it is possible to encounter both transnational businesses and households.

The Cheng family, natives of Qingtian, comprises a married couple and two children, a boy and a girl, aged seven and 10, respectively. The children live with their paternal grandparents in their country of origin. The couple have had a general store in the metropolitan area of Barcelona for four years. Previously, during the capital accumulation phase, the husband – the first member of the family to arrive in Spain – worked for Chinese and Catalan employers for four years. His wife arrived two years later, as until then she had been in Qingtian raising the children. The two children have never visited their parents, but their parents have travelled individually in order to see them. The children are studying in a private school that is considered to be the best in the area. The parents are very proud of their children's performance at school and think that the best they can do for them is to provide them with a good education in China, which they value more highly than a Spanish education. They have not yet planned their future and do not know whether the children will come to Spain or they themselves will return to China permanently. At the moment their business in Spain is doing well and allows them to invest in human capital and in the industrial sector in China, where their investments are managed by a paternal uncle of the husband who lives in China.

This is not the only case found during fieldwork in which there is a financial investment in China with income obtained from operating the family business in Spain. The Zhou family comes from the province of Fujian and information about possible investments in China and their management is handled by the husband's sister. The husband arrived first (in 1999) and the wife in 2004. Their four-year-old son was born in Barcelona and is currently being looked after by his grandparents in their country of origin. The husband worked for several years for his uncle in a garment workshop in the metropolitan area of the city. The wife also worked for other Chinese employers until, in 2008, they decided to open their own business, a typical Spanish bar. Since 2004 they have invested in China and for this reason a part of the start-up capital came from money that they had earned in China:

> We have investments there. In China, for example, when this business opened, we invested a little money and asked for some shares and if they earn money, we divide the profits among us . . . it is an iron and steel factory. Used in the construction of housing . . . (Husband of the Zhou family, who arrived in 1999)

His sister manages their investments in China:

> My sister-in-law's family has earned a lot because they have invested in property and in the iron and steel industry. Years ago these two sectors made a lot of profit. . . . As China is a developing country it needs a lot of iron and steel to build flats, as well as other buildings. So a few years ago they needed a lot of iron and steel. (Wife of the Zhou family, who arrived in 2004)

The Cheng and Zhou families are examples of new transnational monetary routes. This type of circulation maintains an economic link with the past but changes its direction and purpose. If the *qiaoxiang* have developed locally thanks to the remittances and investments of their fellow citizens abroad, the fruit of these (re)investments is the financing of businesses in the destination country. In addition, China's economic potential makes it a focus for investment by migrants, not only in terms of local development but also as the capitalization and search for direct monetary benefits for the business families.

THE VERSATILITY OF REMITTANCES

At a family and local level, remittances are the most obvious manifestation of the benefits produced by international migration (Douw et al., 1999). There is no doubt that the migration from southern Zhejiang Province, the oldest flow of Chinese residents to Spain, has contributed to local development. A walk around Qingtian and its surroundings shows the transformation experienced by this region over the past 20 years – new homes, construction and repair of roads, primary and secondary schools, hotels, shops and the consequent increase in housing prices – which have contributed to a substantial improvement in the quality of life for its inhabitants. In Changle, Fujian Province, the impact of migration on local development is less in relation to the age of the flow. Furthermore, as illustrated by the case of the Zhou family, the transnational economic relations of Chinese family businesses have become more complex. On the other hand, remittances and their use in the country of origin respond to criteria that go beyond the logic of rational use of economic capital.

Strengthening Transnational Family Ties

Family relationships are the first circle of what Fei Xiaotong (1947 [1992]) called the 'differential mode of association' in Chinese rural social structure. Each individual is 'surrounded' by a series of concentric circles that are interrelated. The first circle is that of kinship, followed by the circle of community and so on. The set of circles, of associations, forms the person's social network, their social capital or *guanxi*, whose practice requires 'the exchange of gifts, favours, and banquets; the cultivation of personal relationships and networks of mutual dependence; and the manufacturing of obligation and indebtedness' (Yang, 1994, p. 6).

Family relationships are not exempt from the logic of social practices. Given the vital importance of family networks in the migration project of the family business, it is essential to keep the bonds of kinship alive. Unlike the ideal Chinese family model, which favours the patriarchal line, transnational business families feed both kinship allegiances. This is demonstrated by remittances.

The money transfers that are intended for the upbringing and education of children in the country of origin are more regular and of a greater amount before reunification, when children are young and remain in the care of their grandparents and/or other relatives, that is, when the family business in the country of destination transnationalizes the reproductive labour. The money is usually administered by the women in charge of raising the children, for example, the mother or grandmother. After the nuclear family's reunification, this remittance becomes a token, its purpose being to strengthen kinship networks.

Wherever possible migrants' parents are sent money for their personal use. This gesture is a demonstration of filial piety towards their parents, one of the family values that persist in Chinese society, despite the transformations and cultural renewal that have taken place in China in the late twentieth century. Reference to the need to address the care of parents in Chinese culture (养 *yang* is the term that refers to this obligation of filial piety) is a constant, especially for the women interviewed:

> To make money in Spain. My family needs money to care for my parents. In China, we need to look after parents from both sides. My parents are old and don't earn money. We have to send them money to live on. We also send money to my husband's parents, we have to look after them. (Wife of the Wang family, arrived in 2009)

However, not all of the parents in China are in the same financial situation. Some have a pension and can maintain a standard of living independent of monetary remittances from their sons and daughters. In other cases, the parents divide their time between their children's various residences in Europe. This is a new pattern, a variant of and development in temporary transnational residence. In this case it is the parents of Chinese migrants who stayed in the country of origin who now make up a small flow of temporary mobility in Europe. The socioeconomic status of parents, the generation that did not migrate originally, is heterogeneous, as are the economic responses of their children, except with regard to healthcare:

> Yes, yes, some people send money. They send it to the family to use the money. But here there are things that are much better. For instance, when you are unwell and have to go to the doctor you do not need to pay. It is different for us in China. If you have any problem in China and go to the doctor, you always have to pay. So in China you need the money for this, to go to the doctor. (Husband of the Zhang family, arrived in 2001)

Moreover, parents are at the centre of the kinship networks of extended transnational families, they have greater moral authority and can therefore be more influential in family mediation on the occasion of conflicts of interest that may arise between the various family branches. They also channel the financial assistance required by members of the extended family. It is important not to confuse the 'filial remittances' sent to and intended for parents, from those sent – due to previous formal requests – to meet the economic needs of the kinship network. Both cases are current examples of the traditional criteria for the organization of family structure – generation and age, as well as gender – of the *qiaoxiang*.

Another ritual money transfer is made during the Chinese New Year celebration. The wife of the Li family (native of Qingtian, resident in Spain for 14 years, owner of a restaurant and a clothing store) states that they also send 'filial remittances' during this celebration. The wife of the Wang family adds the custom of giving a 'red envelope' containing money to the children of the family, and the wife of the Yang family (native of the province of Zhejiang, resident in Spain for 14 years and the owner of a bar) draws a link between feelings and finances in the most family-centred celebration in the whole Chinese calendar:

> Sure. The Chinese New Year, positive. Because Chinese New Year is a hongbao tradition [红包 red envelope]. Sure. This Spring Festival is for giving red envelopes to children, to the family, so they can have a good year.
>
> Q: So people who work here send money to China?
> A: Yes, you have to do something to demonstrate your feelings for the celebration. (Wife of the Yang family, arrived in 1998)

In summary, the remittances classified as familial are intended to cultivate, maintain and strengthen kinship networks. Transfers for the upbringing and education of children affect the strength of transnational family ties, with transnational maternity (paternity) being fostered by remittances intended for raising children. 'Filial remittances' are sent by male offspring or the firstborn child, whether male or female, due to the prevalence of patrilineal descent. This emphasizes women's sense of belonging to their natal families, countering the ideological effect of patrilineality. The money sent to meet family needs and the red envelopes nurture transnational family ties. Given the importance of the family network within the Chinese settlement in Spain, familial remittances are an indirect investment in social capital that also has repercussions in the country of destination for the nuclear family that transferred the money.

Investment and Social Capital

Economic transactions between transnational Chinese families have diversified and become more complex. To existing traditional remittances intended to support the family, increase the human capital of the next generation[4] and create a legacy of property, should be added financial capital, dedicated exclusively to the financial profitability of the families' work effort.

Investing in China while living and working in Spain is made possible by the financial management carried out by relatives in the country of origin. As we have seen, parents, paternal uncles and sisters raise capital from profits for their children, nephews and brothers in China while living and working in the destination country. They invest in building new housing for the family and in businesses in the town of origin, or in any of the thriving sectors in China such as the iron and steel industry, mining, construction or property. Financial management impacts on the whole family, as well as on local and national development:

> According to the newspaper, they say that a certain percentage of Changle's economy [Fujian] depends on money transfers from immigrants. In my village, Changle, some immigrants have made money and sent it to their relatives in China. These transfers have a great influence on the economic development of Changle. Specifically, the villagers can buy a flat in the city, and can also take their children to study in the city, they do not study in the village . . . in recent years the Chinese have also invested in property, iron and steel, in factories. (Wife of the Zhou family, arrived in 2004)

It also has negative repercussions. The least-valued consequences of the local impact of this money stem from the increased cost of living, including the investment in symbolic capital required by return journeys to the migrants' country of origin:

> Meat is very expensive in restaurants. It's true, eating in restaurants in Lishui [Zhejiang] is very expensive. I was surprised by the high prices. Once I ate with five or six people in a restaurant and we spent a total of 500 or 600 euros, more or less 5,000 or 6,000 RMB. (Wife of the Li family, arrived in 1998)

Another investment in social capital is where affordable loans are made available to members of the extended family to raise the capital needed to establish the business of the nuclear family unit in a European country. This economic practice draws an economic circuit that goes beyond the linearity of the country of origin/destination vector, diversifying the economic transnationalization of family businesses with a direct effect on the local development of the cities in which their businesses are located. Thus, economic circularity refers not only to the path followed by the money but also to its intended use, including investment and loans.

Frank Pieke (2004) states that the local authorities in Fujian Province have encouraged emigration as a political measure to foster development in the area, in line with the government policy launched in the 1980s of modernization, economic growth and development of the country. However, the *qiaoxiang* predate this era and their existence is more a response to the local cultural and economic situation than to the implementation of state policies, although they may have coincided at a specific point in time. The remittances that are invested in the community of origin are those that achieve greater direct local impact and demonstrate the success of the migration project. Thus the sum invested reverts to the extended family in social capital and is administered by those who remain in the country of origin, who also benefit from it as symbolic capital due to increased social prestige.

Donations

In addition to the capital intended for reproduction and in local and national investment, economic transfers are intended as donations of capital. These are not destined for economic capitalization although they are considered to be assets in the categories of social and symbolic capital.

Donations of money to the community of origin are administered by the extended family in the same way as some family remittances and investments. Such donations are intended to improve the local collective infrastructure that represents the present and future of the location, generating for all those – present and absent – a collective sense of identity. Over the decades, schools, temples, roads, and so on, have all been financed by migrant *qingtianeses*. In general, donations are intended for local development in the realms of education, health and religion. They constitute a special form of what Beltrán Antolín (2004) calls 'generalized redistribution'. In the Chinese context economic success is not synonymous with social success from the point of view of prestige. Thus, people who do not demonstrate solidarity with the family setting are criticized and rejected socially. According to this logic, donations administered by the family in the country of origin also have a bearing on the social capital of the family business at both poles of the transnational space, as this economic behaviour of sharing a part of the success with the community, of social reciprocity according to Chinese cultural values, reveals people's virtue and morality.

Other donations are made to alleviate the human tragedy resulting from natural disasters, such as the Sichuan earthquake of 2008 or the annual floods suffered during the Chinese monsoon season. This transfer features as an investment in social prestige, mentioned previously, when raised by Chinese associations operating in the countries of origin and destination.

Other donations are altruistic, individual and anonymous, when made via the internet, or to associations unrelated to the Chinese community in both the origin and destination countries. By not directly benefiting the town of origin, their potential for investment in symbolic capital is annulled, because it remains beyond the reach and control of the family and of the logic of social relations characteristic of the rural culture of the *qiaoxiang*.

GENDER IN DEVELOPMENT

The narrative of Chinese migration combines the collective epic with the individual. Annals,[5] murals, commemorative plaques, newspaper articles and so on are some of the records of the geographical and economic success of people who have contributed to local development. In those areas where migration is a way of life, both men and women feed images of success into the collective imagination, the reasons for the struggle and what can be achieved (Beltrán Antolín, 2003). Women are not excluded from the historical construction of migration or from local development.

Chinese historians (Du and Cai, 2005) have established that, throughout history, the Chinese gender system has swung between two concepts: the canon and convenience. The first concept (*jing*, 经) refers to the fundamental principles of gender relations such as the *gendered* division of labour between public and private arenas. That is, between what happens beyond the domestic sphere (*wai*, 外 public) and inside it (*nei*, private 内),[6] marriage and family systems based on patrilineality, and so on. According to Du and Cai, these principles remain more or less the same over time, with no change in customs. However, the gender system has shown itself to be flexible, with the existence of the concept of convenience – *quanyi* 权宜 – of being responsible for finding solutions at a specific time and place in accordance with the needs of the person (*ren* 人) and not those of the gender system. One example proposed by Du and Cai refers to those Chinese families in which women have room for action, where the impact of gender on the family structure, combined with age, helps them gain status in the family. According to their argument, not only does the convenience of the system relieve the oppression of women under a restrictive canon, but it also reflects the complexity of gender relations in China. In other words, as opposed to the ideal model of gender, reality imposes another logic in which women develop an important role not only in the family but also in the public domain.

Nevertheless, the canon moulds social order and is enforced at a discursive level. In a study of rural women, Ellen Judd (1990) observed that in many aspects women felt more competent than men. In the words of the famous slogan of the Maoist era, 'women hold up half of Heaven', meaning that they can do the same things as men and many more – such as salting and preserving vegetables, producing charcuterie, and so on – domestic tasks that men were themselves unable to perform. However, in public, in the presence of other men or of people outside the family group, the canon is assumed, affirming to anyone who might hear them that men are of greater value. In short, rural women are aware of their worth and contribution to the family and their discretion in this regard is a further indication of their expertise. This model, where the canon enforces the gender relations narrative of social practice, frames the discourse of Chinese businesswomen living in Spain.

During the Chinese New Year red envelopes arrive from Europe, enabling migrant members to participate in the family unit's celebration, the main objective of this key event in the Chinese calendar. The delivery of red envelopes allows people to be in emotional contact with their country of origin and makes sense of the distance and separation caused by migration:

> At New Year or on my parents' birthdays. I always send red envelopes at New Year. We Chinese have a tradition of caring for the elderly. Here in Spain the young do not need to care for the old. (Wife of the Wang family, arrived in 2009)

> The thing is, my father-in-law has his own business. What he earns is enough for the expenses of the family in China, even more than is needed. So, if my in-laws do not ask us, we only give them money during celebrations, for example, Chinese New Year. (Wife of the Zhou family, arrived in 2004)

The envelopes containing money also strengthen intra-familial gender ties, as shown by the case of the previous informant. Following Chinese family logic, the generational hierarchy is in charge of the allocation and circulation of money, as manifested here by means of an example that demonstrates respect and the strengthening of family ties:

I only transfer money to my parents. But, for example, I told my mother that there is a part (200 RMB, for example) of the transfer that is for my sister. When my mother received the transfer at Chinese New Year, she put the money in the red envelope for my sister so she could buy what she wanted or so that my mother could buy a dress for her for the celebration. If I want to give someone money, I always tell my mother, so that she can do it. (Wife of the Zhang family, arrived in 2008)

The envelopes also maintain extended family relationships, still important in the realms of Chinese social structure and of the transnational family business:

For example, if they get married I will send money to offer my congratulations. Because when I got married my relative also gave me a red envelope. So I need to give them a red envelope as well. Sometimes my mother gives some red envelopes to my relatives as if they were from me and I return the favour. (Wife of the Zhang family, arrived in 2008)

The monetary circulation to the country of origin entitles women separated from their natal family to form part of it, without breaking the ties prescribed by the dominant ideology. Women assume economic behaviour traditionally associated with the obligation of sons due to the patrilineal descent of rural Chinese families, a pattern that still prevails in family organization but does not eliminate other possibilities. The disposable income of women enables them to provide funds for their family in China, strengthening their position in the family and community structure, given the value awarded to money in different spheres.

CONCLUSIONS

China's presence in Spain has a long history. The immigration processes that have taken place over time overlap with the arrival of new population flows, which complete the phases of social integration developed by the earliest Chinese residents, particularly those from Qingtian and Wenzhou. These towns currently benefit from the economic impact of remittances received from their fellow citizens in Europe, improving the health of China's economy, allowing them to profit from investments in the country of origin and also to use these profits to expand their businesses in the destination country. The original remittances intended for subsistence and local development become transnational investment of family capitalization on both sides of the line that unites Spain and China. In other words, the economic development in the country of origin that results from migration has evolved and become a process of transnational monetary circulation.

The case study in this chapter is an analysis of Chinese remittances predominantly from small family businesses. Through them, a special relationship between migration, gender and development is articulated, one that complements and is more complex than the usual perspective applied to the study of remittances that views them as an individual phenomenon associated with situations of subsistence and dependence. The Chinese example of the small family business places remittances on another level: the phenomenon is familial, not individual, and livelihood and dependence have given way to circulation and investment on a global scale seeking higher returns on capital.

As a result of the family business sector – social capital – built up over the years, business families are able to benefit from this structure in the different geographical locations in which they operate. China's economic potential has made it a focus of investment by migrants, no longer just for local development in a strict and limited sense, but also for the capitalization of family businesses and search for direct financial benefits.

From a perspective of gender, decisions about sending money and what it is to be used for are usually made by both spouses, men and women. At the level of discourse women adopt the traditional role that allocates the position of head of family to the man, carrying with it the associated decision making role with regard to monetary issues. However, in practice the rules are less strict, especially when both contribute to the development of the family business and the wife also comes from an extended migrant family.

Finally, remittances impact directly, forming part of a family's social capital and prestige, their significance and use goes beyond the strictly economic, as they have social consequences. Remittances forge and strengthen family ties, provide social prestige and possess a symbolic component beyond economic subsistence.

NOTES

* This chapter was written within the framework of the R&D research project 'El impacto de la inmigración en el desarrollo: Género y transnacionalismo' (SEJ2007-63179/SOCI) of ESOMI at the Universidad de A Coruña; and the R&D MCI research project 'El impacto de Asia Oriental en el contexto español: Producción cultural, política(s) y sociedad' (FFI2011-29090) of the InterAsia research group at the Universidad Autónoma de Barcelona.
1. Wenzhou has a total area of 11,784 square kilometres. Migratory behaviour differs

across the region, with some places, such as the districts of Ouhai, Wencheng and Rui'an being more *qiaoxiang* than others, that is, emigration is not uniform across all zones (Beltrán Antolín, 2003).
2. Research into Chinese migration in Spain and Catalonia dates from early 2000 (see Beltrán Antolín, 2003, 2004; Sáiz López, 2006, 2007, 2010; Beltrán Antolín and Sáiz López, 2009). The quotations in this chapter correspond to specific 'Migration, Gender and Development' fieldwork carried out in Catalonia in 2010. The combination of the two variables that structure the present study – the length of stay in the destination country and transnational ties – indicate family profile. With respect to length of stay, the cases analysed correspond to three points in the recent history of migration to Spain, the 1990s and the first decade of the twenty-first century. A total of 16 interviews (10 women and six men) were conducted in Catalonia. Among those interviewed were four married couples, with both spouses being interviewed. The overrepresentation of women does not relate to a statistical reality but rather to the accessibility of subjects for interview. Given the familial nature of this migration it is important to bear in mind that economic practices alter according to family decisions and requirements. Interviews were conducted by Irene Masdeu Torruella, PhD student at the Universidad Autónoma de Barcelona. Names have been changed to protect identity.
3. According to the *Avance de la Explotación Estadística del Padrón* (Census) of 1 January 2012 of the National Institute of Statistics, 27,695 (15.7 per cent of nationalized Chinese) people were born in Spain, 14,574 male and 13,121 female.
4. 'I have no idea about education in Spain. In China, for example, I have the ability to send my child to good schools if I want. In this respect, there is no problem' (Wife of the Zhou family, arrived in 2004).
5. For example, that edited by Chen Murong, *Qingtian xianzhi* 青田县志 (Annals of Qingtian District), published by Zhejiang People's Publishing House in 1990, or the most recent collective work *Qingtian huaqiao shi* 青田华桥史 (The History of the Migrants of Qingtian) produced by the same publisher in 2011.
6. The phrase that sums up this division of gender is *Nanren zhu wai, nüren zhu nei* 男人主外，女人主内, meaning that men belong to the public, outdoor realm, and women to the inside, domestic realm.

REFERENCES

Anthias, F. and G. Lazaridis (eds) (2000), *Gender and Migration in Southern Europe: Women on the Move*, Oxford: Berg.
Asis, M.B.A., N. Piper and P. Raghuram (2010), 'Migration and development in Asia: knowledge frameworks', *International Migration*, **48** (3), 76–106.
Beltrán Antolín, Joaquín (2003), *Los ocho inmortales cruzan el mar: Chinos en Extremo Occidente*, Barcelona: Edicions Bellaterra.
Beltrán Antolín, Joaquín (2004), 'Remesas y redes familiares desde China a España', in A. Escrivá and N. Rivas (eds), *Migración y desarrollo*, Córdoba: Consejo Superior de Investigaciones Científicas, pp. 285–312.
Beltrán Antolín, Joaquín and Amelia Sáiz López (eds) (2009), *Empresariado asiático en España*, Barcelona: Fundación CIDOB.
Ceccagno, Antonella (2007), 'Compressing personal time: ethnicity and gender within a Chinese niche in Italy', *Journal of Ethnic and Migration Studies*, **33** (4), 635–54.
Douw, Leo, Cen Huang and Michael Godley (eds) (1999), *Qiaoxiang Ties: Interdisciplinary Approaches to 'Cultural Capitalism' in South China*, London: Kegan Paul International.
Du Fangqin and Cai Yiping (2005), 'A history of the patriarchal system and gender relations', in Du Fangqin and Wang Zheng (eds), *Women's Studies in China: Mapping the Social, Economic and Policy Changes in Chinese Women's Lives*, Seoul: Ewha Woman's University Press, pp. 33–52.

Ehrenreich, B. and A.R. Hochschild (eds) (2002), *Global Woman: Nannies, Maids and Sex Workers in the New Economy*, New York: Henry Holt & Company.
Fei Xiaotong (1947 [1992]), '*Chaxu geju*: the differential mode of association', in Fei Xiaotong, *From the Soil: The Foundations of Chinese Society*, Berkeley, CA: University of California Press, pp. 66–70.
Hoe Yow Cheun (2004), 'Detraditionalised and renewed Qiaoxiang areas: case studies of Panyu and Wenzhou in the reform period since 1978', paper presented at the 5th Conference of the International Society of the Study of Chinese Overseas, Elsinore, Denmark, 10–14 May.
INSTRAW (2006), *Potencial de las remesas para el desarrollo desde una perspectiva de género: Metodología de investigación cualitativa*, México: Secretaria de Relaciones Exteriores.
INSTRAW (2007), 'Feminization of migration: gender, remittances and development', Working Paper, 1, UN–INSTRAW.
Jacka, Tamara (2009), 'The impact of gender on urban-to-rural migration in China', in *Gender and Labour Migration in Asia*, Geneva: International Organization for Migration, pp. 263–91.
Judd, Ellen R. (1990), '"Men are more able". Rural Chinese women's conceptions of gender and agency', *Pacific Affairs*, **63** (1), 40–61.
Li Minghuan (1999), '"To get rich quickly in Europe!" Reflections on migration motivation in Europe', in F. Pieke and H. Malle (eds), *Internal and International Migration: Chinese Perspectives*, Richmond, UK: Curzon, pp. 181–98.
Luo Guifen (2006), 'China's rural–urban migration: structure and gender attributes of the floating rural labor force', *Finnish Yearbook of Population Research*, **42**, 65–92.
Murphy, Rachel (2002), *How Migrant Labor is Changing Rural China*, Cambridge: Cambridge University Press.
Murphy, Rachel (2005), 'Helping migration to improve livelihoods in China', in F. Lacko (ed.), *Migration, Development and Poverty Reduction in Asia*, Geneva: International Organization for Migration, pp. 223–42.
Murphy, Rachel (ed.) (2008), *Labour Migration and Social Development in China*, London: Routledge.
Parreñas, Rhacel (2001), *Servants of Globalization: Women, Migration and Domestic Service*, Stanford, CA: Stanford University Press.
Parreñas, Rhacel (2002), 'The care crisis in the Philippines: children and transnational families in the new global economy', in B. Ehrenreich and A.R. Hochschild (eds), *Global Woman: Nannies, Maids and Sex Workers in the New Economy*, New York: Henry Holt & Company, pp. 39–54.
Pieke, Frank and Hein Malle (eds) (1999), *Internal and International Migration: Chinese Perspectives*, Richmond, UK: Curzon.
Pieke, Frank (2004), *Transnational Chinese: Fujianese Migrants in Europe*, Stanford: Stanford, CA University.
Ping Huang and Zhan Shaohua (2005), 'Internal migration in China: linking it to development', in F. Lacko (ed.), *Migration, Development and Poverty Reduction in Asia*, Geneva: International Organization for Migration, pp. 65–84.
Reis Oliveira, Catarina (2010), 'La actividad empresarial china en Portugal', *Revista CIDOB d'Afers Internacionals*, **92**, 223–42.
Sáiz López, Amelia (2001), *Utopía y género: Las mujeres chinas en el siglo XX*, Barcelona: Edicions Bellaterra.
Sáiz López, Amelia (2006), *Procesos de socialización de los hijos e hijas de las familias de origen chino*, Barcelona: Fundació Jaume Bofill.
Sáiz López, Amelia (2007), 'Mujeres en la empresa familiar: El caso de las empresarias asiáticas', *Revista CIDOB d'Afers Internacionals*, **78**, 57–76.
Sáiz López, Amelia (2010), 'Procesos, convergencias y variaciones en el empresariado femenino de origen asiático en España', *Revista CIDOB d'Afers Internacionals*, **92**, 57–76.
Yang, Mayfair Mei-Hui (1994), *Gifts, Favors, and Banquets: The Art of Social Relationships in China*, Ithaca, NY: Cornell University Press.

8 Back to Africa: second chances for the children of West African immigrants*
*Caroline H. Bledsoe and Papa Sow***

INTRODUCTION

This handbook focuses on the connections among gender, migration, development and transnationalism. This chapter takes up a highly focused topic – what appears at first to be a counterintuitive practice on the part of African immigrant parents in the United States who send their children, particularly boys, back to the home country to be raised. In the process, however, it raises several broader issues. First, it draws our attention to youth from African immigrant families and the heightened risks they can face not only in places like Europe, but in a country that prides itself as being a nation of immigrants, the contemporary US. Indeed, because of recent changes in its laws governing criminal sentencing, the United States has within a very short time produced shockingly high rates of incarceration of its own citizens and legal residents: particularly of young black men. Second, it addresses the formation of a socially ascribed gendered identity: in this case, a specific version of masculinity – a dangerously aggressive one with which black boys in particular seem particularly likely to be associated. Finally, it considers simultaneously aspects of the richest and poorest places on earth: the recent immigrants of Sub-Saharan African origin living in the United States.

This chapter, first published two years ago in the *Journal of Marriage & Family*, underscores the importance of the US as a site that poses vital analytical challenges for the study of how impressions of gender are formed, legitimated and acted upon. Though it is still by far the world's largest annual recipient of foreign immigrants, the US increasingly represents a complex mix of views of immigrants that are shaped by fears of terrorist attacks, concerns about competition over jobs in a struggling economy, and an overall hardening of views about who should be allowed to enter and under what conditions. All bear directly on debates about gender.

Recent decades have seen a sharp rise in the number of West African nationals in Europe and North America. Most have been young men seeking work or a degree, though women have come in greater numbers as well, whether independently or, under family reunification provisions, to join a husband (Sow, forthcoming). More thinly documented have been the West African children who are directly affected by international migration to the West. Some of these children are left behind when a parent travels abroad for work; others come as migrants themselves, whether as the dependants of a working parent or, in more extreme cases, unaccompanied by an adult.

Among the most puzzling cases are those of the children of West African immigrants in Europe or North America who are sent back to Africa, particularly boys of older school age. Leaving places that seem to offer every advantage – established health and educational systems; the likelihood of a stable, prosperous future; and so on – these children effectively return to countries with levels of privation that most Europeans and Americans would find unacceptable for their own children (Ariès, 1962). When asked to explain their actions, immigrant parents may point to lower costs of living and abundant childcare back home. Alternatively, they may declare that a child is adapting poorly to the new place or needs to grow up knowing the family's ancestral roots. If pressed, though, nearly all West African immigrant parents living in Europe and the United States, which we describe collectively as 'the West', insist that they want their children to gain a secure footing in the West. Observations like these raise two questions. First, what might immigrants of recent West African origin find so objectionable about countries usually described as the pinnacles of African immigrant ambition, to the point that they would send their children back, and in such heavily gender-weighted numbers, to live in one of the poorest regions on earth? Second, why would parents so often send these children back to the home country at just the point when they should be preparing most intensively for a successful professional life in the new home?

Stripped of their wider social and cultural contexts, we believe that the apparent facts in this case are misleading. Drawing from our past and present studies in Africa and Europe and from a range of secondary sources, we examine two related concerns voiced by West African parents about life in Europe and the United States alike. One is what they see as a Western tendency to coddle and spoil children and to restrict parents' access to measures they deem necessary to bring an unruly child into line. A child with an easy life, they fear, may lose all ambition for school and career achievement, possibly the main reason why the parents made the international move in the first place. Even more serious to parents and, by extension, to the extended families that rely on their remittances, may be the repercussions of an undisciplined child's involvement in gangs, violence and crime in a place that can manifest acute hostility to the

African immigrant presence on the one hand and, on the other, take a dim view of how they try to avert trouble. Forbidden to levy the kind of discipline they deem necessary to control a child who may begin to draw the attention of authorities, immigrant parents may send the child back home, whether to relatives or to a boarding school, to wait for the risk to abate.

In choosing a lens through which to see the phenomenon of sending back older children, we focus on parents' perspectives rather than on those of children or of guardians or authorities. Under US law, parents usually have exclusive authority over their children, even though the entire extended family may have invested heavily in them. And although we make few direct references to age, our analysis implies a focus on children in their early- to mid-teens, an age that usually corresponds to a demanding phase of formal education during which much can go wrong, especially for male children.

Definitions

Cases of children living apart from their biological parents manifest enormous variation across time and space. Children's separation from their parents may last from a month to the entirety of childhood; and they may live down the street or on different continents. Some children in the formal care of others see their parents every day; others have no memory of them. Relationships to carers can range from rural grandmothers who care for newly weaned toddlers to service in the household of elites who seek low-cost household or farm labour.

Western societies, tend to see children as fragile creatures who need the stable parental figures best created by a nuclear family structure; they see a child's transfer to a household headed by non-biological parents as a risk the child and hence as a likely response of last resort to an intolerable situation.

In Africa, by contrast, most transfers of children are taken as normal, or even beneficial, for a child's progress in life, in part because most such transfers involve relatives. Indeed, a promising child may move among several households before reaching adulthood. The exceptionally rare transfers involving the formal process of adopting African children (as understood in Euro-American legal systems) seem to arise only in cases involving Western adoptive parents or in which a destination country allows reunification only of children who belong legally to the destination family.

Child transfers in Africa, then, are not intended to be permanent legal transfers to another family or institution. Quite the contrary: they are often undertaken to reaffirm social connections between parents and guardians. In the view of authors such as Goody (1982) and Alber (2003), in fact, they largely represent residential variations on everyday practices of distributing parenting roles within the lineage. The idea that kin who care for the child of a kinsman would simply be 'fostering' them, implying minimal family connection, would be anathema.

Data

If these definitional matters pose challenges to conventional understandings of families and relationships, the data problems encountered in trying to study cases of children who are sent home from Europe and America pose even more challenges. Almost without exception, every adult of recent West African origin living in Europe and the United States knows about the practice of sending children back to Africa; many know a family who has done so. But most national censuses and vital registries exclude non-resident family members, and few surveys are designed to capture instances of children who were sent back. Nevertheless, the phenomenon appears in many ethnographies of West African immigrant family life (for example, Barou, 2001) and Farjas i Bonet (2002) suggested that nearly one-third of children of the 625 children of Gambian origin she recorded in Catalonia, Spain had been sent back to Africa for a significant amount of time.

In our studies, extraordinarily rich and abundant sources have come from research usually termed 'qualitative': interviews, written texts and ad hoc conversations. The studies from which we draw fall into two broad categories. The first is an ongoing anthropological demographic study of reproductive and family life among transnational Gambians in Spain (see Bledsoe et al., 2007; Empez Vidal, 2007; Fleischer, 2010). The other is a series of earlier studies in West Africa (for example, Bledsoe and Isiugo-Abanihe, 1989; Bledsoe, 1990; Sow, 2010). Although we draw a number of explicit examples from the current study of Gambians in Spain and use past studies' published results to set the African cultural context, the process of analysis in this chapter led us to draw on aspects of the past studies that were not previously published. We also launched a series of open-ended, exploratory forays into secondary materials for illuminating accounts: scholarly books and journals as well as online media; news stories, editorials and newsletters. Because the phenomenon of sending children back to Africa from the West is so thinly documented in the scholarly sources, we opened the search to personal histories and quotes in journalistic or 'discussion group' media. In fact, the ease with which relevant sources from the internet can now be discovered was largely what led us to focus on the abundant materials from North America, mainly the United States, where West African immigrant populations have grown rapidly in the last decades, and where theories of ethnicity and integration have been extensively developed and debated (see, for example, Suarez-Orozco and Suarez-Orozco, 2001).

To be sure, drawing on materials from a wide array of places, with very different immigration histories and policies carries certain interpretive risks. In both Europe and North America, for example, children from West African families are much more likely than their counterparts in Europe to be citizens or legal residents. For many, this is because they were born in the US, which automatically accords citizenship to children who are born on its soil, in contrast to Europe, where children's citizenship generally follows that of their parents: a practice that may help to explain why the status of 'immigrant' can be carried for generations in the 'new' place. But it is also the case that for Africans, getting to the US is much more difficult than to Europe, both logistically and financially. For those without legal status in the US, trying to come from such a distant locale is usually regarded as far too problematic to risk.

The forms that legality takes and what facets of them are emphasised also seem quite different. 'Legal residence' appears most often in discussions of West Africans in Europe, and 'citizenship' in those from the United States. At the same time, there are some striking thematic consistencies across the continents: most notably, in concerns about the risk that trouble with the law can generate, both for individual immigrants and for their families, and in the new place as well as back home. Particularly, we sense, in the wake of the 2001 al-Qaida attacks on New York City, concerns among immigrant families about their rights to stay now suffuse every aspect of life, even among families whose members have been considered 'legal' for some time.

LITERATURE AND CULTURAL CONTEXT

Well before social science research began to focus on transnationalism as an explicit theme, scholarly opinion about the impact on children of separation from parents was divided. Outcomes for older children were generally described as mixed, though students of the family usually linked their health as well as economic and emotional well-being to physical proximity to parents, especially to mothers. For younger children, authors such as Ainsworth (1967) and Thomas (1981) linked separation from parents or mothers to higher risks of mortality and morbidity, whether because these children were weaned too soon, making them vulnerable to nutritional deficit or infectious disease, or simply because they slipped through the cracks of health programmes targeting mothers and their children (Bledsoe et al., 1988).

Recent studies of the consequences of parent–child separation have taken a more explicitly political and economic orientation. Studies influenced by theories of globalization and transnationalism have tended to emphasize the risks to children with the rise in global demands for low-cost domestic service. Anderson (2000), Parreñas (2001) and Ehrenreich and Hochschild (2002), among others, identify 'caring gaps' for the children of women who left to care for children of the affluent in other countries. Similar observations have arisen within Europe, as thousands of new EU-citizen parents from the former Soviet bloc departed for work in wealthier countries, often leaving children with relatives or simply to fend for themselves (Bilefsky, 2009). In the Philippines, authors such as Battistella and Conoco (1998), D'Emilio et al. (2007) and Reyes (2008) have suggested that although parents' work abroad can alleviate familial poverty, children left behind still risk emotional distress, faltering physical development, disrupted school progress and abuse. The same could certainly be said to apply to older children sent home from Europe or North America. Spending these years in poor educational conditions would appear to put them at a sharp competitive disadvantage for future employment opportunities in the West, where their parents nearly always want them to return and take up a productive adult life. Reporting on her research in Spain, Farjas i Bonet (2002) mentions the frustration of Spanish school officials whose Gambian pupils were sometimes sent back to Africa for extended periods; these officials complained that the students, when they returned, had lost ground in their academic and language training and suffered a general cultural disorientation.

The overall impact on children of separation from their parents is far from clear, though. Few would disagree that arranging for care by a non-parent can be good for a young child in a situation of 'crisis fostering' (Goody,1982) such as the death of a parent or pregnancy for a girl whose return to school would be jeopardized by the presence of a baby. Sending young children elsewhere is also a common strategy for removing them from tensions arising in the wake of a divorce. Most people declare that being out of sight and mind is usually far better for young children than staying behind in the care of a woman who may have been instrumental in driving their mother away. Such practices can also bring benefit to extended family members. In West Africa, relatives commonly give a barren woman a child to rear. Even more commonly, a woman with a new baby may leave her newly weaned toddler with an elderly 'granny', whether her own mother or a fictive one, so that she can sustain her farm crop or try to conceive a new child.

As these observations suggest, some children living away from their parents may experience hardship, but we must not lose sight of the many parents who follow what are considered quite ordinary childcare practices that draw on other adults (Panter-Brick, 2001; Madhavan and Townsend, 2007; Leinaweaver, 2008; Mazzucato and Schans, 2008). In Africa, well into the colonial period, parents seeking protection for the family from enemy raiders frequently sent children to a powerful chief (Murphy and Bledsoe, 1987). Boys were expected to become his bodyguards or servants and eventually take up arms for him, while girls, trained in domestic work by senior women in his household, would become wives for him or one of his clients. (For parallels in Western history, see Demos, 1970; Laslett, 1977, p. 111; McCracken, 1983.) In the present, children continue to be expected to be grateful for such opportunities, working hard, producing and marketing goods for their guardians, performing domestic chores and so on (for Ghana, see Goody, 1982; Coe, 2008). Consequently, guardians across the social spectrum see much to gain from taking in outside children. Especially for a promising child, simply giving him a meal when he is hungry could lay the basis for future claims on a powerful patron.

For older children in West Africa, who are charged with helping their families to advance, cultural epistemologies of achievement are pivotal. Linking advancement and wealth to properly approved personal struggle, they have held that valued knowledge is not free but is owned by others. In the past, acquiring such knowledge required children to earn it through 'training' or morally disciplined struggle; accordingly, children were exhorted with phrases like 'No success without struggle' (Bledsoe, 1990). Such struggles required them to fulfil obligations to benefactors and accept with gratitude whatever costs or conditions their benefactors might impose. For ambitious children, moving away from the comfortable yet confining homes where they were born might be the best thing they could do. Not only did the outside world offer them contacts and sophistication, but more distant guardians were regarded as less likely to tolerate disobedience or insolence. Headstrong, impertinent children might be dispatched to a remote village and placed under the authority of an Arabic master renowned as much for his exacting discipline as for his command of the mystical powers of the Qur'an, which properly trained children might be allowed to access. This child training ideology thus provided that deserving children, steeled to hardship, would rise to the surface regardless of the situation. Stories abounded of chiefs who, when seeking close counsellors, brushed aside their own spoiled, bickering sons in favour of young men from humble roots who had proven their unflinching loyalty in the face of harsh adversity. Further, patrons who had seen a child's merit shine through the challenges might send that child on to his own patrons in larger settlements and so on, in a seamless trajectory of geographical, social and ritual advancement. Children who were not made to submit to discipline at the hands of their benefactors, who were pampered and fed to satisfaction, were alleged to grow up lazy and arrogant. Becoming a burden rather than a blessing to their families, they would produce no useful good for the family (see also Coe, 2008). Indeed they would hoard gains for themselves and leave their families vulnerable to enemy predation and impoverishment. Earning not the family's blessings but its curses, they would see all the knowledge and patronage they had gained come to naught.

Training was seen as quite different from formal schooling, which continues to be regarded in West Africa as necessary but insufficient for lasting success. The problem with modern schooling, especially government-supported schooling, according to many, is that it dispenses valued knowledge too freely, eroding proper channels of personal obligation and respect towards those who impart it. Untrained schoolchildren, it is felt, even those with the most impressive educational achievements, will almost certainly fail to rise beyond their present conditions. If Western schooling is seen as a weak link in the chain of discipline, however, it is above all grandmothers who are seen as most ruinous to child training and discipline (Bledsoe and Isiugo-Abanihe, 1989). Grandmothers are notorious spoilers of children, doting on them, feeding them on demand, indulging their impertinence and allowing them to play while elders work. Children raised by grannies are seen as incapable of coping with hunger and hardship. If they are later given the chance to go to a guardian to attend school, they will spend their school hours daydreaming about food. Worse, they will complain about hunger and the hard work demanded of them. A child who displays such an appalling lack of gratitude to his benefactors, it is feared, may well be sent home in disgust.

In the West African cultural sense, 'child development' refers less to children's passive acts of physical maturation than to adult efforts to help them advance in skills and knowledge so that they can, in turn, further 'develop' the family. Such efforts might be most facilitated by arranging for children to be trained by those who are better placed to develop their potential. In contrast, therefore, to the Western convictions that a person needs one stable set of parental figures throughout childhood and that sending a child to distant guardians is necessarily damaging, most West Africans would probably argue the opposite. Such a child may be the one upon whom family hopes rest. Indeed, particularly for boys, a rural child who has not been fostered out to a guardian of higher status or sent to a more urban area is viewed as either unworthy or dull.

None of this is to say that discipline or any other ideological recipe for raising children actually produces the results it promises. Nevertheless, probing the cultural frames surrounding these intergenerational relations provides insight into how Africans try to cope with the precariousness of economic and political life, and why squandering the future of a promising child is described as such a loss for the family.

OPPORTUNITY AND RISK FOR WEST AFRICAN CHILDREN IN NEW LANDS

At the beginning of the twenty-first century, West African families are arguably even more vulnerable than before to the vicissitudes of economic, political and ecological fortune. Family welfare rests more than ever on new generations' successes in establishing a strong foothold in the knowledge, skills and contacts in the outside world. Nevertheless, it would seem to make little sense to send older children back from the West to West Africa at precisely the moment when they should be preparing most intensively to enter the global labour market. What might West African parents find so objectionable about such otherwise desirable places that they would send children away at such a critical phase of life?

Getting to the West to help ease the burdens of family members back home is seldom an easy matter. Nor is being able to stay there. West African immigrants confront an increasingly contentious world of struggle over rights to enter and work in Europe and North America. Most parents would like to stay long enough to see their children safely through a good education and build a house back home where they can eventually retire. To keep their return options open, immigrants, regardless of their educational or professional achievements, must try to maintain ties of goodwill with families back home, whether through remittances, phone calls or visits, or through sponsoring other people to migrate (Levitt and Jaworsky, 2007; Mazzucato, 2008). In the United States, post-9/11 concerns about foreigners and security have raised entry controls to unprecedented levels. In the European Union, where citizens of any member state can travel, work and live freely in other member states and where American tourists can enter with only a passport, restrictions on the movements of citizens of less-favoured countries have escalated. Economic troubles have only intensified these challenges. In Spain, for example, the national economy until recently generated more than half of all new EU jobs (Tremlett, 2006), attracting hundreds of thousands of immigrants each year to work in the booming real estate, tourism and construction industries. But with growing global recession, tourists were leaving, property owners were defaulting on mortgages, and construction jobs were disappearing. By May 2009, Spain's unemployment had reached 18.7 per cent ('Eurozone unemployment reaches 15 million', 2009). Many observers believe that these economic troubles have heightened suspicion of immigrants, exposing them to increased risk of harassment.

West African immigrant parents living in the West want their children to succeed abroad. These new places, however, rife with what immigrants see as drugs, crime, sexual licentiousness, rampant violence and contempt for adult authority, present a most unpromising environment for successful child rearing. Families believe that Western influences corrode youths' moral fibre, posing formidable challenges for their efforts to keep children on track to meet the obligations that family members on both continents expect of them. A Senegalese man in Barcelona we interviewed, for example, reported that many of his countrymen had found living in Spain so damaging to children's training and discipline that they believed they had lost all control of their children.

In both France and Spain, African immigrant families sometimes say that children who have experienced their formative years in Europe become *vacas locas*, in Spanish (*vaches folles* in French) or 'mad cows', a direct reference to the bovine encephalopathy that first surged to world attention in Britain in the late 1980s and early 1990s. Compared to children trained in good manners and discipline, *vacas locas*, most of whom have been born in Europe and have not been back to the home country, are said to be far more vulnerable to leaving school and joining gangs that roam the streets, uncontrolled and confrontational. They also form the frontlines of what their parents see as an unsettling new hostility towards the older generation of immigrants.

Swept into the world of violence and illegality, these children are said to engage in drugs, theft and, in the case of girls, prostitution and even begging on the streets. The spectre is the same in the United States. In several online articles (2002, 2007, 2008), Alex Kabba, publisher of *African Abroad !– USA*, a prominent newsletter for US-resident African immigrants, blames Western media – television, movies, music and videos – for saturating international youth culture with images of violence, insubordination and depravity. All this, he charges, undermines children's respect for elders' authority, and lures them into drugs, truancy and sexual licentiousness (see also Scott, 2000, p.16, on African and Caribbean immigrant parents in Ontario, Canada). Parents also point to pressure from peers, often from broken homes that offer negligible supervision for children (Kabba, 2008). Most of all they blame what they see as a culture of unconscionable laxity that pervades Western culture, persuading child protection authorities that children's bad behaviours should be indulged. This laxity, in their view, not only penetrates homes but also poisons public schools, transforming them into sites of institutionalized permissiveness, breeding grounds for gangs, and surveillance gateways into the home for legal authorities. Sounding almost as if he were reading the words recorded in the early 1980s of Sierra Leoneans who complained about the havoc wrought among their youth by the arrival of 'White men's' schools (Bledsoe, 1990), a Senegalese man we interviewed in Spain railed against what he saw as the corrosive influences of permissiveness in European schools: 'I do not want [my children] to be educated here. Education here is not good. I saw people here who lost control over the training and discipline of their children'. In Swigart's (2001) Philadelphia-area interviews with African immigrants, a Sudanese refugee declared that even refugee camp schools in Kenya were more disciplined than American schools.

Growing up in this environment, parents say, the children in whom they have invested so much may lose both their career ambition and the enormous advantage their parents' immigration to the United States handed them in accessing the resources of the West. Kabba (2008) describes the bewilderment of a Nigerian-origin father in Brooklyn with three professional degrees who imagined that his three sons would grow up to be doctors, lawyers, or other professionals. Instead, reports Kabba, the first son dropped out of college and began wearing braids like the other boys in the neighbourhood; the second, at age 20, dismissed education as 'overrated' and said he wanted to become a barber; and the third, at 16, announced his intention to become a dancer. Where, the parents asked themselves, had they gone wrong? In other cases, however, the consequences are far worse. Kabba (2007) describes the case of middle-class Liberian immigrant parents in Minnesota whose 16-year-old son joined an urban gang to counter the taunts of his schoolmates who called him a 'dumb African', and began to threaten his parents and hang out on street corners, sporting gang tattoos and bandanas. Arrested for robbery, according to Kabba, he was sentenced to six months' incarceration in a juvenile correctional facility. On the day he was to be released, moreover, as he walked out to hug his mother, three armed policemen from a neighbouring jurisdiction seized him, announcing that his fingerprints had turned up in a robbery in their area and took him in to face the fresh charges. He received another 12 months' detention.

The problem, as parents see it, is their inability to deploy the discipline required to raise their children, including, when necessary, physical punishment. Because they were specifically delegated by the family back home to establish a new base of security abroad, these parents feel enormous pressure to protect their children from the new dangers that threaten to derail children and ruin the chances the family struggled so hard to give them (Arthur, 2008, p. 47). Although Western child-rearing authorities advocated strict discipline in the past (Ariès, 1962), warning parents against sparing the rod and spoiling the child, the situation has now changed entirely. Western authorities take a dim view of measures that West African immigrants could deploy back home, especially corporal punishment and withholding food from children. Adopting the language of psychiatry and of human rights, most authorities now cast such measures as abuse or as breaches of children's rights:

> For an African family, armed with the tools used by their parents to raise them, once in America those tools are rendered obsolete. In some cases they are labeled 'dangerous weapons' that could not be used on a child. With the only tools at their disposal taken away, African parents are at a loss as to what to do. The [American] concepts of Reinforcement and Time Out are foreign and less effective. (Kabba, 2008)

In Kabba's view (2002), American laws go too far by tying the hands of parents who are desperate to intervene to save their children from serious trouble.

Trying to protect their children from what they see as the destructive effects of Western culture on children's moral character can have devastating consequences for parents. In Spain, a doctor threatened to report a father after finding evidence that led him to suspect the man had beaten his 12-year-old son, a boy who family friends had come to see as heading for trouble. Despite the parents' efforts to control him, he habitually went out into the streets and came home late. When the police brought him home one night, the father beat him. The next day, the teacher saw the marks and denounced the family, and the school took the boy to the hospital and alerted the social services, where a file was opened on the case.

Child protection agencies in the United States and Europe urge children to report their parents for abuse, and they train police, teachers and medical workers to look for signs of it, evidence that children may exploit in the heat of an argument. Parents who try to correct their children's misbehaviour through physical punishment thus risk losing their children to the child protection authorities. In Spain, our findings suggest that the contradictory demands on parents are now explicit: they feel compelled to go to whatever extreme is required to enforce child discipline, while simultaneously avoiding the risk of their own destruction.

Parents risk arrest or even, for those who are not citizens or permanent residents in the new place, deportation, with catastrophic financial repercussions for the extended family members who rely on their remittances. Nevertheless, some immigrants are so determined to keep their children on track that they knowingly put themselves at risk (Arthur, 2008). Kabba (2002) reports the case of a Nigerian-born computer science professor who, to escape American permissiveness, took his two American-born children back home and left them, but did so against the wishes of his former wife, the children's mother. She alerted the authorities that her husband had 'kidnapped' the children. When he refused the order of a New Jersey court to bring them back from Nigeria, he was held in contempt of court for four years, until the remaining minor child informed the judge that she wanted to complete her education in Nigeria.

African immigrant parents badly want their children to succeed in Europe and America. Ironically, they feel, the good life in the West that fueled their efforts to immigrate now may undermine their ability to provide it. At just the moment when children's opportunities seem within easy reach, the Western culture of indulging youth insolence threatens to destroy children's ambitions and bars parents from deploying measures that they could have used back home to bring their children back into line (Kabba, 2008; see also Scott, 2000, pp. 18–19, for the case of immigrants in Ontario).

Permeating many of these accounts of the dangers Western society can pose to West African immigrant families are concerns about race. It is no secret to anyone, least of all to West African immigrants, that in Europe and America, black youth are more susceptible to authorities' scrutiny than are their white counterparts. Every black parent in Europe and America knows the consequences of discrimination fall disproportionately on racial minorities (US National Council on Crime and Delinquency in the Justice System, 2009). Any youth can have run-ins with school authorities and the police, but white children can flaunt the rules with greater impunity than black children. The problem for West African immigrants, then, is that they see their children subjected to the same forms of discrimination from employers, landlords, real estate agents and law enforcement officers that black youth in the United States have endured for generations (Arthur, 2008, p. 146). Vivid accounts of African immigrants' encounters, as blacks, with the law and legal authorities come from Ghanaian-born sociologist John Arthur's ethnography of Ghanaian immigrants in the United States. Ghanaian immigrant youth, Arthur observes, charge that police see them as guilty of lawlessness and crime simply because they are black. Immigrant Ghanaian youth, according to Arthur, see a thin line separating them from cases with chilling consequences:

> When we go to the mall, the police watch us with an eagle's eyes. . . . [A]s Black kids, we are always singled out and harassed by the mall security officers. Sometimes our encounter with them is fatal. Remember Ahmadou Diallo, the West African immigrant who was gunned down [in 1999] by New York City police. (p. 109)

Boys in particular are said to be the targets of this discrimination. Using equally vivid cases, Kabba (2007) holds that the struggles of immigrant youth not only echo the dysfunction in general of raising black boys in America; they are intensified by it. Taken together, he argues, the paucity of security-providing parent figures, the damage to a boy's self-esteem and a national media that promotes violence and a disdain for the law and social authorities all 'kill . . . the can-do attitude that saw his parents through the pangs of immigration' (Kabba, 2008). Terrified of losing their children to the criminal justice or foster-care systems that so readily come into play in cases involving minorities, or simply of watching their children's academic ambitions dissolve into apathy, many African immigrant parents charge that 'the problem of rearing Black children [in general] has crept into the African family in America' (Kabba, 2007).

According to Arthur (2008, p.144), African immigrants, despite their efforts to achieve success, come to sense that irrespective of their origin or character, their black skin colour may preclude them from achieving full membership in a country that proclaims itself a democracy of equals. This sense, says Arthur, casts a shadow over their desire to remain in the United States once their working years are over. They do not 'see the need to stay in America permanently only to be marginalized and exposed to the deep-seated legacy of racial tension that characterizes Black–White relations in the United States' (Arthur, p.146). For them, the possibility of returning to Africa may in fact offer new advantages. They believe that when they go back they will be hailed as successful returnees. They also hope to benefit from the Ghanaian government's efforts to lure them and their foreign earnings back through tax breaks and housing subsidies. Using their accumulated earnings, foreign bank accounts and networks of overseas friends and associates to start a business, they envisage sending their children to the best preparatory and secondary schools and living the life in Ghana that they might have lived abroad, if race were not a factor. In the words of one returnee:

> I returned home because in Ghana I am treated with dignity and I am not constantly reminded in subtle ways about my blackness. Here, my blackness does not count against me and I am free of this poverty of dignity that America tags its Black population with irrespective of their accomplishments. Being Black in America is a lot of baggage and a heavy load to bear. (Quoted in Arthur, p.146)

BACK TO AFRICA: PARENTS' RESPONSES TO CHILD DISCIPLINE TROUBLES

Our own data as well as the secondary sources we have explored describe a number of efforts by West Africans immigrant parents in Europe and North America to try to solve problems of discipline and build resilience in their children, while avoiding what they see as harmful interference by legal authorities. These strategies effectively exploit channels for mitigating harm to children in ways that more formal institutional practices cannot, or are unlikely to, enact. Studies of what are called 'second chances' have focused on measures that assist individuals who have committed wrongdoings or failed in school or business, but not to the extent that would preclude their future redemption. The goal is to offer the opportunity to 'get it right this time' to people who, because of their perceived youth or inexperience, may yet be able to avoid permanent stigma and discouragement. In the United States, for example, the most common form of a second chance for high school dropouts has been the General Educational Development (GED) test of high school equivalence (see, for example, Kasinitz et al., 2008, pp. 172, 344, on immigrant youth in New York City). Dispatching errant children to boarding school, a religious or military academy or even a wilderness 'boot camp' has drawn considerable interest in popular media. For immigrant youth as well, the texts we have found prominently mention the possibility of taking them out of public school and enrolling them, much in the tradition of European aristocratic youth, in a private school or even a boarding school: preferably one with a conservative, even religious, disciplinary orientation. According to one of Swigart's African interviewees in Philadelphia, many Muslim parents actually prefer Catholic to public schools because they perceive that for Catholic schools, 'discipline is number one' (2001, p. 61).

Sending children back to Africa is the solution to problems of child discipline of chief interest to African immigrant parents. Kabba's articles offer particularly vivid descriptions of the struggles of middle-class professional West African doctors, nurses, writers, professors and business owners who sent a child back to Africa or who came to regret not doing so. In one case (Kabba, 2007), a Ghanaian–American couple in New York refused to let their 15-year-old son bring his girlfriend home. In revenge, the boy complained to his public school that his father had punished and molested him, resulting in jail for the father on charges of child endangerment. When the charges were eventually cleared, the parents took their son back to Ghana to continue his education, lest he bring disaster on the family. Before leaving him, however, the father gave him a thorough beating for the suffering he had caused.

Back in Africa, children are dispatched to a wide variety of settings. Some stay with a relative and enrol in whatever school other children in the family attend. In other cases, parents seek out situations that promise tough discipline, including the possibility of apprenticing them to Arabic masters, so they will be resilient enough when they return to the West to avoid trouble from gangs, violence and the police. Often, however, reports suggest, somewhat contrary to the image of immersing wayward children in the harsh discipline to strengthen their character, parents use their hard-currency income to send their children to private schools, often those patronized by expatriate families or local elites. The intent is to allow the children to continue their education in an unbroken sequence, so that they can move on almost seamlessly to the next phase of schooling when they return to their parents in Europe or North America.

Situations that combine these agendas appear to be ideal. A 2007 story in the London *Sunday Times* titled, 'African cane tames unruly British pupils' (McConnell, 2007) provides a riveting example. According to this article, scores of British schoolchildren of Ghanaian parentage who return to Africa are sent to institutions such as the Faith Montessori boarding school in Accra, in the hope that they will exchange truancy and gangs for traditional teaching and strong discipline. Faith Montessori's director, when queried, traced the troubles of British pupils of African descent in London to a lack of good role models and adult supervision. With most Africans in the United Kingdom having jobs requiring them to be out of the house all day, he asserted, 'the devil finds work for idle hands' (see also Kabba, 2008). By contrast, the director related, youth in Ghana are surrounded by serious black professional lawyers, doctors, and so on, who can inspire youth to higher achievements. The other problem with London for children from African families, he went on, involves gangs, stealing and violence. All, he believes, incite parents of recalcitrant youth in London to send their children home. Getting back on track towards the rigorous education they lacked in Britain, the children may become so polite, articulate and accomplished that they can return to Britain to compete in A-level exams for a university place, as many previous pupils in his school have done, to jobs in business, industry and the theatre in the United Kingdom. He attributes the success of his graduates who were sent back from London to the extraordinary discipline he applies, to a degree that has fallen out of favour in Britain: 'I believe in caning,' he declared. 'I tell the parents: if you don't want your child punished, then your child doesn't belong here'.

So desperate are some parents to remove their children from the context of failure and violence, they may even send their children back to a homeland that is embroiled in war. An article in the *New York Times* titled 'Exiled to a war zone, for his safety' (Barry, 2007) reported that a Liberian refugee mother in New York made an agonizing decision to send her oldest son back to what was then a war zone in Liberia to protect him from what she saw as a worse situation in the United States. Their neighbourhood had filled with waves of refugees over the last 30 years, many of them from Liberia, and immigrant youth daily encountered the lures of drug dealers who sought them as conduits, knowing they were less liable to legal sanction than adults. Ugly turf wars had arisen with a nearby neighbourhood of African Americans, and by his teen years the son had joined a gang and was pushing drugs. Promising to bring him back from a summer visit to relatives, his mother took him to Liberia and left him with her brother. She knew very well, according to the article, that her thoroughly Americanized son would face an empty belly and the possibility of capture and maiming by warlord gangs. In her view, though, he was better off in a Liberian war zone than in their Staten Island neighbourhood. Even when he found himself in the crossfire of battle and begged to come home, she did not relent until she saw clear signs of change – four years later.

In cases of children sent back to Africa, some returnees stay for just a few months; others for much longer. Arthur (2008, p. 48) reports that children of Ghanaian descent who are US citizens may even stay in Ghana for the entirety of their primary and middle school years, coming back only when it is time to start high school, an observation paralleled by some of Smith's (2007, p. 177) observations of Mexican youth and US-born people of Mexican origin living in a small village in southern Mexico. Smith showed that a small but apparently growing number of these youths had been sent back to Mexico from New York in the hope that family members in Mexico would discipline them or at least 'calm' them by giving them a job and a safe space in which to mature.

Such importance is now placed on the option of sending children back to avoid trouble that parents may 'strike early', sending their children back well before they reach adolescence. Other parents now refuse to bring children in their formative years at all. The Senegalese man in Spain we referred to earlier offers a case in point. Although he could have brought his 13 children to live with him, he saw living in a place that promoted such undisciplined laxity among children not as a blessing for them but as potentially career-ending. While he fully intended to bring them later, he had left them in Senegal with their respective mothers to attend schools that followed the French curriculum, well known for its rigour and excellence. Equally noteworthy in this case, however, were the exceptions: two of his children did live in Spain with him, where they were being looked after by a female relative he had brought from Senegal for this purpose. The mother of these children, he explained, had died and he deemed them safer with him rather than with one of his co-wives back in Senegal, who were caring for their own children. Were it not for this extraordinary circumstance, he asserted, he would not have brought them to Europe at all. Observers such as Kabba (2002) see the need to send children back to Africa for disciplinary purposes as becoming so important that the practice has intensified in recent years. Again, reliable quantitative estimates are few. In Farjas i Bonet's (2002) study in Spain, however, in which nearly one-third of the children of Gambian origin had been sent home for significant amounts of time, she commented that most of the older ones who had been sent home appeared to have been sent for disciplinary reasons. Less direct, but possibly equally telling, is a study by Whitehouse (2009) of West African labour migrants in Brazzaville, Congo. Whitehouse reported that 39 out of 99 his respondents said they had sent small children back home. Moreover, they explained their actions as an effort to shield their children, before the children reached an impressionable age, from what they saw as pernicious influences in the host society. In offering this explanation, of course, Whitehouse raises the provocative possibility that migrants everywhere may see their host society, no matter how desirable its appeal for work or education, in ambivalent terms. It may offer a better livelihood than they could earn back home, but at the cost of corrupting children in whom proper cultural foundations have not been laid.

DISCUSSION

This chapter began with two questions. The first was why West Africans living in Europe or North America, places often identified as the global centres of safety and opportunity for children, might suddenly find these places so objectionable that they would send their children back to live in Africa, one of the poorest regions on earth. The second was why they might send children to West Africa at a crucial moment in their educational trajectories, when the children should be preparing most intensively to succeed in the new home their parents have tried so hard to create for them. The material we have found, despite the diversity of its sources, tells a remarkably consistent story of West African immigrant parents' despair at being denied adequate disciplinary means to protect their children from the destruction that Western society's indulgent attitude towards children can precipitate.

For parents caught in a Catch-22 that threatens to undermine the goals for which they came, it should not be surprising that they might send their children away from the places where they so urgently want them to succeed. Nor should it be surprising that they should do so not despite the hardship they know their children will surely confront back home, but specifically to ensure that they will confront it. Back in the home country, appropriate disciplinary action can be taken. Even more important, perhaps, children who are sent home to Africa can simply grow out of the phases in which Western society is most inclined to expect trouble among black youth. Rather than see their children become uncontrollable *vacas locas* within a normative system they see as encouraging youth delinquency – but as interpreting it very differently for black and white youth – many West African parents prefer to send their children back to Africa before serious trouble can even occur at all. Sending children back to Africa, in sum, is seen not as disrupting children's progress towards a career back in Europe or North America, but as an attempt to keep it on course.

Much as they did in the African past, African families living in the West today must prepare their children to confront an external world that, while it may offer them far greater possibilities than their parents had, is also fraught with dangers and unequal playing fields. It is notable, then, that what appear to be the same cultural emphases on hardship, privation and discipline that are associated with rural African philosophies of raising children have not disappeared among West African families now living in the United States and Europe. In our view, however, these patterns do not represent simple carry-overs from African 'traditions', but highly strategic attempts to cope with structured discrimination in the new places.

Certainly some African children growing up in Europe and North America achieve success, some possibly by taking advantage of the assistance programmes established for native ethnic minorities, as the findings of Massey et al.(2007) may imply for the United States. However, West African immigrant parents in both Europe and the United States, as hard as they struggled to clear their children's path to Western education and the benefits it promises, now perceive a more complicated trajectory. For them, protecting children from the risks posed by the forces of discrimination that have long plagued black groups in the West may only be possible by sweeping them temporarily out of the way of the authorities who would deny parents the means to control them. The possibility that African families must try to protect their children in the West by sending them away underscores the need to probe beneath vague rationales of sending children back home to know their kin or to become familiar with the traditions of the homeland. It also underscores the daunting odds of a black child succeeding in the West. In a cultural milieu that both tolerates their children and yet can be so ambivalent about them, West African immigrants living in Europe and North America have every reason to fear trouble. Many authors have emphasized the role of second chances for youth after earlier bouts of trouble or failure, or for shielding them from the most stringent penalties of the law. It is also well known, however, that a native-born black child who drops out of school or runs afoul of the law will almost certainly find second chances harder to come by than white children, whose misbehaviours may be so casually dismissed as manifestations of what Western culture sees as the temporary *Sturm und Drang* of adolescent turbulence. In so far as they have such a readily available 'exit' alternative, therefore, the children of West African immigrants share with many children of recent Mexican origin in the US an enormous advantage over their African-American counterparts: they can simply leave the country. Once the likelihood of trouble has abated, whether because of discipline or simply because of the lapse of time, those children allowed to return do so to an unblemished record and a very strong likelihood of success.

In a similar way, the escalating border control and security measures that Western authorities devise in order to exclude – the same ones that can strain and distort families by enforcing unwanted separation – also hold a paradoxical advantage for their parents. Parents who can take advantage of viable 'exit' options like these for their children may effectively turn the tables, exploiting the same forces of separation to keep serious problems out of sight and mind.

NOTES

[*] The original version of this chapter first appeared in a special issue of *Journal of Marriage & Family*, **73** (4), 2011, 747–62 (Valentina Mazzucatto, ed.) under the same title. It is re-published with the kind permission of the journal and of the publisher, John Wiley & Sons Ltd.
[**] The authors thank Jalika Jammeh and Andreu Domingo for their help on this chapter. For project support, we thank the Max Planck Institute for Demographic Research (Rostock, Germany); the Woodrow Wilson International Center for Scholars (Washington, DC); the Centre for Demographic Studies at the Universitat Autònoma de Barcelona, and the Centre for Research in Ethnic Relations at the University of Warwick (Coventry, United Kingdom).

REFERENCES

Ainsworth, M.D.S. (1967), *Infancy in Uganda*, Baltimore, MD: Johns Hopkins University Press.
Alber, E. (2003), 'Denying biological parenthood: fosterage in Northern Benin', *Ethnos*, **68**, 487–506.
Anderson, B. (2000), *Doing the Dirty Work? The Global Politics of Domestic Labour*, London: Zed Books.
Ariès, P. (1962), *Centuries of Childhood*, New York: Vintage Press.
Arthur, J. (2008), *The African Diaspora in the United States and Europe: The Ghanaian Experience*, Aldershot, UK: Ashgate.
Barou, J. (2001), 'La famille à distance: Nouvelles strategies familiales chez les immigrés d'afrique sahélienne', *Hommes et Migrations*, **1232**, 16–25.
Barry, E. (2007), 'Exiled to a war zone, for his safety', *New York Times*, front page, 14 December.
Battistella, G. and C.G. Conaco (1998), 'The impact of labor migration on the children left behind: a study of elementary school children in the Philippines', *Journal of Social Issues in Southeast Asia*, **13**, 220–41.

Bilefsky, D. (2009), 'In Romania, children left behind suffer the strains of migration', *New York Times*, world, 9 February.
Bledsoe, C. (1990), '"No success without struggle": social mobility and hardship for Sierra Leone children', *Man*, n.s., **25**, 70–88.
Bledsoe, C.H., D. C. Ewbank and U.C. Isiuge-Abanihe (1988), 'The effect of child fostering on feeding practices and access to health services in rural Sierra Leone', *Social Science and Medicine*, **27**(6), 627–36.
Bledsoe, C.H., R. Houle and P. Sow (2007), 'High fertility Gambians in low fertility Spain: mutually entailed lives across international space', *Demographic Research*, **16**, 375–412.
Bledsoe, C. and U. Isiugo-Abanihe (1989), 'Strategies of child fosterage among Mende grannies in Sierra Leone', in R. Lestheaghe (ed.), *Reproduction and Social Organization in sub-Saharan Africa*, Berkeley, CA: University of California Press, pp. 442–75.
Coe, C. (2008), 'The structuring of feeling in Ghanaian transnational families', *City & Society*, **20**, 222–50.
D'Emilio, A.L., B. Cordero, B. Bainvel, C. Skoog, D. Comini, J.G.M. Dias, R. Saab and T. Kilbane (2007), *The Impact of International Migration: Children Left Behind in Selected Countries of Latin America and the Caribbean*, New York: UNICEF.
Demos, J. (1970), *A Little Commonwealth: Family Life in Plymouth Colony*, New York: Oxford University Press.
Ehrenreich, B. and A.R. Hochschild (eds) (2002), *Global Woman: Nannies, Maids, and Sex Workers in the New Economy*, New York: Metropolitan.
Empez Vidal, N. (2007), 'Social construction of neglect: the case of unaccompanied minors from Morocco to Spain', Working Paper 2007-007, Max Planck Institute for Demographic Research, Rostock, Germany, available at: http://www.demogr.mpg.de/.
'Euro zone unemployment reaches 15 million' (2009), Canadian Broadcasting News, 2 July, available at: http://www.cbc.ca/news/business/story/2009/07/02/euro-zone-unemployment-may.html (accessed 14 April 2011).
Farjas i Bonet, A. (2002), 'El process migratori Gambià a Comarques Gironines: El cas de Banyoles, Olot i Salt', unpublished doctoral dissertation, Department de la Pedagogia, Universitat de Girones, Girones, Spain.
Fleischer, A. (2010), 'Making families among Cameroonian "Bush Fallers" in Germany: Marriage, migration, and the law', unpublished doctoral dissertation, Freien Universität, Berlin.
Goody, E. (1982), *Parenting and Social Reproduction: Fostering and Occupational Roles in West Africa*, Cambridge: Cambridge University Press.
Isiugo-Abanihe, U. (1985), 'Child fosterage in West Africa', *Population and Development Review*, **11**, 53–73.
Kabba, A. (2002), 'Daddy, don't be a fool!', *African Abroad!–USA, Gotham Gazette*, 15 April, available at: http://www.gothamgazette.com/citizen/june02/african-aboard.shtml (accessed 21 March 2013).
Kabba, A. (2007), 'Difficulties raising African children in U.S.', *African Abroad!–USA*, Voices that Must Be Heard, New York Media Alliance, 30 March, available at:http://nycma.fcny.org/nycma/voices/266/news/news_1/ (accessed 21 March 2013).
Kabba, A. (2008), 'Problems of raising African boys in America – a clash of culture?', *African Abroad!–USA*, Voices that Must Be Heard, New York Media Alliance, 15 March, available at: http://www.nycma.fcny.org/nycma/voices/314/editorials/editorials_1/ (accessed 21 March 2013).
Kasinitz, K., J.H. Mollenkopf, M.C. Waters and J. Holdaway (2008), *Inheriting the City: The Children of Immigrants Come of Age*, Cambridge, MA: Harvard University Press.
Laslett, P. (ed.) (1977), *Household and Family in Past Times*, Cambridge: Cambridge University Press.
Leinaweaver, J.B. (2008), *The Circulation of Children: Kinship, Adoption, and Morality in Andean Peru*, Durham, NC: Duke University Press.
Levitt, P. and N. Jaworsky (2007), 'Transnational migration studies: past developments and future trends', *Annual Review of Sociology*, **33**, 129–56.

Madhavan, S. and N. Townsend (2007), 'The social context of children's nutritional status in Agincourt', *Scandinavian Journal of Public Health*, **35**, 107–17.

Massey, D.S., M. Mooney, K.C. Torres and C.Z. Charles (2007), 'Black immigrants and Black natives attending selective colleges and universities in the United States', *American Journal of Education*, **113**, 243–73.

Mazzucato, V. (2008), 'Informal insurance arrangements in Ghanaian migrants' transnational networks: the role of reverse remittances and geographic proximity', *World Development*, **37**, 1105–15.

Mazzucato, V. and D. Schans (2008), 'Transnational families, children, and the migration–development nexus', Paper No. 20, presented at the Social Science Research Council Migration and Development Conference, on Migration and Development: Future Directions for Research and Policy, New York, March.

McConnell, T. (2007), 'African cane tames unruly British pupils', The Times Online, London, 4 November, available at: http://www.timesonline.co.uk/tol/news/world/africa/article2800904.ece (accessed 14 April 2011).

McCracken, G. (1983), 'The exchange of children in Tudor England: an anthropological phenomenon in historical context', *Journal of Family History*, **8**, 303–13.

Murphy, W.P. and C.H. Bledsoe (1987), 'Territory and matrilateral kinship in the history of a Kpelle chiefdom', in I. Kopytoff (ed.), *The African Frontier: The Reproduction of Traditional African Societie*, Bloomington, IN: Indiana University Press, pp. 121–47.

Panter-Brick, C. (2001), 'The bodily costs of childbearing: Western science through a West African lens', in H. Schwartzman (ed.), *Children and Anthropology: Perspectives for the Twenty-first Century*, Westport, CT: Bergin & Garvey, pp. 57–81.

Parreñas, R. (2001), *Servants of Globalization: Women, Migration and Domestic Work*, Stanford, CA: Stanford University Press.

Reyes, M. (2008), 'Migration and Filipino children left behind: a literature review', Miriam College/UNICEF, Quezon City, Philippines available at: http://www.unicef.org/philippines/ Synthesis_StudyJuly12008.pdf (accessed 21 March 2013).

Scott, J.L. (2000), 'English language and communication issues for African and Caribbean immigrant youth in Toronto', Coalition of Visible Minority Women (Ontario), available at: from http://ceris.metropolis.net/Virtual%20Library/education/scott1.html (accessed 21 March 2013).

Smith, R.C. (2007), *Mexican New York: Transnational Lives of New Immigrants*, Berkeley, CA: University of California Press.

Sow, P. (2004), 'Practicas comerciales transnacionales y espacios de acción de los Senegaleses en España', in A. Escrivá and N. Ribas-Mateos (eds), *Migración y desarrollo: estudios sobre remesas y otra practicas transnacionales*, Córdoba: CSIC, pp. 235–54.

Sow, P. (2010), 'La "diáspora" comunica, o cómo hacer el codesarrollo mediante el teléfono móvil y el email: Ejemplo de los Senegaleses en Cataluña'; *Migraciones y desarrollo. El codesarrollo: Del discurso a la práctica Anthropos, Editorial del Hombre* (Barcelona), **75**, 151–82.

Sow, P. (forthcoming), 'Management of remittances and family compound by the first spouses: evidence from Gambian and Senegalese women', in J. Oucho, D. Owen and T. Lacroix (eds), *The Role of the African Diaspora in Homeland Development: African Migrant Communities in Africa and Europe*, London: Palgrave Macmillan.

Sow, P. and K. Tete (2007), 'Cajas de ahorro populares africanas en Cataluña: tipos y formas de prácticas financieras sumergidas de los inmigrantes', Grupo de Estudios y de Reflexión sobre Africa, NIF:G63081301, available at: http://www.zef.de/module/register/media/c9aa-AHORR0S%20POPULARIES%20INMIGRANTES%20EN%20EUROPA.pdf (accessed 21 March 2013).

Suarez-Orozco, C., and M. Suarez-Orozco (2001), *The Children of Immigration*. Boston: Harvard University Press.

Swigart, L. (2001), *Extended Lives: The African Immigrant Experience in Philadelphia*, Philadelphia, PA: Balch Institute for Ethnic Studies, Historical Society of Philadelphia, available at: http://www.hsp.org/node/2660 (accessed 14 April 2011).

Thomas, G.C. (1981), 'The social background of childhood nutrition in the Ciskei', *Social Science & Medicine*, **15A**, 551–5.
Tremlett, G. (2006), 'Spain attracts record levels of immigrants seeking jobs and sun', *The Guardian* (London), 26 July, available at: http://www.guardian.co.uk/world/2006/jul/26/spain.gilestremlett (accessed 14 April 2011).
US National Council on Crime and Delinquency in the Justice System (2009), 'Created equal: racial and ethnic disparities in the U.S. criminal justice system', available at: http://nicic.gov/Library/023643 (accessed 21 March 2013).
Whitehouse, B. (2009), 'Transnational childrearing and the preservation of transnational identity in Brazzaville, Congo', *Global Networks*, **9**, 82–99.

9 Transnational return and pendulum migration strategies of Moroccan migrants: intra-household power inequalities, tensions and conflicts of interest*

Hein de Haas and Tineke Fokkema

INTRODUCTION

Since the mid-1960s and following the signing of agreements with northwest European countries to recruit guest workers, Morocco has experienced large-scale emigration of mostly unskilled migrants. Moroccan migration was initially mainly oriented towards France but also increasingly towards Belgium, Germany, the Netherlands and, since the mid-1980s, Italy and Spain. Contrary to expectations and despite the economic recession after the 1973 oil embargo, relatively few Moroccan migrants returned and many ended up settling in their new countries. This process was accompanied by large-scale family reunification. The unfavourable political and economic prospects in Morocco, combined with the discontinuation of the 'return option' to Europe through increasingly restrictive immigration policies, explain why many migrants decided to stay in Europe. So, paradoxically, the freeze on recruitment of new guest workers beginning in the early 1970s stimulated settlement rather than discouraging it (Entzinger, 1985; Fargues, 2004; de Haas, 2007).

While family reunification was largely complete at the end of the 1980s, family formation gained significance as a major source of new migration from Morocco over the 1990s. At least until recently, a large proportion of first-generation Moroccans and their descendants preferred to marry a partner – preferably kin – from the region of origin (Lievens, 1999; Hooghiemstra, 2001; Reniers, 2001; de Valk et al., 2004). In addition, restrictive immigration policies led to increasingly irregular (that is, undocumented) labour migration to the classic destination countries in northwest Europe and to Italy and Spain. The combined effects of family reunification and family formation, natural increase, undocumented migration and new labour migration to Italy and Spain explain why the official number of persons of Moroccan origin living in Europe has increased more than sevenfold: from 300,000 in 1972 to an estimated 2.4 million in 2004. Moroccans now form one of the largest and most dispersed migrant communities in Western Europe (de Haas, 2007).

The first generation of Moroccan migrants is now approaching retirement age. The majority of this generation is currently not working because of early retirement, unemployment or incapacity to work. Close to retirement age, the question of whether to stay or return arises again. While many do not return (Schellingerhout and de Klerk, 2007), some migrants return to Morocco after the end of their active working life. More striking is the increasing proportion of migrants who adopt pendulum migratory strategies, spending several months a year in Morocco while maintaining official residence in Europe – a practice that can be classified as neither permanent settlement in Europe nor return to Morocco. This raises a question of broader theoretical interest: how can we explain such patterns of residential mobility and the decision making processes underpinning them? By analysing the migration behaviour and transnational residential strategies of first-generation ageing migrants in a particular Moroccan sending region, this study focuses on the role of intra-household power inequalities, tensions and conflicts of interest in migration decision making. In addition, we explore the consequences that such migratory strategies may have for intra-household power relations.

This chapter contributes to a conceptual critique of migration theories that identify the household as the most relevant decision making unit. Such theories typically conceptualize migration as the outcome of collective household decisions based on consensus and mutual benefit. Focusing on a particular Moroccan setting, we argue that by disregarding intra-household conflicts of interest along the lines of gender, generation and age, conventional household approaches cannot explain many of the patterns of return and pendulum migration.

THEORETICAL BACKGROUND: INTRODUCING CONFLICT INTO HOUSEHOLD MODELS

Consensus seems to be increasing in literature that migration is a part of livelihood strategies pursued by *households* to spread income risks and, if possible, to generate income and remittances that can be used to improve living standards or to invest in housing, education or commercial enterprises. This particularly applies to developing countries, where credit and insurance markets often fail and many people are poor (Stark, 1991; de Haan, 1999; Taylor, 1999; de Haas, 2010). This perspective, which has been particularly explored within the 'new economics of labour migration' (Stark, 1978; Stark and Bloom, 1985), represented an advance over theories that conceptualized migration as the result of a cost–benefit calculation of income-maximizing *individuals* operating in perfect markets (Todaro, 1969, Harris and Todaro, 1970).

The conceptualization of migration as part of a family or household strategy creates analytical room to move beyond the income-maximizing paradigm and include motives such as risk avoidance and risk sharing. In addition, such perspectives allow migration to be seen as an investment in which household members pool resources to facilitate the migration of one member and shed light on the reasons why migrants send remittances, beyond pure altruism. Conceptualizing individual migration as part of broader household strategies to improve well-being, increase income and raise investment capital also compels us to reinterpret return migration. Return migration has been commonly viewed as a failure of migration strategies or, at best, as a stage following retirement. However, if the main motive for migrating is to improve the situation at home, migrants will return once they have succeeded in amassing, saving or remitting enough financial and human capital to realize their investment plans. Failure to achieve this goal due to low income, unemployment or high costs will prolong the stay in the receiving country. This means that return migration can, under certain circumstances, also be associated with *successful* migration and integration strategies (see, for example, Constant and Massey, 2002).

Notwithstanding their more realistic character, the inherent flaw of household-centred migration theories is that they tend to 'reify' the household, that is, to construct it as an entity, with clear plans, strategies and aims, one that makes unanimous decisions, based on equality of power and commonality of interests among household members, to the benefit of all. This characterization is likely to mask significant intra-household inequalities along gender and generational lines. Particularly in patriarchal societies, of which Morocco is one, women lack an equal stake in migration decision making, while children are almost inevitably in a weaker position *vis-à-vis* their parents. Hence, it is likely that women and children have generally less agency with regard to migratory behaviour. This pertains not only to migration by fathers and male spouses but also to women's and children's own migration: they can either be put under considerable pressure to migrate (alone or in the context of family migration) or be excluded from access to mobility against their will. What is often presented as *the* household strategy can alternatively be seen as the outcome of a struggle for domination between male and female, old and young, powerful and powerless (Rodenburg, 1997). There are also instances in which decisions on migration are taken entirely individually, without consulting and sometimes even without informing other household members. Moreover, when migration decisions reflect intra-household power inequalities, this makes it likely that powerful household members benefit most from migration-generated resources such as remittances and educational opportunities for themselves and, particularly, their children. Migration can under certain circumstances reinforce and reproduce gender inequalities (Day and Içduygu, 1997; King and Vullnetari, 2006; de Haas and van Rooij, 2010).

It would be erroneous, however, to depict women and children as passive victims. Although generally not as powerful as men, women and children (especially adolescents) do exert a certain influence on household decisions. General processes of women's emancipation explain why an increasing share of 'independent' labour migrants are women, even from predominantly patriarchal societies such as Mexico or Morocco (Chant and Radcliffe, 1992; Fadloullah et al., 2000; Salih, 2001; Jureidini and Moukarbel, 2004). Moreover, women's migration is likely to increase their negotiating power by improving their access to employment, education, residency and citizenship rights abroad.

Such acquisition of social, human and material resources may shift the intra-household balance of power and generate substantial intra-household conflict pertaining to (return) migration decision making. This exemplifies how an analysis through the perspective of intra-household power relations can contribute to a better understanding of the intrinsic links between gender, migration and broader development issues. While intra-household gender inequalities will affect access to mobility and the development benefits (such as remittances) of migration, the migration process itself can, in its own turn, affect gendered power relations as well as the allocation of migration-related resources within households. In other words, gendered intra-household inequalities are both affected by and affect migration processes and, hence, influence the distribution of remittances and other benefits derived from migration.

DATA AND METHODS

This study explores the causes and motives for return and pendulum migration by focusing on the Todgha valley, a region of emigration located in the province of Ouarzazate in southern Morocco. Data were collected through quantitative, qualitative and participatory fieldwork conducted by the authors on several occasions between 1998 and 2008. Following an initial participatory appraisal, survey data were collected by the first author between September 1998 and June 2000 among 507 households containing 3,801 individuals, including 237 international (150 current and 87 returned) migrants, in conjunction with continuous participant observation (see de Haas, 2006). The household survey was conducted in six villages located across the Todgha valley. The respondents were selected on the basis of a spatially clustered sample, such that the survey covered the different migratory, ethnic, agricultural and geographical settings in the valley.

The questionnaire contained pre-coded and some open-ended questions on demographic household composition, individual migration histories, educational levels, activity status as well as household-level questions on land and livestock ownership, remittances and non-remittance income, expenditures and investments. Because of the importance of trust, the survey was largely conducted by research assistants from the same ethnic groups as the respondents. We determined that, in this context, the advantages of using 'insiders' outweighed the potential disadvantages of such an approach. Given local ethnic rivalries, the quality of responses would probably have suffered from appointing 'outsider' assistants from other ethnic groups. Interviewers were trained and supervised in the field by the first author and the questionnaire was tested and revised numerous times. Most interviews did not last longer than one hour in order to minimize respondent fatigue. Some questions that proved to be too sensitive or difficult to answer had to be omitted. Surveys were conducted with self-declared household heads, overwhelmingly men. The non-response rate was 5 per cent.

In 1999 open interviews were conducted with 20 migrants aged 30–65 years who were on return visits during the summer holidays. Additional qualitative data were collected through 27 open interviews (25 men, two women) among prospective and return migrants in 2003. These interviews were conducted in French and Moroccan colloquial Arabic by the first author, regularly aided by assistants if translation was needed. Chance meetings during participant observation (1998–2000) and snowball sampling (for other interview rounds) were used to identify respondents for the open interviews. The goal of the open interviews was to gain further insight into the respondents' migration histories, their motives for migrating, their experiences and future plans concerning migration. It offered the opportunity to develop a more complete understanding of why migrants make certain migration decisions.

Because almost all interviews were conducted with men and because we sought insight into the gendered impacts of migration, in 1999 semi-structured interviews took place with 12 women (aged 26–50) married to international migrants and 20 women (aged 22–60) married to non-migrants in one village (van Rooij, 2000). Respondents were approached informally through local contacts. Because most women did not speak French, these interviews were conducted with the help of a local female interpreter. During three months of fieldwork the female interviewer stayed with a guest family in the village. All interviews were conducted in the women's homes in the absence of men. The interviews focused on women's daily lives, tasks and responsibilities, their involvement in migration decision making and how their lives had changed after the migration (and/or return) of the husband.

In 2007 and 2008, semi-structured interviews were guided by the second author with 25 male return migrants (aged 54–73) and 26 sons of return migrants (aged 20–31).[1] The participants were recruited using the snowball method and through personal contacts of the interviewer. To ensure the quality of data, they were interviewed by a male local community member in their Berber language (Tamazight), with regular debriefings with the second author. The questionnaire was circulated among several local community members in advance before drafting a final version. All interviews were recorded and, after translation into English, transcribed verbatim. These interviews covered a range of topics related to three stages of migrants'/fathers' migration history – the situation before emigration, settlement in Europe and linkages with home country and the situation after return – with a particular emphasis on experiences, attitudes and perceptions related to intra-household tensions and conflicts of interest.

Although both quantitative and qualitative data informed the analysis for this study, most findings are based on the semi-structured interviews. These interviews were primarily designed to obtain detailed information on migration decision making; the household survey provided the contextual setting of general patterns and trends of migration from this region. The interviews did not aim to achieve statistical representativity but rather to explore the range of different experiences and motivations among different types of migrants. The use of qualitative methods is particularly appropriate in addressing and exploring issues that are not easily quantifiable: in our case the motives and decision-making processes underlying return and pendulum migration strategies.

RESULTS

The Todgha valley is an oasis with an official population of some 68,500 inhabitants in 2004 (of whom 36,400 are classified as urban). The population has participated intensively in labour migration since the mid-1960s, primarily to France, Morocco's former colonizer. Significant secondary destinations are Belgium and the Netherlands. Following general Moroccan patterns, migration to Europe has been perpetuated since the recruitment freeze in 1973 through family reunification and new marriages between migrants' offspring and non-migrants. After family reunification was largely completed in the 1980s, family formation through new marriages with children of the first generation of migrants has become virtually the only way to enter northwest European countries legally. Our survey data show that, while most labour migrants left Morocco in the 1960s and 1970s, both new labour migration (to Italy and Spain) and return migration (from northwest Europe) have increased markedly since 1990.

General Migration Characteristics of the Todgha Valley

Migration has become a widespread occurrence in the Todgha valley. Of the surveyed active male population (aged 15–65 years) 15 per cent have been or are involved in international migration. Only 35 per cent of all households have no migration history. In total, some 40 per cent of all surveyed households are involved in international migration and/or receive international remittances.

Whereas most international migrants from the Todgha valley still living in northwest Europe have eventually reunified their families at the destination, most migrants who left their family in Morocco have eventually returned. Returnees account for 4 per cent of the total active male population, while current international migrants represent 11 per cent of all active males. Our data indicate that over 70 per cent of the surveyed international migrants who returned to the Todgha valley stayed more than seven years abroad before their return, and the average stay abroad was 18 years.

The average age of the surveyed international return migrants to the Todgha valley is 48 years at the time of their return. However, if we take the mode as the measure of central tendency, 60–64 years is the most typical age of return. Two-thirds of the returnees returned in the 1990s. This corresponds to the ageing of the first-generation migrants who left for Europe during the late 1960s and early 1970s. Twenty-four per cent of current international migrants stayed in Morocco for three months or longer in the year prior to interview.

The lengthy average stay in Morocco can largely be explained by the extended period spent each year in Morocco by elderly international migrants who officially reside abroad but no longer work. Whereas among migrants aged 15–29 years only 7 per cent spent at least three months per year in Morocco, this proportion increases with age, amounting to

20 per cent among those aged 30–44 years and 33 per cent among those aged 45–59. Among migrants over age 60, 56 per cent spent at least three months per year in Morocco and 22 per cent (almost exclusively male) at least six months per year.

The tendency for unemployed, retired and (partially) incapacitated migrants to stay in Morocco for extended periods becomes even clearer if we examine those households participating in international migration in which all household members were declared to be living in Europe. In 12 per cent of those 'empty' households one of the, usually older, 'commuting' household members was in fact present at the time of the survey. While many migrants who maintain official residence in Europe stay in Morocco for extended periods, 55 per cent of all self-declared return migrants have travelled to Europe at least once since their return to Morocco.

Drawing on interview data, the following subsection explores the motivations and decision-making process underlying migration from and return migration to the Todgha valley. Our central research aim is to explore the role of intra-household power conflicts and inequalities in migration decision making. To gain insight into these dynamics, relevant dimensions and stages of the life course of the returnees and pendulum migrants are reviewed, starting with migration to Europe.

Motivations and Decision Making Underlying Migration to Europe

Largely consistent with the new economics of labour migration, migration from the Todgha valley to Europe has been a significant part of livelihood strategies pursued by households. Although most of the migrants did work before migration, mainly in agriculture, their emigration was essentially prompted by economic motivations: improving the living standard of the household, especially for those barely surviving financially, was the main driving factor. For example, one of the interviewees said:

> Why I did leave? Do you think that life here was comfortable? If there was no sea between Morocco and Europe, the cows would not stay either. It was the misery that pushed us to Europe, like birds leaving their children in the bird's nest in search for food. It was difficult to go to Europe and leave the family behind but we had no choice, we had no money, I had to support the family. Before leaving, I was working for seven dirham[2] per day. Do you think I could have built this house if I stayed here?

Emigration of one or more household members to Europe functioned as income insurance for households. While Europe faced a relative labour shortage, there was a high likelihood of finding a relatively well-paid job (compared to Moroccan standards). As one interviewee stated:

At that time [mid-1960s to early 1970s], it was easy to go to Europe and find a job, not like now. Europe needed workers to build Europe, we were the tools. There were a lot of jobs on the one hand and few workers on the other. Bosses were competing for workmen. You could find four jobs in one day. You were working for one [employer] until another one was offering a higher salary.

In general, the household migration strategy coincided with the personal interest of the migrants. Influenced by the positive experiences of those who had already migrated, other Moroccans were generally eager to emigrate. Those who did not emigrate by themselves were happy to be selected by labour recruiters, although the recruitment process was sometimes humiliating:

They were coming here to look for those who could do the heavy jobs. I was lucky that I was selected by Mogha [a renowned French recruiter]. He came here to select those who could work in the French mines. All the men had to undress and he was looking at them. He put a stamp on the ones he thought could work hard. You had to be at least 170 cm tall. We were with 22 from my village, he selected only four and I was among them. We were like sheep. He refused the rest of our friends because some of them were too short, others were not strong enough to work in the mines.

With an abundant supply of jobs, those entering the destination country without a job contract easily found work. However, the living conditions migrants found on their arrival were generally less favourable than expected and the working conditions were difficult and sometimes dangerous. Most worked in mines, car factories, hotels/restaurants or the construction industry. They frequently worked double shifts to earn as much money as possible. In the early years migrants often stayed in overcrowded boarding houses.

Decision Making Related to Family Reunification

Before leaving Morocco, almost all interviewees lived in extended family households. A sizeable proportion was already married and some had children; none of the interviewees, however, initially migrated together with their family. The initial plan was to go abroad to work for some years and return with the savings. Because of the persistent adverse economic and political situation in Morocco and the increasing difficulty re-entering European countries as immigration policies grew more restrictive, many decided to prolong their stay. Eventually many stayed two or more decades.

Consequently, their emigration was followed in many cases by family reunification in the country of immigration. A sharp contrast emerges between those still living in Europe and the eventual returnees. Migrants who decided not to reunify their families in Europe often cited fears that their wives and offspring would become 'Westernized' and lose their religious faith. As one migrant put it:

> I did not want to do so because it is not an easy place to raise your children. You are in their country so you have to respect their rules. The system there is teaching children to be Europeans. If they are young and not thinking about Morocco and their religion, that's not good. There is a lot of freedom which is normal for Europeans but difficult for Moroccans. Moroccans always understand freedom in a wrong way, they turn everything upside down. I am not generalizing the case because there are some young people who succeed. There are engineers, doctors, but the percentage is not that high. I saw so many cases of problems between parents and children and one of them was going to prison. I wanted to raise my children in my own way. That's why I did not bring them to France.

Having experienced the problematic economic position of migrants and mounting racism in Europe over the recession-prone 1980s, many returnees also argued that it would be better not to expose their children to potentially humiliating circumstances.[3] Instead of bringing them to Europe, they reasoned that it would be better to invest in the higher education of their sons in Morocco, which often leads to a secure and comfortable life as a civil servant. As one of the respondents stated:

> I thought that it is better for them to be in Morocco. In Europe there are no rules and we will never really be accepted. I thought I will let them finish school in Morocco and send them to university. Here in Morocco everything is cheaper and you are with your people. If you get a good job as a civil servant in Morocco, you have a lot of money and nothing to worry about. So I thought it is better if they stay in Morocco.

The above-mentioned motives might suggest that the decision not to reunify their families was exclusively taken in the supposed interest of the household. However, these socially acceptable responses sometimes conceal other motives. Failure to fulfil the financial (that is, sufficient income) and legal (that is, status as a permanent resident) conditions for family reunification are important reasons that migrants were reluctant to admit. Other, more personal motives opposing family reunification are marital conflict, estrangement and fear of losing freedom of movement and control. As two migrants stated:

> If you try to control their lives, it is not easy because you are not in Morocco. At school they teach them that they are free to do whatever they want, to come home with whom they want, so you can't control their life anymore. The European system is always trying to drive a wedge between you and your children if there

is something wrong. I know, for example, that if my son would do something wrong and I would beat him, they would arrest me because it is not Morocco.

No, it was not difficult to leave my wife behind because I have experienced what women are doing there. They have too much freedom. If you want to control her, she will go to the police.

Although most interviewed women stated that they agreed with their husbands' decision to migrate, several women also indicated that they had 'no choice other than to agree', which reflects the domination of men in household decision making regarding migration to Europe.[4] On the one hand, thanks to remittances, women left behind tend to live in much better material circumstances than their neighbours. On the other, they experience the separation as very difficult. Besides the perceived burden of carrying double (male and female) responsibilities and the social and psychological stress that this might involve, conflicts between migrants' wives and their in-laws over the use of remittances were frequent, especially for those women living in extended families. The wives and children missed their husbands and fathers. One of the children we interviewed expressed his feelings as follows:

We were satisfied with his financial support, we were living comfortably compared to non-migrant families but the father role was missing in our family for so many years so we suffered as well. I missed him because I need my father as I need my mother. He was coming once per year, in the summer, for one and a half months. For us, as children, it was not enough. When you started to know and get used to him he left for France again. That was hard because most of us were born when he was abroad. Everyone was crying when he left because you knew that he would go for a long period.

The large majority of women wished to join their husband in Europe, pressuring, often successfully, for family reunification. The children interviewed invariably expressed the wish to be reunited with their father in Europe. However, they did not have any voice in the family reunification decision:

My father was 100% against the idea to bring his family to France. He was always speaking about Europe in a negative way. He told us: 'If I am taking you there, you will behave in a bad way, it is so easy to be spoiled. I don't want to be guilty because if you are doing something wrong, I'm responsible'. When we were young we could not be against our father. You know, our tradition, culture is that you have to respect someone who is older. When we became teenagers and wanted to discuss with him, he always escaped. He did not like when we started to talk about this subject.

Most of the interviewed migrants who did not return in the 1970s and 1980s ended up reunifying their families. Some return migrants applied a strategy that has been referred to as 'relay migration' (see Arizpe, 1981). In this case of partial family reunification, the migrant did not reunify his entire household at the destination but allowed only one or two unmarried sons to come to Europe before they reached the age of legal adulthood.[5] These sons then take over their father's role as the migrant breadwinner after his active working life ends or he returns home. Sometimes families can be torn apart through 'now or never migration'. One young man we interviewed, 20 years old, was left alone in Morocco:

> My father worked in Nice since 1969. He never wanted to take his family to France. He was afraid that we would become Nsara [Christians] until he suddenly changed his mind when he realized there was no future in Morocco for us. But I was already too old. My mother, brothers and sisters left me here alone. I do not know what to do. I see no solution.

The young man now lives alone in the family's large house. He put all his hopes on obtaining a scholarship to a French university, which would allow him to join his family.

The Role of Migration in Improving Livelihoods and Investment

From an economic point of view, the migration of one household member to Europe was generally a wise decision. Remittances have come to play an important role in the region's economy. The average income of remittance-receiving households is more than double that of other households and international remittances account for about one-third of the income of all surveyed households. While remittances have increased income inequality, migrants' expenditures on housing and other investments have stimulated the diversifying and urbanizing regional economy of the Todgha valley (see de Haas, 2006).

Most of the migrants interviewed provided substantial support to family members left behind. They sent money on a regular basis, which confirms the notion that migration is part of an implicit social contract and co-insurance strategy of households. The additional income was used for daily necessities, to construct a house, to finance children's education or, sometimes, to set up a small business. In addition, most of the migrants brought home goods (including clothes, electronics, food items and toys) during their yearly visit. Most households have been able to dramatically improve their income and standard of living as a result of remittances and investments.

The interviewed children of returnees considered the supportive role their fathers fulfilled as obvious: after all, the purpose of emigration was to improve the living standards of the household. At a young age, they noticed their privileged position compared to non-migrant households:

> When he was coming in the summer, most of the neighbours visited our house. Besides presents for the neighbours, like tea and coffee, he brought clothes, things for the house, radio, television and toys. We were one of the first families in our town that had bicycles. All my brothers, everyone got his own bicycle.

The lasting and unyielding support was also seen as obvious by the migrants themselves. Nevertheless, some of them regretted that their focus was limited to their country of birth. In this respect, one of the interviewees said:

> At that time there was competition between us. We were not wasting money. We were always buying things second-hand and eating in cheap places, just to be able to build a house in Morocco. We saved money and we lost it in Morocco. In those days, houses were not expensive in France. I could buy five houses for letting out. But we were always thinking about Morocco, we built houses here and they are now useless.

After their return, only a few migrants realized the investment projects they initially contemplated. Besides a lack of money, experience and interest, administrative and institutional constraints were the main reasons for not pursuing such projects.

Motivations and Experiences of Return Migrants

Almost all returnees declared that they came back to Morocco on their own initiative, that their return has been relatively unproblematic and that they do not regret their decision, at least not for themselves. As we noted before, supporting the family was the main driving factor behind migrants' departure to Europe and most of them did not reunify their families. Hence, after their working life ended, there was no reason for those who did not reunify their family to stay in Europe. They had longed to return to Morocco and expressed happiness at being home to enjoy their retirement and be reunited with their family. Almost none of them wishes to settle in Europe again. One of the interviewees described the return decision as follows:

> Why did I return? I am old, I can't work anymore. Do you want me to die there? I went to France to work and I had always in mind to return. Morocco is my country, my land and my home. I'm now old and retired and all I want is to relax. Living in Europe means living in nostalgia, it's hard to live far from the family. I am happy to be home, to live with my family.

In order to explain the returnees' statements about the unproblematic character of their return, it is important to stress that the sample is biased towards those migrants who maintained strong links with Morocco and who returned voluntarily.[6] The fact that the large majority of them did not reunify their families in Europe obviously facilitated the return process. However, the statements by male returnees might reflect a degree of self-justification and might also conceal the lack of agency of their spouses and/or children in the return migration decision and, in the case of those returning as a family, the sometimes less voluntary nature of the return of the other family members.

Relatively few returnees expressed concern about their future financial situation. Their state pension or social (for example, disability) benefits, sometimes supplemented by earnings from one or more investments, are generally sufficient to live comfortably in rural Morocco, where costs of living are much lower than in Europe. As two interviewees stated:

> I worked many years and now I am retired, *hamdulillah*. It was a good experience although we had hard times. You have to sacrifice if you want to live in good conditions. When I was in Europe, I built some houses here and now I have sufficient money for the rest of my life and my family.

> I'm retired and happy to be home. With the amount of money I now receive, it is difficult to live in Europe. Everything is expensive, you cannot buy anything for one Euro, you have to pay a lot just for the house. In Morocco daily life is cheap, I can live here like a king.

Although the returnees generally experienced a fairly smooth re-adaptation, this does not mean that their return was simply a matter of 'going home'. As other studies on return migration have shown, feelings of belonging needed to be renegotiated upon return, both at the community and family levels (Albers, 2005; de Bree et al., 2010). Migrants' decades-long stay in Europe nurtured social norms and expectations that often led to some disappointment upon their return. Some returnees complained about lack of trust, the sharp socioeconomic inequalities, the poor work ethic and what they perceived as the selfish, materialistic mentality of Moroccans in general and public authorities in particular, as the following statements exemplify:

> If you want to succeed in life, you need to be patient with people. I learned how to be honest with people but it is not working here in Morocco. If you want to practice what you learned there, you will be the enemy of the people here. So you have to swim with the current, not against the current.

> The main problem I have is with the administration. What I was used to in Europe is totally different than what I see here. In Europe you can fix your papers just in one day, they serve you in a nice way and people are treated equally. If you are standing in a queue, the first one is the first one, no matter if you are an immigrant or native. The opposite holds in Morocco, there are

no rights, rich people are dominating, that's what I don't like here. If you want to have just one document, it takes many days. They don't appreciate human beings. Here in Morocco, keep your dog hungry and he will follow you, this is the policy of Morocco.

The negative experiences of the interviewed returnees with the Moroccan public authorities in particular have to be put in perspective, as such feelings are obviously not exclusive to returnees. Moreover, exposure to European media and public discourse is likely to have influenced migrants' attitudes towards Moroccan lifestyle and bureaucracy. Also, migrants might attempt to present themselves as more modern and superior by dissociating themselves from Moroccan authorities and society. Furthermore, returnees were explicitly asked about the main problems they faced after their return and the main differences between Europe and Morocco.

At the family level, returnees sometimes experience difficulties regaining a position in the family. The mother–child relationship evolved during the father's long absence. For some sons the father's absence entailed more rights and greater freedom of movement. Unpleasant moments and irritations occur when the father wants to regain the pivotal role in the family. As one of the interviewed children stated:

> We are not free anymore to act as we did with our mother. He is thinking in another way, he executes his orders and he is like a dictator in his arguments. He thinks he is the only one who knows more about the family. In reality, he doesn't know us well but we have to respect him because he has the financial power. He also doesn't like that he gets less attention than my mum. For example, sometimes we have fun with our mum in the kitchen and he is sitting alone in the living room. Then, when we sit together for the dinner, he becomes angry, leaves the room to sleep because there is no conversation with him like we have with our mum.

Although most of the interviewed children were happy their father had finally come home, this decision has frequently not been to their own benefit. The most common conflicts seem to revolve around the father's previous decision not to bring his family to Europe. As we argued above, many fathers had thought it would be preferable to offer their children a better, often higher education, with the expectation of greater employment prospects in Morocco. However, this strategy often failed because it has become increasingly difficult for Moroccan university graduates (*licenciés*) to find a job as a consequence of budget cuts in the public sector, the general economic recession, misguided educational policies, the mediocre quality of higher education and the rise in the number of young people holding higher degrees. Unemployment rates among more highly educated people in households of international migrants range from 18 to 25 per cent.

Many jobless university graduates returned from the cities where they studied to the Todgha valley to live with their family. This is generally perceived as an extremely frustrating if not humiliating experience. The graduates find it dishonourable to remain dependent on their parents and to be unable to marry. Boredom and bitterness often characterize their existence. The unemployed sons (and sometimes daughters) of return migrants tend to resent their father for not allowing them to join them in Europe and are often obsessed by the wish to migrate themselves, as these two comments indicate:

> What is hurting me, and I still remember, is that one time my father came with his boss to Morocco and the boss said: 'I will arrange everything so that you can bring your family to France' but my father refused. He was always giving the same reasons: 'There is nothing to do in Europe, it is hard to live there, difficult to find a good job, I don't want to see you suffer as I did. It is better to stay here, to focus on education, I am sure you will get a good job here in Morocco'. It was easy to convince us when we were still young. But those reasons are now making me upset because I'm looking to my generation that is living in Europe. They have a well-paid job, especially those with a diploma, not like here. I regret all the years I spent here without any result, always quarrels at home. I also want to have a good life and safe future. Life here is dead, nothing to do. Spain or France, it doesn't matter, I just want to be out of Morocco.

> My father told us about the hard time they were having in Europe, how they sacrificed in order to give their family a better life. At that time, we thought that he knew what's the best for us. But as you can see, there is nothing to do here, no jobs, low salary. As a child I was proud of my father. Now I realize that he was making a big mistake not to bring us to Europe. We are like cat and mouse, every time arguing and trying to avoid him. The quarrels and discussions about this subject will always be there.

Confronted with the frustrated ambitions of their children, who find themselves in a situation of 'involuntary immobility' (Carling, 2002), some returnees regret their decision not to reunify their families in Europe:

> To be honest, I regret I did not take my family to Europe, we did not know that life would change in such a fast way. If I did so, my sons could have a good job and be out of the misery. Now they have a diploma and they are doing nothing. Those who brought their children enjoy four or five salaries. If you have a job and respect their law, life in Europe is much better than here.

The majority, however, stick to the opinion that their decision to leave the family behind was the right one. In justification, they cite problems faced by reunited migrant households in Europe, the increased discrimination in the labour market, racism (particularly towards Muslims), the current less favourable employment opportunities in Europe and the sharp contrast between expectations young people have of Europe and migrants' own experiences:

> The problem of young people is that they think Europe is paradise. They are only dreaming and looking to nice cars and they think that immigrants have a lot of money, but they don't realize that it takes a long time and hard work. When you see that someone is having something, a car or a house, you should ask yourself how he managed to get those things. I was patient and working hard. Those two characteristics make one's future, also here, no matter whether or not you went to school. If you want to go from the first floor to the second floor, you have to use stairs. But the problem is that they are not listening to us.

Some of the interviewed returnees held a pessimistic view of the chances of success in Europe among Moroccan jobless youth but also complained about young people's refusal to work in Morocco:

> How can they be successful in Europe if they are not working here? Over there it's hard, you have to wake up early in the morning, you have to be on time but they are sleeping here till ten, having breakfast and going to the [town] centre. During lunch time they are coming back home to eat, take a nap and then they are going out again till they want to eat couscous. If you work here, you will work there as well. But if you are a loser here, you will be a loser there, I saw so many cases.

Despite these assessments by their fathers, a large proportion of adult children want to emigrate. They believe that it is now their turn to experience life in Europe. If they cannot go to Europe through a job contract or marriage, they frequently try to emigrate illegally, sometimes with financial help from the family. Many young men (and, increasingly, women) who now emigrate to Italy and Spain, often irregularly, are children of relatively well-off, elderly return migrants who decided not to reunify their families.

Patterns and Rationale of Emerging Pendulum Migration

In contrast to migrants who did not reunify their families, migrants who did so typically do not return to Morocco towards the end of their working years. The main reason is the reluctance of migrants' spouses and, in particular, children to return. This observation indicates that migration to Europe (in the case of women) and the transition from youth to maturity (in the case of children) have strengthened women's and children's position within the family and, hence, their negotiating power with regard to subsequent moves – including the decision not to return. Women often do not want to return owing to fear of restriction in their freedom of movement and their wish to live close to their children and grandchildren in Europe. Migrants' children generally oppose the idea of returning because they anticipate only limited prospects and problems of integration in Morocco. While mothers and children often form a 'non-return' coalition, most migrants themselves also realize that return of their children is not viable in view of the superior educational and job opportunities in Europe.

Instead of definitively going back to Morocco, a substantial and apparently growing group of elderly 'non-permanent returnees' have developed multi-local residential strategies, in which they spend several months per year in Morocco, while retaining legal residence in Europe. The restrictive European immigration policies imply that migrants have little incentive to give up their residency rights. Maintaining residency in Europe is often also required to maintain access to various social benefits. In practice, obtaining dual citizenship is perceived as the surest way to secure residency and other rights. The majority of these pendulum migrants are men, who typically leave their spouse and children behind in Europe for shorter or longer trips back to Morocco. However, ageing migrant women with adult children seem to increasingly join their spouse for extended 'holiday' stays in Morocco, which might last several months.

While social ties, nostalgia and perceived health benefits (such as the warmer climate in the case of rheumatism, which is often cited by migrants) play an important role in migrants' long stays in Morocco, some of these 'transnational commuters' are active in trade in which they bring consumer goods or cars from Europe and take back from the Todgha local products such as olive oil. Other migrants give people paid rides back to Europe or sometimes smuggle new migrants across the Gibraltar Strait in their vans. It is worth noting that pendulum migration is not confined to migrants who reunified their family in Europe. Some ageing migrants who did not reunify their family and have not returned commute between the destination country and their family left behind in Morocco. Moreover, a substantial proportion of the elderly returnees go back to Europe on a regular basis, to visit family and friends or to do business but also to satisfy a legal requirement to maintain residency and social security rights in Europe.

CONCLUSION

This study has explored the role of intra-household power inequalities and conflicts in migration decision making as well as the effects of migration decisions on inequalities. Insight was gained through a qualitative case study among first-generation ageing Moroccan migrants born in the Todgha valley. While drawing on a variety of empirical sources as well, the methodology of this study contains some shortcomings. This particularly pertains to the potentially biased sample of return migrants in Morocco. Because interviews were conducted in Morocco, the sample is biased towards those migrants who returned and misses most migrants who permanently settled in Europe and return only occasionally. Assuming that the nature of migration decision making is linked to the return rate, this study cannot identify all aspects of migration decision making. Ideally, future research should aim at interviewing matched samples of migrants in both the origin and destination countries.

Despite the limited scope of this study, our findings clearly highlight some weaknesses and contradictions in the existing migration literature and suggest challenges for future research. The evidence presented here seems to support the general hypothesis of the new economics of labour migration that migration from developing to developed countries is often part of broader livelihood strategies pursued by households that tend to benefit collectively from migration through significant improvements in standards of living. From a non-material point of view, however, emigration appears to be less beneficial to some or all household members: while the family members left behind miss their husbands and fathers, the migrants often lead a solitary existence. Moreover, although all household members reap some material benefits from migration, this does not mean that these benefits are equally distributed within households or that labour migration and possible subsequent moves by other household members are the outcome of consensus among all household members. On the contrary, migration decisions often seem to reflect intra-household inequalities along lines of gender and generation.

Some migrants who left in the 1960s and 1970s believed that they would do better to invest in Morocco and in their children's education there. For this reason, along with fear that their wives and offspring would become Westernized and lose their religious faith by living in Europe, they did not reunify their family. The majority of these migrants also decided unilaterally to return home towards the end of their working life. However, their unilateral decision to return also blocked legal entry into Europe for younger family members, an outcome that has generated considerable intergenerational tensions within families. Because of large-scale unemployment and the lack of prospects in Morocco, the unemployed sons (and sometimes daughters) tend to resent their fathers for not bringing them to Europe.

The majority of labour migrants, however, *did* bring their families to Europe. Although they had always cherished the wish to return after retirement, most of them do not return permanently, not least because their children (who were mostly raised and educated in Europe) and spouses (who generally enjoy more legal rights and social freedoms abroad) generally oppose the idea of returning. The limited social and economic opportunities in Morocco and the integration of migrants' children in European societies may explain why the expectation of returning as a family has vanished for most migrants who reunified their households in Europe.

Instead of a definite return, a growing number of ageing Moroccan migrants developed specific forms of pendulum migratory behaviour. While officially residing abroad and often living on social security benefits and pensions, they return to live in Morocco for several months per year. Pendulum migration by elderly Moroccan migrants can be interpreted as a strategy to reconcile the reluctance of children and spouses living in Europe to return to Morocco and the interest migrants have in maintaining social and economic ties with Morocco while maintaining a firm legal, social and economic foothold in Europe to avoid falling back into poverty. This emerging form of transnational mobility defies conventional migration categories since these migrants can be classified neither as permanent settlers nor as returnees and are usually ignored by official migration statistics. Because of these mobility patterns of transnational commuting, classic distinctions between permanent and return migration are becoming increasingly blurred.

In fact, a striking reversal of residential strategies has evolved over time. Whereas in the 1960s and 1970s a sizeable proportion of male guest workers left their families behind in Morocco and visited them during their summer holidays, we now witness the re-emergence of transnational, multi-local households after a phase of reunification in Europe, in which elderly migrant workers leave their spouses and children behind in Europe for part of the year. In both cases, it is the migrant's spouse who maintains the domestic and kin-keeping role. There is one major difference, however. While women and children have an inferior position *vis-à-vis* their spouses and fathers as well as in the decision concerning their own migration to Europe through family reunification, they do exert substantial influence on the decision to stay in Europe, balanced by visits to Morocco for shorter or longer trips instead of returning permanently.

The results of this study are relevant to migration research and theory. First, they suggest that more attention has to be paid to the non-material consequences of migration. While this study provides support for the hypothesis that migration is part of livelihood-improvement strategies pursued by households, it has also shown that migration decision making is typically not egalitarian. In particular, unilateral decisions by migrants not to reunify families can have negative consequences and can be the source of conflicts and tensions. On the other hand, family reunification can empower women and children who generally oppose return and it seems to have pushed many men into strategies of pendulum migration. Without rejecting the household as a unit of research, our findings point to the need to also take into account intra-household power inequalities, tensions and conflicts of interest related to migration behaviour.

The exploratory findings presented in this chapter also lead to new research questions. For instance, are our findings exclusively applicable to guest worker migration or to other types as well? While migration to Europe was part of broader household strategies, which family members dominate which type of migration decisions? Which types of migration are most associated with intra-family conflicts? And will pendulum migration be a sustainable alternative to either permanent settlement or return or is it a temporary phenomenon that will persist only as long as income and health allow migrants to carry it out?

NOTES

* A slightly different version of this chapter was published in 2010 in *Population and Development Review*, **36** (3), 541–61, under the title 'Intra-household conflicts in migration decision-making: return and pendulum migration in Morocco'.
1. The recruitment of respondents and translation of the interviews were done by Jamal Ouahi, a local graduate student who is fluent in English. We are very grateful for his generous efforts.
2. In 2008, one Moroccan dirham was equal to about €0.10.
3. However, there is likely to be a selection bias because migrants who have not reunified their households also tend to have more negative experiences living and working in Europe.
4. The dominance of men in household decision making does not automatically imply full consensus among male adult members. Power inequalities, conflicts and competition might exist both between generations and between siblings. However, these topics were beyond the scope of this study.
5. Adult children generally do not have the right to migrate to European countries on the legal basis of family reunification.
6. This contrasts with the situation of migrants who returned as a consequence of failing to find work or with the experiences of women and children, who often had little say in the return migration process (see, for example, de Bree et al., 2010).

REFERENCES

Albers, S. (2005), 'Terug naar het verbeelde land: Levensverhalen en herinneringen van Nederlands-Marokkaanse remigranten in de Rif', MA thesis University of Amsterdam, Amsterdam.
Arizpe, L. (1981), 'Relay migration and the survival of the peasant household', in J. Balan

(ed.), *Why People Move: Comparative Perspectives on the Dynamics of Internal Migration*, Paris: UNESCO Press, pp. 187–210.

Carling, J. (2002), 'Migration in the age of involuntary immobility: theoretical reflections and Cape Verdean experiences', *Journal of Ethnic and Migration Studies*, **28** (1), 5–42.

Chant, S. and S.A. Radcliffe (1992), 'Migration and development: the importance of gender', in Chant (ed.), *Gender and Migration in Developing Countries*, London: Belhaven Press, pp. 1–29.

Constant, A. and D. Massey (2002), 'Return migration by German guestworkers: neoclassical versus new economic theories', *International Migration*, **40** (4), 5–38.

Day, L.H. and A. Içduygu (1997), 'The consequences of international migration for the status of women: a Turkish study', *International Migration*, **35** (3), 337–71.

de Bree, J., T. Davids and H. de Haas (2010), 'Post-return experiences and transnational belonging of return migrants: a Dutch–Moroccan case study', *Global Networks – A Journal of Transnational Affairs*, **10** (4), 489–509.

de Haan, A. (1999), 'Livelihoods and poverty: the role of migration', *Journal of Development Studies*, **36** (2), 1–47.

de Haas, H. (2006), 'Migration, remittances and regional development in southern Morocco', *Geoforum*, **37** (4), 565–80.

de Haas, H. (2007), 'Morocco's migration experience: a transitional perspective', *International Migration*, **45** (4), 39–70.

de Haas, H. (2010), 'Migration and development: a theoretical perspective', *International Migration Review*, **44** (1), 227–64.

de Haas, H. and A. van Rooij (2010), 'Migration as emancipation? The impact of internal and international migration on the position of women in rural Morocco', *Oxford Development Studies*, **38** (1), 43–62.

de Valk, H.A.G., A.C. Liefbroer, I. Esveldt and K. Henkens (2004), 'Family formation and cultural integration among migrants in the Netherlands', *Genus*, **60** (3/4), 9–35.

Entzinger, H. (1985), 'Return migration in Western Europe: current policy trends and their implications, in particular for the second generation', *International Migration*, **23** (2), 263–90.

Fadloullah, A., A. Berrada and M. Khachani (2000), *Facteurs d'Attraction et de Répulsion des flux Migratoires Internationaux. Rapport National: Le Maroc*, Rabat: Commission Européenne.

Fargues, P. (2004), 'Arab migration to Europe: trends and policies', *International Migration Review*, **38** (4), 1348–71.

Harris, J.R. and M.P. Todaro (1970), 'Migration, unemployment and development: a two-sector analysis', *American Economic Review*, **60** (1), 126–42.

Hooghiemstra, E. (2001), 'Migrants, partner selection and integration: crossing borders?', *Journal of Comparative Family Studies*, **32** (4), 601–25.

Jureidini, R. and N. Moukarbel (2004), 'Female Sri Lankan domestic workers in Lebanon: a case of "contract slavery"?', *Journal of Ethnic and Migration Studies*, **30** (4), 581–607.

King, R. and J. Vullnetari (2006), 'Orphan pensioners and migrating grandparents: the impact of mass migration on older people in rural Albania', *Ageing and Society*, **26** (5), 783–816.

Lievens, J. (1999), 'Family-forming migration from Turkey and Morocco to Belgium: the demand for marriage partners from the countries of origin', *International Migration Review*, **33** (3), 717–44.

Reniers, G. (2001), 'The post-migration survival of traditional marriage patterns: consanguineous marriages among Turks and Moroccans in Belgium', *Journal of Comparative Family Studies*, **32** (1), 21–45.

Rodenburg, J. (1997), *In the Shadow of Migration: Rural Women and their Households in North Tapanuli, Indonesia*, Leiden: KITLV Press.

Salih, R. (2001), 'Moroccan migrant women: transnationalism, nation-states and gender', *Journal of Ethnic and Migration Studies*, **27** (4), 655–71.

Schellingerhout, R. and M. de Klerk (2007), 'Allochtone ouderen: teruggaan of blijven?', *Gerōn*, **9** (4), 12–4.
Stark, O. (1978), *Economic–Demographic Interactions in Agricultural Development: The Case of Rural-to-Urban Migration*, Rome: FAO.
Stark, O. (1991), *The Migration of Labor*, Cambridge, MA and Oxford: Blackwell.
Stark, O. and D.E. Bloom (1985), 'The new economics of labor migration', *American Economic Review*, **75** (2), 173–8.
Taylor, J.E. (1999), 'The new economics of labour migration and the role of remittances in the migration process', *International Migration*, **37** (1), 63–88.
Todaro, M.P. (1969), 'A model of labor migration and urban unemployment in less-developed countries', *American Economic Review*, **59** (1), 138–48.
van Rooij, A. (2000), 'Women of Taghzoute: the effects of migration on women left behind in Morocco', MA thesis, University of Amsterdam, Amsterdam.

PART IV

A PERSPECTIVE ON MIGRATION AND TRANSNATIONALISM

PART IV

A PERSPECTIVE ON MIGRATION AND TRANSNATIONALISM

→ segmented assimilation

→ labor migration
→ professional class migration

10 New directions in gender and immigration research*
Pierrette Hondagneu-Sotelo

INTRODUCTION

Immigration studies have burgeoned in the last 30 years, but a glance at the principal journals and publications in the United States makes it clear that gender is still ghettoized in immigration scholarship. Basic concepts such as gender, sex, power, privilege, sexual discrimination and intersectionalities are regularly absent from the vocabulary and the study designs. The cottage industries of segmented assimilation, transnationalism and citizenship – with a few significant exceptions – remain like hermetically sealed steam trains from another century, chugging along oblivious to developments in gender scholarship of the last 30 years. I went through all of the recent issues of *International Migration Review* (*IMR*), the premier social science journal in this field, and I found that in 2007, 2008 and 2009, there were a total of seven articles with 'women' or 'gender' in the title. In 2006, there were none except those included in a special issue on gender. Why is that? Gender remains one of the fundamental social relations that anchors and impacts immigration patterns, including labour migration as well as professional class migrations and refugee movements. Gender is deeply implicated in imperialist, military and colonial conquests, which are widely recognized as the roots of global international migration flows. Once immigration movements begin, they take form in markedly gendered ways. In addition, immigration processes bring about life-impacting changes, destabilizing and remodelling the gendered way daily life is lived.

Sociology experienced an increase in feminist research in the 1980s and 1990s. In the 1970s, feminist research projects had emphasized the ways in which institutions and social privileges are constructed in ways that favour men. Since then, most feminist-oriented scholars have dispensed with unitary concepts of 'men' and 'women'. Multiplicities of femininities and masculinities are recognized today as interconnected, relational and intertwined in relations of class, race-ethnicity, nation and sexualities. The focus on intersectionalities in immigration studies is palpable in gender and immigration studies elsewhere around the globe, too, but it is perhaps less institutionalized in Europe, Asia and Latin America.

233

Outside the United States, there is also less focus on men and masculinities, and on sexualities (with the exception of trafficking, which I discuss below).

In the scholarship on gender and migration today, there are two seemingly contradictory trends. On the one hand, there is still an androcentric blindness to feminist issues and gender. It is business as usual, the missing feminist revolution. Morokvasic made this observation in 1984, and Silvia Pedraza in 1991. That's now an old song and I don't want to sing it here. On the other hand, there *is* a vibrant scholarship on gender and migration; however, not only is it not reaching or shaping some of the debates at the core, but it is also balkanized. In fact, there are several distinctive arenas of gender and migration scholarship and there appears to be a lack of communication among these arenas. Researchers working on, for example, the subject of migration and transnational sexualities may not be aware of the research on migration and care work. There are at least five different streams of gender and migration research. In this chapter I provide a brief overview of these areas.

GENDER AND MIGRATION: CARRYING THE FLAG

In the first category of 'gender and migration' scholarship, researchers – almost all of them women – are pursuing what some might call a mainstream social science approach. Here, the goal is to make gender an institutional part of immigration studies. It is not, as is often mistakenly suggested, solely about gauging gender gains for immigrant and refugee women. Rather, a small group of intrepid scholars are carrying the flag to establish legitimacy for gender in immigration studies. In the United States this includes prominent scholars such as sociologist, demographer and co-editor of the *American Sociological Review*, Katharine Donato, as well as historian and former president of the Social Science History Association, Donna Gabbacia, and anthropologists Patricia Pessar (deceased in 2012) and Sarah Mahler.

Some of these authors edited a special issue of *International Migration Review* in 2006, with the title 'A glass half full? Gender in migration studies'. This was a 20-year follow up to a 1986 special issue of *IMR* that had focused on the category of immigrant *women*. By the 1990s, the research had shifted away from a focus on 'women' and was emphasizing migration as a gendered process. This research sought to break simplistic gender binaries and drew attention to gendered labour markets and social networks, the relationship between paid work and household relations, changes in family patriarchy and authority that come about through migration, and gendered and generational transnational life (Grasmuck and Pessar, 1991; Kibria, 1993; Hondagneu-Sotelo, 1994). Later, Stephanie Nawyn (2010) emphasized the ways in which refugee resettlement NGOs shape refugee women's ability to challenge patriarchy in the home, yet simultaneously reaffirm patriarchal capitalism in the workplace, and Cynthia Cranford's (2007) research emphasized how economic restructuring and workplace and union politics allow Latina immigrant janitors to challenge gendered constraints in multiple spheres. All of these works emphasize that gender is a dynamic and constitutive element of migration and immigrant integration.

In the special issue of *IMR*, Donato et al. (2006) addressed some of these key themes and offered a multidisciplinary review of the field of migration and gender. The results reflect the pattern identified by Stacey and Thorne (1985) more than two decades ago: more openness in anthropology, less change in the more quantitative fields of demography and economics. Scholars such as Katharine Donato and Donna Gabbaccia seek to discover what they call the 'gender balance' of major migration movements around the world and in different time periods. They seek to measure when migration flows tip from being primarily male to majority female. In the US, that happened at an aggregate level in the early twentieth century.

In Europe, there is burgeoning new research on women's labour migration and transnational motherhood. In Europe, research has focused on gender, migration and welfare politics (Kofman, 2000), gendered transnationalism in Moroccan migration (Salih, 2001), and generationally distinctive patterns of gender order formation among Chechen refugee women (Szczepanilova, 2012). In Spain, we have seen the development of scholarship on South American women's labour migration to Spain and their roles as pioneers in family migration (Escrivá, 2000; Pedone and Araujo, 2008). Research in Asia focuses on gender, migration and the state (Piper and Roces, 2003; Oishi, 2005), and there is diverse gender research in Mexico, the nation with the longest continuously running transnational labour migration (for example, Woo Morales, 1995, 2007; Arias, 2000; Ariza, 2000; D'Aubeterre, 2000; Oehmichen, 2000). In the US, a new book by Gordillo (2010) focuses on Mexican women's gendered transnational ties and a 2009 book edited by Seyla Benhabib and Judith Resnick carries the gender flag into the territory of debates about citizenship, immigration law, sovereignty and legal jurisdiction. The topic of domestic violence in immigrant women's lives has also garnered deserved attention (Menjivar and Salcido, 2002). These are some of the varied and ongoing efforts that seek to reform immigration scholarship so that it acknowledges gender as fundamental to migration processes.

Seyla Benhabib & Judith Resnick

MIGRATION AND CARE WORK

A second stream has focused exclusively on the relation between women's migration, paid domestic work and family care. The key concepts here are 'care work', 'global care chains', 'care deficits', 'transnational motherhood' and 'international social reproductive labour'. The development of this literature has been made possible by theories of intersectionality. Beginning in the 1980s, and guided by paradigm-changing work of feminist scholars of colour in the US, the unitary concepts of 'men' and 'women' were replaced with the idea that there are multiplicities of femininities and masculinities and that these are interconnected, relational and intertwined with inequalities of class, race-ethnicity, nation and sexualities.

In this body of research, the focus shifts away from relations between women and men, to inequalities between immigrant women and nation, the way these are constituted by the international unloading of domestic reproductive work from women of the post-industrial, rich countries to women from the less-developed, poor countries of the Global South. Often, this mandates long-term family separations between migrant women and their children. This is a big literature and still growing, but key contributors have included Hondagneu-Sotelo and Avila (1997), Chang (2000), Hondagneu-Sotelo (2001, [2007]) and Parreñas (2001) on the US; Constable (1997) and Lan (2006) in Asia; Anderson (2000), Escrivá (2000), Parreñas (2001) and Lutz (2002, 2008) in Europe and the UK; and Hochschild and Ehrenreich's (2002) edited book, covering global ground. Newer research examines the integration of immigrant men in domestic jobs, such as Polish handymen in London (Kilkey, 2010) and Mexican immigrant gardeners in Los Angeles (Ramirez and Hondagneu-Sotelo, 2009).

Why did this literature begin to emerge around 2000? The late twentieth century was marked by the rapid increase in women migrating for domestic work. During the peak periods of modernization and industrialization, migrants were mainly men – usually men from poorer, often colonial societies – recruited to do 'men's work'. Chinese, Filipino, Japanese, Irish, Italian and Mexican men, for instance, all took turns in being recruited and brought to build infrastructure in the industrializing US. In some instances, family members were allowed to join them but in many cases, especially those involving immigrant groups perceived as non-white, the family members (women and children) were denied admission. Government legislation enforced these prohibitions on the permanent incorporation of these workers and their families. The Bracero Program and the Guest Worker Program are the exemplars of these modern gendered systems that relied on male labour recruitment and subjugation, and the exclusion of families.

Things have changed today. Factories migrate overseas in search of cheaper labour and hi-tech and highly educated professionals have joined labour migrants. But among them are legions of women who criss-cross the globe, from south to north, from east to west in order to perform paid domestic work. Consequently, in some sites, we are seeing the redundance of male migrant labour and the saturation of labour markets for migrant men. In places as diverse as Italy, the Middle East, Taiwan and Canada, Filipina migrant women caregivers and cleaners far outnumber Filipino migrant men. The demand is activated in different ways by different nations, raising questions of how state policies facilitate women's migration, and here there is a lot of variation. What is clear is that: women from countries as varied as Peru, the Philippines, Moldavia, Eritrea and Indonesia are leaving their families, communities and countries to migrate thousands of miles away to work in the new worldwide growth industry of paid domestic work and elder care. What remains puzzling is the marginalization of this literature in immigration scholarship, but it could be explained because the topic draws together three elements usually thought to be unimportant: women, the domestic sphere and care work.

SEXUALITIES

A third branch of gender and immigration research has been more related with the humanities, queer studies and cultural studies. Here, the focus is on sexualities, including gay and queer identities, as well as heteronormativity and compulsory heterosexuality, employed both as a form of legal immigration exclusion as well as inclusion. The posthumously published book by Lionel Cantu, *The Sexuality of Migration* (2009), edited by his former mentor Nancy Naples and colleague Salvador Ortiz, shows how sexual relationships among Mexican gay men are related to international tourism, transnational networks and, sometimes, legal asylum. The debates over gay marriage also resonate in immigration policies that deny entry to lesbian, gay, bisexual and transgender (LGBT) immigrants. Eithne Luibheid (2002) takes up these themes in *Entry Denied: Controlling Sexuality at the Border*, where she shows how implicit and explicit definitions of heteronormativity have been integral to laws that govern immigration control. In most nations, heterosexual citizens can sponsor their foreign partners for legal residence. But only 19 countries around the world permit lesbian and gay citizens to sponsor their foreign partners. The US is not among those 19 nations. As sociologists Danielle Hidalgo and Carl Bankston (2010) point out, the 1965 Immigration Act made heterosexual marriage the most important avenue for legal entry into the US. We usually think of the 1965 Immigration Act as liberalizing immigration legislation as it ended the Asian racial exclusions and institutionalized legal family immigration – but it is also exclusionary because it reifies a narrow heterosexual definition of family. Another book that addresses the longstanding invisibility of gay and queer immigrants is Martin Manalansan's (2003) *Global Divas: Filipino Gay Men in the Diaspora,* an ethnography conducted in New York City.

Too often 'sexualities' gets translated as a focus on queer sexualities, and a book that makes an important intervention in studying this topic is Gloria Gonzalez-Lopez's (2005) *Erotic Journeys: Mexican Immigrant Women and their Sex Lives.* This book looks at normative heterosexual practices and values of Mexican immigrant working-class women in order to reveal how processes of invisible power organize Mexican immigrant women's lives. Rather than taking the familiar approach of focusing on social problems such as teen pregnancy, or the transnational transmission of HIV, Gonzalez-Lopez examines Mexican immigrant women's sexual practices and how they feel about them. It is sociological imagination at its best, making visible the socially constructed and problematic nature of something previously taken as normative and acceptable.

SEX TRAFFICKING

The fourth stream of gender and migration research is centred on debates about sex trafficking and migrant women working in sex work. In Europe, this is a vibrant area of scholarship and activism, one where the moral crusade often masks structures of labour exploitation (Anderson and Davidson, 2003; Anderson and Andrijasevic, 2008; Oso, 2010). One of the strongest critics of the 'rescue industry' is the scholar/activist Laura Agustín, author of *Sex at the Margins: Migration, Labour Markets and the Rescue Industry* (2007). Originally from Latin America, but based in the UK, she examines connections between sex tourism, sex work migration and crackdowns by police and immigration authorities. Sex work draws migrant women from Eastern Europe, the Caribbean and Latin America, Asia and Africa. Highly influenced by Gloria Anzaldúa's borderlands thinking (Anzaldúa, 1987), Agustín seeks to break down the duality of seeing migrants as unwanted intruders or powerless victims. She views migrant women's sex work through the lens of labour markets and informal economies and she favours a perspective that is devoid of moralizing, one that favours agency over victimization.

The US-based scholar, Rhacel Salazar Parreñas, is best known for her work on transnational Filipina domestic workers and their family formations and relations, but her most recent research focus is on Filipina migrant entertainers and hostesses in Japan. Some of this writing has already appeared as a chapter in her 2008 book *The Force of Domesticity*, but it is most comprehensively presented in the monograph *Illicit Flirtations: Labor, Migration and Sex Trafficking in Tokyo* (2011). Rather than victims of trafficking, she relies on the concept of 'indentured mobility' to show how these Filipinas are exploited by structures of poverty and a migration industry composed of a complex web of managers, talent agents and club owners. Like Agustín, she views migrant women sex workers through the lens of labour markets and structural constraints, rather than as immoral women or hapless victims of exploitation. Unlike Agustín, Parreñas provides close-up ethnography of the Japanese sex industries' reliance on Filipino women and transgender hostesses and entertainers. Until very recently, there was an entire visa system set up to facilitate temporary labour contracts for Filipina/o hostesses in Japan, but this ended with US pressure from the 'war on trafficking' which assumes that all commercial sex transactions are tantamount to exploitation, regardless of consent. The US funds over 100 projects around the world to stop sex trafficking. Parreñas and Agustín are in agreement: many of the US campaigns are tools to control women and to disperse American colonialist culture and morality.

BORDERLANDS AND MIGRATION

The fifth arena is a broad one that owes its legacy to Anzaldúa's classic *Borderlands/La Frontera: The New Mestiza*, published in 1987. The scholarship that it generated brings together a Chicana studies focus on the hybridity of identities and the hybrid space of borderlands. Influenced by socialist feminist thought and internal colonialism, the focus here is on both mestiza identity and on spaces that defy easy opposition between dominant and dominated, here and there. *Women and Migration in the US–Mexico Borderlands*, edited by Denise Segura and Pat Zavella (2007), best exemplifies this stream. Here the contributors argue that there are feminist borderlands and theoretical emphases: structural, discursive, interactional and agentic. New destinations research that focused on the gendered reception for Mexican immigrants in the South and Midwest also highlights diverse borders and crossings (Smith, 2005; Deeb-Sossa and Binkham Mendez, 2008; Schmalzbauer, 2009 Estrada and Hondagneu-Sotelo, 2011).

The notion of 'gendered borderlands' reverberates in research far beyond the US–Mexico border zone. As already noted, Agustín, the scholar/activist who focuses on sex trafficking, is also inspired by Anzaldúa. She very deliberately employs border thinking, challenging the supposed oppression and victimization of migrant women sex workers and rethinking women's migration rights in a broader framework. Bandana Purkayastha's (2003) research on South Asian immigrant women also brings together intersectionalities and transnational social life. And Yen Le Espiritu (2003), underscoring the role of US imperialism, military intervention and multinational corporations in fomenting refugee movements and labour and professional class migration, also calls attention to the US as the primary border crosser. It is a scholarly twist on the old Chicano T-shirt slogan: 'We didn't cross the border. It crossed us'. And it resonates with the political slogan used by Caribbean and South Asian immigrant activists in the UK, signalling the colonialist legacies of contemporary migration and demographic transitions: 'We're here because you were there'.

CONCLUDING THOUGHTS

Gender and migration research momentum continues to advance in many directions. This includes new and continuing research on the global care chains, on labour market processes and activism around sex work and anti-sex trafficking campaigns, on women and borderlands hybridity, continuing projects on the gendered and generational processes of transnational migration, gendered social constructions of childhood, and sophisticated tabulations in demography. These are all valuable. But two trends are notable: first, researchers in these different spheres are mostly not in conversation with one another; and second, there is a continued and near total deafness from scholars working on other core areas of immigration studies, on segmented assimilation, immigrant religion, transnationalism and citizenship. The former is due to the increasingly specialized and balkanized nature of social science research today and the latter remains a concern that should be remedied.

In addition to a 'migration and development' paradigm, we can detect the emergence of a perspective on gender and migration that focuses on 'immigrant integration'. The US and all of the major post-industrial nations in Europe are facing a demographic transition whereby ageing, white, native-born citizens (the 'baby boomers') will be retiring, and a younger population of labour migrants and their children, most of them from the Global South, are standing in line to take their positions. We need research and policies to promote the political, economic and social integration of immigrants and their children. Yet the so-called 'age of migration' is also an age of relentless xenophobia and nativism. Future scholarship in gender and migration must grapple with the fact that we are living in a national and global crisis of immigration restrictionism. Transnationalism is a way of life for many, but unlike some of the celebratory commentators, transnationalism or post-nationalism does not provide a viable framework for immigrant rights. We do not appear to be approaching the erosion of nation-state borders, so with that reality it is important to focus on immigrant integration. And in this regard, we need new, young feminist scholars dedicated to unravelling the gendered processes and institutions that promote immigrant restrictionism, exclusions and violence, and prohibit immigrant integration.

Therefore, I shall conclude by noting how gender is used in the current vilification of immigrants. Since the beginning of the US immigration legislation, gender and race have been used as central categories of exclusion. The Page Act of 1875, the first precursor to US federal immigration law, excluded Chinese women who were held to be immorally suspect prostitutes. The big mid-twentieth-century contract labour programmes in the United States and Western Europe, the Bracero Program and the Guestworker Program, prohibited women and selected prime-working-age men as the ideal labour migrants, as they would not bring social reproduction costs or, it was thought, contribute to demographic transformations. During the 1980s and early 1990s, the 'immigrant danger' was largely seen as a feminine one. The bodies of immigrant women – namely poor immigrant women, women of colour and especially Mexican women – were seen as a threat to the US. Perceived as prolific breeders, they were also construed as racial threats to demographic homogeneity, social welfare drains on public schools and hospitals and as the culprits responsible for the social reproduction of immigrant children and entire communities (Chavez, 2008).

In the last decade, we have seen a switch in the gendered construction of immigrant danger. The new danger is a masculine one, one personified by terrorist men and 'criminal aliens'. These are racialized men. Muslim terrorists, Mexican narco-traffickers and 'gang bangers' are the new racialized and gendered immigrant danger. In US deportation statistics, men far outnumber women and the 10 countries to which deportees were sent in 2010 are all Latin American and Caribbean nations (Golash-Boza and Hondagneu-Sotelo, 2013). As Tanya Golash-Boza and I have suggested, what is occurring during the global financial crisis in the US suggests a gendered racial removal programme, one intent on removing Latino immigrant men from the United States. The majority of criminologists agree that there are no obvious connections between criminality and the foreign born, but in spite of this, we have seen a rapid increase in the number of immigrant men incarcerated, detained and deported. Why? It is largely due to draconian immigrant restrictionist legislation, the Illegal Immigration Reform and Immigration Responsibility Act (IIRIRA) of 1996 and the expansion of 'secure communities', aggressive practices of imprisoning those awaiting asylum decisions, and ways in which many drug crimes – even possessing a small amount of marijuana or cocaine – are now considered deportable crimes for legal immigrants. The increasing rate of incarceration of immigrant men also corresponds with the rise of private, for-profit prisons run by corporations (Golash-Boza, 2012). The popular mass media has covered these issues in such a way that leads to the conflation of undocumented immigrants, 'criminal aliens', and terrorists – all of them configured as dangerous men.

It is a moment in history where racialized and gendered xenophobia have greased the chutes of deportation and blocked the ladders of immigrant integration. This is an issue of great urgency for women, men and children of all nations. As this chapter suggests, gender and migration scholarship has flourished, but it has remained somewhat balkanized. The next generation of gender and migration scholars has a strong scholarly foundation on which to build, and given the current social and political climate, the challenges of understanding the gendered dimensions and repercussions of immigrant restrictionism and immigrant rights should emerge as among the most pressing new arenas of focus.

NOTE

* Earlier versions of this chapter appeared as 'Gender and migration scholarship in the 21st century', in Steve Gold and Stephanie Nawyn (eds), *Handbook on International Migration* (London: Routledge, 2012) and 'Gender and migration scholarship: an overview from a 21st century perspective', *Migraciones Internacionales*, Colegio de la Frontera Norte (Colef), Mexico, January 2011, **20**, 219–33.

REFERENCES

Agustín, Laura (2007), *Sex at the Margins: Migration, Labour Markets and the Rescue Industry*, London: Zed Books.
Anderson, Bridgit (2000), *Doing the Dirty Work: The Global Politics of Domestic Labour*, London and New York: Zed Books.
Anderson, Bridgit and Rutvica Andrijasevic (2008), 'Sex, slaves and citizens: the politics of anti-trafficking', *Soundings*, **40**, 135–45.
Anderson, Bridgit and Julia O'Connell Davidson (2003), *Is Trafficking in Human Beings Demand Driven? A Multi-country Pilot Study*, Geneva: International Organization for Migration.

Anzaldúa, Gloria (1987), Borderlands/La Frontera: The New Mestiza, San Francisco, CA: Aunt Late Books.
Arias, Patricia (2000), 'Las migrantes de ayer y de hoy', in Dalia Barrera and Cristina Oehmichen (eds), *Migración y relaciones de género en México*, Cuiclad de México: GIMTRAP/UNAM/IIA, pp. 185–202.
Ariza, Marina (2000), 'Género y migración femenina: dimensiones analíticas y desafíos Metodológicos', in Dalia Barrera and Cristina Oehimichen (eds), *Migración y relaciones degénero en México*, Ciudad de México: GIMTRAP/UNAM IIA, pp. 33–62.
Benhabib, Seyla and Judith Resnick (eds) (2009), *Migrations and Mobilities: Citizenship, Borders and Gender*, New York: New York University Press.
Cantu, Lionel (2009), *The Sexuality of Migration: Border Crossings and Mexican Immigrant Men*, edited by Nancy A. Naples and Salvador Vidal-Ortiz, New York: New York University Press.
Chang, Grace (2000), *Disposable Domestics: Immigrant Women Workers in the Global Economy*, Cambridge, MA: South End Press.
Chavez, Leo (2008), *The Latino Threat: Constructing Immigrants, Citizens and the Nation*, Stanford, CA: Stanford University Press.
Constable, Nicole (1997), *Maid to Order in Hong Kong: Stories of Filipina Workers*, Ithaca, NY: Cornell University Press.
Cranford, Cynthia J. (2007), '"It's time to leave machismo behind!": challenging gender inequality in an immigrant union', *Gender & Society*, **21** (3), 409–36.
D'Aubeterre Buznego, María Eugenia (2000), *El pago de la novia. Matrimonio, vida conyugal y prácticas transnacionales en San Miguel Acuexcomac, Puebla, Zamora*, El Colegio de Michoacán, Benemérita Universidad Autónoma de Puebla, Instituto de Ciencias Sociales y Humanidades.
Deeb-Sossa, Natalia and Jennifer Binkham Mendez (2008), 'Enforcing borders in the Nuevo South: gender and migration in Williamsburg, Virginia and the Research Triangle, North Carolina', *Gender & Society*, **22** (5), 613–38.
Donato, Katharine M., Donna Gabaccia, Jennifer Holdaway, Martin Manalansan IV and Patricia R. Pessar (2006), 'A glass half full? Gender in migration studies', *International Migration Review*, **40** (1), 3–26.
Escrivá, Angeles (2000), 'Empleadas de por Vida? Peruanas en el Servicio Doméstico en Barcelona', *Papers*, **60**, 327–42.
Espiritu, Yen Le (2003), *Homebound: Filipino American Lives across Cultures, Communities and Countries*, Barkeley, CA: University of California Press.
Estrada, Emir and Pierrette Hondagneu-Sotelo (2011), 'Intersectional dignities: Latina immigrant adolescent street vendors in Los Angeles', *Journal of Contemporary Ethnography*, **40** (1), 102–31.
Golash-Boza, Tanya (2012), *Immigration Nation: Raids, Detentions and Deportations in Post-9/11 America*, Boulder, CO: Paradigm.
Golash-Boza, Tanya and Pierrette Hondagneu-Sotelo (2013), 'Latino immigrant men and the deportation crisis: a gendered racial removal program', *Latino Studies*, forthcoming.
Gonzalez-Lopez, Gloria (2005), *Erotic Journeys: Mexican Immigrant Women and their Sex Lives*, Berkeley, CA: University of California Press.
Gordillo, Luz Maria (2010), *Mexican Women and the Other Side of Immigration: Engendering Transnational Ties*, Austin, TX: University of Texas Press.
Grasmuck, Sharri and Patricia R. Pessar (1991), *Between Two Islands: Dominican International Migration*, Berkeley, CA: University of California Press.
Hidalgo, Danielle Antoinette and Carl Bankston III (2010), 'Reinforcing polarizations: US immigration and the prospect of gay marriage', *Sociological Spectrum*, **30** (1), 4–29.
Hochschild, Arlie and Barbara Ehrenreich (eds) (2002), *Global Woman: Nannies, Maids and Sex Workers in the New Economy*, New York: Henry Holt and Metropolitan Books.
Hondagneu-Sotelo, Pierrette (1994), *Gendered Transitions: Mexican Experiences of Immigration*, 4th edn, Berkeley, CA: University of California Press.
Hondagneu-Sotelo, Pierrette (2001 [2007]), *Domestica: Immigrant Workers Cleaning and*

Caring in the Shadows of Affluence, Berkeley, CA: University of California Press. (New edition, with new preface 'The domestic goes global', 2007; Spanish language translation, Porrua Editorial, Mexico, 2011).

Hondagneu-Sotelo, Pierrette and Ernestine Avila (1997), '"I'm here, but I'm there": the meanings of Latina transnational motherhood', *Gender & Society*, **11**, 548–71.

Kibria, Nazli (1993), *Family Tightrope: The Changing Lives of Vietnamese Americans*, Princeton, NJ: Princeton University Press.

Kilkey, Majella (2010), 'Domestic-sector work in the UK: locating men in the configuration of gendered care and migration regimes', *Social Policy and Society*, **9**, 443–54.

Kofman, Eleonore (2000), *Gender and International Migration in Europe: Employment, Welfare and Politics*, London and New York: Routledge.

Lan, Pei-Chia (2006), *Global Cinderellas: Migrant Domestics and Newly Rich Employers in Taiwan*, Durham, NC: Duke University Press.

Lubheid, Eithne (2002), *Entry Denied: Controlling Sexuality at the Border*, Minneapolis, MN: University of Minnesota Press.

Lutz, Helma (2002), 'At your service Madam! The globalization of domestic service', *Feminist Review*, **70**, 89–104.

Lutz, Helma (ed.) (2008), *Migration and Domestic Work: A European Perspective on a Global Theme*, London: Ashgate.

Manalansan, Martin (2003), *Global Divas: Filipino Gay Men in the Diaspora*, Durham, NC: Duke University Press.

Menjivar, Cecilia and Olivia Salcido (2002), 'Immigrant women and domestic violence: common experiences in different countries', *Gender & Society*, **16** (6), 898–920.

Morokvasic, Mirjana (1984), 'Birds of passage are also women ...', *International Migration Review*, **18** (4), 886–907.

Nawyn, Stephanie J. (2010), 'Institutional structures of opportunity in refugee resettlement: gender, race/ethnicity, and refugee NGOs', *Journal of Sociology and Social Welfare*, **37** (1), March, 149–67.

Oehmichen, Cristina (2000), 'Las mujeres indígenas migrantes en la comunidad Extraterritorial', in Dalia Barrera and Oehmichen (eds), *Migración y relaciones de género en México*, Ciudad de México: GIMTRAP UNAM IIA, pp. 319–49.

Oishi, Nana (2005), *Women in Motion: Globalization, State Policies, and Labor Migration in Asia*, Stanford, CA: Stanford University Press.

Oso, Laura (2010), 'Money, sex, love and the family: economic and affective strategies of Latin American sex workers in Spain', *Journal of Ethnic and Migration Studies*, **36** (1), 47–65.

Parreñas, Rhacel (2001), *Servants of Globalization*, Stanford, CA: Stanford University Press.

Parreñas, Rhacel (2011), *Illicit Flirtations: Labor, Migration and Sex Trafficking in Tokyo*, Stanford, CA: Stanford California Press.

Pedone, Claudia and Sandra Gil Araujo (2008), 'Maternidades transnacionales entre America Latina y el Estado espanol: El impacto de las politicas migratorias en els estrategias de reagrupación familiar', in Carlota Sole, Sonia Parella and Leonardo Cavalcanti (eds), *Nuevos retos del transnacionalismo en el estudio de las migraciones*, Madrid: Observatorio Permanente de la Inmigracion.

Pedraza, Silvia (1991), 'Women and migration: the social consequences of gender', *Annual Review of Sociology*, **17**, 303–25.

Piper, Nicola and Mina Roces (eds) (2003), *Wife or Worker? Asian Women and Migration*, Oxford: Rowman & Littlefield.

Purkayastha, Bandana (2003), 'Skilled migration and cumulative disadvantage: the case of highly qualified Asian Indian immigrant women in the US', *Geoforum*, **36** (2), 181–96.

Ramirez, Hernan and Pierrette Hondagneu-Sotelo (2009), 'Mexican immigrant gardeners in Los Angeles: entrepreneurs or exploited workers?', *Social Problems*, **56** (1), 70–88.

Salih, Ruba (2001), 'Moroccan migrant women: transnationalism, nation state, gender', *Journal of Ethnic and Migration Studies*, **27** (4), 655–71.

Schmalzbauer, Leah (2009), 'Gender on a new frontier: Mexican migration in the rural Mountain West', *Gender & Society*, **23** (6), 747–67.
Segura, Denise and Patricia Zavella (2007), *Women and Migration in the US–Mexico Borderlands*, Durhan, NC: Duke University Press.
Smith, Robert Courtney (2005), *Mexican New York: Transnational Lives of New Immigrants*, Berkeley, CA: University of California Press.
Stacey, Judith and Barrie Thorne (1985), 'The missing feminist revolution in sociology', *Social Problems*, **32** (4), 301–16.
Szczepanilova, Alice (2012), 'Becoming more conservative? Contrasting gender practices of two generations of Chechen women in Europe', *European Journal of Women's Studies*, **19** (4), 475–89.
Woo Morales, Ofelia (1995), 'Las mujeres mexicanas indocumentadas en la migración internacional y la movilidad transfronteriza', in Soledad González, Olivia Ruiz, Laura Velasco and Ofelia Woo Morales (eds), *Mujeres, migración y maquila en la frontera norte*, Ciudad de México: COLEF-COLMEX, pp. 65–87.
Woo Morales, Ofelia (2007), 'La experiencia migratoria de las mujeres urbanas hacia el norte', in Patricia Arias and Woo Morales (eds), *Campo o ciudad? Nuevos espacios y formas de vida*, Guadalajara: Universidad de Guadalajara.

11 Women, gender, transnational migrations and mobility: focus on research in France
Christine Catarino and Mirjana Morokvasic

INTRODUCTION: THE NEED FOR A RETROSPECTIVE AND A COMPARATIVE PERSPECTIVE

This chapter provides a brief overview of the literature in France focusing on gender and women in migration since the beginning of the 1990s. The timespan covered corresponds to a turning point and a new phase in the European migration landscape triggered by the end of the bipolar world, its subsequent European enlargement, increasing globalization, transnationalization and the feminization of migratory flows. In order to avoid being trapped in the discourse on 'rethinking migration', on 'new trends' and 'discoveries', we cannot ignore the production of knowledge which has shaped the current highly interesting and multifaceted debate. The next section addresses the debates preceding the period we are focusing on, namely from the 1970s onwards. The subsequent sections will provide an overview of selected issues and trends in research. In spite of the diversity of origins, profiles and patterns of migration, paradoxically there is a persistence in stereotyping women as 'passive victims'. Research on agency and migrant women's mobilization challenges such images. Further, we present research focusing on the integration of migrant women in different sectors of the labour market, predominantly in domestic service and care, sex work and related activities.[1] The following section draws on studies which relate the spatial and the social mobility in an attempt, for some of them, to address the question of migration and empowerment. In order to answer that question, an intersectional perspective is increasingly recognized as being of prime importance (Yuval-Davis, 2006). We draw some conclusions regarding migration, gender and development and finally point to some gaps in research and suggest possible topics to be dealt with in the future.

In the globalized world of social sciences the debates and exchange increasingly take place across national boundaries. Therefore, aware of the difficulty of reducing the relevant literature in our field to a 'national container', we have all along felt the need to contextualize the

French production of knowledge within the European and international debates.

PRECEDING DEBATES

The 1970s and 1980s

The pioneering works of the 1970s and 1980s on women in migration appeared in a context marked by a male bias in mainstream migration studies, themselves marginalized in social sciences. The aim of these first studies was to draw attention to migrant women in areas where they were thought to be absent and to point to the vast diversity of migration patterns, migrant profiles and experiences against the misleading stereotypes and representations which imposed a global unified picture of exclusively masculine migration. Providing statistical evidence of their presence (Wisniewski, 1974; Taravella, 1980) especially on their labour market participation (Morokvasic, 1976; Paperman and Pierrot, 1978) was necessary to make migrant women visible in a context which was focusing primarily on labour migration and in which a migrant was 'legitimate' as a worker only. The feminist questioning about women's position in society indirectly provided an undeniable impetus to the studies on women in migration (Golub et al., 1997). However, for a long time mainstream feminism and studies on the social relations between the sexes ('*rapports sociaux de sexe*') remained ethnicity- and migration-blind. They had other priorities and focused on what they considered the primordial form of domination: patriarchy. The voice of migrant women themselves, their gradual organizing into associations and their mobilizing for their rights further contributed to increase their visibility (*Des femmes immigrées parlent*, 1978).

In the 1970s, the migration context changed: the labour recruitment suspended in 1974 was followed by family immigration (in reality, family migration occurred in parallel with labour recruitment but it became noticeable when that recruitment stopped). The focus shifted from *migrant worker* to *migrant family* and to *women and children*. Several studies more or less directly responding to public policy demands examined integration issues and adopted a culturalist perspective, focusing on migrant women as mediators for the adoption of French society values (Taboada-Leonetti and Lévy, 1978). Whereas the studies in this period were essential in raising awareness about the presence of immigrant women in French society, they also contributed to forging and maintaining a stereotype of these women as isolated, illiterate, unadapted to modern society and in need of assistance. The emerging institutional support structures providing assistance functioned as a self-fulfilling prophecy along with this stereotype in order to justify their existence and survive: they needed problem-burdened, helpless, isolated women, lost in the modern urban world. The demand-driven research and production of knowledge focused on those issues which confirmed this very stereotypical profile.

In the 1980s, the coming of age of the 'second generation' produced on the one hand migration researchers, as well as, on the other, a myriad of intercultural mediators and self-organized social workers who gradually contributed to modifying the prevalent image by treating women as 'actors'.[2] But, as we shall see in the overview of more recent literature, even today the stereotypes are hard to dismantle; they have survived and keep surfacing over and over again.

These are some of the main facets of the literature from the period preceding the one on which we shall focus. Because it aimed at providing evidence about immigrant women when they were either 'absent' or represented in a reductionist way, one can call this period a 'compensatory stage'.

The New Context at the Turn of the Century

At the beginning of the 1990s, the European migration landscape began changing rapidly: the flows became more and more diversified; the regions of departure and arrival often overlapped; the EU states proceeded to selective inclusion and exclusion of newcomers (Wihtol de Wenden and de Tinguy, 1995). The production of knowledge we are looking at now takes place in a very different context, one which is more favourable to the problematic of women and migration:

- Migration issues are no longer marginalized in social sciences or limited to the concerns of local policy-makers. More than ever, they are on the agenda of public policy-makers not only at local and national levels, but also at the European and international levels. Later migration has become a global governance issue (Thiollet, 2010).
- This context is also marked by gender-mainstreaming, which necessarily facilitates a given output, reception and impact. None the less, it can sometimes have a perverse effect: even where specific measures for disadvantaged categories of women exist, they may actually *exclude* immigrant women (Morokvasic and Catarino, 2007a).
- French (mainstream) feminists who already had a serious problem with 'class' and were divided on the issue of articulating class and

gender were long reluctant to contextualize the social relations of gender. Finally, they opened up and took over the already existing discussion on the articulation of gender, class and ethnicity (see the intersectional analysis below).
- There has been worldwide interest in the issue of women/gender in migration and an increasing number of studies and publications in journals of leading publishers setting up standards of reference and excellence non-existent 10 to 15 years ago.[3]

This context has had a considerable impact on research in France. Over the past 20 to 30 years, there has been an abundant literature, special issue publications and teaching modules devoted to women and migration and more recently to *gender* and migration.[4] To sum this up, we make some transversal observations:

- The gender perspective in migration has become necessary, a *sine qua non* in studying migration phenomena. In migration studies, in line with those on development, the research on gender often tended to focus on women only. In both academic areas, there 'has been a growing awareness of this bias' and a 'move from women *per se*' to 'women in relation to men' (visible in development studies in the shift from a 'women in development' (WID) to a 'gender and development' (GAD) perspective) (Bjerén, 1997 quoted by Carling, 2005; Catarino, 1999). But as underlined by Carling (2005, pp. 2–3), only recently were men included as men and masculinities and femininities mirrored. In the policy domain as well, gender has become a 'fuzzword', a consensual and depoliticized concept (Verschuur, 2009) explaining how it was brought into the mainstream. Focusing on women has been an important phase in acknowledging the necessity of a gender perspective, and it can be argued that it will remain a necessary contribution to a gendered perspective on migration as long as the gender bias exists (Morokvasic, 2008). As Parreñas (2001, p. 30) puts it: 'A sole focus on the experiences of women in various institutional settings can still advance gendered migration research. Such studies can continue the new directions in migration research that accounts for the intersections of race, class, gender and foreign status in the lives of male and female migrants'. Indeed, Donna Gabaccia's comprehensive historical analysis of immigrant life in the US (1994), though centred on women, 'does not stop with them. Immigrant women cannot be studied apart from men of their own backgrounds, not apart from American women' (1994, p. xi).

- It would have been logical to expect that the accumulation of knowledge and wide distribution of studies would diminish the amount of stereotyping and misleading representations. They have always been easy cover-ups for existing knowledge gaps and ignorance, and one could assume that the wide availability of research evidence and data would make resorting to them irrelevant. However – and the literature review confirms this – the stereotypes are stubborn and persistent.
- In the context of globalization and changing migration patterns, the focus of research today is seldom 'Franco-French', that is on France only. Rather, migrations are increasingly approached as transnational phenomena, involving more than one or two countries. French scholars are now turning their attention towards phenomena beyond France as well, to other countries or even continents. This was still exceptional 20 or 30 years ago, but in our increasingly globalized world social sciences have had to, and will further have to, 'globalize' themselves – not in order to abandon the nation-state logic, but in order to combine and include transnational and trans-state developments.

DIVERSITY OF PATTERNS: DIMENSIONS OF TRANSNATIONAL EXPERIENCES

Transnational Families

After the pioneering studies in the 1990s (Basch et al., 1994; Ong, 1999) which focus on multi-site families, their links and 'flexible citizenship', a number of publications, mainly English speaking, contributed to the debates and interrogations on transnational motherhood and transnational families (for example, Bryceson and Vuorela, 2002; Parreñas, 2005), The issue of 'living apart together' of spatially dispersed families has lately attracted attention in France as well. 'Transnational families' defined as those living some or most of the time separated from each other, yet holding together and contributing to the feeling of collective welfare and unity, a 'familyhood' even across the borders (Bryceson and Vuorela, 2002) are in the focus of a collection of essays in the journal *Autrepart* (Razy and Baby-Collin, 2011). Authors highlight multiple experiences in different parts of the world: mobile kin communities and how they are transformed by communication technologies, organization of intergenerational solidarities, transnational motherhood, and the impact of tightening of borders on family links, are some of the dimensions analysed. They tackle the questions relative to the recomposition of these families, to rethinking of the relationships (gender, intergenerational) in a discontinued but connected space and highlight the ways in which the transnational spaces can be both obstacles and sources of opportunities. Elodie Razy and Virginie Baby-Collin, the editors of the issue, stress that the freedom of circulation, presently often restricted by migration policies, is fundamental for enabling transnational life '*modi*' and thus achieving the right to a family life, today often obstructed (2011, p. 55).

Settling in Mobility and Circulatory Territories

In the context where 'the freedom to move has become the main stratifying factor of our late modern and post-modern times' (Bauman, 1998, p. 2), mobility and the ability to be mobile play an important part in the strategies of these migrants. Rather than trying to immigrate and settle in the target country, migrants 'settle in mobility' (Morokvasic, 1992), staying mobile as long as they can in order to improve and maintain the quality of their life at home. Migration thus becomes a lifestyle, an occupation, whereby leaving one's home paradoxically becomes a strategy of staying at home, an alternative to emigration. This transnational short-term mobility can be a resource and an important dimension of these migrants' social capital. Hence, remaining in control of one's own mobility is a *sine qua non* for achieving the original target of social promotion or status preservation at home: the more they have control over their mobility, the more they are able to use it as a resource, whereas vice versa, the less control they have, the less likely they are to benefit from the returns of their mobile strategies (Morokvasic, 1999, 2004).

Circulation is facilitated for those who do not have to cope with obstacles such as visas and to worry about temporary permits. Therefore, it is important to regularize one's situation and obtain resident permits. A stable status is not only instrumental for easier mobility, but it also enables greater control over that mobility (Morokvasic, 1999; Riccio, 2003; Weber, 2007). Women are more likely to rely on family reunification channels or marriage in order to obtain stable status (Giabiconi, 2005).

Comparing Circulation Patterns of Women from Central-Eastern Europe and those from the Euro-Mediterranean Space and Africa

North African migrant women develop a specific 'know-how to circulate' – Alain Tarrius (1992) – which differs, for instance, from the self-managed rotation strategies of Polish domestic workers and traders (Morokvasic, 1999). Polish domestic workers function as a group but travel individually and substitute for each other at weekly or monthly intervals. In contrast, North Africans travel in groups: this has a socializing function for newcomers and the group itself, as social control minimizes the possibilities for transgressing the gender code implied in geographical mobility. Groups of women traders from Tunisia manage not only to invest in public spaces in cities such as Naples but also to transform them (Schmoll, 2005). Women moving within the world of men often have a male 'protector'; but while among Eastern Europeans the protector regulates and manages the services – including sexual services – that some women of the group might provide as part of trade negotiations (Irek, 1998), the protector of Tunisian women ensures that the moral code is preserved and that the women are not sexually assaulted.

In a society where, according to the prevailing gender norm, the man is the breadwinner and women working outside are transgressing that code, women handle this major transformation carefully. Although it eventually may become a primary source of income for the family, it continues to be considered as complementary only. Women make sure that men 'do not lose face' in the process: men are often formally associated with women's businesses. Men assist the women, and when they do not, outside forces are cited as an excuse for men's non-participation in cross-border trading: 'they have obstacles in getting visas' (Schmoll, 2005).

Marie Sengel (2000) provides further evidence about transnational commercial activities of women between Africa and Europe. In a very competitive context they engage in partnerships in order to increase their social capital and recruit persons of different nationalities to enlarge their circle of customers. In order to avoid risking the non-renewal of their residence papers or work contracts and so as not to be declassed because of unrecognized credentials, they also instrumentalize intimate relationships, as is the case for some women from Central and Eastern Europe studied by Serge Weber (2007).

EMERGING ISSUES: THE UNDERSIDE OF GLOBALIZATION

Prostitution, Trafficking, Care and Domestic Services

French feminists and scholars have long focused their interests on women's work while omitting to include immigrant women in their analyses (Chaib, 2003; Zaidman, 2003). They drew attention to women's unpaid work in the household (Delphy, 1970). They also widely mobilized against prostitution as sexual exploitation and against trafficking in women. This might in part explain their late interest in externalized housework performed by women (who happen to be immigrant or of immigrant origin) as well as their special concern and focus on migrant women mainly as victims of prostitution and trafficking (rather than as sex workers). These developments have shaped a situation where considerable attention has been paid to sexual/sexualized issues – sexual violence, mutilations, polygamy, forced marriages, prostitution, trafficking. This has taken place in a context in which:

- the feminist debates have shifted away from women's unpaid domestic work which was in the forefront in the 1970s,[5] when it opposed feminists in their explanation of women's exploitation (capitalism versus patriarchy)[6] and in which social class as the prime category for explaining social phenomena has declined along with the influence of Marxism in social sciences in France. Recourse to ethnicity and intersectionality in order to explain social practices and representations has become more frequent (Catarino, 1999). In other words, the emphasis has shifted from (unpaid) work to sexual/sexualized issues and from class *per se* to ethnicity and increasingly to intersectionality (including class divisions but combined with others).
- there is an increasing intervention of public policies in such private and intimate issues as sexuality and sexualities. Legislation against domestic violence has been passed;[7] the Law on Internal Security of March 2003[8] directly affects prostitutes and in particular immigrant prostitutes; international and national organizations have organized against trafficking. In France, this has also been reflected in demand-driven research which tends to focus on sexual/sexualized issues.

In contrast, in particular given their considerable representation in that sector, there are few studies on immigrant women in domestic service. Indeed the research on domestic work and care focusing on migrant women specifically remains, comparatively to issues such as prostitution and trafficking, relatively scarce. Public policies may partly be held accountable for this: until recently they failed to recognize the specific demand for immigrant women to work in domestic service (either in terms of a specific entry channel, as is the case in Italy or in terms of quotas). Immigrant women in the personal services sector were made invisible: the discourse on the professionalization of these activities (focusing on agencies and the so-called 'service employment cheques') refered to *all* potential workers, irrespective of their nationality or origin (Scrinzi, 2003).

Lately, a new generation of researchers (Guillemaut, 2005, 2006; Darley, 2006; Jaksic, 2008) has deconstructed the victimization discourse on prostitution and trafficking. Some of these researchers draw on Paola Tabet's (2004) concept of 'sexual–economic exchanges' to address an array of sexual paid and non-paid activities such as prostitution, migration cross-border marriages, sexual arrangements as well as the sexual exploitation of domestic workers (Moujoud and Pourette, 2005; Lévy and Lieber, 2009; Moujoud and Falquet, 2010; Pian, 2010). Indeed, feminist debates and research rather concentrate on different forms of sexuality and gender, thereby increasingly questioning the heterosexual norms of society. At the same time, research has demonstrated that questions about sexuality are racialized and racial issues sexualized. 'Prostitution' refers both to sexuality and to immigration. Sexual violence also tends to be racialized – the perpetrators of sexual violence tending to be racialized. Likewise, some of the issues related to immigration are treated as sexual issues: the 'Islamic' head-scarf is seen as a form of 'rape', and questions of polygamy and of forced marriages are racially and ethnically stigmatized in the name of gender equality.[9] Some authors even see the emergence of a kind of 'state feminism' (some feminists and public authorities being of the same mind).[10]

On the other hand, research on domestic work has also depicted internal migration in non-French contexts (Drouilleau, 2009; Jacquemin, 2009) and reframed the demand for those sexual, domestic and care activities showing their blurred lines within the new international division of labour (NIDL).

Development of Services and an Ethnic Division of Labour: Global Causes

A number of studies shed light on the structural causes leading to the development of service activities, including commercial sex, in which immigrant women increasingly take part (Handman and Mossuz-Lavau, 2005).

Jules Falquet (2006) claims that the international and sexual division of labour sustains the joint development of the phenomenon of 'armed men' on the one hand and 'domestic women' such as prostitutes on the other. The increase in the production and circulation of weapons, numerous ongoing conflicts, the increasing number of militarized peacekeepers, the growth in informal or illegal activities (drug dealing, money laundering) as well as terrorist activities, create a labour market for sex by raising the demand and supply of sexual services. The supply ensues from capitalist, racist and patriarchal social relations through migration and sex tourism. Public policies foster the development of globalized sexual services: development policies accompanied by sex tourism and militarized peacekeeping contribute to creating and constructing labour markets for sexual services.

Commercial sex activities are characterized by an ethnic division of labour where female migrants are mostly positioned at the bottom of the hierarchy. This holds especially true for street prostitution, where the recently arrived and undocumented prostitutes tend to be relegated to the insecure areas of city outskirts (Deschamps, 2006).[11] Class and ethnicity create the sex workers' profiles based on their kind of customer: among North African prostitutes Nasima Moujoud (2005) distinguishes those who practise on the streets or in workers' hostels and those who target rich Middle East bachelors. The latter are young, urban, educated girls engaged in transnational prostitution between France and the Middle East.

There is also evidence of an ethnic division of labour in other service sectors. In the cleaning sector, for instance, the most recently arrived women (black women from Africa) are hired by placement agencies as hotel cleaners, while women belonging to older migration waves (Spanish, Portuguese) are directly recruited by hotel groups and are granted better and more stable working conditions (Puech, 2006).

Mobilizing Categories of Otherness

Francesca Scrinzi (2003) analysed processes of 'othering' while observing the behaviour of instructors on training courses for domestic workers. Migrant women taking these courses are taught norms supposedly foreign to them, such as punctuality. On the one hand, their culture is assumed to be homogeneous and they are expected to conform to the dominant culture (for instance, one employer talking about her employee says: 'my culture in which she lives'). On the other hand, they are taught about the plurality and diversity of the living modes in their employers' homes.

In her study of domestic workers from the Philippines in France, Liane Mozère (2005) shows how they manage to mobilize categories of otherness to their own advantage. She underscores the empowerment of these women, who become '*entrepreneures d'elles-mêmes*', that is, their own entrepreneurs. By capitalizing on the attributes that distinguish them as exceptionally good for personal services, in particular for the care of the elderly and children (a good education and knowledge of English, a Catholic patriarchal upbringing, docility and deference), they create an employment niche in the sector.

Trafficking: Denouncing Criminalization and Victimization

In line with other critical research which aims at deconstructing the discourse on trafficking (Andrijasevic, 2005), Françoise Guillemaut claims that the overall focus on trafficking essentially serves the purpose of anti-immigration policies in the Schengen space and discredits immigrant women by constructing them as powerless victims. She shows how the victimization of women is produced and vehicled in official texts and international recommendations: the reference to migrant women is limited to the problematic of violence against women (prostitution and trafficking), to the detriment of other issues such as the defence of human rights (free circulation of persons and so on) or women's work. As for the protection of victims, it is instrumentalized for the purpose of testimony in denunciating 'criminal' networks (2005 and 2006) (see also Jaksic, 2008).

Within their humanitarian discourse, NGOs consider trafficking as the violation of fundamental rights, whereas the states focus on security issues and treat it as a dimension of organized crime and illegal immigration that should be eradicated. But despite these differences, both share a certain image of the victims of trafficking as persons incapable of developing strategies of resistance. The victim is socially constructed as 'innocent', a 'Madonna', forced and deceived and as such deserving protection by the state. Those who know and accept what they are getting into are, on the contrary, excluded from such protection (Darley, 2006). The representatives of NGOs advocating prostitutes' rights and in charge of trafficking issues in France nevertheless argue that police officers have a stereotyped, victimizing, paternalistic and discriminating image of migrant women seen as 'victims' of trafficking. Psychological and behavioural characteristics are not the only elements which make up the definition of a victim in the eyes of the authorities, but also ethnicity, colour of skin, and other phenotypical characteristics: being white, Eastern European and blonde helps in order to be defined as a victim (Morokvasic and Catarino, 2007b).

SPATIAL MOBILITY AND SOCIAL MOBILITY: CAN MIGRATION BE EMPOWERING?

Research evidence suggests that crossing borders for work purposes can be empowering and open up opportunities for challenging the established gender norms, but it can also lead to new dependencies and reinforce existing gender boundaries and hierarchies.

Assessing Social Mobility in/between Different Spaces

In order to assess migrants' social mobility over time it is important not only to apply a longitudinal perspective, but also to take into account both its objective and subjective dimensions. Migrants compare their social mobility to the socioeconomic situation of those who stayed behind, that is, the 'reference group' of relatives who were either unable or unwilling to migrate (Oso, 2005). The social mobility should then be evaluated by taking into account both spaces, the sending and the receiving one. Transnational living between two countries, two space–time dimensions, might help in restoring or achieving upward mobility, in enduring and accepting one's condition and in getting empowered. The migrant women from northern China studied by Lévy (2005) show signs of a 'split psychology': they oppose their lives in China where they are 'good and respectable women' and in France, a suspended timespan in which 'nothing matters, everything is allowed' (Lévy, 2008). This enables them to justify and to endure prostitution while at the same time sustaining or restoring their self-esteem. Filipino domestic workers (Mozère, 2005) invest in their children's education or in real estate projects, or open up businesses in their home country. Above all they have access to liberties hitherto unknown to them, which they would not willingly renounce. One of the signs of these women's higher social status and social recognition in their home country lies in their capacity and practice of giving gifts.[12] In contrast, the Spanish domestic workers depicted by Laura Oso (2005), who in the past used to display their wealth once a year during a vacation to those of their compatriots who did not migrate, at the cost of innumerable deprivations in France, no longer had this possibility. The booming Spanish economy as well as high consumption levels cancelled out migrants' advantage, making these migrant women believe that their compatriots and relatives who did not migrate enjoyed greater social mobility than themselves. A new comparative research in the current Spanish and international crisis context could question whether it has in the meantime restored migrants' advantage over non-migrants.

Migration and Gender Order

The outsourcing of domestic tasks (rather than sharing them within the family) has an emancipating effect on working middle-class women while preserving the status quo, hence, the presence of migrant women in personal services enables the gender hierarchies to be preserved in their employer's household. The typical traditional gender order remains unchallenged, even though (or precisely because) the father or the partner had actually taken over the household in the wife's absence. When the new post-socialist superwoman mother worker is back, things have to 'return to normal' and, of course, it is she who does everything, even though it may take half of her vacation. 'When I go home to Poland, I do not rest; there is so much to do. Imagine a man alone with two kids . . . If I go to stay one month for instance, the first two weeks I do nothing but cleaning, housework' (Kuzma, 2003, p. 124).

The gender order is not only resistant to change, but under certain circumstances its intersection with class, migrancy and legality can be intensified. Is there nevertheless a potential for agency behind the unchallenged, preserved gender order? Migrant women negotiate the contradictions between economic gains and downward social mobility, how they turn their 'handicaps' into advantages in response to stigmatization and blame, how they disconnect norms and behaviour or use traditional patterns to follow their own objectives, and so on. For instance, the capital earned by Tunisian women on their trading trips (Schmoll, 2005) is invested in their daughters' dowries, but also in their education. Thus, mothers are dealing with the contradiction between keeping some gender norms intact while trying to promote the emancipation of their daughters.

APPLYING AN INTERSECTIONAL PERSPECTIVE

Migrants are situated within power hierarchies – which shape the ways people think and act – which they have not themselves constructed (class, race, ethnicity, nationality, gender, immigrant status and so on). But they also develop different types of agency *vis-à-vis* these hierarchies depending on their own social location within these structural conditions. Feminist researchers have long been stressing that gender processes cannot be understood independently of class, race, immigrant status and so on, with which they intersect (Anthias and Yuval-Davis, 1983). An intersectional perspective has increasingly been adopted in research on migration experiences, representations/identities and collective mobilizations of migrants (for special issues, reviews of the literature and critics, see, for example, Dorlin, 2005 and 2012; Falquet et al., 2006; Palomares and Testenoire, 2010): the focus has been mainly on the articulation of gender, class and ethnicity, the three most-cited dimensions of social hierarchies and modes of identification.

Intersectionality and Modes of Identification

The typology of North African prostitution in France, proposed by Nasima Moujoud (2005) indicates that social class determines not only the type of prostitution practised but also the social representations about clients and about the potential risks of contamination by sexually transmissible diseases. Women practising in workers' hostels believe, for instance, that belonging to the same ethnic or religious group protects them against these illnesses. Others engaged in 'luxury prostitution' sometimes accept unprotected intercourse for financial reasons, and some imagine that the economic capital of their clients is a guarantee of their health.

Another way of underscoring the impact of ethnicity and class is to look at what is going on between women of different origins practising prostitution. According to Catherine Deschamps (2006) there is a latent conflict between 'established' and foreign prostitutes detectable through spreading of rumours and the uttering of insults. In 2002, the NGO Hétaïra en colère, an association of female prostitutes, demanded the prohibition of prostitution among minors and young people. Furthermore, insults between French prostitutes and young prostitutes from East European countries, and pejorative nicknames given to African prostitutes, are constitutive of ways that women use to defend their territory. The reputation of violence attributed by the 'established' prostitutes to the new pimps coming from Eastern European countries and above all from China serves the same purpose. The aim is to convince the public authorities of the necessity to eliminate young competitors without valid papers from the market, justifying this by the violence they allegedly suffer.

Immigrants may be engaged in practices of social distinction. The northern Chinese used to be well educated and regarded southern Chinese as peasants and uneducated persons. In France, these social hierarchies are reversed. Whereas southern Chinese have often become business owners, the northern Chinese have few other opportunities but to work for the southerners in their shops or as domestic workers. Northern Chinese women may subsequently opt to enter prostitution rather than having to work and bear humiliating working relationships in the ethnic economic niches dominated by the southern Chinese (Lévy, 2005; Lieber, 2007; Lévy and Lieber, 2009). This in turn nourishes stereotypes about northern Chinese women and stigmatizes them as prostitutes accused by southern Chinese of 'betraying their country' (Lieber, 2007).

Intersectionality and Social Mobilization

A question and difficulty arises in the sphere of political activism: how to determine the priority of claims or alliances in the coalition of identity organizations? This is the purpose of Helen Schwenken's research (2005), where she explores the difficulty of articulating different social positionings in collective mobilizations and struggles. She analyses the RESPECT network, which defends the interests of immigrant domestic workers lobbying in EU institutions and shows that the claims prioritized by the defence organizations are not necessarily based on the most obviously and ad hoc politically resonant themes such as trafficking issues.

In line with research showing an absence of sisterhood, Nasima Moujoud (2012) examines class and race divisions of labour and hierarchies within women's activist milieu. She explores some undocumented minority women's reluctance to join the activist organizations. They feel instrumentalized by non-migrant/French/white women who are eager to use them as proof of their cause, asking them to provide testimony in public meetings. While some refuse to join activist organizations, others (those who are more educated) do join and experience both discrimination and assistance from the organizations.

GENDER, MIGRATION AND DEVELOPMENT

Christine Verschuur (2009) distinguishes three phases regarding the inclusion of gender in development studies and which could be applied to the analysis of the gender and migration field/nexus: the first, in the wake of Ester Boserup's seminal work (1970), has been devoted to making women's work visible; the second explores gender transformations related to the new international division of labour in the globalized context and mainly addresses domestic and care work (as well as commercial sex activities); and the third, mainly dedicated to identity and struggles analysis, has been spearheaded by migrant as well as Global South scholars and is a revival of the intersectional perspective. As highlighted in this chapter, French research about migration and gender roughly falls into these three non-linear steps: rendering migrant women's labour visible; studying the NIDL; and incorporating intersectional concerns in the domain/realm of identities/social representations and struggles (social mobilizations). Nevertheless, with regard to the NIDL, a specificity of French research as compared to European research and beyond, is its late and relatively scarce interest in migrant paid domestic and care work issues.

The recent 'rediscovery' or refashioning of the migration and development nexus has been increasingly concerned with remittance issues, supposed to instigate the sustainable socioeconomic development of migrant sending countries and to dry up the flow of immigrants. Research on gender patterns in the sending and use of remittances is deficient. As a matter of fact, the growing body of literature on gender remittances has revolved around Latin American and Asian migrant origins while migrants in France come mainly from North African and other African countries. French research on the migration and development nexus has mostly included studies on circular migration and development (Péraldi, 2001; Tarrius, 2002), as well as studies assessing the impact of African migrants' remittances – sent through migrant associations channels – on the development of countries of origin (Lacroix, 2009). These studies focus primarily on male migrants.[13]

Although women moving on their own have recently and increasingly caught the attention of researchers in France, and given that female migrants reuniting with their families have attracted more interest, research has rather documented the situation of the family left behind than that of migrant female-headed households, while there is a great amount of literature on this topic in Spain for instance (Oso, 2008). As a result, there is no steady tradition within the French academic literature of developing approaches which combine production and reproduction aspects within transnational households such as gendered patterns of sending remittances or transnational parenthood practices. We can hypothesize that the so-called 'articulationist theories' (see Kearney, 1986; Oso, 2008) have been more prominent in EU countries with a larger – and more visible – proportion of highly feminized flows of migrants and migrant female-headed households than France, such as Spain (see Oso, 1998; Gregorio Gil, 1998; Herrera, 2006; and Gonzálvez, 2007, for a review). Research in France none the less combines production and reproduction issues when showing that women get involved in commercial sex in order to sustain their families abroad.

GAPS IN RESEARCH AND FUTURE ORIENTATION SUGGESTIONS

In the context of a diversification of research themes and perspectives, there are some gaps and certain orientations can be followed and developed further in the future. Among the evident needs is the deconstruction of persisting stereotypes. One way to do this would be to turn away from 'trendy' and demand-driven topics covered by the media anyway, namely to target those issues unlikely to contribute to representations maintaining immigrant women in the position of assisted persons in need of help and support; to focus not only (or less) on the reproductive sphere where migrant women can find work more easily than elsewhere and shift their attention to production, entrepreneurship and businesses; and to investigate women in highly skilled professions, in managerial positions; and so on. This would shed light on so far less explored sectors such as unskilled mixed-gender activities (the garment industry for instance), as well as on the processes of de-skilling.

Studies should focus on men *and* women (labour insertion, transnational parenthood, social construction of masculinity and femininity in migration and correlative social identifications and so on).

Monographs focusing on one community would be interesting because they provide an in-depth perspective that some transversal studies cannot offer. One could imagine comparative studies of the same immigrant group in two or more destination countries (for instance, the Chinese in 'old' destination countries such as France or Germany and in a 'new' country such as Spain or Hungary); Latin Americans or Eastern Europeans are two other groups that have been investigated extensively in one country (Latin Americans in Spain, Eastern Europeans in Germany) but not comparatively. Research could embrace the analysis of gender remittance practices, one new feature of the migration/development nexus.

NOTES

1. Giving priority to these issues is directly related to the objectives of our EU-funded FeMiPol research (Integration of Female Immigrants in Labour Market and Society. Policy Assessment and Policy Recommendations) (2006–08) and its selective focus on the labour market, see: http://www.femipol.uni-frankfurt.de/ (accessed 28 November 2012). The present text is a modified and updated version of Morokvasic and Catarino (2010).
2. See the overviews of literature in France and internationally (Morokvasic, 1976, 1983, 1984; Kofman, 1999; Donato et al., 2006). For a retrospective view in France, see Morokvasic (2008, 2011). For Germany see Gutiérrez (1999).
3. An example of this new trend is Mathilde Darley's article on prostitution clubs in the border region of the Czech Republic in the top French journal *Revue française de sociologie*, 2007.
4. Special issues of periodicals dedicated to either immigration or gender have been devoted to women in migration and to gender or to both: *Migrations Société*, 1997 and 2005; *REMI*, 1999 and 2005; *Cahiers du CEDREF*, 2000, 2003 and 2008; *Hommes & Migrations*, 2004; see Barison and Catarino, 1997; Golub et al., 1997; Falquet et al., 2000, 2008; Zaidman and Bachelet, 2003; Hersent and Zaidman, 2003; Catarino et al., 2005; Rigoni and Séhili, 2005.
5. Another important issue was women's right to have control over their own bodies (abortion rights and sexual orientation).
6. Feminists such as Christine Delphy have prioritized patriarchy.
7. For instance, Law No. 2006-399 of 4 April 2006 on the prevention and repression of domestic violence.
8. Law No. 2003-239 of 18 March 2003.
9. *Journée d'étude Féminisme, sexualité et (post-)colonialisme*, 3 February 2006, available at: http://calenda.revues.org/nouvelle6346.html (accessed 17 July 2008).
10. This 'state feminism' was strongly criticized by Sylvie Tissot (2007) in the special issue of *Plein Droit* because it obfuscates gender inequality. The title of that issue: 'Femmes et étrangers, des causes concurrentes?' (Women's and foreigners' claims

in competition?), is indicative of the marginalization of social class as a category of analysis.
11. Note that under the cover of 'curbing the spread of crime', the Law on Internal Security of March 2003 (see above, note 8) introduced the notion of 'passive solicitation': this sanctions women and men who practise street prostitution, obliging them to move to remote areas where they are increasingly vulnerable to assaults by clients and pimps. This criminalization of prostitution has an additional effect on foreign prostitutes, whose residence permit can be confiscated at any time, thus increasing their risk of being expelled.
12. Liane Mozère, spontaneous speech at the Journées d'Étude 'Migrations: Nouvelles pratiques, approches plurielles', EHESS, Paris, 8 October 2008.
13. Even at the international level, research on gender and remittances in Africa is scarce and recent. Part of it was promoted by the IOM (Alvarez, 2009; IOM, 2010); see also Dodson et al. (2008).

REFERENCES

Alvarez Tinajero, Sandra Paula (2009), *Angola: A Study of the Impact of Remittances from Portugal and South Africa*, IOM Migration Research Series 39, IOM, Geneva.
Andrijasevic, Rutvica (2003), 'The difference borders make: (il)legality, migration and trafficking in Italy among Eastern European women in prostitution', in S. Ahmed, C. Castañeda, A.-M. Fortier and M. Sheller (eds), *Uprootings/Regroundings: Questions of Home and Migration*, Oxford: Berg, pp. 251–72.
Anthias, Floya and Nira Yuval-Davis (1983), 'Contextualizing feminism – gender, ethnic and class divisions', *Feminist Review* (15), November, 62–75.
Barison, Noella and Christine Catarino (eds) (1997), 'Les femmes immigrées en France et en Europe', *Migrations Société*, **9** (52), 15–130.
Basch, Linda, Nina Glick Schiller and Cristina Szanton Blanc (1994), *Nations Unbound: Transnational Projects, Postcolonial Predicaments, and Deterritorialized Nation-States*, Amsterdam: Gordon & Breach.
Bauman, Zygmunt (1998), *Globalization. The Human Consequences*, New York: Columbia University Press.
Bjerén, Gunilla (1997), 'Gender and reproduction', in T. Hammar, G. Brochmann, K. Tamas and T. Faist (eds), *International Migration, Immobility and Development: Multidisciplinary Perspectives*, Oxford: Berg.
Boserup, Ester (1970), *Woman's Role in Economic Development*, New York: St Martin's Press.
Bryceson, Deborah and Ulla Vuorela (2002), *The Transnational Family: New European Frontiers and Global Networks*, Oxford: Berg.
Carling, Jørgen (2005), 'Gender dimension of international migration', Global Commission on International Migration, *Global Migration Perspectives*, **35**, May, 2–7.
Catarino, Christine (1999), 'L'insertion sociale des immigrés capverdiens et angolais dans l'aire métropolitaine de Lisbonne: une étude de cas des relations et rapports sociaux de sexe, de classe et ethniques', doctoral thesis, IEDES-Université Paris I Panthéon-Sorbonne, September.
Catarino, Christine, Mirjana Morokvasic and Marie-Antoinette Hily (eds) (2005), 'Femmes, genre, migration et mobilités', *Revue Européenne des Migrations Internationales*, **21** (1), 7–27.
Chaib, Sabah (2003), 'Women, migration and the labour market: the case of France', in J. Freedman (ed.), *Gender and Insecurity: Migrant Women in Europe*, Burlington, VT: Ashgate, pp. 107–17.
Darley, Mathilde (2006), 'Le statut de la victime dans la lutte contre la traite des femmes', *Critique Internationale*, **1** (30), January–March, 103–22.

Darley, Mathilde (2007), 'La prostitution en clubs dans les régions frontalières de la République tchèque', *Revue française de sociologie*, **48**, 273–306.
Delphy, Christine (1970), 'L'ennemi principal', *Partisans* (54–5), July–October, 157–72.
Des femmes immigrées parlent (1978), Paris, Genève: L'Harmattan, CETIM.
Deschamps, Catherine (2006), *Le sexe et l'argent des trottoirs*, Paris: Hachette.
Dodson Belinda, Simelane Hamilton, Tevera Daniel, Green Thuso, Chikanda Abel and Fion de Vletter (2008), 'Gender, migration and remittances in Southern Africa', Southern African Migration Project, *Migration Policy Series*, **49**.
Donato, Katharine M., Donna Gabaccia, Jennifer Holdaway, Martin Manalansan IV and Patricia R. Pessar (2006), 'A glass half full? Gender in migration studies', *International Migration Review*, Gender and Migration Revisited, **40** (1), February, 3–26.
Dorlin, Elsa (2005), 'De l'usage épistémologique et politique des catégories de "sexe" et de "race" dans les études sur le genre', *Cahiers du Genre*, **2** (39), 83–105.
Dorlin, Elsa (2012), 'L'Atlantique féministe: l'intersectionnalité en débat', *Papeles del CEIC*, **2** (83), 1–16.
Drouilleau, Félicie (2009), 'Exode et domesticité à Bogotá', *Travail, genre et sociétés*, Domestiques d'ici et d'ailleurs (22), November, 75–96.
Falquet, Jules (2006), 'Hommes en armes et femmes "de service": tendances néolibérales dans l'évolution de la division sexuelle et internationale du travail', *Cahiers du Genre*, Travail et mondialisation, Confrontation Nord/Sud, **1** (40), 15–38.
Falquet, Jules, Annette Goldberg-Salinas and Claude Zaidman (eds) (2000), 'Femmes en migrations. Aperçus de recherches', *Cahiers du CEDREF* (8–9).
Falquet, Jules, Emmanuelle Lada and Aude Rabaud (eds) (2006), '(Ré)articulation des rapports sociaux de sexe, classe et 'race'. Repères historiques et contemporains', *Cahiers du CEDREF* (14).
Falquet, Jules, Aude Rabaud, Jane Freedman and Francesca Scrinzi (eds) (2008), 'Femmes, genre, migrations et mondialisation: un état des problématiques', *Cahiers du CEDREF* (16).
Gabaccia, Donna (1994), *From the Other side: Women, Gender, and Immigrant Life in the U.S. 1820–1990*, Bloomington, IN: Indiana University Press.
Giabiconi, Dominique (2005), 'Les mariages mixtes franco-polonais: contours et enjeux', *Revue Européenne des Migrations Internationales*, Femmes, genre, migration et mobilités, **21** (1), 259–73.
Golub, Anne, Mirjana Morokvasic and Catherine Quiminal (1997), 'Evolution de la production des connaissances sur les femmes immigrées en France et en Europe', *Migrations Société*, **9** (52), 19–36.
Gonzálvez, Herminia (2007), 'Familias y hogares transnacionales: Una perspectiva de género', *Puntos de Vista. Cuadernos del Observatorio de las Migraciones y de la Convivencia Intercultural de la Ciudad de Madrid*, **3** (11), September, 7–26.
Gregorio Gil, Carmen (1998), *La migración femenina y su impacto en las relaciones de género*, Madrid: Narcea.
Guillemaut, Françoise (2005), 'Les femmes migrantes dans l'étau des politiques publiques en Europe', talk given at 'Mobilités au féminin', Laboratoire Méditerranéen de Sociologie, Maison Méditerranéenne des Sciences de l'Homme, Tangiers, 15–19 November.
Guillemaut, Françoise (2006), 'Victimes de trafic ou actrices d'un processus migratoire? Saisir la voix des femmes migrantes prostituées par la recherche action (enquête)', *Terrains et Travaux*, **1** (10), 157–76.
Gutiérrez Rodriguez, Encarnación (1999), *Intellektuelle Migrantinnen – Subjektivitäten im Zeitalter von Globalisierung. Eine postkoloniale dekonstruktive Analyse von Biographien im Spannungsverhältnis von Ethnisierung und Vergeschlechtlichung*, Opladen: Leske & Budrich.
Handman, Marie-Elisabeth and Janine Mossuz-Lavau (2005), *La Prostitution à Paris*, Paris: La Martinière.
Herrera, Gioconda (2006), 'Precarización del trabajo, crisis de reproducción social y migración femenina: ecuatorianas en España y Estados Unidos', in G. Herrera (ed.), *La*

persistencia de la desigualdad. Género, trabajo y pobreza en América Latina, FLACSO Ecuador, pp. 199–214.
Hersent, Madeleine and Claude Zaidman (eds) (2003), 'Genre, travail et migrations en Europe', *Cahiers du CEDREF* (12).
Hommes & Migrations (2004), 'Femmes contre la violence' (1248), March–April.
International Organization for Migration (IOM) (2010), 'A study on remittances and investment opportunities for Egyptian migrants', IOM Cairo.
Irek, Małgorzata (1998), *Der Schmugglerzug. Warschau-Berlin-Warschau: Materialien einer Feldforschung*, Berlin: Das Arabische Buch.
Jacquemin, Mélanie (2009), '"Petites nièces" et "petites bonnes" à Abidjan: les mutations de la domesticité juvénile', *Travail, genre et sociétés*, Domestiques d'ici et d'ailleurs (22), 53–74.
Jaksic, Milena (2008), 'Figures de la victime de la traite des êtres humains: de la victime idéale à la victime coupable', *Cahiers Internationaux de Sociologie*, Questions d'ici et d'ailleurs (124), 127–46.
Kearney, Michael (1986), 'From the invisible hand to visible feet: anthropological studies of migration and development', *Annual Review of Anthropology*, **15**, October, 331–61.
Kofman, Eleonore (1999), 'Birds of passage a decade later: gender and immigration in the European Union', *International Migration Review*, **33** (2), Summer, 269–99.
Kuzma, Elzbieta (2003), 'Les immigrés polonais à Bruxelles', Rapport de recherche, Université de Bruxelles, Bruxelles.
Lacroix, Thomas (2009), 'Migration, développement, codéveloppement: quels acteurs pour quels discours?', Rapport de Synthèse Européen, Informer sur les migrations et le développement (IDEM), Institut Panos, Paris.
Lévy, Florence (2005), 'Les migrations des femmes du Nord de la Chine: l'exil, alternative à une situation de déclin?', paper presented at 'Mobilités au féminin', Laboratoire Méditerranéen de Sociologie, Maison Méditerranéenne des Sciences de l'Homme, Tangiers, 15–19 November.
Lévy, Florence (2008), '"Faire ça": la prostitution comme adaptation résignée à la précarité de migrantes chinoises à Paris', paper presented at the Journées d'Étude: 'Migrations: Nouvelles pratiques, approches plurielles', Paris, EHESS, 8 October.
Lévy, Florence and Marylène Lieber (2009), 'La sexualité comme ressource migratoire: Les Chinoises du Nord à Paris', *Revue française de sociologie*, **50** (4), 719–46.
Lieber, Marylène (2007), 'Au-delà des migrations féminines ou comment penser le genre: Une réflexion à partir du cas des Chinois de France', in C. Audebert and E. Ma Mung (eds), *Les Migrations internationales: enjeux contemporains et questions nouvelles*, Bilbao: Université de Deusto, pp. 241–56.
Morokvasic, Mirjana (1976), 'L'immigration féminine en France: état de la question', *L'Année Sociologique*, **26** (2), 563–75.
Morokvasic, Mirjana (1983), 'Emigration féminine et femmes immigrées: discussion de quelques tendances dans la recherche', *Pluriel* (36), 20–51.
Morokvasic, Mirjana (1984), 'The overview: birds of passage are also women', *International Migration Review*, **18** (4), 886–907.
Morokvasic, Mirjana (1992), 'Une migration pendulaire: les polonais en Allemagne', *Hommes & Migrations* (1155), June, 31–7.
Morokvasic, Mirjana (1999), 'La mobilité transnationale comme ressource: le cas des migrants de l'Europe de l'Est', *Cultures & Conflits* (33–34), 105–22.
Morokvasic, Mirjana (2004), 'Settled in mobility: engendering post-wall migration in Europe', *Feminist Review*, **77** (1), 7–25.
Morokvasic, Mirjana (2008), 'Femmes et genre dans l'étude des migrations: un regard rétrospectif', in J. Falquet, A. Rabaud, J. Freedman and F. Scrinzi (eds), 'Femmes, genre, migrations et mondialisation: un état des problématiques', *Cahiers du CEDREF* (16).
Morokvasic, Mirjana (2011), 'L'(in)visibilité continue', *Cahiers du Genre*, Migrantes et Mobilisées (51), 25–47.

Morokvasic, Mirjana and Christine Catarino (2007a), 'Une (in)visibilité multiforme', *Plein Droit*, 'Femmes, étrangers: des causes concurrentes?' (75), December, 27–30.
Morokvasic, Mirjana and Christine Catarino (2007b), 'Between policies and the praxis: state administration and the NGOs discourse – the French case', FeMiPol Working Paper 4 – WP2, FeMiPol.
Morokvasic, Mirjana and Christine Catarino (2010), 'Women, gender, transnational migrations and mobility in France', in K. Slany, M. Kontos and M. Liapi (eds), *Women in New Migrations. Current Debates in European Societies*, Cracow: Jagiellonian University Press, pp. 51–82.
Moujoud, Nasima (2005), 'Prostitution et migration des Maghrébines', in M.-E. Handman and J. Mossuz-Lavau (eds), *La Prostitution à Paris*, Paris: La Martinière, pp. 199–233.
Moujoud, Nasima (2012), 'Femmes sans-papiers et exilées dans des mobilisations féministes. Les limites de la solidarité formelle', in C. Cossée, A. Miranda, N. Ouali and D. Séhili (eds), *Le Genre au cœur des migrations*, Paris: Éditions Pétra, pp. 255–70.
Moujoud, Nasima and Jules Falquet (2010), 'Cent ans de sollicitude en France. Domesticité, reproduction sociale, migration et histoire coloniale', *Agone* (43), 169–95.
Moujoud, Nasima and Dolorès Pourette (2005), '"Traite" de femmes migrantes, domesticité et prostitution: A propos de migrations interne et externe', *Cahiers d'Études Africaines*, **45** (3–4), (179–80), 1093–121.
Mozère, Liane (2005), 'Les domestiques philippines à Paris: un marché mondial de la domesticité défini en termes de genre?', *Migrations Société* (99–100), May, 217–28.
Ong, Aihwa (1999), *Flexible Citizenship: The Cultural Logics of Transnationality*, Durham, NC: Duke University Press.
Oso, Laura (1998), *La migración hacia España de mujeres jefas de hogar*, Madrid: Instituto de la Mujer, Ministerio de Trabajo y Asuntos Sociales, Serie Estudios 52, p. 438.
Oso, Laura (2005), 'La réussite paradoxale des bonnes espagnoles à Paris: stratégies de mobilité sociale et trajectoires biographiques', *Revue Européenne des Migrations Internationales*, Femmes, genre, migration et mobilités, **21** (1), 107–29.
Oso, Laura (2008), 'Migration, genre et foyers transnationaux: un état de la bibliographie', in J. Falquet, A. Rabaud, J. Freedman and F. Scrinzi (eds), 'Femmes, genre, migrations et mondialisation: un état des problèmatiques', *Cahiers du CEDREF* (16), pp. 125–46.
Palomares, Elise and Armelle Testenoire (2010) (eds), 'Prismes féministes. Qu'est-ce que l'intersectionnalité?', *L'homme et la société*, **2–3** (176–7).
Paperman, Patricia and Liliane Pierrot (1978), *Le travail ambigu*, Paris: Cerfise, Cordes, no. 74–8.
Parreñas, Rhacel Salazar (2001), *Servants of Globalization: Women, Migration and Domestic Work*, Stanford, CA: Stanford University Press.
Parreñas, Rhacel Salazar (2005), *Children of Global Migration: Transnational Families and Gendered Woes*, Stanford, CA: Stanford University Press.
Péraldi, Michel (2001), *Cabas et containers, activités marchandes informelles et réseaux migrants transfrontaliers*, Paris, Aix en Provence: Maisonneuve et Larose, Maison Méditerranéenne des Sciences de l'Homme.
Pian, Anaïk (2010), 'La migration empêchée et la survie économique: services et échanges sexuels des Sénégalaises au Maroc', *Cahiers du Genre* (49), 183–202.
Puech, Isabelle (2006), 'Femmes et immigrées: corvéables à merci', in M. Maruani and I. Puech (eds), *Travail, genre et sociétés*, Les dégâts de la violence économique (16), Ivry Sur Seine: Armand Colin, pp. 39–51.
Razy, Elodie and Virginie Baby-Collin (2011), 'La famille transnationale dans tous ses états', *Autrepart* (57–58), 7–22.
Riccio, Bruno (2003), 'From "ethnic group" to "transnational community"? Senegalese migrants' ambivalent experiences and multiple trajectories', *Journal of Ethnic and Migration Studies*, **27** (4), 583–99.
Rigoni, Isabelle and Djaouida Séhili (eds) (2005), 'Femmes dans la migration', *Migrations Société*, **17** (99–100), June.
Schmoll, Camille (2005), 'Pratiques spatiales transnationales et stratégies de mobilité des

commerçantes tunisiennes', *Revue Européenne des Migrations Internationales*, Femmes, genre, migration et mobilités, **21** (1), 131–54.
Schwenken, Helen (2005), 'The challenges of framing women migrants' rights in the European Union', *Revue Européenne des Migrations Internationales*, Femmes, genre, migration et mobilités, **21** (1), 177–94.
Scrinzi, Francesca (2003), '"Ma culture dans laquelle elle travaille". Les migrantes dans les services domestiques en Italie et en France', in M. Hersent and C. Zaidman (eds), 'Genre, travail et migrations en Europe', *Cahiers du CEDREF* (12), pp. 137–62.
Sengel, Marie (2000), 'Nana-Benz de Noailles', *Hommes & Migrations* (1224), March–April, 71–8.
Tabet, Paola (2004), *La grande arnaque: Sexualité des femmes et échange économico-sexuel*, Paris: L'Harmattan, Bibliothèque du Féminisme.
Taboada-Leonetti, Isabel and Florence Lévy (1978), *Femmes et immigrées: l'insertion des femmes immigrées en France*, Paris: La Documentation française.
Taravella, Louis (1980), *Bibliographie analytique sur les femmes immigrées: 1965–1979*, Paris: CIEMM.
Tarrius, Alain (1992), *Les fourmis d'Europe: migrants riches, migrants pauvres et nouvelles villes internationales*, Paris: L'Harmattan.
Tarrius, Alain (2002), *La mondalisation par le bas: les nouveaux nomades des économies souterraines*, Paris: Balland.
Thiollet, Hélène (2010), 'Migrations et relations internationales: Les apories de la gestion multilatérale des migrations internationales?', *Transcontinentales, Sociétés, Idéologie, Système Mondial*, Dossier: Des migrations aux circulations transnationales, **8/9**, available at: http://transcontinentales.revues.org/787 (accessed 8 October 2012).
Tissot, Sylvie (2007), 'Bilan d'un féminisme d'État', *Plein Droit*, 'Femmes, étrangers: des causes concurrentes?' (75), December, 15–18.
Verschuur, Christine (2009), 'Quel genre? Résistances et mésententes autour du mot "genre" dans le développement', *Revue Tiers Monde*, **4** (200), 785–803.
Weber, Serge (2007), 'Liens intimes, liens utiles? Les avatars de la sexualité au cours des trajectoires migratoires féminines', *Migrances*, Construction des sexualités et migration, (27), 48–59.
Wihtol de Wenden, Catherine and Anne de Tinguy (1995), *L'Europe et toutes ses migrations*, Bruxelles: Éditions Complexe.
Wisniewski, Jean (1974), 'Les travailleuses immigrées': panorama statistique, *Hommes & Migrations* (862), April.
Yuval-Davis, Nira (2006), 'Intersectionality and feminist politics', *European Journal of Women's Studies*, **13** (3), August, 193–209.
Zaidman, Claude and Patricia Bachelet (2003), 'Introduction', in M. Hersent and C. Zaidman (eds), 'Genre, travail et migrations en Europe', *Cahiers du CEDREF* (12), pp. 10–22.

12 The gendered dynamics of integration and transnational engagement among second-generation adults in Europe
James D. Bachmeier, Laurence Lessard-Phillips and Tineke Fokkema

INTRODUCTION

Within the social science literature on contemporary immigration and immigrant incorporation, considerable theoretical debate has revolved around the notion of immigrant transnationalism (Glick-Schiller et al., 1995; Portes et al., 1999; Kivisto, 2001; Joppke and Morawska, 2003; Waldinger and Fitzgerald, 2004; Levitt and Jaworsky, 2007; de Haas, 2010). During the 1980s, migration scholars began emphasizing the extent to which international migration consisted of mutually reinforcing processes unfolding in both sending and receiving communities (Massey et al., 1987, 1994; Grasmuck and Pessar, 1991). This bi-directional flow of people, goods and ideas across borders appeared inconsistent with classical perspectives of 'assimilation' and called into question traditional notions of citizenship and the state (Bloemraad et al., 2008). In light of this, based on ethnographic research in migrant communities, many scholars argued that a theory of transnationalism, rather than assimilation, more adequately described the dynamics of international migration in a world that is increasingly interconnected owing to technological change.

Subsequent survey-based research, however, revealed that the share of the immigrant population maintaining intensive transnational engagements was quite small (Guarnizo et al., 2003; Schans, 2009; Beauchemin et al., 2011) and that the majority of immigrants become less oriented to the home country with increasing duration spent in the host country (Snel et al., 2006; Soehl and Waldinger, 2010; Cela et al., 2013). While this has tempered assertions that transnationalism represents an alternative form of immigrant integration or incorporation (Portes, 2006), research focused on the transnational engagements and orientations of immigrants has nevertheless provided important insights into understanding how immigrants' orientation to their country of origin is related to their integration into the host society. Although the transnational engagements of immigrants appear largely to conform to a pattern stressed by the assimilation perspective, research on transnationalism indicates that the maintenance of transnational ties is largely complementary to rather than a substitute for socio-cultural and economic incorporation into the host society (Portes et al., 2002; Guarnizo et al., 2003; van Dalen et al., 2005; Beauchemin et al., 2011; de Haas and Fokkema, 2011; Cela et al., 2013). In addition, research on immigrant transnationalism has demonstrated that the relationship between migrants' transnational orientations and their host-country incorporation outcomes depends significantly on gender (Grasmuck and Pessar; 1991; Hondagneu-Sotelo, 1994; Salih, 2003; Itzigsohn and Giorguli-Saucedo, 2005).

Because immigrant adaptation is an intergenerational process (Gordon, 1964), evaluating the extent to which transnational ties are associated with host-country incorporation outcomes requires an analytical focus on the second generation (Levitt and Waters, 2002; Levitt, 2004; Thomson and Crul, 2007). Little is known about the extent to which the gendered dynamics of incorporation and transnational engagement observed in the immigrant population also apply to the experiences of their adult children. While the limited amount of existing evidence seems to support the notion that these dynamics are transmitted intergenerationally, these preliminary conclusions are based largely on ethnographic research of second-generation children and young adults deeply embedded within the transnational social world of their parents (Smith, 2006). Moreover, initial examinations of survey samples of the adult second generation have placed little analytical emphasis on gender and are almost exclusively focused on the second-generation immigrant population in the United States (Kasinitz et al., 2002; Rumbaut, 2002; Haller and Landolt, 2005; Tamaki, 2011).

Using survey data from a sample of adult second-generation immigrants in 13 European cities, this chapter examines the extent to which the gendered dynamics of host-country integration and the maintenance of transnational ties are also observed among second-generation adults. Investigating the transnational ties of the second generation is likely to yield important insights into the prospects for successful host-country integration (Levitt and Waters, 2002; Haller and Landolt, 2005; Jones-Correa, 2012). This is particularly crucial in the European context where concerns over the implications of immigration and multiculturalism for social cohesion have loomed especially large (Foner and Alba, 2008). Finally, the research presented in this chapter has potentially important implications for theoretical and public policy discussions of immigrant integration as they pertain to gender, since the status of women in immigrant communities has been an oft-cited factor underlying integration concerns (Kastoryano, 2006; Korteweg and Yurdakul, 2009).

Studying second-generation transnationalism also has implications for researchers and policymakers concerned with the relationship between migration and development in sending countries. More specifically, and analogous to research on migration and development, origin-country development outcomes will likely depend on the prevalence and selectivity of second-generation transnationalism (Massey et al., 1998; de Haas, 2010). With respect to remittances, even if the rate of remitting in the second generation is low compared to the immigrant generation, simply by virtue of coming of age in a developed society, second-generation immigrants possess significantly higher levels of human capital and therefore are capable, at least hypothetically, of sending larger remittances on an individual basis. And in non-monetary terms, their retention of ties and involvement in the origin country may lead to the cultural transmission of norms and expectations held in more-developed host societies. Finally, development effects are likely to depend on the selectivity of second-generation transnationalism. Development outcomes may vary depending on whether, for example, high-achieving women show greater interest in the affairs of the origin country, or by contrast, economically discouraged second-generation men are relatively more likely to sustain attachment to the origin country.

BACKGROUND

Migration, Host-country Integration and Gender

In order to derive a tentative set of hypotheses pertaining to transnationalism among the European second generation, we build on three empirically supported conclusions from existing research on immigration, integration, and gender. The first is that rather than representing a postmodern, alternative mode of immigrant integration, transnational engagement among immigrants appears to take place within a larger context of assimilation in which home-country ties diminish with increasing exposure to the host society (Portes et al., 2002; Guarnizo et al., 2003; Portes, 2006; Waldinger, 2007; Soehl and Waldinger, 2010; Cela et al., 2013). Only a relatively small proportion of immigrants exhibit meaningful transnational engagement and as immigrants are increasingly tied to life in the host country, attachments to the country of origin tend to weaken (Massey et al., 1987; Snel et al., 2006; Schans, 2009; Soehl and Waldinger, 2010). Given this tendency among members of the immigrant generation, it is not surprising that early analyses also find little evidence of widespread, intensive transnationalism in the second generation (Rumbaut, 2002; Fokkema et al., 2012).

The second important finding from previous research is that immigrant transnationalism, when it does occur, is *positively* related to indicators of integration in the host society (Portes et al., 2002; Guarnizo et al., 2003; Itzigsohn and Giorguli-Saucedo, 2005; Marcelli and Lowell, 2005; van Dalen et al., 2005; Snel et al., 2006; Carling, 2008; Jayaweera and Choudhury, 2008; Mazzucato, 2008; Schans, 2009; Beauchemin et al., 2011; de Haas and Fokkema, 2011; Cela et al., 2013). Net of the inverse effects of duration of residence on home-country attachments, integration, especially economic mobility, facilitates migrants' capacity to engage simultaneously in life in the country of origin through investment, remittances and social visits. Similarly, increased ethno-cultural and civic integration in the host-country can facilitate transnational engagement through greater access to passports and travel documents that comes with host-country language, legal status and citizenship acquisition (Al-Ali et al., 2001; Singer and Gilbertson, 2003; Molina, 2008; Fresnoza-Flot, 2009).

The third important finding comes from research focusing on the gendered dynamics of immigrant integration and transnationalism. Female migrants tend to experience gains in status by virtue of migration to developed societies with a relatively greater institutional commitment to gender equality than exists in developing countries of origin (de Haas and Fokkema, 2010). Immigrant men, on the other hand, tend to experience a concomitant 'status loss', both in relation to immigrant women and with respect to their position within the status hierarchy of the receiving society relative to that of their home country. This dynamic can lead to conflicting orientations with respect to host-country settlement, with immigrant women expressing a greater desire to settle permanently in the receiving country in contrast to immigrant men, who are more likely to desire an eventual return to the home country (Grasmuck and Pessar, 1991; Hondagneu-Sotelo, 1994; de Haas and Fokkema, 2010).

Male status loss, however, does not necessarily lead to lower *levels* of transnational engagement among women, but rather gender differences in the *type* of transnational engagement and gender differences in the relationship between host-country integration and transnationalism. Emphasizing women's traditional role of 'kin keeping', research suggests that the transnational engagements of immigrant women tend to be focused on family life in the country of origin (Menjivar, 2000; Salih, 2003; Itzigsohn and Giorguli-Saucedo, 2005). By contrast, the home-country engagement of immigrant men tends to be concentrated in the male-dominated realm of local politics (Goldring, 2003) and the sending of remittances which confers status and prestige in the home-country

(Johnson and Stoll, 2008; Schans, 2009). This implies gender differences in the underlying motivations for home-country engagement, which in turn is likely to result in a gendered relationship between host-country integration and transnational engagement. Quantitative evidence from the United States supports the notion that the transnational engagement of female migrants is more likely to be 'resource based' and therefore is more strongly related to their level of host-country economic integration (Itzigsohn and Giorguli-Saucedo, 2005). The home-country engagement of immigrant men, however, is more likely to be 'reactive' and varies to a greater extent with experiences of discrimination and dissatisfaction with opportunities available in the host society (ibid.).

Evidence from the Second Generation

As indicated at the outset of the chapter, little empirical work has been done to document the prevalence and nature of transnationalism among children of immigrants *as adults*. The limited body of empirical evidence that has thus far emerged indicates that the first two research findings discussed above for the immigrant generation appear to apply to the US and European second generations as well. A recent comparative study of transnationalism among second-generation adults in Los Angeles, New York and eight European cities indicates that a majority of adult children of immigrants report having made at least one visit to their parents' country of birth as an adult (Fokkema et al., 2012). The same study, however, also found that a small (though non-negligible) proportion of the second generation exhibited more-intensive forms of transnational engagement. Research based on a sample of adult children of US immigrants in Miami and San Diego reports similar findings (Rumbaut, 2002; Haller and Landolt, 2005).

This same small number of studies also suggests that the relationship between host-country integration and transnational engagement among second-generation immigrants runs generally parallel to those reported for their immigrant parents. Not surprisingly, ethno-cultural factors, such as the maintenance/loss of their parents' language, explain a considerable share of variation in second-generation transnational engagement. However, as with their parents, home-country engagement increases significantly among more economically integrated second-generation adults as their upward mobility affords them relatively more resources to devote to international travel and remitting (Kasinitz et al., 2002; Rumbaut, 2002; Haller and Landolt, 2005; Tamaki, 2011; Fokkema et al., 2012).

Finally, to our knowledge, none of the limited number of existing empirical studies of second-generation transnational engagement has placed analytical focus on gender, and the information that can be gleaned from the results of these studies is inconclusive. Fokkema et al. (2012), for example, find no differences between second-generation men and women in Europe or the US with respect to the *level* of transnational engagement, measured using a composite index. However, consistent with the 'status loss' dynamic discussed above for the immigrant generation, they do find that second-generation men in Europe, but not the US, are significantly more likely than their female counterparts to engage in more-intensive *types* of home-country engagement. Rumbaut (2002) and Haller et al. (2005) find that second-generation men in San Diego and Miami, respectively, are significantly more likely to remit to parents' birth country. Still other studies report no gender differences with respect to remitting (Kasinitz et al., 2002; Rumbaut, 2002), and inconsistent results in terms of gender differences in home visits (ibid.; Tamaki, 2011). On balance, the lack of analytical emphasis on gender coupled with differences in contexts, the focal population being examined, and the operationalizing and measurement of transnational engagement, precludes drawing any firm conclusions about gendered dynamics of integration and second-generation transnationalism on the basis of existing evidence.

Study Hypotheses

While there continues to be considerable debate over what constitutes transnational engagement, adjudicating this debate lies beyond the scope of this chapter. Nevertheless, prior to positing a tentative set of hypotheses, it is necessary to clarify how transnationalism is operationalized here. We examine three types of transnational involvement (the measurement of which is described in greater detail below) and conceptualize them as being positioned on a hypothetical continuum ranging in intensity from low to high. *Visiting* parents' country of origin constitutes a relatively low-intensity form of transnational engagement because international travel to visit family and friends does not require a sustained commitment to life in the origin country. *Remitting* to parents' country of origin signifies a relatively more committed stake in the affairs of kin and family remaining in the origin country. Finally, the *intention to return* to live in the parents' origin country constitutes an even greater attachment to the origin country.

Owing to the lack of available evidence and the underdeveloped nature of theorizing about gender, host-country integration and second-generation transnationalism, only tentative hypotheses can be drawn at this point for empirical testing. All of the hypotheses offered here assume that the gendered dynamics discussed above with respect to the immigrant generation also carry over to influence the transnational behaviour and orientations reported by second-generation adults in Europe. More specifically, we expect that status gain/loss will lead to more 'resource-based' transnationalism among second-generation women while 'reactive' transnationalism should be more prevalent among second-generation men (Itzigsohn and Giorguli-Saucedo, 2005). While it may at first seem illogical to speak of gender status losses and gains among the second generation, transnational theorists point out that the children of immigrants are nevertheless raised within a transnational social field in which the process of shifting and renegotiation of gender roles plays out (Levitt, 2009). In his 15-year study of Mexican immigrants in New York, Smith (2006) describes how adolescent boys, struggling with growing up as a racialized minority in New York, experience status gains during trips to their parents' home community in Mexico, while their female counterparts experience status losses. This implies that growing up within a transnational social field fosters a gendered orientation to host-country integration and transnational attachment among the second generation that parallels the experiences of their parents.

To the extent that these gendered mechanisms are operating within the adult second generation, we expect:

Hypothesis 1 The transnational engagements reported by second-generation women will be disproportionately low intensity in nature, while those second-generation adults exhibiting stronger attachments to the country of origin will be disproportionately male.

While 'kin-keeping' roles may dispose second-generation women to engage to a greater degree than their male counterparts in maintaining connections to family in the parental country of origin (Menjivar, 2000; Itzigsohn and Giorguli-Saucedo, 2005), differences between sending and host countries in gender relation regimes are likely to elicit greater reluctance to forge more committal ties with their parents' country of origin among women as compared to men (Hondagneu-Sotelo, 1994; de Haas and Fokkema, 2010). Stated differently, Hypothesis 1 implies that gender differences in transnationalism will vary depending on the type of transnational engagement in question.

With respect to integration and transnationalism, using the same European data employed in this chapter, Fokkema et al. (2012) find a strong inverse relationship between host-country ethno-cultural integration and second-generation transnational engagement. Net of ethno-cultural integration, however, Fokkema et al. also find that economic integration is positively associated with second-generation transnationalism, consistent

The gendered dynamics of integration and transnational engagement 275

with findings among first and second-generation immigrants in the US (Kasinitz et al., 2002; Rumbaut, 2002; Guarnizo et al., 2003; Itzigsohn and Giorguli-Saucedo, 2005). However, if female transnationalism is disproportionately resource based while male transnationalism is disproportionately reactive in response to status loss, we would expect to find that the relationship between economic integration will be moderated by gender *and* that the nature of the gender–integration interaction will depend on the intensity of transnational engagement. More specifically:

Hypothesis 2 The effect of economic integration on low-intensity forms of transnationalism (for example, visiting) will be stronger and more positive among women.

When both men and women lack the resources needed to visit family and friends in the home country, we expect men and women to be equally unlikely to engage transnationally. But if female transnational engagement is driven by their traditional 'kin-keeping' role, we would expect their rate of informal transnational engagement to increase more precipitously with gains in resources as compared to men. By contrast, we expect:

Hypothesis 3 The effect of economic integration on high-intensity forms of transnational engagement (for example, return intention) will be stronger and more negative among men.

These expectations stem from the processes of male status loss and 'reactive' transnationalism stressed in existing literature (Hondagneu-Sotelo, 1994; Itzigsohn and Giorguli-Saucedo, 2005; Schans, 2009; de Haas and Fokkema, 2010). Experiences of status loss are likely to be felt most acutely among second-generation men who have struggled to attain economic integration and frustration with the opportunities available in the host society may, in turn, foment a reactive transnational attachment. While second-generation women may also be frustrated by a lack of economic integration, they may not perceive their prospects to be much better in the 'home' country owing to the fact that gender inequality and segregation is much more pervasive compared to developed host countries (Wessendorf, 2007).

The framework developed here suggests that the gendered dynamics of transnationalism may be less discernible when it comes to moderately intensive forms of transnational engagement, in this case remitting. This is because remitting can simultaneously represent kin-keeping *and* status-seeking transnational behaviour. Thus, female remitting, motivated disproportionately by kin-keeping motivations, may not differ significantly in prevalence from remitting among their male counterparts, motivated to a greater extent by status seeking. Moreover, regardless of gender, remitting necessarily depends on the availability of resources and thus it is likely that economic integration will be equally positively associated with remitting for both men and women. It follows that:

Hypothesis 4 Men and women will not differ in their likelihood of remitting, nor will the positive association between economic integration and remitting vary by gender.

Finally, it is not immediately clear, however, whether this same logic should be expected to apply with respect to gender differences in the relationship between *ethno-cultural* integration and transnationalism, and while we test for such differences in our analyses, we do not derive specific hypotheses. Ethno-cultural integration, at least conceptually, is relatively more multidimensional compared to economic integration. The former consists of language use, religiosity and other culturally related practices that are based in large part on choices made by individuals, while economic integration is governed to a greater extent by opportunity structures and the extent to which immigrants have access to the education and occupations necessary to achieve economic parity with natives (Bean et al., 2012).

DATA, MEASURES AND METHODOLOGICAL APPROACH

Data

To test these hypotheses, we use the Integration of the European Second Generation Survey (TIES; see www.tiesproject.eu for more information). The TIES survey, covering 15 European cities in eight countries,[1] focused on the lives of second-generation young adults of Turkish, Moroccan and former Yugoslavian descent compared to native-born young adults with native-born parents living in similar neighbourhoods, when possible (Crul et al., 2012). By means of cross-section surveys using various sampling and interviewing methods, 9,971 individuals aged 18–35 were sampled and interviewed between 2006 and 2008 (Groenewold and Lessard-Phillips, 2012). The immigrant groups included in city-specific samples varied according to the predominant groups in the individual countries.[2] The analyses presented in this chapter include only those second-generation respondents out of full-time education with non-missing information on all variables in all countries except Belgium, yielding an analytical sample of 2,595 observations across 13 cities in seven European countries. Post-stratification weights based on the age–sex distribution of the groups at the city level are used in the analyses for all countries except Spain.

Measurement

Transnational engagement

As mentioned above, we examine three types of second-generation transnational engagement. *Visiting* is measured by the number of times second-generation immigrants travelled to their parents' country of birth in the previous five years. Scores on this variable range from zero (no visits during the previous five years) to six (six or more visits). This outcome is analysed using negative binomial regression models, commonly employed for count variables. *Remitting* is operationalized as a binary indicator equal to one for persons reporting that they send money to their parents' country of birth and zero otherwise, and we analyse this outcome using logit models. Finally, *return intention* is measured by the respondents' intentions to live in their parents' birth country for at least one year or longer in the future. The four response categories are: 'certainly not', 'possibly', 'likely' and 'certainly'. We analyse this outcome using multinomial logit models comparing the probability of choosing each of the last three categories over the first one (the reference category).

Economic and ethno-cultural integration

We include numerous indicators of economic and ethno-cultural integration and use principal components analysis (PCA) to reduce these items to single-factor indicators of each of these dimensions of integration, respectively. The ethno-cultural factor includes the following items: proficiency with parents' language of origin; use of host-country language; ethnic media consumption; ethnic background or generation of spouse or partner; religious worship services attendance; and feelings of belonging to the host country. The economic integration factor includes: indicators of educational attainment; occupational prestige (with individuals without a score imputed at zero); and respondents' experience with financial hardship. All of the indicators are coded so that higher values indicate greater integration.

PCA provides several analytical benefits. First, based on factor loadings, it tests empirically the extent to which ethno-cultural and economic indicators, respectively, bundle together and thus constitute a multidimensional approximation of latent ethno-cultural and economic factors. The results of our PCA (shown in Appendix Table 12A.1) indicate that our ethno-cultural and economic indicators do in fact load on two distinct factors. A second benefit of PCA is that it allows for the calculation of factor scores that measure a person's overall level of ethno-cultural and economic integration. For each person, the factor score is calculated as the weighted sum of standardized values for each integration indicator with the PCA factor loading serving as the weight for each indicator. These scores are distributed with a mean of zero and a standard deviation of one. Thus, a score of zero indicates an average relative level of economic or ethno-cultural integration, higher scores represent higher relative levels of integration. The use of factor scores eases the interpretation of the extent to which economic and ethno-cultural integration are associated with second-generation transnationalism. Rather than interpreting the coefficients for each individual integration indicator, the magnitude and direction of which may vary across indicators, PCA reduces the integration indicators to two factors approximating individuals' *overall* levels of ethno-cultural and economic integration, thus allowing for more parsimonious analyses and facilitating the interpretation of model results.

Covariates of transnational engagement
We include in our models several demographic and contextual control variables that are likely to influence transnational engagement. First, we include a control for age since transnational engagement has been shown to vary over the life-course (Smith 2006; Levitt 2009), though we may see little evidence of an age effect given the limited age range of the TIES sample. Also, as young adults, it is not uncommon to find TIES respondents living with their parents. To the extent that such persons are more likely to be transnationally engaged by virtue of their immigrant parents' home-country orientation, we account for this exposure using a dummy-coded indicator (1 = lives with parents). Another life course factor that may influence transnational behaviour is child rearing. While the birth of a child may lead to increased motivations to visit family members abroad, over the long run raising children in the host country entails immersion into activities, institutions and organizations that is likely to be at odds with the simultaneous maintenance of transnational ties. We thus include a dummy variable for which second-generation parents are coded one.

Recent studies have demonstrated that the dynamics of second-generation integration and transnational engagement vary across local and national integration contexts (Glick-Schiller, et al., 2006; Fokkema, 2011; Bean et al., 2012; Fokkema et al., 2012). We account for differences in local integration contexts by including city dummies that contrast the transnational engagement reported by second-generation adults in Vienna (the reference category) to the other 12 TIES cities. Controlling for survey city will account for differences in transnational behaviour that are the result of local integration contexts, but will also adjust for the fact that the national origin mix of the second generation varies across cities.[3] Given that our emphasis in this chapter is not on contextual effects, we do not report the city dummies in the results.

RESULTS

Descriptive Results

Means and percentages for all of the variables described above are presented in Table 12.1 for the sample as a whole and separately by sex. Eighty per cent of second-generation adults reported making at least one visit to their parents' country of birth during the previous five years and the proportion is significantly higher for women (82 per cent) compared to men (78 per cent). Among those who reported making at least one trip home, the number of visits reported is virtually the same for men and women. With respect to remitting, about one-fifth of second-generation adults reported sending money to the origin country during the previous five years. The percentage is slightly higher for men (21.6 per cent compared to 19.5 per cent for women), but this difference is not statistically significant.

Turning to the more permanent form of return migration, nearly two-thirds (63.5 per cent) of second-generation adults have no intention of ever taking up long-term residence in their parents' birth country. The magnitude of foreclosure on the possibility of return, however, varies significantly by gender, as 68 per cent of women have no intention of returning compared to 59 per cent of men. Among those not entirely opposed, return migration appears to be viewed as merely a 'possibility'; this proportion is higher among men. Only about one-third of those who are not steadfastly against returning view return migration as a likely or certain outcome and this holds for both sexes. Thus, there is a gender distinction with respect to return intention, yet at higher levels of return commitment there is no gender difference.

With respect to ethno-cultural and economic integration, the mean for the total sample is zero due to the way in which the factor scores are calculated, as described above. Gender comparisons reveal that second-generation adult men are disadvantaged relative to their female counterparts in terms of both ethno-cultural and economic integration. These differences are small in magnitude and not statistically significant, however.

Finally, the mean age of the sample is about 26, overall, and for men and women separately. Because the TIES sample is relatively young, it is not surprising to find that just over a third of second-generation adults (34.8 per cent) reside with their parents. Men (38 per cent) are significantly more likely to reside in their parents' home than women (31 per cent). Women are probably less likely to be living with their parents because they are more likely than men to be married (not shown) and thus, as Table 12.1 shows, are significantly more likely to have children. Overall,

Table 12.1 Weighted means and percentages of variables used in analyses of transnationalism among second-generation adults in Europe (2006–2008)

	Total (N = 2,595)	Men (n = 1,252)	Women (n = 1,343)
Visits to parental country of birth (last five years)			
% Never	20.2	**22.2**	**18.3**
% Once	11.1	11.2	11.0
% Twice	16.0	**14.4**	**17.6**
% Three times	14.5	14.7	14.2
% Four times	8.2	7.9	8.5
% Five times	21.5	20.5	22.5
% Several times	8.6	9.1	8.0
Remittances to parental country of birth (last five years)			
% Remitting	20.6	21.6	19.5
Return intention to parental country of birth			
% Certainly not	63.5	**59.1**	**67.9**
% Possibly	23.7	**26.7**	**20.7**
% Likely	7.7	8.4	7.0
% Certainly	5.1	5.8	4.4
% Male	50.6		
Mean age	26.3	26.3	26.3
% Living with parents	34.8	**38.2**	**31.3**
% With children	30.9	23.7	38.2
Mean ethno-cultural integration score	0.000	−0.052	0.053
Mean economic integration score	0.000	−0.085	0.087

Note: Proportions in **bold** indicate a significant gender difference in proportions between men and women at the 0.05 level.

Source: The Integration of the European Second Generation (TIES).

31 per cent of the sample has children (24 per cent among men compared to 38 per cent for women).

Multivariate Results

Home country visits
We turn now to the presentation of multivariate results for second-generation transnationalism, starting with home-country visits. Coefficients from negative binomial models of the number of home-country visits made during the last five years are presented in Panel A of Table 12.2 and reflect the change in the log of the expected number of trips associated with a unit change in the independent variable, holding other factors constant. Because this interpretation is not necessarily straightforward, we concentrate instead on the direction and statistical significance of the coefficients.

Model 1 includes only city dummies (not shown), gender and the other demographic control variables. Consistent with our first hypothesis, holding other demographic factors constant, the number of visits is lower among men, but the difference is not statistically significant. Not surprisingly, the number of visits is significantly higher among second-generation adults living with their parents. Men report a significantly smaller number of visits when we hold ethno-cultural and economic integration constant in Model 2. As expected, ethno-cultural integration is inversely and significantly related to the number of visits, while economic integration is positively associated with visiting.

Finally, Models 3 and 4 examine whether the effects of ethno-cultural and economic integration, respectively, on visiting vary by gender. Neither model indicates that these associations are gendered. Thus, with respect to visiting, we do not find support for our second hypothesis predicting a stronger association between economic integration and visiting among women.

Remittances
Next we examine corresponding model results for second-generation remitting behaviour in Panel B of Table 12.2, where we present coefficients from logit models predicting the sending of remittances in the five years prior to the survey. In Model 1 we find that men are significantly more likely to remit than second-generation women. Model 1 also indicates that age and the presence of children are both positively and significantly associated with the probability of remitting. The gender difference in remitting is no longer significant, however, when the two integration factors are held constant in Model 2. Consistent with the pattern observed for home-country visits, ethno-cultural integration is inversely associated with the

Table 12.2 Coefficients from negative binomial models of the number of visits (A) and from logit models of remitting (B) to parents' country of birth among second-generation adults in Europe (N = 2,595)[a]

	A. Visits (negative binomial)				B. Remitting (logit)			
	Model 1	Model 2	Model 3	Model 4	Model 1	Model 2	Model 3	Model 4
Age	0.01**	0.01	0.01	0.01	0.09***	0.09***	0.09***	0.09***
	(0.00)	(0.00)	(0.00)	(0.00)	(0.01)	(0.02)	(0.02)	(0.02)
Living with parents	0.15***	0.15***	0.15***	0.15***	0.03	0.04	0.02	0.03
	(0.04)	(0.04)	(0.04)	(0.04)	(0.16)	(0.16)	(0.16)	(0.16)
With children	0.07*	−0.04	−0.04	−0.04	0.42**	0.14	0.13	0.15
	(0.04)	(0.04)	(0.04)	(0.04)	(0.14)	(0.15)	(0.15)	(0.15)
Male	−0.05	−0.07**	−0.08**	−0.07*	0.28*	0.18	0.13	0.21
	(0.03)	(0.03)	(0.03)	(0.03)	(0.12)	(0.12)	(0.12)	(0.12)
Ethno-cultural integration		−0.24***	−0.23***	−0.24***		−0.57***	−0.48***	−0.57***
		(0.02)	(0.02)	(0.02)		(0.07)	(0.08)	(0.07)
Economic integration		0.11***	0.11***	0.11***		0.18**	0.18**	0.24**
		(0.02)	(0.02)	(0.02)		(0.06)	(0.06)	(0.09)
Male*Ethno-cultural integration			−0.02				−0.18	
			(0.03)				(0.12)	
Male*Economic integration				0.00				−0.12
				(0.03)				(0.11)
Constant	0.68***	0.78***	0.78***	0.78***	−4.26***	−4.27***	−4.25***	−4.29***
	(0.13)	(0.12)	(0.12)	(0.12)	(0.44)	(0.46)	(0.46)	(0.46)
lnalpha	−1.83***	−2.42***	−2.42***	−2.42***				
	(0.14)	(0.21)	(0.22)	(0.21)				
Pseudo-R^2					0.08	0.12	0.12	0.12

Note: *** $p < 0.001$; ** $p < 0.01$; * $p < 0.05$ (standard errors in parentheses); [a] controlled for survey city.

source: The Integration of the European Second Generation (TIES).

probability of remitting while economic integration is positively associated with remitting.

Model 3 tests for gendered variation in the association between ethno-cultural integration and remitting and, while suggesting that the inverse effect is somewhat stronger among second-generation men than it is for women, the coefficient for the interaction term is not statistically significant. Similarly, in Model 4 we find no significant gender difference with respect to the association between economic integration and remitting. Taken as a whole, the results in Panel B of Table 12.2 lend support to our fourth hypothesis, which predicted that because remitting represents kin-keeping behaviour *and* confers status on remittance senders, observed gender differences in remitting may be obscured by gender-specific motivations that encourage remitting.

Return intention
Finally, we turn to results testing whether second-generation men are more likely to entertain the possibility of 'return' migration (Hypothesis 1), and whether this gender difference is most pronounced at lower levels of economic integration (Hypothesis 3). These hypotheses are tested in Table 12.3, which reports results from multinomial logit models. The coefficients for each model reflect the change in the logit from the reference (certainly no return intention) to the response categories associated with unit change in the independent variable. Consistent with Hypothesis 1, men are significantly more likely than women to entertain the possibility of return in Model 1, as their probabilities of selecting one of the three categories other than 'certainly not' is higher than that of their female counterparts. This conclusion holds in Model 2, which adds the two integration factors. In this case, however, men are only significantly more likely to choose the 'possibly' category over 'certainly not', as the male coefficients for the two more certain categories are no longer significant.

As with other forms of transnational engagement, the probability of return intention decreases with increases in ethno-cultural integration. However, although economic integration has been shown to increase less-intensive forms of transnational engagement, in this case visiting and remitting, Model 2 suggests that economic integration is largely unrelated to return intention and, if anything, more economically integrated members of the second generation are *less* likely to have strong return intentions as compared with having no intention whatsoever. And finally, the coefficients for the other demographic variables that are significantly associated with return intentions – parental co-residence and the presence of children – are in the expected direction. All else being equal, return intentions tend to be significantly stronger among members of the second

Table 12.3 Coefficients from multinomial logit models of origin country return intentions among second-generation adults in Europe (N = 2,595; comparison category: 'Certainly not')

	Model 1			Model 2			Model 3			Model 4		
	Possibly	Likely	Certainly	Possibly	Likely	Certainly	Possibly	Likely	Certainly	Possibly	Likely	Certainly
Age	-0.01	-0.01	-0.01	-0.00	0.01	0.02	-0.00	0.01	0.03	-0.00	0.01	0.02
	(0.01)	(0.02)	(0.03)	(0.01)	(0.03)	(0.04)	(0.01)	(0.03)	(0.04)	(0.01)	(0.03)	(0.04)
Living with parents	0.32*	0.67**	1.09***	0.31*	0.69*	1.16***	0.32*	0.71**	1.12***	0.31*	0.69*	1.15***
	(0.14)	(0.25)	(0.30)	(0.15)	(0.27)	(0.32)	(0.15)	(0.27)	(0.32)	(0.15)	(0.27)	(0.32)
With children	0.04	0.63**	0.49	-0.38*	-0.06	-0.28	-0.38*	-0.06	-0.29	-0.41**	-0.08	-0.28
	(0.14)	(0.22)	(0.38)	(0.15)	(0.24)	(0.37)	(0.15)	(0.24)	(0.35)	(0.15)	(0.24)	(0.37)
Male	0.38***	0.38*	0.53*	0.28*	0.16	0.23	0.29**	0.29	-0.09	0.27*	0.16	0.23
	(0.11)	(0.17)	(0.24)	(0.11)	(0.18)	(0.24)	(0.11)	(0.22)	(0.30)	(0.11)	(0.18)	(0.25)
Ethno-cultural integration				-0.81***	-1.37***	-1.38***	-0.84***	-1.46***	-1.18***	-0.81***	-1.37***	-1.38***
				(0.06)	(0.12)	(0.15)	(0.09)	(0.16)	(0.18)	(0.06)	(0.12)	(0.15)
Economic integration				-0.04	-0.11	-0.27*	-0.04	-0.11	-0.28*	-0.19*	-0.19	-0.26
				(0.06)	(0.10)	(0.12)	(0.06)	(0.10)	(0.12)	(0.08)	(0.14)	(0.19)
Male*Ethno-cultural integration							0.06	0.16	-0.32			
							(0.12)	(0.21)	(0.26)			
Male*Economic integration										0.27*	0.15	0.01
										(0.11)	(0.17)	(0.24)
Constant	-0.72	-1.75*	-3.61***	-0.81	-2.37**	-4.61***	-0.82	-2.46**	-4.48***	-0.80	-2.36**	-4.60***
	(0.40)	(0.71)	(0.99)	(0.43)	(0.78)	(1.08)	(0.43)	(0.79)	(1.10)	(0.43)	(0.78)	(1.08)
R-squared	0.07			0.15			0.15			0.15		

Note: *** $p < 0.001$; ** $p < 0.01$; * $p < 0.05$ (standard errors in parentheses); [a] controlled for survey city.

Source: The Integration of the European Second Generation (TIES).

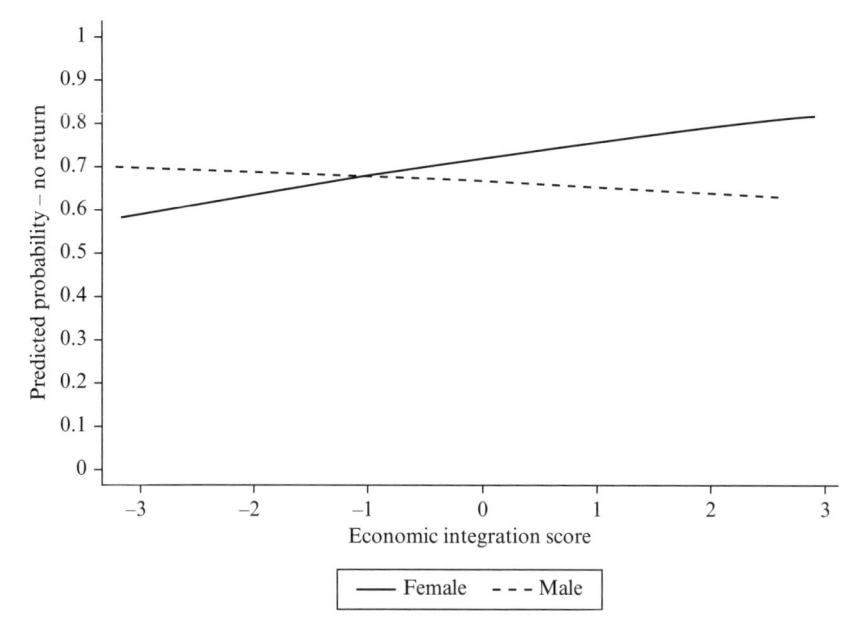

Figure 12.1 Predicted probability of return by economic integration and sex

generation who reside with their parents, while those with children tend to be less likely to express a possibility of return.

Model 3 tests for gendered variation in the relationship between ethnocultural integration and return intention; the results indicate that ethnocultural effects operate similarly for men and women. In Model 4, we test the third hypothesis, which predicts that economic integration will be more strongly related to return intention among men than among women and that men experiencing economic frustration will be the most likely to desire return. Model 4 provides mixed support for this hypothesis. The relationship between economic integration and return intention varies significantly and runs in the opposite direction for men and women, as illustrated in Figure 12.1. For women, increases in economic incorporation are inversely related to return intention, while conversely it is the most highly integrated men who are the most likely to entertain the possibility of return.

DISCUSSION AND CONCLUSIONS

Research focusing on the transnational nature of immigration and immigrant integration has made significant progress over the past several decades towards understanding the scale of immigrant transnationalism (Portes et al., 2002; Guarnizo et al., 2003; Portes, 2006), the nature of the association between host-country integration and transnational engagement among immigrants (Guarnizo et al., 2003; Snel et al., 2006; de Haas and Fokkema, 2011) and the extent to which the dynamics of immigrant transnationalism and integration are gendered (Hondagneu-Sotelo, 1994; Goldring, 2003; Itzigsohn and Giorguli-Saucedo, 2005; de Haas and Fokkema, 2010). Focusing on the European context, the aim of this chapter has been to explore the extent to which the interpretations of integration, transnationalism and gender growing out of the rich tradition of research studying the immigrant population can also be applied to explain patterns observed among the second generation coming of age in immigration countries across Europe.

The results of this empirical exploration suggest that many of the conclusions drawn from research on the first generation apply as well to their children. For instance, our results support the conclusions drawn by other recent quantitative studies of the second generation in the US and Europe demonstrating that, as with the first generation, transnationalism is the exception rather than the rule, as most second-generation adults are oriented overwhelmingly to life in their country of birth (Kasinitz et al., 2002; Rumbaut, 2002; Tamaki, 2011; Fokkema et al., 2012). This varies, however, depending on how restrictive one is in defining behaviour as transnational. Thus, second-generation transnational engagement occurs on a scale that warrants further research aimed at understanding the determinants of transnational engagement, its implications for the integration of the second generation and its impacts on both sending and host societies.

Also in keeping with research on immigrant transnationalism, we find evidence suggesting that transnational engagement is complementary to host-country economic integration among members of the second generation. Second-generation immigrants in Europe make visits and remit to their parents' country of origin only as economic attainments in the host country afford them the resources to do so. Also, the relatively low prevalence of transnational engagement can be explained in large part by the rapid pace at which the second generation adopts host-country cultural norms and orientations.

We also find evidence indicating that the gendering of integration and transnationalism, widely documented in the first generation, operates in the second generation as well. Consistent with interpretations stressing differences in gender relations regimes in host versus origin countries, second-generation women in Europe are less likely than their male counterparts to entertain the possibility of return migration. However, we find mixed evidence implying that female transnational engagement is disproportionately 'resource based' and driven by mechanisms specified by 'kin-keeping' explanations of transnational engagement among immigrant women (Menjivar, 2000; Itzigsohn and Giorguli-Saucedo, 2005). On the one hand, second-generation women visit the home country with somewhat greater frequency than their male counterparts, but their visiting behaviour does not hinge more strongly on economic integration than it does for men, as the resource-based theory suggests. On the other hand, men are *more* likely than women to remit, but there is very limited evidence suggesting that the probability of remitting among women increases at a faster rate as economic integration increases than for men, which would be consistent with the 'resource-based' theory.

The transnational engagement outcome that paints perhaps the clearest picture of the gendered dynamics of second-generation integration and transnationalism is return intention. Consistent with expectations, second-generation men are more likely than women to entertain the possibility of return to their parental country of birth. And as expected, the magnitude of the gender difference in return intention varies with the level of economic integration, but *not* in the pattern predicted by interpretations of 'reactive' transnationalism among male immigrants who respond to economic marginalization in the host society by strengthening their orientation and attachment to the home country (Hondagneu-Sotelo, 1994; Itzigsohn and Giorguli-Saucedo, 2005). Rather, second-generation men who are highly integrated into the host-country economy are the most likely to entertain the possibility of return. This may reflect a scenario in which highly skilled second-generation men are more likely to experience discrimination than low-skilled men (a testable hypothesis), perhaps because their higher degree of structural integration exposes them to such 'opportunities'. Alternatively, this finding might reflect a greater tendency for highly skilled men to respond to perceptions of blocked mobility pathways by considering the extent to which they would not face such ceilings in the labour market of the origin country and where the cost of living is considerably lower. Low-skilled men, by contrast, may conclude that their limited skills would not yield much improvement in their economic position in the origin country, especially considering access to social welfare (Fokkema, 2011).

In contrast to the integration dynamics of male return intentions, the gendered nature of second-generation integration and transnational attachments is reflected most clearly in the finding that economic integration exerts the opposite influence on the return intentions of women. Thus, overall, the economic integration of the second generation is unrelated to return intentions (ibid.), but this is entirely due to the fact that economic integration works in opposite directions for men and women.

The results presented here carry potentially important implications as well for origin-country development dynamics. To the extent that migrant sending countries rely heavily on remittances for revenue, it is important to note that (a) a non-negligible share of second-generation adults remit to their parental birth country and (b) second-generation adults who are more upwardly mobile in the host society are more likely to be engaged in life in the origin country. These results suggest that origin-country efforts to maintain ties with the children of emigrants are a potentially important development strategy. However, these implications may be qualified by the fact that our results suggest that origin-country attachments among the second generation are significantly gendered. Most importantly, because more economically integrated second-generation women are *less likely* to sustain origin-country attachments while more economically integrated men are *more likely* to sustain meaningful attachments, it is possible that development strategies focused on second-generation immigrants may have little impact on gender relations regimes in origin countries.

While this chapter has contributed some important findings to the effort of developing empirically based theoretical explanations of the dynamics of second-generation integration and transnationalism, there are, of course, a number of research questions that remain unaddressed. Little is yet known about the variation of transnational engagement across multiple subdimensions of the broader dimension of ethno-cultural integration. Theoretically, ethno-cultural integration entails the reduction in ethnic-native differences in language, religious beliefs and practices, choice of marriage partners and numerous other norms and value orientations. Because so much of the academic and public discussion revolves around such concerns, which might pose a potentially insurmountable obstacle to social integration, 'unpacking' the various components of ethno-cultural integration may be especially important in the European immigration context (Alba, 2005; Foner and Alba, 2008).

Also, considerably more theorizing is needed to specify and test the mechanisms underlying the emerging relationship between integration and transnationalism among the second generation and their gendered variation. Such theoretical development, which will continue to rely heavily on mixed methods research approaches, will help to elucidate questions about the meaning and motivations behind second-generation immigrants' transnational engagements, whether and how studies of second-generation transnational engagement might adjudicate between competing claims of contemporary assimilation perspectives and how research on second-generation transnationalism might inform policies related to immigrant incorporation and development in migrant sending countries.

NOTES

1. The eight countries are: France (Paris and Strasbourg); Germany (Berlin and Frankfurt); Spain (Madrid and Barcelona); Austria (Vienna and Linz); the Netherlands (Amsterdam and Rotterdam); Belgium (Brussels and Antwerp); Switzerland (Basel and Zurich); and Sweden (Stockholm).
2. Turks and Moroccans are the target groups in the Netherlands and Belgium; Turks and former Yugoslavs are the target groups in Germany, Austria and Switzerland; Turks are the target group in France and Sweden; and Moroccans are the target group in Spain.
3. We are unable to include *both* city *and* ethnic group dummies in our models due to the fact that the group or groups sampled varies depending on the city.

REFERENCES

Al-Ali, Nadje, Richard Black and Khalid Koser (2001), 'The limits to "transnationalism": Bosnian and Eritrean refugees in Europe as emerging transnational communities', *Ethnic and Racial Studies*, **24** (4), 578–600.

Alba, Richard (2005), 'Bright vs. blurred boundaries: second-generation assimilation and exclusion in France, Germany, and the United States', *Ethnic and Racial Studies*, **28** (1), 20–49.

Alba, Richard and Victor Nee (2003), *Remaking the American Mainstream: Assimilation and Contemporary Immigration*, Cambridge, MA: Harvard University Press.

Bean, Frank D., Susan K. Brown, James D. Bachmeier, Tineke Fokkema and Laurence Lessard-Phillips (2012), 'The dimensions and degree of second-generation incorporation in US and European cities: a comparative study of inclusion and exclusion', *International Journal of Comparative Sociology*, **53** (3), 181–209.

Beauchemin, Cris, Hugues Lagrange and Mirna Safi (2011), *Transnationalism and Immigrant Assimilation in France: Between Here and There?*, Documents de Travail 172, INED.

Bloemraad, Irene, Anna Korteweg and Gökçe Yurdakul (2008), 'Citizenship and immigration: multiculturalism, assimilation, and challenges to the nation-state', *Annual Review of Sociology*, **34** (1), 153–79.

Carling, Jorgen (2008), 'The determinants of migrant remittances', *Oxford Review of Economic Policy*, **24** (3), 581–98.

Cela, Eralba, Tineke Fokkema and Elena Ambrosetti (2013), 'Variation in transnationalism among Eastern European migrants in Italy: the role of duration of residence and integration', *Southeast European and Black Sea Studies*, available at: http://dx.doi-org/10.1080/14683857.2013,789671.

Crul, Maurice, Jens Schneider and Frans Lelie (eds) (2012), *The European Second Generation Compared: Does the Integration Context Matter?*, Amsterdam: Amsterdam University Press.

de Haas, Hein (2010), 'Migration and development: a theoretical perspective', *International Migration Review*, **44** (1), 227–64.
de Haas, Hein and Tineke Fokkema (2010), 'Intra-household conflicts in migration decisionmaking: return and pendulum migration in Morocco', *Population and Development Review*, **36** (3), 541–61.
de Haas, Hein and Tineke Fokkema (2011), 'The effects of integration and transnational ties on international return migration intentions', *Demographic Research*, **25** (24), 755–82.
Fokkema, Tineke (2011),'"Return" migration intentions among second-generation Turks in Europe: the effect of integration and transnationalism in a cross-national perspective', *Journal of Mediterranean Studies*, **20** (2), 365–88.
Fokkema, Tineke, Laurence Lessard-Phillips, James D. Bachmeier and Susan K. Brown (2012), 'The link between the transnational behaviour and integration of the second generation in European and American cities', *Nordic Journal of Migration Research*, **2** (2), 111–23.
Foner, Nancy and Richard Alba (2008), 'Immigrant religion in the US and Western Europe: bridge or barrier to inclusion?', *International Migration Review*, **42** (2), 360–92.
Fresnoza-Flot, Asuncion (2009), 'Migration status and transnational mothering: the case of Filipino migrants in France', *Global Networks*, **9** (2), 252–70.
Glick-Schiller, Nina, Linda Basch and Cristina Szanton-Blanc (1995), 'From immigrant to transmigrant: theorizing transnational migration', *Anthropological Quarterly*, **68** (1), 48–63.
Glick-Schiller, Nina, Ayse Caglar and Thaddeus C. Guldbrandsen (2006), 'Beyond the ethnic lens: locality, globality, and born-again incorporation', *American Ethnologist*, **33** (4), 612–33.
Goldring, Luin (2003), 'Gender, status, and the state in transnational spaces', in Pierrette Hondagneu-Sotelo (ed.), *Gender and US Immigration*, Berkeley, CA: University of California Press, pp. 341–58.
Gordon, Milton M. (1964), *Assimilation in American Life: The Role of Race, Religion, and National Origins*, New York: Oxford University Press.
Grasmuck, Sherri and Patricia R. Pessar (1991), *Between Two Islands: Dominican International Migration*, Berkeley, CA: University of California Press.
Groenewold, George and Laurence Lessard-Phillips (2012), 'Research methodology', in Maurice Crul, Jens Schneider and Frans Lelie (eds), *The European Second Generation Compared: Does the Integration Context Matter?*, Amsterdam: Amsterdam University Press, pp. 39–56.
Guarnizo, Luis Eduardo, Alejandro Portes and William Haller (2003), 'Assimilation and transnationalism: determinants of transnational political action among contemporary migrants', *American Journal of Sociology*, **108** (6), 1211–48.
Haller, William and Patricia Landolt (2005), 'The transnational dimensions of identity formation: adult children of immigrants in Miami', *Ethnic and Racial Studies*, **28** (6), 1182–214.
Hondagneu-Sotelo, Pierrette (ed.) (1994), *Gendered Transitions: Mexican Experiences of Immigration*, Berkeley, CA: University of California Press.
Itzigsohn, Jose and Silvia Giorguli-Saucedo (2005), 'Incorporation, transnationalism, and gender: immigrant incorporation and transnational participation as gendered processes', *International Migration Review*, **39** (4), 895–920.
Jayaweera, Hiranthi and Tufyal Choudhury (2008), *Immigration, Faith and Cohesion: Evidence from Local Areas with Significant Muslim Populations*, York: Joseph Rowntree Foundation.
Johnson, Phyllis J. and Kathrin Stoll (2008), 'Remittance patterns of Southern Sudanese refugee men: enacting the global breadwinner role', *Family Relations*, **57** (4), 431–43.
Jones-Correa, Michael (2012), 'The study of transnationalism among the children of immigrants: where we are and where we should be headed', in Peggy Levitt and Mary C. Waters (eds), *The Changing Face of Home: The Transnational Lives of the Second Generation*, New York: Russell Sage Foundation, pp. 221–41.

Joppke, Christian and Ewa T.Morawska (2003), *Toward Assimilation and Citizenship: Immigrants in Liberal Nation-States*, Basingstoke: Palgrave Macmillan.
Kasinitz, Philip, John H. Mollenkopf, Mary C. Waters and Jennifer Holdaway (2008), *Inheriting the City: The Children of Immigrants Come of Age*, New York: Russell Sage Foundation.
Kasinitz, Philip, Mary C. Waters, John H. Mollenkopf and Merih Anil (2002), 'Transnationalism and the children of immigrants in contemporary New York', in Peggy Levitt and Mary C. Waters (eds), *The Changing Face of Home: The Transnational Lives of the Second Generation*, New York: Russell Sage Foundation, pp. 96–122.
Kastoryano, Riva (2006), 'Religion and Incorporation: Islam in France and Germany', *International Migration Review*, **38** (3), 1234–55.
Kivisto, Peter (2001), 'Theorizing transnational immigration: a critical review of current efforts', *Ethnic and Racial Studies*, **24** (4), 549–77.
Korteweg, Anna and Gökçe Yurdakul (2009), 'Islam, gender, and immigrant integration: boundary drawing in discourses on honour killing in the Netherlands and Germany', *Ethnic and Racial Studies*, **32** (2), 218–38.
Levitt, Peggy (2004), 'Redefining the boundaries of belonging: the institutional character of transnational religious life', *Sociology of Religion*, **65** (1), 1–18.
Levitt, Peggy (2009), 'Roots and routes: understanding the lives of the second generation transnationally', *Journal of Ethnic and Migration Studies*, **35** (7), 1225–42.
Levitt, Peggy and B. Nadya Jaworsky (2007), 'Transnational migration studies: past developments and future trends', *Annual Review of Sociology*, **33**, 129–56.
Levitt, Peggy and Mary C. Waters (2002), 'Introduction', in Levitt and Waters (eds), *The Changing Face of Home: The Transnational Lives of the Second Generation*, New York: Russell Sage Foundation, pp. 1–32.
Marcelli, Enrico and B. Lindsay Lowell (2005), 'Transnational twist: pecuniary remittances and the socioeconomic integration of authorized and unauthorized Mexican immigrants in Los Angeles county', *International Migration Review*, **39** (1), 69–102.
Massey, Douglas S., Rafael Alarcon, Jorge Durand and Humberto Gonzalez (1987), *Return to Aztlan: The Social Process of International Migration from Western Mexico*, Berkeley, CA: University of California Press.
Massey, Douglas S. Joaquín Arango, Graeme Hugo, Ali Kouaouci, Adela Pellegrino and J. Edward Taylor (1998), *Worlds in Motion: Understanding International Migration at the End of the Millennium*, New York: Oxford University Press.
Massey, Douglas S. Luin Goldring and Jorge Durand (1994), 'Continuities in transnational migration: an analysis of nineteen Mexican communities', *American Journal of Sociology*, **99** (6), 1492–533.
Mazzucato, Valentina (2008), 'The double engagement: transnationalism and integration: Ghanaian migrants' lives between Ghana and the Netherlands', *Journal of Ethnic and Migration Studies*, **34** (2), 199–216.
Menjivar, Cecilia (2000), *Fragmented Ties: Salvadoran Immigrant Networks in America*, Berkeley, CA: University of California Press.
Molina, Raul Sanchez (2008), 'Modes of incorporation, social exclusion and transnationalism: Salvadoran's adaptation to the Washington, DC Metropolitan area', *Human Organization*, **67** (3), 269–80.
Portes, Alejandro (2006), 'Conclusion: theoretical convergencies and empirical evidence in the study of immigrant transnationalism', *International Migration Review*, **37** (3), 874–92.
Portes, Alejandro, Luis Eduardo Guarnizo and William J. Haller (2002), 'Transnational entrepreneurs: an alternative form of immigrant economic adaptation', *American Sociological Review*, **67** (2), 278–98.
Portes, Alejandro, Luis Eduardo Guarnizo and Patricia Landolt (1999), 'The study of transnationalism: pitfalls and promise of an emergent research field', *Ethnic and Racial Studies*, **22** (2), 217–37.
Rumbaut, Ruben G. (2002), 'Severed or sustained attachments? Language, identity, and

imagined communities in the post-immigrant generation', in Peggy Levitt and Mary C. Waters (eds), *The Changing Face of Home: The Transnational Ties of the Second Generation*, New York: Russell Sage Foundation, pp. 43–95.

Salih, Ruba (2003), *Gender in Transnationalism*, New York: Routledge.

Schans, Djamila (2009), 'Transnational family ties of immigrants in the Netherlands', *Ethnic and Racial Studies*, **32** (7), 1164–82.

Schneider, Jens, Tineke Fokkema, Raquel Matias, Snežana Stojcic, Dušan Ugrina and Constanza Vera-Larrucea. (2012), 'Identities: urban belonging and intercultural relations', in Crul et al. (eds), *The European Second Generation Compared: Does the Integration Context Matter?*, Amsterdam: Amsterdam University Press, pp. 285–340.

Singer, Audrey and Greta Gilbertson (2003),'"The blue passport": gender and the social process of naturalization among Dominican immigrants in New York city', in Pierrette Hondagneu-Sotelo (ed.), *Gender and US Immigration: Contemporary Trends*, Berkeley, CA: University of California Press, pp. 359–78.

Smith, Robert Courtney (2006), *Mexican New York: Transnational Lives of New Immigrants*, Berkeley, CA: University of California Press.

Snel, Erik, Godfried Engbersen and Arjen Leerkes (2006), 'Transnational involvement and social integration', *Global Networks*, **6** (3), 285–308.

Soehl, Thomas and Roger Waldinger (2010), 'Making the connection: Latino immigrants and their cross-border ties', *Ethnic and Racial Studies*, **33** (9), 1489–510.

Tamaki, Emi (2011), 'Transnational home engagement among Latino and Asian Americans: resources and motivation', *International Migration Review*, **45** (1), 148–73.

Thomson, Mark and Maurice Crul (2007), 'The second generation in Europe and the United States: how is the transatlantic debate relevant for further research on the European second generation?', *Journal of Ethnic and Migration Studies*, **33** (7), 1025–41.

van Dalen, Hendrik P., George Groenewold and Tineke Fokkema (2005), 'The effect of remittances on emigration intentions in Egypt, Morocco, and Turkey', *Population Studies*, **59** (3), 375–92.

Waldinger, Roger (2007), 'The bounded community: turning foreigners into Americans in twenty-first century LA', *Ethnic and Racial Studies*, **30** (3), 341–74.

Waldinger, Roger and David Fitzgerald (2004), 'Transnationalism in question', *American Journal of Sociology*, **109** (5), 1177–95.

Wessendorf, Susanne (2007), '"Roots Migrants": transnationalism and "return" among second-generation Italians in Switzerland', *Journal of Ethnic and Migration Studies*, **33** (7), 1083–102.

APPENDIX

Table 12A.1 Results from principal components analysis of indicators of ethno-cultural and economic integration among second-generation adults in Europe (N = 2,595)

	Rotated loadings	
	Ethno-cultural	Economic
Education	0.090	**0.754**
Occupational prestige	0.074	**0.717**
Difficulties with income	0.028	**0.680**
Speaking parents' language	**0.534**	0.092
Survey country language spoken at home	**0.732**	0.070
Ethnic media use	**0.682**	0.085
Visit to place of worship	**0.539**	0.168
Partnership status	**0.396**	0.242
Feelings of belonging to survey country	**0.562**	0.205
Eigenvalue	2.24	1.52
Proportion of variance explained	0.249	0.169

Source: The Integration of the European Second Generation (TIES).

13 Gendered and emotional spaces: Nordic–Hellenic negotiations of ethno-cultural belongingness in narrating segmented selves and diasporic lives of the second generation

Anastasia Christou

INTRODUCTION: GENDERING AND EMOTIONALIZING MOBILITIES OF HOMING AND BELONGING: SITUATING AND STUDYING THE SECOND GENERATION IN EUROPE

Multi-varied mobilities through multiple time-spaces are the quintessential characteristic of our era, and contemporary narrative urban ethnographies reveal the fascinating social interactions that take place in city spaces in everyday life when migrants arrive, settle or simply exist in these locales.

Over the last two decades an emergence of intensive research on the second generation in the United States (Portes and Zhou, 1993; Portes, 1996; Portes and Rumbaut, 2001; Levitt and Waters, 2002; Kasinitz et al., 2004; Louie, 2006) has also only recently surfaced in Europe (Christou, 2006; Potter and Phillips, 2006; Crul, 2007; Wessendorf, 2007; Zontini, 2007; Christou and King, 2010; Baldassar, 2011; Reynolds, 2011; Teerling, 2011; Vathi, 2011). Research on the second generation has focused mostly on issues of 'home', 'identity' and 'belonging'; all three rather fluid concepts often linked to processes of 'integration'. All these concepts, from 'generation' to 'integration', are not only complex, contested and ambiguous but also location specific where specificities of particular societies shape both policy and everyday life of migrants and their descendants. In research with second-generation Greek-German women returnees, for some the ancestral homeland becomes 'a utopian quest of escape from the patriarchy of their family situation in the diaspora, but the enduring economic, emotional and socio-cultural difficulties of creating a satisfying life in modern-day Greece bring elements of dystopia to this quest' (Christou and King, 2011, p. 310); whereas for others the return becomes an embodiment of an action of renunciation of the Greek diasporic family setting through the emergence of an autonomous self and a sense of agency (Christou, 2011b, p. 146).

Contemporary mobilities evolve within a spatial and temporal context inclusive of sets of social relations (for example, gender, ethnicity, class) that each extends to a social system of such intersectionalities (Walby, 2007). Second-generation ancestral homeland return migration is one such phenomenon. Second-generation returnees' lives replicate ancestral journeys characterized by a process of grieving for a lost home and the anticipation of an imagined home to be discovered. These journeys seem to be the quintessential fulfilment of the 'dream of return', which is often mythologized by the migrant first generation in longing for belonging (Christou, 2006; Christou and King, 2011; King and Christou, 2011).

Through ethnographic and life story narratives this chapter[1] examines second-generation Greek-Danish women's portrayals of their fluid sense of self and blurred sense of place in negotiating their emotions and their impact on their diasporic lives. The analysis addresses issues of cultural marginality and the emotionally embodied context of belonging. I examine scripted and storied lives in exploring how intimate attachments, desires and emotionalities shape mobility experiences. Within a gendered and affective approach to diasporas, my focus is primarily on women while acknowledging the repeated critique that gender encompasses an attention to both men and women, for example, Cornwall (2000) and Carling (2002). My explicit focus on women coincides with the need to contribute to a rounded theory of subjectivity and agency, which is one of the principal aims of a feminist project, that is, according to McNay (1992, p. 3), 'to rediscover and re-evaluate the experiences of women'. For example, in drawing from Teresa de Laurentis' (1987) concept of 'gendered subjectivity' in relation to concrete habits, practices and discourses while at the same time recognizing the fluidity of these, Alcoff (1988) develops a concept of positionality which recognizes the importance of identity politics. According to Alcoff, women are not merely passive recipients of an identity but part of the historicized, fluid movement of experiences. In this respect, the chapter aims to present the lived experiences of women in understanding their agency but also as part of the narrative they advance in a dynamic context of speaker–audience interactions. In this respect, extracts from women's focus groups will also be analysed by embracing a more holistic understanding of how both lives and identities are disrupted by the fragments of mnemonic and experiential articulations of their spatial encounters.

The chapter endeavours to present some of the emotional geographies of these diasporic women, who, for the most part are invisible as their trajectories are those of a relatively unnoticed group of migrant women who in many ways have become well 'integrated' into Danish society. Nevertheless, as offspring of Greek migrants to Denmark, they continue to struggle in reconciling the matrix of 'roots' and 'routes' in celebrating a self that is no longer anchored in the ethnos; one that is truly post-national and liberated by the constraints of culture. Such struggles stimulate an agonistic and agonizing pathway to the shaping of identities that highlights the complexity of contemporary mobilities. These internal and external processes are intermingled with the emotional stuff that characterizes everyday life in any context and setting. But such emotionalities are heavily loaded by layers of family/social/political histories and ethnic/cultural/gendered geographies. It is such an inter/intra-penetration of institutions, structures and agencies in the particularities of spatialities and temporalities of the 'home' and 'host' countries that make these women's narratives insightful and interesting.

Furthermore, in addition to the research approach and study being innovative, the study of a North–South mobility venture with the intention of a permanent relocation and not just a holiday visit is an intriguing case study. The case of North–South migration is a unique phenomenon. Migration research regarding North–South flows and movements reveals that only a few case studies exist and those primarily within the retirement migration literature (for the so-called 'heliotropic migrants' refer to King et al., 2000; O'Reilly, 2000). There has been a general observation of a type of lifestyle migration in this direction by younger people who, although not on a massive scale, for climatic and other personal lifestyle reasons choose to move from the northern to the southern regions and who for livelihood reasons end up opening a business or providing other services mainly to the ex-pat community. However, second-generation mobilities are intriguing by the very core of the reasons for relocation to the ancestral homeland and therefore should be viewed as new (cultural) geographies of movement. Such geographies of mobilities are also geographies of identities in situating 'home' and belonging.

During both collective (focus group) discussions and individual sessions with the women participating in the study, testimonials unfolded as narrative performances where embodied representations of the affective aspects of diasporic experiences were visibly expressed through body language, emotions and demonstrative acts of feelings. Although two of the participants were actors who admittedly asserted that their everyday lives were an escape from their professional scripts and acting roles, the gatherings that took place despite their spontaneity, to me, appeared as staged performances of diasporic lives. Those encounters were saturated with layers of emotionalities; anger, pain, joy, hope, despair, disillusionment, anticipation, delight. These affective dimensions of our encounters were the result of my probing into spaces of diasporic lives where uncertainty reigns. The reactions varied in intensity, length and duration but also expression, from laughter to sobbing to silence to noise.

Such affective reactions offered an opportunity for both myself and the participants to deal with emotional dilemmas in the context of reflective 'sharing' groups (rather than strictly methodologically organized focus groups) whereupon in the midst of pot-luck dinners and in the typical Danish candlelight tradition (*'hygge'*) we would share 'food–feelings–fieldwork'. These participant–researcher get-togethers would be followed by my subsequent reflective journal writing sessions where a textual interaction/filtering of events would take place (Christou, 2011a).

Such textual and performative representations are filtered through subjectivity; they are acted out through a narrative performance and they are shaped by specific historic, socio-cultural contexts. I approach the interpretation of the narrative material with a conscious awareness of the limits of the analytical parameters. I analyse the narratives through the cultural significance and socially specific filters of agency, self, gender and emotion that surround the participants' stories.

In the following sections I shall examine how emotionalities become entangled in how ethnicities and identities are negotiated in cultural spatialities. I shall focus on how place-making emerges through the unmaking of translocalities as women situate their lives within terrains of the 'here' and 'there'.

ETHNICITIES, SPATIALITIES AND IDENTITIES: THE UNBEARABLY AFFECTIVE NEGOTIATION OF CULTURE

Everyday social relations constitute an important and insightful conceptualization in the study of migration (Ho and Hatfield, 2010) and the focus on everyday matters in the mundane context of sociality conveys the depth and extent of lived experiences in understanding both people and places. Moreover, everyday life is entangled in a web of emotions as experiences stimulate feelings, and feelings account for how people process those experiences in an affective and embodied manner. The emotional dimensions of human mobility are often underpinned by experiences of loss and homelessness as migration sets a series of predicaments that have to do not only with single lives but also with families. Second-generation Greek-Danish women's intimate predicaments seem to point to what Herzfeld (1997) has termed 'cultural intimacy'. Herzfeld's notion of cultural intimacy is a concept that refers to the tensions emerging when a collectivity's self-knowledge is in direct conflict with its collective self-representation. 'Cultural intimacy' is an explanatory framework for how ethnic groups and nations maintain a homogeneous and harmonious identity to present externally to others while degrees of escalating contestation exist in their internal core, yet this is safeguarded from the outside world. More specifically, Herzfeld defines 'cultural intimacy' as:

> The recognition of those aspects of a cultural identity that are considered a source of external embarrassment but that nevertheless provide insiders with their assurance of common sociality, the familiarity with the bases of power that may at one moment assure the disenfranchised a degree of creative irreverence and at the next moment reinforce the effectiveness of intimidation. (p. 3)

For instance, Herzfeld explains a common attitude in Greece where people believe that private matters of the household should not be exposed to the public sphere and hence to open scrutiny (p. 95). As Herzfeld argues, 'the house guards intimate secrets that are themselves the basis for family solidarity and that, from within, do not necessarily appear in a negative light at all' (p. 169). In protecting and guarding 'cultural intimacy' from outsiders, members of the collectivity fit in and become part of the nation.

Discussions with the women underscored a continuous struggle with reconciling a 'North/Nordic' and 'South/Hellenic' sense of self with all the imbued features of the contested meanings of both those cultural categories that signify more than territorial difference and contain distinct cultural geographies of each. This negotiation of self-making and place-making, what I have previously referred to as the 'who I am' in the 'where I am' (Christou, 2006) is more often than not an unbearable struggle of a balancing act between culture, lifestyle, desires and pragmatics. Undeniably, both the process and the outcome (if there is one?) of such a struggle are highly emotional. Ultimately, the end goal is both the preservation of one's well-being and the maintenance of well-balanced personal and family relationships.

The following lengthy extract from Trudy's narrative illustrates some of these issues discussed here. Trudy is a 40-year-old medical doctor married to a Palestinian doctor she met when she was living on a Greek island during a planned gap year. As Trudy's relationship evolved over the year or so, they both decided to move to Denmark where they could embark on their medical studies.

Trudy's story reflects very many similarities with other second-generation Greek-Danish women. Several of the women decided to take a gap year upon completion of secondary school and before they proceeded with their university studies, and opted to relocate to Greece in order to improve their language skills and to have a 'Greek experience'. Some of those women also met their partners/husbands in Greece who were not all necessarily Greek. However, in all those cases the partners/husbands 'convinced' the women that it would be wise to move to Denmark where the social welfare system would be supportive in both pursuing studies and having children at the same time. The plan was then to find employment upon graduation and to save enough money to relocate to Greece a few years later. Yet, the latter kept being postponed and, for many, indefinitely or until retirement, as their lives had taken a different path in securing mortgages and purchasing property in desirable areas where school placements for their children were possible in the type of schools and neighbourhoods they sought. Trudy's narrative below encapsulates the journey, both emotional and physical, in how those plans were conceived but fell through or were postponed until the distant future:

> Well, I met my husband during summer vacations while on my gap year on my native Greek island and although I wanted to remain in Greece he convinced me that we should go back to Denmark and finish our studies and then relocate to the Greek island and the Greek life of our dreams. Well, it has been over two decades now and I don't see that dream materializing and that makes me depressed. I mean, don't take me the wrong way – my husband and my children are the source of my overwhelming happiness and I love my job in being a medic and saving lives but I also want to save my life from this grey and depressing landscape that is not just physical but psychological. . . . Anyway, the Danes are very proud of their country and they think it is perfect. But it is not. And I feel squeezed between a rock and a hard place. I guess because the system works here and with the anarchy that exists in Greece it would be very difficult for me to work there. So, I am counting the days and years until retirement when we will be able to return and live in Greece. Until then, it is an emotional struggle every day, at work, at home, with friends, with the children's friends and their parents. (Trudy, 40)

Although Trudy insinuates that the kaleidoscope of culture and belonging often traps individuals in a challenging and frequently competitive match of which side should prevail in order to simplify life, she seems to reconsider in suggesting that such a challenge builds resilience.

For other participants the quest to maintain their ancestral cultural sense of self and belonging is a conscious effort. Alex talks about a specifically planned effort by herself and her husband to act as 'cultural transmitters' for their children, who effectively are the third generation. More specifically she explains:

> Yes, to maintain one's Greekness, it must happen consciously. I cannot talk about everyone in public but in my life it is impossible and I try to maintain my Greekness as much as I can. . . . So consciously we both try very much but due to what happens in reality I see that there is a withdrawal and this kind of

> withdrawal somebody would characterize as small and others as big, meaning how much can somebody remain Greek. ... It is a very subjective issue and it depends on the family and the circumstances as in every country. (Alex, 43)

Alex's narrative offers an account of how the second generation perceives its role as cultural transmitters. Throughout the collection of life stories and narrative biographical data the second-generation returnees dwelt on their experiences in Greece. They included critical as well as positive commentary about 'life lived' in Denmark as well as 'living life' in Greece. However, on a deeper psychic level, the return migratory project is also characterized as a self-actualization process of introspection. It is actually an identification project and a reflective experience of belongingness:

> And for me you know it was very good because it was Greece and even now it is like a country you go on vacation. I hadn't lived the regular life in Greece. So I went and it was a tremendous experience because I understood then that I belong to Denmark rather than Greece. (Daphne, 27)

But when they do spend time in the ancestral homeland and they are confronted by experiences that stimulate their introspection, how do the participants identify? What sense of belongingness do they express? Some of the most characteristic responses are the following:

> I am lucky I think because I have two of everything: two idiosyncrasies, two cultures, two languages. I am lucky; others have only one language, one culture and they don't know anything else. I feel very lucky. (Dina, 30)

> I think it is completely subjective. It depends on where you have lived, with whom you have lived, who your parents are, if your parents agreed on things or if each one had their own opinion, where your siblings are. There are a lot of things in the middle, you can't say something general about identity and belonging. (Michaela, 25)

It is clear that, as a complex notion, identity in the case of the participants occupies a sense of duality; it is always in the making, non-stable, not fixed and constantly under negotiation between the 'here' and 'there'. On occasions it exacerbates confusion and anger but it also offers a richness of experiences, endurance and resilience along with a wider sense of one's surroundings and 'place' in the world; a wider context than a confined cultural space. However, above all, belonging and identity are subjectively mediated cultural notions translated through personal, experiential and emotional circumstances.

Returnees' thoughts about how migrants perceive their state of migrancy upon relocation to the ancestral homeland provide a series of questions that characterize the lives of migrants. First, is all this critical reflection necessary? If so, is it fruitful or potentially harmful? Second, does it provide any avenues towards happiness and inner stability or would it be preferable to ignore the psychological, social and cultural implications of one's migration venture?

In examining the life stories of Greek female returnees who maintain transnational mobility and their narrativization of home, belonging, self and diaspora life in how they envisage their roles as mothers, wives, professionals and so on, in between the everyday spaces of sociality in Denmark and those of the ancestral homeland that they mentally, emotionally and physically inhabit, we come to realize that what underpins any sense of cultural change is the women's agency and their conscious acts of self-development and self-ascription. In this sense, we as researchers need to capitalize on the strengths of narratives in unveiling the cultural connotations of migrancy but we also need to steer clear of the essentializing and dehumanizing weaknesses of such narrations that do not historically and politically locate the self in the production of cultural space, otherwise those stories will not become dialogic and will remain anchored in culturally fabricated monologues. In the next section I discuss how agentic place-making is shaped by the biographicities of women who are confronted by the dilemmas of migration and the emotions of a self-searching project to belong.

REFLECTING ON BIOGRAPHICITIES AND THE MEANINGS OF PLACE-MAKING

At the heart of the theoretical concept of 'biographicity' is the synthesis of structure and individuality. 'Biographicity' is the intuitively available genetic structure of a biography. It is the ability of the individual to shape that which is social 'self-referentially' and to place oneself in relation to society. 'Biographicity' means that individuals can continually reinterpret their life in the contexts in which they experience it, contexts which they themselves experience as 'mouldable' and 'shapeable'. When individuals as social actors relate to their life-world in such a way that their self-reflexive activities begin to shape social contexts, this establishes an act of biographicity, which is a very important notion in documenting patterns of coping and ways of organizing lives and composing identities across various social groups (West et al., 2007).

In her research with young return migrants, Hatfield (2010, p. 155) illustrates 'the value of exploring the small-scale places of importance to the everyday lives of young migrants', where meanings of such everyday micro-spaces become negotiated by migrants and so place-making unfolds in relation to belonging. Such relationships are complex and often contradictory (Hatfield, 2010) but they highlight the importance of context and the elements involved in deciphering everyday experiences. Catrina, below, talks about the messiness of everyday life that can become a pristine act of organization and compartmentalization of the personal/private/domestic and the professional/public/social in maintaining a balance between the two cultural worlds, namely that of 'Greekness' in contrast to that of 'Danishness':

> When I returned back to Denmark, I returned the same way I was when I left for Greece and I think that things should remain that way but unfortunately they have changed. Everything has changed a great deal. Very much so, extremely so. But when I am there I try to be Greek; a Greek like them. But, it is a hard act to follow and causes me a great deal of pain, a lot, because it is very difficult to have two faces. I feel Greek inside me; I cannot change my ethnicity and culture at all. (Catrina, 56)

Migration is a phenomenon that often interferes with how life plans are carried out and the continuity and linearity that some people strive to achieve as the life-course progresses. Migration is a form of displacement as migrants' lives shift in locale and their established social and familial relations may be disrupted by their translocal and transnational lives. All these changes in space and time mediate differing meanings in how connections and disconnections are entangled with emotions, relations and institutions in various cultural settings. At times migrants experience rifts, reconciliations and ruptures. At other times the interruptions in their lives are pleasing, albeit challenging. Sometimes the disruptions are insurmountable and lives become shattered. What triggers and sustains particular emotional responses may be in the domain of more psychoanalytic research, but here, the social science interest is in the broader sociocultural processes and structures as embedded and connected with migrant emotional narratives. The cultural themes of sameness and difference are the focus of migrant emotional worlds and how these shape particular gendered responses to be/longing. In this chapter I have also reflected on how cultural spaces shape the way emotional experiences in the context of migration impact on how belonging is articulated by migrants.

Nancy, 43, spent almost a decade in Greece when she went there at the age of 18, initially on a gap year and then remaining to complete a university degree in Modern Greek studies despite a passion for design and architecture. When I asked her why she opted for Modern Greek studies, she elaborated on a deeply emotional need to connect with her Greek roots as she grew up in a 'mixed' family environment in Copenhagen and Aalborg, with a large Danish family on her mother's side and her Greek father who had migrated to Denmark as a political dissident during the Greek dictatorship. This is what she had to say:

> This was a deeply emotional need to connect with my ancestral background and to learn what it means to be Greek. But it was a complete failure. I thought that it would be easy for me but it was very difficult. Very painful. I was disappointed. But it was interesting as long as it lasted. And despite that I still have this unfulfilled dream of return. I always think about it. It is lodged in my brain and my heart. I always think about it because I always imagined myself living in Greece permanently. And it was a difficult decision to return to Denmark because I didn't return for emotional reasons but just for financial. . . . But when you are here in Denmark you find everything Greek to be ideal. It's all this emotional abundance. A wealth of emotions, all that emotional stuff that goes on all day, every day, and here in Denmark people are cold, they are lonely, they are isolated, there is so much loneliness and that is awful. So it doesn't really bother me when I hear that Greeks live with their parents beyond the age of 40. It has its drawbacks but there is a lot of bonding going on.

Nancy then elaborated on the 'emotional stuff' that goes on in Greece when children keep living with their parents despite getting married and having families. On the one hand, she contended that it had its practical benefits of free childcare and domestic assistance, not to mention an opportunity to save money by sharing household expenses. On the other, she anxiously dwelt on her own experience, which resulted in her separating from her first (Greek) husband when living under similar conditions. One of her main issues was what she refers to as the 'Greek cultural establishment', which she deconstructed as a mixture of overprotection, superstition, shame, honour, old-fashioned ideas and hypocrisy. She referred to the stigmatization of women/daughters who, in her own words, were more liberated, fashionable and autonomous but who were repressed from going out and having sexual relationships. Meanwhile the men/sons were free to go from one (hetero) sexual relationship to another, while parents were proud of having their 'virgin daughters locked up at home'. Nancy recalled her experiences of living in Greece in the mid to late 1980s when stereotypes of morality were pronounced and hegemonic along with extreme patriarchal social rules.

But, Nancy asserted, all these 'distressing and annoying backward behaviours' are in a sense counterbalanced by some of the very positive experiences she had while living in Greece. In Nancy's words:

> One of the positive things that Greeks have is their overwhelming sense of hospitality to the degree that they will share the last morsel of bread with whoever sits at their table. They are not stingy and penny-pinching, miserable people like

the Danes, who are so cheap and only think of themselves and nobody else. The degree of miserable stinginess, the lowlife repulsive frugality that these people have is beyond description. I mean they will make sure that they calculate and divide and multiply the very last kroner and for me as a Greek-Dane to see them buying and selling one cigarette from each other is completely ridiculous. I mean it makes me sick and angry; it really, really bothers me that they are not hospitable like the Greeks. It really gets me so upset and embarrassed.

During similar conversations with the women participants, a degree of 'cultural translation' occurred which aimed at situating their account of the dichotomies they experienced in their migrant family worlds. In the next section I reflect on the layers of 'cultural translation' in the research and writing process in developing migration research that is attentive to notions of gender and emotion as well as power in the field, in society and the academy.

DISLOCATING DIASPORAS, GENDERING EMOTIONALITIES, NARRATING WOMEN'S LIVES IN SPACE AND TIME: SOME CONCLUDING THOUGHTS

In another publication (Christou, 2009) on biographical methods in migration research I outlined how a narrative approach in the collection of life stories explores the biographicity of everyday life in the diaspora.

In agreement with Stacey (1997, p. 115) who explains that 'most feminist scholars advocate an integrative, trans-disciplinary approach to knowledge which grounds theory contextually and in the concrete realm of women's everyday lives', I advocate that in order to unpack the hidden layers of oppression and difference that women are faced with on a daily basis, it is important that we study the intimate space-scapes where social relationships and social subjectivities emerge. It is within the realm of ethnographic study and narrative ethnographies in particular, that places, people, communities and experiences of the lived and built environment come to the fore. The ethnographic research process is where a shared subjective experience between researcher and researched becomes situated in the issues and experiences examined and where the production of (feminist) knowledge is situated. Again, as Stacey (p. 116) explains: 'In ethnographic studies the researcher herself is the primary medium, the "instrument" of research, this method draws on those resources of empathy, connection, and concern that many feminists consider to be women's special strengths and which they argue should be germinal in feminist research'.

Additionally, for feminist geographers research is an inherently

Gendered and emotional spaces 305

embodied and performative social practice and this is at the crux of a positionality that seeks to challenge masculinist visions of objectivity that have drawn on repressions of bodies (Rose, 1993, p. 3). Such a relationship between bodies and performances entails attention to emotionalities. As Gregson et al (1997, p. 196) eloquently illustrate:

> The process through which bodily performances are constituted through particular spaces is beginning to be explored in more detail by some feminist geographers concerned with the process of subjectivity. The ways in which bodies themselves are imagined as spaces, and the spaces which they are imagined as inhabiting, are being examined by some feminist geographers in relation to a range of subjective, emotional and psychic processes.

There are clearly parallels between translocal, transcultural and transnational practices that require translation. In these, translation is no longer considered mimetically, as the product of a linear activity – that of migration – but as a plurilinear constellation of activities across not only territorial but also imaginative and emotional geographies of mobilities that are gendered and performative enactments of cultural translations.

As the product of pluridimensional agency, such experiences and identities are mediated through cultural difference when subjects cross borders but also create novel (ethnic and cultural) boundaries in their new social worlds, be that in the 'host' country during immigration or in the ancestral homeland during return migration. In this respect we depart from the notion of 'translation' in the philological sense and arrive at a conceptualization of translation as a salient category of social and cultural theory as well as a central signifier in the politics of culture and difference.

This kind of approach to translation focuses attention on questions that attempt to redefine 'translation between cultures', 'translation between subjects and researchers' as well as 'translation in the academy'[2] and highlights, among other things, those factors of translation relevant to the construction of 'culture'. Among others, factors are embodied, performative and gendered in the crossroads of 'power' and 'agency' and in a dialogic relationship to research and researchers.

Against this background, the research I have been conducting with migrants and return migrants provides an insightful platform to problematize the conditions underlying features of transcultural translation. Furthermore, in the very research process there are obstacles and constraints involved that require a range of translations and negotiations. In the narrative extracts there are several layers of emotional (inter)subjectivities, power and gender in the participants' everyday lives in diasporic settings and wider social life. This section of the chapter aims to expand a narrow view of transcultural and translation processes in migration research into a dialogic and reflective critique of methods, research practice, hierarchies, dichotomies and interdisciplinarity. Critical and feminist geographies concerned with the 'crisis of ethnographic representation', ethnocentrism, racializations and inequalities brought to the fore considerations of positionalities and the politics of research (and writings). Work within cultural studies examining heterogeneous concepts of difference in the formation of cultural identities illuminates core issues of transcultural and translation perspectives in migration research. Homi Bhabha's endeavour to develop a new concept of translation can serve as a basis for this: in the context of the debate on centre/periphery and cultural overlaps, Bhabha (2004, p. 247) proposes a 'translational culture' as a new point of departure for the study of cultural encounter, thus revealing translocal and translation potentials to construct culture:

> Culture . . . is both transnational and translational. . . . The transnational dimension of cultural transformation – migration, diaspora, displacement, relocation – makes the process of cultural translation a complex form of signification. The natural(ized), unifying discourse . . . cannot be readily referenced. The great, though unsettling, advantage of this position is that it makes you increasingly aware of the construction of culture and the invention of tradition.

Hybridity, as the central conceptualization of Bhabha's cultural theory, is seen as an active challenge to the dominant cultural power, a force that transforms the cultural from a source of conflict into a productive element and thereby opens up a 'third space'. The in-betweenness of cultural and social (transnational and translocal) migrant spaces and their imaginings allows us to mediate meaning of the 'incompatible, the silenced, the unconscious' as this kind of 'third space' should not be understood as a static, fixed and identity-bestowing unity but as a process, one that can be re-written and translated. However, tensions do emerge as such spaces are not necessarily those of a liberating and empowered potential but may involve disruptures and hegemonies, exclusions and marginalizations for both subjects and researchers. Moreover, antagonistic and oppositional spaces may emerge for both migrants and researchers that require negotiations, a location and a voice in the translation and mediation process. Yet, 'hybridity' also needs to be problematized and contextualized beyond universalized models that uncover discursive contradictions. Hybridity is not rootless, it is often grounded in national discourses and may not reflect deeper contradictions in social realities. Although Papastergiadis (1997, p. 261), in viewing hybridity, optimistically claims that, 'hybrids were conceived as lubricants in the clashes of culture; they were the negotiators who would secure a future free of xenophobia', hybridization should also be viewed within the realms of 'westernized' ethnocentric and patriarchal perspectives of purity and hierarchy that need to be addressed further in order for research to appropriate an enhanced awareness of the processes of transformation due to cultural translation. Thus, the historical components and political forces along with symbolic practices addressed in this chapter need to be taken into consideration. What are the complexities involved? What types of cultural entanglements emerge? What does it mean for a subject and a researcher to negotiate polyphonic, dialogic and interacting voices? Here attention is required to unveil power relations and socio-biographic mechanisms within processes of cultural translation. For migration studies the application of a gendered and reflexive frame of reference means, first and foremost, expanding the perspective of the field of research from the 'self/other' dichotomy to a more collaborative, collective, inclusive and transcultural viewpoint that encompasses reflective elements while questioning 'authority' and 'authenticity' as a capable means of transforming research into transcultural political praxis. Can we follow a research programme that involves procedures of transformation that can be applied beyond the theoretical and conceptual level to a politics of action? Such scholarship should aim to trace those relations from the field and the academy to the social world in interpreting conditions that may constitute an arena of change and/or discontent in practice.

This chapter has presented theoretically informed empirical insights into diasporic feelings, embodied experiences and migrant encounters in considering how second-generation Greek-Danish women's cultural understandings of place, home and belonging are practised, performed, negotiated and narrated in the diaspora. The focus is on how gendered identities are appropriated within gendered (power) diasporic relations. The chapter reflected on spatialized performativities of gendered participation and experiences in the diaspora in order to examine how cultural processes take place in diasporic settings. The analysis is guided by a qualitative and narrative turn in migration studies and an emphasis on new mobility pathways to account for the embodied and emotional dimensions of migration and return migration. Interrogating gendered migration narratives in the 'here' and 'there' of women participant lives, I scope the emotionally embodied context of belonging and being. I looked at the participant narrative accounts of their experiences as stories of be/longing and explored how emotions, desires and intimate attachments have shaped their mobilities and ultimately their sense of self and identity – the latter being always in the making as the journey of counter return to the ancestral homeland is still an expectation for a future life. As the participants are still shuffling the fragments of memory of an ancestral past Greek life while coping with the present life of Danish/Greek context, the ultimate expectation is the attainment of equilibrium between the 'cultural stuff' of Danishness and of Greekness that gets in the way of finally accepting the self, neither coherent, nor split but in the making. After all, isn't this the pathway of adulthood as the life course progresses and stages follow one after the other, don't we all yearn to 'settle' somewhere and somehow?

In order to conclude with a reflective account of how we can operationalize gender, development and migration in a context of socioeconomic crises with Greece as a case study focus, it is important to come to the realization that, while theoretically appropriate and socially imperative, it is only through governmental and policy avenues combined with a thorough transformation of social consciousness and praxis that any difference can be made in Greece today. While researching gender, migration and development in Greece offers a wide range of conceptual and empirical opportunities to address debates on these issues, the current context of domestic and international crises presents additional challenges to reconsider in both academic and policy terms. Furthermore, contemporary neoliberal migration/economic management regimes pose added ethical as well as ideological challenges to be considered. While situating this chapter within the context of the current crisis in Greece, it is imperative to incorporate inscriptions of historical marginalizations and social exclusions in Greece as well as reflections on what kind of change can be mobilized in theory and practice to tackle inequalities and polarizations.

The gendered developmental mobilities contribution in the literature has, in stages, produced powerful analytical tools from feminist empowerment to policy-focused perspectives published in both migration studies and gender/development studies journals. As King et al. note:

> When we examine gender's bilateral links first with migration and then with development, we see a much more active, synergetic relationship in the respective literatures. . . . Likewise 'gendering development' has an established tradition of academic and policy-focused research, which Sassen (2000) neatly traced through the phases of agricultural and industrial development to a third phase in which women, largely through their migratory initiatives, are protagonists of 'counter-geographies of globalisation', enabling the survival of households in the global South. (2011 p. 396)

In both sending and receiving countries, migrants are an essential component of economies and societies and so the link between migration and a sustainable future of global governance and development for a future of equality and prosperity is beyond any doubt. Societies have the capacity to unlock and unblock the potential of migrants, to build upon their social and economic capital and remittances and to take steps forward collectively. An efficient framework for such type of governance for the years of precarity and uncertainty to come is to harness the collective potential and to implement it productively. For instance, care work is important to development, as well as the transnational care implications of ageing and retired migrants. There is a clear necessity to address policy considerations in relation to transnational caregiving, mobility of care, aged care, social capital of older migrants, retirement migration in relation to medical care, pensions, taxation and so on. Yet, I dare argue that the missing link to an effective contribution to development by migrants is an affective one, that is, affect and emotion can be harnessed in not only understanding the psychosocial elements of the extent of trauma and rupture that crises mark on societies but, above all, to utilize the core of the migration experience as a 'moving' phenomenon, one that mobilizes change through emotion/compassion.

Academics can be very useful in stimulating change that governments and policy makers can implement through the positive (emotional) inter/action of migrant and non-migrant groups. Sustainable coexistence entails the co-presence, comprehension and compassion for others, who themselves as transformative agents will transmit this to subsequent generations.

NOTES

1. This chapter forms part of a wider research project exploring first- and second-generation Greek-Danes and their experiences of migration, identity, gender, home and belonging in Denmark and Greece. The study used a multi-method approach based on qualitative, ethnographic, life history, narrative and biographical methodologies. During participant life-story narrations, experiences, feelings, thoughts, reflections and personal information were shared and recorded. From 2004 to 2005 a total of 40 participants contributed to the study. I provide a very detailed overview of all methodological and theoretical aspects of the project in Christou (2011a) and for reasons of length limitations I cannot duplicate that discussion here.
2. With regard to my use of the term 'Academy' versus the Anglophone 'Academia', I would point readers to the etymological origin from the Greek ('Ακαδημία'), as that of an institution of higher learning, research, or honorary membership. The name traces back to Plato's school of philosophy, founded approximately 385 BC at 'Ακαδημία', a sanctuary of Athena, the goddess of wisdom and skill, north of Athens, Greece. In the 'western' world 'academia' is the commonly used term for the collective institutions of higher learning. However, here, I am not referring simply to the institutions of higher learning but on the contrary to the establishment of scholarly knowledge as the output of wisdom and so the academy here reflects the collective establishment of scholarship as an institutional constellation of not solely information transfer but above all, as the transmission of knowledge production. My point here is not to elaborate on symbolic markers of Greek history and language but to signify defiance to the Anglophone hegemony in publishing which also does not accurately capture what I want to say.

REFERENCES

Alcoff, Linda (1988), 'Cultural feminism versus poststructuralism: the identity crisis in feminist theory', *Signs: Journal of Women in Culture and Society*, **13** (3), 405–36.
Baldassar, Loretta (2011), 'Italian migrants in Australia and their relationship to Italy: return visits, transnational caregiving and the second generation', *Journal of Mediterranean Studies*, **20** (2), 255–82.
Bhabha, Homi (2004), *The Location of Culture*, London: Routledge.
Carling, Jorgen (2002), 'Review of F. Anthias and G. Lazaridis (eds), *Gender and Migration in Southern Europe: Women on the Move*', *Asian and Pacific Migration Journal*, **11** (3), 399–401.
Christou, Anastasia (2006), *Narratives of Place, Culture and Identity: Second-generation Greek-Americans Return 'Home'*, Amsterdam: Amsterdam University Press.
Christou, Anastasia (2009), 'Telling diaspora stories: theoretical and methodological reflections on narratives of migrancy and belongingness in the second generation', *Migration Letters*, **6** (2), 143–53.
Christou, Anastasia (2011a), 'Narrating lives in (e)motion: embodiment, belongingness and displacement in diasporic spaces of home and return', *Emotion, Space and Society*, **4**, 249–57.
Christou, Anastasia (2011b) 'Translocal geographies: multi-sited encounters of Greek migrants in Athens, in New York and Berlin', Katherine Brickell and Ayone Datta (eds), *Translocal Geographies: Spaces, Places, Connections*, Ashgate: Aldershot, pp. 145–61.
Christou, Anastasia and Russell King (2010), 'Imagining "home": diasporic landscapes of the Greek second generation', *Geoforum*, **41**, 638–46.
Christou, Anastasia and Russell King (2011), 'Gendering diasporic mobilities and emotionalities in Greek-German narratives of home, belonging and return', *Journal of Mediterranean Studies*, **20** (2), 283–315.
Cornwall, Andrea (2000), 'Missing men? Reflections on men: masculinities and gender in GAD', *IDS Bulletin*, **31** (2), 18–27.
Crul, Maurice (ed.) (2007), *The Second Generation in Europe*, Special Issue, *Journal of Ethnic and Migration Studies*, **33** (7), 1025–193.
de Lauretis, Teresa (1987), *Technologies of Gender*, London: Macmillan.
Gregson, N., L. Crewe and B. Longstaff (1997), 'Excluded spaces of regulation: car-boot sales as an enterprise culture out of control?', *Environment and Planning, A* **29** (10), 1717–37.
Herzfeld, Michael (1997), *Cultural Intimacy: Social Poetics in the Nation-State*, New York: Routledge.
Ho, Elaine and Madeleine E. Hatfield (2010), Introduction to special issue: 'Migration and everyday matters: sociality and materiality', *Population, Space and Place*, DOI:10.1002, p. 636.
Kasinitz, Philip, John Mollenkopf and Mary Waters (eds) (2004), *Becoming New Yorkers: Ethnographies of the New Second Generation*, New York: Russell Sage.
King, Russell, Adriana Castaldo and Julie Vullnetari (2011), 'Gendered relations and filial duties along the Greek–Albanian remittance corridor', *Economic Geography*, **87** (4), 393–419.
King, Russell and Anastasia Christou (2011), 'Of counter-diaspora and reverse transnationalism: return mobilities to and from the ancestral homeland', *Mobilities*, **6** (4), 451–66.
King, Russell, Alan Warnes and Allan Williams (2000), *Sunset Lives: British Retirement Migration to the Mediterranean*, Oxford: Berg.
Levitt, Peggy and Mary Waters (eds) (2002), *The Changing Face of Home: The Transnational Lives of the Second Generation*, New York: Russell Sage.
Louie, Vivian (2006), 'Second-generation pessimism and optimism: how Chinese and Dominicans understand education and mobility through ethnic and transnational orientations', *International Migration Review*, **40** (3), 537–72.

McNay, Lois (1992), *Foucault and Feminism: Power, Gender and Self*, Boston, MA: Northeastern University Press.
O'Reilly Karen (2000), *The British on the Costa del Sol*, London: Routledge.
Papastergiadis, Nicos (1997), 'Tracing hybridity in theory', in Prina Werbner and Tarik Modood (eds), *Debating Cultural Hybridity: Multi-Cultural Identities and the Politics of Anti-Racism*, London: Zed Books, pp. 257–81.
Portes, Alejandro (ed.) (1996), *The New Second Generation*, New York: Russell Sage.
Portes, Alejandro and Ruben Rumbaut (2001), *Legacies: The Story of the Immigrant Second Generation*, Berkeley, CA: University of California Press.
Portes, Alejandro and Min Zhou (1993), 'The new second generation: segmented assimilation and its variants among post-1965 immigrant youth', *Annals of the American Academy of Political and Social Science*, **530**, 74–98.
Potter, Rob and Joan Phillips (2006), '"Mad dogs and international migrants?" Bajan-Brit second-generation migrants and accusations of madness', *Annals of the Association of American Geographers*, **96** (3), 586–600.
Reynolds, Tracey (2011), 'Caribbean second-generation return migration: transnational family relationships with "left-behind" kin in Britain', *Mobilities*, **6** (4), 483–501.
Rose, Gillian (1993), *Feminism and Geography: The Limits of Geographical Knowledge*, Minneapolis, MN: University of Minnesota Press.
Sassen, S. (2000), 'Women's burden: counter-geographies of globalization and the feminization of survival', *Journal of International Affairs*, **53**, 503–24.
Stacey, Judith (1997), 'Can there be a feminist ethnography?', in Linda McDowell and Joanne Sharp (eds), *Space, Gender, Knowledge: Feminist Readings*, London: Arnold, pp 115–23.
Teerling, Janine (2011), 'The "return" of British-born Turkish Cypriots to Cyprus: narratives of a fractured homeland', *Journal of Mediterranean Studies*, **20** (2), 315–41.
Vathi, Zana (2011), 'A context issue? Comparing the attitude towards return of the Albanian first and second generation in Europe', *Journal of Mediterranean Studies*, **20** (2), 343–64.
Walby, Sylvia (2007), 'Complexity theory, systems theory and multiple intersecting social inequalities', *Philosophy of the Social Sciences*, **37** (4), 449–70.
Wessendorf, S. (2007), 'Local attachments and transnational everyday lives: second-generation Italians in Switzerland', *Gobal Networks*, **10** (3), 365–82.
West, Linden, Peter Alheit, Anders Siig Anderson and Barbara Merrill (eds) (2007), *Using Biographical and Life History Approaches in the Study of Adult and Lifelong Learning: European Perspectives*, Frankfurt am Main: Peter Lang.
Zontini, Elisabetta (2007), 'Continuity and change in transnational Italian families: the caring practices of second-generation women', *Journal of Ethnic and Migration Studies*, **33** (7), 1103–20.

14 Bolivian migrants in Spain: transnational families from a gender perspective
Sònia Parella

INTRODUCTION

According to Basch et al. (1994, p.238), 'family processes and relations between people defined as kin constitute the initial foundation for all other types of transnational social relations'. Migratory flows generate micro-social processes that require families to make adjustments over time and across space within the constraints exercised by broader, complex and interconnected economic, political and social processes. This chapter has two objectives:

1. to analyse the transnational practices of Bolivian migrants, trying to identify whether there are distinctive patterns based on gender and migrants' family structure; and
2. to examine the impact of Bolivian families' transnational arrangements on the perception of family gender roles and on practices based on the sexual division of labour for both the migrants as well as for the family members left behind in Bolivia.

The results presented here are based on two types of data:

- data from a survey of 200 Bolivian migrants residing in the province of Barcelona carried out during the second quarter of 2010; and
- qualitative data that form part of a broader project, entitled 'Transnacionalismo económico: remesas y empresas de los migrantes bolivianos en España' (Economic transnationalism: remittances and businesses of Bolivian migrants in Spain) (Reference SEJ2007-60734) financed by Spain's Ministry for Research and Science.[1] The data were obtained based on a qualitative and multi-local methodology that takes the transnational family as a unit of analysis to incorporate the perspective of both migrants and family members 'left behind'. This is done through the use of semi-structured interviews.

First, we discuss the theoretical foundations underlying analysis from a gender perspective of transnational family structures as configured by migratory processes. Following this, the recent migratory flows from Bolivia to Spain are analysed in the context of the dynamics that have transformed these recent migrations in comparison with 'traditional' Bolivian migratory patterns. Next, we present the main results. The quantitative analysis permits us to identify the main characteristics of the Bolivian men and women surveyed regarding their migratory projects and transnational practices from a gender perspective. These data are supplemented with an analysis of the transnational adjustments made by Bolivian migrants in Spain to gender roles, taking the transnational family as the unit of analysis. The analysis of the in-depth interviews of the migrants and their Bolivian counterparts permits us to articulate economic and kinship links, as well as those related to caregiving, while incorporating the relational (between men and women) and situational character of the perspective of gender. The chapter concludes by assessing how migration impacts the various family members from a gender perspective and the more significant implications for a migration–development nexus (Mazzucato and Schans, 2011).

MIGRATORY PROCESSES AND TRANSNATIONAL FAMILIES FROM A GENDER PERSPECTIVE

Gender as a Constituting Element of Migration

Hondagneu-Sotelo (2000, p. 428) points out that gender determines the social relations and practices that articulate migrations and should be considered in the analysis of all stages of the migratory cycle, in both immigrants' place of origin and their place of destination, and for both men and women. According to this author, gender dynamics articulate the decision to emigrate (who emigrates and who stays); the employment patterns that integrate individuals in the labour market in both the place of origin and destination; the tension between circularity, return or definitive settlement; the patterns of participation in community organizations and political parties; the roles of family members that remain; as well as family arrangements after migration and transnational economic links (economic remittances).

According to Herrera (2005, p. 12), 'the transnational family should be understood as a locus of social and emotional support, but also as a field of conflictive power relations between its members'. For this reason it is necessary to avoid approaching the family as a uniform entity or unified object of analysis, and to take into account the unequal power relations within it (gender relations, intergenerational relations), as well as the differentiated allocation of roles in processes of identity construction and in the reproduction of the welfare of its members (Herrera, 2004; Suárez and Crespo, 2007). Conceiving the migratory process from the perspective of the family group as a unit of reference permits us to understand how the division of functions between genders (men and women) and members of different generations takes place.

The migration of women is due to many factors, among which stand out the lack of job opportunities, the difficult socioeconomic situation of their families in their country of origin, the devastating impact of structural adjustment plans in many regions and the increase in single-parent households headed by women and other conditions related to gender. However, these migratory processes are not only the result of the feminization of so-called 'global survival circuits' in the words of the sociologist, Saskia Sassen (2003). They are also the consequence of transformations in the labour markets of destination countries, major recruiters of women for work in low-paying jobs, primarily in the service sector and in economic activities that provide care for dependent persons (Parella, 2007). In this sense, the globalization of care work constitutes a necessary starting point in analysing the current feminization of international migrations and their impact on gender inequalities in the context of crises in social reproduction (Zimmerman et al., 2006).

Women play a key role as the cornerstone in maintaining family bonds despite the physical distance that separates family members when one member migrates (Baby-Collins et al., 2008; Zontini, 2010). The articulation between economic links and those of caregiving and kinship is strongly conditioned by gender. Baby-Collins et al. (2008) find that women are pivotal in maintaining family ties, as family breadwinners and as the persons in the family responsible for transmitting the cultural values of their place of origin. Consequently, they constitute the intergenerational 'node' that maintains the cohesiveness of the family and migratory networks. When they emigrate, in addition to the economic and productive functions they assume (sending remittances), they are also the primary articulators of transnational social spaces through their daily reproductive work (Pedone, 2004).

The factors conditioning gender are situated in a new setting, one in which migration, as a family response, is increasingly feminized. This pioneering female migration transforms and re-orients marital and mother–child relations, which are shifted onto a transnational social space. The international migration of women with family responsibilities permits us to advance the feminist debate over the connections between the conditions under which women participate in the labour market and their concentration and responsibilities in reproductive work. At the same time it is an opportunity to make reproductive work more visible and to situate it in a more prominent place within the economy and within general social welfare (Benería, 2008).

The Transnational Family as an Object of Study from a Gender Perspective

The family constitutes a central axis in the social organization of migrants' lives, its importance increasing in transnational contexts (Ariza, 2000). According to Zontini (2010, p. 52), transnational families are multi-local families, families with members distributed in different spaces across national borders and who participate in family events and decisions from a distance. With regard to this concept, Bryceson and Vuorela (2002) defines transnational families as 'families that live some or most of the time separated from each other, yet hold together and create something that can be seen as a feeling of collective welfare and unity, namely familyhood even across national borders' (p. 3). Based on this definition we can see that geographical distance is only one element defining transnational family structure. A sense of belonging on the part of family members must exist and members must participate collectively in managing the well-being of the family beyond national borders (Levitt and Glick Schiller, 2004).

To understand the family in its 'transnational life' implies the study of forms and meanings that homes use, through the transnational actions of migrant and non-migrant actors, to create social spaces that permit the interweaving of different types of links (Faist, 2000). Economic activities (principally monetary remittances) have been widely studied and constitute a key pillar of all the typologies that try to describe the heterogeneity of transnational activities and practices (Guarnizo, 1997; Portes et al., 2003).

However, beyond family economic transfers, there are other types of links, grounded in the overlapping of the productive and reproductive spheres. First, links between the management of affect and care, also known as caring work (Alicea, 1997; Gonzálvez, 2005; Parella, 2007; Zontini, 2010); second, kin work, defined by Di Leonardo (1992, p. 248) as the totality of activities oriented towards the maintenance of kinship bonds within the family group (visits, ritual celebrations, telephone calls, gifts, and so on).

Functions concerning affect and care are reconstructed with migration and also form part of the resources that flow through family networks. Therefore, they give form to the relationships of 'reciprocity' that govern migratory chains and the transnational ties between migrants and their counterparts (Parella and Cavalcanti, 2008). Although family reciprocity is a continuous chain of obligations (gender and generational) that are disrupted by spatial and temporal family separation, transnational links bring about a redefinition of family relations and exchange of support. These are relationships and exchanges of resources, both tangible and intangible, which involve those who leave and those who stay behind (family arrangements) (Parreñas, 2001; Ho, 2002). All these roles and relationships change family structures and the transnational lifestyle has effects for the different members (between spouses, parents, children and elderly parents).

The spread of the concept of 'transnational family' ('motherhood at a distance' or 'transnational motherhood') began at the end of the 1990s as a body of research which, from a gender perspective, analyses the dynamics of the globalization of care and how migrant women from poor countries participate as 'pioneers' of the migratory process to provide domestic reproductive work for families in destination societies. This situation often means long-term separations between migrant women and their children (Parreñas, 2001; Hochschild, 2003; Bernhard et al., 2005; Sørensen, 2007).

The tension between the productive role that the woman migrant adopts and her reproductive role increases with her absence. The allocation of reproductive work to women implies increased workloads and responsibilities for other women in the family when it is a woman who migrates to another country (Vidal et al., 2002; Tapia, 2010). Unfortunately, certain political, academic and media discourses have pointed to the separation of families when the 'pioneering' migrant is a woman as triggering negative effects, such as an increase in divorce, male alcoholism, teen pregnancies and the poor academic performance of children in school (Hochschild, 2003; Parella, 2007; Sørensen, 2007).

Women who migrate are stigmatized based on emphasizing the devastating consequences of their 'abandoning the home' (Parreñas, 2000; Poggio and Woo, 2000; Woo, 2001; Vidal et al., 2002; Pedone, 2008; Wagner, 2008). The discourse on 'bad migrant mothers' is a response to the need to renegotiate gender relations in the context of female migration, which, according to different studies, is threatening the very pillars of patriarchy (Parreñas, 2001, 2003; Wagner, 2008). In contrast, for men, although migration also involves significant changes in the exercise of fatherhood, their mobility reinforces their role as economic breadwinners and grants them social prestige (symbolic capital) (Pedone, 2004). This is why most research in this area focuses mainly on the study of mothers and the mother–child bond and little attention is paid to fathers who emigrate. According to Pribilsky (2004) and Mazzucato and Schans (2011), the inclusion of fathers in the analysis is necessary to get a complete overview of transnational families and their impacts.

THE CONTEXT OF BOLIVIAN MIGRATION TO SPAIN

In recent years, Bolivia has been one of the main sending countries of emigrants to Spain during its consolidation as 'immigrant Spain' (Cachón, 2009).[2] This was especially the case in 2006, as a consequence of visa requirements for entry into the EU that would go into effect in April 2007 (Whitesell, 2008; Hinojosa, 2008b; Gadea et al., 2009). Data from Spain's National Statistics Institute's (INE) Municipal Registers reveals that there were 202,657 persons born in Bolivia registered in Spain as of 1 January 2011 (this is down from a maximum of 242,496 on 1 January 2008, a consequence of the economic crisis). Longitudinal analysis of the Municipal Registers' data shows the significant and rapid increase in these migratory flows from Bolivia, especially since 2005, as well as their marked feminization (on 1 January 2011, 58.3 per cent of the persons of Bolivian origin included on the Municipal Registers were women).

Based on data from the 2007 INE National Immigrant Survey, 31.4 per cent of Bolivians were employed in domestic services and 20.3 per cent in construction (ibid.). This is a feminized flow, with a high percentage being undocumented and concentrated in 'employment niches' commonly associated with economic immigration and characterized by poor working and living conditions. Based on data from 1 January 2011, almost 30 per cent of Bolivian migrants in Spain live in Madrid, Barcelona and L'Hospitalet de Llobregat.[3] The majority of Bolivians that reside in Spain are from the departments of Cochabamba and Santa Cruz de la Sierra. However, as flows from Bolivia have consolidated, places of origin have diversified and migrants have also come from rural areas in Bolivia's valleys, the east and the highlands (Hinojosa, 2009b).

Migratory flows to Spain should be situated within Bolivia's long historical experience with socio-spatial mobility inside and outside of the country (Hinojosa, 2009a). Spain, as a destination country, reveals a new model for movement that cannot be understood if it is not analysed within the context of survival strategies in Bolivian society, based on established family and community practices regarding mobility, which different authors have referred to as a 'culture of mobility' (De la Torre, 2006; Hinojosa, 2009a).

During the final decades of the twentieth century, the primary destinations of international migration from Bolivia were the bordering countries of Argentina and Brazil, with the United States as another important destination. Argentina was, and continues to be, the main destination and was the source of many of the migrants from the first wave of Bolivian migration to Spain, particularly during 2001 and 2002 (Hinojosa, 2009b).[4] There are diverse reasons for this change in orientation (Bastia, 2007; Gadea et al., 2009), among which are the strong demand in Spain for workers in domestic services and low-skilled workers in other service sectors and the influence of migratory networks. Coinciding with Argentina's economic crisis at the end of the 1990s, this led to a significant number of Bolivian migrants who had returned to Bolivia from Argentina deciding to invest their savings in emigrating to Spain (Bastia, 2007; Hinojosa, 2009a).

One of the major changes in these migratory flows is, for the first time in Bolivia's history, their marked feminization, which has altered gender relations in a significant manner (Cortes, 2004). For the Bolivian this means a potential change in family care structures. Women, who historically were less likely than men to participate in migration (mainly young single women and women following a family unification process through cross-border circular migrations), now move to seek work independently. This change is the consequence of transformations in the labour markets of destination countries, which have become recruiters of women workers to work as caregivers and in other low-wage jobs, primarily in the service sector (Parella, 2007). Therefore, the migration of Bolivian women, primarily to Spain and the United States, should be placed with the dynamics of the feminization of other international migratory flows that have been described as the consequence of the globalization of care work (Zarembka, 2003). The feminization of Bolivian migration challenges the assumptions and practices that had predominated until then, based on the organization of predominantly male international migratory projects (Pedone, 2008). This was a feminine migration that was no longer primarily of single women, but was constructed as part of families' survival strategies.

Another transformation to take into account is the impossibility of maintaining the circular patterns that had characterized interregional migrations (to Argentina and Brazil). The visa requirement for Bolivian immigrants in Europe and the recent character of the migratory flow to Spain has led to a significant population of undocumented migrants. Their resulting difficulty in returning to Spain if they leave keeps many of these migrants from travelling back to Bolivia. The inability to design circular patterns of mobility has a significant effect on family structures and on strategies to readjust gender relations and relations between generations. The migrations of Bolivians to Argentina, by contrast, allowed migrants to periodically return to their home of origin, as they occurred in a legal context with greater flexibility for leaving, returning and residing in the destination country (Dandler and Medeiros, 1991).

QUANTITATIVE APPROACH TO THE TRANSNATIONAL LINKS OF BOLIVIAN MIGRANTS IN SPAIN FROM A GENDER PERSPECTIVE

The quantitative data we present in what follows are from a survey carried out with 200 Bolivian migrants aged between 20 and 65 and residing in the province of Barcelona. The sample was chosen based on the composition of the Bolivian population by sex and age as revealed by data from Spain's Municipal Registers for 1 January 2010. The 200 in-person interviews were carried out from April to June 2010 at cultural and sporting events where a significant attendance of Bolivian migrants was expected.[5]

Table 14.1 shows the main characteristics of the sample: type of family structure, migratory project and legal and economic status in Spain by sex.

Regarding family structure, the data do not reveal notable differences between men and women. Some 14.5 per cent of the respondents stated that they have a partner residing in Bolivia and almost 36 per cent of the respondents have some or all of their children living in Bolivia, which could be an indicator of family structures of a transnational character if the welfare of family members is managed in a collective manner. In contrast, approximately one-fifth of respondents (19.8 per cent) have no children. Almost 30 per cent have brought over a child during their migratory stage in Spain.

The data reveal differences between men and women with regard to when they arrived in Spain and the reasons behind their decision to emigrate. Some 61.5 per cent of men arrived in Spain after 2004, while the figure for women was 55.6 per cent. The reasons for deciding to emigrate show that influences on the migratory process differ for men and women. While women identify factors that have to do with the economic situation of the family (half of the women surveyed mentioned this reason), or with improving the family's quality of life (38.1 per cent); men, by contrast, more often mention factors that are directly concerned with the productive dimension (such as the lack of work in Bolivia), and are more likely to be motivated by 'individual economic projects'.

The segregation of Bolivian women migrants in domestic service jobs is clear (57.1 per cent). The men, on the other hand, are employed in diverse sectors and a much higher percentage is self-employed (21.2 per cent). The unemployment rate is higher among men than women (8.7 versus 1.7 per cent), which can be explained by the fact that the care sector where women

Table 14.1 Basic data on Bolivian migrants in Barcelona

	Men	Women	Total
Family structure			
% Civil status 'married' or 'with partner'	68.0	56.3	61.0
% Spouse or partner in Bolivia	15.6	13.8	14.5
% Spouse or partner in Spain	55.4	46.4	50.0
% No children	21.8	18.5	19.8
% More than two children	24.7	34.8	30.6
% All children reside in Bolivia	28.2	31.1	29.9
% All children reside in Spain	35.9	39.5	38.1
% Some children reside in Bolivia	6.4	5.0	5.6
% Who have brought a child to join them	28.4	29.7	29.2
Arrival in Spain			
% Arrival after 2004	61.5	55.6	57.9
% Migrated alone	51.3	50.0	50.5
Reasons for migrating*			
Individual economic projects	31.6	24.6	27.4
Economic reasons related to the family	30.4	50.0	42.1
Lack of work	30.4	18.6	23.4
To improve quality of life	35.4	38.1	37.1
Employment status in Spain			
Private sector employee	55.0	23.5	36.2
Domestic service	6.2	57.1	36.7
Self-employed	21.2	7.6	13.1
Unemployed	8.7	1.7	4.5
Other situations (inactive)	8.9	10.1	9.5
	(100%)	(100%)	(100%)
Income level in Spain			
% Income over 1,000 euros/month	64.1	39.1	49.5
Education level			
Primary school	6.3	5.1	5.6
Secondary school	64.9	63.2	64.0
University	26.3	25.6	25.9
Unknown/No answer	2.5	6.1	4.6
	(100%)	(100%)	(100%)
Current legal status			
Only passport (undocumented)	19.8	7.6	12.6
Temporary residence status	46.9	42.4	44.2
Permanent residence status	14.8	23.7	20.1
EU resident	2.5	2.5	2.5
Spanish nationality	3.7	5.1	4.5
Others (pending or students)	12.3	18.7	16.1
	(100%)	(100%)	(100%)

Note: * Multiple responses.

Source: Based on data from the Survey 'Transnational practices of Bolivian migrants in Barcelona', 2010.

are concentrated has been more resistant to the loss of jobs during this economic crisis (Pajares, 2010). Despite this finding, the monthly income of men is clearly higher than that of women. Some 64.1 per cent of the men surveyed have an income over 1,000 euros a month, while only 39.1 per cent of the women reach this amount.

Regarding legal status, a much higher percentage of men are undocumented than women – almost one in every five men compared to only 7.6 per cent of women. The women reveal a high percentage with stable legal status (almost one in four women have permanent residency). These differences may be partly explained by the fact that women have, on average, accumulated more time as residents in Spain. In addition, 2005 was the last year in which a so-called 'process of normalization' of the status of undocumented immigrants occurred, and this has to be taken into consideration. This process (between 7 February and 7 May 2005) led to a total of 687,138 applications for residency in Spain. In the case of Bolivia, there were a total of 47,202 applications (making Bolivia the country with the fifth-highest number of applicants); more women took advantage of this process than men, many of them through job offers in domestic service. Bolivian men, in contrast, not only migrated to Spain in greater measure after this regularization (mainly between 2005 and 2007), but have also been concentrated in job sectors where it is more difficult to obtain a legal job offer (for example, in construction).

Table 14.2 shows the main results of the survey regarding the transnational practices of migrants by sex and type of family structure. For family structure we distinguish only between those persons with children in Bolivia at the time they participated in the survey and those who have no children or whose children reside with them in Spain.

An initial block of indicators entails the sending of remittances, their frequency, quantity and the use to which they are put. Men and women do not differ much in their propensity to send remittances, the frequency with which they do so and the quantity sent (measured by the percentage that send more than 200 euros a month). However, if we take into account that the women in our survey earn less than their male counterparts (see Table 14.1), these data reveal that Bolivian women have a greater potential to save money for sending to Bolivia.[6] Having children or not is a determinant of the frequency and quantity of money sent. In almost 62 per cent of the cases, money is directly sent to parents. However, if there are children, men send the money to them in 53.8 per cent of the cases and women in 48.7 per cent of the cases.

The variable 'use of remittances' reveals clear differences between men and women; this is in line with the different migratory projects that have been identified in table 14.1. More of the money women send is spent on

Table 14.2 Transnational practices of Bolivian migrants by sex and family structure

	Men	Women	Men Children in Bolivia	Men Without children in Bolivia	Women Children in Bolivia	Women Without children in Bolivia	Total
Send remittances							
% Send money to Bolivia	92.6	89.7	100.0	88.9	95.2	86.7	90.9
% Send money every month	61.6	63.8	92.3	44.7	90.0	47.7	62.9
% Send more than 200 euros/month	38.5	40.4	75.0	17.1	84.4	13.5	60.4
Who gets the money*							
% Spouse or partner	12.3	14.4	30.8	2.1	35.9	1.5	13.6
% Parents	65.8	58.7	30.8	85.1	33.3	73.8	61.6
% Children	23.3	21.2	53.8	–	48.7	–	22.0
% Siblings	13.7	17.3	0.0	21.3	2.6	26.2	15.8
Use of remittances*							
% Pay debts in Bolivia	13.5	13.7	11.1	14.9	15.0	12.9	13.6
% Family consumption	86.5	90.2	92.6	83.1	95.0	86.7	88.6
% Pay private school for children in Bolivia	4.1	18.6	11.1	–	42.5	–	12.5
% Buy land or property	12.2	16.7	22.2	6.4	27.5	9.7	14.8
% Business investment	10.8	7.8	18.5	6.4	7.5	8.1	9.1

Trips to Bolivia							
% Has not visited Bolivia since arriving in Spain	50.0	41.2	50.0	50.0	38.1	43.1	44.8
% Has visited Bolivia at least once a year	11.5	20.2	23.1	5.8	28.6	15.3	16.7
Intention to return (next five years)							
Intention to return to Bolivia	32.5	36.2	48.1	24.5	38.1	35.1	34.7
Intention to stay in Catalonia	38.8	53.4	33.3	41.5	50.0	55.4	47.4
Move to another part of Spain or another country	25.1	6.0	14.8	30.2	4.8	6.8	13.8
Unknown/No answer	3.6	4.4	3.8	3.8	7.1	2.7	4.1
	(100%)	(100%)	(100%)	(100%)	(100%)	(100%)	(100%)

Note: * Multiple responses.

Source: Based on data from the Survey 'Transnational practices of Bolivian migrants in Barcelona', 2010.

family consumption, paying for private school for the children and buying land or property. In all cases, the propensity of migrants to allocate remittances for an investment in their country of origin (buying land, buying property or investing in a business) is much more frequent (three times more) among migrants with children in Bolivia than among those who have no descendants there, with one exception: the percentage of women who say they invest their remittances in a business is similar for both women who have children in Bolivia and women who do not (7.5 and 8.1 per cent, respectively).

Regarding the frequency of trips to Bolivia, the data show that women maintain greater contact with their families than men. Only 41.2 per cent of women have not travelled to Bolivia since they arrived in Spain, compared to 50 per cent of men. This difference of almost nine percentage points could be explained by the higher percentage of men who are undocumented, which would prevent them from leaving the country. However, among those migrants who can travel, a much higher percentage of women than men return to Bolivia at least once a year (20.2 versus 11.5 per cent).

A similar percentage of men and women state that they intend to return to Bolivia in the next five years, 32.5 per cent of men and 36.2 per cent of women. Where we do find greater differences between men and women is in the intention to stay in Catalonia. A much higher percentage of women than men state that they intend to stay – 53.4 versus 38.8 per cent, respectively. However, a much larger proportion of men state that they intend to move to another part of Spain or to another country. The higher unemployment rate among men may explain this predisposition for geographical mobility that does not include a return to Bolivia. In addition, although intentions to return to Bolivia or to remain in Spain in the case of men clearly depend on whether they have children in Bolivia (a much higher percentage of men with children in Bolivia state that they intend to return than men without children in Bolivia), among women we find practically no differences in their intentions concerning family structure.

QUALITATIVE APPROACH

Some Methodological Notes

Given that data from the survey have showed some differences in the way that men and women migrants manage transnational families – with regard to the reasons for emigrating, the use of remittances and the frequency of trips to Bolivia – the qualitative approach places emphasis on studying the changes in perceptions and practices of gender roles caused by transnational family structure, depending on whether it is men or women who emigrate.

The qualitative data referred to in the analysis of transnational families form part of a bi-local design that begins with the family as the unit of analysis. This type of design permits us to analyse the migratory process (pre- and post-migratory stages) from the perspective of how it is perceived by different members of the transnational family. According to Mazzucato and Schans (2011), to understand the effects on all family members requires following them to where they are located, to where migrants live and where their family members reside. In addition, by incorporating men and women from a conception of gender as a relational process, this study overcomes the bias towards only the experiences of women of many studies that address the construction of gender and migratory processes (Hondagneu-Sotelo, 2000; Rosas, 2010).

Given that the family is the unit of analysis, one of the key methodological decisions was to identity what type of transnational family structure is best for studying the Bolivian case, in the sense of considering nuclear structures or, in contrast, extended families. According to Dandler and Medeiros (1991, p. 21), Andino family structure is usually nuclear, although nuclear family members are strongly connected to extended family relationships. Families with parents and married children usually live closely together, in the same group of houses, and they participate in exchanging products and informal work even though each nuclear family unit manages their own resources (Balán, 1990, p. 278). This study has used the nuclear family structure, based on the definition of transnational family of Leonardo de la Torre (2006, p. 126) as that which 'participates in the migratory phenomenon through one or more members of the nuclear family unit, composed of a father, mother, siblings or children, husband and wife'. Despite this operative definition, our study takes into account that transnational practices (remittances, demonstrations of family migrant community solidarity and so on) are managed not only from the necessary nuclear connection with migrant family members, but also in a framework of wider kinship (De La Torre and Alfaro, 2007).

The research from which the data have been extracted used a typological classification system that guided the selection of 20 transnational Bolivian families based on three criteria: type of family structure, region of origin (Cochabamba, La Paz, Oruro and Santa Cruz) and migrant's place of residence in Spain (Madrid or Barcelona as main destinations). With regard to the type of family structure, for the analysis we take into account only the data referring to nuclear families in which the mother or father emigrated as pioneers, while all or some of the children remained in

Bolivia.[7] Thus we shall consider the cases in which children are raised by either their biological mother or their biological father – in this last case, sometimes with the support of a carer in the extended family (Mazzucato and Schans, 2011).

For this qualitative stage, we proceeded by carrying out semi-structured interviews with migrants in Madrid and Barcelona between June 2008 and June 2009. Afterwards, in a second phase, we contacted members of the transnational families of the migrants we had interviewed who had remained in Bolivia (either the wife or the husband) and they were subsequently interviewed in their homes in Bolivia (Santa Cruz, Cochabamba, Oruro and La Paz).

Transnational Adjustments and their Impact from a Gender Perspective

Gender conditioning impacts on the migratory projects of both men and women as both are 'gendered' subjects. In reconstructing the subjects' migratory processes, we find differences between men and women. When it is men who initially emigrate, the decision is made within the family and reinforces the social representation that associates the carrying out of an international migratory project with the figure of the male 'head of household' (the 'man of the house'). It is assumed that the emigration of the 'father' is not going to cause a serious disruption in the family (Pedone, 2004).

When it is women who emigrate as 'pioneers', economic motivations aimed at improving family living conditions (primarily to achieve a better education for the children – private school or university – or to pay-off debts) appear as the triggers of the migratory process. The knowledge that it will be easier for women than for men to find employment in Spain, along with the greater potential to save money by working in domestic service – particularly if employment is live-in – are some of the reasons put forward for migration by the respondents. These are bi-directional projects (round trip), constructed with the idea of an eventual return to Bolivia, that describe female mobility as a result of household strategies, in which women assume the economic responsibility for the family (spouse, children and other family members) (Oso, 2007).

For the case of the families studied in which the father emigrates, the discourse of our respondents emphasized the costs that migration had for the father, who misses his children, although the negative impact on the children is barely mentioned. In this sense, the emigration of the father does not substantially alter the family structure, which continues to be nuclear, or the responsibility of the mother for care work.

The negative effects of the absence of the mother on the children, in contrast, are mentioned explicitly, both by the emigrant women and their partner or spouse 'left behind'. These effects are closely connected to the age of the children during the period of separation and range from a decline in school performance (especially during the first years of separation), to a rejection of the mother as a response to feelings of 'abandonment'. In addition, these transnational families also face the social stigma of the mother's absence reflected in the discourse of teachers and educators in the schools, who blame low academic performance on women's migration (Fe y Alegría, 2010). The capacity of the mother to maintain contact from a distance is fundamental in modulating the effects of separation, although this contact is not always enough to compensate for the 'affective' functions that the father, in charge of the children back home, is often incapable of assuming.

Although it can be stated that migration involves a renegotiation of gender roles and leads to a restructuring of gender asymmetries, as argued by Rosas (2010, p. 246), these modifications and changes do not necessarily 'nullify inequality'. In other words, migration potentially leads to changes in gender relations; however, it is not possible to establish, a priori, their occurrence or what they might look like, their direction or results – whether these asymmetries will be reduced or, on the contrary, reinforced (Gregorio, 1998; Ariza, 2000, p. 226; Oso, 2007).

For this study we used two categories of analysis which permit us to address the discursive perspective of both men and women located in different social and territorial spaces:

1. changes in perceptions of gender roles in relation to the pre-migratory period; and
2. changes in practices regarding the sexual division of labour in relation to pre-migratory practices.

With regard to the emigration of men, the results of the interviews reveal a discourse that maintains the role of the male breadwinner as the 'authority figure', as well as that of the woman as responsible for social reproduction. The role of the man is not necessarily weakened by distance, thanks to the possibilities that new technologies offer to enable him to make certain decisions, for example, about how to spend the money that he sends. However, the transnational situation that the family faces can lead to changes in the role of the women left behind.

With the prospect of the return of their spouse, in some cases women perceive the recomposition of their relationship as a complicated process, as the period of separation may have permitted them to gain autonomy and freedom of movement.

It is pioneering feminine migration, however, that has the greatest impact on gender roles in the family. Women 'pioneer' migrants, in general, have to face the pain and stigma of not living with their children. At the same time, they achieve greater levels of emancipation and face new spheres of socialization. This emancipation is expressed not only explicitly, but primarily through allusions to a greater degree of control over their migratory projects. This may take the form of a desire to delay their return and stay in Spain longer or, despite the initial migratory project not contemplating such a possibility, a proposal for the reunification of the family in Spain, which often faces opposition from family members in Bolivia.

For Bolivian women who have emigrated, prestige comes not from the type of work they carry out (the most common job they hold is as a domestic worker, an occupation with low status in Bolivia), but from the fact that they become the principal breadwinner in their family. Their discourse combines economic success for their family with an active form of constructing their own emancipation, drawing on the competencies gained through migration (Baby-Collins et al., 2008).

Pioneering women's emigration, as was previously mentioned, generates cracks in the traditional role of the woman as 'spouse' and 'mother', as the male spouse maintained by his partner's remittances faces the questioning of traditional masculinity (Oso, 2007). For the man, his partner's emigration means having to deal with the stigma of the 'kept man' who does not exercise his masculinity according to traditional standards. These 'new' feminized migratory patterns undoubtedly require a more flexible masculinity, as men face difficulties fulfilling their role as the family breadwinners (Rosas, 2010). But not all men follow the same strategies when dealing with the pressures of gender roles. In some cases they reinforce their control over their partner from a distance, through a discourse of blaming and being alert to possible and eventual changes in their partner's attitudes or behaviour after migration (way of speaking, of dressing and so on), which may lead to questioning their role as 'man of the house'.

Regarding changes in practices concerning the sexual division of labour, no significant changes take place when the man emigrates, as responsibility for the home and providing care continue to devolve to women. However, as Pribilsky (2004) shows, women left behind take on new responsibilities when their husbands emigrate and take on tasks that only the man did before he emigrated. The results of the interviews show that women not only see their role in managing the family economy reinforced (thanks to the remittances they receive), but, additionally, they are responsible for maintaining family cohesion through the discursive reconstruction of the migratory project of the 'absent father' as something shared by and beneficial for the whole family. In addition, some of the women interviewed took on functions that had previously been the responsibility of their spouse – for example, negotiating with creditors or picking up children after a night out. In any case, the results show that the 'kin work' of the women who remain in their country of origin is essential in maintaining the father as a symbolic figure and authority.

Parreñas's reasearch (2005, p. 332) on the emigration of women reveals how the economic contributions of Philippine women who emigrated to the United States did not result in a reconfiguration of the sexual division of labour in the family. In the case of Bolivia, the interviews show that when the woman emigrates this leads to an increase in the involvement of men in reproductive tasks, although always as 'support' for other women in the family, generally mothers-in-law, as they are the ones who take responsibility for the majority of these tasks.

CONCLUSIONS

As the results show, whether the family member who emigrates is a man or a woman is a key determinant of the migratory project and the transnational adjustments the family makes. In the case of Bolivia, the influence of gender should be framed in the context of the recent feminized migratory patterns from Bolivia to Spain (and Europe), which have substantially altered the canons of Bolivian society's 'migratory culture', characterized by its masculinization, its circularity and its intra-regional character. The quantitative results presented show that the existence of a transnational family structure conditions both the maintenance of transnational ties (the sending of money, trips to Bolivia) and the intention of the migrant to return. From a gender perspective, we find that women's migratory projects are more often motivated by family welfare than by individual advancement, which translates into a greater potential to save and send money home, the primary use of which in the case of women is for things concerning the family (family consumption or the children's education).

The qualitative results drawn from the interviews with transnational families show the impacts that these migratory processes have when it comes to readjusting perceptions of gender roles and the sexual division of labour. Both in regard to families in which the woman remains in the country of origin, as well as in cases when the woman has been the pioneer in the migratory process, the transnational adjustments based on gender that the migratory process involves confirm the key role of women in maintaining family ties and the cohesion of the family (Baby-Collins et al., 2008).

Without a doubt, the disruption caused by the migratory process affects women more than men, as migration makes it difficult for women to maintain their productive and reproductive tasks from a distance, which can place their maternal role in question. Despite this pressure on gender roles and with the added burden that many women work in the worst-paid jobs – principally in domestic services – an emancipatory discourse regarding gender and their migratory projects emerges, connected to their achievement of autonomy. This emancipatory discourse could explain why we find a greater propensity among women respondents in our survey not to return to Bolivia, independent of their family situation.

All these questions have undoubtedly important effects on the migration and development nexus. The implications of transnational families on the development of sending countries have largely focused on the economic effects of remittances on the household as a single unit. But according to Mazzucato and Schans (2011), most of the studies from the area of migration and development barely explore the different impacts of migration on the various family members and they do not take into account the non-economic effects on migrants, spouses, children and the elderly who are left behind. From a gender perspective, these analyses should require a study of how these family structures alter traditional roles and sexual division of labour. Further more, in order to capture all these development outcomes, it is necessary to take into consideration – and at the same level of importance – both migrant sending and receiving countries, instead of focusing on either one context or the other and offering just a partial view that leaves out some of the family members (ibid., p. 706).

NOTES

1. Study directed by Professor Carlota Solé, Director of the Immigration and Ethnic Minorities Research Group (GEDIME) at the Universidad Autònoma de Barcelona. The second, third and fifth sections of this chapter are a slightly revised version of my 2012 article 'Familia transnacional y redefinición de los roles de género: El caso de la migración boliviana en España', published in *PAPERS, Revista de Sociologia*, **97** (3), 661–84.
2. For a detailed analysis of the causes of the formation of 'immigrant Spain', see Cachón (2009).
3. However, in recent years there has been a gradual process of geographical dispersion towards other autonomous regions in Spain, with an important Bolivian presence in the Valencian Community and Murcia, as well as in the Andalusian provinces of Granada, Malaga and Seville (Hinojosa, 2009b)
4. This migration has also expanded towards other European countries (Italy, the UK and

Switzerland) and even towards destinations such as Japan and Israel (Hinojosa, 2008a). This tendency towards dispersion in Europe is intensifying as a result of the loss of jobs in Spain.
5. The Vive Latinoamérica Fair (L'Hospitalet de Llobregat); the Feria de Abril (Sant Adrià del Besós); matches of the Eurolatinoamericano basketball league (Badalona); the Bolivian Mother's Day Festival (Badalona); the Asamblea de la Federación de Entidades Bolivianas (Barcelona) and the Taller de Mujeres organized by the Asociación de Mujeres Bolivianas de Cataluña (Barcelona).
6. Women's greater propensity to save may be explained by the fact that many of them work as live-in domestic employees, which means that they do not have to dedicate part of their salary to food and lodging.
7. Based on the adaptation of the typologies of Oso (1998) and Parreñas (2001), the research incorporates two other family structures: single-parent families in which the parent emigrates, and nuclear families in which the adult children emigrate. We chose not to include the transnational family where both partners emigrate and the children remain in the care of other members of an extended family (generally the grandparents).

REFERENCES

Alicea, Marixsa (1997), '"A chambered Nautilus". The contradictory nature of Puerto Rican women's role in the social construction of a transnational community', *Gender & Society*, **11** (5), 597–626.
Ariza, Marina (2000), '*Ya no soy la que dejé atrás . . .*': *Mujeres migrantes en República Dominicana*, México: Editorial Plaza y Valdés.
Baby-Collins, Virginia, Geneviève Cortes and Susana Sassone (2008), 'Mujer, movilidad y territorialización. Análisis cruzado de las migraciones internacionales en México y Bolivia', in H. Godard and G. Sandoval (eds), *Migración transnacional de los Andes a Europa y Estados Unidos*, Lima, La Paz: IFEA/PIEB/IRD, pp. 135–66.
Balán, J. (1990), 'La economía doméstica y las diferencias entre los sexos en las migraciones internacionales: un estudio sobre el caso de los bolivianos en la Argentina', *Estudios Migratorios Latinoamericanos*, **15–16**, 269–95.
Basch, Lina, Nina Glick Shiller and Cristina Szanton Blanc (1994), *Nations Unbound: Transnational Projects, Postcolonial Predicaments and Deterritorialized Nation-states*, Amsterdam: Gordon & Breach Science.
Bastia, T. (2007), 'From mining to garment workshops: Bolivian migrants in Buenos Aires', *Journal of Ethnic and Migration Studies*, **33** (4), 655–69.
Benería, L. (2008), 'The crisis of care, international migration and public policy', *Feminist Economics*, **14** (3), 1–21.
Bernhard, Judith, Patricia Landolt and Luin Yoldring (2005), 'Transnational, multi-local motherhood: experiences of separation and reunification among Latin-American families in Canada', CERIS WP 40, available at: http://www.ryerson.ca/%7Ebernhard/documents/WorkingPaperSeries.pdf (accessed 10 November 2012).
Bryceson, Deborah and Ulla Vuorela (eds) (2002), *The Transnational Family: New European Frontiers and Global Networks*, Oxford: Berg.
Cachón, Lorenzo (2009), *La 'España inmigrante': marco discriminatorio, mercado de trabajo y políticas de integración*, Barcelona: Anthropos.
Cortes, Geneviève (2004), *Partir para quedarse: Supervivencia y cambio en las sociedades campesinas andinas de Bolivia*, La Paz (Bolivia): IRD, Plural, IFEA.
Dandler, Jorge and Carmen Medeiros (1991), 'Migración temporaria de Cochabamba, Bolivia a la Argentina: patrones e impacto en las áreas de envoi', in P.R. Pessar (ed.) *Fronteras permeables: Migración laboral y movimientos de refugiados en América*, Buenos Aires: Planeta, pp. 19–54.

De la Torre Ávila, Leonardo (2006), *No llores, prenda, pronto volveré: migración, movilidad social, herida familiar y desarrollo*, La Paz (Bolivia): PIEB.
De la Torre, Leonardo and Yolanda Alfaro (2007), *Caminos y sendas de desarrollo en los municipios migrantes de Arbieto y Toco*, La Paz (Bolivia): PIEB.
Di Leonardo, Micaela (1992), 'The female world of cards and holidays: women, families, and the work of kinship', in B. Thorne and M. Yalom (eds), *Rethinking the Family: Some Feminist Questions*, Boston, MA: Northeastern University Press, pp. 246–61.
Faist, Thomas (2000), *The Volume and Dynamics of International Migration and Transnational Social Spaces*, New York: Oxford University Press.
Fe y Alegría (2010), *Los efectos de la migración de los progenitores en el desempeño escolar de los niños y adolescentes en Bolivia*, Madrid: Entreculturas.
Gadea, Elena, Roberto Benencia and Germán Quaranta (2009), 'Bolivianos en Argentina y en España: De la migración tradicional a las nuevas rutas', *AREAS, Revista Internacional de Ciencias Sociales*, **28**, 30–43.
Gonzálvez, Herminia (2005), 'Familias y hogares transnacionales: una perspectiva de género', *Puntos de Vista*, **11**, 7–26.
Gregorio, Carmen (1998), *La migración femenina y su impacto en las relaciones de género*, Madrid: Editorial Narcea.
Guarnizo, Luis Eduardo (1997), 'Going home: class, gender and household transformation among Dominican return migrants', in P.R. Pessar (ed.), *Caribbean Circuits: New Directions in the Study of Caribbean Migration*, New York: Center for Migration Studies, pp. 13–60.
Herrera, Gioconda (2004), 'Elementos para una comprensión de las familias transnacionales desde la experiencia migratoria del Sur del Ecuador', in F. Hidalgo (ed.), *Migraciones: Un juego con cartas marcadas*, Quito: ILDIS-Abya Yala, pp. 215–32.
Herrera, Gioconda (2005), 'Mujeres ecuatorianas en las cadenas globales del cuidado', in Herrera, Cristina Carrillo and Alicia Torres (eds), *Migración ecuatoriana: Redes, transnacionalismo e identidades*, Quito: FLACSO-Plan Migración Comunicación y Desarrollo, pp. 281–304.
Hinojosa, Alfonso (2008a), 'Transnacionalismo y multipolaridad en los flujos migratorios de Bolivia. Familia, comunidad y nación en dinámicas globales', in H. Godard and G. Sandoval (eds), *Migración transnacional de los Andes a Europa y Estados Unidos*, Lima, La Paz: IFEA/PIEB/IRD, pp. 77–101.
Hinojosa, Alfonso (2008b), 'España en el itinerario de Bolivia. Migración transnacional, género y familia en Cochabamba', in Susana Novick (ed.), *Las migraciones en América Latina, Consejo Latinoamericano de Ciencias Sociales*, Buenos Aires: CLACSO, pp. 93–112.
Hinojosa, Alfonso (2009a), 'Buscando la vida. Familias bolivianas transnacionales en España – Estado de situación', La Paz: CLACSO, Fundación PIEB.
Hinojosa, Alfonso (2009b), 'Migración boliviana a España: antecedentes, caracterización y perspectives', in AA.VV, *Migraciones contemporáneas: Contribución al debate*, La Paz: CIDES-UMSA, pp. 157–80.
Ho, Elsie (2002), 'Multi-local residence, transnational networks, Chinese astronaut families in New Zealand', *Asian and Pacific Migration Journal*, **11** (1), 145–64.
Hochschild, Arlie Russell (2003), *The Second Shift*, New York: Penguin Group.
Hondagneu-Sotelo, Pierrette (2000), 'La incorporación del género a la migración: no sólo para feministas ni sólo para la familia', in Dalia Barrera and Cristina Oehmichen (eds), *Migración y relaciones de género en México*, México DF: Grupo Interdisciplinario sobre Mujer, Trabajo y Pobreza (GIMTRAP)/UNAM, Instituto de Investigaciones, pp. 423–51.
Levitt Peggy and Nina Glick Schiller (2004), 'Conceptualizing simultaneity: a transnational social field perspective', *International Migration Review*, **38** (3), 1002–38.
Mazzucato, Valentina and Djamila Schans (2011), 'Transnational families and the well-being of children: conceptual and methodological challenges', *Journal of Marriage and Family*, **73** (4), 704–12.
Oso, Laura (1998), *La migración hacia España de las mujeres jefas de hogar*, Madrid: IMU.

Oso, Laura (2007), 'Migración, género y hogares transnacionales', paper presented at the 4th Congreso sobre la Inmigración en España, Valencia, 21–23 March.
Pajares, Miguel (2010), *Inmigración y mercado de trabajo: Informe 2010*, Madrid: OPI/Ministerio de Trabajo e Inmigración.
Parella, Sònia (2007), 'Los vínculos afectivos y de cuidado en las familias transnacionales migrantes ecuatorianos y peruanos en España', *Migraciones Internacionales*, **4** (2), 39–76.
Parella, Sònia and Leonardo Cavalcanti (2008), 'Aplicación de los campos sociales transnacionales en los estudios sobre migraciones', in C. Solé, S. Parella and L. Cavalcanti (eds), *Nuevos retos del transnacionalismo en el estudio de las migraciones*, Madrid: OPI, pp. 219–47.
Parreñas, Rhacel Salazar (2000), 'Migrant Filipina domestic workers and the international division of reproductive labor', *Gender & Society*, **14** (4), 507–24.
Parreñas, Rhacel Salazar (2001), *Servants of Globalization: Women, Migration and Domestic Work*, Palo Alto, CA: Stanford University Press.
Parreñas, Rhacel Salazar (2003), 'The care crisis in the Philippines: children and transnational families in the New Global Economy', in B. Ehrenreich and A. Russell Hochschild (eds), *Global Woman: Nannies, Maids, and Sex Workers in the New Economy*, London: Granta Books, pp. 39–54.
Parreñas, Rhacel Salazar (2005), *Children of Global Migration: Transnational Families and Gendered Woes*, Palo Alto, CA: Stanford University Press.
Pedone, Claudia (2004), 'Negociaciones en torno al asentamiento definitivo de las familias migrantes ecuatorianas: construcción de espacios sociales transnacionales', paper presented at the 4th Congreso sobre la Inmigración en España, Gerona, 10–13 November.
Pedone, Claudia (2008), '"Varones aventureros" vs. "Madres que abandonan", reconstrucción de las relaciones familiares a partir de las migración ecuatoriana', *REMHU Revista Interdisciplinar da Movilidades Humano*, **30**, 45–64.
Poggio, Sara and Ofelia Woo (2000), *Migración Femenina hacia EUA: Cambio en las relaciones familiares y de género como resultado de la migración*, México: ENDAMEX.
Portes, Alejandro, Luis Eduardo Guarnizo and Patricia Landolt (2003), *La globalización desde abajo: transnacionalismo inmigrante y desarrollo*, México D.F.: FLACSO.
Pribilsky, Jason (2004), '"Aprendamos a convivir": conjugal relations, co-parenting and family life among Ecuadorian transnational migrants in New York City and the Ecuadorian Andes', *Global Networks*, **4** (3), 313–34.
Rosas, Carolina (2010), *Implicaciones mutuas entre el género y la migración*, Buenos Aires: EUDEBA, Universidad de Buenos Aires.
Sassen, Saskia (2003), *Contrageografías de la globalización. Género y ciudadanía en los circuitos transfronterizos*, Madrid: Traficantes de Sueños, available at: http,//www.edicionessimbioticas.info/IMG/pdf/contrageografias.pdf (accessed 10 November 2012).
Sørensen, Nina (2007), 'La Vida de la Familia Transnacional a través del Atlántico, La Experiencia de la Población Colombiana y Dominicana Migrante en Europa', *Puntos de Vista*, **9**, 7–28.
Suárez, Liliana and Paloma Crespo (2007), 'Familias en movimiento: El caso de las mujeres rumanas en España', *Migraciones*, **21**, 235–57.
Tapia, Marcela (2010), 'Yo venía con un sueño . . . Relaciones de género entre inmigrantes de origen boliviano en Madrid', doctoral thesis, UCM/IUOG, Madrid.
Vidal, Laura, Esperanza Tuñón, Martha Rojas and Rameis Ayús (2002), 'De Paraíso a Carolina del Norte. Redes de apoyo y percepciones de la migración a Estados Unidos de mujeres tabasqueñas despulpadoras de jaiba', *Migraciones Internacionales*, **1** (2), 29–61.
Wagner, Heike (2008), 'Maternidad transnacional: discursos, estereotipos y prácticas', in G. Herrera and Jacques Ramírez (eds), *América Latina Migrante: Estado, familia, identidades*, Quito: Facultad Latinoamericana de Ciencias Sociales (FLACSO), pp. 325–42.
Whitesell, Lily (2008), 'Y aquellos que se fueron: retratos del éxodo boliviano', in J. Schultz and M. Crane Draper (eds), *Desafiando la globalización. Historias de la experiencia boliviana*, La Paz: El Centro para la Democracia, Plural Editores, pp. 279–317.

Woo, Ofelia (2001), *Las mujeres también nos vamos al norte*, Guadalajara (México): Universidad de Guadalajara.
Zarembka, Joy M. (2003), 'America's dirty work: migrant maids and modern-day slavery', in B. Ehrenreich and A.R. Hochschild (eds), *Global Woman: Nannies, Maids, and Sex Workers in the New Economy*, London: Granta Books, pp. 142–53.
Zimmerman, Mary K., Jacquelyn S. Litt and Christine E. Bose (2006), *Global Dimensions of Gender and Carework*, Palo Alto, CA: Stanford University Press.
Zontini, Elizabetta (2010), *Transnational Families, Migration and Gender: Moroccan and Filipino Women in Bologna and Barcelona*, Oxford: Berghahn Books.

PART V

GLOBAL PRODUCTION

15 The internationalization of domestic work and female immigration in Spain during a decade of economic expansion, 1999–2008*

Elena Vidal-Coso and Pau Miret-Gamundi

INTRODUCTION

During the decade covered by our study, Spain experienced an important growth in the volume of its female immigrant workers. According to the Spanish Labour Force Survey (SLFS), from 1999 to 2008, the number of employed immigrant women increased from 226,639 to 1,530,926. In relative terms, that is an increase from 4.4 to 18 per cent of all employed women in Spain. We believe that this recent influx of females is the product of the extraordinary upward labour and social mobility of young Spanish women. This mobility has generated a new labour demand to fill the lower-level positions left vacant by the Spanish population. These new vacancies are predominantly in domestic and other personal services and are due to the increase of Spanish female participation in the labour market. Effectively, the massive arrival of immigrant women is largely in response to the externalization of domestic tasks. A large number of foreign women have entered the labour market through domestic services and, as a consequence, their social image is mainly derived from their position in this labour market. Thus, although the analysis considers the causes and implications of female immigration within the receiving society, Spain, we framed our analysis on the existing links between migration, gender and development. In fact, it is not possible to understand the arrival and labour integration of immigrant women in Spain without taking into account the emerging trends played out by women in contemporary mobility flows in the age of globalization, particularly the migratory movements of women caused by the existence of global production and reproduction chains. The employment dynamics we analyse in this chapter therefore consists of an obvious example of the essential role that immigrant women play in the labour market and in the development process of the receiving society, given the familistic welfare state and the imperfect transition towards gender equity in Spain. Thus, following

Moreno-Fontes (2008), we aim to demonstrate that immigrant women provide human resources in jobs that Spanish women do not want but that are essential for the receiving economy and also play key roles in the care economy, freeing Spanish women to take up higher-status jobs. Our analysis also demonstrates, however, that the contribution of immigrant women to the Spanish economy is at the expense of their own skills as they end up in occupations below their level of qualification. In terms of development, this process represents not only a loss to the workers themselves, but also a waste of valuable human resources to both origin and destination countries (ibid.). Furthermore, we can only understand the expansion of female domestic work in Spain as the consequence of the transfer of reproductive work to immigrant women (Sørensen, 2005). The addition of the demand for domestic immigrant helpers simply entails the continuing gender inequality of the receiving society.

Previous studies in the late 1990s and early twenty-first century have shown that the arrival of immigrant women in Spain is explained by a very specific labour demand in domestic services and other highly female and unskilled occupations (Solé, 1994, 2001b, 2003; Oso, 1998, 2003; Catarina and Oso, 2000; Parella, 2000, 2002, 2003, 2007; Colectivo IOE, 2001, 2003; Ribas-Mateos, 2004). These investigations coincide with this process being set against a weak welfare state, with women's enhanced working and economic autonomy and with the existence of other structural and segmentation dynamics in the labour market. For these authors, the outcome is that the occupational characteristics of immigrant women in Spain would be according to their country of origin and to the specificities of the Spanish labour market, whereas their educational level or previous work experience are less decisive factors.

Using the SLFS for the years from 1999 to 2008, a period of extraordinary economic growth, and following a quantitative and demographic perspective, this chapter revisits the main contributions of previous researchers with regard to the dynamics of labour supply and integration in the employment structure of female immigrants from developing countries. We strongly believe that these years of exceptional economic boom and of increasing labour demand are also a period of intensification in the segmentation of female employment by birthplace, and of an accentuation of the process of socio-demographic substitution in domestic occupations. The main contribution of this chapter, therefore, is to update the analysis for the period from 1999 to 2008, just as the Spanish economic miracle had come to an end.

Consequently, for the years under consideration we reintroduce the hypotheses concerning the process of labour complementarity by birthplace and of socio-demographic substitution in domestic occupations:

Hypothesis 1 The existence of a *labour complementarity* by birthplace explains why young Spanish women are mainly in skilled occupations, whereas immigrant women, regardless of their human capital, are over-represented in those more gendered and unskilled labour positions.

Hypothesis 2 A process of *socio-demographic substitution* exists in domestic occupations: from mature Spanish women with low educational attainment, to younger immigrant women with higher educational levels.

Finally, Hypotheses 1 and 2 lead to:

Hypothesis 3 The initial demand for domestic helpers is not sufficient to explain the acceleration of female immigrant flows during recent years. Therefore, it is the arrival itself of a cheap and ready immigrant labour force that has caused the *addition effect*, generalizing the hiring of domestic workers within the middle classes, multiplying this labour demand. This effect was especially obvious during the economic miracle experienced by the Spanish economy during the decade under consideration.

The target population is the female population living in Spain, both native and immigrant. We shall emphasize the characteristics of non EU25[1] women. Birthplace will be a central variable in the analysis, differentiating native women and those who are foreign born, who will be grouped by area of origin. Results will refer to the Spanish territory as a whole.

At this point, we need to clarify that although this investigation will be limited to the study of two different groups of women, native and immigrant, and does not use sex as an independent variable, it is based on the importance of gender relations and on the existence of a labour market segmented by sex. We therefore adopt the gender perspective by considering female labour market participation and the role of domestic work in female international immigration and within the logic of the internationalization of domestic tasks. Only with the inclusion of this gender viewpoint is it possible to understand those processes that lie hidden in the labour and socio-demographic complementarity of the female labour force by national origin.

THEORETICAL PERSPECTIVES AND RESEARCH HYPOTHESES

Prior to focusing on the occupational characteristics of female immigrant women, we begin by contextualizing the causes of their arrival in

Spain. The existence of a labour complementarity between national-born and immigrant labour force within a segmented labour market is the theoretical approach that guides this analysis (Piore, 1979a, 1979b). This research assumes that this approach applies to the way the Spanish labour market functions, where a divide exists between the primary – or capital-intensive – segment, and the secondary – or labour-intensive – segment. In this chapter we interpret the labour demand for immigrant women as a consequence of the insufficient supply of native women for unskilled jobs – an argument that would go hand in hand with the complex and general process of labour complementarity (Colectivo IOÉ, 1998; Martinez Veiga, 1999; Juliano, 2000; Solé, 2001a; Abad, 2002; Cachón, 2002, 2003, 2004, 2006, 2009; Arango, 2004; Domingo and Houle, 2005; Pajares, 2007). As Piore (1979b) pointed out, international migration is caused by a permanent demand for an immigrant labour force that is inherent in the economic structure of developed countries, as well as by the demographic factors that explain the scarcity of labour supply in the secondary segment.

This labour demand explains why the recent female immigration in Spain has different causes and consequences from the arrival of immigrant women in Western Europe after the Second World War. During that period, female immigration was largely the result of the family reunification process. In Spain, however, as in other countries of Southern Europe, female international migration must be framed in the globalization of the market economy as a response to a specific female labour demand caused by the *internationalization of domestic work* (Morokvasic, 1984; Sassen, 1984, 1988, 1991; Nakano Glenn, 1992; Lim, 1996, 1997; Reyneri, 1996, 2004; Kofman, 1999; King and Zontini, 2000; Parreñas, 2001; Izquierdo, 2003; Solé, 2003; Ribas-Mateos, 2004; Parella, 2007). This is characterized by the demand for female immigrant labour from rich countries as a way of easing deficits in the reproduction sphere caused by the generalized labour participation of women in those countries. As Parreñas (2000) pointed out, the international transfer of care taking refers to a social, political and economic relationship between women in the global labour market. For this author, this division of labour is a structural relationship based on the class, race, gender and citizenship of women.

The situation in Spain is especially relevant because of the extraordinary increase in the number of Spanish women participating in the labour market, and the massive female immigration that this social process has promoted over the past few years. The existence of this labour demand explains, in part, the high labour participation rates of immigrant women in destination labour markets. The origins of this process are related to a weak welfare state in Spain, as well as to the spectacular transformation of women's role in Spain during the last decades of the twentieth century. Therefore, far from the common image of immigrant women as inactive and dependent subjects, in this investigation immigrant women are understood to be a diverse population with regard to their socio-demographic characteristics and migratory project. The common feature such migratory projects share, at least during the first stage post-arrival, is that their labour insertion depends on their country of origin and the specificities of the Spanish labour market. Their individual characteristics, such as educational level or previous labour experience, are less influential (Vidal-Coso, 2009). Following Martín Díaz (2008) Spain is another example of 'new colonialism' based on the transnationalization of labour and the reproductive task.

In line with other researchers, such as Boyd (1984), Solé (2001b, 2003), Oso (1998, 2003) and Parella (2000, 2002), we adopt the concept of 'ethnic and gender discrimination' of immigrant women in the labour market. This concept points to the fact that female labour positions of immigrants are limited to those in the secondary segment and that foreign-born women compose a subsegment within the female labour force. In other words, gender discrimination is added to migrant discrimination. From this perspective, while immigrant men occupy those gaps in the male labour market, immigrant women hold those jobs that native women no longer want to do.

Within a highly gendered Spanish labour market, women are restricted to those labour positions considered typically female oriented, despite their national origin. However, beyond this gender segmentation, we hypothesize the existence of a *labour complementarity* by birthplace (Parella, 2000, 2003, 2007; Solé, 2003, Colectivo IOÉ, 2001). Indeed, Spanish women aim for those more-skilled labour positions in social services, health services or in education and other good positions in sales or management. For all these jobs, a secondary education or university degree is required. By contrast, labour insertion of immigrant women is limited to those unskilled jobs in cleaning services, in hotels and restaurants and, especially, in domestic services. There is therefore a key element: worker demand for unskilled labour positions has increased to cover those reproductive tasks that, as a result of their new careers, skilled young Spanish women no longer want to do.

A further key element in understanding the arrival of female immigrant flows is the imperfect transition towards gender equity in Spain (Parella, 2002). Although young women have equalled, or even exceeded, men in their educational attainment, the labour participation of women is similar to that of men and their presence in the labour market is no longer interrupted by marriage or childbearing. However, the formal equity between men and women is not accompanied by an actual equity within the domestic sphere: reproductive responsibilities are still, almost exclusively, undertaken by women. Given the family-oriented nature of the Spanish welfare state, with insufficient services to reconcile work and family when both members of the couple are working, families have opted to externalize domestic tasks. Moreover, in the context of an ageing Spanish population, the demand for carers for the elderly dependent population has also increased. However, although there is a general increase in the demand, there is a scarcity of native women on the supply side, as Oso (1998, 2003) and Catarina and Oso (2000) pointed out. Additionally, native domestic workers are not willing to provide those services under the same conditions as immigrant women (Colectivo IOÉ, 2001), primarily as a result of their demand for higher salaries and better labour conditions, especially during the economic boom of our study period. For that reason, a widespread solution was to hire immigrant women for these domestic services, as they were willing to do this work and obtain legal residency in Spain as part of a wider migration strategy towards better social and labour positions. The flexibility of labour contracts in domestic services, together with the insufficient economic and family support that immigrant women have in Spain, are the most important reasons for their temporary acceptance. This explains the *socio-demographic substitution* of mature and less-skilled natives for younger and more-skilled immigrant workers in those occupations – our second hypothesis. Furthermore, to understand the acceleration of female immigrant flows it is also necessary to identify the *addition effect*. The initial demand for domestic helpers is not sufficient to explain the acceleration of these flows during recent years. In fact, the very arrival of immigrant women increases this labour demand. Therefore, our third hypothesis is that the existence of a cheap and ready immigrant labour force has caused the addition effect, generalizing the hiring of domestic workers within the middle and lower-middle classes, multiplying this labour demand, particularly during the recent period of economic growth, low unemployment rates and increasing family wealth.

DATA AND METHODS

In this investigation we used data from the SLFS for the 1999–2008 (second wave) period. In each wave, the survey interviews approximately 200,000 people from 65,000 households and is representative of Spain's working-age population. The survey contains a great number of variables concerning the population's socio-demographic and labour characteristics at individual level, which makes its analysis the best option for the purpose of this chapter.

To overcome some historical problems of the under-representation of foreign populations (Cachón, 2004) and the unequal representation of foreigners by origin (Africans and EU foreigners were more under-represented than people from other origins), and because of the rapid and recent growth of foreigners living in Spain, the SLFS was modified in 2005 and adapted to the new demographic and labour context. One of the most significant changes was the substitution of the sampling frame based on the 1991 Census with a new frame based on the 2001 Census and its successive population revisions (García, 2005). The most important consequence of this change is that new weight factors applied to the sample are now more coincident with a recent volume of population, a recent age and sex structure in every region and recent volume of population by nationality. Obviously, this update to the sample frame has special importance in calculating percentages of foreigners, since their numbers in Spain grew significantly between 1991 and 2001 (INE, 2005). In fact, estimates from the SLFS in 2007 are very similar to the official volume of immigrant population obtained from the Municipal Registers. For example, in 1999 the SLFS estimated that there were 277,970 immigrant women aged 16–64 (2 per cent of total women aged 16–64 estimated by the SLFS) – a value very close to the 296,908 registered immigrant women in that year (1.7 per cent of total women registered). In 2007, the SLFS estimated 2,067,384 (10.8 per cent) immigrant women, ahead of the actual 1,705,746 (11 per cent) registered.

Following demographic and sociological perspectives and through quantitative analysis, this chapter aims to contribute to a better knowledge of the dynamics of labour supply and integration in the employment structure of female immigrants and of the complex process of complementarity between women in Spain by national origin. The analysis focuses on the period of economic expansion (1999–2008), which ends with the eruption of the current economic crisis and its effects on employment opportunities. The target population is the female population living in Spain, both native and immigrant, emphasizing the characteristics of those non-EU25 women.

Birthplace will be the central explanatory variable in the analysis: foreign-born women will be grouped by area of origin. As Cortina et al. (2008) pointed out, country of birth is used as opposed to citizenship because place of birth is, by definition, invariable whereas citizenship can be modified. The choice of birthplace instead of nationality as a key variable should therefore obtain a greater sample and introduce into the study those immigrant women who have obtained Spanish citizenship. The resulting groups are as follows: EU25, Rest of Europe, Latin America, Africa, Asia and North America and Oceania. Since very few women from Asia, North America and Oceania were interviewed, differences for these two groups were not always statistically significant.

RESULTS

Although the presence of female foreign-born workers in Spain is not a new phenomenon, the real acceleration of female immigration occurred in the last years of the twentieth and the beginning of the twenty-first centuries. The most obvious consequence of this rapid and recent increase of immigrant flows has been the extraordinary growth and diversification by birthplace of the female labour force. Indeed, in Table 15.1 we can observe that during the decade from 1999 to 2008, female employment has dramatically increased. Effectively, in 2008 there were 3,323,196 more female workers than in 1999 (64 per cent in relative terms). Although the contribution of native women to this increment is considerable – 2,018,883 more employed women – the immigrant contribution is even more significant as approximately one-third of this increment, 1,304,286, must be attributed to the entry of immigrant women into the labour market. The share of immigrant women within total female employment has grown from 4.4 to 18 per cent. This first result, then, highlights the non-existent negative effects of immigration on native employment, on the basis that the latter would compete directly with immigrant women for a fixed number of jobs. Contrary to this thesis, female employment, both native and immigrant, has increased extraordinarily during the period.

By birthplace, we can observe that the Latin American group is the most numerous and growing collective of immigrant women, representing 10 per cent of total female employment in 2008. This increment was even more obvious in absolute terms: in 2008 there were 785,839 more women born in Latin America employed than in 1999. None the less, we must emphasize that women from the rest of Europe are those who have most recently and rapidly entered into Spanish female employment. Indeed, from being almost non-existent in 1999 (only 10,452 women born in non-communitarian Europe or 0.2 per cent of total female employment), their presence in 2008 is the second most important. The opposite is true of African women, as in 2008 they only represent 1.3 per cent of female employment, in line with the lower activity rates of that group (Vidal-Coso, 2009).

Continuing our analysis, and in order to assess the complementarity and segmentation of the labour market, we recognize that the structure of the labour market is unequal, ordered by differentiated labour positions. These positions are ordered within the occupational scale by the human capital, skills and experience required, as well as by the social status and economic rewards they provide. Figure 15.1 gives evidence of the complementarity by native–migrant origin within the female occupational structure. In 2008, approximately 60 per cent of native

Table 15.1 Absolute and relative growth of female employment by area of birthplace, Spain (1999–2008)

Employed	Spanish born	Immigrant	African	Latin American	EU25	Rest of Europe	Asian	North American and Oceania	Total
Total									
1999	4,956,997	226,639	24,181	85,777	86,857	10,452	12,755	6,619	5,183,636
2008	6,975,880	1,530,926	109,293	871,616	183,748	311,887	44,293	10,089	8,506,806
Total increment									
1999–2008	2,018,883	1,304,286	85,112	785,839	96,891	301,436	31,538	3,470	3,323,169
Relative increment									
1999–2008 (%)	40.7	575.5	352.0	916.1	111.6	2884.1	247.3	52.4	64.1
% Immigration (Immigrant/total women)									
1999 (%)	–	4.4	0.5	1.7	1.7	0.2	0.2	0.1	–
2008 (%)	–	18.0	1.3	10.2	2.2	3.7	0.5	0.1	–

Source: Spanish Labour Force Survey (1999–2008).

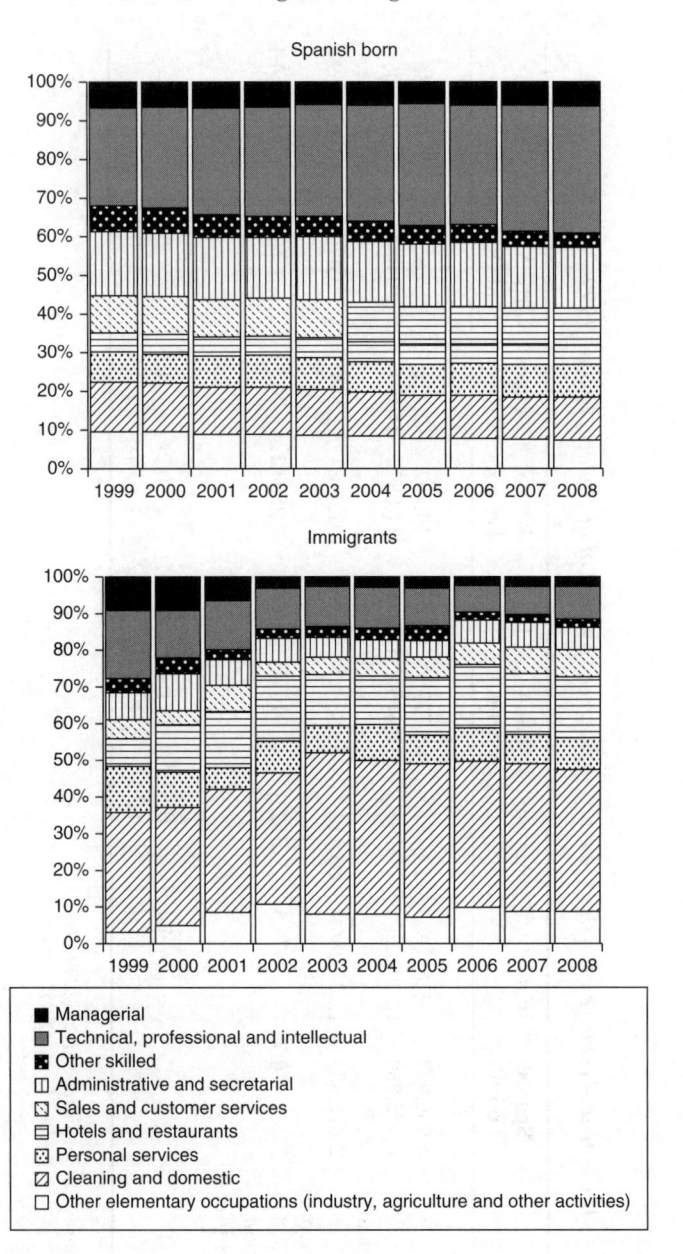

Source: Spanish Labour Force Survey (1999–2008).

Figure 15.1 Female occupational structure by birthplace, Spain (1999–2008), employed women aged 16–64

women were employed in the most skilled occupations, those with higher requirements of human capital: managerial, technical, professional and intellectual occupations; other skilled occupations (in agriculture, arts and crafts, construction and industry), and administrative and secretarial occupations. When we add sales and customer service occupations, which are situated in the middle of the scale, the figure rises to 70 per cent. By contrast, only 30 per cent of Spanish-born women held jobs in the secondary segment: in hotels and restaurants, personal services, cleaning, domestic and other elementary occupations, whereas 65 per cent of immigrant women employed in 2008 were concentrated in those secondary labour positions.

Moreover, by 2008 the employment structure of native women was 10 per cent more qualified than in 1999, just 10 years before. Effectively, in 1999, 25 per cent of Spanish-born women were employed in technical, professional or intellectual positions, rising to 35 per cent in 2008. The opposite evolution is true of immigrant employment. During the same period, there was a relative increment of those less prestigious labour positions. That is, if in 1999 approximately a quarter of immigrant women were employed as cleaning and domestic helpers, by 2008, more than a third of them were. The relative growth of immigrant employment in hotels and restaurants has also been significant – from 7 to 15 per cent. Meanwhile the relative percentage of immigrant women working as managers or in professional, technical and intellectual roles decreased from 25 to 12 per cent. Figure 15.2 corroborates the complementary role of employed women from outside the European Union. Thus, whereas the distribution of EU25 women within the occupational structure is similar to that of Spanish-born women, the rest of the non-communitarian groups follow the immigrant occupational distribution described above: about 70 per cent are concentrated in the categories at the bottom of the occupational scale.

From this analysis we conclude that there is a complementarity and segmentation between native and immigrant female employment, which has been accentuated during the years of economic expansion. However, these aggregate percentages do not indicate that immigrant women, at an individual level, have been experiencing a worsening in their labour position during that period. Rather, they reflect how the newly arrived flows of immigrant women have been absorbed into those less-prestigious and less-skilled occupations in the labour market (ibid.).

Figure 15.3 reinforces the occupational differences by birthplace and describes the accentuation of a native–immigrant duality within female employment. It shows how many immigrant women are in every occupational category for every 100 native women. Therefore, columns to the

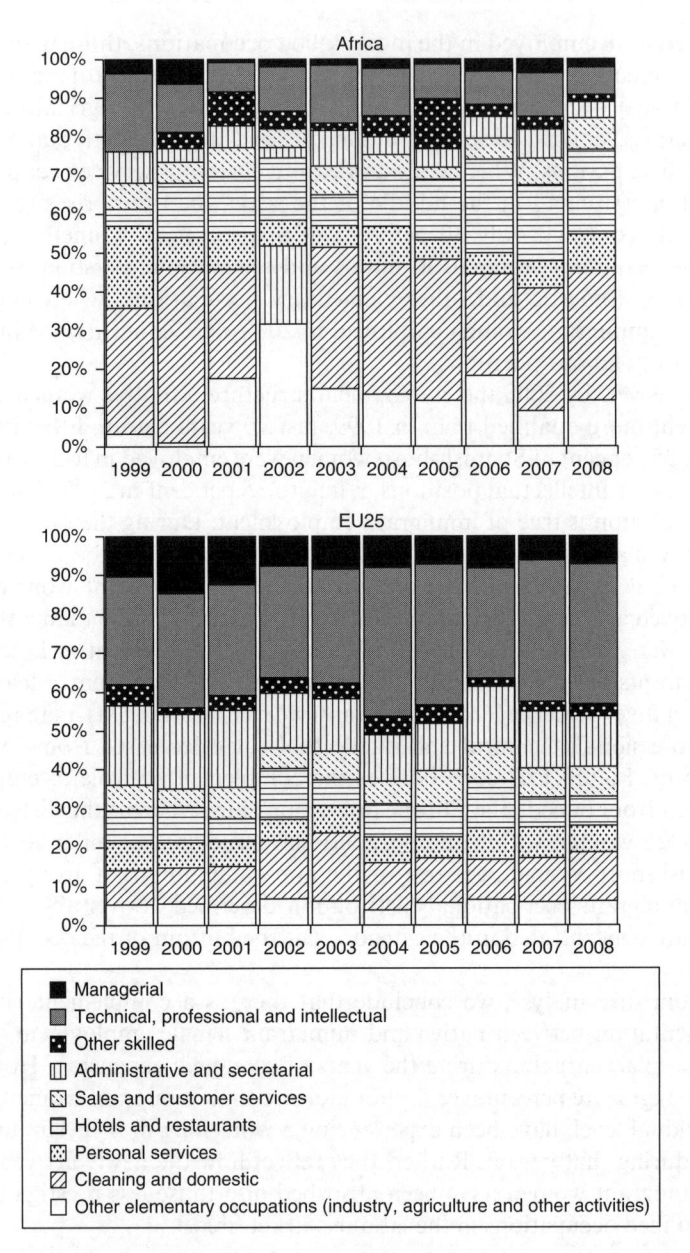

348 *International handbook on gender, migration and transnationalism*

Source: Spanish Labour Force Survey (1999–2008).

Figure 15.2 Female occupational structure by area of birthplace, Spain (1999–2008), employed immigrant women aged 16–64

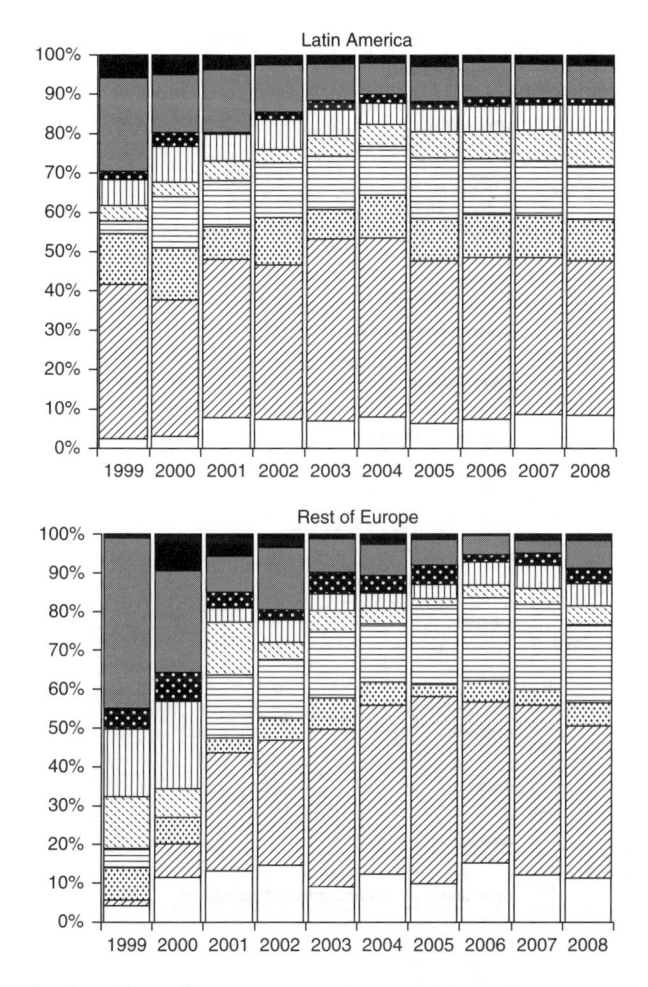

Internationalization of domestic work and female immigration in Spain 349

Figure 15.2 (continued)

right of the black line represent high concentrations of immigrant women in the occupational category and those to the left of the line indicate a presence of foreign-born women below what was expected according to the relative weight of these groups within female employment. At first sight we can see that during these 10 years, there has been an intense concentration and over-representation of the immigrant female labour force in just two occupational niches: *cleaning and domestic occupations* and *hotel and restaurant occupations*. In fact, in 1999 there were approximately 180 immigrants for every 100 natives in domestic work. However, it is interesting to note for that same year that some groups were already

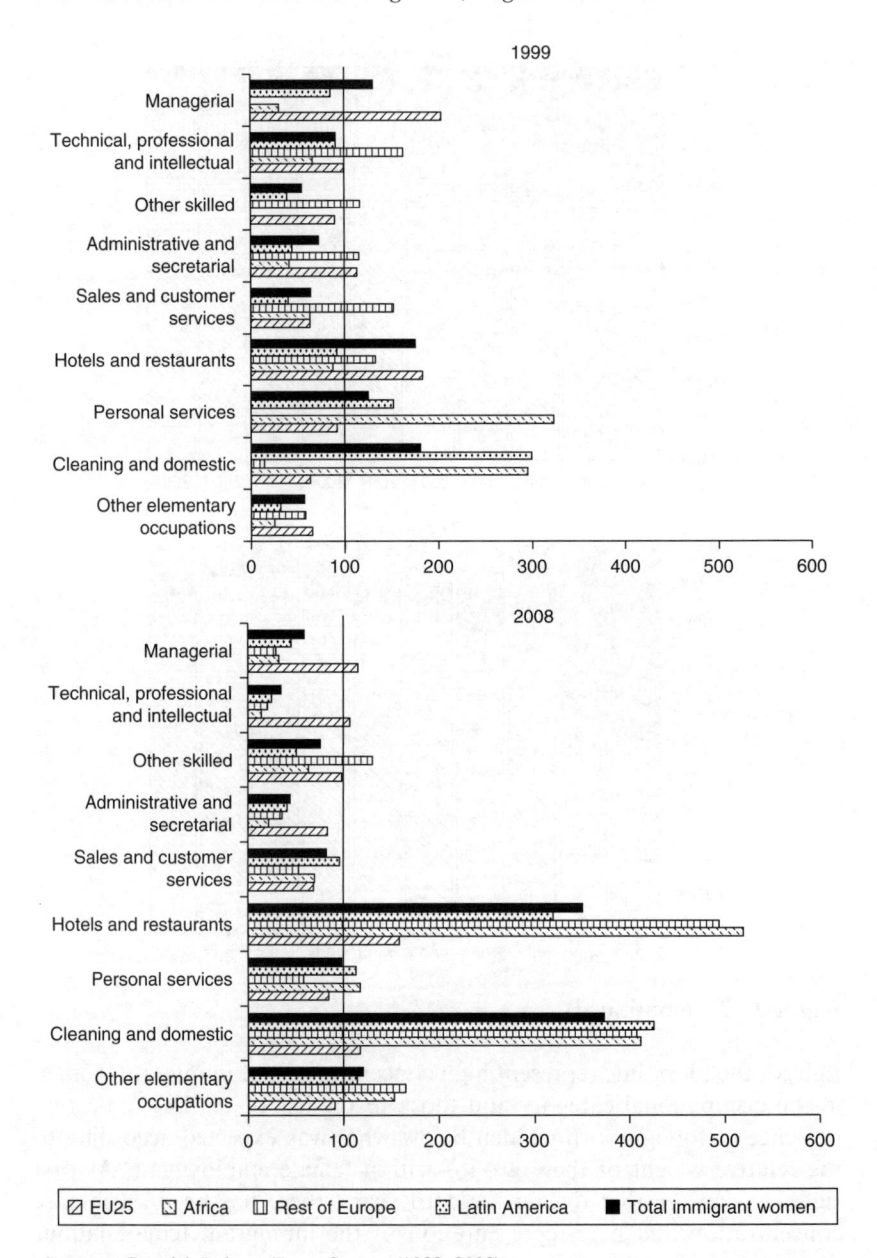

350   *International handbook on gender, migration and transnationalism*

Source: Spanish Labour Force Survey (1999–2008).

Figure 15.3   Immigrant–native rates in occupational categories, natives = 100 (1999 and 2008), employed women aged 16–64

concentrated in those occupations: 299 Latin Americans and 295 Africans for every 100 natives. In 2008 the ratio increased abruptly: 373 immigrant women for every 100 natives (426 Latin American, 412 African and 408 non-communitarian European women). And in contrast, the immigrant–native ratios in those more-skilled and -prestigious labour positions have clearly dropped.

Finally, the over-representation of immigrant women has also risen significantly during 1999–2008 in the *hotel and restaurant occupations*, from 175 to 350 for every 100 native workers. By area of origin the ratios were: 520 African women, 494 women from the Rest of Europe, and 319 Latin American women, for every 100 Spanish-born women.

After describing the growing segmentation of female employment by birthplace, we try to identify the process of *socio-demographic substitution* by analysing the age and educational structure of Spanish-born and immigrant women in domestic occupations during 2008 (Figure 15.4). The absolute number of immigrant women working as domestic helpers in 2008, 574,631, is close to the number of native women in the same labour positions, 747,054, and is the first evidence that some kind of substitution has occurred. Differences in the age and educational structure may also be observed. Indeed, most of the native domestic workers were aged 40–54, with a mean age of 46, and they were generally low-skilled workers, as the percentage of women with secondary or tertiary education was practically residual – respectively, 14 and 0.9 per cent of the total. In sum, the socio-demographic structure of Spanish-born women working as domestic helpers was that of a middle-aged and poorly skilled population. By contrast, immigrant domestic helpers were younger, with a mean age of 37, and generally more skilled. Effectively, taking into account the lack of requirements in human capital, it is significant that the immigrant group in domestic work had a higher percentage of women with secondary education (42 per cent) and a university degree (10 per cent).

In Figure 15.4, appreciable heterogeneity could also be observed between the different groups of immigrants regarding these socio-demographic features. Indeed, bearing in mind that approximately half of immigrant domestic helpers, 342,587, were Latin American women, it is easy to understand why this group presented an age and educational structure very similar to that of the total immigrant group. On the other hand, the African group, with 36,644 domestic workers, presented the youngest age structure, with a mean age of 36. Therefore, we can conclude that the age structure of African domestic workers represents the opposite end of the scale to that of native domestic workers. However, the educational structure of African female immigrants is the most similar to the native-born women's, with a small proportion of women with

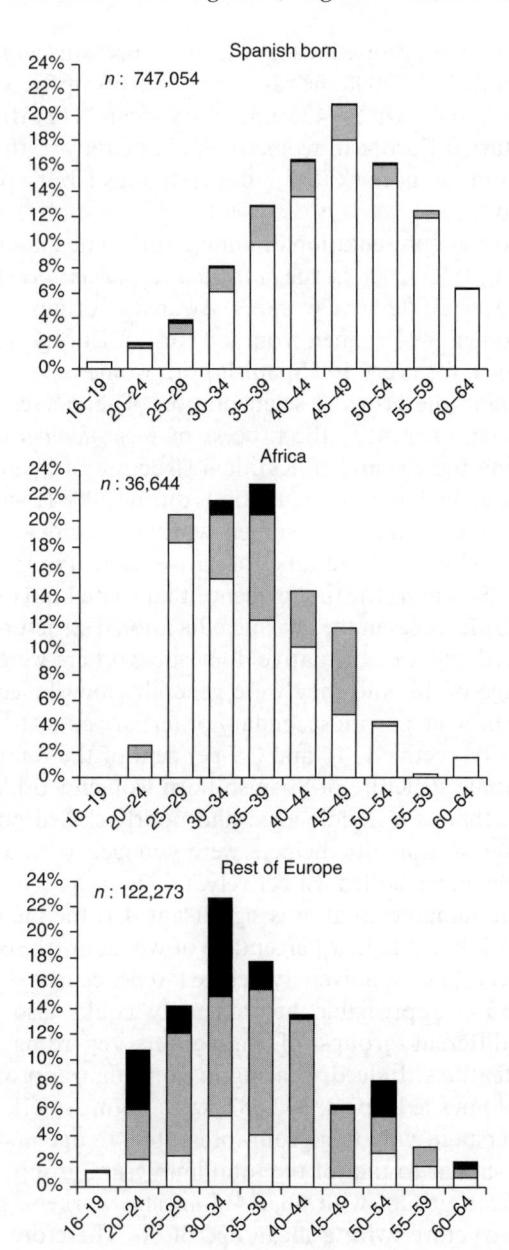

Source: Spanish Labour Force Survey (1999–2008).

Figure 15.4 Age and educational structure of cleaning and domestic employed women by birthplace (2008)

Internationalization of domestic work and female immigration in Spain 353

[Immigrants chart: n: 534,631, age groups 16–19 through 60–64, stacked bars showing University degree, Secondary level, Compulsory level]

[Latin America chart: n: 342,587, age groups 16–19 through 60–64, stacked bars showing University degree, Secondary level, Compulsory level]

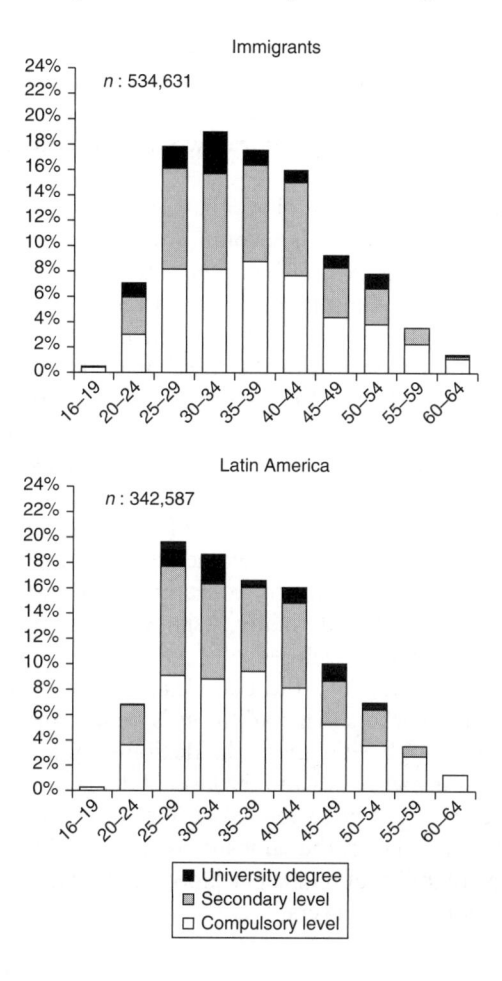

Figure 15.4 (continued)

secondary education (27.6 per cent) or a university degree (3.4 per cent). Our interpretation is that, whereas among Spanish-born women there is a selection process and the higher the educational attainment, the lower the probability of working as a domestic assistant, in the case of African women living in Spain, this structure is representative of the educational levels of the group.

Female domestic workers from the Rest of Europe were the furthest removed from the socio-demographic structure of the native group, which in part may be explained by their most recent entry into the Spanish labour market. Indeed, they were on average younger, generally below 34, with a modal age of 25–29 years. Moreover, they had higher educational attainment – 54 per cent with secondary education and 20 per cent with a university degree – indicating the overqualification of women from those non-communitarian European countries working as cleaning and domestic helpers.

Finally, we tested the last of our hypotheses regarding the *addition effect*. In Table 15.2 we can observe the evolution of domestic female employment. We interpreted this extraordinary growth as the real reason behind the acceleration of female immigrant flows into Spain in recent years, and we believe that the initial demand for domestic helpers is not sufficient to explain the evolution observed in the table. In 2008 there were 591,031 more domestic helpers than in 1999 which, in relative terms, represents an increment, in just one decade, of 64 per cent. Moreover, the protagonists of the rise in cleaning and domestic employment between 2000 and 2008 were immigrant women, especially Latin American women. In fact, Spanish-born women account for only 19 per cent of the increment. By birthplace the percentages are: Latin American women 52 per cent; women from the Rest of Europe 21 per cent (mostly concentrated in more recent years); African women 5 per cent; and, finally, Asian women 1 per cent.

Therefore, from this growing evolution of cleaning and domestic employment, we may identify the complex process of addition in the demand for female workers. This addition is believed to be a two-sided process. From the supply side, given the flexibility of labour contracts in domestic and cleaning activities and the level of demand, this kind of work has become the easiest way to regularize the legal status of immigrant women. On the demand side, the same intensification of female immigrant flows and the availability of a cheaper labour force has acted to increase the demand for domestic workers.

CONCLUSIONS AND DISCUSSION

The work highlighted in this chapter confirms for the 1999–2008 period the existence of the labour and socio-demographic complementarity between immigrant and native women in Spain, a society with a segmented and gendered labour force. This complementary role of immigrant women in Spanish society is part of the internationalization of domestic work, characterized by the female immigrant labour demand caused by the general labour participation of native women.

The polarization or segmentation of the female structure has been especially evident during the last 10 years. Native occupational distribution has been compared with that of immigrant women and reveals an

Table 15.2 Absolute and relative growth of cleaning and domestic female employment in Spain (1999–2008)

Cleaning and domestic female employment	Occupational growth	Contribution to the occupational growth by area of origin						Total
		Spain	EU25	Asia	Africa	Rest of Europe	Latin America	
1999–2000 (%)	8.0	73.4	1.6	1.2	10.5	2.3	11.1	100
Freq.	55,101	40,431	896	645	5,762	1,265	6,102	
2000–2001 (%)	3.6	−55.0	6.7	−4.3	−13.0	39.9	125.8	100
Freq.	26,593	−14,614	1,775	−1,146	−3,467	10,605	33,441	
2001–2002 (%)	9.2	23.0	14.6	0.5	−3.4	5.4	59.8	100
Freq.	70,675	16,271	10,335	344	−2,373	3,810	42,288	
2002–2003 (%)	10.7	11.6	4.6	−1.3	12.2	24.8	48.1	100
Freq.	90,522	10,515	4,144	−1,207	11,076	22,466	43,528	
2003–2004 (%)	5.0	−15.9	−14.4	2.6	−0.8	31.9	96.6	100
Freq.	47,055	−7,499	−6,762	1,213	−389	15,019	45,474	
2004–2005 (%)	12.0	16.5	2.5	5.2	7.3	33.9	34.6	100
Freq.	117,991	19,412	2,987	6,182	8,665	39,958	40,787	
2005–2006 (%)	8.0	35.5	−2.7	0.7	−2.3	9.7	59.2	100
Freq.	87,455	31,024	−2,368	587	−2,019	8,462	51,768	
2006–2007 (%)	5.5	10.1	6.2	1.6	9.8	34.9	37.5	100
Freq.	65,356	6,592	4,025	1,072	6,397	22,782	24,488	
2007–2008 (%)	2.4	27.9	1.7	−9.1	16.9	−7.4	70.0	100
Freq.	30,285	8,436	529	−2,758	5,132	−2,251	21,196	
Total period (1999–2008) (%)	64.0	19.0	3.0	1.0	5.0	21.0	52.0	100
Freq.	591,031	10,568	15,561	4,932	28,783	122,116	309,071	

Source: Spanish Labour Force Survey (1999–2008).

evolution towards an increasing segmentation of employed women by their migrant or native origin during the years of economic and labour expansion. The results highlight how the evolution during this period of the occupational distribution of native women has moved towards higher proportions of those more-qualified occupations. This process has taken place in parallel to the large inflow of immigrant women working in those labour positions at the bottom of the occupational structure.

By area of origin, the occupational characteristics of women from the EU25 are similar to those for native women. In contrast, Latin American, African and non-EU European women are mostly concentrated in the four areas of occupation at the bottom of the structure.

The *substitution* dynamic of native by immigrant female worker has its clearer expression in domestic service. The absolute number of immigrant domestic workers is closer to that of native workers, thus giving evidence of a clear replacement in this specific labour position. Moreover, the age and educational structure of these two distinct labour forces is very different. While native domestic women are mostly middle-aged and of a low educational attainment, immigrant domestic women are younger and more educated. The main groups that are replacing native domestic helpers are Latin Americans and non-EU European women.

The unprecedented growth of immigrant women with occupations in domestic services points to the confirmation of the initial hypothesis of the *addition* of the immigrant demand, one of the main contributions of our research. We interpret this rapid increase in the number of domestic helpers not only from the initial demand, but also from the very existence of cheap immigrant labour undertaken by women who accept such work. This tendency has broadened the demand for domestic helpers, not only from higher social classes, but from the middle and lower-middle classes, too. Moreover, the exceptional nature of the socioeconomic context during 1999–2008 is a key element in explaining this growth in demand for domestic help from Spanish families. From the supply side this additional dynamic is explained by the flexibility of labour contracts in domestic services. As a consequence, immigrant women are prone to lowering their social and labour status in the initial stage of their residence in Spain as a way of obtaining legal status. Therefore, the addition in demand for immigrant domestic helpers is a two-sided dynamic.

Since the inflow of immigrant women is too recent in Spain, we can interpret the observed complementarity between native and immigrant women within the segmented and gendered Spanish labour market as a consequence of the arrival, in and of itself, of foreign-born workers. If such a statement were true, we would expect an improvement in their labour position and a confluence with the natives' occupations, according to their educational attainment. In this case, we would interpret this initial complementarity in terms of what the young population experience in the labour market; they aim for higher positions as they gain work experience. The opposing situation would be one in which immigrant women were maintaining the same labour positions despite their educational attainment and independent of the length of time they have lived in Spain. In such a case, we would expect an ethnic segmentation of the labour force. However, from this analysis we cannot conclude which scenario is more likely. We shall need to wait some years until immigrant women are well established in the Spanish labour force and in society in order to obtain a better picture about what the future holds for immigrant women.

None the less, our analysis was focused on a context of exceptional economic growth and of increasing labour demand. It is unclear in the current situation, with a general rise in unemployment rates, whether competition dynamics between those less-skilled native and immigrant women will become more obvious. It is not possible to know, at this stage, which of these two groups of women would be most affected. If the labour market evolves towards an ethnically segmented market, immigrant women or even their children will be the losers. On the other hand, if the labour market were to reward human capital, then the best-educated immigrant women will converge on the same labour positions as skilled native women. Finally, although demand for immigrant domestic helpers will depend heavily on the amount of assistance provided by the welfare state programmes, the evolution of the employment crisis is also a crucial factor. In fact, in the most recent phase of the economic crisis, unemployment is starting to damage the traditionally female occupations, especially in education, health services and other public administration positions. We therefore expect deterioration in the job opportunities for native women that, in the medium to long terms, may affect labour demand in domestic services, too.

NOTES

* This research has received economic support from the 2010 R+D Programme of the Spanish Ministry of Sciences and Innovation as part of the following projects: 'Labour market dynamic and family formation in Spain during the turn of the century' (Dinámica del mercado de trabajo y formación familiar en España durante el cambio de siglo) (Reference CSO2010-21028/SOCI) and 'Multiple equilibrium analysis of family' (Análisis de múltiples equilibrios en la família) /(Reference CSO 2010-19062/SOCI).
1. In this investigation, Bulgarian and Romanian women are considered as non-communitarian women as the incorporation of their countries into the European Union did not occur until 2007. Moreover, the volume and the labour characteristics of immigration from these countries made it necessary to differentiate these women from other communitarian immigrants.

REFERENCES

Abad, L. (2002), 'Contradicciones de la globalización: migraciones y convivencia interétnica tras el 11 de septiembre', *Migraciones*, **11**, 225–68.
Arango, J. (2004), 'La inmigración en España a comienzos del siglo XXI', in Leal Maldonado, J. (ed.), *Informe sobre la situación demográfica en España*, Madrid: Fundación Fernando Abril Martorell, pp. 161–86.
Boyd, M. (1984), 'At a disadvantage: the occupational attainments of foreign-born women in Canada', *International Migration Review*, **18** (4), Special Issue: Women in Migration, 1091–119.
Cachón, L. (2002), 'La formación de la "España inmigrante": mercado y ciudadanía', *Revista española de investigaciones sociológicas*, **97**, 95–126.
Cachón, L. (2003), 'La migración en España: los desafíos de la construcción de la nueva sociedad', *Migraciones*, **14**, 219–304.
Cachón, L. (2004), 'Inmigrantes y mercado de trabajo', *Índice. Revista de estadística y sociedad*, **3**, 16–17.
Cachón, L. (2006), 'Los immigrantes en el mercado de trabajo en España', in E. Aja and J. Arango (eds), *Veinte años de inmigración en España: Perspectivas jurídica y sociológica (1985–2004)*, Barcelona: Fundació CIDOB, pp. 175–201.
Cachón, L. (2009), *La 'España inmigrante': marco discriminatorio, mercado de trabajo y políticas de integración*, vol. 66, Rubí (Barcelona): Anthropos, Migraciones Proyecto Editorial, Autores, Textos y Temas, Ciencias Sociales, pp. 49–73.
Catarino, C. and L. Oso (2000), 'La inmigración femenina en Madrid y Lisboa: hacia una etnización del servicio doméstico y de las empresas de limpieza', *Papers, revista de sociología*, **60** (Special Issue: Inmigración femenina en el sur de Europa), 183–207.
Colectivo IOÉ (1998), 'Inmigración y trabajo: hacia un modelo de análisis: Aplicación alcaso de la construcción', *Migraciones*, **4**, 35–70.
Colectivo IOÉ (2001), *Mujer, inmigración y trabajo*, Ministerio de Trabajo y Asuntos Sociales, Madrid: IMSERSO.
Colectivo IOÉ (2003), 'Mujeres inmigradas y trabajo', in F. Checa (ed.), *Mujeres en el Camino: El fenómeno de la migración femenina en España*, Barcelona: Icaria Editorial, pp. 15–54.
Cortina, C., A. Esteve and A. Domingo (2008), 'Marriage patterns of the foreign-born population in a new country of immigration: the case of Spain', *International Migration Review*, **42** (4), 877–902.
Domingo, A. and R. Houle (2005), 'Situación laboral de la población de nacionalidad extranjera censada en España', *Papers de Demografia*, **266**, 1–34.
García, M.A. (2005), 'Cambios en la Encuesta de Población Activa en 2005', *Índice. Revista de estadística y sociedad*, **11**, 6–10.
INE (2005), 'Encuesta de Población Activa 2005', *Cifras INE. Boletín informativo del Instituto Nacional de Estadística*, March, 1–8.
Izquierdo, A. (2003), 'La inmigración en Europa: flujos, tendencias y políticas', in Izquierdo (ed.), *Inmigración: Mercado de trabajo y Protección Social en España*, vol. 141, Madrid: Consejo Económico y Social, pp. 401–23.
Juliano, D. (2000), 'Mujeres estructuralmente viajeras: estereotipos y estrategias', *Papers, revista de sociologia*, **60** (Special Issue: Inmigración femenina en el sur de Europa), 381–9.
King, R. and E. Zontini (2000), 'The role of gender in the South European immigration model', *Papers, Revista de Sociologia*, **60** (Special Issue: Inmigración femenina en el sur de Europa), 35–52.
Kofman, E. (1999), 'Female "birds of passage" a decade later: gender and immigration in the European Union', *International Migration Review*, **33** (2), 269–99.
Lim, L.L. (1996), *More and Better Jobs for Women. An Action Guide*, Geneva: International Labour Office.
Lim, L.L. (1997), 'Flexible labour markets in a globalising world: the implications for

international female migration', paper presented at the 23rd General Population Conference, Beijing, 11–17 October.
Martín Díaz, E. (2008), 'El impacto del género en la migraciones de la globalización: Mujeres, trabajo y relaciones interculturales', *Scripta Nova*, **12** (270), available at:http://www.ub.es/geocrit/sn/sn-270-133.htm.
Martínez Veiga, U. (1999), 'Immigrants in the Spanish labour market', in M. Baldwin Edwards and J. Arango (eds), *Immigrants and the Informal Economy in Southern Europe*, London and Portland, OR: Frank Cass, pp. 105–28.
Moreno-Fontes, G. (2008), 'Migration, gender equality and development', ILO overview paper presented at the international conference on gender, migration and development: 'Seizing Opportunities, Upholding Rights', Manila, Philippines, 25–26 September.
Morokvasic, M. (1984), 'Birds of passage are also women . . . ', *International Migration Review*, **18** (4), 886–907.
Nakano Glenn, E. (1992), 'From servitude to service work: the historical continuities of women's paid and unpaid reproductive labor', *Signs: Journal of Women in Culture and Society*, **18** (1), 1–44.
Oso, L. (1998), *La migración hacia España de las mujeres jefas de hogar*, Madrid: Ministerio de Trabajo y Asuntos Sociales, Instituto de la Mujer, Estudios, **52**.
Oso, L. (2003), 'Las jefas de hogar en un contexto migratorio. Modelos y rupturas', in F. Checa (ed.), *Mujeres en el camino: El fenómeno de la migración femenina en España*, Barcelona: Icaria Editorial, pp. 85–104.
Pajares, M. (2007), *Inmigración y mercado de trabajo: análisis de datos de España y Cataluña. Informe 2007*, **14**, Madrid: Ministerio de Trabajo y Asuntos Sociales, Documentos del Observatorio Permanente de la Inmigración.
Parella, S. (2000), 'El trasvase de desigualdades de clase y etnia entre mujeres: los servicios de proximidad', *Papers, revista de sociología*, **60** (Special Issue: Inmigración femenina en el sur de Europa), 275–89.
Parella, S. (2002), 'La internacionalización de la reproducción: La inserción laboral de la mujer inmigrante en los servicios de proximidad', doctoral thesis, Departament de Sociologia, Universitat Autònoma de Barcelona, Bellaterra.
Parella, S. (2003), *Mujer, inmigrante y trabajadora: la triple discriminación*, Barcelona: Anthropos.
Parella, S. (2007), 'Mujeres inmigrantes en el mercado de trabajo español: La división internacional del trabajo reproductivo', in I. Diz Otero and M. Lois González (eds), *Mujeres, instituciones y política*, Bellaterra (Barcelona): Edicions Bellaterra, pp. 361–86.
Parreñas, Rhacel Salazar (2000), 'Migrant Filipina domestic workers and the international division of reproductive labor', *Gender and Society*, **14** (4), 560–80.
Parreñas, Rhacel Salazar (2001), *Servants of Globalization: Women, Migration and Domestic Work*, Stanford, CA: Stanford University Press.
Piore, M. (1979a), *Birds of Passage: Migrant Labour and Industrial Societies*, Cambridge: Cambridge University Press.
Piore, M. (1979b), 'Los trabajadores extranjeros', in M. Piore (ed.), *Paro e inflación: Perspectivas institucionales y estructurales*, Madrid: Alianza Editorial, pp. 273–89.
Reyneri, E. (1996), *Sociologia del mercato del lavoro*, Bologna: Il Mulino.
Reyneri, E. (2004), 'Immigrants in a segmented and often undeclared labour market', *Journal of Modern Italian Studies*, **9** (1), 71–93.
Ribas-Mateos, N. (2004), 'How can we understand immigration in Southern Europe?', *Journal of Ethnic and Migration Studies*, **30** (6), 1045–63.
Sassen, S. (1984), 'Notes on the incorporation of Third World women into wage-labor through immigration and off-shore production', *International Migration Review*, **18** (4, Special Issue: Women in Migration), 1144–67.
Sassen, S. (1988), *The Mobility of Labor and Capital: A Study in International Investment and Labor Flows*, Cambridge: Cambridge University Press.
Sassen, S. (1991), *The Global City: New York, London, Tokyo*, Princeton, NJ: Princeton University Press.

Solé, C. (1994), *La mujer inmigrante*, Madrid: Ministerio de Asuntos Sociales, Instituto de la Mujer, **40**.
Solé, C. (2001a), 'La inserción de los inmigrantes en el mercado de trabajo: El caso español', in Solé (ed.), *El impacto de la inmigración en la economía y en la sociedad receptora*, **27**, Rubí (Barcelona): Anthropos, pp. 11–51.
Solé, C. (2001b), 'La mujer inmigrante en la era de la globalización', in R. Radl (ed.), *La mujer en la nueva era de la globalización*, Madrid: Centro de investigaciones sociológicas (CIS).
Solé, C. (2003), 'Inmigración, mercado de trabajo y género', *Documento de Trabajo, Serie Sociología*, S2003/01.
Sørensen, N. (2005), 'Migración, género y desarrollo: el caso dominicano', in N. Zúñiga García-Falcés (ed.), *La migración, un camino entre el desarrollo y la cooperación*, Madrid: Centro de Investigación para la Paz, pp. 163–82.
Vidal-Coso, E. (2009), 'La complementarietat sociodemogràfica entre les dones immigrades i les no immigrades a Espanya', doctoral thesis, Departament de Geografia, Universitat Autònoma de Barcelona, Bellaterra.

16 Towards a gender-sensitive approach to remittances in Ecuador*
Diana Mata-Codesal

REMITTANCES AND GENDER IN ECUADOR

In the era of globalization, migrants' remittances are pictured as the most reliable source for funding development many countries have. Unsurprisingly then, remittances have been assigned a central place in the so-called 'migration–development nexus'. They are currently a fashionable topic in both political and academic milieus where they are usually portrayed in a very positive light. However, against a background of overenthusiastic discourses and grand images of remittances, it is clear that there is a need for sharper research questions and more contextualized analyses on the topic. This is even more urgent in the case of discussions of remittances in relation to gender. As Morokvasic pointed almost three decades ago, women are also birds of passage (1984). Not only are migrant women receiving more scholarly attention since Phizacklea edited her book about migrant women (1983), but there is also growing recognition that migration and remittances are highly gendered social processes (King et al., 2004, p. 33).

The academic debate has traditionally oscillated between accounts that portray remittances as empowering devices for receiving women and accounts highlighting their burdening effects. Recently more-tempered accounts bring to the fore the importance of inserting remittances' effects into the broader socio-cultural and economic contexts in which they are deployed (see, for instance, de Haas and van Rooij, 2010). Research in this chapter follows the same reasoning, providing an ethnographic micro-perspective on international remittances to Ecuador that incorporates gender as a key variable. By focusing on the family dynamics involved in remittance processes, a topic that remains largely unresearched, the aim is to start opening the black box of the household to investigate the negotiations, tensions, continuities and changes triggered by remittances.

In 2011, Ecuador received US$2.67 billion from its citizens abroad (BCE, 2012). Financial remittances to Ecuador are the country's second-highest income after oil exports. Remittances are macro-economically important as well as being at the core of the survival and improvement strategies of a high number of Ecuadorian families. Ecuador provides a unique field for studies on remittances because of the country's two different traditions of international migration to the US and to Europe. The different gender composition of each flow, male led to the US and female pioneered to Europe, has stimulated academic interest on gender and migration in Ecuador (see, for instance, Gratton, 2007; Pribilsky, 2007; Herrera, 2008). In regions where women represent an important share of their total migrant population (for example, South America, Central and Eastern Asia), researchers have produced an extended bibliography on gender and migration/remittances. This is even more intense when the gender composition of the migration flow has experienced changes in a short period, as has been the case for Ecuador. The quick feminization of international migration from Ecuador took place in the 1990s when the ageing Southern European countries demanded female care workers. It was in marked contrast with the older migration to the US, predominantly male. Remittances from the US, Spain and Italy systematically account for over 95 per cent of the total received amounts in Ecuador (BCE, 2012).

Methodologically this research draws on quantitative data (from a purpose-designed questionnaire), as well as qualitative data from interviews and nine months of participant observation carried out in 2009 in two small Ecuadorian villages, Xarbán and Pindo (pseudonyms), and a short follow-up in migrants' places of current residence in the US and Spain in 2010.[1] I interviewed 83 people in four different settings (the two villages in Ecuador, the state of New York, and Spain), and surveyed 15 per cent of each village's population (according to the 2001 Ecuadorian Population Census), 306 villagers in Xarbán and 370 in Pindo, as well as gathering information about 213 migrants from the first village and 185 from the second.

Xarbán and Pindo are two rural parishes[2] in the Ecuadorian provinces of Azuay and Loja, respectively, with very different international migration profiles. Migration from Xarbán is predominantly of young males to the US. According to the latest available population census except one, all migrant villagers are in the US, with 75 per cent of them being males (INEC, 2010). Data from my own questionnaire reports that virtually none of these migrants holds regular legal status in the US (only 11 out of 213 migrants hold legal status abroad) and their chances of ever achieving it are very slim as they entered the country irregularly crossing the Mexico–US border, and there is currently no route to regularization for them. International migration from Pindo shows a wider range of destinations although Spain is the most preferred one (71 per cent of migrants from Pindo are in Spain according to the 2010 census), followed by Italy (15 per cent). Migration to Spain and Italy was initially pioneered by female villagers although the gender composition of the flow was later balanced when many of these women reunified or facilitated their male relatives' migration. My questionnaire data indicate that 87 per cent of Pindo migrants abroad in 2009 held regular legal status. These two villages are cases in point of the two international migration traditions in Ecuador.

The villages' migration profiles have a mirror image in their remittance panoramas. In both cases, almost every household with international migrants is receiving money from abroad, usually on a monthly basis. Money is sent from the US in the case of Xarbán and from Spain and to a lesser extent from Italy in the case of Pindo. A point of difference is that international migration is older and more pervasive in Xarbán than in Pindo (as it is Ecuadorian migration to the US). In Xarbán almost every household in the village is or has been involved in international migration at some point. Data from the questionnaire indicate that Xarbán's households receive, on average, US$285 per month while Pindo's receive only US$175.

After this brief sketch, the next section will focus on the gender of remittance senders and receivers and the links between these two groups. The third section outlines a refined definition of remittances that takes into account senders' and receivers' perceptions. In the final section, the main uses of financial remittances in Xarbán and Pindo are presented under a gender reading.

RELATIONSHIPS BETWEEN REMITTANCE SENDERS AND RECEIVERS

Studies looking at remittances have traditionally focused on the sender and/or the receiver. Some recent scholarly work has produced gendered perspectives on remittances (Piper, 2005; Sørensen, 2005; García and Paiewonski, 2006; King et al., 2006; Kunz, 2008; Ghosh, 2009; King and Vullnetari, 2010) that focus on the relationship between the sender (or senders) and the receiver (or receivers). Following Carling (2007, p. 17) I use the tag 'dyad' to convey this relationship. Remitters can send money to more than one person, and one non-migrant can receive money and gifts from more than one migrant. To capture this complexity, I use the term 'main dyad' and 'secondary dyad(s)'. As not all relationships are equally strong or bonding, 'main dyad' represents the strongest and most stable of the relationships between a remittance sender and receiving household(s). While each migrant can only belong to a main dyad, they can have weaker and less stable links within 'secondary dyads'. A married male Xarbán migrant in the US whose wife and children live in Xarbán can have them as his main dyad, while at the same time also sending occasional amounts of money or gifts to his elderly parents (secondary dyad).

The gender of migrants combines with their civil status to explain different remittance behaviours. Single migrants tend to form a main dyad with their parents, and sometimes also their younger siblings living in the parental house. Once female migrants marry they are more likely to stop sending money to their parents, in contrast to their husbands. In patriarchal societies, as Smith found for Albania (2009, p. 559), daughters are not expected to make contributions to their parents while sons do so even after they marry. Married migrants' main dyad is usually their spouse and children, unless these family members are abroad with the migrant. As I shall show later on, the fact of having young children encourages the settlement of stronger and more stable dyadic relations.

In Xarbán the most common dyads consist of married male migrants sending money to their spouse and children and migrant couples sending money to their children in the village. Children can live on their own if they are old enough or with a relative who takes care of them. Quite often grandchildren are taken care of by their maternal grandmother. In Xarbán, dyads do not tend to challenge traditional gender roles, as men are still the breadwinners, albeit from afar, and women stay at home taking care of the children. In Pindo there is a wider variety of dyadic relationships as family arrangements are more complex because of female and male migration but also because of irresponsible paternity that led many mothers to migrate in the first place. The fact that in Pindo female villagers pioneered the flow directly attacks the traditional gender role structure in the village. Migrant mothers are portrayed as mothers who abandoned their children (Pedone, 2008, p. 47), while those husbands who receive money from their wives abroad are subjected to a lot of social pressure as a result of this change in the traditional gender roles. In Pindo, fathers are very often absent, hence children of migrant mothers are taken care of by female relatives (the maternal or the paternal grandmother, older sisters or aunts), creating female-only dyads.

Contrary to literature on migration that identifies the household as a harmonious unit as in the new economics of labour migration approach pioneered by Lucas and Stark (1985) dyadic relations are not problem free (de Haas and Fokkema, 2010, p. 543). There are power imbalances that need to be taken into account. Following Sanz Abad (2009, p. 390), it is useful to think about who decides what to do with the remittances (decision power), who manages them (management) and who eventually enjoys the consequences that ensue (enjoyment). It is also important to look at the control mechanisms available for decision takers.

Towards a gender-sensitive approach to remittances in Ecuador 365

The issue of enjoyment, as straightforward as it may seem, requires acknowledgement and engagement with the literature dealing with the motivations to remit. Under the altruism approach the concept of enjoyment is broader. In a less economic jargon than the one used by Lucas and Stark (1985), migrants' enjoyment can be derived from the enjoyment of those they love or care for. Hence, enjoyment would be a shared and self-perpetuating situation. However, I am referring not so much to vague feelings of happiness and accomplishment, as to the concrete act of enjoyment. Migrants can be happy because a relative is wearing proper shoes, whereas the actual enjoyment of having warm and comfortable feet goes to the person who is wearing the shoes.

There are decisions to be taken regarding four aspects of material remittances: the nature of the remittance, the frequency of the sending, the sending channel and the uses of those remittances. Depending on the transfer, the sender or the receiver – or both – agree what and when to send. Migrants usually decide how to send the money, as they have a better knowledge of the available channels, although the type of transfer very much determines the channel. Depending on the transfer as well, senders or receivers decide what to use it for. Some sending is clearly targeted while other resources are sent with no clear aim. In the case of in-kind remittances, it makes little sense to talk about untargeted in-kind remittances. Gifts such as a washing machine or clothes can seldom be used for other than their original purpose. With regard to financial remittances, sometimes the receivers make the decisions, do the actual management and enjoy the consequences. In other cases, senders decide what to do with the sent resources and will enjoy (or suffer) the consequences of their decision. Nonetheless they cannot implement their decisions by themselves and need to rely on other people.

Control is irrelevant when the person who decides how to use remittances also does the actual management. This is the case of the small regular amounts sent by migrants to cover their direct relatives' daily expenses in Ecuador. Non-migrants decide how to distribute the relatively small amounts they receive among their competing needs for food, transport, utilities, education, or healthcare. As non-migrants do the actual management and they will enjoy the consequences of their decisions and management, migrants do not usually supervise this type of transfer. Control is also irrelevant in the case of in-kind remittances as these gifts can hardly be used for other than their intended use. Sending in-kind remittances is a type of control mechanism where senders ensure that their decisions will bring the expected outcome. However, control is crucial in the case of migrants' savings sent to Ecuador, money sent quickly to cope with unexpected emergencies, and money sent to repay debts (particularly debts incurred to make the journey, or to pay the monthly instalments of loans or mortgages).

Some supervision mechanisms are in place for senders to monitor receivers' behaviour. Gossiping is perhaps the mechanism par excellence, particularly in the case of Xarbán due to migrants' and non-migrants' residential concentration and the fact that everybody knows everybody else. Telephone calls enable gossip to fly back and forth in Xarbán in what Dreby labels 'transnational gossiping' (2009). However, it can become distorted, making gossiping potentially very destructive. Videos and photos are also an important supervision mechanism for migrants who can thereby check on non-migrants' management of their money. This is very important in the case of remittances to build houses (Carrillo Espinosa, 2007, p. 291). Migrants can also implement disciplinary measures, such as withdrawal of remittances or retaining savings abroad, if they suspect that their relatives are not following their instructions or mismanaging.

It might appear naive but, as Pribilsky found (2004, p. 324), those families who learn to *convivir* (live side-by-side) and have better relationships are more likely to perform better economically and socially. There is nothing better than having a good relationship, which usually implies that migration and remittances are a joint venture between husband and wife or among siblings or between children and parents. Because decisions are agreed, there is less need to control and monitor.

After examining the household in some detail, in the next section I shall question the taken-for-granted definition of remittances. Is it too generic a term? Does it accurately describe the reality of people in villages such as Xarbán and Pindo?

REFINED DEFINITION OF FINANCIAL REMITTANCES

Fieldwork data are unequivocal about the need to disaggregate remittances in order to work with a definition more in tune with the reality of senders and receivers. The broad term 'remittances', used prolifically by researchers, policy makers and politicians, obscures a more complex reality and prevents academics from researching the accommodations and ruptures taking place within remittance dyads. In this section I extend and enhance our working definition of remittances by identifying two different types of transfers that are subsumed and homogenized under the main 'remittances' umbrella: emic remittances and savings (the comprehensive six-item typology is fully developed in Mata-Codesal, 2011).

The first transfer is what I have labelled 'emic remittances' using the anthropological difference between 'emic' (insider's viewpoint) and 'etic' (observer's viewpoint). My decision is based on the fact that it is this transfer that receivers themselves identify as 'remittances'. Xarbán and Pindo villagers have internalized the term 'remittances' and use it, but they also feel that it does not quite fit their reality. By 'remittances' villagers understood the small amounts of money sent periodically to them by their close relative migrants abroad to pay for food and utilities, and cover the normal expenses in a household including children's education and recurrent small medical expenses (unexpected high medical expenses are not met by this type of transfer). Money is sent every month or with specific periodicity. My informants often use the expression *'no más para la comidita'* (only for the food) meaning for their physical reproduction. As this transfer is intended for the basic physical reproduction of the household members, there are no remaining resources to be saved or invested. The circularity in the definition creates a tension that has policy implications. When policy makers and academics complain bitterly about the overwhelming share of 'remittances' spent on daily expenses, they are overlooking the fact that (emic) remittances are such because they are sent to cover daily expenses. Emic remittances are being drip fed into many households in Xarbán and Pindo and as such they can be considered maintenance funds.

Thanks to this transfer, receiving villagers' levels of well-being have increased dramatically. This huge increase is partly the consequence of very low initial levels of material well-being. This improvement in material well-being does not come without a negative side. Loneliness and family separation are often mentioned as painful drawbacks by remittance receivers. There is a tension between money and family: either to migrate and earn money for the family but without the family, or to stay put in Ecuador with the family but without access to stable sources of income. This discourse is verbalized by both migrants and non-migrants, each group praising their decision but aware of the intrinsic trade-off.

The issue of power imbalances inherent to the sender–receiver dyad is very important. Non-migrants are aware of their precarious condition and there is always the possibility that emic remittances will stop. Migrants can either evade their family financial responsibilities (if married migrants become involved with someone else, for instance), or they can become unable to meet them (if unable to work). However, non-migrants are not powerless victims, since they develop different strategies to cope with this uncertainty and vulnerability, such as self-imposed restrictions on expenses in order not to get used to a lifestyle that is unsustainable without international remittances.

Single migrants usually send emic remittances to their parents and younger siblings living in the household. This situation changes when migrants marry. They acquire obligations towards their spouse ('*ser de obligación*' meaning being married), and their parents' household usually stops being their main household of reference, although if migrants' income is sufficient, they can still send some residual remittances to their parents or siblings. Emic remittances to old parents profoundly disrupt generation roles. Bajic documented how disruptive this unintended consequence of remittances can be for receivers in a Serbian urban context (2007). Parents who are traditionally portrayed as their children's providers, become remittance receivers and, as such, dependent on their children.

When there are several migrants from the same household, the financial burden of sending emic remittances is shouldered by all of them, which lightens considerably the financial responsibility. In the case of parents with migrant and non-migrant children, the former are usually in charge of providing the money while the latter do the actual physical care of elderly parents.

Emic remittances usually take place within the spouses' dyad, with or without children in Ecuador. When migrants have children in Ecuador all respondents (remittance senders and receivers alike) agree that the obligation to send emic remittances becomes stronger than when married migrants are still childless. Having a child, and particularly if it is a boy, is very important for women whose husbands are abroad, particularly in Xarbán where women seldom migrate. A baby boy means more reliable and higher emic remittances. Non-migrants with children do not usually need to ask for emic remittances. There is an agreement (either implicit or explicit) between migrants and their families in Ecuador regarding the amount and the regularity of the sending.

The second item in this typology is of an 'anything else' nature: any money transfer not intended to cover the daily expenses of the receiving household in Ecuador. I label it 'savings' in the interests of simplicity although I am aware of the connotations of this label. In contrast to emic remittances, considered by migrants as part of their expenses, migrants' savings are possible if, and only if, there is any remaining money after migrants have paid for their living expenses in their new place of residence, paid debts and sent emic remittances to their direct relatives in Ecuador. Migrants can either keep their savings with them abroad or send them to Ecuador. In Ecuador, money can be kept as such or spent. Most migration from Xarbán and Pindo is targeted to build or buy one's own house in Ecuador. Hence building a house is the first main expenditure made by migrants once they manage to save. The range of business opportunities available in Xarbán and Pindo, after building a 'proper' house, is rather narrow. Many migrants and returnees opt for setting up a small shop that is very time consuming and yields low profit. Owning a vehicle provides male villagers with a stable job as a taxi or bus driver. These uses have a gender reading that I shall examine in the next section.

The issue of control is key for this type of transfer. Theoretically migrants are the ones who decide how to use this money. Obviously they can be advised by their relatives in Ecuador regarding investment opportunities or the bank accounts with the most favourable conditions, as their non-migrant relatives have a more up-to-date knowledge of the context situation in the country. However, migrants' decisions are not always adhered to. Control is a two-way issue: non-migrants can use the money for purposes other than that intended; and migrants can also conceal information about their real earnings and expenses while keeping money in bank accounts in their new place of residence.

Refining the definition of remittances is not mere academic entertainment; it also has development implications. In order to understand and design policies to enhance the developmental impact of the money migrants send to their families, the presence of these diverse types of money transfers must be acknowledged and incorporated into the analysis. This disaggregation also facilitates surveying changes over time regarding power balances within remittance dyads while applying gender readings. Gender not only permeates ethnographic definitions of remittances, but the effects of remittances in Xarbán and Pindo show equally marked gendered effects. In the next section I apply a gender lens to the most frequent ways of using financial remittances in the two villages to show how the effects are different for male and female receivers and how, in some cases, remittances affect the relations between both.

GENDERED EFFECTS OF FINANCIAL REMITTANCES

Some of the main changes experienced as a result of receiving financial remittances have a gender dimension. In this section I deal with the gender implications of emic remittances, money for education, house construction, and vehicle acquisition in Xarbán and Pindo.

Most studies on the use of remittances tend to classify them as either consumption or investment (see, for example, Adams, 1989; Lucas, 2005; Gupta et al., 2007). Consumption (often labelled 'conspicuous') is regarded in most of these studies as a waste of resources, to the detriment of investment ventures. Consumption might be positive in terms of poverty alleviation, but it does not set the basis for future development independent of remittances. Following this line of reasoning and given that what has been labelled in this research as emic remittances is traditionally considered as non-productive consumption, financial remittances are broadly speaking not a source of sustainable development on their own. Mahler's powerful critique of the underlying ideas behind explanations of the 'productive use of remittances' highlighted that on one hand most of these studies use a conservative and narrow definition of 'productive use' (2000, p. 30). Under such a heading only 'remittances invested in business ventures or placed in savings accounts where the capital can be invested by the banking system' are considered as yielding productive use (ibid., p. 31). On the other hand, she also notes that definitions of investment are not only too narrow, they are also laden with infelicitous socio-cultural connotations, particularly regarding gender, given that women are often the receivers of emic remittances:

> When remittances are spent on consumption then a subtle gendered critique emerges, one in which women are portrayed – albeit inadvertently – as failing to put remittances to their best use, or inhibiting investment. One reason for this characterization is the fact that remittances are not studied holistically. (p. 31)

As mentioned, emic remittances also include money to pay for the education of migrants' children in Ecuador. This specific use of emic remittances has gender consequences, particularly in the case of Xarbán. Although financial remittances are used in both villages for pursuing education beyond primary school, the presence of a culture of migration in Xarbán affects young villagers' educational aspirations. Migration to the US, instead of education, is seen in Xarbán as a path to social and economic mobility. This situation has a gender reading because female Xarbán villagers are not expected to migrate and they have the financial resources (in the form of remittances) to pursue further education. Young female villagers in Xarbán are getting ahead in education terms compared with their male peers. All the cases of successful educational investment in Xarbán were women who, supported financially by their parents in the US, have finished university education and currently have a career of their own (a more detailed analysis of the impact of remittances on education is in Mata-Codesal, 2013).

Remittances have dramatically changed the housing landscape of both villages, especially in Xarbán. Migration is quite often targeted at building one's own house and migrants endure much hardship in order to save enough to build a concrete house. This is usually the first big expenditure made by migrants after daily expenses are covered and debts repaid. Both in Xarbán and in Pindo, building a house is one of the initial motivations to migrate and save money. However, while Xarbán migrants almost always decide to build their house in Xarbán, Pindo migrants show different and diversified behaviour regarding their housing decisions. Housing is perceived as a secure investment in a highly insecure investment environment because 'brick lasts'. Due to the insecurity in some parts of Pindo, few houses are built in the more isolated parts of the village.

The effects of remittance houses are gendered. They have a direct impact on job opportunities for male villagers. Construction work is available for non-migrant male villagers or returnees as construction workers tend to be hired locally, with a strong preference for relatives. Remittance houses have a different set of effects on female villagers' lives. Before migration it is quite common for newly married couples to live in their parents' house (usually with the rest of the family). These houses tend to be small (one or two rooms for several family members), well away from the main paths and roads, and built in adobe. Remittances allow remittance receivers to move away from their parents' or their parents-in-law's house. The new house built with money earned abroad is bigger, with longer-lasting materials (concrete and blocks), and better located by the main roads and in the parish centre. Particularly in the case of Xarbán, these three features allow migrants' spouses and children to live in more comfortable dwellings in terms of independence, size and location. Remittance houses also have effects beyond the migrants' nuclear family. This is, for instance, the case of mothers of migrants abroad who endured abusive marital relations and who have been able to move away from that situation into the empty remittance houses of their children abroad or with their daughter/son-in-law and grandchildren.

On a side note, the issue of the family-in-law is crucial in the villages. The family-in-law can either smooth the hardships of physical separation between spouses or, on the contrary, make unbearable the life of the spouse who stays put. My research clearly shows that having a child (specially a male) makes the lives of migrants' wives more stable. Remittances arrive in a more regular way. If possible, the wife is allowed to live on her own with her children. In this case the family-in-law has less impact on migrants' wives and children. Pauli, who conducted research in Mexico (2008), states that migration mitigates in-laws' control. My data strongly support Pauli's explanation.

The final use I present here within a gender framework is that of remittances for vehicle acquisition. In Xarbán 14 per cent and in Pindo 18 per cent of surveyed households have bought a vehicle since they started receiving remittances, usually a car, but also buses, coaches and trucks. The percentage is higher in Pindo because cars are high on the list of priorities of migrants' relatives and returnees due to the village isolation. Often, the money earned abroad by a female migrant is used upon return to buy a taxi. The fact that remittances earned by female migrants are used to buy vehicles has a very interesting gender reading given that women do not traditionally drive in rural Ecuador. In Xarbán but especially in Pindo where more women migrated, some female migrants and returnees opt to use their savings to buy cars and cooperative memberships for their male relatives. As Bastia found in Bolivia (2011), the women who challenged traditional gender roles with their international migration were as a result subjected to much criticism in Ecuador. Upon their return these women are willing to comply with the gender status quo in order to be able to convert their economic success gained abroad into local upwards social mobility. Many of the women interviewed by Bastia 'use the taxi to reinstate their husband's role and confirm his identity as the main breadwinner while at the same time positioning herself as a housewife' (ibid., p. 1525). Thus, female migrants' remittances and savings reinstate male domination that had been touched by female migration. This suggests that 'women migrants prefer to barter the gender gains accrued abroad for upward social mobility' (ibid. p. 1526).

It is clear then that the effect of remittances is highly gendered but it would be oversimplistic to conclude that, overall, remittances are increasing gender equality in receiving areas. As seen, change is not linear and unequivocal, but rather convoluted.

FINAL REMARKS

This chapter has contributed to the topic of, gender, migration and transnationalism, by showing how remittances are a gendered, socioeconomic phenomenon. Using a case study of international migration from two rural areas in Ecuador, it has addressed the pressing need to start opening the black box of family dynamics regarding remittances, introducing and applying the term 'dyad'. Such re-conceptualization is based on the fact that the household, conceived as a harmonious whole, is not the most convenient unit of analysis to inquire about remittances. Moreover, focusing only on the sending or receiving part of the equation can also lead to accounts that miss the dynamic interplay between the involved parts. The relationships between sender and receivers – the sender(s)–receiver(s) dyad – provides a fruitful research locus. The 'dyad' is a methodological device that facilitates micro-readings of remittances, principally in terms of gender and generation. Dyadic relationships do not have to be necessarily symmetrical, nor does it mean that one extreme is completely powerless. Both ends (which could comprise more than two people) are immersed in constant negotiations. The dyad provides the focus to analyse the empowering or burdening potential of remittances. The methodological device of the 'dyad' sheds light on the fact that quite often these two processes are not mutually exclusive. In some cases, processes of empowerment and burdening are simultaneously taking place in different realms, or both processes take place in a dyad but at different points in time.

Broadly speaking, and in line with Pribilsky's findings (2004), those remittance dyads, both in Xarbán and Pindo, that have managed to build a relationship of trust and mutual support are more likely to perform better at several levels. This type of relation is of course more rewarding in emotional terms for all those involved, but they also perform better socially and economically. Because of the presence of a shared project and mutual trust, there is little need to supervise each other's behaviour.

Clear from the accounts above, it is unwise to conclude that, overall, remittances in rural Ecuador are disrupting traditional gender roles. Their effects must be understood within broader dynamics and structural changes taking place in migrants' places of origin. Remittances deploy their full significance if read stemming and affecting specific socio-cultural and economic environments, which include gender regimes and roles.

NOTES

* This research was funded by the Basque Country government under its FPI-AK programme.
1. At the time of the data collection the worst effects of the financial crisis that was unleashed in 2008 were still to come, particularly in Spain. While in 2009 migrant villagers in Spain were waiting for the economic situation to improve, in 2012 after their unemployment benefits dried up and unsure of when the situation will eventually improve, they are returning to Ecuador. As a consequence, the total amount of financial remittances received from Spain has diminished (BCE, 2012). In the case of migration to the US, the situation in Mexico in 2012 is perceived by migrants and migrants-to-be as too dangerous to travel. Hence, migrants in the US are unwilling to return while no villagers in 2012 risk migrating irregularly to the US. In aggregated terms this situation does not have such a dramatic effect on remittance transfers from the US.
2. A parish is the smallest administrative unit in Ecuador.

REFERENCES

Adams, R.H. (1989), 'Worker remittances and inequality in rural Egypt', *Economic Development and Cultural Change*, **38** (1), 45–71.
Bajic, I. (2007), 'Serbian remittances: from development myths to ethnographic reality', paper presented to the Remittances and Transnational Livelihoods Conference, Peace Research Institute, Oslo, 31 October.
Bastia, T. (2011), 'Migration as protest? Negotiating gender, class and ethnicity in urban Bolivia', *Environment and Planning A*, **43** (7), 1514–29.
BCE (2012), 'Evolución Anual de las Remesas', Ecuadorian Central Bank, Quito.
Carling, J. (2007), 'The prevalence and substance of transnational ties: a model applied to the study of remittances', Working Paper, Peace Research Institute, Oslo.

Carrillo Espinosa, M.C. (2007), 'Foto de Familia. Los Usos Privados de las Fotografías Entre Familias Transnacionales Ecuatorianas: El Caso de la Migración Hacia España', paper presented to the 50th FLACSO Conference, Facultad Latinoamericana de Ciencias Sociales, Quito, 29–31 October.

de Haas, H. and T. Fokkema (2010), 'Intra-household conflicts in migration decision-making: return and pendulum migration in Morocco', *Population and Development Review*, **36** (3), 541–61.

de Haas, H. and A. van Rooijb (2010), 'Migration as emancipation? The impact of internal and international migration on the position of women left behind in rural Morocco', *Oxford Development Studies*, **38** (1), 43–62.

Dreby, J. (2009), 'Gender and transnational gossip', *Qualitative Sociology*, **32** (1), 33–52.

García, M. and D. Paiewonski (2006), 'Gender, remittances and development: the case of women migrants from Vicente Noble, Dominican Republic', Working Paper, United Nations International Research and Training Institute for the Advancement of Women, Santo Domingo.

Ghosh, J. (2009), 'Migration and gender empowerment: recent trends and emerging issues', Human Development Research Paper 2009, **4**, United Nations Development Programme, New York.

Gratton, B. (2007), 'Ecuadorians in the United States and Spain: history, gender and niche formation', *Journal of Ethnic and Migration Studies*, **33** (4), 581–99.

Gupta, S., C. Pattillo and S. Wagh (2007), 'Impact of remittances on poverty and financial development in Sub-Saharan Africa', Working Paper, International Monetary Fund, Washington, DC.

Herrera, Gioconda (2008), 'Políticas Migratorias y Familias Transnacionales: Migración Ecuatoriana en España y Estados Unidos', in Herrera and Jacques Ramírez (eds), *América Latina Migrante: Estado, Familia, Identidades*, Quito: FLACSO, pp. 71–87.

INEC (2010), 'VII Censo de Población y VI de Vivienda', Instituto Nacional de Estadística de Ecuador, Quito.

King, R., M. Dalipaj and N. Mai (2006), 'Gendering migration and remittances: evidence from London and Northern Albania', *Population, Space and Place*, **12**, 409–34.

King, R., M. Thomson and T. Fielding (2004), 'Gender, age and generations', State-of-the-art Report IMISCOE Cluster C8, Sussex Centre for Migration and Population, Brighton.

King, R. and J. Vullnetari (2010), 'Gender and remittances in Albania: or why "Are women better remitters than men?" is not the right question', Working Paper, Sussex Centre for Migration Research, Brighton.

Kunz, R. (2008), '"Remittances are beautiful?" Gender implications of the new global remittances trend', *Third World Quarterly*, **29** (7), 1389–409.

Lucas, R. (2005), *International Migration and Economic Development: Lessons from Low-Income Countries*, Cheltenham, UK and Northampton, MA, USA: Edward Elgar.

Lucas, R. and O. Stark (1985), 'Motivations to remit: evidence from Botswana', *Journal of Political Economy*, **93** (5), 901–18.

Mahler, S.J. (2000), 'Migration and transnational issues: recent trends and prospects for 2020', Working Paper, Institut für Iberoamerika-Kunde, Hamburg.

Mata-Codesal, D. (2011), 'Material and social remittances in Highland Ecuador', PhD thesis in Migration Studies, University of Sussex, Brighton.

Mata-Codesal, D. (2013), 'Linking social and financial remittances in the realms of financial know-how and education in rural Ecuador', *Migration Letters*, **10** (1), 23–32.

Morokvasic, M. (1984), 'Birds of passage are also women', *International Migration Review*, **18** (4), 886–907.

Pauli, J. (2008), 'A house of one's own: gender, migration, and residence in rural Mexico', *American Ethnologist*, **35** (1), 171–87.

Pedone, C. (2008), '"Varones Aventureros" vs. "Madres Que Abandonan": Reconstrucción de las Relaciones Familiares a Partir de la Migración Ecuatoriana', *REMHU-Revista Insterdisciplinar da Mobilidade Humana*, **16** (30), 45–64.

Phizacklea, A. (ed.) (1983), *One-way Ticket: Migration and Female Labour*, London: Routledge.
Piper, N. (2005), 'Gender and migration', Working Paper, Global Commission on International Migration, Geneva.
Pribilsky, J. (2004), '"Aprendemos a Convivir": conjugal relations, co-parenting, and family life among ecuadorian transnational migrants in New York City and the Ecuadorian Andes', *Global Networks*, **4** (3), 313–34.
Pribilsky, J. (2007), *La Chulla Vida: Gender, Migration, and the Family in Andean Ecuador and New York City*, New York: Syracuse University Press.
Sanz Abad, J. (2009), 'Entre "Cumplir" y "Hacer Cosas": Estrategias Económicas y Simbolismo en el Uso de las Remesas de la Migración Ecuatoriana en España', PhD thesis in Anthropology, Universitat Rovira i Virgili.
Smith, E. (2009), '"Gap-fillers" or "clan-destroyers": transnational female solidarity towards kin in the region of Fier', *Southeast European and Black Sea Studies*, **9** (4), 555–73.
Sørensen, N.N. (2005), 'Migrant remittances, development and gender', DIIS Brief, Danish Institute for International Studies, Copenhagen.

17 Remittances in the Spain–Ecuador corridor: a gendered estimation through Bayesian networks
Pilar Campoy-Muñoz, Melania Salazar-Ordóñez and Carlos R. García-Alonso

INTRODUCTION

Under contemporary globalization, migration has emerged as a response to the reorganization of production among and within world regions (Orozco, 2002). Over 215 million people are currently living and working outside their country of birth, of which more than 171 million come from developing countries (World Bank, 2010). These migratory flows produce economic and social repercussions in their country of origin through migrant remittances (Orozco, 2002). The rising remittance flows constitute the second-largest and most stable source of foreign currency for the developing world (World Bank, 2010), but empirical evidence has shown that they can also produce an increase in inflation, appreciation of the real exchange rate, reduction in the labour supply and mixed reactions in the economic growth of receiving economies (Chami et al., 2008). At the household level, studies have found that remittances increase the recipient household expenditure on consumption and investment (Adams and Cuecuecha, 2010) and reduce the incidence of child labour and infant mortality (Zhunio et al., 2012), although mixed results are reported with respect to the rate of school enrolment (Calero et al., 2009; Giannelli and Mangiavacchi, 2010) and entrepreneurship (Amuedo-Dorantes and Pozo, 2010; Woodruff and Zenteno, 2007).

The global processes of migration are paralleled by the feminization of these flows, not only because of an overall increase in women migrants, from 47 per cent in 1960 to 49 per cent in 2010 (ILO, 2010), but also because more women are migrating independently of their male relatives (Sørensen et al., 2002). However, in most cases the feminization implies the transfer of reproductive work from qualified native women, with difficulties in reconciling work and family responsibilities, to migrant women working in an informal economy, therefore perpetuating the existing class and ethnic group inequalities among migrant women (Parella, 2006). Even so, the emergence of women as active protagonists in these migratory flows has made them both primary breadwinners in their own household and relevant contributors to the development of their community of origin through the sending of remittances.

Although female migrants send approximately the same amount of remittances as male migrants at the global level, recent studies highlight that gender influences the remittance process and therefore their impact in receiving countries (Ramírez et al., 2005). In this regard, researchers found that female migrants remit smaller amounts of money than their male counterparts (Semyonov and Gorodzeisky, 2005), but these represent a greater percentage of their salary (Rahman and Fee, 2009). Studies also showed that women remit money to a wider circle of family members (De la Cruz, 1995) and over longer periods of time than men (Orozco, 2006). Furthermore, female migrants seem to exhibit deeper commitment than male migrants to delivering economic support to the relatives they leave behind (Ribas-Mateos, 2004). Females and males also have different preferences when implementing the remittances. Women send money for family food, health and education, and female-headed households have greater expenditure related to overall family welfare, while men remit for investment and asset accumulation and spend significantly more on housing and durable goods (Guzmán et al., 2008).

In addition, remittances contribute to the economic and social empowerment of women, which is in turn transforming relationships between women and men. When females become migrants and providers of remittances, their bargaining power within their household increases and new models of gender relations are discussed and agreed upon, which in turn generates a better environment for other women in the household and community (Levitt and Lamba-Nieves, 2011). On the other hand, male migration often implies that women achieve access to the labour market, increasing their involvement in decision making and participating fully in the community and wider swathes of society, despite the fact that they take on the responsibilities of reproductive work (Ramírez et al., 2005).

Although the above findings show that remittance flows and expenditure patterns can be highly gender specific, there is relatively little research on independently estimating remittances sent by women and men, thus hindering their correct factoring in policy design. There are two major reasons that explain the lack of such studies. First, the statistics on recorded remittance flows are not broken down according to the gender of the remitter. And second, there are few databases containing information on individual remitters, making it difficult to disentangle female and male behaviour (Orozco, 2006). This lack of data is even more severe in specific migratory corridors linking destination and origin countries of migration flows, even though these corridors seem to be some of the most pertinent units for analysis in the study of remittances (Carling, 2010).

In this regard, the Spain–Ecuador corridor is an interesting case study due to the recent feminization of migratory flows (UN, 2005) and the increasing number of remittances recorded (Central Bank of Ecuador, 2011). This phenomenon has led to a growing body of scientific literature covering aspects such as: the role of monetary and social remittances in family asset accumulation strategies and the relationships in Ecuadorian transnational households (Parella and Cavalcanti, 2006; Oso, 2011); time patterns of the remitters (Echazarra, 2010); the socio-demographic characteristics (Reher et al., 2009) and labour activities of Ecuadorian migrants (IOE, 2007); as well as the reason for their migration to Spain (Bertoli et al., 2011). However, to the best of our knowledge, there are only a few studies focused on estimating remittance flows from Spain (IOE, 2001; Moré et al., 2008), of which only Moré et al. offered results disaggregated by gender, but limited to 2006.

Within this last strand of literature, this chapter aims to design and develop a Bayesian network for estimating remittance flows sent by female and male migrants in the Spain–Ecuador corridor during the 2000–10 period. In this way, we contribute to the existing studies in at least two ways. First, our Bayesian network comprises not only the key determinants of remittance flows, but also the relationships among them, capturing the gender-specific aspects. And second, the joint use of simulation and fuzzy inference techniques to solve the network addresses the problem of insufficient or disaggregated information. This point allows us to yield results that are broken down by gender, as well as related to specific migratory corridors, and over longer periods of time than previous works.

The remainder of the chapter is organized as follows. The following section develops the Bayesian network for remittance flows. The third section presents a brief description of the methodology applied. The data and results derived from analysing the corridor selected are shown in the fourth section. The final section offers a review of the main conclusions.

THE BAYESIAN NETWORK FOR REMITTANCES

Bayesian networks (Pearl, 2009) are probabilistic graphical models where the nodes depict variables and the arrows denote causal relationships among them. These graphical models are considered an efficient and intuitive framework for understanding complex real systems under uncertainties such as the migrants' remittance process (Griffiths et al., 2008). Figure 17.1 shows the corresponding Bayesian network model for

Remittances in the Spain–Ecuador corridor 379

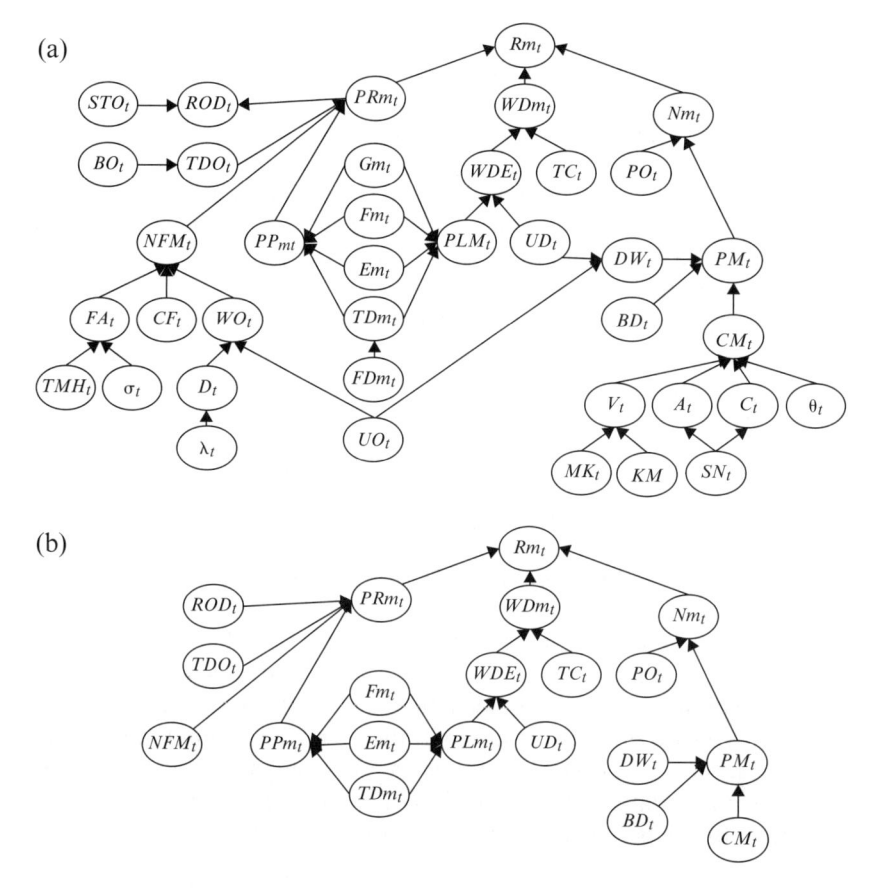

Source: Authors' elaboration.

Figure 17.1 Bayesian network for remittance flows and gender: complete (a) and simplified (b) models

estimating remittance flows between two countries, both the complete and the simplified models discussed in the empirical section. Variables and causal relationships were obtained from the vast body of empirical literature about the determinants of remittance flows. These determinants were considered from both microeconomic and macroeconomic perspectives as in previous research done by, for example, Adams (2009). Causal relationships among those variables always implied a real dependence relationship (DR), which can formally be positive or negative. In the former case, an increase in variable A (cause) implies another increase in variable B; while in the latter case, an increase in A supposes a decrease in B.

According to García-Alonso et al. (2012), the remittance flows received in a given country can be calculated by:

$$Rm_t = f(PRm_t, WDm_t, Nm_t) = PRm_t \times WDm_t \times Nm_t, \quad (17.1)$$

where Rm_t is the amount of money received in the migrant's home country in year t; PRm_t is the corresponding propensity to remit wages; WDm_t is the wage of the migrant in the host country and, finally, Nm_t is the stock of migrants in the host country.

The propensity to remit wages PRm_t is defined as the percentage of the migrant's wage that is sent back home (Orozco, 2006). This variable can be obtained by a fuzzy relationship u (17.2) of the migrant's remitting profile PPm_t, the migrant's family monetary needs NFM_t, the cost of sending money TDO_t, and the interest rate differential between home and host country ROD_t. The PRm_t is influenced positively by PPm_t and NFM_t as well as by ROD_t and negatively by TDO_t:

$$PRm_t = u(PPm_t, NFM_t, TDO_t, ROD_t). \quad (17.2)$$

The migrant's remitting profile PPm_t is given by another fuzzy relationship u (17.3) that relates four variables (Adams, 2009): gender, Gm_t; age, Em_t; educational level, Fm_t; and length of stay in the host country, TDm_t. Thus, in the case of a female migrant, the older she is (Em_t), the greater her educational level (Fm_t), and the shorter her length of stay (TDm_t), the greater her migrant's remitting profile (PPm_t). In turn, TDm_t is influenced positively by the presence of the migrant's family in the host country, FD_t (17.4):

$$PPm_t = u(Gm_t, Em_t, Fm_t, TDm_t) \quad (17.3)$$

$$TDm_t = u(FD_t). \quad (17.4)$$

Family monetary needs, NFM_t (Osili, 2007) are estimated (17.5) by comparing the cost of purchasing basic goods and services CF_t (INEC, 2011) and their incomes, given by the wages (WO_t) of the family members (FA_t) in the home country. Wages (WO_t) are negatively conditioned (17.6) by the level of unemployment in the home country (UO_t). Natural disasters (D_t) also influence the family income due to the loss of wages (Yang and Choi, 2007). The magnitude of D_t is approximated by the number of people affected (λ_t) (17.7). Finally, FA_t is calculated (17.8) using the number of people living at home (TMH_t) and their economic dependency ratio (σ_t) (Hoddinot, 1994):

$$NFM_t = f(CF_t, WO_t, FA_t) = CF_t - (WO_t \times FA_t) \qquad (17.5)$$

$$WO_t = u(OU_t, D_t) \qquad (17.6)$$

$$D_t = u(\lambda_t) \qquad (17.7)$$

$$FA_t = f(TMH_t, \sigma_t) = TMH_t \times (1 - \sigma_t). \qquad (17.8)$$

The transaction costs (TDO_t) (Freund and Spatafora, 2008) comprise the exchange rate, courier and bank fees (17.9); in this case the smaller the size of the banking system (BO_t) in the home country, the greater the TDO_t.

$$TDO_t = u(BO_t). \qquad (17.9)$$

The interest rate differential between the home and the host countries (ROD_t) (Amuedo-Dorantes and Pozo, 2010) positively affects the propensity to remit (PRm_t). High interest rates in the home country increase remittance flows (17.10), but too high an interest rate at home tends to reduce these flows because it is a sign of political or economic instability (STO_t) (Aydas et al., 2005):

$$RDO_t = u(STO_t). \qquad (17.10)$$

The wage of migrants in the host country (WDm_t) (Osili, 2007) is the second variable that determines remittance flows (Rm_t). The countries involved may use different currencies, so WDm_t is the multiplication of the migrant's wage in the host country (WDE_t), and the exchange rate (TC_t) (17.11). In turn, WDE_t is determined (17.12) by the migrant's labour profile (PLm_t) (Chiswick et al., 1997) and the unemployment rate in the host country (UD_t) (Bratsberg et al., 2006):

$$WDm_t = f(WDE_t, TC_t) = WDE_t \times TC_t \qquad (17.11)$$

$$WEm_t = u(PLm_t, UD_t). \qquad (17.12)$$

The migrant's labour profile (PLm_t) is determined by the same four variables as the migrant's remitting profile (17.13). Thus, the greater the age, educational level and length of stay of a female migrant, the greater her labour profile will be:

$$PLm_t = u(Gm_t, Em_t, Fm_t, TDm_t). \qquad (17.13)$$

Finally, the stock of migrants in the host country (Nm_t) is the third and last variable that influences the remittance flows (Rm_t). This can be calculated (17.14) as the product of the population in the home country (PO_t) and the propensity of this population to migrate (PM_t) (García-Alonso et al., 2012):

$$Nm_t = f(PO_t, PM_t) = PO_t \times PM_t \qquad (17.14)$$

$$PM_t = u(BD_t, DW_t, CM_t), \qquad (17.15)$$

where BD_t is the social benefits in the host country (17.15), such as subsidies or free education and health (Borjas, 2000), DW_t is the differential on wages between the host and home country (Harris and Todaro, 1970), and CM_t is the cost of migration (Clark et al., 2004). Both BD_t and DW_t have a positive effect on the propensity to migrate while CM_t, affects it negatively.

$$DW_t = u(UO_t, UD_t) \qquad (17.16)$$

$$CM_t = f(V_t, A_t, C_t, \theta_t) = V_t + A_t + (C_t \times \theta_t) \qquad (17.17)$$

$$V_t = u(KM, Mk_t) \qquad (17.18)$$

$$A_t = u(SN_t) \qquad (17.19)$$

$$C_t = u(SN_t). \qquad (17.20)$$

DW_t depends on (17.16) the unemployment rates in the home (OU_t) and the host (UD_t) countries and CM_t depends on (17.17) several costs linked to the migration process, such as: travel costs (V_t), the administrative costs of acquiring legal status in the host country (A_t) and living expenses (C_t) during the time span θ_t. The time span θ_t goes from the date of arrival to the date of finding a first job. Finally, V_t increases (17.18) with the distance (KM) between the host and home countries as well as with market factors (MK_t) such as fuel prices, seasonal sales and so on, while A_t and C_t decrease (17.19 and 17.20) due to the existence of migrant social networks (SN_t) in the host country (Ziesemer, 2009).

EXPERT KNOWLEDGE IN MONTE CARLO SIMULATION AND FUZZY LOGIC

Expert knowledge is widely used to structure and parameterize system models (Ford and Sterman, 1998). In the model described above, the lack of data makes it necessary to employ expert knowledge for: (i) the selection of an appropriate statistical distribution (StD) for the variables (nodes) in the Bayesian network; and (ii) the definition of the dependence relationship (DR) between them (*f* and *u* functions). The behaviour of random variables (nodes) depends on their corresponding StD (García-Alonso et al., 2012). Where there is not enough raw data, the expert-based selection (Law, 2008) of the StD is crucial to determine the outputs expected from the simulation process (Kuhl et al., 2008). On the other hand, two types of DR have been used in our model: algebra-based DR, noted by *f*, and expert-based DR – fuzzy functions based on fuzzy logic – identified by *u*. In the latter type, the relationship is defined by a set of causal rules with a standard *IF... and... THEN* semantic structure, because the lack of data makes it difficult to define their functional forms.

Expert-based DRs (fuzzy functions *u*) are evaluated by a fuzzy inference engine (García-Alonso et al., 2012). This engine 'fuzzifies' numeric variable values (inputs, left-hand side of the *IF... and... THEN* rule) by translating them into linguistic labels, called a membership function (MF) or a fuzzy set. Once input MF_i are identified ($i = 1, 2, \ldots, m$; where *m* is the number of inputs for the corresponding *u* function), their combination identifies the MF_o for the output (17.21) which is finally 'defuzzified' and translated to a numerical value (output, right-hand side of the *IF... and... THEN* rule) using the product-sum-gravity with a superposition method (Cox, 2005):

$$MF_o = round\left[\left(\sum_{i=1}^{m} w_i MF_i / \sum_{i=1}^{m} w_i\right) + Q + D\right]. \quad (17.21)$$

Additional parameters related to the input variables must be established by experts to make this process automatic. So, for each variable in the model (inputs and outputs in all the *u* functions), experts have to select: (i) its feasible value range; (ii) its variation throughout the time span (increasing, decreasing, constant, following a specific tendency, and so on); (iii) its orientation (positive: the greater the input value, the greater the output value or, conversely, negative: the greater the input value, the lower the output value) – its type (*Q*) moves MF_o to the right/left, increasing/decreasing the standard effect of MF_i in (17.21), its intensity (*D*) showing nuances in rule fulfilment (*D* moves the resulting MF_o at random when experts are not sure about its value); and, finally, (iv) its weight (w_i) on the output.

A Monte Carlo simulation engine calculates the input values using their StD and evaluates the algebra-based DR (*f*). Moreover, the fuzzy inference engine, which is hybridized within the Monte Carlo engine, evaluates

u functions. This methodological approach allows us to estimate the final value of the corresponding outputs in complex and uncertain models.

THE SPAIN–ECUADOR CORRIDOR: A GENDER APPROACH

The Case under Study

This research focuses on the Spain–Ecuador remittance flows during the 2000–10 period. During that decade, Ecuador received increasing remittance flows from Spain, reaching a maximum of US$1.28 billion in 2006–07. However, by 2010 remittances had declined to about US$945 million (Central Bank of Ecuador, 2011) due to the global economic crisis and the resulting loss of jobs for those who had migrated seeking a better standard of living.

Nearly two out of 12 million Ecuadorian inhabitants migrated in the last decade (INEC, 2011), of whom 50 per cent were women in 2000–05 (UN, 2005), fleeing from the poverty caused by the 1998–99 economic downturns and the dollarization process that tried, unsuccessfully, to resolve it (Vos, 2002). Spain became their foremost destination as they were drawn by both the easier entry conditions compared to the US, and the high number of low-skill jobs on offer for non-native workers stemming from the Spanish economic boom in the early 2000s (Bertoli et al., 2011).

However, at the beginning of 2008, prosperity began to fade and Spain fell into recession towards the end of that year. As a result, migrants lost their jobs in stagnating and contracting sectors such as construction, manufacturing, domestic care and agriculture, on which the previous economic growth was based (Papademetriou et al., 2010). Despite the rising rates of unemployment and the return programs of the Spanish and Ecuadorian governments, many migrants still remain in Spain, relying on the social benefits provided by the public welfare system and 'pro-immigrant' civil society initiatives (Boccagni and Lagomarsino, 2011). This fact is confirmed by the Spanish Census that set the Ecuadorian migrant stock at 480,626 people in 2011 (INE, 2012), making them the third-largest immigrant group after Romanians and Moroccans.

The Ecuadorian community in Spain comprises young people, 80 per cent aged between 18 and 40, and low–medium-skilled people, 50 per cent of whom have primary education and 30 per cent secondary (Reher et al., 2009). Their wages are about 30 per cent lower than those of native workers with similar jobs (Izquierdo et al., 2009). Male migrants are mainly concentrated in construction, services and agriculture, while

Table 17.1 *Dependence relationships in the Bayesian network: simplified model*

Equation	Equation number
$Rm_t = PRm_t \times WDm_t \times Nm_t$	(17.1)
$PRm_t = u(PPm_t, NFM_t, TDO_t, ROD_t)$	(17.2)
$PRm_t = u(Gm_t, Em_t, Fm_t, TDm_t)$	(17.3)
$WDm_t = WDE_t \times TC_t$	(17.11)
$WDE_t = u(PLm_t, UD_t)$	(17.12)
$PLm_t = u(Gm_t, Em_t, Fm_t, TDm_t)$	(17.13)
$Nm_t = PO_t \times PM_t$	(17.14)
$PM_t = u(BD_t, DW_t, CM_t)$	(17.15)

Source: Authors' elaboration.

females are employed in health and care services, especially domestic service, small businesses, catering and hotels. The migrants remit about 23 per cent of their wages, but females send a higher percentage, despite the fact that their wages are about 30 per cent lower than those of migrant males (Moré et al., 2008).

Data

A simplified Bayesian network based on the theoretical model described above was used to analyse remittance flows from Spain to Ecuador in the 2000–2010 period (Figure 17.1b). To simplify the calculations, the model was reduced by removing some low-level DR, as shown in Table 17.1.

Table 17.2 summarizes the input variables for the selected DR. Their *variation* indicates the evolution of the variables throughout the time span and their StD show their feasible value ranges. The selection of the StD and the range for each input variable are based on secondary data and expert knowledge. Gender differences are taken into account through different StD.

Table 17.3 shows the StD for output variables in the Bayesian network. This is only used by a Monte Carlo engine to calculate the output value when the fuzzy rules are not instantiated. Our instantiation probability is 0.98, which means that only 2 per cent of the simulations are solved randomly. Both type (Q) and intensity (D) are neutral, which means that there is no distortion in the inference process ($Q = 0$ and $D = 0$).

The relative importance/weight of each input (w_i) in its corresponding output is shown in Table 17.4. Their values are determined by the Monte Carlo engine according to their StD. The input *orientation* indicates the

Table 17.2 Expert-based structure of input variables in the Bayesian network

Variable[a] (unit)	Variation[b]	StD[c] Women	StD[c] Men	Source
Fm_t (scale)	Increasing	U [45, 60]	U [40, 50]	IOE (2007)
Em_t (scale)	Increasing	T [22, 28, 35]	T [22, 28, 35]	Reher et al. (2009)
TDm_t (years)	Increasing	U [0, 10]	U [0, 10]	Reher et al. (2009)
NFM_t (percentage)	Decreasing	U [5, 50]	U [5, 50]	INEC (2011)
TDO_t (percentage)	Fluctuating	T [2, 6, 9]	T [2, 6, 9]	Remesas.org (2011)
ROD_t (percentage)	Increasing	U [1, 5]	U [1, 5]	Bank of Spain (2011) and Central Bank of Ecuador (2011)
UD_t (percentage)	Increasing	U [13, 32]	U [8, 40]	INE (2012)
TC_t (€/US$)	Increasing	U [0.87, 1.55]	U [0.87, 1.55]	Bank of Spain (2011)
DW_t (times)	Decreasing	U [3.70, 4.90]	U [3.70, 4.90]	World Bank (2011)
BD_t (€/person)	Increasing	U [1,800, 3,600]	U [1,800, 3,600]	OECD (2011)
CM_t (US$/person)	Decreasing	U [1,500, 5,000]	U [1,500, 5,000]	Bertoli et al. (2011)
PO_t (inhabitants)	Increasing	U [3.65, 4.29]	U [3.71, 4.29]	INEC (2011)

Notes:
[a] t is the year analysed.
[b] Variation throughout the time span.
[c] Statistical distributions: U – uniform; T – triangular.

type of relation between it and its corresponding output. Positive orientation means that the greater the input value, the greater the output value; whereas a negative influence indicates that the greater the input value, the lower the output value.

In DR2 (see 17.2), the migrant-remitting profile PPm_t is what most affects (0.55) migrant propensity to remit PRm_t, followed by the families' monetary needs NFM_t (0.3). It indicates that, although altruistic motivation works (Lucas and Stark, 1985), it is modulated by migrant characteristics. Regarding DR12 (see 17.12), the migrant's labour profile PLm_t (0.4) is less relevant than unemployment UD_t (0.6) for determining wages in the host country WDE_t followed by the families' monetary needs

Table 17.3 Characteristics of dependence relationships: outputs and structure

Variable[a]	Unit	Probability	StD[b] Women	StD[b] Men
PPm_t	Scale	0.98	U [10, 90]	U [10, 90]
PRm_t	Percentage	0.98	U [10, 40]	U [10, 20]
PLm_t	Scale	0.98	U [10, 90]	U [10, 90]
WDE_t	€ per person	0.98	U [5,000, 10,000]	U [9,000, 12,000]
PM_t	Percentage	0.98	U [1, 5]	U [1, 5]

Notes:
[a] t is the year analysed.
[b] Statistical distributions: U – uniform, T – triangular.

Source: Authors' elaboration.

Table 17.4 Characteristics of dependence relationships: inputs and structure

Variable[a]	DR	Weight	Orientation
NFM_t	2	T[0.29, 0.30, 0.31]	Positive
PPm_t	2	T[0.54, 0.55, 0.56]	Positive
ROD_t	2	T[0.04, 0.05, 0.06]	Positive
TDO_t	2	T[0.09, 0.10, 0.11]	Negative
Em_t	3	T[0.09, 0.10, 0.11]	Positive
Fm_t	3	T[0.09, 0.10, 0.11]	Positive
TDm_t	3	T[0.79, 0.80, 0.81]	Negative
PLm_t	12	T[0.39, 0.40, 0.41]	Positive
UD_t	12	T[0.59, 0.60, 0.61]	Negative
Em_t	13	T[0.09, 0.10, 0.11]	Positive
Fm_t	13	T[0.29, 0.30, 0.31]	Positive
TDm_t	13	T[0.59, 0.60, 0.61]	Positive
BD_t	15	T[0.04, 0.05, 0.06]	Positive
DW_t	15	T[0.14, 0.15, 0.16]	Positive
CM_t	15	T[0.79, 0.80, 0.81]	Negative

Note: [a] An output variable of one DR can be the input variable in another DR; t is the year analysed.

Source: Authors' elaboration.

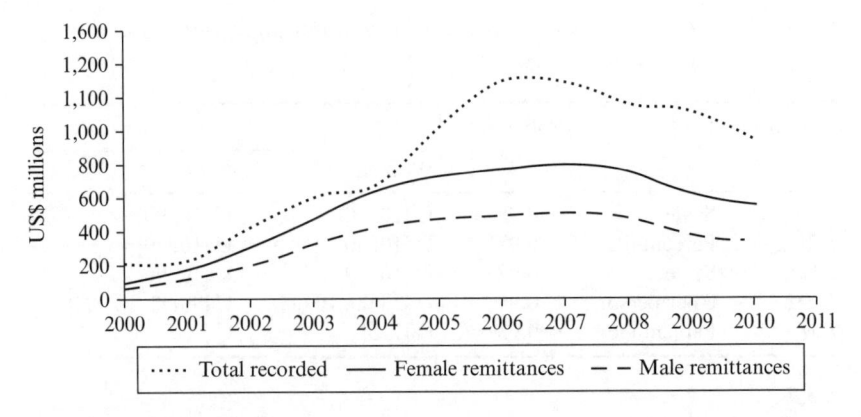

Figure 17.2 Remittance flows Rm$_t$ *in Spain–Ecuador corridor: estimated values (calculated by gender) versus real values (total recorded)*

NFM_t (0.3). The above statement indicates that migrants are employed in jobs with low levels of protection, as firms tend to set wages according to the unemployment rate (Sanromá and Ramos, 2005). Finally, in DR15 (see 17.15), high migration costs CM_t (0.8) reveal that poverty constrains international migration.

Finally, the number of simulations chosen was 5,000 (five batches of 1,000 simulations each). Results obtained in each replication were statistically compared to the real data available.

Results

Figure 17.2 shows the estimated remittance flows Rm_t (see 17.1) sent by Ecuadorian female and male migrants in Spain during the 2000–10 period. Final Rm_t, calculated by the Monte Carlo simulation engine and fuzzy inference, were compared to the real values recorded by the Central Bank of Ecuador (2011).

Our model adjusts the tendency of the recorded remittances. It tends to overestimate the total flows received in Ecuador during the 'dollarization period', when remittances increased from US$200 million in 2000 to almost US$1300 million in 2006, while it underestimates the 'crisis period' flows, from 2007 until the end. This behaviour is due to the difficulty in fine-tuning parameters for all the StD of model variables. The amount of remittances sent by women is higher than that sent by men;

to be more specific, 59.3 per cent of the remittances received in Ecuador during 2006 were sent by women. This result is quite similar to the 60.3 per cent obtained by Moré et al. (2008), which is the only study that has been carried out on remittances, gender and nationality in Spain.

Based on these facts: (i) the designed Bayesian network adjusted the tendency of remittance real values, thus correctly reflecting the evolution of the variables selected throughout the time span; and (ii) the percentage of remittances sent by women is similar to that mentioned in the study, so we assume that the model reproduced the behaviour of remittance flows sent by female and male migrants during the period under study.

The evolution throughout the time span of WDE_t, PRm_t, UD_t and Nm_t explains the estimated differences between women's and men's remittances. Taking into account that: (i) the percentage of women and men in the migrant stock Nm_t was balanced (Figure 17.3, Nm_t); (ii) females' wages WDE_t were lower than those of males (Figure 17.3, WDE_t); and (iii) during the crisis period, wages of females fell less than those of males because the female unemployment rate UD_t was lower (Figure 17.3, UD_t), Ecuadorian women remitted a higher percentage of their wages than men. This rose from about 20 per cent in 2000 to 30 per cent at the end of 2010, while men's propensity to remit varied from 10 to 15 per cent in the same period.

CONCLUSIONS

The research presented above points out that gendered estimation of remittance flows is possible and, at the same time, necessary to correctly factor them into the design of policies and programmes aimed at leveraging their potential benefits for receiving communities and for women themselves. This task is especially relevant during times of crisis, when the decline in remittances can threaten the sustainability of the social and economic transformations reached in terms of gender equality.

With this in mind, we presented an alternative approach that allows the estimating of remittances sent by female and male migrants. Our approach improves on existing studies about remittances in the Spain–Ecuador corridor in at least two ways. First, the Bayesian network offers a conceptual model that comprises both the key determinants of remittances and the relationships among them, capturing gender specific aspects. Second, the joint use of artificial intelligence techniques deals with the problem of insufficient and disaggregated data in migratory corridors, allowing us to yield results that are not just broken down according to gender, but also cover longer periods of time than previous studies.

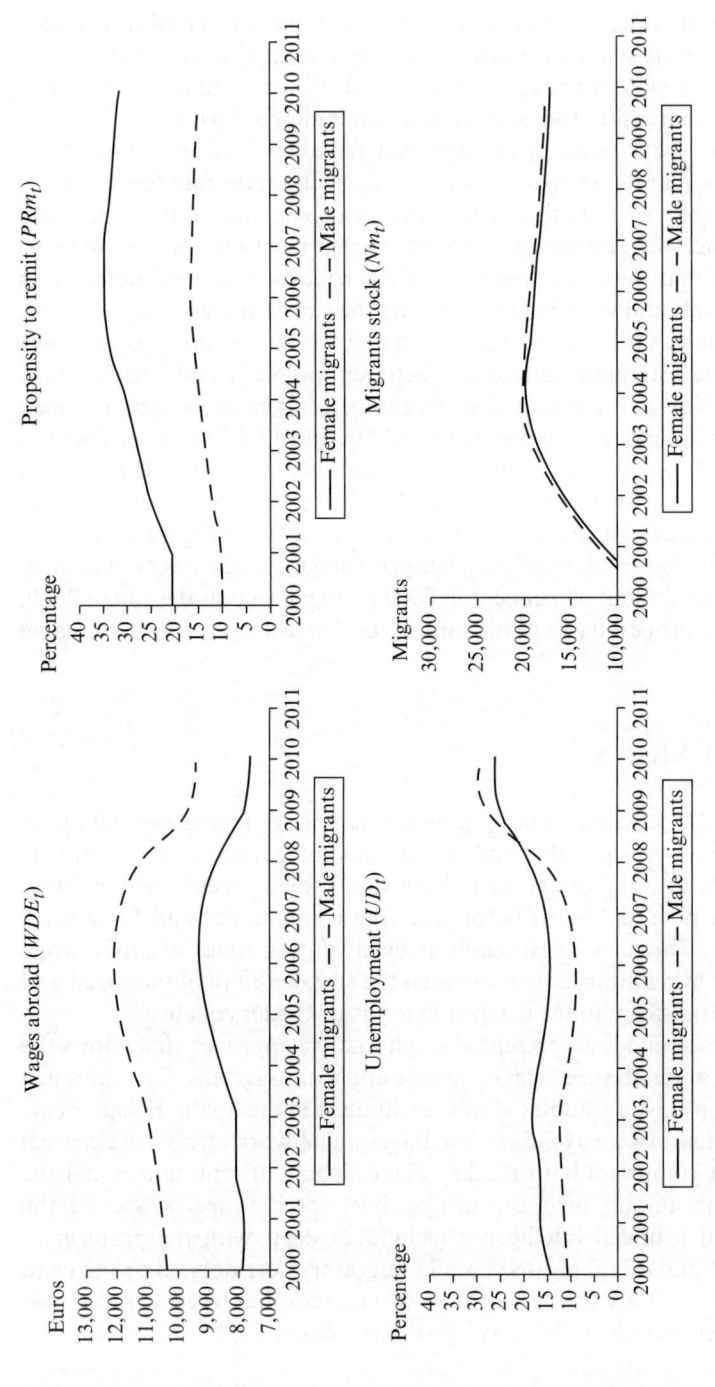

Figure 17.3 Estimated values of some relevant variables: WDE_t, PRm_t, UD_t *and* Nm_t

Source: Authors' elaboration.

In the case of the Spain–Ecuador corridor during the 2000–10 period, the results show that Ecuadorian women were more likely to send money than men. Men's propensity varied from 10 to 15 per cent throughout the time span, while women's propensity to remit rose from about 20 per cent in 2000 to 30 per cent at the end of the period. These results underlined the relevant contribution of Ecuadorian females in supporting their families back home, although the economic crisis has struck them severely.

Thus, Ecuadorian women as well as other female migrants are a driving force for economic recovery and progress in the developing world, so they should be fully and significantly included in economic and labour development strategies. Female migrants must be considered not simply as economic beings, but as human beings with full rights, so that they are protected from abuses and discrimination by laws and governmental initiatives that contribute to their economic and social empowerment on both sides of the migratory corridor.

REFERENCES

Adams R.H. (2009), 'The determinants of international remittances in developing countries', *World Development*, **37** (1), 93–103.
Adams, R. and A. Cuecuecha (2010), 'Remittances, household expenditure and investment in Guatemala', *World Development*, **38** (11), 1626–41.
Amuedo-Dorantes, Catalina (2006), 'Remittances and their microeconomic impact: evidence from Latin America', in Jeffrey F. Hollifield, Pia M. Orrenius and Thomas Osang (eds), *Migration, Trade and Development*, Dallas, Tx: Federal Reserve Bank of Dallas, pp. 187–97.
Amuedo-Dorantes, C. and S. Pozo (2010), 'Remittances and their response to portfolio variables', Discussion Paper Series 1021, Centre for Research and Analysis of Migration (CReAM), Department of Economics, University College London.
Aydas, O., K. Metin-Ozcan and B. Neyapti (2005), 'Determinants of workers' remittances: the case of Turkey', *Emerging Markets Finance and Trade*, **41** (3), 53–69.
Bank of Spain (2011), available at: http://www.bde.es/webbde/es/estadis/tipos/tipos.html (accessed May 2011).
Bertoli, S., J. Fernandez-Huertas Moraga and F. Ortega (2011), 'Immigration policies and the Ecuadorian exodus', *World Bank Economic Review*, **25** (1), 57–76.
Boccagni, P. and F. Lagomarsino (2011), 'Migration and the global crisis: new prospects for return? The case of Ecuadorians in Europe', *Bulletin of Latin American Research*, **30** (3), 282–97.
Borjas, G.J. (2000), 'Foreign-born teaching assistants and the academic performance of undergraduates', *American Economic Review*, **90** (2), 355–9.
Bratsberg, B., E. Barth and O. Raaum (2006), 'Local unemployment and the relative wages of immigrants: evidence from the current population surveys', *Review of Economics and Statistics*, **88** (2), 243–63.
Calero, C., A.S. Bedi and R. Sparrow (2009), 'Remittances, liquidity constraints and human capital investments in Ecuador', *World Development*, **37** (6), 1143–54.
Carling, J. (2010), 'Migration corridors: conceptual and methodological issues', Memo for the NORFACE-funded THEMIS Project 1, Peace Research Institute, Oslo.

Central Bank of Ecuador (2011), 'Estadísticas sobre remesas', available at: http://www.bce. fin.ec/frame.php?CNT=ARB0000985 (accessed May 2011).
Chami, R., A. Barajas, T. Cosimano, C. Fullenkamp, M. Gapen and P. Montiel (2008), 'Macroeconomic consequences of remittances', International Monetary Fund Occasional Paper 259, Washington, DC.
Chiswick, B., Y. Cohen and T. Zach (1997), 'The labor market status of immigrants: effects of unemployment rate at arrival and duration of residence', *Industrial and Labor Relations Review*, **50** (2), 289–303.
Clark, X., T.J. Hatton and J.G. Williamson (2004), 'What explains emigration out of Latin America?', *World Development*, **32** (11), 1871–90.
Cox, Earl (2005), *Fuzzy Modeling and Genetic Algorithms for Data-Mining and Exploration*, San Francisco, CA: Elsevier.
De La Cruz, B.E. (1995), 'The socioeconomic dimensions of remittances: case studies of five Mexican families', *The Berkeley McNair Journal*, **3**, 1–10.
Echazarra, A. (2010), 'Accounting for the time pattern of remittances in the Spanish context', FUNCAS Working Paper 553, Fundación de las Cajas de Ahorros, Madrid.
Ford, D.N. and J.D. Sterman (1998), 'Expert knowledge elicitation to improve formal and mental models', *System Dynamics Review*, **14** (4), 309–40.
Freund, C. and N. Spatafora (2008), 'Remittances: transaction costs, determinants, and informal flows', *Journal of Development Economics*, **86** (2), 356–66.
García-Alonso, C.R., E. Arenas-Arroyo and G.M. Perez-Alcalá (2012), 'A macro-economic model to forecast remittances based on Monte-Carlo simulation and artificial intelligence', *Expert Systems with Applications*, **39** (9), 7929–37.
Giannelli, G.C. and L. Mangiavacchi (2010), 'Children's schooling and parental migration: empirical evidence on the "left-behind" generation in Albania', *Labour*, **24** (1), 76–92.
Griffiths, Thomas L., Charles Kemp and Joshua B. Tenenbaum (2008), 'Bayesian models of cognition', in Ron Sun (ed.), *The Cambridge Handbook of Computational Cognitive Modeling*, Cambridge: Cambridge University Press, pp. 59–100.
Guzmán, Juan C., Andrew R. Morrison and Mirja Sjöblom (2008), 'The impact of remittances and gender on household expenditure patterns: evidence from Ghana', in Morrison, Maurice Schiff and Sjöblom (eds), *The International Migration of Women*, Basingstoke, UK and New York: World Bank and Palgrave Macmillan, pp. 125–52.
Harris, J. and M.P. Todaro (1970), 'Migration, unemployment and development: a two-sector analysis', *American Economic Review*, **60** (1), 126–42.
Hoddinott, J. (1994), 'A model of migration and remittances applied to Western Kenya', *Oxford Economic Papers*, **46**, 459–76.
ILO (2010), 'International labour migration: a rights-based approach', International Labour Organization, Geneva, available at: http://www.ilo.org/global/publications/books/ WCMS_125361/lang--es/index.htm (accessed February 2011).
INE (2012), 'Explotación Estadística del Padrón Municipal de Habitantes 2011', National Statistics Institute, Madrid, available at: http://www.ine.es/inebmenu/mnu_cifraspob.htm (accessed September 2012).
INEC (2011), 'Statistical data', National Institute of Statistics and Censuses, Ecuador, available at: http://www.inec.gob.ec/home/ (accessed May 2011).
IOE (2001), 'Las remesas de los inmigrantes ecuatorianos. Funcionamiento y características de las agencias de envío de dinero', Plan Migración, Comunicación y Desarrollo Ecuador-España, Informe 1.
IOE (2007), 'La inmigración ecuatoriana en España: una visión a través de las fuentes estadísticas', available at: http://www.colectivoioe.org/index.php/publicaciones_colaboraciones/show/id/40 (accessed May 2011).
Izquierdo, M., A. Lacuesta and R. Vegas (2009), 'Assimilation of immigrants in Spain: a longitudinal analysis', *Labour Economics*, **16** (6), 669–78.
Kuhl, Michael E., Emily K. Lada, Natalie M. Steiger, Mary Ann Wagner and James R. Wilson (2008), 'Introduction to modeling and generating probabilistic input processes for simulation', in Scott J. Mason, Raymond R. Hill, Lars Mönch, Olivier Rose, Thomas

Jefferson and John W. Fowler (eds), *Proceedings of the 2008 Winter Simulation Conference*, Piscataway, NJ: Institute of Electrical and Electronics Engineers Inc, pp. 48–61.
Law, Averill M. (2008), 'How to build valid and credible simulation models', in Scott J. Mason, Raymond R. Hill, Lars Mönch, Olivier Rose, Thomas Jefferson and John W. Fowler (eds), *Proceedings of the 2008 Winter Simulation Conference*, Piscataway, NJ: Institute of Electrical and Electronics Engineers Inc, pp. 39–47.
Levitt, P. and D. Lamba-Nieves (2011), 'Social remittances revisited', *Journal of Ethnic and Migration Studies*, **37** (1), 1–22.
Lucas, R. and O. Stark (1985), 'Motivations to remit evidence from Botswana', *Journal of Political Economy*, **93** (5), 901–18.
Moré, I., A. Echarraza, B. Halloufi and R. Petru (2008), 'Cuantificación de las remesas enviadas por mujeres desde España', available at: http://www.remesas.org/files/RemesasMujeresBrief.pdf (accessed January 2011).
OECD (2011), 'Social expenditure dataset', Organisation for Economic Co-operation and Development. Paris, available at: http//stats.oecd.org/Index.aspx (accessed May 2011).
Orozco, M. (2002), 'Globalization and migration: the impact of family remittances in Latin America', *Latin American Politics and Society*, **44** (2), 41–66.
Orozco, M. (2006), 'Gender remittances: preliminary notes about senders and recipients in Latin America and the Caribbean', *Proceedings of the 50th session of the United Nations Commission on the Status of Women, High-level Panel on the Gender Dimensions of International Migration*, New York: UN.
Osili, U.O. (2007), 'Remittances and savings from international migration: theory and evidence using a matched sample', *Journal of Development Economics*, **83** (2), 446–65.
Oso, Laura (2011), 'Plata y/o amor: Remesas, acumulación de activos y movilidad social de las familias de migrantes ecuatorianos', in Jorge Ginieniewicz (ed.), *La migración latinoamericana a España: una mirada desde el modelo de acumulación de activos*, Quito: FLACSO, pp. 129–51.
Papademetriou, Demetrios G., Madeleine Sumption and Aaron Terrazas (2010), *Migration and Immigrants Two Years after the Financial Collapse: Where Do We Stand?*, Washington, DC: Migration Policy Institute.
Parella, S. (2006), 'Some reflections on female migration and the internationalisation of social reproduction', *Quaderns de la Mediterrània*, **7**, 147–52.
Parella, S. and L. Cavalcanti (2006), 'Una aproximación cualitativa a las remesas de los inmigrantes peruanos y ecuatorianos en España y a su impacto en los hogares transnacionales', *Revista Española de Investigaciones Sociológicas*, **116** (6), 241–57.
Pearl, J. (2009), *Causality: Models, Reasoning and Inferences*, New York: Cambridge University Press.
Rahman, M.M. and L.K. Fee (2009), 'Gender and the remittance process: Indonesian domestic workers in Hong Kong, Singapore and Malaysia', *Asian Population Studies*, **5** (2), 103–25.
Ramírez, C., M. García Domínguez and J. Míguez Morais (2005), 'Crossing borders: gender, remittances and development', United Nations International Research and Training Institute for the Advancement of Women (UN-INSTRAW) Working Paper, New York.
Reher, D., M. Requena and L. Rosero-Bixby (2009), 'Ecuatorianos en España', in David-Sven Reher and Miguel Requena (eds), *Las múltiples caras de la inmigración en España*, Madrid: Alianza Editorial, pp. 117–52.
Remesas.org (2011), available at: http//www.remesas.org/precioremesas.html (accessed May 2011).
Ribas-Mateos, Natalia (2004), 'Barrios y familias tangerinas dependientes de remesas', in Angeles Escrivá and Natalia Ribas (eds), *Migración y Desarrollo. Estudios sobre remesas y otras prácticas transnacionales*, Córdoba: Consejo Superior de Investigaciones Científicas e Instituto de Estudios Sociales de Andalucía, pp. 213–33.
Sanromá, E. and R. Ramos (2005), 'Further evidence on disaggregated wage curves: the case of Spain', *Australian Journal of Labour Economics*, **8** (3), 227–43.
Semyonov, M. and A. Gorodzeisky (2005), 'Labor migration, remittances and household

income: a comparison between Filipino and Filipina overseas workers', *International Migration Review*, **39** (1), 45–68.
Sørensen, N., N. Van Hear and P. Engberg-Pedersen (2002), 'The migration–development nexus: evidence and policy options state-of-the-art overview', *International Migration*, **40** (5), 3–47.
UN (2005), 'Trends in total migrant stock: the 2005 revision', available at: http://www.un.org/esa/population/publications/migration/UN_Migrant_Stock_Documentation_2005.pdf (accessed January 2011).
Vos, Robert (2002), 'Ecuador: economic liberalization, adjustment and poverty, 1988–99', in Vos, Lance Taylor and Ricardo Paes de Barros (eds), *Economic Liberalization, Distribution and Poverty: Latin America in the 1990s*, Cheltenham, UK and Northampton, MA, USA: Edward Elgar, pp. 259–313.
Woodruff, C. and R. Zenteno (2007), 'Migration networks and microenterprises in Mexico', *Journal of Development Economics*, **82** (2), 509–28.
World Bank (2010), *Migrations and Remittances: Factbook 2011*, Washington, DC: World Bank.
World Bank (2011), Data Catalog, available at: http//data.worldbank.org/ (accessed May 2011).
Yang, D. and H. Choi (2007), 'Are remittances insurance? Evidence from rainfall shocks in the Philippines', *World Bank Economic Review*, **21** (2), 219–48.
Zhunio, M.C., S. Vishwasrao and E.P. Chiang (2012), 'The influence of remittances on education and health outcomes: a cross-country study', *Applied Economics*, **44**, 4605–16.
Ziesemer, T. (2009), 'Remittances, lagged dependent variables and migration stocks as determinants of migration from developing countries', UNU-MERIT Working Paper Series 007, New York.

PART VI

GLOBAL CARE CHAINS

18 Care and feminized North–South and South–South migration flows: denial of rights and limited citizenship
María Luisa Setién and Elaine Acosta

INTRODUCTION

Migration has become a prevalent topic in debates on the social organization of care and the progress towards fairer care systems. The so-called 'care crisis' is one of the key factors explaining the increasing numbers of immigrant women carrying out this work in both the northern and southern hemispheres. However, while work in this sector affords job opportunities for many immigrant women, it also evinces a great lacuna of social and labour rights regarding work carried out by individuals who are socially marginalized or undervalued.

The analysis presented in this chapter is part of a wider debate on gender, migration and development. There has been a propensity to neglect gender as a relevant analysis variable in studies on international migration. However, today it is widely accepted that gender is a decisive element in the migratory experience, both in shaping and in reaching the decision to migrate. The decision of when, who, how and where to migrate is conditioned by gender, that is, it crucially depends on the immigrant's roles and responsibilities associated with gender. Of course, other factors such as age and social class must also be taken into account. The inclusion of the gender variable has also helped us to understand that migration today is more often an economic survival strategy for whole families than an exclusively personal project undertaken individually.

Thanks to gender analysis, it has been possible to establish that the drivers and development of feminine migratory flows and the appearance of transnational households headed by women respond to a set of structural factors, which in turn are the cause and result of the problems linked to the development of sending and receiving societies. Changes in the job markets in receiving nations have been pointed out as the most significant factor. More specifically, aspects such as the increase in the number of women working outside their home in these countries; the growing demand in developed nations – and more recently, in developing nations – for women to do the most menial work (domestic service, caring for dependants and sexual services); the transfer of social reproduction tasks resulting from the globalization of production in international business; the impact of structural adjustment policies and programmes on the social situation of women (Oso, 2008), have all been highlighted.

The current care 'crisis' is clearly a determining factor in the boom of feminine migration and also makes evident the connection between this phenomenon and development problems. When we refer to this crisis, we are in fact alluding to a variety of social problems that affect different sectors (education, health, social benefits, employment and so on), taking place at different levels (micro and macro), and involving a heterogeneous group of public and public players (state, markets, family, community and non-profit organizations). Therefore, the crisis refers not only to the conspicuous *deficit* observed in the private care sector due to the shortage of people and support networks that would guarantee that dependent family members are looked after, but also to the public sphere, in which there is a lack of state policy regarding the situation of these groups.

The recent social changes that have caused the increase in demand for care have clearly shown the lack of alternatives to informal care. Families have been compelled to reorganize their strategies in response to this crisis. They have tried out different possibilities and most often decided to externalize care by hiring immigrant women. All things considered, this solution proves partial and insufficient since it means a transnational transfer of paid care from poorer and emerging economies – such as South America, Asia, Africa and Eastern Europe – to the more-developed Western nations.

This contribution is part of a broader research project[1] which aims to explore the rights – and obligations – that working in the care sector implies, with special emphasis on the care provided by immigrant women. A comparative approach will be taken to examine how South–North and South–South migratory flows have recently evolved. The first flow we shall study is immigration to Spain and the second is to Chile. Both countries, Spain and Chile, are notable cases showing a sustained growth in and an increasing participation of women in the labour market, concurrent with an ageing population and significant changes in family structures and dynamics. Notwithstanding the particularities of each case, the higher rates of dependence and of potential demand for care pose similar challenges for Spain and Chile, concerning the social organization of care. This derives from the fact that not only are the numbers of elderly requiring care growing larger but there will also be fewer people able to meet this need. In addition to the incidence of these socio-demographic factors, the segmentation job markets and migration state policies, as well as the insufficient supply of care services provided by institutions, are all contributing to a higher concentration of immigrant women on domestic and care markets. For all these reasons, the care sector has become an employment niche for this group, especially for Latin American women.

With regard to methodological specifications, this study has used 67 in-depth interviews with different actors who play a role in the domain of care (women immigrant carers, employers and dependants) in Spain and Chile. Assessment and perception of how rights are achieved and exercised in the social relationship of care support the hypothesis of a combined – or concatenated – denial of rights in this context, as shown in earlier studies. This denial results in the exercise of limited citizenship in the case of women immigrant care workers as well as dependants who find themselves in a highly precarious situation.

The first aim of this chapter is to examine some of the main issues in the theoretical discussion of care, especially in relation to the problems of exercising rights and citizenship in the context of the feminization of international migrations. Second, we shall explore the interviewees' discourse – particularly that of immigrant women carers – focusing on the different areas in which their rights are expressed: political and legal citizenship rights, labour rights, and the right to self-care and professionalization in care jobs. Finally, we consider some conditions that would possibly expand the exercise of rights in the transnational context of care work.

CARE WORK, RIGHTS AND CITIZENSHIP IN THE CONTEXT OF FEMINIZED INTERNATIONAL MIGRATIONS

The concept of 'care' is relatively new in social sciences and is still the object of much discussion in the discipline. Its emergence can be traced back to the debates on domestic work in Anglo-Saxon countries after the 1970s, due mainly to the attention it received from the feminist movement in social sciences (Letablier, 2007; Aguirre, 2008). The subject gained visibility in feminist discourse and was finally introduced into academic discussions, despite some initial resistance to accepting it as an area of study (Carrasco et al., 2011).

In spite of this early resistance, the concept of care has been widely adopted by the scientific community and has become the subject of many studies, most of which have been carried out in Europe, particularly in the United Kingdom and Scandinavia. Carrasco et al. explain that its higher degree of acceptance in these countries is due to the attention it has always received in the Anglo-Saxon tradition and the interest it arouses among welfare policy specialists, who are rarely suspicious of feminist ideas and unlikely to see eye to eye with studies taking a gender perspective.

The so-called 'care crisis' has been one of the key factors in the feminization of today's migratory flows. This crisis has opened up job opportunities in the fields of domestic service and care, which increasingly have been taken up by immigrant women. The dynamics resulting from this process have given rise to what specialized literature calls the 'care-drain' problem. In this context, a female and flexible workforce (mostly composed of immigrant or indigenous women or Third World African women) replaces unpaid domestic and care work formerly done by women in developed nations (Bettio et al., 2006; Parella, 2007; Martínez Buján, 2010).

The concept of global care chains has come to problematize the issue of replacement as one of the strategies used by women to solve the care crisis. Moreover, it has also been identified as a structural cause of gender inequality, thus becoming an urgent topic of social research since it provides insights into the organizing dynamics of globalization and how the gender dimension operates within them (Pérez Orozco, 2007).

In Spain, studies covering the problems of the feminization of today's migratory flows, their characteristics, causes and effects and so on, are relatively recent – beginning in the mid-1990s – although a considerable amount of research has been done since then. The role these women, especially Latin Americans, have played in compensating for the care deficit is crucial. A recent monographic study directed by Oso and Parella (2012) notes that studies on feminine migration and domestic service in recent years have shifted their emphasis to a more specific focus on care work. Cristina Vega's (2009) work departs from the analysis of the crisis and reorganization of care as the starting point to consider the working conditions of women carers in the different types of care contexts and the increasing presence of foreigners in the sector. Raquel Martínez Buján's (2010, 2011) research centres on the increasing demand for immigrant women carers in Spain in recent years, and demonstrates that it is immigrant women who accept the most precarious jobs in the domestic sector, thus becoming the first link in the chain into this secondary labour market segment.

Based on more recent data and still in a much earlier stage of development, social research in Chile is slowly making progress towards identifying the care deficit problem and how it is being partly solved by importing female immigrant workers. One of the pioneer studies that has connected care with feminine migrations also incorporates contributions considering the concept of global care chains. This project includes joint research that analyses Chile as a destination for female Latin American immigrants.[2]

In their results, the authors, Irma Arriagada and Marcela Moreno (2011), insist on the great difficulties in identifying and visualizing feminine immigration and the care provided by female immigrants in the receiving country. They also underline the point that the immigrant women's participation in work of this type has a great influence on the formation of the so-called 'global care chains', which once again places migration under the forces of globalization. The authors describe the working conditions of domestic workers and how this work is perceived by employers and the workers themselves.

The degree to which research on care and migrations has progressed in Spain and Chile reveals that a comparative approach has rarely been used. This is especially the case in the area of qualitative research. Besides this comparative approach, an intersubjective perspective has also been missing from the studies. This perspective would provide us with the 'sense' and value that each of the players involved in the social relationship of caring grants to this activity. While it is true that knowledge has been gained on migrant women's motivations, projects and migratory experiences, and evidence on their living conditions and work trajectories at their destinations has also been gathered, these issues are not usually studied in relation to other players involved, such as those who receive care or the employers. Likewise, the perspective of rights has been introduced only very recently. This perspective considers not only the migrant women as carers but also the persons requiring care and the family members responsible for managing that care. This chapter aims to offer a comparative approach to care issues from an intersubjective perspective, giving special attention to the issue of rights. We undertake an important line of research that the feminists have studied in depth, that is, women's access to social rights and, also, the notion of social citizenship (Letablier, 2007).

According to Pautassi (2008), the problems posed by caregivers and care issues in general raise issues such as the exercise of rights, reproduction of inequalities and implementation of public policy, in which empirical evidence shows the perpetuation of inequalities related to social responsibility. This is evidenced, in particular, by the difficulties women – mainly immigrants – face when integrating into the labour market and seeking to enjoy equal opportunities, as well as how roles and the responsibility of care work are distributed among the state, the family, and the labour market: who meets the costs and the extent to which these activities are socially valued.

In addition to the problem of social exclusion faced by migrant workers resulting from their limited material resources, their gender responsibilities and racial stereotypes, there is also the gender bias associated with care. This prejudice, based upon the widespread belief that women possess the natural skills to perform these tasks, is reinforced by the devaluation of care. This, in turn, appears to be closely related to the rights of the actors involved in the social relationship of care and the circumstances and conditions under which they exercise their citizenship.

Social research has revealed significant violations, not only of the right to care but also of labour and reconciliation rights of immigrant caregivers. Such violations are closely linked, on the one hand, to the fragile structures that characterize care work, which are similar to those of domestic work. On the other hand, the increased vulnerability of those providing it is intensified among especially vulnerable groups such as immigrant women. In their case, the physical separation from their families, which sometimes lasts longer than expected because of strict immigration policies and poor working conditions, especially if they are live-in domestic workers, poses great difficulties and even a complete inability to reconcile their work and family life.

In practice, there has been clear evidence of what Pérez Orozco (2006) has called a 'concatenated denial of rights' in the social relationship of care. This process is broad and complex. Its breadth derives from the number of actors whose rights are violated, which in this case includes not only the dependent population. Its complexity is related to the mechanisms and conditions that allow – or prevent – access to and exercise of these rights on an equal footing:

> There is no full right to care (e.g., to leave the labour market driven by a desire or need to care) or not to care (e.g., places available in nursery schools). Nor is there a combined right to choose the type of care work, that is, one that combines care work in decent conditions with a certain degree of defamilization. It is, therefore, a concatenated denial of rights. (Ibid., pp. 21–2)

This complexity is also conditioned by the irregular way in which this denial works. Other researchers (Stefoni and Fernández, 2011; Rogero García, 2010) agree that this denial of rights does not apply equally to all social groups or even within the same group. On the contrary, there are different levels of recognition, regulation and exercise that intervene in each individual's specific right of access. Thus the link between the individuals involved in a social relationship of care[3] and the social status of the individual subject of rights – as determined by gender, social class, ethnic group, immigrant status, socioeconomic status, place of residence and level of 'dependency', among others – establishes the possibilities of access, recognition and exercise of rights. In practice, there is evidence that the main constraints are experienced by women and, in particular, by immigrant women and women with disabilities (INSTRAW, 2009; Zavala and Rojas, 2005).

Table 18.1 Rights and duties with regard to care

	Dependent persons	Caregivers	Other citizens
Rights	To be cared for	To care	To care/to be cared for in the future
	To decide the conditions of their care	To decide the extent of their duty of care To decide how to care	To decide how and to what extent they will care/will be cared for
Duties	To make being cared for easy	To care properly	To care (if applicable) To contribute to protection systems

Source: Rogero García (2010, p. 44).

In addition to this inequality, according to Rogero García (2010), the care of dependent people involves not only a number of *rights* but also obligations, or *duties*,[4] from those individuals directly engaged in such an activity, including state and institutional actors (see Table 18.1). They are involved in a *dynamic* relationship and that relationship changes constantly, both in political (rules, services, and so on) and social (distribution of responsibilities within households, public awareness, role of volunteering, and so on) terms. At the same time, these rights and obligations are determined by the social structure, deriving from the individuals' position with regard to care work generally – caregivers, dependants or society – thus determining the way in which citizenship is expressed.

'Citizenship' has generally been defined as a set of practices that define a person as a full member within a society, who acquires rights and duties, depending on the socio-historical context. Glenn (2000) examines the scope of the concept of citizenship within care work. In this context, the concept of citizenship must be understood in terms of the 'public/private' dichotomy, which usually views the private aspect as being not only outside the public sphere but also in opposition to it. As a result, care work in the private sphere is considered to be done outside society and citizenship.

Thus, Glenn underlines the low social status of caregivers and care recipients, which results in the devaluation of caregiving as a 'double devaluation'. Seen in this light, both caregivers and care recipients would be excluded from citizenship status due to their greater dependence on other care providers and the particular environment in which these services are offered, which is generally the domestic sphere.

The way in which the relationship between rights and duties is expressed is the result of social practices that reflect how individuals interpret their relationships and define what is known as 'substantive citizenship':[5]

> To analyse substantive citizenship, it is necessary to go beyond the visible, as crystallized by the State ... It is imperative to resort to inter-individual strategies, to underlying social relations, since it is social practices that define the actual state of citizenship. These vital experiences shape and are a result of both rights and duties to which every citizen is subject, and are expressed in living conditions and in both individual and group discourse. (Rogero García, 2010, p.43)

In line with this premise, this analysis will use 'discourse' and 'practice' to understand the way in which the rights and duties involved in care work have an influence on the exercise of citizenship for immigrant women caregivers. Based on the above, this chapter aims to examine to what extent the individuals involved in the social relationship of care – in our case, dependent people, immigrant women caregivers and employers[6] – perceive the knowledge and application of the rights of the immigrant women who work in this activity. The aim is to establish whether there are differences between the views held by the actors involved, on the one hand, and the different target contexts, on the other. Spain and Chile[7] have been chosen as receiving contexts, since they are representative of the processes that occur in two South–North and South–South migration flows, respectively.

In recent years, Spain and Chile have experienced an intense growth in immigration, although the scope is clearly different in each case (Table 18.2). It is important to note that, in spite of a slight decrease in the last few years, 12 per cent of Spain's total population is foreign compared to only 2 per cent of Chile's. These figures mean that the impact of migration on demographic growth is different in each country. In the case of Spain, it is clear that it has been a positive contribution to population replacement, while the opposite could be said of Chile.

When we compare immigrant women's access to labour in Spain and Chile, the group tendency towards heavy concentration and labour segregation in domestic work and care is confirmed. Although female migrants share similar educational levels, their qualifications are usually higher than those of the native women involved in the same activity. Thus, immigrant women arrived in both countries to fill a gap in the job market that had previously been abandoned by local women who found better job opportunities – and more social recognition – in other economic sectors. Latin American women – with some nationalities outnumbering others, in each case – are particularly visible in domestic and care work, while their presence is not perceived as much in other occupations.

Table 18.2 Most relevant indicators of increased feminine migratory presence in Spain and Chile

Indicators	Spain	Chile
Size of the foreign population (percentage of foreigners in the total native population)	12%	2.08%
Growth rate of the foreign population	75% of Spain's population increase in the last decade is attributable to immigration With a slight decrease (0.3%) between 2010 and 2011	Absolute growth of the immigrant population (144.4% between 2002 and 2009) By 2009, an increase of nearly 72% in comparison to the 2002 census
Weight of the Latin American immigrant population (percentage of Latin American immigration)	*Latin Americanization* of flows (an increase of 256%, accounting for 35% of foreign residents in the country between 2001 and 2007) Slight decrease by 2010: 30.6% of total foreigners	*Latin Americanization* of flows (accounting for 66% of the foreign population; it has risen by 8% since 2002) *Peruvianization* of immigration (intercensal variation of 394%, 1992–2002 and 245% between 2002 and 2009)
Weight and evolution of the foreign female population	Quantitative feminization: increase of 162% between 1997 and 2003 Significant increase of Latin American female group: it quadruples between 2001 and 2008	Quantitative feminization: prevalence of women in the total foreign population and in seven of the main migratory stocks
Impact of migration on demographic growth	Positive	Negative

Source: Authors' own study.

While growth and feminization changes and new trends are seen in the make-up of the domestic work force in both countries, there are also clear differences regarding the weight of the foreign female presence in the total population involved in this activity. In Chile, they account for only 3.6 per cent of the total population in this sector, while in Spain 18.47 per cent of women within the social security system are registered under the special provisions for domestic workers. Nevertheless, hiring immigrant women is in both cases an increasingly common strategy that native families use to respond to the booming demand mentioned above and in the absence of care provided by institutions – public and private – which is prominent in both care systems.

This analysis will also explore whether the aforementioned actors' discourse confirms a trend that has been revealed by previous research carried out in Europe and Latin America. On the one hand, this research shows that the denial of rights that is occurring is much broader and more complex than one that could be corrected simply by putting an end to the vulnerability generated by the absence of the right to be cared for, or in cases of dependency. This would have negative consequences for both the development and exercise of substantive citizenship. On the other hand, research also proves that the feminist claim for individualization and universalization of rights has made it possible to make progress in the promotion and respect of rights for those mainly engaged in care work – namely, immigrant women.

POLITICAL AND LEGAL CITIZENSHIP RIGHTS: 'IT IS BETTER TO BE A "LEGAL" IMMIGRANT BECAUSE ONE CAN THEN MAKE A CLAIM'

When assessing their rights, immigrant women caregivers in private households are aware that they start from a doubly disadvantaged situation that prevents both access to and enforcement of their rights. On the one hand, there is their status as immigrants and, on the other, as workers belonging to a sector widely known for its low wages: 'As an immigrant, you need to have some rights' (WIC_SP_PER_018 and 019).[8] For an immigrant to obtain political and legal citizenship rights, regularization of the migration process is essential, in addition to registration, a procedure required only for immigrants residing in Spanish territory.[9] Both in Chile and in Spain, the immigrant women we interviewed were aware of the difficulties they faced in trying to gain access to regularization and registration procedures, and the consequences that this entailed in terms of their labour market insertion and subsequent integration into the host society: 'When they refuse to register you here, you don't exist and as a worker, you are not entitled to anything' (WIC_SP_ECU_012); 'When you are illegal, they don't pay you, they take advantage of you because you don't have any legal papers' (WIC_CHI_PER_60). As a result of these restrictions or obstacles, immigrants are denied civil and political rights. This also fosters the violation of labour and social rights, such as access to health and housing services, education for their children or social security.

On the other hand, employers recognize that the (il)legal status of immigrant caregivers has a decisive effect on immigrant women's possibilities of gaining access to care work and their subsequent working conditions. This has a bearing on their employment rights, too, intertwining paid work and unpaid work, and self-care issues:

> Migrants are less able to negotiate the conditions, especially when they are in the country illegally. If she had had a choice she would have probably chosen an employer that did not make her work on Saturdays. Perhaps if she had had her 'residence permit', she would have tried to find better working conditions. (EMP_CHI_062)

However, the 'immigration status' variable does not affect women in each receiving country in the same way. In the case of Peruvian immigrants in Chile, both employers and immigrant women consider that the regularization process of immigrants is easier and faster than in other countries: 'In Chile, getting legal status is easier, compared to other countries' (EMP_CHI_062). The difficulties arise, however, with the 'subject to contract' visa, which requires immigrant women to stay with the same employer for two consecutive years to be able to obtain 'permanent residency' status. This situation affects, at least temporarily, the ability to enjoy labour rights as workers try to avoid conflicts with their employers so as not to be dismissed, which would oblige them to start a new visa process. 'She, the employer, did not want to have illegal workers in her house. I was "legal" when I arrived here, but then I became "illegal" when I changed jobs and then it is very difficult to get out of that circle. You have to start from scratch again' (WIC_CHI_PER_60).

In spite of these initial difficulties, once they can regularize their immigration status, the different actors involved can see a change of attitude in immigrant women. The fact that they can obtain this status is regarded as positive in terms of enforcement of labour rights: 'It is better to be "legal" because one can claim for one's rights' (WIC_SP_ECU_012). As the immigration project is gradually developed and consolidated, immigrant women, both those who arrive in Chile and those settling in Spain, show a personal perception of increasing self-confidence that encourages them to demand their labour rights:

> When I first arrived here, I didn't know anything about working conditions, what they are like here. But as time went by, I learnt that you should not work

without an employment contract; there are laws and I found out where I have to go to complain if something happens to me in a job, if I don't get paid. You start learning because you can't keep quiet all the time; the longer you live in a country, the more you learn. (WIC_CHI_PER_60)

However, the problem is that not many immigrant women caregivers understand their rights. Their vulnerability is therefore perpetuated over time and transferred to newly arrived immigrant women. A perverse effect is triggered among immigrant women, since violations of rights are attributed to the limited capacity of certain subgroups performing this work – from other places or newcomers – to enforce their rights rather than to the structural factors preventing it: 'People do not complain about this mainly because they do not have a contract and are not legal' (WIC_SP_PER_018Y019); 'There is always that friction because they state that we are submissive and do everything they, the employers, tell us' (WIC_CHI_PER_056).

LABOUR RIGHTS OF IMMIGRANT CAREGIVERS: THEY 'PUT UP WITH A LITTLE BIT MORE'

Social research brought to light significant violations for immigrant women caregivers, not only of their labour rights but also of those concerning reconciliation of work and family life. Such violations are closely linked, on the one hand, to the structural instability that characterizes care work, which is similar to that found in domestic employment and, on the other, to the increasing vulnerability of those providing it. This perverse situation becomes even worse in the case of certain groups that are particularly vulnerable, such as immigrant women.

The labour scenario in Spain and Chile, featuring transnational conditions in which immigrant women have found themselves since the mid-1990s, is marked by the tension between what has been called a 'servile pole' and another that recognizes labour rights as vital to formalizing employment relations. In Chile, 'the arrival of immigrant women reproduced the servile pole at first, as it introduced women's racialization and nationality as a new axis of discrimination and subordination' (Stefoni and Fernández, 2011, p.68). In Spain, it is also argued that 'there is a boundary between servitude and neo-servitude and this boundary has a gender, ethnicity, social class and place-of-origin character' (Tobío et al., 2010, p.141). As the migratory project progresses, this tension is resolved in favour of the pole of rights, in which the social capital that immigrant women have (mostly their educational level and social networks at their destination), and the existing rights they manage to obtain, play a significant role.

Some of the variables included in the servile pole include the worker's origin (national or immigrant). This determines whether more abuse and violations affecting immigrant women occur, since the latter would be the group with less power to make claims. This perception is very similar in the two receiving countries under analysis here: 'the people who live here do not have much to lose; for example, sometimes there is something they do not like and they just say: "You know what? I'm not coming to work tomorrow"' (WIC_CHI_PER_064).

The preference for hiring immigrant women in the domestic and care sector is related not only to a shortage of 'national labour', but also to the 'comparative advantage' that this group would have when it comes to making fewer labour-related claims than national workers, as other empirical studies have shown.[10] This state of affairs is explicitly recognized in the employers' discourse:

> I think that immigrants are at a disadvantage because they are less able to establish specific conditions when it comes to signing a contract. They are willing to work under conditions that others, national citizens, would normally not accept. They 'put up with a little bit more'. (EMP_CHI_062)

> Chilean carers make many more demands. They may want to have their breakfast served in bed, say that they will be going to work from and to a certain time, or if you want me to do that, it's extra. They are much more difficult. (EMP_CHI_080)

The recognition of immigrant women's labour rights by their employers is also affected by the 'cultural traits' variable. The existence of a number of stereotypes attributed to the immigrant women's culture of origin affects the employers' perception regarding the greater or lesser capacity of immigrant caregivers to claim or demand their labour rights. For example, Chilean employers perceive that what they call the 'servile trait' of the Peruvian culture would help immigrant women to accept working conditions without major objections. However, such a feature begins to lose its relevance when they come in contact with the Chilean labour culture, and also to the extent that the rights related to immigration status are consolidated:

> They, Peruvian immigrants, come with such a strong mental scheme of servility that, at first, they can hardly look you in the eye. But you know what? They become so 'Chilean' that in the end they take advantage of it. It depends on your relationship with your social networks here and the attitude you have. (EMP_CHI_ 059)

In spite of these difficulties in accessing and exercising their labour rights, the migrant women involved recognize major advances in their knowledge of the rights that performing care work has provided them with. Positive self-assessment of the work experience acquired can be observed in immigrant women caregivers and they regard it as a contribution to their own professional and personal development, which has a positive impact on their self-esteem. Phrases like 'I can do it', 'I'm sure I can do it', or 'I've learned a lot', are recurrent in their discourse, although they become much more habitual in those who have been immigrants for a longer time.

Their employers, who behave in a very similar way in the two destination contexts studied, showed an ambivalent assessment of these advances regarding labour rights. They recognize their importance, provided that the exercise thereof does not come into conflict with other rights related to persons in a situation of dependency, or the employer's own family:

> About ten or 15 years ago, they were rather shy, but now they are much more self-confident, more talkative. But I also see another other side to this, 'I am entitled to it and it belongs to me'. They know what their rights are and what belongs to them down to the very last detail, but they are unaware of what needs to be given in return for it. I see that they are more legally informed but I don't think this attitude is fair. (EMP_SP_040)

> They keep on referring to the issue of law here, as if they were threatening you. It is very sad, as if we were faced with two worlds, as if they felt that their employer were an enemy. (EMP_CHI_059)

In other words, from the shared perception of Chilean and Spanish employers, there is not always a correlation between labour rights and duties, in particular the duty to care properly. Employers report that immigrant women caregivers often ask them to change the agreed terms: a pay rise, shorter working hours, and so on, and providing proper care for their families depends on this. The frequent request to change their working conditions has a negative effect on the work environment, thus creating mistrust between employers and caregivers:

> They are always changing their conditions or demanding more and more . . . when they start they just say 'yes' to everything and do everything alright; they do not see anything wrong with anything you suggest, and two years or a year and a half later, they start making demands. I think their idea is, I'll go there and I'll just do whatever they tell me without complaining and, a year and a half later, they start making demands. (EMP_SP_047)

> And then, one day, they leave without notice, they are not straightforward about things, they do everything behind your back ... lack of responsibility, demanding their rights in a somewhat aggressive way. (EMP_CHI_059)

The increase in care work contracts, as a result of a greater enforcement of labour rights, is not always highly regarded by employers, considering the specific nature of the type of work and environment – households – where it is done. Immigrant women's labour rights intersect with other rights, for example, those of employers to decide on how and to what extent they will care/be cared for. The problem lies in the fact that the exercise of this right by employers may come into conflict with the rights of other groups that do not have the choice or negotiation skills to establish a labour relationship that respects and protects the rights of immigrant workers and their own families.

In general, there is a widespread negative perception of an increased enforcement of rights in so far as immigrant women consolidate their migration project and regulate their employment status: 'Right now the story goes: I am entitled to it, it belongs to me, how much I will earn, what time I will go to work. I wonder to what extent this is even likely to have adverse effects for them' (EMP_SP_040). Undoubtedly, those most affected by this view are newly arrived immigrants and live-in domestic workers whose employers expect them to have no right to claim.

Employers express some difficulty in meeting their obligations or duties when it comes to providing adequate means to ensure or facilitate care work, once they have decided to employ an immigrant woman caregiver in their home. They are aware of the changes now taking place and some – although certainly a minority – place positive value on the immigrant caregivers' greater knowledge and demand for labour rights. However, the culture of servitude when it comes to agreeing on and ensuring their carers' labour rights, still prevails in most of them:

> She seemed a sensible person; you could tell she was a person who had worked before, who had experience here. She did not say 'yes' to everything, she also asked me about the working conditions, how she was expected to work, she even tried to negotiate some terms. She had more experience; she wasn't a newcomer like some of the others I had interviewed, who would say 'yes' to everything, whatever they were offered. They were in such need or they wanted the job so badly that they did not even think they could choose. (EMP_SP_047)

Table 18.3 presents a summary of how the interviewees perceive the main spheres of violation of labour rights for immigrant women who are

Table 18.3 Spheres of violation of labour rights in care work and their relationship with other rights, as perceived by immigrant caregivers and employers

	Immigrant women	Employers
Violation of rights: main spheres or aspects	Working hours per day Break time (during working day and weekly) Social security Contract Professional status of work	Proper care Privacy Provision of adequate means to facilitate care work To decide how and to what extent they will care/will be cared for
Spheres or aspects of increasing recognition	Knowledge of rights Positive self-assessment of work experience for professional and personal development	Need for greater professionalization Ambivalent assessment of the recognition of the labour rights of immigrant women caregivers
Interrelationship with other rights	Right to self-care Right to care and combine paid and unpaid care work Right to privacy Political/legal citizenship rights	Right to privacy and inviolability of the home Tension between labour rights and duties ('to care properly')
Variables that influence access and exercise of labour rights	Origin (national or immigrant) Immigration status Number of years on the immigration project Level of association (labour or immigrant) of women caregivers Cultural traits Level of participation or relationship with family or social networks	Prevalence of a servitude culture Low social recognition of care work Low social status of workers of immigrant origin

Source: Authors' own study, based on the analysis of interview responses.

engaged in paid care work. It also shows how they relate to other rights of those involved in the social relationship of care – dependent persons and employers. The table includes a set of variables that may be affecting access to and exercise of those rights.

RIGHT TO SELF-CARE: 'WHEN YOU GIVE FREEDOM TO THE PEOPLE YOU WORK FOR, YOU HAVE LESS FREEDOM YOURSELF'

Research has increasingly recognized the importance of 'self-care' and although it has not been studied as frequently, it is expressed in a wide range of habits ranging from eating and hygiene or finding time for oneself, to risk behaviours. Care work is a job, but it is also a complex activity because it requires both physical and psychological skills. It is often difficult to develop these skills adequately because the way we care for ourselves has a negative impact on our physical and mental health, while at the same time being a condition of caring for others. This often results in what is known as 'caregiver syndrome or stress' (Tobío et al., 2010).

Although there is no socially guaranteed right to quality time, one's own leisure time affects our well-being (Pérez Orozco and López Gil, 2011), and it is important to recognize the way it is used and distributed. This is an important indicator, especially in the case of someone who has experienced migration. It helps to understand the differential use of time by the native and immigrant populations in the host country and the personal and social impacts on both. This negative perception of the lack of leisure time available to caregivers[11] is shared by both employers and immigrant women in both receiving countries. This situation has a negative effect on their personal and social life, particularly for live-in domestic workers: 'When you give freedom to those you work for, you enjoy less freedom yourself' (WIC_SP_ECU_012).

Despite this lack of leisure time, Spanish employers in particular recognize and view positively the fact that immigrant women devote time to self-care, to improving their personal appearance, to broadening their education, or simply to enjoying their free time, all of which have a positive impact on their self-esteem:

> She pays more attention to her looks, she looks more attractive . . . she now has such eagerness to learn things and gain self-confidence that she believes she is able to do things that she did not dare to do before. Back then, she just cared for the children, did things for her husband and nothing else. (EMP_SP_047)

However, labour rights collide with the right to self-care, which in turn, in the case of care work undertaken in the private home, may clash with the right to privacy and inviolability of the home. With regard to privacy, employers themselves acknowledge the difficulties that immigrant workers face, especially live-in domestic workers, in having not only their own space in which to rest, eat or fulfil other basic needs, but also the freedom to move around the home or outside:

> I still find that home care work is terrible because they have little freedom when working indoors. They have their own room but they don't always move freely in it, or say 'I have finished work and I'm going to a shopping centre for a walk'. Their work is very difficult, unappreciated; we try to make it pleasant but who knows to what extent we succeed? (EMP_CHI_ 065)

THE RIGHT TO PROFESSIONALIZATION OF CARE WORK AND ITS SOCIAL ACKNOWLEDGEMENT

Professional levels of care work both in Spain and Chile are still low, since there is much diversity with regard to the qualifications and working conditions, as well as the ways to provide care (Martínez Buján, 2010; Arriagada and Moreno, 2011). The growing struggle for recognition of labour rights in the sector is a way to give professional status to the service and to acknowledge and reappraise, at least indirectly, its social function, especially that performed in the family household.

These interviews reveal the need for immigrant caregivers to see their work as enjoying professional status. They demand that their employers recognize many of the skills and knowledge acquired in the performance of care work. However, their discourse reveals a number of variables that affect the professional status of the service. These include the degree of knowledge and access to sources of information on rights. Factors such as lack of time and digital accessibility, lower educational levels or the presence of few immigrant associations, mean that this recognition is taking place slowly and unevenly. Institutionalized care work has so far benefited more from the professional status of the service than work carried out in private homes.

On the other hand, employers are aware of the importance of reappraising care work, changing the existing prejudices about the activity and those who perform it. The discriminatory view on immigrant women and the consequent attribution of a lower social status prevents the recognition of their potential as workers and people:

> I think the work of a maid or of those providing care for elderly people is as worthy as any other profession. Employers have to be shown and told to value this type of work. In my opinion, this is urgently needed. I think the feeling of being a slave should disappear from the worker's mind once and for all, and if you have it, then there is something wrong in the relationship. (EMP_SP_38)

FINAL REMARKS: A NEGATIVE BALANCE FOR RECOGNITION AND ENFORCEMENT OF RIGHTS IN THE TRANSNATIONAL CONTEXT OF CARE WORK?

Any analysis of immigrant women carers' rights and their possibilities of enjoying citizenship must be carried out taking into account the specificities and inequalities that are distinctive of domestic work in both of the countries under consideration and the large number of factors that generate and reproduce them. As the results of recent studies show, special systems or labour laws in both destinations have established different conditions for workers in this sector: 'Instead of thinking of the particularities as reasons for additional protection, they are used as an argument to limit their rights' (Pérez Orozco and López Gil, 2011, p. 102).

Social research has given consistent and in-depth evidence of how the *place/spatial setting* in which domestic work and care are performed – private homes – is in itself a vulnerability factor. The isolation in which carers, especially live-in workers, work in households and the lack of regulations in this space, which is closely linked to another feature that negatively affects women workers' rights – the right to the inviolability of the home – are all factors that increase the vulnerability of the people performing these activities (Stefoni, 2009; Pérez Orozco and López Gil, 2011).

Last, but equally important, is the factor concerning the carer's *social position*. This position fosters an attitude of subordination when exercising labour rights in conditions which, in principle, are similar to those of other workers. This attitude is reinforced not only because the carer is a woman and a worker but also by her national/ethnic origin and her irregular legal status. In short, the wide variety of working conditions to be found and the different assessments they generate are closely related to the specific characteristics of domestic work which 'condenses all the vulnerability factors: the space of invisible activity, an individual work relationship, discriminatory regulations, etc.' (ibid., p. 95).

As this study demonstrates, the assessments and perceptions concerning the access and exercise of rights in the social relationship of care reinforce the idea, established in earlier research in Chile and Spain, of the existence of a concatenated denial of rights and hence, of the exercise of limited citizenship among immigrant women caregivers. Throughout the analysis of the responses on the access and exercise of political and legal citizenship rights, it has been noted that both immigrant women and their employers met serious difficulties in accessing the procedures related to regularization processes. As can be seen, this difficulty is closely related to the double vulnerability of those who require legal immigrant status and employability in a sector marked by high instability. However, the 'immigration status' variable does not show the same incidence in each of the receiving countries under analysis, since they face fewer difficulties in the case of Chile. This has in fact become an explanatory variable of the increasing intra-regional migration in Latin America.

The work experience of immigrant caregivers, the duration of their immigration project, their immigration status and the role of social networks are factors that have a positive influence on the knowledge and exercise of their rights. However, since this is an economic sector that operates with a large number of deficits in social and labour rights and has socially invisible and underprivileged actors, this breach in the guarantee of rights still continues to have a negative impact on newly arrived immigrants.

The employers' perception of workers' rights – which proves very similar regardless of the direction of migration flows – is quite contradictory. They recognize the importance of these rights, provided that the exercise thereof does not conflict with other rights related to persons in a situation of dependency or the employer's family. On the other hand, employees are aware of the importance of their work and their contribution to the household. Consequently, they find it difficult to understand why their work is not fully regularized with regard to such important aspects as respect for labour rights, the professional status of their work or the right to self-care.

As a result of the tension between a pole of servile tradition and one of incipient development of a human rights culture, it can also be observed that, in practice, some dimensions of the rights we have discussed above come into conflict with each other. For instance, labour rights clash with the right to self-care, which in turn, in the case of care work undertaken in the domestic sphere, may easily be incompatible with the right to privacy and inviolability of the home. In addition, this study also confirms that these tensions are exacerbated by the influence of variables such as race and nationality, which further increase the subordination and discrimination already present in the sector, thus limiting the possible achievement of a substantive citizenship.

As a conclusion, and based on the analysis of the discourse of the three types of actors directly involved in the social relationship of care, it can clearly be said that the traditional perception of domestic and care work as an activity that is socially undervalued still prevails, with no significant differences between the two receiving societies studied here. At the same time, it has become evident that the relationship between rights and duties is not static but, rather, the values and attitudes of employers and immigrant caregivers tend to change according to the work experience gained at their destination, the duration of the immigration project, the immigrants' possibilities of gaining access to training and social capital, and social networks – among other factors. More attention will need to be paid to these issues to consolidate a rights culture with regard to the social relationship of care and progressing towards the development of a substantive citizenship for immigrant caregivers.

NOTES

1. 'Crisis del cuidado y migración. Análisis comparativo de flujos migratorios feminizados: sur-norte y sur-sur', funded by the Spanish Ministry of Science and Innovation, 2010–2012 (Project FEM2009-09007-SUBPROGRAMME FEME).
2. The title of this project is 'Construyendo Redes: Mujeres latinoamericanas en las cadenas globales de cuidados', and it was coordinated by INSTRAW.
3. This link defines who is entitled to care (or not to care), for whom, and what forms of social coexistence acquire social legitimacy.
4. Pautassi (2008) also highlights the importance of considering care as an obligation arising from the right to care. The right to care, to be cared for, and to take care of oneself correlates with the duty to care.
5. In the analysis of citizenship, literature on the subject has distinguished between what is called 'formal citizenship' and 'substantive citizenship' (Brubaker, 1989; Rogero García, 2010). The first refers to belonging to a nation-state and the second to all civil, social and political rights that ensure participation in government affairs.
6. With regard to the methodology of the qualitative part of this study, we used an in-depth interviewing technique, which was applied to a total of 67 people (39 in Spain and 28 in Chile). For the sample design, interviews were conducted among three types of actors in each case of the migratory flows under study: (a) immigrant women providing paid care to dependent persons in private households (28 interviews); (b) employers of immigrant women who perform paid care work with dependent persons in private households (26 interviews); and (c) dependent persons who are cared for by immigrant women in private households (13 interviews). With regard to the location of the study: for interviews in Spain, two metropolitan areas were chosen (Madrid and Bilbao) – Madrid, for its high levels of immigration and the metropolitan area of Bilbao, where the relative percentage of Latin American people in proportion to the total number of immigrants is very high. In the case of Chile, interviews were conducted entirely in the metropolitan area of Santiago de Chile, where most Ecuadorean and Peruvian immigrants live. In Spain, interviews were conducted from March to June 2010 and in Chile in November 2010.
7. Spain and Chile are countries that have seen a high increase in immigration in recent years and, at the same time, they have received highly feminized migrant groups that are usually absorbed into domestic and care work, among other activities.
8. Codes have been used to protect the identity of the interviewees. These codes indicate the origin of the interviewed individuals as follows: the first letters of the code stand for the type of actor (WIC: Woman immigrant carer, EMP: Employer); the second abbreviation identifies the destination (SP: Spain or CHI: Chile); the third shows the immigrant carer's country of origin (PER: Peru, ECU: Ecuador). The figure closing each entry just indicates the number assigned to each interview.
9. Registering one's personal data officially with the local municipal census office, which keeps a written record of all the residents in a town. Apart from being useful to check how long a person has been living in Spain, registration also enables citizens to apply for the Social Security card, providing schooling for their children or gaining access to

social services in the municipality. It can be a requirement for many official procedures, social assistance and financial aid.
10. Chilean employers, for example, prefer Peruvian women to work in the domestic and care sector on the grounds that they make fewer demands than Chilean workers and they are 'more devoted, caring or submissive' (Hill-Maher and Staab, 2005). On the other hand, social research in Spain has revealed that employers 'are especially fond of "servants" from Latin America'. In addition to the arguments regarding language, religion and cultural proximity, the analysis has shown the 'existence of a relationship between Latin women and certain personality traits such as "patience" and "affection" that are perfectly related to the care of elderly people' (Martínez Buján, 2010, p. 121). The preference for specific nationalities and an irregular legal situation determine care work in the domestic-family sphere.
11. In Spain, the 2003 data from the National Statistics Institute show that the foreign population invest more time in paid work and less in all those activities that are not regarded as strictly necessary (social life, hobbies and so on). In general, they devote the same time to their home life and families as the Spanish population. From the above, the studies conclude that the foreign population has less freedom to choose what to do with their free time (INSTRAW, 2009). On the other hand, Fernández Cordón and Tobío (2007) also show that the lack of time to engage in social and leisure activities has very serious effects on care work.

REFERENCES

Aguirre, Rosario (2008), 'El futuro del cuidado', in Irma Arriagada (ed.), *Futuro de las familias y desafíos para las políticas*, Serie Seminarios y Conferencias no. 52, Santiago: CEPAL, pp. 23–34.
Arriagada, Irma and Marcela Moreno (2011), 'La constitución de cadenas globales de cuidado y las condiciones laborales de las trabajadoras peruanas en Chile', in Carolina Stefoni (ed.), *Mujeres inmigrantes en Chile. ¿Mano de obra o trabajadoras con derechos?*, Santiago: Ediciones Universidad Alberto Hurtado, pp. 149–54.
Bettio, F., A. Simonazzi and P. Villa (2006), 'Change in care regimes and female migration, the "care drain" in the Mediterranean', *Journal of European Social Policy*, **16** (3), 271–85.
Brubaker, William Rogers (1989), *Immigration and the Politics of Citizenship in Europe and North America*, Lanham, MD: University Press of America.
Carrasco, C., C. Borderías and T. Torns (eds) (2011), *El trabajo de cuidados: Historia, teoría y políticas*, Madrid: Catarata.
Fernández Cordón, J.A. and C. Tobío (2007), *Andalucía: Dependencia y solidaridad en las redes familiares*, Seville: IEA, Council of Economics and the Treasury, Government of Andalusia.
Glenn, Evelyn N. (2000), 'Creating a caring society', *Contemporary Sociology*, **29** (1), 84–94.
Hill-Maher, Kristen and Silke Staab (2005), 'Nanny politics: the dilemmas of working women's empowerment in Santiago, Chile', *International Feminist Journal of Politics*, **7**, 71–88.
INSTRAW (2009), *Reorganización social de los cuidados: Nodos de vulneración de derechos*, Madrid: UN-INSTRAW.
Letablier, Marie-Térese (2007), 'El trabajo de "cuidados" y su conceptualización en Europa', in C. Prieto (ed.), *Trabajo, Género y tiempo social*, Madrid: Editorial Complutense, pp. 64–84.
Martínez Buján, Raquel (2010), *Bienestar y cuidados: el oficio del cariño: Mujeres inmigrantes y menores nativos*, Madrid: Consejo Superior de Investigaciones Científicas (CSIC).
Martínez Buján, Raquel (2011), 'La reorganización de los cuidados familiares en un contexto de migración internacional', *Cuadernos de Relaciones Laborales*, **29** (1), 93–123.
Oso, Laura (2008), 'Migración, género y hogares transnacionales', in Joaquín García Roca

and Joan Lacomba (eds), *La inmigración en la sociedad española: una radiografía multidisciplinar*, Madrid: Ediciones Bellaterra, pp. 561–86.
Oso, Laura and Sònia Parella (2012), 'Inmigración, género y mercado de trabajo: una panorámica de la investigación sobre la inserción laboral de las mujeres inmigrantes en España', *Cuadernos de Relaciones Laborales*, **30** (1), 11–44.
Parella, Sònia (2007), 'Los vínculos afectivos y de cuidado en las familias transnacionales: migrantes ecuatorianos y peruanos en España', in *Migraciones Internacionales*, **4** (2), 151–88.
Pautassi, Laura (2008), 'Nuevos desafíos para el abordaje del cuidado desde el enfoque de derechos', in Irma Arriagada, *Futuro de las familias y desafíos para las políticas*, Serie Seminarios y Conferencias, no. 52, Santiago: CEPAL, pp. 59–76.
Pérez Orozco, Amaia (2006), 'Amenaza tormenta: la crisis de los cuidados y la reorganización del sistema económico', Revista de Economía Crítica, **5**, 7–37.
Pérez Orozco, Amaia (2007), 'Cadenas globales de cuidado', Documento de trabajo 2, INSTRAW.
Pérez Orozco, A. and S. López Gil (2011), *Desigualdades a flor de piel: cadenas globales de cuidados. Concreciones en el empleo de hogar y políticas públicas*, ONU Mujeres, Madrid.
Rogero García, Jesús (2010), *Los tiempos del cuidado: el impacto de la dependencia de los mayores en la vida cotidiana de sus cuidadores*, Colección de Estudios Serie Dependencia, no. 12012, Madrid: Instituto de Mayores y Servicios Sociales (IMSERSO).
Stefoni, Carolina (2009), 'Migración, género y servicio doméstico: mujeres peruanas en Chile', in C. Mora and M.E. Valenzuela (eds), *Trabajo doméstico y equidad de género en Latinoamérica: desafíos para el trabajo decente*, Santiago: OIT, pp. 191–232.
Stefoni, Carolina and Rosario Fernández (2011), 'Mujeres inmigrantes en el trabajo doméstico: entre el servilismo y los derechos', in Carolina Stefoni (ed.), *Mujeres inmigrantes en Chile. ¿Mano de obra o trabajadoras con derechos?*, Santiago de Chile: Ediciones Universidad Alberto Hurtado, pp. 43–72.
Tobío, Constanza, M.S. Agulló, M. Victoria Gómez and M. Teresa Martín (2010), *El cuidado de las personas: un reto para el siglo XXI*, Colección de Estudios Sociales, no. 28, Barcelona: La Caixa Foundation.
Vega, Cristina (2009), *Culturas del cuidado en transición: Espacios, sujetos e imaginarios en una sociedad de migración*, Barcelona: Editorial UOC.
Zavala, Ximena and Claudia Rojas (2005), 'Globalización, procesos migratorios y estado en Chile', in *Migraciones, globalización y género en Argentina y Chile*, Buenos Aires: Centro de Encuentros Cultura y Mujer, pp. 150–91.

19 What has Polanyi got to do with it? Undocumented migrant domestic workers and the usages of reciprocity
Anna Safuta and Florence Degavre

INTRODUCTION

The entire *œuvre* of the Hungarian economist Karl Polanyi is widely critical of the so-called 'economistic fallacy' (also known as the 'catallactic fallacy') according to which human beings are by nature market-oriented (read 'profit-making oriented') beings. Polanyi endeavoured to demonstrate that in pre-modern Europe and more generally in most pre-industrial societies, the importance of (market) exchange has been only marginal – a complementary source of income for certain categories of the population (Polanyi, 1944, 1957a and b, 1966, 1977). People's livelihoods in these societies were guaranteed mostly through reciprocity and redistribution. In contemporary market societies, however, it is the contrary: men and women are expected to be 'commodified' – to survive on resources stemming primarily from market exchange. Resources originating from redistribution (the welfare state) and reciprocity (social links and obligations) supplement or temporarily replace market resources when individuals are unable to take part in market exchange (due to pregnancy, old age, disability or unemployment, for example).

In this chapter we investigate usages of Polanyian reciprocity in contemporary Western societies, using as our example those migrants staying illegally in Belgium (hereafter referred to as 'undocumented migrants') who are or have at a certain point in time been employed in domestic services (including home-based care). We distinguish between undocumented migrants whose livelihood in the host country is mainly or exclusively guaranteed through reciprocity, and those for whom reciprocity only complements wages and other resources accessed through market exchange. The functions that reciprocity fulfils for employers of undocumented migrant domestic workers will be investigated by the authors in another contribution.

Polanyi identified three logics – what he called 'forms of integration' – according to which goods or services circulate: (market) exchange, reciprocity and redistribution (to which householding is sometimes added, but we consider it here as a subcategory of reciprocity). The idea of applying a Polanyian framework to home-based care services was first developed by Degavre (2005) and Degavre and Nyssens (2008, 2009) in their studies of formal care services in Wallonia (Belgium). Their work shows that to function, these services use resources stemming from the three Polanyian logics. Extending their approach, we apply here a Polanyian-inspired framework to study domestic services as provided without a legal contract by undocumented migrants.

Undocumented migrants have been chosen as the research group for methodological reasons. Since they do not have access to redistribution in the host country (that is, Belgium's welfare system), all the resources that undocumented migrants access outside of the strict exchange of their labour power against money, goods or services can, in fact, be considered as stemming from reciprocity.[1] However, we do not claim that those categories of the population that have access to redistribution do not use or need reciprocity.[2]

Domestic services have been chosen as the focus of the investigation because the functions that reciprocity fulfils are easier to observe in such a setting, where the relationships between migrant workers and employers are longer lasting and usually more personalized than in other sectors of the economy where migrants are present.[3] However, we do not claim that there is no reciprocity involved in other sectors of the economy where migrants are present.

Based on exploratory semi-structured interviews with undocumented migrants currently or formerly employed in the domestic services sector in Belgium and experts dealing with the phenomenon of undocumented migration in this country,[4] we distinguish between two types of usage of reciprocity by undocumented migrants. For 'commodified' migrants, reciprocity only complements market exchange as the main form of integration used to survive in the host country. The livelihood of 'non-' or 'de-commodified' migrants is guaranteed mainly through reciprocity. The sociological literature on migration in Belgium seems to suggest that this dichotomy is also operational for migrants who worked or are now working in other sectors of the economy and across all existing entry categories (see 'Discussion', below).[5]

This binary approach is an improvement on the initial framework, in which we reproduced the economistic fallacy described above. We initially endeavoured to study the de-commodifying effects of Polanyian reciprocity for undocumented migrant domestic workers. Such an approach assumed that, in order to earn a living in the host country, undocumented migrants had to be commodified, while goods and services accessed through reciprocity constituted only a complement to market-earned resources. In our initial conceptual framework, resources accessed through reciprocity in a way constituted a palliative in the absence of the de-commodifying effects that redistribution offers citizens and/or legal residents of the host country. Data collected through interviews with (previously) undocumented migrants currently or previously employed in the domestic work sector, however, quickly showed us that, for some of them, reciprocity – and not market exchange – is what enabled them to survive in the host country. Some of our respondents subsisted for several years exclusively or mainly on resources originating in reciprocity, while they resorted to market exchange only once their subsistence in the host country has been guaranteed through reciprocity, or as a source of 'pocket money'.

After briefly outlining the Belgian migration regime and policies pertaining to domestic and care work, we summarize those elements of the Polanyian heritage that are necessary to understand the subsequent discussion of the empirical evidence. The Discussion section starts with an outline of different usages of reciprocity among undocumented migrant workers. We then detail the functions that reciprocity fulfils for commodified undocumented migrants, using the example of those employed in domestic services: put employees in contact with (potential) employers, help migrants find stable employment, and alleviate the lack of access to redistribution.

THE CONTEXT

The Belgian shadow economy is relatively large (Schneider and Klinglmeir, 2004) and Belgian society seems quite tolerant towards informal employment of undocumented migrant workers, as Grzymała-Kazłowska's (2005, p. 680) study of Polish undocumented workers in Brussels suggests. Immigration to Belgium is mostly a two-tier phenomenon: on the one hand Westerners (mostly citizens of the 'old' EU) working legally in skilled occupations, on the other, migrants from Poland, Romanians (who cannot freely access the Belgian labour market[6]) or undocumented migrants from outside the European Economic Area (EEA) working in low-skilled sectors, mainly agriculture, the hotel and catering industry, construction and domestic services.

Belgium is an 'old' immigration country, but most migrant domestic workers are part of the wave of female 'autonomous migration', which started in the late 1980s and flowed into housework jobs in private houses or offices, and less often into home-based 'live-in' or 'live-out' care of children, the elderly, and disabled or chronically ill adults. Official statistics report that in 2008, 1,069 individuals were newly registered as domestic workers in Belgium. In principle this figure also includes foreign domestic workers who first had to obtain a type B work permit in order to work legally.[7] However, this figure is only an estimate of all those legally employed in the sector because – even when they have a legal contract – workers for whom employers do not pay social security contributions are not registered anywhere (OR.C.A, 2010, p. 14).

The national and ethnic origin of migrant domestic workers in Belgium is quite diverse (Eastern Europe, Latin America, North and Sub-Saharan Africa, the Philippines). Migrant domestic work is also a two-tier phenomenon because the service voucher scheme introduced in 2004 had a segregating effect: those female migrants who can freely access the Belgian labour market (or succeeded in obtaining a stay/work permit) would rather work within the service voucher scheme, while irregular domestic work became a niche mostly for nationals of the Philippines, Brazil or South American Spanish-speaking countries, for whom it is virtually impossible to obtain a stay permit outside of the periodic regularization-through-work campaigns.[8]

There are few studies of irregular domestic work in Belgium and no statistical data showing how many individuals/households in the Brussels Region illegally employ a migrant domestic worker.[9] It is not always clear to what extent the findings of existing analyses of migrants' living and/or working conditions fit the particular situation of undocumented migrants employed in domestic services.

Undocumented migrant domestic workers have usually outstayed the expired diplomatic ID (Filipinos) or tourist visa (Brazilians and Filipinos) with which they legally entered Belgian territory. Among Filipino domestic workers in Brussels, it is common to start working legally for an expat household with a diplomatic passport, slip into illegality after employers leave Belgium (ibid., p. 47) and subsequently apply for a stay permit.

For migrants who cannot freely access the Belgian labour market, possibilities for legal employment as domestic workers include a type B work permit, au pair status or a diplomatic passport. The type B work permit allows one single household to hire a domestic worker only on a live-in (and thus full-time) basis. The imposed minimum wage is then a monthly €1,400, which is too high a sum for most households to bear on their own. The au pair status does not allow the benefiting individual to work more than 20 hours a week and four hours per day, while only diplomats can hire a migrant worker on the basis of a diplomatic passport.

Third-country nationals who could face persecution when sent back home can apply for asylum, but procedures are very lengthy. It is quite rare to meet domestic workers who are asylum seekers since authorities examine the applicant's case and assess whether the asylum seeker is entitled to material help at the 'reception centre' to which they have been assigned. When they arrived in Belgium, the migrant service voucher workers interviewed by Rosenfeld et al. (2010, p. 156) who had applied for refugee status focused on the administrative requirements linked to their application: wage work was a secondary consideration since asylum seekers are entitled to board and lodging as long as their application has not been accepted or rejected. Our respondent Ai, who also applied for refugee status, explains that despite her willingness to work (she has not worked full-time since her arrival in Belgium in 2006) and the 18-month care assistant training she successfully completed while living in a federal reception centre, she is forced to search for informal work because of the difficulty in finding an employer willing to go through the process of applying for the work permit necessary to hire her.[10]

Previously a characteristic of mainly upper-class/better-off families, the 'internal outsourcing' of domestic work has now spread beyond the elite sections of society. This tendency has been acknowledged by public authorities, albeit not for care work. Since 2004, Belgium has had a publicly subsidized voucher scheme allowing households to outsource certain tasks to employees of companies or agencies operating within the scheme.[11] Service users can choose to use vouchers to outsource tasks such as house cleaning, doing the laundry, ironing, meal preparation or transport of less mobile individuals. Unlike similar schemes in France and Sweden,[12] childcare, long-term care and gardening cannot be provided through this scheme. Clearly, the scheme is not aimed at elderly users: while 30 per cent of a voucher's costs are tax deductible, pensioners do not benefit from this tax break, since it applies only to taxable income (Sansoni, 2009, p. 18).

Social policy literature has offered some tentative explanations as to why households choose to hire migrant carers for children and the elderly privately, without establishing a legal contract and paying social security contributions. Among factors explaining why certain households choose this solution, social policy literature cites the lack of public care services,[13] insufficient market supply (in the case of elder-care provision – be it public or market based – both institutional and home-based services have to be taken into account), a care culture which privileges care within the private sphere by relatives, a tradition of informality in society, a migration regime supplying cheap migrant labour, a country's migration history, and a broad affluent middle class (Bettio et al., 2006; Williams and Gavanas, 2008). Studies that focus specifically on elder care cite unconditional (untied) dependency/care allowances as an important factor behind the spread of undeclared migrant care work (Bettio et al., 2006; Ungerson, 2006; Simonazzi, 2009).

As noted above, despite the Belgian shadow economy being relatively large, and the social tolerance towards the informal employment of migrant workers, it seems unlikely that undeclared migrant care work will spread in Belgium as it has in the last 30 years in other European countries. Among the EU27, Belgium has the highest level of satisfaction with regard to the quality, availability, access and affordability of publicly funded care services for dependent people.[14] In terms of care for the elderly, both home-based and institutional supply is deemed to be good throughout the country. While there is also good coverage in terms of childcare institutions, the situation is less positive in terms of after-hours structures. Existing legal solutions in terms of home-based childcare also seem ill suited to the demands of users who privilege this mode of care over childcare in institutions (OR.C.A, 2010, p. 18). According to the study conducted by the NGO OR.C.A (p. 51), individuals who illegally employ a migrant childminder do not do it because they were unable to find a place in publicly subsidized nurseries, but because this mode of care corresponds to their professed ideal of care.[15]

It seems that in Belgium, ideals of care for children and for the elderly differ. When 'devoid of educational content' (as stated in the law), childcare can be provided by individuals without ad hoc training (notably the long-term unemployed, activated by local employment agencies, or au pairs). This is not the case for elder care: as mentioned above, personal care to elderly or dependent adults has been explicitly excluded from the services offered within the service voucher scheme.

CONCEPTUAL FRAMEWORK

Polanyi originally identified four 'forms of integration'[16] that have characterized economies through history: redistribution, reciprocity, householding and (market) exchange. By focusing on market exchange, contemporary neoclassical, Marxist and neo-institutional economics tend to overlook other forms of integration present in contemporary Western societies, perceived either as auxiliary (redistribution) or residual (reciprocity) (Lemaître, 2009, p. 58). Leaving aside the discussion around the relative prevalence of those four forms of integration at the macro level (is it really that most inhabitants of Belgium sustain a livelihood mainly through market exchange and redistribution?), in this chapter we examine how individuals use reciprocity and how they combine it with market exchange in a given sectoral and national context. This contribution adopts the conceptual approach put forward by Degavre (2005) and Degavre and Nyssens (2008, 2009) in their studies of publicly supervised (and thus formal) care services in Wallonia. Adopting a feminist approach of Polanyian forms of integration, these authors demonstrate how market exchange, redistribution, reciprocity and householding combine in the social innovation processes at work in formal care services. While Degavre and Nyssens' approach focused on the organizational level and formal care services, our contribution examines domestic services from the perspective of migrant individuals and examines provision without a (legal) contract (and thus informal). We start by defining market exchange and reciprocity. Redistribution and householding will also be briefly outlined, as they appear in this study.

(Market) exchange is a two-way movement between willing transactors (individuals, groups or institutions), 'neither of whom is required to transact with the other after completion of the agreed-upon exchange' (Schaniel and Neale, 2000, p. 92). In other words, once a transaction is fulfilled, there are no further obligations between the parties.

Reciprocity is a flow of resources from one unit (again, an individual, a group or an institution) to one or more other units (ibid., p. 91). In fact reciprocity is a way of enacting the social relations that link us to others:

> In Polanyi's conception, the paradigmatic reciprocal relationship is gift exchange, which is in central aspects antithetical to market exchange: in the latter, the relationship is entered into for the sake of the commodity, in the former, the product is exchanged for the sake of the relationship. (Dale, 2010, p. 116).

It is very rare that the law forces us to practise reciprocity, which is most often voluntary.[17] However, social institutions such as politeness, religion, charity, kinship or friendship most often encourage or force us to give to others or to reciprocate.

A reciprocal gesture does not always call for a 'counter gift' (Servet, 2007) and should also be distinguished from barter, which is a form of market exchange in the Polanyian conceptual framework. Reciprocity should not be restricted to symmetry understood literally: the person I give to in a reciprocity flow did not necessarily give something to me previously and will not necessarily repay me later. Intergenerational flows are generally cited as an example of reciprocity: we give to the next generation, who give to the following generation and so on (Schaniel and Neale, 2000, p. 92). It is also how reciprocity is often studied: in the context of solidarity between family members. Reciprocity between unrelated workers and employers or fellow migrants, such as examined here, is more rarely investigated using a Polanyian framework. In the particular case of home-based elder care, which we consider as a subcategory of domestic services, reciprocal flows can be identified between the caring migrant and the elderly cared-for person and/or between the migrant and the cared-for person's family or guardian.

In methodological terms, we distinguish between reciprocity and market exchange by determining whether a given movement of goods or services between migrants and their employer occurs because one or both parties aims at sustaining the relationship existing between them (in which case we are confronted with a reciprocity mechanism) or whether the objective of the considered transfer of goods or services is the transfer in itself.

Redistribution is a form of integration where goods flow to a central authority, which then redistributes them according to collective political criteria (ibid., p. 92; see also Servet, 2007, p. 262), such as with social policy. Following Polanyi (1957b) himself, householding is sometimes presented as a particular form of redistribution ('redistribution writ small': Schaniel and Neale, 2000, p. 92).[18] We tend to consider it here rather as a particular form of reciprocity – reciprocity between relatives or assimilated.

DISCUSSION

Methodology

In this section, we examine data collected in 2012 in the wider Brussels conurbation through 14 semi-structured interviews with 12 migrant respondents and two experts in undocumented migration in Belgium. The aim of this section is to examine how undocumented migrants use reciprocity in Western European contexts. We interviewed migrants who were undocumented in the past or are still, and who worked or are still employed in domestic services without a legal contract. Respondents were found through the authors' personal contacts or by contacting trades unions and local NGOs working with migrants.

The age structure of our small sample (see note 4) does not correspond to what Van Meeteren et al. (2009, p. 888) call 'the general image of irregular migrants', namely the fact that they are generally younger than 40. This might be due to this study's focus on domestic services or to the average length of stay of our respondents in Belgium. Besides being dominated by women, some types of domestic services such as childcare might attract middle-aged and older migrants, unable or unwilling to engage in other, heavier kinds of physical labour. That most of our respondents are older than 40 is more likely to be linked with the fact that all of them (except two) arrived in Belgium five or more years ago.

As noted above, we have chosen to focus on domestic services because the role that reciprocity plays for undocumented migrants is easier to observe in this sector. Due to the fact that they work mostly in domestic services, female migrants are said to have an overall better position in the labour market than their male counterparts, who are mostly employed in other sectors, such as construction, renovation or agriculture (Hagan, 1998; Grzymała-Kazłowska, 2005, p. 678; Rosenfeld et al., 2010, p. 158). 'Women's situation on the job market is more stable [than men's] due to the fact that they usually work "permanently" for the same households, whereas men are continuously forced to look for new odd jobs' (Grzymała-Kazłowska, 2005, p. 678). Ro[19] explains:

> If you need to have a work, permanent work, you have to clean. Because painting and the other work is not permanent . . . But the cleaning it's a big difference [compared to] painting, because the cleaning is always to clean, every week, until employer will expire or what [laughs]. (Ro, male, Filipino, 47)

Usages of Reciprocity

A first fundamental distinction in the usages of reciprocity by migrants has to be made between undocumented migrants for whom reciprocity only complements market exchange as the main form of integration used to survive in the host country ('commodified' migrants), and those whose livelihood in Belgium is guaranteed mainly through reciprocity ('non-commodifed' or 'de-commodified' migrants). This distinction is introduced here only for analytical reasons and does not imply that individuals are once and for all commodified, non- or de-commodifed. We do not intend to construct a typology of migrants, but rather to distinguish between differing usages of reciprocity. In fact, it appears that migrants can change over time from non-commodification to commodification (as has been the case for my respondent Fa) or from commodification to de-commodification (as shown in Mostowska, 2012).

Among our respondents, we consider that Fa from Morocco and MaCha from Cameroon initially belonged to the 'non-commodifed' category because after arriving in Belgium they resorted to market exchange only as a source of 'pocket money' or once their subsistence had been guaranteed thanks to reciprocity. For several years after their respective relationships with the men with whom they came to Belgium proved different from what they had envisaged, both Fa and MaCha subsisted almost exclusively on resources originating in reciprocity. They benefited from the help and support of Belgian and international NGOs working with migrants, individuals and informal organizations, as well as religious institutions (namely a mosque and a convent). After several years of non-commodification, Fa is now earning a living for her two children and herself through stable, legal employment. Conversely, in her article on homeless Polish migrants living in Brussels, Mostowska describes previously commodified individuals who, after losing their job because of seasonal unemployment, illness, alcohol problems or other life circumstances, are now de-commodified and survive mainly through reciprocity. Some of them are occasionally employed doing menial jobs, but mostly they beg, collect empty bottles or steal. They sleep at friends' houses, in squats, homeless shelters or on the streets, eat in soup kitchens, collect free food packages or discarded food and, when necessary, use free emergency medical help. Van Meeteren et al. (2009, p. 896) also describe undocumented migrants unwilling to commodify themselves because 'working informally could prevent them from getting papers' and thus surviving thanks to reciprocity.

Finally, for commodifed migrants, the reciprocity component of undeclared domestic work has limited de-commodifying effects and thus appears as a palliative to their lack of access to de-commodification through redistribution. Resources stemming from reciprocity are not always employment related, such as in the case of employers financing the education or holidays of the worker's child or when employers help their undocumented employee obtain a stay permit. However, in this contribution we concentrate on the rudimentary de-commodifying effects of reciprocity, neglecting for example the way reciprocity can be used to help legalize one's stay in the host country. We also use the Polanyian-inspired conceptual framework we developed to shed light on the importance of reciprocity for finding and securing jobs, a theme previously explored using the 'social capital' approach (Granovetter, 1995; Aguilera, 2002, 2003).

Finding a Job

Among our respondents, the Filipino Ro and MaCha from Cameroon explicitly mention the difficulty of finding a job when one has no papers. The Filipino Jo explains that after arriving in Belgium in 2005 she stayed at home for one year taking care of the children of domestic worker friends from the Philippines because she could not find a job herself.

Filipino respondents in particular stress the importance of a recommendation from fellow Filipino churchgoers, neighbours, friends or family, sometimes from an employer who hired a friend or a relative and hence trusts you 'by extension'. They emphasize that the person who has been recommended would not like to disappoint the recommending party:

> When they found out that we are very hardworking, when there is somebody coming, they will recommend us: 'Oh, you have to take this guy, they are very, very good, they don't lie, they don't cheat to you.' (Al, male, Filipino, 42)

But when the employer . . . well (ehh) observed you the first time you work, and they found that you are a good cleaner, they will recommend you, with their friends, their colleagues, relatives, something like that . . . My first regular employer until now, he has a son, and then he gave me to his son, to work with the son. And then the son, his son, give me to that lady . . . She's very proud for me, about my work. Every time she recommends me [to] her friends. (Ro, male, Filipino, 47)

Ri from the Philippines found her current job in a French nationals' household (cleaning and taking care of the family's children after school) thanks to her previous employer recommending her to this new employer. She mentions that her current employers knew her already because their children attend the same French school in Brussels as the offspring of her previous employer. The sporadic cleaning and babysitting offers with which she supplements her 8am–12pm Monday to Friday position and regular Saturday cleaning job also come from Filipino friends recommending her to potential employers.

From the jobs the Moroccan Fa got while undocumented, the only two that she did not find through friends or acquaintances were negative experiences. She quit a waitressing job she found herself, because the owner asked her to stand in front of the café in order to attract clients (the café was located in a street known for being a place where potential clients can accost prostitutes). The job offer Fa found in the classifieds of a free newspaper was as bad an experience as the waitressing. The man in his sixties whom she was caring for started to ask for sexual favours and stopped paying her when she refused. By contrast, a Belgian man she met when he helped her to get on the metro with her pram found her a job as the replacement for an incapacitated cleaning lady. She found her third job through her mother's friend – cooking and cleaning for an elderly lady as a replacement while the friend was on holiday in the country of origin.

Replacing a family member or friend who has travelled to the country of origin with the intention of coming back (or who is pregnant) is a very common way of finding employment among undocumented migrants. Jo and Ro also started with replacements before finding steady jobs. Ro and Ri, respectively male and female Filipino nationals, explain that after their arrival in Belgium, and before they had established a client base, migrant domestic worker friends took them to their own workplace and shared their hours (and thus wages). Ro learned to clean because his friend showed him what to do and how to finish within the timeframe agreed upon with the employer.

Positive experiences of how reciprocity works between members of the same ethnic community must be moderated, however. While compatriots exchange information about jobs, bargains (that is, secondhand cars or furniture), possibilities for regularization, affordable accommodation and so on, in her study on undocumented Polish migrants in Brussels, Grzymała-Kazłowska (2005) also mentions cases of cheating and exploitation:

> Deceptions, thefts and taking over somebody else's job in an unfair way are quite frequent occurrences within the community of undocumented workers. ... Some of the undocumented workers deduct a part of the wages of recruited persons (sometimes even relatives or acquaintances) for putting them into contact with future employees. (pp. 678 and 690)

Improving Employment Conditions and Securing Stable Employment

Research has already shown how employers of migrant domestic workers use reciprocity to their advantage (see Anderson, 2000, 2007; Hondagneu-Sotelo, 2001; Parreñas, 2001; Romero, 2002). Literature claims that 'some employers use close personal relations with their employees as a means of exerting pressure on them to do tasks or hours that the worker would otherwise refuse or for wages that they would otherwise deem too low' (Anderson, 2007, p. 256). According to Anderson (pp. 255 and 259), good personal relations with employers are of crucial importance for undocumented workers, since they are one of the only means (with labour withdrawal) of limiting employers' power over them.

The data we collected confirm Anderson's findings. The Polish cleaner, An, recalls the following story from the time she was working without a legal contract for private households in Belgium. It seems that the good personal relations she established with one of her employers allowed her to refuse to perform a task without risking her job. An explains that one of her employers – for whom she had by then been working for a long time – one day unexpectedly left her a long list of things to do during her usual working hours. An refused and stormed out of her employer's home:

> No, but, you know, when you already know someone well and that person confides in you, sharing the most secret things with you, everything is OK and then suddenly, I don't know why, because she's in a bad mood or just, I don't know, all of a sudden she wants to act ... as a great 'lady of the house' and so on, so I thought that, you know, she went a bit too far. (An, female, Polish, 44, translated from Polish)

An recalls that the employer in question ended up calling her to apologise and asked her to come back. When asked whether she genuinely liked her employer, An admits that it wasn't really the case. Therefore it seems that she strategically allowed the employer to personalize the employee–employer relationship, in order to be able, if needed, to tap into the resources offered by reciprocity, that is, in order to protect herself against what she considered as abusive treatment by her employer.

Developing good personal relations with employers can also be a way of improving one's employment conditions. The trust, attachment, solidarity or friendship building between migrant domestic workers and their employers can be a source of goods and/or services, such as:

- being paid on bank holidays or during employers' annual holidays;
- being paid without having to come to work (in the absence of the employer or of the cared-for person);
- being paid the same sum as usual despite having been asked to leave the workplace earlier;
- being able to refuse to do certain tasks without risking dismissal;
- getting help from the employer when acquiring a stay/work permit or with other administrative procedures;
- getting help from the employer with finding and/or funding training, changing jobs or transferring from undeclared work into the legal service voucher scheme; and
- non-pecuniary in-work benefits such as holidays financed by the employer.

The Filipino Ro explains the importance of resources stemming from reciprocity when one does not have access to the resources that legally employed workers draw from redistribution:

> You have to avoid that you get sick. You have to take care of yourself that you are not sick because if you are sick, you lose how many . . . yeah, work. You know, before, even if I had a headache or fever, something like that, I work, I still work . . . For example one day, you have to think 'Ah, for this day I receive 60 euro and then I have a fever, if I don't work today, I lose my 60 euro', you know, just imagine. So that's why I work even if I have fever, yeah. . . .
>
> When I was working in black [that is, moonlighting], you have to work, even if it is a holiday, because if you don't have the work, you don't have money. . . . sometimes the employer didn't give you money if you are not working. Even if you said:
> – Madame, it's a holiday, so are you paying me?
> – No!
> Yeah, sometimes it's like that. But sometimes they have also employer, a good, a good employer, he can understand if there's a holiday. He will pay you, even if you don't have to work . . . (Ro, male, Filipino, 47)

According to OR.C.A's estimates (2010, p. 8), around half of migrant domestic workers employed illegally in the Brussels Region work for only one employer. Most of our respondents aim to reduce the number of employers for whom they work, but having few employers can also mean increased vulnerability and commodification, hence the importance of the de-commodifying effects of reciprocity. Jo explains that the parents of the children she babysits every afternoon after school pay her even when she does not work because the children are on holiday or have a playdate outside of home. She explains it was not initially the case, but she complained to her employer:

> 'You should understand my situation, every day I have to eat and then we have to pay our bills, pay our apartment, like that'. So maybe they understand that, what I said, and now she pays me if sometimes they did ask me not to come, she pays me 25 euros instead of [the usual] 40 [per day]. And then, like, they spend the holiday for one week, they pay me also like 25 euros per day. (Jo, female, Filipino, 58)

Ri also mentions that when she leaves her four hours a day/five days a week job earlier than usual because her employer has stayed at home that day (which is the case every week for at least one day out of the five she has been working for that family), she is still paid as if she worked four full hours.

Grzymała-Kazłowska (2005, p. 693) explains that the best way to get a new job is to maintain good relations with actual and former employers. 'Therefore, the migrants interviewed often tried to strengthen their relationships with employers and transform them into friendship or patronage'.

As mentioned above, finding a holiday replacement is common practice among migrant domestic workers, allowing, in a truly reciprocal manner, a friend or acquaintance to access employment; in the same way, new arrivals benefit from the help of more experienced colleagues. Second, far from creating competition for the recommending employee, it allows them to secure their employment position. Indeed, ensuring that employers will not look for another cleaner or carer (who could permanently replace the employee concerned) sustains the longer-term trust relationship established with the employer. Third, in the case of pendular migration:

> The informal institutions of 'substitution' and 'shift work' enable women with permanent employment in Belgium to combine their job abroad with life [in the country of origin]. During holidays, pregnancies and illness, they ask trusted relatives to replace them in their jobs abroad. The substitute earns money and works in place of the replaced person. In the case of 'shift work' two women make an agreement that they will do one job and rent one room alternately. When one of them works in Belgium, the other takes care of her family [in the country of origin]. After a couple of weeks or months, they change places. (Ibid., p. 683)

CONCLUSIONS

In contemporary market societies men and women are expected to be 'commodified' – to survive on resources stemming primarily from what Polanyi called 'market exchange'. Redistribution (the welfare state) and reciprocity (social links and obligations) are said only to supplement or temporarily replace market resources when individuals are unable to take part in market exchange. Because they do not have access to the safety net offered to citizens and legal residents by redistribution, reciprocity is of utmost importance for undocumented migrants. In this chapter we thus examined how undocumented migrants use Polanyian reciprocity within and outside of employment relations, with reference to those who are or have in the past been employed in domestic services without a legal contract.

Based on exploratory semi-structured interviews with undocumented migrants currently or formerly employed in the domestic services sector in Belgium and experts dealing with the phenomenon of undocumented migration in this country, we uncovered two main categories of usages of reciprocity by undocumented migrants. For 'commodified' migrants, reciprocity merely complements market exchange as the main form of integration used to survive in the host country, while the livelihood of 'non-' or 'de-commodified' migrants is largely guaranteed through reciprocity.

Above, we cited the case of Fa and MaCha, who resorted to market exchange only as a source of 'pocket money' or once their subsistence had been guaranteed thanks to reciprocity; they subsisted almost exclusively on resources originating in reciprocity and thus remained non-commodified. Conversely, Mostowska (2012) described migrants who became unemployed for a variety of reasons, and are now de-commodified and surviving mainly through reciprocity. Unlike non- and de-commodified migrants, commodifed migrants sustain a livelihood mainly through engaging in market exchange. With its limited de-commodifying effects, reciprocity appears to be a palliative to offset their lack of access to the de-commodification offered to citizens and legal residents by redistribution.

Reciprocity thus fulfils several functions. Undocumented migrants need it to survive when they are unable to enter the labour market (because their life situation has changed suddenly and there is no time to find work, because of illness, lack of language skills, alcohol problems, or simply because it is not always easy to find employment when one is undocumented). Undocumented migrants also need reciprocity when they are unwilling to commodify themselves because working informally could prevent them from getting papers. Reciprocity is also necessary to commodify oneself, since undocumented migrants need it to find and maintain jobs. Additionally, the trust, attachment, solidarity or friendship building between migrant domestic workers and their employers is a way of improving one's working conditions and securing some of the resources that citizens and legal residents of the host country access through redistribution.

We do not claim, however, that migrants always use reciprocity instrumentally. As underscored by Ambrosini (2011, p. 368) in his study of undocumented migrants working in domestic and home-care services in Italy, 'involvement in some kind of family relationships with the Italian families that employ them may also respond, to a certain extent, to the emotional needs of the migrants themselves, who are separated from their loved ones'.

This contribution does not explicitly tackle unequal power relations between migrant domestic workers and their employers. However, it is important to note that reciprocity does not necessarily redress these inequalities. In Polanyi's definition reciprocity is not an egalitarian form of integration *per se*; it is a way of enacting social relations, and thus can be used to create dependencies or perpetuate existing power inequalities.

NOTES

1. Of course there are exceptions to these rules: Grzymała-Kazłowska (2005) reminds us that some Polish migrants still have access to welfare benefits or pensions in Poland.
2. Studies show that reciprocity, in the form of social networks, is crucial for labour market access for all low-skilled workers, not only undocumented foreigners.
3. Because they work mostly in domestic services, female migrants are said to have an advantage over men, mostly employed in other sectors, such as construction, renovation or agriculture. Women's situation on the labour market 'is more stable due to the fact that they usually work "permanently" for the same households, whereas men are continuously forced to look for new odd jobs' (Grzymała-Kazłowska, 2005, p. 678). The personalized relationships developing between worker and employer in undeclared household and care jobs bring this type of employment close to an open-ended contract (Rosenfeld et al., 2010, p. 158).
4. This first sample includes 12 migrant respondents, of which seven come from the Philippines, one from Poland, one from the Democratic Republic of Congo, one from Ecuador, one from Morocco and one from Rwanda; 10 are women and two are men; they all work and live in the wider Brussels conurbation. Most respondents were aged 40–50, except one in her 20s, two aged 30 and one, aged 62. The migrants interviewed in this study here entered Belgian territory through different legal routes (asylum application, overstaying a tourist visa or diplomatic ID, legal economic migration based on EU citizenship) and have a variety of legal statuses. At the time of interview most respondents had a stay permit obtained after several years of being undocumented. One respondent was an asylum seeker who lodged an appeal after having been formally ordered to leave Belgian territory.
5. Migration studies differentiate between types of migration and between migrants

according to entry categories such as labour (or 'economic') migration, political migration, family reunification, irregular migration and so on. Entry categories create a hierarchical differentiation between the social rights to which migrants have access in the host country (Sainsbury, 2006, p. 230).
6. After Bulgaria and Romania's accession to the EU, Belgium chose to restrict the access of Bulgarian and Romanian citizens to its labour market until December 2013.
7. Non-EEA (and, until December 2013, also Romanian and Bulgarian) workers who wish to work in Belgium as employees must hold a work permit, of which there are three different types: type A is valid for all salaried professions and all employers, for an unlimited period; type B is valid for only one year and allows the holder to work only for the employer who introduced the work permit application; and type C, is for students and asylum seekers.
8. We have, however, encountered migrants who claim to prefer illegal domestic work to legal employment in the service voucher scheme because of the regulations linked to the latter type of employment.
9. See, however, the following studies of migrant domestic services: OR.C.A. (2010); Rosenfeld et al. (2010), as well as Degavre and Langwiesner (2011) for irregular childcare.
10. Since 2010, asylum seekers whose application remains unaddressed for longer than six months have had the right to work (in some cases while simultaneously retaining the right to stay in a reception centre and/or to help in-kind) after obtaining a type C work permit.
11. 'The firms or agencies whose role it is to employ the *titres services* workers are admitted to the arrangement only after they have been approved by the federal government. . . . Several types of firms or agencies may be approved, including local employment agencies (ALE), temping agencies, other private commercial firms, labour market insertion agencies, non-profit associations, local authorities, public social action centres, but also individual persons in the capacity of self-employed employers' (Sansoni, 2009, p. 19).
12. France introduced vouchers allowing private households to purchase domestic and personal care services (Chèque Emploi Service Universel), while Sweden introduced tax credits allowing households to claim back up to 50 per cent of the costs of this type of services.
13. Kofman and Sales (2001, p. 102) speak of the 'absence or withdrawal of the state' from care provision.
14. See questions QA3.5, QA4.5 and QA29.2 in the Special Eurobarometer 283/Wave 67.3 (December 2007), 'Health and long-term care in the European Union', Luxembourg: Eurostat.
15. In Kremer's (2005, p. 14) definition, 'ideals of care' define the kind of care deemed appropriate and morally acceptable for the child's well-being.
16. Alternatively called 'socioeconomic principles', 'socioeconomic logics', 'transactional modes', also 'modes of circulation' and/or 'allocation of resources', by his followers and critics.
17. However, there are exceptions, such as the alimony obligation that children have towards their elderly parents in some countries, for example in Poland.
18. Mentioned in *The Great Transformation* along with the three other forms of integration, 'householding had disappeared from Polanyi's analyses by the time that *Trade and Market* was written' (Schaniel and Neale, 2000, p. 102), but re-entered the picture once again in the posthumously published *Dahomey and the Slave Trade*. In 'The economy as an instituted process', Polanyi redefined redistribution so that it 'may apply to a group smaller than society, such as a household' (Polanyi, 1957b, p. 254).
19. All names have been changed.

REFERENCES

Aguilera, Michael Bernabé (2002), 'The impact of social capital on labor force participation: evidence from the 2000 Social Capital Benchmark Survey', *Social Science Quarterly*, **83** (3), 854–74.
Aguilera, Michael Bernabé (2003), 'The impact of the worker: how social capital and human capital influence the job tenure of formerly undocumented Mexican immigrants', *Sociological Inquiry*, **73** (1), 52–83.
Ambrosini, Maurizio (2011), 'Surviving underground: irregular migrants, Italian families, invisible welfare', *International Journal of Social Welfare*, **21** (4), 361–71.
Anderson, Bridget (2000), *Doing the Dirty Work? The Global Politics of Domestic Labour*, London: Zed Books.
Anderson, Bridget (2007), 'A very private business: exploring the demand for migrant domestic workers', *European Journal of Women's Studies*, **14** (3), 247–64.
Bettio, Francesca, Annamaria Simonazzi and Paola Villa (2006), 'Change in care regimes and female migration: the "care drain" in the Mediterranean', *Journal of European Social Policy*, **16** (3), 271–85.
Dale, Gareth (2010), *Karl Polanyi: The Limits of the Market*, Cambridge: Polity Press.
Degavre, Florence (2005), *Enjeux du développement dans les contexts Nord: le rôle des femmes dans le care et la reproduction du lien social*, Louvain-la-Neuve: PUL (published dissertation).
Degavre, Florence and Gertraud Langwiesner (2011), 'Le care dans les stratégies migratoires au début du XXIème siècle: quel gain d'autonomie pour les femmes migrantes en Belgique?', in M.-P. Arrizabalaga, D. Burgos and M. Yusta (eds), *Femmes et stratégies transnationales (XVIIIe-XXIe siècles)*, Brussels: Pieter Lang, pp.67–91.
Degavre, Florence and Marthe Nyssens (2008), 'L'innovation sociale dans les services d'aide à domicile: les apports d'une lecture polanyienne et féministe', *Revue française de socio-économie*, **2** (2), 79–98.
Degavre, Florence and Marthe Nyssens (2009), 'L'innovation sociale dans les services d'aide à domicile: normes et processus', in C. Nicole-Drancourt and I. Jonas (eds), *Conciliation famille/travail: Attention Travaux!*, Paris: L'Harmattan, pp.145–54.
Granovetter, Mark (1995), *Getting a Job: A Study of Contacts and Careers*, Chicago, IL: Chicago University Press.
Grzymała-Kazłowska, Aleksandra (2005), 'From ethnic cooperation to in-group competition: undocumented Polish workers in Brussels', *Journal of Ethnic and Migration Studies*, **31** (4), 675–97.
Hagan, Jacqueline Maria (1998), 'Social networks, gender, and immigrant incorporation: resources and constraints', *American Sociological Review*, **63** (1), 55–67.
Hondagneu-Sotelo, Pierrette (2001), *Doméstica: Immigrant Workers Cleaning and Caring in the Shadows of Affluence*, Berkeley, CA: University of California Press.
Kolfman, Eleonore and Rosemary Sales (2001), 'Migrant women and exclusion in Europe', in J. Fink, G. Lewis and J. Clarke (eds), *Rethinking European Welfare*, London: Sage.
Kremer, Monique (2005), 'How welfare states care: culture, gender and citizenship in Europe', thesis, University of Utrecht, available at: http://igitur-archive.library.uu.nl/dissertations/2005-1116-200003/index.htm (accessed 15 March 2013).
Lemaître, Andreia (2009), *Organisations d'économie sociale et solidaire. Lectures de réalités Nord et Sud à travers l'encastrement politique et une approche plurielle de l'économie* (Thèse en sciences politiques et sociales UCL/CNAM), Louvain-la-Neuve: Presses Universitaires de Louvain.
Mostowska, Magdalena (2012), 'Homelessness abroad: "place utility" in the narratives of the Polish homeless in Brussels', *International Migration*, published online on 30 July.
OR.C.A. (2010), 'Le personnel domestique: un autre regard', OR.C.A., Brussels.

Parreñas, Rhacel Salazar (2001), *Servants of Globalization: Women, Migration, and Domestic Work*, Stanford, CA: Stanford University Press.
Polanyi, Karl (1944), *The Great Transformation: The Political and Economic Origins of Our Time*, New York: Farrar & Rinehart.
Polanyi, Karl (1957a), 'Aristotle discovers the economy', in Polanyi, M. Conrad Arensberg and Harry W. Pearson (eds), *Trade and Market in the Early Empires*, New York: Free Press, pp. 64–94.
Polanyi, Karl (1957b), 'The economy as an instituted process', in Polanyi, M. Conrad Arensberg and Harry W. Pearson (eds), *Trade and Market in the Early Empires*, New York: Free Press, pp. 243–70.
Polanyi, Karl (1966), *Dahomey and the Slave Trade: An Analysis of an Archaic Economy*, Seattle, WA: University of Washington Press.
Polanyi, Karl (1977), *The Livelihood of Man*, New York: Academic Press.
Romero, Mary (2002), *Maid in the USA*, London: Routledge.
Rosenfeld, Martin, Hélène Marcelle and Andrea Rea (2010), 'Chapitre 4: Opportunités du marché de l'emploi et carrières migratoires. Études de cas', in M Martiniello, A. Rea C. Timmerman and J.Wets (eds), *Nouvelles migrations et nouveaux migrants en Belgique*, Ghent: Academia Press, pp. 119–75.
Sainsbury, Diane (2006), 'Immigrants' social rights in comparative perspective: welfare regimes, forms of immigration and immigration policy regimes', *Journal of European Society Policy*, **6** (3), 229–44.
Sansoni, Anna Maria (2009), 'Limits and potential of the use of vouchers for personal services: an evaluation of *titres-services* in Belgium and the CESU in France', ETUI Working Paper 2009.06, ETUI, Brussels.
Schaniel, William C. and Walter C. Neale (2000), 'Karl Polanyi's forms of integration as ways of mapping', *Journal of Economic Issues*, **34** (1), 84–104.
Schneider, Friedrich G. and Robert Klinglmeir (2004), 'Shadow economies around the world: what do we know?', IZA Discussion Paper series **1043**, Bonn.
Servet, Jean-Michel (2007), 'Le principe de réciprocité chez Karl Polanyi, contribution à une definition de l'économie solidaire', *Revue Tiers Monde*, **2** (190), 255–73.
Simonazzi, Annamaria (2009), 'Care regimes and national employment models', *Cambridge Journal of Economics*, **33** (2), 211–32.
Ungerson, Clare (2006), 'Gender, care, and the welfare state', in Kathy Davis, Mary Evans and Judith Lorber (eds), *Handbook of Gender and Women's Studies*, London: Sage, pp. 272–86.
Van Meeteren, Masja, Godfried Engbersen and Marion Van San (2009), 'Striving for a better position: Aspirations and the role of cultural, economic, and social capital for irregular migrants in Belgium', *International Migration Review*, **43** (4), 881–907.
Williams, Fiona and Anna Gavanas (2008), 'The intersection of childcare regimes and Migration regimes: a three-country Study', in Helma Lutz (ed.), *Migration and Domestic Work*, Aldershot: Ashgate, pp. 13–28.

20 Temporary female migrations through transnational family networks: the ethnographic case of the caregiver in Riffian Imazighen women*

Irina Casado i Aijón

INTRODUCTION

I shall start this chapter by introducing two ethnographic cases which allow me to illustrate and raise its main subject. Both of them were collected during my fieldwork (2006–11) among Riffian Imazighen residents in the *comarca* of Osona (Catalonia):[1] the cases of Nadia[2] and of Amina.

Nadia was a single Riffian girl who lived in Nador, the biggest city in the Rif, northern Morocco, with her parents and her other single siblings. She was 18 years old when her older sister, Rachida, became pregnant with her second child. After Rachida had got married she had migrated to Vic, Catalonia, in the final step of a large family reunion process initiated by her husband. In the seventh month of Rachida's pregnancy Nadia travelled to Vic to take care of her sister during the final months of her pregnancy and once the child was born. Nadia travelled alone from Nador to Vic, not only to take direct care of Rachida but also to replace her in her motherhood role during this period.

Amina, the oldest daughter of Habib, got married in the early 1970s in Nador, where all six of her children were born before they migrated to Vic. The migration processes that Amina and her children followed are typical in the context of contemporary Riffian migrations. In the mid-1960s, Habib (Amina's father) had already decided to migrate to Spain to look for work and, consequently, to improve his and his family's economic situation. However, the Spanish political and economic scene at the end of Francisco Franco's dictatorship made Spain a poor settlement option compared to other European countries, so Habib migrated to the Netherlands. During these years, his first wife died and he then married a local woman from Nador. Habib and his second wife lived in the Netherlands while Amina, her husband and their children settled in Vic. Habib was 63 when he travelled for the first time from Rotterdam to Amina's home in Vic. He suffered from heart disease, for which he had initially been treated under the Dutch public health system, but due to the high costs of healthcare and drug treatment he decided to seek more accessible and affordable care in Catalonia. However, he also had another reason for going to Spain: Habib, a widower and married for a second time, was also hoping to be cared for by his oldest daughter. He lived in Amina's home during the entire treatment period and registered as a resident in order to have the right to Catalonian public healthcare. Amina's domestic unit, which includes the whole extended family located in any transnational space, provided him with the direct care and support that Habib needed during his treatment.

During Habib's therapeutic sojourn in Catalonia, the migration movement was unidirectional, from the Netherlands to Vic and to the Catalonian public healthcare system, but it had a dual purpose. On the one hand, he was looking for a specific person to be responsible for his care and, on the other, for a more economic biomedical healthcare system. However, Habib's therapeutic journey did not end there. Back in the Netherlands his heart disease underwent critical periods and he alternated between hospital care and rest at home. During these periods, a second temporal migration movement took place, through Amina's various trips to the Netherlands to take care of her father in his own home.

As we can see in both cases presented, among the Riffian people temporary migrations for health reasons are quite usual, either between Nador and Europe or within European countries. In both our examples it is possible to differentiate between two types of temporary migration movements according to the person who migrates: those undertaken by the sick person and those undertaken by the carer. In the first instance, temporary migrations are undertaken regardless of whether the sick person is male or female; however in the second, the migrating carer is always female. Social and cultural gender rules operate and attribute roles and tasks to both men and women. I shall focus on the latter type of migration, that of the women carers, but even though the traveller is a woman, it is difficult to categorize any migratory process as exclusive to that individual.

We must judge not only the impact that migrations have on the nearest family group but also their impact on society as a whole. When the number of cases is large, we cannot describe them as individual migrations, at least not when considering their consequences. Any group that loses members through migration will need to adapt or modify its sociocultural organization in the same way that a person has to when he or she settles in a new migratory context. The adaptation process to the new reality of migration is produced by the changes, continuities and adjustments carried out on the basis of representation of each specific sociocultural model. These adjustments are not static but change according to two factors: the duration of the migration process within the society of origin, and the cultural and socioeconomic characteristics of the settlement destination.

The main aim of this chapter is the analysis of the socio-cultural phenomenon resulting from migratory processes undertaken by Riffian Imazighen women. I shall study the adaptations, changes and continuities introduced into the society of origin and all its components: temporary female migrations for assistance purposes, support and care of sick family members (the case of Amina) or pregnant relatives and/or postpartum periods (the case of Nadia). Necessarily, the analysis must be based on factors that have been modified not only as a result of migration processes but also by the development of Riffian society in its place of origin. The understanding of the basic structure of Riffian organization, the *familia*,[3] and the gender roles that are attributed to its members is very important in such a study. Gender and age are the two variables that determine roles of responsibility and authority within the *familia*. The analysis will take into account the perspective of those parts of extended families residing in Catalonia and consequently I shall focus on data that has emerged from five years of ethnographic research among the Riffian Amazigh immigrants in Catalonia, specifically in the *comarca*[4] of Osona.[5]

In order to understand these types of female migrations they must be placed in the context of the different phases of contemporary Riffian migrations to Catalonia. It is also important to study the consequences that these migrations have had in the *familia* structure, based on families that are articulated through patrilineality and patrilocality principles, which give rise to extended families with transnational, multi-situated domestic units, especially in European countries such as France, Belgium, Germany and the Netherlands. Adaptations in the structure and necessary changes produced by physical distance to the *familia* members have also involved an adaptation of their roles – determined by gender and age – and of the tasks, responsibilities and authority associated with each member. In this case, the adjustments have given rise to new forms and practices – temporary migrations of certain female family members – but have not changed the representative models – the attribution of responsibilities and tasks associated with marked gender segregation within Riffian society and the determination of figures of authority[6] within the group. Thus while the *familia* model has remained the same over the course of migration processes, the family's settlement in various destinations and the fulfilment of basic needs (legal regulation, housing, employment, education, health) have allowed it to recover some of its forms of expression – whether changed, adapted or with recognizable continuity.

CONTEMPORARY MIGRATION PROCESSES OF RIFFIAN PEOPLE: BETWEEN NADOR, CATALONIA AND EUROPE

During the twentieth century, Morocco and Spain enjoyed a very close relationship. From the establishment of the Protectorate in the Rif region in 1912 until Morocco's independence in 1956, bonds and relations between the two sides of the Mediterranean were based not only on economics but also on demographics. The Spanish Protectorate in Rif largely determined the characteristics of Moroccan migration waves to the Spanish state, since during that time a large number of Riffian people worked in Spanish industry and most of them spoke Spanish. After independence in Morocco, the political and economic scene in Spain – the Franco dictatorship – instigated the spread of Riffian migration processes to other European countries with more stability and more favourable situations. Often, members of the same *familia* went to several European countries, while some stayed in their place of origin, and this triggered the start of the separation of extended families throughout Europe. Advantages offered by the knowledge of Spanish, along with a previous working relationship between Spanish companies and Riffian workers, made Spain, and especially those areas with the most important industrial development, the destination for most of that labour force. One of these areas was Catalonia.

The first Riffian migrants arrived in Catalonia roughly towards the end of the 1950s. The intensity of migration was very low at that time and continued to be so into the 1960s: the situation in Spain did not favour migration, and the few Riffians who arrived were often encouraged by previous labour relations established in Morocco. From the late 1950s and throughout the 1960s, most immigrants were men travelling alone, single or married, who had left their families in their place of origin and migrated with a clear working objective. The success of these processes along with the liberalization towards the end of the Francoist period intensified the Riffian migratory projects throughout the 1970s. It was as a result of this great migratory wave that Riffian people settled in the *comarca* of Osona and thus we can distinguish some phases in the whole process that are determined by the characteristics of the migrants and the reasons for migration.

Following the migratory dynamics of the late 1950s and 1960s, during the 1970s and early 1980s it was common for men to arrive in Osona alone. They were mostly young single men, but some were married men who had left their wives and children in Morocco. They settled especially in the capital city of the *comarca*, Vic, where many of them shared accommodation between five or more. The migration characteristics of Osona are determined by the fact that the first successful processes provided an example for starting new ones, and over the course of the decade people came from the same area of Rif, Nador, to Osona. They were relatives and neighbours of the first male migrants and they profited by the network of Riffian people from Nador that was gradually taking shape in Osona. This network eased the process of arrival and settlement in the *comarca*. The newly arrived Riffian men found jobs in the dynamic pig meat industry of the region, in construction and in leather-related industries. Throughout the decade, the networks were strengthened at the same time as settlement was becoming more and more established: it was relatively easy to satisfy the main basic needs such as employment and housing, and later, legal regulation.

In the early 1980s the men who arrived with the first migrant wave that had left their families in Nador began the regrouping process. The regroupment comprised the second phase of the Riffian migration process, which was still weak in the 1980s but grew in intensity during the 1990s. The settled men then began preparing to buy homes in Vic, some of them regrouping with their wives and children, while others returned to Morocco to find a wife and, after the wedding, to organize the paperwork to obtain Spanish residency for her. The second phase, therefore, consisted mainly of women and children, something that differs from the first phase as do the reasons for migration: economic and employment reasons in the first instance, family reasons in the second. At the same time individual men continued to arrive and seek work during this second phase.

By the end of the 1990s the third phase started, but slowly. The reasons and characteristics of migration in the third phase are extensions of the two previous phases. Many of the children who had arrived from Morocco in the second phase, and those already born in Osona, began to look for a spouse. Consequently, a new form of social promotion was established, especially for the young women born in Osona or those who had arrived when they were very little, in which marriage with Riffian males, residents in other European countries, was a way to move up the social ladder. Thus began another kind of migration, undertaken in this case by young Riffian females. Meanwhile, the males of this generation continued to seek a wife in Morocco. The reasons for this difference are clear: women socialized and educated in Osona had changed their expectations towards marriage and family, that is, towards the gender roles attributed to them, while Moroccan women still remained true to traditional values. Along with the migrations of men for occupational reasons, family reunions and these new migrations for the social promotion of women by marriage, a map of Osona was being drawn on which most of the immigrants were Riffian

Imazighen from Nador who tapped into more complete networks to find the support they needed on their arrival. This *comarca* provided the same neighbourly relations that they had had in Morocco: people who were neighbours in Nador might now be neighbours in Osona. Therefore, there is a stable and compact settlement of Riffian people in Osona – in most cases with legal status and some with Spanish nationality.

As a result, since the beginning of the contemporary migration wave, the diversity of destinations (mainly Catalonia, France, the Netherlands, Belgium and Germany) has drawn a map on which *familia* are distributed throughout European space in far-flung domestic units that become transnational. But, at the same time, this physical distance between households becomes a clear set of networks which connect them, link them and hold them together.

TRANSNATIONAL *FAMILIAT*[7]

The separation of the *familia* members through European space does not necessarily require a change in the representation of the Riffian family model, which is based on the principles of patrilineality. But the model also follows patrilocality, that is, that the newly married couple reside in the home of the husband's family after marriage. Thus, the model modifies the pattern of residence after marriage to become, by migratory necessity or by choice of the new couple, neolocal[8] but not the kind of *familia* which remains extended. While most couples in Osona create their own domestic unit after marriage, these homes must be placed within the extended family household units even though they are physically separated – from apartments in the same block of flats to homes in other countries. However, the distance between family members does not equal a change in roles. The new geographical reality does not affect the status of its members, nor does it change the allocation of responsibilities or authorities for gender and age within the group. This therefore involves the addition of two new phenomena: the flow of information through telephone and internet connections and the circulation of family members through the network tracks laid down by the transnational establishment of domestic units.

In Riffian society, a change in the representation model of the *familia* does not happen often, although a change in practices does occur – not in all of them, but in those necessary to install its members in the context that provides migration processes and in the various European host societies. The principles of patrilineality and patrilocality are maintained whenever possible and in those cases when they are not, the practice is changed with the establishment of neolocal residences close to the original family of the male, with neolocal transnational residencies which remain joined to the rest of the *familia* through patrilineality. But above all, even when the families are separated by distance, they maintain the roles established for the variables of gender and age. It consists then of patrilineal extended families with domestic units, in most cases neolocals, transnationally located between Nador, Catalonia and certain European countries that maintain their structure and organization. They do so by establishing a network with the necessary information to maintain both the unity of the *familia* and its members with specific roles of authority and responsibility when they are required.

CHANGES, ADAPTATIONS AND CONTINUATIONS OF ROLES AMONG *FAMILIA* MEMBERS

The organization of the Riffian *familia* is founded on two principles that are their main strengths: the identification of certain activities to which roles of authority are attributed and specific tasks within the group, which result in an internal group hierarchy. It is an organization in which both genders, male and female, are perceived as complementary in terms of roles and tasks that are assigned to them. It is possible to describe the Riffian *familia* model as a group with a hierarchical but also complementary internal organization, characteristics coherently articulated although at first sight they seem to be opposed to one another.

From the hierarchy and complementarity, we find an organization of family members among Riffians that is a reflection of the whole social structure. The hierarchical system is formed, as we have already seen, using two variables, gender and age, with gender being the more important. Thus, within the family group – and by extension within the whole society – men take up roles of authority that will be graduated and blended according to their age. In any case, they have authority over women, at least those of the same age or younger. When gender articulates with age, older men occupy positions of major authority, which other group members respect and obey.

The place of women within the group is also determined by gender and age. It should be noted that the place of women and their roles are subject to a *feminine hierarchy* in which women have a certain status within the group that is linked to their virginity, marriage and motherhood. These variables act to place the women in positions of authority *vis-à-vis* themselves and give them social status among the rest of the family group and society.[9] Over the last decade, a new way has been established by which women acquire status and power within the group: by being the ones who regroup with their husbands in Spain in those cases where the female finds a partner in Morocco.

Although one form of social promotion is the marriage of Riffian women from Catalonia with Riffian men residing in other parts of Europe, the fact that these women already established in Catalonia regroup for marriage with a man who lives in Morocco gives them new power, new authority. The value of the woman's signature on her new husband's papers is priceless.

Up to now we have discussed roles of authority and of power within the family. The family model, however, has tasks that are associated with these roles; responsibilities within a group that in this case have clear gender segregation. As in other situations, the model does not always fit with what people do on a daily basis. And in this sense, while the model of roles and tasks links the woman to domestic spaces and the responsibility for everything that happens inside the home, housework and childcare in particular, men are linked to the public sphere. It is clear that many Riffian women from Osona work outside their home yet their roles and responsibilities are still measured by the traditional model. Riffian women are responsible for the care of members of the group, of children and adults in cases of illness or dependency. And this responsibility is determined by the bond that exists between the caregiver and the person being cared for, and the degree of proximity attributed which gives more or less responsibility to the carer – by affinity or consanguinity. This model demands, for example, that when a woman needs to be cared for and when the person who is higher in the female hierarchy cannot be held responsible, it must always be another woman in the group who takes that responsibility. What one woman cannot do, another will. But a man is unlikely to do the same since the men are assigned other responsibilities. Above, we talked about hierarchy and also of gender complementarity, but to understand the phenomenon of female temporary migration it is essential that we focus on another basic concept in Riffian society: feminine solidarity. This kind of solidarity is only constructed and nurtured by the women, either of the *familia* or in an extended group within society. Feminine solidarity operates in all life spheres but it has a special presence among women of the same *familia* even if their domestic units are distant, in cases of care and assistance but also in daily domestic tasks such as childcare or housework. It is in this frame of feminine solidarity and distribution of roles by gender where we should understand female temporary migration in the contexts of health, diseases or pregnancy and postnatal periods.

TEMPORARY FEMALE MIGRATIONS

Within the framework that being part of a transnational extended family confers, the maintenance of women's roles as carers has not changed but

Temporary female migrations through transnational family networks 447

has adapted to the new locations of its members and their new realities. The roles adapt with changes in practices and forms of *familia*, and socio-economic and employment situations. These changes also take place in the *familia* model. With regard to gender roles, the forms have changed but not the models of representation. Despite physical distance between domestic units, hierarchical organization with authority figures within the group is still maintained, as is the way of organization and the roles that are related to the specific tasks attributed to each gender.

In the maintenance of the model, and as a result of the network map that can be drawn between stable domestic units transnationally settled in Nador and throughout Europe, it is women who have the responsibility and the obligation to take care of certain *familia* members. Distinctions should be drawn, as mentioned above, between the roles of responsibility and obligation: on the one hand, those who have the responsibility and social obligation to undertake direct care, and on the other, those with authority to take decisions regarding the health of other *famila* members. Authority and responsibility seldom fall to the same person.

In this scenario, we can distinguish from the whole migratory processes a particular type of migration, specific in three characteristics: they are feminine migrations – and in most cases women travelling alone – they are temporary, and they have as their main objective the provision of assistance, care and support in situations where they are required. The female carers circulate through a transnational space that traces the location of *familia* domestic units; a phenomenon that begins once the settlement of these households has stabilized and basic needs have been met. This new transnational spatial distribution of the *familia* members has been changed so that it is the women who are responsible for taking care of it. Although patrilocality allows women such as mothers, unmarried daughters and daughters-in-law to share the tasks of care, neolocality with distance or proximity ensures that these carers do not live in the same domestic unit. Thus, everyday life ensures that the tasks of caring fall to daughters rather than daughters-in-law, or compels others to travel when their role and responsibility towards the person who they have to care for requires it. It should be noted that these kinds of temporary migrations are possible in two instances: when the female carer is unmarried and she does not have the burden of responsibility towards her own husband and children, and when there is another woman from the *familia* who can replace her.

With these characteristics, it is possible to distinguish two kinds of situations in which female carers are required: when a *familia* member is sick and needs caring and assistance, and when a female *familia* member – usually a sister or sister-in-law – is pregnant and/or during the postpartum period. In these situations, female carers who travel carry out two types of care tasks: direct caring where they are responsible for the care of the sick – medical treatment control, hygiene, visits to the doctor – and indirect care. In these cases their tasks are to offer assistance and support, especially to women who are responsible for the direct care and, therefore, they neglect duties for which they would normally be responsible. When the aim of migration is to take care of a female *familia* member who is pregnant and/or going through her postnatal period, the woman who travels is usually her unmarried sister or, sometimes, her husband's unmarried sister, her mother or her mother-in-law.[10] The normal responsibilities of the carer have been replaced by the obligation to help the pregnant woman with housework, and to care for the woman's husband and children. In such cases, this mostly involves indirect care, although there are situations in which female carers have direct care of the new mother and newborn baby.

When the goal of migration is to take care of a sick person, the types of tasks may vary according to who the sick person is, and who the person is who is socially assigned to the direct care of him or her. Thus, travel begins when a person is ill, whether male or female, and there is an obligation to take care of that person because of the kinship bond between them. When the issue is indirect care of sick people, whether they are men or women, the woman who has the closest bond with the direct carer is the one who travels. Therefore, the female carer will travel when the woman responsible for the direct care needs assistance and support in all the tasks she neglects or needs help with during that period.

Faced with these situations, two directions in carers' mobility have been identified: (i) from Nador to Catalonia and Europe, mostly undertaken by women who are going to take care of others during pregnancy and/or post-partum periods (Nadia's case), and (ii) between Catalonia and Europe – in both directions – when the intention is to look after another, directly or indirectly, in periods of illness (the case of Amina and her father, Habib). It is a short-term movement – between two to three months – that occurs by following the network created by the establishment of several domestic units in a transnational context. Right from the beginning of the migration its duration is already determined. In those cases where women travel from Nador, the length is clear – it is the time allowed by the validity of the visa. If care is still required, these women return to Nador, renew the visa and travel again. In cases where the origin of migration is Catalonia, duration is not limited by legal issues, only by occupational ones. This is because women often travel, leaving behind their own responsibilities, a situation that cannot be extended for too long even though there are other women who can replace them in their absence. This set-up allows more flexibility than visits controlled by visas.

CONCLUSIONS

The Riffian *familia*, as a basic institution of social organization, has gone through a process of adaptation whereby as a result of the intensification of the migration of its members to Europe, it has adapted and preserved its features and functions. It is an organization based on two principles: patrilineality, by which group membership and authority figures are established; and patrilocality, which has adapted to the demands of a transnational migratory context where their members have set up domestic units. Once their situation has been regularized and basic needs have been covered, *familia* functions and responsibilities attributed to the roles assumed by its members continue to exist. The roles are assigned by gender and age but also by the existence of female solidarity and hierarchy that differentiates the women of the group by identifiers such as virginity, marriage and motherhood. While ways of representing *familia* and certain principles remain, others are modified by adaptation to a new migratory context. And, despite the new situation of Riffian women outside their homes, the principal role as caregiver is attributed to them. The physical separation of the domestic units of the extended families in a transnational space, the drawing of networks that this separation implies, along with the maintenance of the roles of authority and responsibility in care allow the temporary movement of Riffian women. This occurs so that they can respond to their responsibilities wherever and whenever someone needs them.

These female migrations are only possible when the socioeconomic situation of the domestic unit permits. In this way a form of feminine solidarity is restored by which, if a woman of the group cannot assume the tasks bestowed to her by her role within the group, another woman will. This other woman will very often take on not only assistance and support – indirect care – but also direct care in cases of illness or during pregnancy and/or postnatal periods.

Female temporary migrations are the consequences resulting from the introduction of changes to the domestic units which constituted the extended *familia* spread over in a transnational space. But, at the same time, the Riffian *familia* has maintained ways of representation and functions of the institution as well as the roles and status of its members. For the Riffian people of Osona, the *familia* is still the group of reference which provides for their basic needs. It offers support, assistance, care and help to all its members depending on where they are within the transnational space that the *familia* occupies.

The way of representing and conceiving these female temporary migrations has not changed with regard to the movement of women for care purposes when domestic units are close or when the patrilocality principle prevails. It corresponds to the responsibilities that are attributed by gender according to who the person is who needs direct or indirect assistance. It determines which woman will travel: from bonds between people but also between the places that both of them occupy within the family group. These are new forms of expression of a *familia* model and of gender roles. It is a representation that retains enough flexibility to accommodate family distance, the inclusion of Riffian women into the labour market and new forms of residence by its members.

NOTES

* This work is part of my PhD thesis entitled 'Parentiu i salut entre els imazighen rifenys de Catalunya' (Kinship and Health among Riffian Imazighen of Catalonia), which is in the final phase of writing. The ethnographic data presented arises from the fieldwork carried out between August 2006 and August 2011, within the frame of my participation in two research projects: *Teoría transcultural de la reproducción de los grupos humanos. La Antropología del parentesco como estudio de los modelos socio-culturales de procreación y crianza de los niños*, directed by Dr Aurora González Echevarría (Plan Nacional I+D, Ministerio de Educación y Ciencia. Project: SEJ2006-1086) and *Desigualdades socioeconómicas y diferencia cultural en el ámbito de la salud en barrios de actuación prioritaria de Catalunya*, directed by Dr Teresa San Román (agreement between Departament de Salut de la Generalitat de Catalunya and GRAFO de la Universitat Autònoma de Barcelona).
1. Riffian people are one of the eight heterogenic subgroups in which Imazighen (Amazigh in singular) are divided. Imazighen are considered to be native inhabitants of North Africa. The territory where Imazighen live was Arabized and Islamized in the seventh century. However, they kept their own language, *Tamazight*, their own writing, *T(h)ifinagh*, and other social, economic and culturally specific characteristics. Imazighen spread over a large territory, *Tamazgha*, which is the name of the Imazighen country. *Tamazgha* extends over some areas of Morocco, Algeria, Libya, Tunisia, Mauritania, Egypt, Mali and Niger. Riffian people are natives of the Rif Mountains (northern Morocco): although official statistics do not make it possible to determine how many Imazighen there are in Catalonia because they do not establish ethnic origin, it is estimated that two-thirds of Moroccans in Catalonia are Imazighen. And, specifically, in the *comarca* of Osona where I carried out my fieldwork, it is estimated that 80 per cent of resident Imazighen are Riffian people from the province of Nador.
2. Names have been changed to preserve the informants' identity.
3. I shall use the Riffian term '*familia*' (indicated in italics) to designate the group of people linked to each other especially through consanguinity and affinity bonds, both on the mother's and the father's side, although the model is organized under patrilineality and patrilocality principles.
4. The translation of *comarca* in English is 'region'.
5. Osona is a *comarca* located in central Catalonia, in the province of Barcelona. The major part of the territory is dedicated to rural activities. In Osona there are two main towns with major migrant populations: Vic, which is the capital city of Osona, and Manlleu. Contrary to what one might think, since they are Muslims, Osona has a semi-rural population with an extended pig meat industry where a large number of Riffian men and women work.
6. Among Riffian people, authority and responsibility do not fall on the same person.

According to Riffian gender and age rules which operate as transversal variables to social organization, it is usual – and a social basis too – that the oldest man has the authority and responsibility. In this case it is to take charge of matters relating to the care of dependent members of the family group, such as the sick and young children – and this responsibility falls on women, without age discrimination.
7. In Tarifit, the plural of *familia*.
8. Among Riffian people there are other types of postnuptial residence that are not so common but they do exist: feminine monoparental, especially after divorce; unipersonal, especially male following divorce or as a consequence of a boy's emancipation before marriage; and, finally, neolocal domestic units formed by reconstituted families.
9. In this feminine hierarchy related to a woman's situation in terms of her sexuality and her marital status or her capacity to become a mother, feminine authority is held by those women who will become a grandmother, especially the husband's mother. This means that motherhood is important within this specific hierarchy but not more important than virginity. Although getting married is essential in the social order, once a woman marries, she loses her virginal condition and remains in a weak position until she becomes a mother. But virginity has a double meaning since age becomes an important variable in feminine hierarchy: young virgin girls have a higher social and more important feminine status than single women over 25, even if they remain virgins.
10. Note that very often these women (mothers, mothers-in-law, sisters and unmarried sisters-in-law) live in Nador because they were not able to realize family reunion due to the restrictions of the Spanish Aliens' Law approved in 2010.

BIBLIOGRAPHY

Artal, C., A. Pascual and M. Solana (2006), 'Trajectòries migratòries de la població estrangera a Catalunya: les poblacions marroquina, equatoriana i pakistanesa', Grup de Recerca sobre Migracions, Departament de Geografia, Universitat Autònoma de Barcelona, Study with financial support from Secretaria per a la Immigració de la Generalitat de Catalunya and Fundació Jaume Bofill.

Boughali, M. (1974), *La representation de l'espace chez le marocain illettre*, Casablanca: Editions Anthropos.

Bourdieu, Pierre (2007), *La dominación masculina*, Barcelona: Anagrama.

Bramón, Dolors (2007), *Ser dona i musulmana*, Barcelona: Editorial Cruïlla.

Casado i Aijón, Irina (2012), 'Cuidadoras y enfermos en el espacio transnacional de la familia. Migraciones temporales por salud entre los imazighen rifeños', in Actas VII Congreso, *Migraciones internacionales en España. Movilidad humana y diversidad social*, Universidad del País Vasco, Bilbao, 11–13 April, digital support, 12 pages.

Chatou, M. (2000), 'La noción de pertenencia tribal en el seno de los rifeños', in V. Moga and Ahmed R. Raha (eds), *Estudios amaziges: Sustratos y sinergias culturales*, Melilla: Servicio de Publicaciones, Consejería de Cultura Ciudad Autónoma de Melilla, pp. 121–33.

Eguren, J. (2004), 'De Marruecos a España: la comunidad transnacional rifeña', *Migración y desarrollo*, April, 49–61.

Espona, A. and Mireia Rosés (2002), *Osona i la immigració: estudi diagnòstic i línies estratègiques de futur*, Pla comarcal d'integració dels immigrants d'Osona, Vic: Consell Comarcal d'Osona, available at:http://www.ccosona.net/admin/uploads/htmlarea/osona. pdf (accessed 4 January 2009).

Grasshoff, M. (2006), 'The central position of women among the Berber people of Northern Africa, exemplified by Kabyle women', in *Societies in Peace*, 2nd World Congress on Matriarchal Studies, Texas (USA), 29 September–2 October, available at:www.second-congress-matriarchal-studies.com/grasshoff.html (accessed 17 May 2010).

Hernández Corrochano, Elena (2008), 'Diferentes perspectivas sobre el estudio de la familia en el norte urbano de Marruecos: un análisis en perspectiva de género', in

Papeles del CEIC, **35** (1), CEIC, Universidad del País Vasco, 19 pages, available at:www.identidadcolectiva/pdf/35.pdf (accessed 7 July 2009).
Karrouch, Laila (2004), *De Nador a Vic*, Barcelona: Columna Edicions.
Mateo, Josep Lluís and Maite Ojeda (2009), 'Repensando las dicotomías sexuales desde las relaciones de poder: un enfoque comparativo', *Quaderns*, **25**, Barcelona: Institut Català d'Antropologia and Editorial UOC, 73–87.
Valcárcel Guitián, Rosa (1999), 'Etnografia de les famílies immigrants marroquines', Master's thesis in Social and Cultural Anthropology, Universitat Autònoma de Barcelona.
Yacine, Tassadit, Maria-Angels Roque, Mansour Ghaki. Mohaned Chafik et al. (2010), *Les Amazighs aujourd'hui, la culture berbère*, Paris: Éditions Publisud.

21 Transnational mobility and family-building decisions: a case study of skilled Polish migrant women in the UK
Anna Cieslik

INTRODUCTION

Krysia says that her decision to migrate was spontaneous. In 2005 she and her husband bought two plane tickets and moved to the UK. She explains that the timing of their departure was important: '[I]t was this moment when you don't have children yet, you don't have an apartment, you don't have a mortgage – this is the moment when you can leave and do something'. Krysia studied marketing in Poland and was determined to find a job in her profession. She managed, and now works as an executive marketing coordinator in a publishing company. She is planning to return to Poland within a year or two because she misses her family and the feeling of stability. She and her husband are planning to have a baby and she believes that her mother's help would be essential.

Magda migrated for the sake of her husband's job in 2006. In Poland she worked for three years in marketing and she felt that her company would 'squeeze her like a lemon'. She says she believed that she had to work those three years, 'to sacrifice', as she put it, in order to find a better job afterwards. In fact, she found a good job immediately after moving to London. She became a planner for a big corporation. She appreciates her employer because he provides excellent benefits for mothers. Magda is worried, however, that pregnancy and childrearing will be too difficult for her in London. She wants to have the support of her mother or her mother-in-law. She is thinking about bringing her parents to London or moving back to Warsaw.

Alicja decided to go to London to learn English. She left in 2003 on an au pair visa. In Poland she had graduated from university with a degree in banking and finance, and had a well-paid job at a bank and could afford an apartment. She had to overcome significant family resistance towards her migration as an unskilled au pair. Once in London, she completed a course in general English and in business English. She found a job at a bank and was quickly promoted from an entry-level administrative position to Clients' Officer in the Compliance Department. Her British employer is paying for her further education in the compliance field. Alicja is considering going back home in two years. She says she is thinking of having children, which is more important for her than her career. She does not want to raise the children in London, which she considers a 'spoilt city'.

These three women made a brave decision to break with their lives in Poland and to start again in a new country. They were determined to find employment commensurate with their education and they succeeded. They all have a fulfilling professional life in London. Yet their stories reveal that, while they are satisfied with their careers, they believe that having a baby and a stable family life requires, at least temporarily, a return to Poland. The women described in this chapter graduated in Poland, some of them worked there for a few years, and subsequently went to the UK to acquire skills in a foreign context. After spending a few years abroad, their plan is to go back to Poland to raise their children in a family-oriented environment with the help of their parents. Their decision to return is, however, not necessarily permanent. The women do not exclude the possibility of migrating to the UK again or of moving elsewhere in the world.

The aim of this chapter is to explore the link between the transnational mobility of skilled women migrants and their childrearing plans. The women in these vignettes are representatives of a successful global elite. They frequently travel between Poland and the UK and take advantage of market opportunities in both countries. One woman that I spoke to had a permanent managerial job in London and flew to Poland every second weekend to complete her studies there. Yet mobility across national borders becomes difficult when one has to take care of a baby. According to these women, childrearing requires the stable, secure environment that most of them expect to find only in Poland. Most of them are willing to return to Poland for a couple of years of childrearing and then stay there, return to England, or migrate elsewhere. Their migration projects fluctuate and are often changed on the basis of the current situation. This trend is reflective of wider tendencies in Polish migration, that is, the readiness to cross borders frequently and maintain transnational lives (Burrell, 2008; White and Ryan, 2008; Ryan et al., 2009).

From the economic perspective, this period of childrearing in Poland could be critical for Polish authorities' efforts to encourage these female migrants to stay in Poland. If the Polish labour market presented them with good employment opportunities and benefits, the women would be more likely to settle there. Unfortunately, as I shall show below, the British labour market is still more attractive than the one in Poland.

This chapter investigates if and how family-building decisions are linked with economic considerations in influencing the international migration trajectories of skilled women. It is directly addressing three areas that would benefit from more academic inquiry. First, we focus on migrants' family-building strategies, as opposed to investigating families where children are already present. The migration literature has recognized that the presence of children in the household influences who migrates, where to, and for how long. For example, in 'astronaut families' (Zhou, 1998; Waters, 2002; Ho, 2002; Chiang, 2008), the mothers accompany their children who pursue education abroad while the fathers remain in the country of origin to keep their jobs there. Other accounts speak about 'transnational motherhood' (Hondagneu-Sotelo and Avila, 1997), or 'global chains of care' (Ehrenreich and Hochschild, 2003), where migrant mothers, drawn to feminized jobs abroad, leave their children behind in the care of relatives. In the context of Polish migration, White (2009) analysed the migration of entire families from small towns in Poland. Yet there are few accounts of the complex interactions between the plans for migration and those for having children, although this issue has become increasingly important in the European context. The emigration of young couples causes concern among officials in many countries struggling with population decline. France, Sweden and Poland, among others, have adopted pro-natalist policies, intended to encourage younger couples to have more children (Grant et al., 2004). This study demonstrates how migration and family-building decisions are intertwined and can serve to improve and streamline existing policies to effectively encourage young people to stay in a country and establish a family there.

Second, this chapter joins numerous arguments that favour a more nuanced understanding of the nexus between development, gender and migration. Development is frequently understood in economic terms, for example as the increase of GDP per capita (Benería et al., 2012), but more-nuanced conceptualizations of development have come to light recently (Raghuram, 2007; Rahman, 2009; Tomei 2011). For example, Piper (2008) emphasizes the social dimension of development and describes the impact of migration on personal development among women migrants in Asia. Dannecker (2009) argues for looking at the notion of development from a multifaceted perspective of the migrants themselves. In this chapter I show that for migrant Polish women, development means more than general economic progress and unemployment reduction. It also entails access to employment opportunities that aim specifically at women re-entering the labour market after childrearing, the availability of flexible work arrangements, and childcare opportunities.

Recent reports, widely circulated in the British media, have pointed out that the birthrate among Polish women in the UK is higher than the birthrate in Poland (Iglicka, 2011). Polish mothers in the UK are more likely to have children than those in Poland. For England and Wales, this means that, between 2005 and 2011, the percentage of Polish babies among all babies born jumped from 0.5 to 2.7 per cent (Doyle, 2011, Department of Health figures). The most frequent interpretation of this phenomenon is that Polish migration to the UK is turning from temporary and circular to permanent, as migrants decide to establish families abroad (Iglicka, 2011). It also indicates that the policies and labour market conditions in the UK are more family friendly. The findings of this chapter confirm both of these theories. Polish women are aware of the better labour market situation in the UK and, while considering a temporary return to Poland for a short period of childrearing, they often express a desire to return and settle in the UK.

Finally, this study illustrates the transformative and politically relevant role of emotion in everyday life. The results show that many skilled migrant women choose to return to Poland temporarily to raise their children, although provisions for working mothers are significantly worse there than in the UK. They explain their decisions in terms of their emotional ties to their families and their homeland. In literature on geographies of emotion and affect a conflict has emerged between the perception of emotion as intensely personal and subjective (and thus less relevant), and the need for politically engaged research (Anderson and Smith, 2001; Thrift, 2004; McCormack, 2007). The disjunction, as many have argued, is based on an artificial classification of emotion as 'private' (Ettinger, 2004; Thien, 2005; Tolia-Kelly, 2006; Sharp, 2009). Emotions have enormous power to transform social and political structures. For example, Bosco (2007) shows that activism in Argentina is a form of emotional labour that helps build networks of resistance to political dominance. This study joins this stream of research in emphasizing the role of emotion in directing international migration.

A focus on skilled migrant women is important because their numbers are on the rise (Ouaked, 2002). In particular, the free movement of labour within the European Union has resulted in an increasing number of women crossing international borders in search of professional jobs. Numerous authors have bemoaned the lack of academic research on skilled women and the reproductive sphere of life (Kofman, 2000; Willis and Yeoh, 2000, 2002; Willis et al., 2002; Raghuram, 2004; Kofman and Raghuram, 2006). While a lot of literature has since been produced on gender and skilled migration (Hardill, 2004; Iredale, 2004; Yeoh and Willis, 2005; Riano and Baghdadi, 2007; Liversage, 2009; Meares, 2010), the inquiry into the interplay between migration, gender and development is not yet complete.

In the following sections, I shall first review the methodology used for this study. The next two sections will elaborate the connection between migration and childrearing plans and examine the role of local incentives in encouraging/discouraging mobility. Finally, in the conclusion I shall highlight the importance of looking at migration and development from the gendered perspective.

METHODS

This research was conducted in the United Kingdom and in Poland in 2007. It is based on 60 semi-structured interviews with migrants and returnees to Poland. For the purpose of this chapter, only interviews with skilled migrant women are analysed (30 interviews). The respondents were approached through the use of the snowball method, as well as through the internet network of Polish professionals abroad. Contacts were first obtained through my participation in Polish immigrant community events in London. This participant observation allowed me to verify that the respondents were indeed the appropriate target population for the interviews, that is, skilled young professionals. Most of the interviews in Poland were conducted by my research assistant, Anna, and utilized her local knowledge and contacts. This qualitative study is not intended to represent general trends in Polish migration to the UK. Rather, it illustrates the importance of particular motivations for migration, which are related to life-course events.

MIGRATION AND CHILDREARING PLANS

The interviews conducted confirm the long-established fact that migration decisions are often influenced by life-course stage and personal events. Factors such as the age of household members, migrants' marital status, the birth of children, entry into the labour force and retirement, determine people's motivations to move, domestically and internationally. In their study of domestic migration in the US, Chen and Rosenthal (2008) show that young migrants are motivated by economic opportunities, while older migrants tend to look at the place-specific amenities of particular places (see also Clark and Onaka, 1983; Clark et al., 1994). On the international level, Massey (1987) shows that Mexican households with a large number of dependants, that is, relatively young households, are likely to send a male worker to the United States. Ley and Kobayashi (2005) argue that the circular movement of migrants between Hong Kong and Canada is determined by the age of the children in the family and by the retirement of migrants.

These studies primarily rely on data established post facto, that is, on migrants' accounts of their move after it has taken place. In this study, I focus on the planning of migratory moves and use qualitative material to highlight the factors relevant to the planning process. In particular, I show that childrearing plans might affect migrants' decisions to leave Poland and to return.

The issue of having versus not having children first arose when women considered moving out of Poland. For many of them, the decision to migrate stemmed from the desire to defy rigid social norms that require women to have children soon after marriage. One of my respondents, Zofia, explained why she decided to leave Poland:

> So I was with my ex-boyfriend, we graduated at the same time and we decided to come for, let's say, two years to earn money for an apartment and then come back to Poland. And other than that, I simply wanted to go because I was driven. I did not want to immediately go to work in an office, and talk to these 50 years old ladies about 'when are you getting married?', 'when are you having children?'. (A9)

Zofia was convinced that staying in Poland would result in her having a boring office job, and a mundane, settled existence. She told me that she did not want stability at that point in her life; she was 23 when she decided to migrate. She was convinced that if she stayed in Poland, she would get a dead-end job and her personal development would be stalled. She was also obviously afraid to be pressured into establishing a family and having children. At the time of the interview she was working in a bank in Manchester and trying to get into a university to study for a two-year graduate degree. She was very happy with her career.

Another woman, Magda, complained about her family pressuring her to have children:

> It's terrible. We are now seven years after our wedding. I'm 27 years old. The Polish standard (for having children) is nine months after the wedding. Before we left there was this pressure from grandmothers and mothers. I believe that you either decide to have a baby very early, in order to have time for yourself later, or the other way round. I feel I still have at least ten years to go. (MM8)

Both Magda and her husband had lived in London for five years and had established successful careers there. They bought a nice apartment, spent vacations in exotic places and dreamed about a trip around the world. Moving out of Poland allowed Magda to escape her family's expectations about childrearing and follow her professional development path.

The migration literature abounds in examples of women escaping conservative social norms. For example, in their book on migration from the Dominican Republic, Grasmuck and Pessar (1991) show that for many women migration is a means of escape from the economic dominance of their husbands. In most cases, such migration decisions are interpreted as the victory of agency over structure and the decision to leave is interpreted as the woman's conscious move towards empowerment. In the Polish case, the key dimensions in deciding to migrate were the stage of the life cycle and individual career progress. The women moved early in their careers, or directly after graduation, because they considered it the only point in life when migration is actually possible. Krysia explained the timing of her move:

> It is not that I wanted to change my job. I simply wanted to do something with my life. . . . You are at such a moment . . . And it was this moment when you don't have children yet, you don't have an apartment, you don't have a mortgage – this is the moment when you can leave and do something. (AA1)

Krysia and her husband both had good jobs in Poland. She had worked in the marketing department of a publishing house for two and a half years. She was young enough in her career that the move to the United Kingdom did not disrupt any potential career options for her. Furthermore, she felt free from any kind of obligations like children or a mortgage. That is why, as she says, it was a good moment to leave.

Iwona bought her flight ticket to London on the day of her graduation. She finished her studies in administration and political science and decided to emigrate. She believes that her decision to move prevented her from following the standard Polish life course: studies, job, marriage, children. When describing her friends in Warsaw she says:

> [If I had stayed in Poland] I would be working in administration 99%. My friends in Poland have a good life standard, they don't starve, they are not in poverty, they have the American lifestyle, the mortgage. It does not scare me, I will probably do that too. They work, they have children. It's the life-stage, [if I had stayed in Poland] I would probably be at a similar stage. (MM16)

In this example Iwona's power and agency manifests itself in her choice to postpone a particular stage in life, which, according to her, involves having children and a mortgage. She believes that if she had not migrated she would find herself in that stage. Her migration was timed in such a way that she was able to explore other options before tying herself to home and family. Iwona does not want to avoid this kind of attachment eternally – it does not scare her, as she explains. She just wants to have the option to enjoy life first. She likes her life in London, and the ability to travel.

Since settling in London, she has visited France, Morocco, Switzerland, Istanbul, Barcelona and Berlin; something she would not have been able to accomplish had she stayed in Poland and had children.

For many of these migrant women, having children means a reduction in mobility. In their accounts, childrearing is linked with being in one place (most likely Poland), having to work and paying off the mortgage. Women like Iwona do not want to avoid this situation completely. They just want to postpone it for a couple of years while working abroad. Frequently, they are planning to go back to Poland and have children there. Return migration is therefore much influenced by childrearing plans. Krysia responded to my question about having children as follows:

> We were thinking about it . . . It would be great, but I will not manage it on my own . . . It would be nice to have your mother by your side, who will tell you what to do when the baby is crying, right?

And later she added:

> I would like to go back already, really, because it is . . . Here you can have fun, but later go back to normal life. Have a normal family and everything. (AA1)

Presented this way, for Krysia her time in London is the moment to have fun and enjoy life before going back to the 'normal life' and a 'normal family' in Poland (for a mother's 'quest for normalcy' in England, see Lopez Rodriquez, 2010; Rabikowska, 2010). The availability of help from her mother also seems to be an essential element in decision making. Magda expressed similar sentiments:

> If I were to get pregnant, it would be very hard for me alone, this is the minus. It is very beautiful and nice to be here as a couple, but when the need for help arises, then there is nobody, because nobody is able to sacrifice their time for you. You have to rely on yourself. My mother or Marek's mother probably would be very happy to help us, but that would mean that either they would have to come here, or we would have to leave for some time. (AA4)

Magda and Marek have not decided what to do should they have children. Magda does not want to go back home, but at the same time she also thinks that it is unrealistic to expect the grandmothers to come to the UK. Her mother does not speak English and would not feel comfortable caring for children in a foreign country. Magda also says that she does not want to impose on her mother-in-law's independence. It is possible, therefore, that Magda and Marek will leave and stay in Poland at least until their children reach the daycare age and then they will return to England.

For some women, going to Poland to have children is not dictated by the pragmatic considerations of childcare. For many it signifies a return to 'normal' life. While life in London is considered a step up on the career path, these migrants see their ultimate goal as having a family in Poland. Alicja, who is single, describes her migration plans as follows:

> I'm thinking about staying two more years. We will see how it goes with my job ... I want to learn as much as I can, and if I get such an offer like the one I had three months ago (for a job in Poland), then I'm going straight back to Poland ... I am not a person concentrated on doing business, money, money and more money. I am a woman, I am thinking about having children. Let the men (make money). (MM6)

Alicja considers motherhood as an essential part of her identity as a woman. Like many others, she has internalized Polish norms about motherhood. She goes as far as to present career and money-making as being a masculine activity. A return to Poland is associated with having children and a focus on the family. At the same time, she is making good use of her time in London. She has been promoted several times in her career and is still expecting to stay for two more years to 'learn as much as she can' about banking.

The stories of these Polish women confirm that childbearing and childrearing are crucial to the making of migration plans. From the timing of the move from Poland through career-making in London to the eventual return, the planning of international mobility is enmeshed in reproductive choices. These findings confirm the feminist argument that the productive and reproductive spheres are inextricably connected (Benería, 1979; Nash and Fernández-Kelly, 1983; Hanson and Pratt, 1988). Women's entry and re-entry into the labour market is determined by their childrearing choices and obligations. Furthermore, the process of making migration decisions depends on women's individual agency, but is also controlled by wider norms of behaviour and social support systems. It is acceptable for Polish women to leave Poland soon after graduation, when they do not have established careers or childcare obligations. The time they spend abroad is often perceived as a time to 'have fun' and to hone one's professional skills. The eventual return to Poland is a result, on the one hand, of the very pragmatic need for childcare and, on the other, of the perception of Poland as being the appropriate place for childrearing.

Life-course progress influences both the productive and reproductive choices of women. It should be borne in mind, however, that all the decisions, including migration decisions, are made in the context of particular places. Pratt and Hanson (1993, p. 30) write: 'Lives are lived through time; they are also lived in place and through space'. Although the timing of particular decisions is important, it is also important to consider the local conditions that influence them. The following section focuses on the two environments relevant for Polish migrants' decision making – Poland and the UK.

CHILDREARING, MIGRATION AND LOCAL INCENTIVES

Places offer the structural context in which decisions are made. This section investigates how migrant women describe the childrearing options in their country of origin and in the UK, and how they link the situation in those countries to their migration decisions. I considered migrants as being 'emplaced', that is, influenced by the physical location of their activities. The evaluation of the local place is always conducted simultaneously with the evaluation of the foreign location. The migrant situation breeds such comparisons. I have not had a single conversation with a female or male migrant, where comparisons between Poland and the UK were not drawn. All aspects of life are dissected in an attempt to understand the differences. Migrants compare everything from people's behaviours and attitudes through to job descriptions and salaries, to the price of grocery items in the two countries. Through comparison they validate or invalidate their choices about migration and make future plans.

Important issues for skilled migrant women are the advantages and disadvantages of having children in Poland and the UK. As discussed above, a primary factor pulling them back to Poland is the availability of childcare help from parents and grandparents. There are, however, other factors that they take into consideration, the most important of which is the availability of childcare benefits. In the case of skilled women, the benefits that they are interested in are not the welfare cheques offered by the government to mothers, but the provisions offered by their jobs. Employment policies in the UK are generally considered more child friendly than in Poland. Krysia describes her company as being very accommodating to future mothers:

> My company currently has this program that when you have a baby you can work at home for two days (a week). You can leave work earlier, you can come to work later. And it does not influence your salary. You have 100% of your salary, completely. They share the cost of daycare, or a babysitter, whatever you prefer. (AA1)

This very advantageous situation is contrasted with Krysia's situation in Poland where she was not entitled to any benefits. Her Polish company did not want to sign a permanent contract with her, leaving her with only short-term contracts. As a result, she could not obtain insurance through her employers and was not entitled to maternity benefits. She was also unable to get a loan for a house. 'In this respect, it is for sure better [in the UK]', she claims.

The difference can be explained partly because of the legal differences between the two countries. In the UK, women are entitled to benefits (statutory maternity pay) for 39 weeks after giving birth, while in Poland they receive maternity pay only for 20 weeks. Krysia also provides an example of her sister in Poland, who had serious problems finding a job after having a baby:

> K: My sister, who had a baby . . . was looking for a job for two years . . .
> A: Is it because she had a baby?
> K: Yes. Everything was OK, she was being invited to the second-stage interviews . . . Right . . . And then the questions: . . . 'How are you with time flexibility?' My sister says she is completely flexible, but she has to be there at 5pm, because at five she is picking up her kid from the kindergarten. So they say 'You are not flexible.' My sister says 'Yes, I am', and they say 'No, no, no'. (AA1)

Krysia's sister faces the typical charge brought by employers against female employees, the supposed lack of flexibility and 24/7 availability. More often than men, women have to coordinate childcare arrangements and job requirements, and frequently childcare needs take precedence over career choices. Hanson and Pratt (1995) show that women in Worcester (MA) looked for jobs in close proximity to their place of residence in order to be able to pick up their children from school and be available for emergencies. Polish employers seem to expect round-the-clock availability from their employees, regardless of their family situation.

In the UK, the law requires employers to be flexible. While paternity leave has been available in the UK since 2003, it was not available in Poland at the time of research and was only introduced in 2010. Alina, a university teacher, explained the situation to me as follows:

> [Here] everybody has the same entitlements. De facto, you have nine months paid by your insurance premiums, the National Insurance, you pay it through the insurance premiums. Men also have a two-week maternity leave. Then some people have 'flexi time', you can start your work between 8 and 10am, this is advantageous, you can choose who takes the kids to school and leave earlier to pick them up. In Poland in some companies it is also like that, but these are foreign companies. My brother works for Siemens, he can come in at 10am. My father works in a state company, if he came in at 8.05am he would be late. (MM12)

Alina's observation is interesting. While foreign companies operating in Poland have adopted more women-friendly standards of flexibility, state-owned businesses and agencies maintain their conservative arrangements. The Polish state, in general, does not promote policies that would enhance women's situation in the labour market. One recently introduced measure, aimed to remedy the demographic decline, is the so-called '*becikowe*', or 'cradle money'. It represents a small sum of money – about US$280 – provided by the state to the family after the birth of a baby. The aim of this incentive is to encourage Polish women to have more children. Most parents, however, realize that this amount is insufficient as a means of helping with the economic and practical difficulties of raising a child. One of my interviewees, Alina, believes that not only is it insufficient, but it is also representative of the general lack of respect for mothers:

> The question of women's status in Poland is not appreciated. Recently they started to worry about the demographic decline, that Polish women don't want to give birth. But there is no incentive. It can't be a one-time help, for show, such a token. The atmosphere is important, how you see the role of a mother, what the woman's salary will be, if she is going to have retirement benefits, or unemployment benefits. (It is about) how you treat this period of maternity. (MM12)

As my interviewees do not have the experience of childrearing in Poland, they frequently rely on accounts from their friends and relatives. Krysia talked about her sister, Alina about her brother. Dorota also mentioned her sister's problems: 'My sister was on maternity leave and she almost got fired because of that. She had problems' (MM7). Yet, despite these negative portrayals of the Polish labour market situation, migrant women still intend to have children in Poland. As discussed in the previous section, return is the preferred option for the majority of respondents. One reason is the practical availability of childcare through grandparents. The other reason, I argue, is the imaginary construction of Poland as a place that is appropriate for raising kids. Poland is traditional, slow-paced, safe and also promotes conservative values. These constructions of place seem to have more appeal for women than the experience-based negative accounts of women's labour market situation.

One of the issues that make Poland more appealing than England is the importance of traditional family values. Barbara, a human resources administrator in one of the major London hotels, told me that she does not like the transitory character of life in England:

> Even relationships here are temporary, the people don't pay attention to each other and to the values ... I still miss the values in which I was brought up. I would be afraid to raise children here, even if I was with an English man I would like us to live in Poland. The values – family, friends. The human being is not an object. (MM10)

Barbara believes that family values are lost in England. She appreciates many things about Poland: the respect shown to older people, obligations towards parents and relatives, and the time spent together as a family:

> People have time to share with others, for family and friends . . . And what an advantage for the children, the grandparents have time to answer children's questions . . . I like this provincial character of Poland. Probably in ten years it is going to look different, I hope I can still catch this traditional lifestyle. Here it no longer exists. Parents are waiting for the children to grow up . . . waiting for the children to move out, the grandparents are somewhere, but nobody even heard about them. (MM10)

Attachment to family and friends was very important when considering return. For Krysia, just like for Barbara, missing her parents was one of the main factors pulling her back:

> This is our idea – to go back home as soon as possible. Because we want to go back to our family as soon as possible. [In Poland] you have an apartment, you have a home, you have an apartment where nobody is knocking on your door . . . and your own bathroom and kitchen; you have friends, you can go visit your mum for a while. Here you live like in a students' house: everything is in motion, the people are changing, because they are coming and going, and you don't have this nest that would be yours, and just yours. And this is something I miss most. I miss stability. (AA1)

For Krysia, residing in Poland represents stability both in the sense of having her own apartment and her place in the world, but also in the sense of having family support. She misses the possibility of dropping by at her mother's place whenever she feels like it. The role of emotional attachments and affective imaginations of places has just recently started to be explored in migration research. Conradson and McKay (2007) argue that emotion is a central aspect of international mobility. Gray (2008) believes that there is an explicit connection between movement and attachment. Aranda (2007) confirms these findings and shows that, for professional Puerto Rican migrants, family was an important factor motivating return migration. She conceptualizes the process of migration decision making through the notion of 'emotional embeddedness', that is, the affect towards one's surroundings and a sense of belonging in a place. Polish migrants seem to be embedded emotionally in their home-places in Poland, where place signifies not only a physical location, but also the social relationships and emotional ties. Their images of localities in Poland are shaped by their migration experiences and are frequently idealized. For example, London would often be presented as a 'corrupt city' while places in Poland exuded security and childhood sentiment. Natasza, who works in a large shipping company in London, expressed her emotional attachment to her home city in Poland as follows:

> I loved it. I miss the sea. I have good memories of the city, it was nice. I love it, I miss it, maybe I will go back there sometimes. It is first of all the city of my childhood. I don't intend to return yet, for at least a year. But my family is there, so I can't imagine another place to go back to. (MM11)

For Natasza, the love of the city and the love for her family blend together to form a dream place of return. She describes London, on the other hand, as a 'violent city'. She is dreaming of having a family and a little cottage in the countryside. Such experiences of places are typical for migration. Svasek (2010, p. 3) writes that 'it should be acknowledged that certain emotional processes are caused by migration-specific issues. These processes do not take place in the isolated minds/bodies of the migrants, but arise in the interaction of individuals with their human and non-human surroundings'. Missing home, a typical migrant experience, results for many migrant women in the decision to return, despite their 'objective' knowledge of the disadvantages of women's labour market situation in Poland.

Asia, a student, does not exactly fit the 'skilled migrant' category. She migrated with her boyfriend during her studies in Poland and was employed in housekeeping and laundry in a small English city. She was the one, however, who explained best her decision to return:

> A lot of people could not understand why I came back from England to Poland when I was pregnant, that I didn't stay there, because it is better there. I came back for other reasons: I simply wanted to be with my family and I did not want to be alone, although their social benefits there [UK] are much better than here [Poland] (C2)

Women's emotional craving for Poland leads them to return there for childrearing. It should be emphasized, however, that some of them indicated the possibility of onward migration. Krysia wants to have a baby in Poland, but her husband has been trying to convince her to move to the United States. Although she is not in favour of living in the US, she does not exclude the possibility of going elsewhere.

> We thought about moving somewhere else (than the US). But we don't know yet. I would like to go to the Czech Republic or somewhere around there. Yes, I don't know what else we will think of. Maybe we will go to Poland for some time, stay there, buy an apartment, rent it out later and travel somewhere else. I don't know. (AA1)

Similarly, Natasza wants to return to Poland eventually, but she does not exclude the possibility of migrating somewhere else, where the quality of life is better than in London. She thought about moving to a place with a better climate, possibly to the Mediterranean region. My findings indicate that skilled migrant women give in to the emotional pull towards Poland and intend to go there for the early years of childrearing. Onward migration, however, remains an option. It is more likely to become a reality if the Polish government fails to create conditions that encourage mothers' participation in the labour market. Going back to work will not only allow women to continue with their fulfilling careers, it will also give them the economic means to increase their quality of life in Poland.

CONCLUSION

European countries are struggling to maintain positive or at least zero population growth. For many young families, the decision whether and when to have children is influenced by their international mobility. The links between migration and family-building decisions have been explored in the research on population movement within countries (Sandell, 1977; Mincer, 1978; Cadwallader, 1992). This study is a call for more such research in an international context, with an emphasis on the gendered nature of mobility. Migration between Poland and the UK has significant consequences for both the population structure of Poland and the personal career development of the women migrants themselves.

An increased feminization of migration has emerged in the context of globalization (Benería et al., 2012). Improved communication and transportation technologies have increased the volume of international flows of women. The European Union provides a very specific context in which the mobility of labour is, in most cases, not curtailed by the state. The women in my research have the economic and political freedom to move freely between Poland, the UK and other member states. This intra-regional mobility may have negative consequences for demographic and fiscal structures in Poland.

The last Eurostat report shows that in 2060 Poland will have the highest percentage of people over 65 years of age – every third national will be retired. These data reflect only prognoses on birth and death rates and do not include the out-migration statistics (in Iglicka, 2011, p. 2). At the same time, Polish women in the UK have higher birthrates than women in Poland. My research indicates that, despite career opportunities being available in the UK, many Polish families want to return to Poland to raise children. A critical policy issue emerges from this phenomenon: how to ensure that women are able to re-enter the Polish labour market after giving birth. In cases where the grandparents' help is unavailable, the Polish inadequate system of maternity benefits does not encourage a return to work. Leaving skilled migrant women out of the labour force leads to a significant loss of foreign-learned skills and experiences. If the labour market in Poland remains unfriendly towards working mothers, return migration may prove to be temporary. The women I interviewed often spoke about returning to Poland for a couple of years to bring up the children and then embarking on further migratory voyages. One migration experience significantly increases the probability of further migration and many skilled women feel empowered by their professional success to look for satisfying jobs in various European and non-European countries.

The findings of this study reiterate the feminist argument concerning the necessity to look at both the productive and reproductive spheres in order to understand economic and demographic processes. The free movement of people in the EU market is directly linked to the reproductive choices made by skilled migrant women. The discriminatory practices of local labour markets, combined with localized social norms, lead to particular migration trajectories and family-building decisions. These decisions are not made in an emotional vacuum. Rather, emotion and personal attachments are critical for understanding both the decision to have children and the decision to move.

REFERENCES

Anderson, K. and Susan J. Smith (2001), 'Editorial: Emotional geographies', *Transactions of the Institute of British Geographers*, **26** (1), 7–10.
Aranda, E.M. (2007), *Emotional Bridges to Puerto Rico: Migration, Return Migration, and the Struggle of Incorporation*, Lanham, MD: Rowman & Littlefield.
Benería, L. (1979), 'Reproduction, production and the sexual division of labour', *Cambridge Journal of Economics*, **3**, 203–25.
Benería, L., C.D. Deere and N. Kabeer (2012), 'Gender and international migration: globalisation, development and governance', *Feminist Economics*, **18**, 1–33.
Bosco, F. (2007), 'Emotions that build networks: geographies of human rights movements in Argentina and beyond', *Tijdschrift voor Economische en Sociale Geografie*, **98**, 545–63.
Burrell, K. (2008), 'Time matters: temporal contexts of Polish transnationalism', in M.P. Smith and J. Eade (eds), *Transnational Ties: Cities, Migrations, and Identities*, New Brunswick, NJ: Transaction, pp. 15–38.
Cadwallader, M.T. (1992), *Migration and Residential Mobility: Macro- and Micro Approaches*, Madison, WI: UW Press.
Chen, Y. and S.S. Rosenthal (2008), 'Local amenities and life-cycle migration: do people move for jobs or fun?', *Journal of Urban Economics*, **64**, 519–37.
Chiang, L.-H.N. (2008), '"Astronaut families": transnational lives of middle-class Taiwanese married women in Canada', *Social and Cultural Geography*, **9**, 505–18.
Clark, W., M.C. Deurloo and F.M. Dieleman (1994), 'Tenure changes in the context of micro-level family and macro-level economic shifts', *Urban Studies*, **31**, 137–54.
Clark, W. and J.L. Onaka (1983), 'Lifecycle and housing adjustment as explanations of residential mobility', *Urban Studies*, **20**, 47–57.

Conradson, D. and D. McKay (2007), 'Translocal subjectivities: mobility, connection, emotion', *Mobilities*, **2**, 167–74.
Dannecker, P. (2009), 'Migrant visions of development: a gendered approach', *Population, Space and Place*, **15**, 119–32.
Doyle, J. (2011), 'More children in Britain born to Polish mothers than those from any other foreign country', *Mail Online*, 19 September (accessed 7 September 2012).
Ehrenreich, B. and A.R. Hochschild (2003), *Global Woman: Nannies, Maids, and Sex Workers in the New Economy*, New York: Metropolitan Books.
Ettinger, N. (2004), 'Towards a critical theory of untidy geographies: the spatiality of emotions in consumption and production', *Feminist Economics*, **10**, 21–54.
Grant, J., S. Hoorens, S. Sivadasan, M. Van het Loo, J. DaVanzo, L. Hale, S. Gibson and W. Butz (2004), *Low Fertility and Population Ageing: Causes, Consequences and Policy Options*, Cambridge: Rand Europe Corporation.
Grasmuck, S. and P.R. Pessar (1991), *Between Two Islands, Dominican International Migration*, Berkeley, CA and Oxford: University of California Press.
Gray, B. (2008), 'Putting emotion and reflexivity to work in researching migration', *Sociology*, **42**, 935–52.
Hanson, S. and G. Pratt (1988), 'Reconceptualising the links between home and work in urban geography', *Economic Geography*, **64**, 299–321.
Hanson, S. and G. Pratt (1995), *Gender, Work and Space*, London: Routledge.
Hardill, I. (2004), 'Transnational living and moving experiences: intensified mobility and dual career households', *Population, Space and Place*, **10**, 375–89.
Ho, E.S. (2002), 'Multi-local residence, transnational networks: Chinese "astronaut" families in New Zealand', *Asian and Pacific Migration Journal*, **11**, 145–64.
Hondagneu-Sotelo, P. and E. Avila (1997), '"I'm here but I'm there": the meanings of Latina transnational motherhood', *Gender & Society*, **11**, 548–71.
Iglicka, K. (2011), 'Migracje Dlugookresowe i Osiedlencze z Polski po 2004 Roku-Przyklad Wielkiej Brytanii: Wyzwania dla Statystyki i Demografii Panstwa', *Raporty i Analizy*, Centrum Stosunkow Miedzynarodowych.
Iredale, R. (2004), 'Gender, immigration policies and accreditation: valuing the skills of professional women migrants', *Geoforum*, **35**, 155–66.
Kofman, E. (2000), 'The invisibility of skilled female migrants and gender relations in studies of skilled migration in Europe', *International Journal of Population Geography*, **6**, 45–59.
Kofman, E. and P. Raghuram (2006), 'Gender and global labour migrations: incorporating skilled workers', *Antipode*, **38**, 282–303.
Ley, D. and A. Kobayashi (2005), 'Back to Hong Kong: return migration or transnational sojourn?', *Global Networks*, **5**, 111–27.
Liversage, A. (2009), 'Vital conjunctures, shifting horizons: high-skilled female immigrants looking for work', *Work Employment and Society*, **23**, 120–41.
Lopez Rodriguez, M. (2010), 'Migration and a quest for "normalcy": Polish migrant mothers and the capitalization of meritocratic opportunities in the UK', *Social Identities*, **16** (3), 339–58.
Massey, D.S. (1987), 'Understanding Mexican migration to the United States', *American Journal of Sociology*, **92**, 1372–403.
McCormack, D. (2007), 'Molecular affects in human geographies', *Environment and Planning A*, **39**, 359–77.
Meares, C. (2010), 'A fine balance: women, work and skilled migration', *Women's Studies International Forum*, **33**, 473–81.
Mincer, J. (1978), 'Family migration decisions', *Journal of Political Economy*, **86**, 749–73.
Nash, J.C. and M.P. Fernández-Kelly (1983), *Women, Men, and the International Division of Labor*, Albany, NY: SUNY Press.
Ouaked, S. (2002), 'Transatlantic Roundtable on High-skilled Migration and Sending Countries Issues', *International Migration*, **40** (4), 153–66.
Piper, N. (2008), 'Feminisation of migration and the social dimensions of development: the Asian case', *Third World Quarterly*, **29**, 1287–303.

Pratt, G. and S. Hanson (1993), 'Women and work across the life course: moving beyond essentialism', in C. Katz and J. Monk (eds), *Full Circles: Geographies of Women over the Life Course*, New York: Routledge, pp. 27–54.

Rabikowska, M. (2010), 'Negotiation of normality and identity among migrants from Eastern Europe to the United Kingdom after 2004', *Social Identities*, **16** (3), 285–96.

Raghuram, P. (2004), 'The difference that skills make: gender, family migration strategies and regulated labour markets', *Journal of Ethnic and Migration Studies*, **30**, 303–21.

Raghuram, P. (2007), 'Which migration, what development: unsettling the edifice of migration and development', Working Paper 28, COMCAD Arbeitspapiere, Bielefeld.

Rahman, M.M. (2009), 'Temporary migration and changing family dynamics: implications for social development', *Population, Space and Place*, **15**, 161–74.

Riano, I. and N. Baghdadi (2007), 'Understanding the labour market participation of skilled immigrant women in Switzerland: the interplay of class, ethnicity, and gender', *Journal of International Migration and Integration*, **8**, 163–83.

Ryan, L., R. Sales and M. Tilki (2009), 'Recent Polish migrants in London: accessing and participating in social networks across borders', in K. Burrell (ed.) *Polish Migration to the UK in the 'New' European Union: After 2004*, Farnham: Ashgate, pp. 149–66.

Sandell, S.H. (1977), 'Women and the economics of family migration', *Review of Economics and Statistics*, **59**, 406–14.

Sharp, J. (2009), 'Geography and gender: what belongs to feminist geography? Emotion, power and change', *Progress in Human Geography*, **33** (1), 74–80.

Svasek, M. (2010), 'On the move: emotions and human mobility', *Journal of Ethnic and Migration Studies*, **36**, 865–80.

Thien, D. (2005), 'After or beyond feeling? A consideration of affect and emotion in geography', *Area*, **37**, 450–56.

Thrift, N. (2004), 'Intensities of feeling: towards a spatial politics of affect', *Geografiska Annaler*, **86B**, 57–78.

Tolia-Kelly, D. (2006), 'Affect – an ethnocentric encounter? Exploring the "universalist" imperative of emotional/affectual geographies', *Area*, **38**, 213–17.

Tomei, G. (2011), 'Cultural and symbolic dimensions of the migration–development nexus. the salience of community', IMI Working Papers 30, International Migration Institute, University of Oxford.

Waters, J.L. (2002), 'Flexible families? "Astronaut" households and the experiences of lone mothers in Vancouver, British Columbia', *Social and Cultural Geography*, **3**, 117–34.

White, A. (2009), 'Family migration from small-town Poland: a livelihood strategy approach', in K. Burrell (ed.) *Polish Migration to the UK in the 'New' European Union: After 2004*, Farnham: Ashgate, pp. 67–85.

White, A. and L. Ryan (2008), 'Polish "temporary" migration: the formation and significance of social networks', *Europe-Asia Studies*, **60** (9), 1467–502.

Willis, K. and B. Yeoh (2000), 'Gender and transnational household strategies: Singaporean migration to Chi', *Regional Studies*, **34**, 253–64.

Willis, K. and B. Yeoh (2002), 'Gendering transnational communities: a comparison of Singaporean and British migrants in China', *Geoforum*, **33**, 553–65.

Willis, K., B. Yeoh and S. Fakhri (2002), 'Introduction: transnational elites', *Geoforum*, **33**, 505–7.

Yeoh, B. and K. Willis (2005), 'Singaporeans in China: transnational women elites and the negotiation of gendered identities', *Geoforum*, **36**, 211–22.

Zhou, M. (1998), '"Parachute kids" in Southern California: the educational experience of Chinese children in transnational families', *Educational Policy*, **12**, 682–704.

Index

African studies 20, 251–2, 351–2; *see also* names of individual countries and regions
Agustín, L. 238, 240
American Sociological Review 234
Andean studies, *see* gender, migration and development (Andean study); names of individual countries
anthropological perspectives, *see* culture and European exclusion
Anzaldúa, G. 239
Arthur, J. 198
articulationist approach 3–4, 32–3, 146, 147–8, 155
Asian studies 235, 240
Autrepart 250–51

Barcelona 320
Basch, L. 312
Bastia, T. 372
Bayesian networks 378–89
Belgium 7, 25, 30, 31, 36, 208, 214, 277, 289, 420, 421–5, 427–31, 433, 434, 436, 441, 444
Belgian studies, *see* domestic workers and usages of reciprocity
belonging 295
Bhabha, H. 306
birth rates
Polish-UK 456
Spanish-Chinese 171–2
Bolivian studies 135, 136, 372
migration to Spain (gendered perspective) 317–29
adjustments and impacts 326–9
interregional circular patterns 318–19
migration flows 317–18
qualitative approach 324–9
quantitative approach 319–24
remittances and return practices 322–4
Bryceson, D. 315

Canadian studies 457–8
Cantu, L. 237
capitalism, *see* globalization of capitalism
care/care work
carers' temporary migrations 439–40, 447–8
concept of 156, 399
development of literature on 236–7
growth factors 50–51
labour and social rights, *see* care work, rights and citizenship
social reproduction and 28–31, 50–51, 153–7, 314
undocumented migrants 53
see also domestic work
'care chains' 50, 154–5, 157, 400
care work, rights and citizenship 397–417
drivers of migration and transnational households 397–8
demand increase 398
labour rights and political/legal registration 406–8
labour rights violations 408–12
'cultural traits' variable 409
positive self-assessment (rights and duties) 410–11
'servile pole' and variables 408–9
spheres (employee and employer perceptions) 412
place/spatial setting factors 415
professionalization and acknowledgement of 414
self-care and 413–14
study approach and data 398–9
conclusions drawn from 415–17
immigrant and native comparison 404–6

471

theoretical discussion on feminized international migration 399–406
  'citizenship' 403
  comparative approach 401
  duties (carers' and states') 403–4
  global care chains 400
  social inequalities/violations and gender bias 401–3, 415
    concatenated denial of rights 402
  studies in Spanish and Chilean immigration 400–401
caring gaps 190
child transfers, *see* West African study on child transfers
childcare services in receiving country 425, 462–3
childrearing 453–68
children left behind 54, 171–2, 190, 217, 219, 326–7
  grown child responses 223–4
children within migrant families 137–8, 210–11, 218
Chilean studies, *see* care work, rights and citizenship
Chinese studies 165–82, 457–8
  literature on 165
  migration to Spain, familial/business nature of 166
    gender in development 179–81
    migration flow overview 167–9
    overview 32
    remittances 174–9
      donations 178–9
      family ties and values 174–7, 180–81
      investment and social capital 173–4, 177–8
    role of government policies 168–9
    transnational family businesses 172–4
    transnational households 170–72
Chronic Poverty Research Centre (CPRC) 115
circulation, strategies and patterns 251–2, 318–19
citizenship 30, 83, 403–4
co-development, Andean countries and Spain 128, 130–31, 137–41

Cohn-Bendit, D. 79
Colombian studies 134, 135–6
colonial order 147–8
commodification 420, 421–2, 428–9
commodity/production chains 5–7, 25–6
conditional cash transfer programmes 102
Congolese studies 202
crime 241–2
'cultural intimacy' 297–8
culture and rhetorics of exclusion in Europe 69–90
  cultural fundamentalism and 76–80
    human nature argument 78–80
    legitimization of exclusion 77–8
  French and British positions on 84–8
    British ethnic integration 86–8
    French Republican assimilation 85–6
  national identity and definition 88–90
  racism versus cultural fundamentalism 80–84
    political exclusion (citizenship) 83
    rationalization of cultural fundamentalism 81–3
    rationalization of racism 80–81
  rhetorical shifting of anti-immigration sentiments 71–2
    economic ills and 73–4
    from racial categories to cultural 74–6
    'us' and 'them' rhetoric 73
    xenophobic reactions and national sovereignty 69–70

Dale, G. 426
Danish studies, *see* gendered and emotional spaces
decision-making, *see* migration decisions
decolonial perspective 147–8
'Defining Gender in the 21st Century' 115
delocalization and global commodity chains 5–7

dependency theory 11–12
development, overview of concept
  conceptualization of feminism and 20, 150–51
  development and its transformations 19–20
  institutional/stakeholder approaches 23–5
  literature overview 20–23, 455
development and governance, *see* globalization and development
development and migration studies, *see* development in sending countries; gender, migration and development (academic and policy overview); gender, migration and development
development in sending countries 52–9
  impact on migration 58–9
  knowledge transfer 58
  labour market impacts 55
  negatives of migration (brain drain) debate 52–5
  remittances and their use 55–8, 177–9, 368–9
  gender and 179–81, 369–72
  second-generation transnationalism and 270
discipline and morality 191–202
division of labour 149, 152, 254–5, 319, 321
  labour complementarity and 338–42, 346–51
domestic work 152, 251–2, 253–4, 255
  internationalization, *see* internationalization of domestic work (Spanish study)
  reciprocity, *see* domestic workers and usages of reciprocity
  social reproduction and 146–7, 148, 153–9
  see also care/care work
domestic workers and usages of reciprocity 420–35
  Belgian context
    child and elderly care 424–5
    immigration history 422–3
    service voucher scheme 423, 424
    undocumented and legal migrants 423
  commodification and non-commodification 420, 421–2, 428–9
  overview 434–5
  Polanyian market exchange, reciprocity and redistribution 30, 420–21, 425
  reciprocity, conceptual framework 425–7
    how reciprocity is studied 426–7
    (market) exchange and reciprocity, definitions 426
    redistribution, definition 427
  reciprocity, usages 428–9
    employment conditions and stability 431–3
    finding a job 429–31
  study methodology 421, 427–8
  see also undocumented migration
Dominican Republic studies 459
Donato, K. 11, 234, 235
Dummett, A. 87

economic factors
  articulation of productive–reproductive spheres 148
  deregulation and crisis (2008) 47–8
  Malthusian 'population bomb' 73
  'smart economics' 97–103, 104
  see also labour market
Ecuadorian studies
  remittances and gender 129, 130–31, 135, 136, 361–73
    data, lack of 377–8
    gendered effects 369–72
      family-in-law effects 371
      vehicle acquisition 371–2
    gendered migration flows 134, 362
    migration and development nexus 137–40
    overview 27, 372–3
    remittance houses 370–71
    remittances as development fund ('savings') 368–9
      control issues 369
    remittances as maintenance funds ('emic') 366–8
      affected by male children 368
      drawbacks and power imbalances 367–8

sender and receiver relationship
(dyad) 363–6
different behaviours 364
motivation, enjoyment 365
power imbalances 364
sender's supervision
mechanisms 366
types and management of
transfer 365–6
study data and methodology
362–3
remittances through Bayesian
networks 376–91
analysis (Spain–Ecuador corridor)
384–9
data 385–8
migrant community in Spain
384–5
migration history 384–9
overview 389–91
results 388–9
existing data 377–8
female generated, and effect on
female recipients 377
model 378–82
remitting profile and family
monetary needs 380–81
stock of migrants in host
country 382
structured through expert
knowledge 382–3
transaction costs 381
wage variable and labour profile
381
educational factors 52–4
Elson, D. 108, 115
European Union and European
countries 235, 238
child transfers 190, 194, 195
circulation patterns 251–2
culture, *see* culture and rhetorics of
exclusion in Europe
domestic workers 352, 353–4
migration cycle 7
Moroccan immigration, *see*
Moroccan study on return
migration and intra-household
power
pro-natalist policies 455
second-generation transnationalism,

see integration and
transnational engagement
'Women in Development' 128
see also names of individual
countries
Evans, D. 109, 111–12

Falquet, J. 255
family as strategic discourse of
co-development 137–41
family dynamics 51, 54
child transfer, *see* West African study
on child transfers
Chinese migration and, *see* Chinese
studies
family reunification decision making
216–19
Herzfeld's 'cultural intimacy' 298
intercultural marriages 298–301
remittance processes 361–73
transnational families, *see*
transnational families
family planning/building decisions 33,
73, 453–68
feminism 20, 147, 253, 295
feminization of migration 14, 49–52,
134–7, 149–52, 362, 376–8
fertility rates 73–4
Filipino studies 51, 190, 237, 239, 255,
429
financial crisis (2008) 47–8
Fordism 7
foreign assistance 58
fostering 190–91
French studies 23, 75–6, 84–6,
246–62

Gabbacia, Donna 234, 235, 249
garment industry 5–6
gender, definition and function 146,
249
gender and immigration, new research
directions 233–42
borderlands and migration 239–40
gender and vilification of
immigrants 241–2
gender as constituent element of
migration 234–5, 313–14
overview 233–4
research needs 240–41

sex trafficking 238–9
sexualities 237–8
transnational families 315–17, 326–9
women's care work 236–7
see also gender, migration and development (academic and policy overview); migration
gender, integration and transnational engagement 271–2, 273–6, 286–7
gender, migration and development (academic and policy overview) 1–35
  development as a result 19–25
    concept of development and its transformations 19–20
    conceptualization of feminism and 20
    international institutional/stakeholder approaches 23–5
    literature overview 20–23
  gender–migration axis 9–19
    empowerment and agency-based discourse 16–17
    care work debate 15
    feminization of migration discourse 14
    global frameworks 9–11
    intersectionality theory 17–19
    review of historical periods of study 11–13
    sexualities-based approach 15
    transnational households debate 15–16
  global context 3–9
    articulated geography 3–4
    asymmetries 8–9
    delocalization and global commodity chains 5–7
    Fordist migration model 7
    nation-state models and 4–5
    transnationalism as opposition to Fordist migration 8
  key chains of debate 25–33
    classic production chains 25–6
    productive and reproductive articulation 32–3
    remittances 26–8
    social reproduction and care 28–31
    linking production and reproduction chains in contemporary mobility 34–5
  migration–development nexus 2
  see also gender and immigration, new research directions; migration
gender, migration and development (Andean study) 127–42
  Andean migration to Spain 127, 134–7
    policies 134–5
    remittances 135–7
  co-development and stereotyping of family 137–41
    remittances strategies 138–41
    gender differences 140–41
  co-development policies and stakeholders 128–9, 138
  overview 24, 141–2
  political construction 129–31
    economic-based view of remittances 129–30
    security/prevention 130–31
  transnational perspective 131–3
gendered and emotional spaces 294–309
  'biographicity' and place-making 301–4
  cultural negotiations 297–301
    case studies (intercultural marriages) 298–300
    displacement and disruption 302
    emotional/experiential struggles (identity) 297–8, 302
  mobilities and belonging 295–6
  North–South mobility 296
  overview, and cultural and political challenges 307–9
  returnee's utopian/dystopian perceptions 294–5, 302–4, 464–7
  study methodology 296–7
  translating narrative extracts 305–7
    bodies and performances 305
    space-scapes and narrative ethnographies 304
  see also integration and transnational engagement
geographically articulated patterning 3–4
German studies 56–7

Ghanaian studies 197–8, 199–200, 201
girls, reasons for investment in 100–101
Glenn, E.N. 403
'global assembly line' 5–7
global context (academic and policy overview) 3–9
　articulated geography 3–4
　asymmetries 8–9
　delocalization and global commodity chains 5–7
　Fordist migration model 7
　nation-state models and 4–5
　transnationalism and 8
Global North 7, 45, 59, 117, 146, 147, 149, 156, 157–8, 159
Global South 6, 7, 9, 10, 26, 45, 51, 52, 56, 58, 59, 99, 116, 146, 147, 148, 149, 158, 159, 236, 240, 260
globalization and development 45–66
　development in sending countries 52–9
　　impact on migration 58–9
　　impacts on labour market 55
　　negatives of migration (brain drain) debate 52–5
　　remittances and their use 55–8
　　return migration 58
　'feminization' of migration 49–52
　forces driving migration
　　acceleration of movement of labour 45
　　care crisis 46
　　financial crisis (2008) 47–8
　　income inequalities 46
　　interregional migration 46–7
　　networks 46
　migration and governance 60–64
　　ILO and UN 62–3
　　incoherence of policy and failures 60–63
　　neoliberal agenda 62
　　policies on migration and finance 48–9
　　rights and market forces 63
　　skill-based selection 60
　national transformations during neoliberal period 45–6
　overview of gender analysis 64–6
globalization and women's work 252–6

globalization of capitalism 147–9
　articulation of productive–reproductive spheres 146, 147–8, 155
　colonial order 148
　domestic economy and 146–8, 157–9
　international division of labour 149, 152, 254–5
　North/South relationship 147, 157–8
　remittances and 140, 158
Gonzalez-Lopez, G. 238
governance 60–64
Greek–Danish studies, *see* gendered and emotional spaces
Gregson, N. 305
Grzymała-Kazłowska, A. 431, 433
Guest Worker Program 236–7
Guillemaut, F. 256

Hatfield, M.E. 301–2
Herrera, G. 313–14
Herzfeld, M. 297–8
Hobsbawm, E.J. 88
Holst, E. 56–7
Honduran studies 57
household migration, *see* Moroccan study on return migration and intra-household power
households 7, 10–11, 13–18, 21–2, 26–8, 30, 51, 53–5, 57, 98, 102, 108, 115, 134, 136, 151, 165–6, 170–73, 187, 191, 208–28, 234, 252, 257, 261, 298, 303, 308, 314, 326, 330, 342, 361, 363–4, 366–8, 371–2, 376–8, 397, 403, 406, 411, 414–16, 420, 423–8, 430–31, 444, 447, 455, 457
Human Development Index 58

identity 297–301
illegal immigrants, *see* undocumented migration
income, *see* wages
inequality and discrimination 17–18
　between women and nation 236
informal economy 10, 49, 127, 146, 149, 376
integration and transnational engagement 268–88

'assimilation' theories and 268
data and study focus 269–70, 276–7
  control variables 278–9
  economic and ethno-cultural integration 277–8, 293
  measurement 277–9
  use of 'transnationalism' 273, 277
existing research as background hypotheses 270–74
  second-generation evidence 272–3
gender differences 271, 286–7
  hypotheses based on 273–6
  status gain/loss 273–4
overview 22, 268–9
results of study 279–85
  descriptive 279–81
  home country visits 281, 282
  overview 285–8
  remittances 281–3
  return intention 283–5
see also gendered and emotional spaces
International Convention on Decent Work for Domestic Workers 154
international financial institutions 56
International Food and Policy Research Institute 115
International Labour Organization 62
International Migration Review 233, 234
international migration, driving forces 45–7
international migration, globalization, development and governance, *see* globalization and development
International Organization for Migration (IOM) 63–4
internationalization of domestic work (Spanish study) 337–57
  data and methods 342–3
  effects of increased immigration 344, 345
  ethnic shares 344
  migration drivers, analysis framework and hypotheses 337–8
    addition effect (growth 1999–2008) 354, 356

complementarity/segmentation by native–migrant origin 344, 346–51
socio-demographic substitution 351–4
overview 26, 354, 356–7
theoretical perspectives and research hypotheses 339–42
  ethnic and gender discrimination 341
  gender equity in Spain 341–2
  labour demand 340–41
intra-regional migration 51–2
investment transfer/circulation 173–4, 219–20, 370–71

Japanese studies 239

Kabba, A. 195, 197–8, 199
knowledge transfer 58

labour complementarity in Spain 338–42, 346–51
labour market
  development in sending countries 55
  employment policies (UK/Poland comparison) 462–4
  global assembly line 5–7
  instability and segregation of women 50
  mobility obstacles, effects of 48–9
  see also economic factors
labour rights
  market imperatives and 63
  political/legal registration 406–8
  violations 408–12, 424
Latin American studies 53, 147, 152, 351, 353
  Andean women immigrants, *see* gender, migration and development (Andean study)
  Bolivian migration to Spain, *see* Bolivian studies
Liberian studies 200–201

Mahler, S.J. 370
market exchange, definition 426
market resources, *see* domestic workers and the usages of reciprocity
marriage 298–301, 446

married couples 298–301
Mediterranean 9, 51, 251, 442, 467
Mexican studies 57, 201, 237, 238, 239, 274
migration
  as a result of recomposition of capital 6
  changing debate and landscape (1970s to the 1990s) 247–50
  classic migration theories 11–13
  feminization of 14, 49–52, 134–7, 149–52, 362, 376–8
    rights and citizenship 399–406
  figures 14, 134, 149, 152, 317, 337, 384
  Fordist migration model 7
  see also gender and immigration, new research directions; gender, migration and development (academic and policy overview)
migration decisions/strategies 457
  childrearing and 453–68
  gendered (Bolivia/Spain) 319
  health care 439–40
  household as most relevant unit 209–11
  household migration (Todgha valley case study) 214–25
    emerging pendulum migration 224–5
    family reunification and 216–19, 223–4
    livelihoods and investment 219–20
    migration characteristics 214–15
    motivations and decision to migrate 215–16
    return motivations and reactions 220–24
      response of children left behind 223–4
  interculturally married couples 298–301
migration policies
  Belgian 423–4
  co-development 128–9
  ILO and UN 62–3
  incoherence of, and failures 60–62
  on migration and finance 48–9
  neoliberal agenda 62

non-governmental organizations and 62–3
rights and market forces 63
rights of care workers 406–8
skill-based selection, and de-skilling processes 53, 60
Spanish 137–8, 321
US prohibitions 236–7, 241
Millennium Development Goal (MDG 3) 99
mobilities 317
  global context 3–9, 31
  labour relative to capital 47–8
  'settling in mobility' and circulation 251–2
  spatial and temporal context 295
monetary and non-monetary resources 31
Monte Carlo simulation engine 382–4
Montevideo Commitment on Migration and Development 135
morality and discipline 191–202
Morocco 6, 25, 31, 70, 208–28, 428, 439, 442–6, 460
Moroccan study on return migration and intra-household power 208–28
  data and methods 211–13, 226
  decision making, household and intra-household inequalities 209–11
  migration flows 208–9
  overview 22, 225–8
  pendulum strategies 209, 224–5, 227–8
  public authorities and 222
  Riffian Imazighen women's experience, *see* Riffian study in temporary migration
  Todgha valley to Europe 214–25
    decisions relating to family reunification 216–19, 223–4
    emerging pendulum migration 224–5
    livelihoods and investment 219–20
    migration characteristics 214–15
    motivations and decision to migrate 215–16
    return motivations and reactions 220–24

response of children left behind 223–4
see also West African study on child transfers
Morrison, A.R. 14
Mostowska, M. 429
motherhood 453–68
Mozère, L. 255

national identity and exclusion 69–70, 74–6, 84, 88–90
networks 13, 31
　Chinese ethnic niche 167, 174–5
　finding a job 429–31
　'social remittances' 133
Nicol, A. 87
non-governmental organizations 62, 137–8, 235, 256
North Africa 25, 86, 251, 252, 255, 258, 261, 450
North American Free Trade Agreement 46
North–South studies, *see* gendered (female) and emotional spaces
Nyssens, M. 30–31, 421, 425–6

OECD 138
Orozco, M. 402

Parreñas, R.S. 1, 27, 45, 51, 165, 190, 236, 239, 249, 250, 316, 329, 340, 431
pendulum migration 209, 224–5, 227–8, 433
People's Global Action on Migration, Development and Human Rights Forum 62
Peraldi, M. 8
Peruvian studies 136–7, 407
Petrozziello, A.J. 57
place 415, 462–67
Plan International, 'The State of the World's Girls 2009' 100
Polanyi, K. 30
Polanyian reciprocity, *see* domestic workers and the usages of reciprocity
policies on migration, *see* migration policies

Polish studies
　domestic workers 251–2
　transnational mobility and family-building decisions 453–68
　case histories 453–4
　employment/childcare issues (UK/Poland comparison) 462–4
　interviews 457–62
　overview 467–8
　sense of (local) place and return migration 462, 464–7
　study focus 454–7
　study methods 457
　UK birthrates 456
poverty alleviation 57–8
Powell, Enoch 74
power relations 146, 224–5, 364, 367–8, 377
production chains 25–6
productive and reproductive articulation 32–3, 146, 147–8, 155

racial organization 146
racism 69–70, 78
　institutional 197–8, 217
　rationalization of 80–81
Razavi, S. 109
reciprocity, *see* domestic workers and usages of reciprocity
redistribution 427, 432, 439–40
refugees/asylum seekers 424
'relay migration' 219
religion 81, 191, 217, 219
remittances
　as part of household strategy 219–20
　effect on sending countries 55–8
　see also remittances and gender; remittances through Bayesian networks 55–8
　gender and, *see* remittances and gender
　migration–development nexus 129–30, 135–7
　　Chinese case study 165, 171–81
　　co-development discourse and interventions 138–41
　　practices of Bolivian migrants in Spain 321–2

production chains 26–8
'social remittances' 133
social reproduction and 158
total volume (2000–2008) 55
remittances and gender 361–73
  data and methodology 362–3
  Ecuadorian receipts 361–2
  gendered migration flows 362
  overview 27, 372–3
  remittance houses 370–71
  remittances as development fund ('savings') 368–9
  remittances as maintenance funds ('emic') 366–8
    gendered effects of 369–72
  sender and receiver relationship (dyad) 363–6
    different behaviours 364
    motivation, enjoyment 365
    power imbalances 364
    senders' supervision mechanisms 366
    types and management of transfer 365–6
remittances through Bayesian networks 376–91
  analysis (Spain–Ecuador corridor) 384–9
    data 385–8
    migrant community in Spain 384–5
    migration history 384–9
    overview 27, 389–91
    results 388–9
  existing data 377–8
  gender differences and impact 377
  models 378–82
    remitting profile and family monetary needs 380–81
    stock of migrants in host country 382
    structured through expert knowledge 382–3
    transaction costs 381
    wage variable and labour profile 381
Renan, Ernest 89
return migration
  as cooperation policy 138

child transfers, *see* West African study on child transfer
family-building decisions 453–4, 460–61, 464–7
  gender differences 271, 279–81, 283–5, 323
  intercultural spouses (case studies) 298–301
  knowledge transfer 58
  reinterpretation of 210
  in Todgha valley 214–15, 220–24
    and family reunification alternative 217
    pendulum migration and 209, 224–5, 227–8, 433
    utopian/dystopian perceptions 294–5, 302–3
Riffian study in temporary migration 439–50
  health care 439–40
  migration processes (Nador, Catalonia and Europe) 442–4
    changing gender roles 443–4
    history of 442–3
    male regrouping 443
  overview 449–50
  social and *familia* impacts and adjustments 440–41
    feminine hierarchy and 445
    feminine solidarity 446
    marriage 446
  study focus and methodology 441
  temporary female migrations and care role 446–8
    differing care requirements and locations 447–8
  transnational *familiat* 444–5
Rogero García, J. 404

Sassen, S. 7
Schmid, T. 79
Scott, J. 146
Scrinzi, F. 255
second-generation immigrants, *see* gendered and emotional spaces; integration and transnational engagement
Segura, D. 239
Senegalese studies 194, 195, 201–2
sex services 254–5

sex trafficking and exploitation 15, 59, 235, 238–9, 254–5
victimization discourse 254, 256
sexual diversity 15, 107–8, 237–8
Sherman, Alfred 74
'smart economics'
  appearing in *World Development Report 2012* 109, 110–11
  Bank discourse 97–9
  stakeholder popularization of 100
  women as 'conduit for policy' 102, 104
'social remittances' 133
social reproduction 145–59
  care, domestic work and 28–31, 50–51, 153–7, 314
  children left behind 54, 171–2, 190, 217, 219, 326–7
    grown child responses 223–4
  concept/definition 155
  employment shares 152
  feminization of migration and globalization of 149–52
  global capitalism and domestic economy (articulation of) 145, 146–9, 157–9
social rights, *see* care work, rights and citizenship
south–south migration 51
Soviet studies 190
Spanish Labour Force Survey 337, 342–54
Spanish studies
  Bolivian migration to Spain, *see* Bolivian studies
  care workers, *see* care work, rights and citizenship
  Chinese immigration, *see* Chinese studies
  domestic workers, *see* internationalization of domestic work (Spanish study)
  economic troubles 193–4
  Gambian immigration 188, 190
  Gender Sectoral Plan 128
  remittances, *see* remittance through Bayesian networks
  Riffian immigration, *see* Riffian study in temporary migration
    West African view of culture 194, 195, 196, 201–2
Sri Lankan studies 152
Stacey, J. 304
'substantive citizenship' 404

Taguieff, P.-A. 75
tax on financial flows 48
Thatcher, Margaret 75
'tied movers' 53
trafficking 15, 59, 63, 238–9, 254, 256
transnational families 312–30
  adjustments and impacts (gendered perspective) 326–9
  Bolivian migration to Spain 317–29
    adjustments and impacts (gendered perspective) 326–9
    interregional circular patterns 318–19
    migration flows (feminized) 317–18
    qualitative approach 324–9
    quantitative data on 319–24
    remittances and return practices 322–4
  concept of 316
  data and methodology 312–13
  diversity of 250–52
  integration, *see* integration and transnational engagement
  migatory processes 313–17
    gender as constituent element 313–14
    gender perspective (stigmatization of women) 315–17
  overview 16, 32–3, 329–30
  transnational return, *see* Moroccan study on return migration and intra-household power
transnational migration, *see* women, gender, transnational migrations and mobility
transnational mobility and family-building decisions 453–68
  case histories 453–4
  employment/childcare issues (UK/Poland comparison) 462–4
  interviews 457–62
  overview 33, 467–8

sense of (local) place and return
    migration 462, 464–7
study focus 454–7
study methods 457
UK birthrates 456
transnationalism 8, 241, 268

underdevelopment 138
undocumented migration 53, 58–9,
    208, 317, 321, 406–8; *see also*
    domestic workers and usages of
    reciprocity
United Kingdom of Great Britain,
    studies 23
  national identity and exclusion 74–5,
    86–8
  Polish immigration, *see* Polish
    studies
United Nations
  Development Fund for Women 62,
    63
  Development Programme
    (2009) 55–6, 58–9
    (2010) 46
  Refugee Convention (1951) 23
  UN Women 108, 112–13
  UNESCO (Educational, Scientific
    and Cultural Organization) 62
  UNFPA, *State of the World's*
    Population (2006) 113
  World Conference (Beijing):
    Enhancing Women's
    Participation in Economic
    Development 98
United States of America, studies
  Bracero and Guest Worker Programs
    236–7
  child transfers, gender and
    legitimization of moral laxity
    185, 194–8, 199, 203
  deportation 241–2
  garment industry 5–6
  mainstream social science approach
    234–5
  migration decisions 457
  policy exclusions 236–7, 241
  second-generation immigrants 272,
    273, 274, 294
  trafficking policy 63, 239
unpaid work 153–4

victimization discourse 254, 256
Vuorela, U. 315

wages
  domestic workers 432–3
  increasing levels of per capita
    income 59
  inequalities 46
  share to total income 48–9
  and unpaid work 153–4
West African study on child transfers
    185–204
  cultural context 189–93
    epistemologies of achievement/
      moral discipline 191–2
    impact on children 190–91
    modern schooling versus training
      192
  data 188–9
  definitions 187–8
  literature on consequences of 189–90
  overview 16, 185–7, 202–4
  parents' responses to discipline
    problems 198–202
    return to home country 199–202
    'second chances' 199, 203–4
    violence 199
  parents' views of opportunity and
    risk 193–8
    corrosion of moral fibre 194–5
    disciplinary deployment 195–6
    institutional racism and 197–8
    willingness to break receiving
      country's laws 196–7
  US, formation and legitimization of
    impressions of gender 185
  see also Moroccan study on return
    migration and intra-household
    power
Whitehouse, B. 202
Women and Migration in the
  US–Mexico Borderlands 239
women, gender, transnational
    migrations and mobility 246–62
  changing approaches and landscape
    (1990s) 248–50
  gender perspective 249
  circulation patterns 251–2, 317–18
  domestic service, scarcity of studies
    253–4

global causes of service activities
  development 254–5
  otherness mobilization 255
'settling in mobility' 251
transnational families 250–51
victimization discourse
  debates (1970s and 1980s) 247–50
  focus on trafficking as counterpart to criminality 256
  shifting/emergent debate 252–4
World Bank 138
  Gender Action Plan (2007–10) 97–9, 101–2
  Gender Action Plan (2010–13) 102–3
  see also World Development Report 2012: Gender Equality and Development
World Development Report 2012: Gender Equality and Development
  consultation period 103–6
  critique of its method, value and contribution 114–17
  draft outline (2011) 104–5
  evolution to completion 106–14
    between draft and final version 112–14
    gendered mobility and migration 113
    draft detail 106–9
    published version 109–12
  'smart economics' 97–103
    Bank discourse 98–9
    investment in girls' focus 100–101
    stakeholder popularization of 100
    women as 'conduit for policy' 102
  team members 105–6
  see also World Bank

xenophobia 61–2, 69–70, 241–2
  cultural exclusion, *see* culture and rhetorics of exclusion in Europe

Zavella, P. 239